America and Vietnam,
1954–1963

America and Vietnam, 1954–1963

The Road to War

MICHAEL M. WALKER,
COL., USMC (RET.)

McFarland & Company, Inc., Publishers
Jefferson, North Carolina

The Central Intelligence Agency has not approved
or endorsed the contents of this publication.

Library of Congress Cataloguing-in-Publication Data

Names: Walker, Michael M., 1956– author.
Title: America and Vietnam, 1954-1963 : the road to war /
Michael M. Walker, Col., USMC (Ret.).
Description: Jefferson, North Carolina : McFarland & Company, Inc., Publishers, 2022 |
Includes bibliographical references and index.
Identifiers: LCCN 2022032938 | ISBN 9781476689555 (paperback : acid free paper) ∞
ISBN 9781476647517 (ebook)
Subjects: LCSH: Vietnam War, 1961-1975—United States. |
Vietnam War, 1961-1975—Causes. | Vietnam—History—1945-1975. |
United States—Relations—Vietnam. | Vietnam—Relations—United States. |
BISAC: HISTORY / Wars & Conflicts / Vietnam War
Classification: LCC DS558.2 .W35 2022 | DDC 959.704/3—dc23/eng/20220720
LC record available at https://lccn.loc.gov/2022032938

British Library cataloguing data are available

ISBN (print) 978-1-4766-8955-5
ISBN (ebook) 978-1-4766-4751-7

On the cover: *inset* Geneva Conference 1954 (U.S Army Photographs);
Crack troops against the Communist Viet Cong guerrillas, 1963 (National Archives)

Printed in the United States of America

*McFarland & Company, Inc., Publishers
Box 611, Jefferson, North Carolina 28640
www.mcfarlandpub.com*

To those on all sides who served honorably

Acknowledgments

No history book is created in isolation, and that is true in this case. First, I wish to thank Colonel David M. Glantz, U.S. Army (Ret.) and Pritzker Prize recipient, who set me on the path to becoming a military historian. Rhonda Herman, president, and Charles L. Perdue, acquisitions editor, for McFarland & Company, need special mention for having the steadfastness to publish what is both an unconventional and controversial presentation of the Vietnam War spanning the years 1954–1963. I also must thank Colonel Andrew R. Finlayson, USMC (Ret.), for his strong encouragement. In the same vein, I wish to acknowledge the support of Steve Sherman of the Vietnam Veterans for Factual History.

Research is heart of history, and technology has revolutionized the process by allowing researchers to dig into primary and secondary sources from anywhere at any time. Of note are Clemson University's Professor Edwin E. Moise's Vietnam War Bibliography website and the invaluable Texas Tech University's Virtual Vietnam Archive. This book benefits greatly from them as well as luck and timing. Only long after the war did many key participants publish memoirs and histories. This was especially true in the case of the Vietnamese—perhaps the most important voices missing from many treatments of the war. Similarly, the U.S. government only began to declassify reams of official diplomatic, military, and intelligence documents decades after the war, a process that continues.

Lastly, my brother, Joseph D. Walker, Jr., proved invaluable. Needless to say, this book would not have been possible without my wife, Megumi, who stood by my side throughout this endeavor.

Table of Contents

Abbreviations

AA—Anti-Aircraft

ADC—Assault Defense Company

ANL—Lao National Army

APC—Armored Personnel Carrier

ARVN—Army of the Republic of Vietnam

BA—Base Area

BSP—Border Surveillance Program

CAT—Civil Air Transport

CCP—Chinese Communist Party

CDNI—Committee for the Defense of National Interests

CEFEO—French Expeditionary Corps in the Far East

CI—Counterintelligence

Chicom—Chinese Communist

CIA—Central Intelligence Agency

CIDG—Citizens (later Civilian) Irregular Defense Group

CINCPAC—Command-in-Chief, Pacific

CJCS—Chairman, Joint Chiefs of Staff

CMPC—Central Military Party Committee

COMINT—Communications Intelligence

Comintern—Communist International

COSVN—Central Office for South Vietnam

CSD—Combined Studies Division

CTZ—Corps Tactical Zone

DMZ—Demilitarized Zone

DRV—Democratic Republic of Vietnam

DTA—Division Tactical Area

FAN—Neutralist Army Forces

FAR—Royal Armed Forces

GI—Infantry Group

GM—Mobile Group

GCMA—Composite Airborne Commando Group

GRSD—General Rear Services Department

GVN—Government of Vietnam

HUMINT—Human Intelligence

ICC—International Control Commission

ICP—Indochinese Communist Party

INR—Intelligence and Research

JCS—Joint Chiefs of Staff

JGS—Joint General Staff

JUWTF—Joint Unconventional Warfare Task Force

LLBD—South Vietnamese Airborne Special Forces

LZ—Landing Zone

MAAG—Military Assistance Advisory Group

MACV—Military Assistance Command, Vietnam

MAP—Military Assistance Program

MAROPS—Maritime Operations

MIS—Military Intelligence Service

MSUG—Michigan State University Group

MR—Military Region

NATO—North Atlantic Treaty Organization

NCO—Non-Commissioned Officer

NLF—National Liberation Front

NRC—National Reunification Committee

NRM—National Revolutionary Movement

NSAM—National Security Action Memorandum

NSC—National Security Council

ODA—U.S. Special Forces Operational Detachment A

OG—Operation Group

OPLAN—Operations Plan

OSS—Office of Strategic Services

PARU—Police Aerial Reinforcement Unit

PAVN—People's Army of Vietnam

PLA—People's Liberation Army

PLAF—People's Liberation Armed Forces

POE—Programs Evaluation Office

PRC—People's Republic of China

PRP—People's Revolutionary Party

PSYOPS—Psychological Operations

RPG—Rocket-Propelled Grenade

RVN—Republic of Vietnam

SCMA—Subcommittee on Military Affairs

SDC—Self Defense Corps

SDECE—Service for Exterior Documentation and Counter Espionage

SEALs—U.S. Navy Special Operations Forces

SEATO—Southeast Asia Treaty Organization

SEPES—Political and Social Studies Service

SIGINT—Signals Intelligence

SMM—Saigon Military Mission

SOV—State of Vietnam

TERM—Temporary Equipment Recovery Mission

TES—Topographical Exploitation Service

TF—Task Force

TRIM—Training Relations and Instruction Mission

TRU—Technical Reconnaissance Unit

UN—United Nations

USAID—United States Agency for International Development

USOM—United States Operations Mission

VC—Viet Cong

VCP—Vietnamese Communist Party

VDP—Village Defense Program

VIAT—Vietnamese Air Transport Company

VNA—Vietnamese National Army

VNQDD—Nationalist Party of Vietnam

VWP—Vietnamese Workers' Party

WSM—Women's Solidarity Movement

Preface

This is a history of America and the Vietnam War during the years 1954–1963, the period when everything that followed had its origins and a history that remains full of challenges and controversy more than half a century after the event.[1] The truth is that even today, too many presentations of the war create a feeling of unease, and here is the difficulty: The military history all too often does not hold together; the tale is too loose, too vague with claims that mostly make sense but never seem fully right. It is akin to trying to view a war reflected off a mirror in a carnival fun house. The image proves too distorted and too many parts too blurry or obscured to offer a satisfactory picture. Attempting to resolve that led to the big question of this book: What really happened?

The surest way to get at the answer remains the best: follow the facts and keep asking questions. Fortuitously, the vast amounts of newly available sources and research finally provided the needed information but offered no obvious path out of the dilemma. That became the next task. Research began with the Americans and their leaders in Washington and Saigon. The exertions gained much but fell short of the goal. That led to looking into how the South Vietnamese conducted themselves. When combined with actions of the Americans, many things began to fall into place, but they still did not offer a way out of the fun house. The war's political history had taken a discernible shape, but the war itself remained an unhelpful blur despite the efforts.

Again, assumptions were discarded to follow facts, and they led to the leaders of the Democratic Republic of Vietnam (DRV) and the history of the People's Army of Vietnam (PAVN). Winston Churchill's quote came to mind: "No matter how enmeshed a commander becomes in the elaboration of his own thoughts, it is sometimes necessary to take the enemy into account." The trip was worth it as it led to a small epiphany: All roads lead to Hanoi. With that, the path forward was revealed, largely due to the works of Pierre Asselin and David W.P. Elliot, Lien-Hang T. Nguyen, and Merle Pribbenow.

Armed with that and striving to approach the problem with a clean slate led to an approach not initially contemplated. The most informative way to present the war was primarily, but not solely, through the actions of the victor, Hanoi. Additionally, when studying the North Vietnamese, another important issue emerged as Laos kept popping up like a bad penny. The centrality of Laos came as a revelation, and understanding what Hanoi accomplished there from 1954 to 1963

1

did more to clarify how the war in South Vietnam evolved than almost any other factor.

After developing the history through the lens of Hanoi, it then was possible to go back and map the corresponding actions of the Americans and South Vietnamese to tell the history of what really happened in a more complete and accurate manner. This was accomplished by examining in detail four areas of the war as it evolved: Part I, "The Path to War"; Part II, "The Combatants"; Part III, "What About Laos?"; and Part IV, "How the War Went and the Fall of Diem." Each part begins with a list of *dramatis personae*.

The first task was to ask three questions: When did the war begin, how, and why? The answers form the basis for Part I, "The Path to War." The most logical answer to when the war began is January 1959 when Hanoi adopted Resolution 15. That act began the reunification struggle in Vietnam. To explain the how required not only a study of Resolution 15 and the state of the revolution in Vietnam but also an introduction to the Vietnamese Workers' Party (VWP) and several of its leaders starting with Ho Chi Minh, General Vo Nguyen Giap, and Le Duan. With the most fitting answers to when and how the war began in hand, answering the bigger question of why came next.

The underlying cause lies at the feet of the July 1954 Geneva agreements to end the 1946–1954 War of Resistance. But again, what really happened? The desperation of France to end the war after its defeat at Dien Bien Phu led to rashly drafted accords. Another flaw that opened the road to war stemmed from the refusal of the United States to act as guarantor or support the 1956 reunification elections unless conducted by the United Nations. That the delegation from the State of Vietnam (as South Vietnam was then called) also refused to be a party to the agreements further damaged the accords' power. Ultimately however, what fully opened the door to future war was the partition of Vietnam at the 17th parallel that left two diametrically opposed states facing each other across a demilitarized zone (DMZ).

While Geneva explains how the door to conflict opened, it does not explain why Hanoi felt compelled to walk through it in 1959. The answer to that is found in the actions of the two rival governments in Hanoi and Saigon during the years 1954–1959, an historic period that often has been both underappreciated and not well understood. Topics covered include the consequences of the 1954 Geneva negotiations along with the VWP's assumption of power in the Democratic Republic of Vietnam and its relentless drive for reunification with the south under the leadership of Le Duan. The rest of the section addresses the more specific question of why war became necessary in 1959: the improbable survival of the State of Vietnam and the rise of its successor, the Republic of Vietnam (RVN) under Ngo Dinh Diem.

That led to another quandary. How could Diem, who is portrayed almost universally as a deeply flawed and inept leader, take a failing state on the brink of collapse in 1954 and build South Vietnam into a functioning and progressing nation by 1959? Again, the answer lay in abandoning assumptions and following the facts. That largely undertold or omitted history comprises the remainder of Part I. The early events center on the 1954 mutiny by General Hinh followed by the outbreak of the 1955 sect war. Both crises were designed to overthrow Diem, initially aided and abetted by the French, who hoped to maintain their influence in, if not dominance over, South Vietnam.

The election controversy is addressed directly as it furthered the rise of the two men who led their countries to war: Diem and Le Duan. In South Vietnam, Ngo Dinh Diem used elections in 1955 and 1956 to consolidate power. In the DRV, a more complex drama played out. Given the disastrous land reform program, the repression of religion, and the crackdown on individual freedoms, the last thing the skeptical VWP leadership wanted was a free and fair election in 1956. For Hanoi, the unfulfilled reunification plebiscite was of greater value as propaganda. The DRV land reform upheavals had even deeper ramifications as they ended with the fall of the VWP secretary general; that opened the path for Le Duan to assume supreme leadership in Hanoi.

As no biography of Ngo Dinh Diem exists, the last chapter serves to draw an informative sketch of Diem. It covers his upbringing, his government career in the 1920s and early 1930s, and his resignation in protest of French overlordship. That defiant stand led to his rise as a voice for Vietnamese independence and opened a political path ending with his appointment as prime minister in 1954. The discussion then moves to his rule as president of the Republic of Vietnam from 1955 until war came in 1959, with an emphasis on the relationship with the Americans. Diem's family is included, not just his controversial brother Nhu, but the profound effect of the murder of the elder brother, Khoi. Also discussed is Madame Nhu, where the foundation is laid to argue that her vilification had less to do with outspokenness and more with her refusal to be treated as inferior to the men she dealt with. She was a woman ahead of her time.

Part II, "The Combatants," seeks to answer the question, How could two small fledgling nations, the Democratic Republic of Vietnam and the Republic of Vietnam, wage a massive war that lasted well over a decade? The most repeated and obvious answer is that Vietnam became an important "hot war" in the bipolar Cold War, an outcome that drew in immense resources from the United States, China, and the Soviet Union. But it is an insufficient explanation as there is more to the story than materiel of war, and in the case of the United States, the commitment of its military forces. To fully appreciate the duration and intensity of the conflict, a deeper understanding of the two combatants is required to address and compare their ability to fight the protracted war they subsequently fought.

The presentation begins with an overview of the RVN and DRV to include a comparative analysis of land reform efforts in the north and south. Things then transition into studies of South Vietnam's security forces, most notably the Army of the Republic of Vietnam (ARVN), whose French colonial legacy left it saddled with a wide range of deficiencies. That is followed by a similar assessment of the People's Army of Vietnam on the eve of war in 1959. It is a tale of two armies, one that began by being straightjacketed by its colonial master, France, and the other forced to create itself overwhelmingly from within. While the French deliberately kept what became the ARVN at the level of dependency, the PAVN became dynamically self-sufficient during the War of Resistance. Throughout the 1954–1959 period, the PAVN developed into a first-rate professional military, while the ARVN, with

American support, attempted to do the same, yet fell short in closing the gap. The ARVN never caught up with the PAVN but came near enough to ensure future conflict would be a hard struggle as long as American assistance was readily available. But there is no doubt that the PAVN entered the Vietnam War as the superior military.

Part II closes with the rise of Viet Cong and then goes into detail to try answer the question, Who were the Viet Cong? The history again is a fascinating and contentious issue and starts with the political face of the Viet Cong and its military command structure, both of which were under the control of Hanoi through the VWP and PAVN from their inception. Next comes a presentation on the challenges the Viet Cong faced in recruiting and training soldiers during the evolving 1959–1963 timeframe. Also covered, as it is for the ARVN and PAVN, is the underaddressed role of uniformed women in the Vietnam War. That is followed by reassessment of Viet Cong intelligence operations with a new emphasis on signals intelligence (SIGINT) and espionage. That transitions into an assessment of Viet Cong weapons and equipment, financing (another often overlooked aspect of the war), and logistics. The study of the Viet Cong ends with a presentation on tactics that also changed significantly over time and reveals the Viet Cong's high degree of skill and ability to improvise and innovate, characteristics that senior Americans often were slow to appreciate.

Part III, "What About Laos?" represents a break with the conventional history of the Vietnam War by delving into the critical role of Laos. The evidence begins with the road to Laotian independence in the late 1940s and the large-scale 1953–1954 PAVN combat operations in Laos that made possible the victory over the French at Dien Bien Phu. It was during that conflict that General Vo Nguyen Giap perfected his use of Indochina as "one battlefield" to wage mobile conventional war supported by insurgency. That Laotian-Dien Bien Phu experience is hard to overstate, as it became the foundation for the military strategy Hanoi used to win the Vietnam War.

As in Vietnam, the 1954 Geneva agreements sowed the seeds of future conflict in Laos. And as in South Vietnam, Hanoi left forces behind in 1954 to strengthen and expand the Pathet Lao. Having made good progress, they returned to the DRV in 1957 and further Pathet Lao training shifted there. And yet again as in South Vietnam, the year 1959 changed everything for Laos. In the wake of Resolution 15, in May Hanoi formed Group 559 to infiltrate VWP and PAVN regroupees along with military supplies into the RVN to include through Laos and in July activated Group 759 for maritime infiltration. In June the VWP Central Committee with Pathet Lao concurrence renewed war in Laos and in September mobilized PAVN Group 959 to assist them.

The fighting that began in 1959 slowly ripped Laos apart into three warring factions: pro–Hanoi, pro–Washington, and after his successful coup in 1960, the neutralists led by paratroop officer Kong Le. Civil war raged across the Kingdom. That triggered a strong reaction in Washington to include preparations for direct military intervention into the region—a first—and Hanoi's far larger military intervention. At that point, the Soviets and China took an active interest. The escalating combat sobered all parties, including the superpowers, to ensure the conflict did not spiral out of control. A ceasefire brokered in May 1961 was followed by reconvened Geneva negotiations to neutralize Laos.

When neutralization talks dragged into 1962 without resolution, Hanoi moved to consolidate its gains in Laos on the battlefield, culminating in the decisive PAVN victory at Nam Tha in May. That broke the diplomatic logjam in Geneva to end the Laotian civil war. The talks were a success for Hanoi as it gained unfettered control over the Laotian border frontier along both the DRV and, more importantly, the RVN. The experience in Laos from 1959 to 1962 again provided a valuable template for the war in South Vietnam. When the Pathet Lao proved incapable of advancing the revolution in 1960, PAVN "volunteers" went to assist in 1961, and when that effort fell short, entire PAVN battalions went in ending with the Nam Tha battle. The Americans did not grasp the lesson. Washington never saw Laos outside the lens of a secondary battleground in the global Cold War and often kept the preservation of its relationship with Moscow the focus. In that regard, the 1962 Geneva protocol was a success for the Americans. For the war effort in the RVN, it was resounding victory for Hanoi and disaster for Saigon.

To fully explain Hanoi's satisfaction, the story shifts to North Vietnam's infiltration into South Vietnam and the consequences of its 1961 decision both to shift to the main Ho Chi Minh Trail to Laos and to make it traversable by truck. Included is a discussion of Group 759's maritime infiltration that got off slowly, but by 1962, the arrival of mortars, machine guns, and rockets in South Vietnam increased the lethality of the war and allowed the Viet Cong to equip Main Force battalions. Similarly, Group 559's expansion of the trail in Laos increased the flow of PAVN regroupees and VWP cadres to include two leadership groups that totaled 900 senior VWP and PAVN officers in 1961.

How infiltration transformed the war can be seen in two statistics. In 1959 about 300 tons of military supplies with 617 PAVN soldiers and VWP cadres entered South Vietnam. By the end of 1963, the infiltration totals exploded to 3,364 tons of war supplies with nearly 40,000 PAVN soldiers and over 1,000 VWP cadres who took charge of the revolution in the south. And the Ho Chi Minh Trail in Laos was only beginning to realize its potential. It is argued that the failure to effectively neutralize Laos was Washington's first strategic blunder of the Vietnam War. That closes out the third part.

Part IV, "How the War Went and the Fall of Diem (1959–1963)," pivots back to South Vietnam and deals with the war through 1963. The goal is to bring a sense of order to the conduct of the war during those years that approaches the presentations of the Allied 1944 campaign in Northern France. Even though insurgencies are chaotic rather than straightforward affairs, armies function under direction—even those composed of guerrillas—and bringing greater clarity is possible. The first two years, 1959–1960, centers on the awakening of the revolution in the south through Hanoi's 1959 Concerted Uprising and 1960 Destruction of Oppression Campaigns. It is through those operations, in combination with the actions taken by Saigon, that the presentation is structured.

Then comes 1961, the year of change. For Hanoi it not only signified switching the Ho Chi Minh Trail to Laos, but also the VWP taking full control of the revolution in the south with the arrival of the leadership groups. Soon, one in six VC Main Force soldiers and guerrillas was a PAVN regroupee, with nearly all filling a leadership or staff officer or technical expert position. With that influx, 1961 witnessed steady gains by the Viet Cong in Nam Bo (southern Vietnam) and especially the Mekong Delta. By year's end, there were some 30,000 Viet Cong serving in Main Force or guerrilla units along with 80,000 militia backed by 200,000 supporters or sympathizers. Le Duan was so pleased with the progress that he ordered the supreme headquarters in the south, the Central Office for South Vietnam (COSVN), to form in 1962 twelve Main Force battalions in Nam Bo and six in Military Region-5 that covered the rest of South Vietnam.

For America, 1961 marked the entrance of the Kennedy administration that made winning in the RVN a priority. That ushered in a new era of significantly increased economic and military aid combined with thousands of military advisors initially following the Staley-Taylor plan developed jointly by economist Eugene Staley and General Maxwell Taylor. Also addressed are the secret wars directed by the Central Intelligence Agency (CIA) to win over the Montagnard populations in the Central Highlands and dangerous missions to insert clandestine South Vietnamese operatives into the DRV by sea and air to form a resistance against the VWP.

For Saigon, the evidence shows that increased support from Washington was a godsend. In 1962, the full implementation of the Staley-Taylor plan, combined with the Strategic Hamlet Program initiated in February, either stifled or rolled back many earlier Viet Cong gains. From a military perspective, the arrival of M113 armored vehicles and U.S. Army helicopters came as hammer blows to Viet Cong operations. While Hanoi continued to hold the strategic initiative in South Vietnam as it had since 1959, by year's end Saigon was on offense tactically against the Viet Cong and contesting the operational initiative on the battlefield. For the Americans and South Vietnamese, 1962 concluded in a mixture of frustration and guarded optimism. The Viet Cong found mainly frustration.

The events of 1963 were and remain some of the most controversial of the war and are treated in some depth. The history begins with a critical reappraisal of 1963's battle of Ap Bac, and beyond some new tactical analyses, the driving point is that the political significance of battle in the United States outweighed its military importance. It marked the first major transition from support of Saigon and Diem to criticism. That is followed by an effort to answer the question: What was the real story behind the Buddhist uprising along with the coup and subsequent assassination of Diem in 1963?

Putting aside the narratives and reevaluating the evidence puts those events in a new light. First and foremost, the role of senior U.S. officials in Washington and Saigon was far greater than most histories contend. The American role was both pervasive and decisive. Trying to explain what the Americans were thinking and why they pursued such extreme solutions is the heart of the presentation. A closer examination of the facts also reveals that the motivation of cleric Thich Tri Quang, who orchestrated the Buddhist uprising, was almost purely political, and his most effective tactic, defining the struggle in terms of religious persecution by Diem, collapses under scrutiny. That he succeeded in destabilizing the Saigon government was due in large measure to American support.

The American role in Diem's murder was equally profound. Washington first learned that the coup leaders intended to assassinate Diem in July and were told so again repeatedly in the months and weeks before the coup. Yet every step of the way, American officials, especially those in the State Department led by W. Averell Harriman, urged the coup leaders forward. Those U.S. officials became convinced that the war could not be won under Diem's leadership and took the unheard-of step of fomenting a coup amongst the ARVN generals to violently overthrow an allied leader—and against the orders of President Kennedy. The critical moment occurred in late August when the Harriman team cabled Saigon pushing for a coup. To those Americans closely involved in the coup, beyond the exact timing, Diem's murder came as no surprise, public denials notwithstanding.

That left one remaining question: What did the bloody November coup mean for the war? The short answer is that it radically altered the course of the war. The year of 1963 became the year that dramatically redefined the Vietnam War. From 1959 with the passing of Resolution 15 into early 1963, the war followed a roughly linear course as the two sides grappled for advantage and violence escalated. With the coup, the Vietnam War spun off onto an entirely different trajectory. The ARVN generals who directed the coup proved useless and divided. Rather than unite the country in the war against Hanoi, they vied for power and ushered in a chaotic period of coup and counter coup while Thich Tri Quang resumed his destructive protests. The Americans watched in dismay as much of what was achieved in over two years of effort and sacrifice evaporated in a matter of months.

Far and away the most significant outcome was Hanoi's decision to exploit the post–Diem instability in the RVN to fully mobilize the PAVN for war and move to launch a General Offensive–General Uprising (GO-GU) to rapidly win the conflict. The plan of action developed in December 1963 was captured in another dynamic document, Resolution 9. Le Duan finally obtained the authority to forcefully reunify Vietnam and finish the revolution, and he would follow General Giap's big unit mobile war strategy to achieve his aims. While Hanoi unified to pursue total victory, Saigon fell into political paralysis. Overthrowing Ngo Dinh Diem was Washington's second strategic blunder.

PART I

THE PATH TO WAR

Part I: Dramatis Personae

The French

Paul Ely—last commander of French forces in Indochina

The South Vietnamese

Ba Cut (Le Quang Vinh)—Hoa Hao general and intractable foe of Diem

Bao Dai—Former emperor of Vietnam and head of the State of Vietnam

Bay Vien—Leader of the Binh Xuyen criminal organization in and around Saigon

Duong Van "Big" Minh—One of South Vietnam's most successful generals in the 1950s who came to Diem's aid

Madame Nhu (born Tran Le Xuan)—Wife of Ngo Dinh Nhu and one of Vietnam's leading revolutionary women

Ngo Dinh Diem—Appointed prime minster by Bao Dai in 1954 who became leader of South Vietnam

Ngo Dinh Nhu—Diem's powerful brother and close confidant

Nguyen De—Bao Dai's fixer who worked behind the scenes to oust Diem

Nguyen Van Hinh—French Air Force officer who became first commander of Vietnamese National Army (VNA) and sought to rule South Vietnam in 1954

Nguyen Van Vy—A senior VNA General and Bao Dai loyalist

Pham Cong Tac—Cao Dai religious sect leader and enemy of Diem

Phan Huy Quat—A Nationalist Party leader seen by many Americans as an alternative to Diem as head of South Vietnam

Tran Kim Tuyen—Diem's head of the intelligence service (SEPES)

Trinh Minh The—Charismatic non-communist guerrilla commander who sided with Diem and was killed during the 1955 battle for Saigon

The North Vietnamese

Ho Chi Minh—Lifelong communist revolutionary and VWP Chairman who ruled over the DRV and party loyalists in South Vietnam

9

Le Duan—The low profile but powerful VWP official who advocated armed struggle to reunify Vietnam

Le Duc Tho—Le Duan's most trusted and ruthless ally

Pham Van Dong—High ranking VWP official and DRV prime minister

Truong Chinh—VWP General Secretary and second in power to Ho. His fall from power opened the way for Le Duan

Vo Nguyen Giap—Ho Chi Minh loyalist, PAVN founder and commander, and rival of Le Duan

The Americans

J. Lawton Collins—Famed World War II combat general and Eisenhower's special representative to South Vietnam in 1954–1955

Donald R. Heath—U.S. ambassador to South Vietnam who opposed efforts to overthrow Diem

Edward G. Lansdale—CIA officer charged by Washington with saving South Vietnam in 1954

1

Going to War in 1959

On 19 January 1959, the order to bring down the Republic of Vietnam (RVN) through political and armed struggle, Resolution 15, was issued in Hanoi. With that act Vietnam, a land largely unknown to rest of the world, began to enter center stage as a key battlefield at the height of the Cold War. To defeat South Vietnam, Resolution 15 stated, "the path is to harness the power of the masses, to rely on the political forces of the masses, to combine them with the power of the armed forces to overthrow the regime."[1] To keep Saigon, Washington, and others in the dark, the resolution remained strictly confidential, held under varying levels of secrecy and only fully revealed to senior Vietnamese Workers' Party (VWP) officials with direct responsibility for implementing it. Even the part intended for publication was kept under wraps until 15 May, and the secret sections were never made public during the war. Neither the public Central Committee communiqué nor the party organ, *People's Daily*, made any mention of armed action in the south; the closest was a vague reference to using "all necessary forms and measures" to advance the revolution.[2] At all costs, the fighting could not be seen as war of aggression waged by Hanoi against Saigon. The official narrative presented the war, especially to the international community, as an internal RVN affair and the fault of the Saigon regime. The cover story held that Hanoi was a natural ally of the southern revolutionaries but did not start and was not directing the war.[3]

The reasons the Democratic Republic of Vietnam (DVR) had been brought to such an extreme were principally twofold: save the southern revolutionaries and restart the reunification struggle. The years following the 1946–1954 War of Resistance against France had not gone well for Hanoi's southern adherents—VWP members and their supporters—many of whom stayed behind after the 1954 Geneva Accords ended the war with France. Hanoi referred to the period as the "ceasefire" or "restored peace" era and more somberly and accurately for the southern cadres as the "dark days" of 1954–1959, for by 1959 the revolution in the south was on the edge of exhaustion.[4]

Dividing the nation in 1954 came as a heavy blow for southern communists to absorb. Had they not won the war against France? Why split the country if the Dien Bien Phu victory had been so decisive? Many were dismayed when partition came. Southern comrades were embittered but remained determined to fight on, and their plight only helped accelerate the restart of the armed struggle. They swallowed their anger, vowed to carry on, and vigorously if secretly sought out new recruits.

A small number continued the military struggle under restricted conditions. The party thinking in 1954 went that the South Vietnamese government was too feeble to survive, and reunification was only months or at most a few years away. And southern cadres' voices still could be heard; their senior VWP officials retained their seats on the Central Committee and other positions of authority within the party. There also was the reality that the loss of life from 1946 to 1954 had been great. Better to be patient and achieve final victory through peaceful means.[5]

The proponents of that theory had been proven badly mistaken. Partition did not just divide the country. It split the revolution. In the north, it progressed along one path while the south faced a very different fate. The party in the south was in disarray from the delta to the highlands and virtually nonexistent in northern South Vietnam. While Saigon's security forces were an imminent threat to VWP revolutionaries, the non-communist anti–Diem opposition groups posed a political threat to party control over the resistance. In that sense, Resolution 15 was enacted to stop the damage. Helping southern comrades to survive, however, was not the driving force behind Resolution 15. Of the two reasons that led to Resolution 15, the goal of reunification dominated. The resolution was not a stopgap to save the VWP in the south—it was much more. It was a call to political-military battle with total victory the aim.[6]

How the Decision Was Made

In January 1959, the 15th Central Committee Plenum of the 2nd VWP Congress, including committee members from the south, met in Hanoi to plan out Vietnam's future. As with everything in the DRV and areas in the south under their sway, the VWP had final authority and controlled events. It did so through the party's leaders appointed by the Party Congress. At that time four veteran VWP members led the nation: Party Chairman Ho Chi Minh[7] with Le Duan as acting Party First Secretary, Prime Minister Pham Van Dong, and General Vo Nguyen Giap, who commanded the armed forces, the People's Army of Vietnam (PAVN).[8]

Their power resided in three organizations: (1) The Central Committee that enacted party and national policies, orders and directives; (2) the smaller but more powerful Political Bureau (Politburo) that formulated policy for the Central Committee; and (3) the Central Committee's Secretariat which answered to the First Secretary and oversaw day-to-day implementation of enacted measures. Party Congressional Conventions, where the leadership for the top committees was elected, were rare and short events—the 1st Congress lasted four days in 1935 and the 2nd Congress convened for nine days in February 1951. To resolve pressing matters until the next convention, Central Committee Plenums were held. The January 1959 session was the fifteenth such occurrence since 1951 and explains why its actions were captured in Resolution 15.[9]

The most powerful VWP leaders were members of all three organizations as they shaped Politburo policy, saw to its enactment by the Central Committee, and then as members of the Secretariat, ensured its implementation. In 1959, beyond acting First Secretary Le Duan and Prime Minster Pham Van Dong, only long serving VWP cadres Pham Hung and Nguyen Duy Trinh were in all three, and both were loyal to and had served under Le Duan in the south during the War of Resistance. There was one last center of power, the VWP Central Organization Committee, which ran the party itself. Le Duc Tho, Le Duan's closest lieutenant since 1948, became its secretary in 1956 and then entered the Politburo. Despite the role of the various leaders, tight party structure, and outward appearance of disciplined unity, there was considerable give-and-take amongst the senior comrades, and on occasion heated disputes over policy and the direction the party and nation should follow.[10]

Given the gravity of the act, the decision to go to war outlined in Resolution 15 had been one of those contentious moments. There were strong divisions within the party over the wisdom of enacting the resolution. Leading the war faction was Le Duan. General Giap, the hero of Dien Bien Phu, headed the rival "North First" faction seeking to postpone any conflict until the DRV became stronger. Giap wanted to keep the peace and focus on developing economic socialism, especially after the damage done by early agricultural reforms and while unanticipated difficulties encountered in industrialization still were being resolved. He was aided by Pham Van Dong. That Ho Chi Minh's two senior comrades headed the "North First" faction should have settled the matter, but Dong was a passive ally. That left Giap to lead the fight, and he largely succeeded—well into 1958 the "North First" faction dominated VWP policy making as witnessed by the passing that year of Resolution 14 that reaffirmed the "North First" economic agenda.[11]

Duan ultimately prevailed in passing Resolution 15 in 1959 for a number of reasons beyond his carefully placed loyalists. By then the hard life lived by Ho Chi Minh was taking a toll, and he took a less prominent role in party matters. Ho also pursued unity and compromise over divisive internal disagreements and vigorously eschewed bloody party purges. That opened the door for an aggressive Duan to push his war agenda. Strengthening him was the hobbled opposition. The failed 1956 agrarian reform opened the way for Le Duan to replace Truong Chinh, and he became acting VWP First Secretary in 1957. Duan now held the most powerful post in the country. That left Giap as his only rival. But Giap had weaknesses; he was a general—not a party leader and organizer like Ho and Duan—and unlike them, he was not a party founder. Further, while Trung Chinh had fallen, he remained a force in the VWP and was Giap's most outspoken critic.[12]

There were other differences that helped Le Duan. When Giap lived the life of an academic during most of the 1930s, Le Duan languished under harsh conditions in French prisons, and amongst VWP leaders, that sacrifice counted for much. Further, Le Duan fought the war in the south against the French, and afterwards the party ordered him to remain behind as the leader of the clandestine VWP resistance. His was the last unfinished battle. Upon his return to Hanoi in 1956, Le Duan forcefully advocated for reunification by whatever means necessary. It was a sentiment shared by all in the VWP, and Giap only could argue against it indirectly.[13]

Further strengthening Le Duan, no one in the North First faction was as convincing or driven or powerful. Gaining one last advantage, Le Duc Tho had become the National Reunification Committee (NRC) secretary in 1955, and the NRC played the central role in directing the revolution in the south as well as infiltration from the north. With all those factors working in his favor, it was not surprising that Le Duan won the day. While he never achieved the fame of either Ho or Giap, Le Duan played the dominant role in waging the Vietnam War.[14]

While passing Resolution 15 proved as momentous as North Korea's invasion of South Korea, the war in Vietnam would be waged in a new manner. That was due to the differing circumstances Hanoi's leaders faced compared to those in Pyongyang in 1950. Dissimilar to the Korean situation, the VWP in the south was already organized, both politically and militarily. That had been achieved during the war with France and provided Hanoi with an alternative to crossing the border with the PAVN. It also stemmed from the Korean War military lesson of 1950: A conventional invasion could trigger a massive response by the Western powers led by the United States. That was the outcome to be avoided, a conclusion shared by China, the DRV's nearest and most essential ally. Resolution 15 triggered an awakening of the resistance in the south, not the start of a massive conventional war.[15]

Understanding Resolution 15

To achieve victory, the resolution laid out the war's strategic objectives: liberate the south, protect the north, and unify the country. The objectives were neither limited in scope nor ambiguous. They aimed to finish the War of Resistance, to struggle until Vietnam was fully independent and reunified under Hanoi's leadership. Le Duan firmly believed that a general uprising akin to the 1945 August Revolution was key to victory, a conviction shared by his Politburo comrades. In true Marxist form, the DRV's leaders had few misgivings about going to war. It saw the enemy as a colonialist, semi-feudal, reactionary, and brutal dictatorship to be eliminated. As 1959 was a year in the heart of the Cold War, Resolution 15 further defined the coming war in a global context that tasked the VWP leadership with identifying the relationship between the revolutionary struggles in the south and north and to align the Vietnamese revolution within the world socialist revolution envisioned by Vladimir Lenin four decades earlier.[16]

What made Resolution 15 significant was the approval of armed struggle, of organized violence, in combination with political struggle, a goal Le Duan had pushed since 1956 when he wrote "The Path to Revolution in the South" that had been adopted by the Central Committee in 1957. Equally important, it was not carte blanche to wage war. The political struggle dominated. To achieve a popular uprising amongst the masses, the resolution ordered the formation of a united front much the same as the Viet Minh in the War of Resistance. Beyond that, Resolution 15 was a product of a divided Politburo that was long on Marxist-Leninist rhetoric—chock full of references to imperialism, feudalism, and the like. The ideological language mattered. Marxism-Leninism was their religion, and they were believers; it was not a superficial doctrine. Ideology provided transcendental guidance that would long outlast issues of day, even one as overwhelmingly critical as reunification, but in terms of details, the resolution raised many unanswered questions. The decisive step had been taken but work remained.[17]

To win, Hanoi had to fight the war according to the unique situation of the revolution both in the north and south as well as in Indochina as whole, what was termed the "one battlefield."[18] But what was the situation? Was peaceful reunification still possible? If not, what was the proper balance between political and military struggles? What was the correct path to build up the people's revolutionary power in the south? The revolution there had not been held in suspended animation since 1954, and Ngo Dinh Diem, South Vietnam's leader, had seen to it that VWP power had been dramatically weakened in the ensuing years. The party challenge in 1959 was not holding on in South Vietnam or even getting back to where the struggle had been but to gain the real prize: national reunification. Without clarity Resolution 15 could do more harm than good. Until detailed orders arrived, only limited actions were to be carried out in the south.[19]

Clarifications and Implementing Instructions

The VWP leadership in Hanoi had to define the revolutionary objectives and methods, and addressing those issues took months of work. The answers, mostly in the form of directives, addressed five sequential steps to be taken by the southern comrades during the new war: (1) propagandize and proselytize the masses, (2) organize guerrilla units and create base areas, (3) begin guerrilla attacks, (4) then create regular forces and increase attacks and finally, (5) carry out large-scale counterattacks by regular forces. And the armed struggle would follow Giap's theory for revolutionary war: (Phase 1) political-military contention, that led to (Phase 2) equilibrium and finally to (Phase 3) the counteroffensive to push out the imperialists. With the precarious situation in the south, they initially authorized the southern comrades and their adherents to use force but only to advance the political struggle. To make things clear, Le Duan personally briefed the Central Military Party Committee (CMPC) in February and, while stressing the political struggle in the population rich Mekong Delta, the Politburo ordered the creation of a "revolutionary base" in the Central Highlands due to its strategic military importance.[20]

The guidelines further explained that armed resistance was justified, not only for defense, but to set the stage for toppling "the dominant regime of the imperialists and feudalists" to be replaced with the people's revolutionary government.[21] Hanoi defined the enemy as an American-Diem alliance (My-Diem) and the struggle as a "special war" where America provided support but not combat troops. Lastly, authority was delineated: Hanoi was in charge, and that authority would not be relinquished. The implementing guidelines were approved in May and arrived in South Vietnam a month later. Resolution 15 marked the beginning of Hanoi's war with Saigon. As historian Douglas Pike noted, the passage of Resolution 15 was and remains the PAVN's "most historically significant moment."[22] The VWP hierarchy felt they had made a prudent and wise decision.[23]

War came to Vietnam but what kind remained unknown. The DRV's basic goals were achieved; the armed struggle would be a gradual and relentless process that needed time to develop and would not present an easy pretext for outside intervention. Resolution 15 also fell considerably short of what Le Duan wanted but did allow him to set in motion forces that would change world history. It would be no exaggeration to call what followed Le Duan's War.

Regardless of its limitations, when Resolution 15 was presented to the southern comrades, VWP leaders reported that it was met with joy and spontaneous displays of excitement and enthusiasm. The problem was that once begun, violence could prove impossible to control, and Vietnam was no exception. The consequences were profound, for Resolution 15 ushered in a terrible conflict.[24]

The VWP, Ho Chi Minh, Vo Nguyen Giap, and Le Duan

An understanding of how the Vietnam War began must include an appreciation for the Vietnamese Workers' Party and its founder, Ho Chi Minh, his general, Vo Nguyen Giap, and Ho's successor, Le Duan. The VWP was established in February 1951 at the 2nd Party Congress as the War of Resistance started to turn in the DRV's favor. The time had come to gradually toss off the united front veneer and re-exert party control over the revolution. The Viet Minh name remained for the time being, but the VWP now was in the "vanguard."[25] It was both a watershed moment and nothing new, for except in name, the new VWP was led by the same Vietnamese Marxists who founded the communist party two decades earlier, and its mission also remained unchanged: to free the Vietnamese and other peoples of Indochina from France and establish a Marxist socialist state. The party's success had been long in coming and from its founding, the fate of the party was inseparable from that of its leader, the capable, charismatic, and life-long communist revolutionary Ho Chi Minh, reverently referred to as Uncle Ho by the people. He was respected by both communists and non-communist Vietnamese alike.

By any measure, Ho Chi Minh lived an extraordinary life. Born as Nguyen Sinh Cung into a Mandarin civil servant family in Trung Bo (Central Vietnam), he attended the

Ho Chi Minh, the revered communist revolutionary who led the Vietnamese people to independence from France (photograph courtesy of Vietnam News Agency).

prestigious Quoc Hoc National Academy at the imperial capital in Hue. In 1911, at age 21, Ho left Vietnam to embark on a 30-year odyssey that would take him across the world and transform him into one of the world's most experienced Marxist revolutionaries. During those years, Ho Chi Minh was known by many names. At age ten, per Confucian tradition, he was renamed Nguyen Tat Thanh and as a young man adopted the name Nguyen Ai Quoc (Patriot Nguyen). During his years with the Communist International (Comintern), he used a myriad of aliases before returning to Vietnam in 1940 to become Ho Chi Minh (Ho who has been enlightened). For the sake of clarity, he will be referred to as Ho Chi Minh.

Although already opposed to French rule when he left in 1911, Ho Chi Minh first surfaced as a Vietnamese nationalist in France during the 1919 Versailles Peace Conference. He was one of the first of his generation to do so and quickly became enamored of radical socialist politics. Ho attended founding meetings of the French Communist Party in 1920. After spending several years as an activist in France, in 1923 Ho traveled to the Soviet Union, graduated from Moscow's University of the Toilers of the East (later the Stalin School), and went to work in the Comintern, the organization that shaped his career over much of the next two decades.[26]

In 1924, the Comintern sent Ho to Canton (Guangzhou), China. Canton at that time was the center of China's united front, the alliance between Sun Yat-sen's Nationalist People's Party (Kuomintang or KMT) and the Chinese Communist Party (CCP). In addition to working with the CCP, Ho advanced the cause in Indochina and recruited Vietnamese revolutionaries through his editorship of the magazine *Youth* (*Thanh Nien*). He excelled in propaganda and political mobilization and remained in China until Chiang Kai-shek ended the Chinese united front and violently suppressed the CCP in 1927. Ho fled to the Soviet Union, where he remained until the Comintern ordered him to Siam (Thailand).[27]

In July 1928, Ho Chi Minh arrived in Bangkok to help organize Thai Marxists while converting exiled Vietnamese and Laotian revolutionaries to communism and serving as the Comintern liaison to CCP exiles. After the French sentenced him to death in absentia in 1929, any hope of an early return to Indochina disappeared. Later that year, Ho reported to the clandestine Comintern Far East Branch cell in Hong Kong and renewed contact with his comrades in Vietnam. Various competing Vietnamese communist groups had been unable to coalesce into a single movement until Ho, having the dual responsibility of being a senior Comintern officer in the Far East and a leading Vietnamese communist revolutionary, finally brought unity. On 3 February 1930 in Hong Kong, Ho Chi Minh oversaw the formation of the Vietnamese Communist Party (VCP).[28]

Soon afterwards, the independence movement in Vietnam exploded with May Day protests that spread across the country and led to violent opposition to French rule. The uprising continued for several months until the French launched a bloody suppression campaign against the communists and other Vietnamese nationalists. The VCP survived, and in October, as the uprising was peaking, Ho headed another Hong Kong meeting where, at Comintern direction, the VCP expanded to become the Indochinese Communist Party (ICP) that included Cambodia and Laos, the name it kept through the 1940s and the onset of the War of Resistance. That year marked the high point of Ho's Comintern career, as he played an instrumental role in the formation of the Malayan and Thai communist parties as well. On 6 June 1931, British authorities in Hong Kong cracked down on the Comintern and arrested Ho. After an extended period of house arrest, he was expelled and put on a ship to Shantou China in January 1933, where he resumed his Comintern responsibilities and reestablished lines of communication with the ICP before his return to the Soviet Union.[29]

Back with the Comintern in Moscow by July 1934, Ho remained there until 1938. The years of demanding duty without respite caught up with him. Physically exhausted, he was sent to Crimea in the fall of 1934 for rest and recuperation. He returned with vigor. In addition to his Comintern duties, Ho completed two years of advanced studies in Marxism and Soviet communism at the International Lenin School—the Western-focused counterpart to the Stalin School. After that, he served as an instructor on Indochina at the Stalin School, and during breaks, visited Western Europe to renew his relationships with leading French communists. During the 1935 7th Congress, which Ho attended as a senior delegate, the Comintern formally admitted the ICP. The winds of war, however, swept aside Ho Chi Minh's academic life.[30]

Sparked by the July 1937 Japanese invasion of China, in 1938 the Comintern sent Ho back to China to help the CCP and strengthen his ties to the ICP. His departure was fortuitous. In 1937 the Great Purge began to focus on the foreign communists in the Comintern. Their arrests and executions tore through the socialist ranks, and by some reports, Stalin had taken a dislike to Ho. If true, Ho Chi Minh probably would have become one more of the hundreds of thousands of forgotten victims of Soviet communism. Had that occurred, not only would the history of Vietnam been changed, but the history of the world would have been altered as well. Those years in the Soviet Union shaped Ho Chi Minh, and as noted above, he adamantly eschewed interparty bloodletting. That policy very likely was rooted in the horrors he witnessed during the Great Purge in Moscow during the mid–1930s.[31]

After arriving back in China, Ho first served at Mao Zedong's headquarters in Yanan and soon became an instructor on guerrilla warfare with the CCP's 8th Route Army. He later worked under Zhou Enlai in Chongqing as part of the renewed KMT-CCP united front. Then came the 1939 German-Soviet pact, followed by the start of World War II that provided the French colonial authorities a pretext to arrest every ICP member they could lay hands on. The ICP reeled under the police onslaught. That was followed by France's defeat by Nazi Germany in 1940, which presented the opportunity to reverse the ICP setbacks. Moscow shifted Ho's duties to focus exclusively on the ICP and to be in close touch with the Bac Bo (northern Vietnam) comrades; he was transferred to Kunming, a city in southern China connected by rail to Hanoi. The Vietnam revolution entered a new and decisive stage.[32]

During June–July 1940, perhaps the most momentous meeting of Vietnamese communist leaders in history took place when the greatly weakened Bac Bo Central Committee sent Giap and Pham Van Dong to China to meet with Ho for guidance. There it was decided to revitalize the ICP and restart the revolution in Vietnam under Ho's leadership. The three would play central roles in Vietnam's history for most of the next three decades, with Vo Nguyen Giap in command of the army and Pham Van Dong as prime minister. During the ICP's 7th party plenum in mid–1941, the leadership was set with the addition of Truong Chinh as party secretary general. Ho's double duty, of being both a senior Comintern official and the leader of the Indochinese communists, had come to an end. Going forward he dedicated himself to the revolution in Vietnam.[33]

Vo Nguyen Giap and Dong were life-long loyalists of Ho Chi Minh, and in Giap's case, the friendship began as soon as they met in 1940. Giap was born on 25 August 1911 into the family of a low-ranking government official. Like Ho, Ngo Dinh Diem, and Pham Van Dong, Giap came from Trung Bo and attended Quoc Hoc Academy. He later studied under Marxist professor Dang Thai Mai. Rejecting French rule, Giap went to prison for participating in the 1930 May Day uprising in Hue. Released in 1932, Giap married Professor Mai's daughter Quang Thai, a fellow revolutionary inmate, and after release they left for Hanoi to rejoin his mentor and father-in-law. In 1934 Giap passed his baccalaureate at Hanoi's elite Lycée Albert Sarraut. With degree in hand, Giap taught history and began his first serious military history studies while pursuing a university degree. In 1936, he renewed his

revolutionary activities, which caught the eye of Pham Van Dong. Dong recruited the bright, energetic, and budding Marxist. Vo Nguyen Giap became an ICP member in 1937.[34]

Ho Chi Minh's relationship with Pham Van Dong went back farther as he had studied under Ho at Canton in 1926. Dong, who was five years Giap's senior, also came from a low-ranking civil servant family but had taken a different road from either Ho or Giap. Having served with the Revolutionary Youth Association (the precursor to the communist party), upon his return to Vietnam from China in 1927, he quickly immersed himself in revolutionary activities. That led to arrest and imprisonment by the French in 1929. Unbroken, he was released in 1936 and joined the ICP leadership in Hanoi. By 1940, Dong and Giap were close comrades and rising within the party when they received the order to meet with Ho in Kunming.

After planning the next steps for the revolutionary struggle, Ho sent Dong to the China border region

The brilliant and tireless General Vo Nguyen Giap photographed after the victory at Dien Bien Phu. Father of the People's Army of Vietnam, Giap overcame his reservations over starting the reunification war in 1959 after arguing for more time to build up strength in the DRV (photograph courtesy of Vietnam News Agency).

to organize the political movement in northern Vietnam. Ho then directed Giap to attend a CCP Red Army school where he became familiar with Mao's theories on guerrilla warfare, and Ho designated Giap as the leader of the ICP armed resistance. Ho and Giap learned in late 1940 of an armed struggle orchestrated by Dong at Bac Son near the Chinese border led by ICP guerrillas, and Ho ordered Giap to the region to take command. Giap arrived, set up a base camp, and took control of the uprising. At the same time, Ho began to organize the Viet Minh, the Independence League of Vietnam (Viet Nam Doc Lap Dong Minh Hoi), to expand the uprising into a broad-based, national movement. The trip to China turned bitter for Giap as the price for struggling against France became clear. Shortly after his departure, the secret police (Sûreté Nationale) rearrested his wife, Quang Thai, and she died in a Hanoi prison during the spring of 1941.[35]

Ho Chi Minh returned to Vietnam in February 1941 after three decades abroad and with his authority over the party unchallenged. The combination of Ho's return, Giap's leadership of the Bac Son guerrillas, and the formation of the Viet Minh on 19 May breathed new life into the revolutionary movement. For the rest of World War II, the Viet Minh battled both the occupying Japanese and Vichy French. Upon the war's end, the Vietnamese people moved for complete independence from France during the August 1945 Revolution. As an unequivocal sign of his popularity, Ho was named the first president of the Democratic Republic of Vietnam that came into being on 2 September.

To further broaden national support of the Viet Minh and unify the Vietnamese independence effort, in November Ho overtly suspended the communist party, claiming it had become the Association for Marxist Studies in Indochina. In reality, the ICP simply went underground and covertly continued. By 1951, it seemed clear that victory over France loomed, at which point it resurfaced as the VWP. From that time until final victory, the single most powerful political entity not just in North Vietnam or Vietnam as a whole but in Southeast Asia was the Vietnamese Workers' Party.[36]

The last great figure was Le Duan, who was less charismatic than Ho but an equally dedicated and more ruthless Marxist revolutionary. Born into a poor family in rural Quang Tri province in 1907—his father was a rice farmer and carpenter—Duan became a member of the Revolutionary Youth in 1929 and later helped found the ICP with Ho. Enriching his knowledge of Vietnam and its people, Duan had worked on the railways and traveled the length of the country. He did not take him long to mature as a revolutionary. In 1931, Duan was arrested during the French crackdown and remained jailed until 1937. Once freed, Duan resumed his party activities, first as party secretary in Trung Bo. He later participated in the ICP's failed November 1940 Nam Bo (southern Vietnam that the French called Cochinchina) uprising. He was arrested again and remained in prison until March 1945, when the Japanese ended French rule and released thousands of political prisoners including many ICP comrades. Le was fortunate; the French executed many party leaders during the 1940 rebellion.[37]

The Nam Bo uprising occurred just months after the Ho-Giap-Dong meeting in China that revitalized the ICP in the north. With the southern leadership decimated, the importance of Ho and his comrades came to the fore. After his release, Le Duan first worked with Ho Chi Minh in Hanoi and, when the War of Resistance began, he was sent back to Nam Bo where he progressively rose in rank and responsibility. In 1951, Le Duan joined the top ranks of the newly formed VWP with his entrance into the Central Committee. He also was appointed to command the Central Office of South Vietnam (COSVN), directing all VWP and PAVN operations in Nam Bo with Le Duc Tho serving as his lieutenant. Inside the party, Le Duan and Le Duc Tho became known as the Two Le's, and Le Duan found himself one of the most powerful figures in Vietnam.[38]

Setting the Stage for War: Geneva 1954

Le Duan in 1957, the aggressive and determined VWP First Secretary who led his country in the war to reunify Vietnam (photograph courtesy of Vietnam News Agency).

The VWP's unfilled expectations resulting from the 1954 Geneva conference to end the War of Resistance against France became one of the underlying causes of the Vietnam War. It is hard to recapture the reality of 1954. The conference took place at the height of the Cold War, where mistrust and inflexibility dominated relations between the communist socialist nations and the Western free-market democracies and their allies. Either confoundingly or predictably, just nine years earlier, all the major powers had been allied in victory after defeating the Axis Powers in World War II. By 1954 they were foes, with the United States, the United Kingdom, and France arrayed against the Soviet Union and the People's Republic of China (PRC) at Geneva.

Often forgotten but importantly, the 1954 Geneva conference convened to end not one but two wars: The 1950–1953 Korea War (meeting from 26 April–15 June) and the Indochina conflict (8 May–21 July). The Korea War talks, agreed to as condition of the July 1953 ceasefire, began and ended without resolving anything of significance—a failure that cast a shadow over the Indochina negotiations. In the Korea talks, an inability to agree to free and fair reunification elections conducted by the United Nations (UN) was a chief reason for the lack of progress. The sticking point was a guarantee of international officials to first verify that conditions for free and fair elections existed throughout Korea for both the pre-election campaign period as well as the conduct of the voting and tallying. Any hope for a solution ended when North Korea rejected international supervision and permission to enter the country, and the Chinese and Soviets backed that stance. The United States refused to accede to anything less.[39]

The Western powers, especially the Americans, could not have been more wary of the communists at Geneva. Free elections conducted in areas they controlled had failed from World War II's end forward. In 1945, Soviet leader Josef Stalin promised the Allies that the Polish people would decide on their post-war government through "free and unfettered" elections.[40] It never happened. Hugh Lunghi of the British Military Mission in Moscow later reflected that there was not a chance in hell that Stalin would allow fair elections in Poland, and the communists took power during corrupt and fraudulent plebiscites in 1946 and 1947. Stalin himself had summed up best the tactics decades earlier: "What is extraordinarily important is who will count the votes and how."[41]

Things did not get better. In 1946, Moscow again rigged elections in Soviet-occupied East Germany, but the German communist Socialist Unity Party in Berlin was defeated in the election supervised by the joint Allied occupation. It was finally undone when the party incited riots in 1948, a pretext the Soviets used to establish communist rule over East Berlin that helped usher in the Berlin Crisis that year. Also, in 1948 Moscow orchestrated a communist coup in Czechoslovakia that overthrew the elected government there. The occupying Red Army ensured its success. Then came the 1949 Korea elections that the UN called off because it was impossible to vote freely in the north. Finally, in March 1952, Stalin duplicitously proposed similar reunification elections for Germany while never intending to allow them; the real objective was to derail West Germany's decision to join the European Defense Community. The Americans deflected the ploy. Those precedents helped lead to the Geneva impasse over Korea in 1954.[42]

Similarly, the talks to end the Indochina war, co-chaired by the United Kingdom and Soviet Union, were fraught with obstacles. And again, arguments over reunification elections in Vietnam became central. Critically, the Americans remained apart from the negotiations. Washington held that as a combatant in Korea, it was a principal party, but that was not true in Indochina, and it attended only in an advisory and assistance capacity. Adding to the diplomatic hurdles, the two Vietnamese governments, Ho Chi Minh's DRV and the State of Vietnam (SOV) led by ex-emperor Bao Dai, were internationally recognized along Cold War lines. Even more exasperating, both claimed to be the sole representative of Vietnam and refused to recognize the other's authority.

The result was that neither the DRV nor SOV were initially invited to sit at the table. The Soviets had let it be known in March 1954 that they would wait for the French to propose inclusion of the Associated States of Indochina (State of Vietnam and the Kingdoms of Laos and Cambodia) before nominating the DRV as a participant. It was not until the week before the talks began that the Bao Dai government realized its DRV boycott would leave it with no say in the outcome and proposed to allow both the SOV and DRV to officially participate. As a failsafe, the Bao Dai government reserved its right to withdraw from the conference if a proposed settlement "would not really bring a lasting peace."[43] Topping off the drama, the talks opened on 8 May, the day following the French surrender to the PAVN at Dien Bien Phu.[44]

The Dien Bien Phu defeat made it clear to Paris that the war had to end promptly. Achieving that goal created many of the same problems that had proven irresolvable during the talks over Korea: how to keep Vietnam unified and how to peacefully create one government. A grim reality intruded into everyone's calculations: the specter of renewed fighting as both the PAVN and French Expeditionary Corps remained potent foes. No matter what, neither France nor the DRV wanted the conflict to continue, and the two big initial questions were: How to disengage the armies and establish a ceasefire?[45]

Politically, the situation was turbulent. Vietnam, like Korea, had a torn population; in Vietnam's case between loyalties to Ho and those opposing his socialist-communist vision. The advantage lay with the DRV. They were united while the SOV was divided, and the Bao Dai government shockingly feeble. Nonetheless, the anticommunists numbered in the millions, were concentrated in the south, and could not be dismissed. The French remained hopeful of retaining influence in the region through formal association and continued membership of Vietnam, Laos, and Cambodia in the French Union while the DVR opposed significant residual French influence. As for an election under those conditions, was it even possible to achieve national reconciliation through a referendum?

Turning the negotiations further into a tangled web, the DRV laid claim to territory in the Kingdoms of Laos and Cambodia to be controlled by its surrogate communist parties. The DRV delegation insisted on the recognition of the Pathet Lao and Free Khmer communists as legitimate governments in Laos and Cambodia equal to their authority in Vietnam. They proposed competing governments not just in Vietnam but also in Laos and Cambodia to be reunified through elections supervised by "local commissions."[46] Beyond Western power objections, the delegations from both Kingdoms rejected the proposal out of hand by claiming that neither the communist Free Khmer nor Pathet Lao possessed real political power. Phoui Sananikone, the head of the Laotian delegation, stated the Pathet Lao represented "absolutely nothing" in the Kingdom.[47]

In the case of Laos, the DRV's claim was not idle—it was backed up by brute force as the PAVN had half a dozen or more regiments in Laos who controlled a large part of the country. But as Phoui Sananikone noted, the DRV's claim had problems. Everyone knew that the Pathet Lao were as weak as the PAVN strong. And the DRV could make no such claim in Cambodia; outside of remote regions of the Mekong Delta and the April 1954 arrival of PAVN troops in the lightly populated and rugged northeast (which Cambodia termed an invasion), the DRV exerted no influence. Nonetheless, Ho Chi Minh had led the Indochina Communist Party—not a Vietnamese Communist Party. His vision of a communist socialist system for all Indochina never wavered, and the fact that Ho helped organize the Lao communists in the 1920s was not forgotten. When the parties were revived in 1951, the VWP announced, "The people of Vietnam are willing to enter into long-term cooperation with the peoples of Laos and Cambodia with the view to bring about an independent, free, strong and prosperous federation."[48] The DRV's Laotian and Cambodian agenda at Geneva was driven by long-standing party strategy.[49]

Laos and Cambodia aside, progress had been made—if not exactly as anyone planned. The path to a ceasefire supervised by an international commission advanced, and it became clear in June that support for partition of Vietnam, an idea all parties initially condemned, became stronger. To stop the fighting, Vietnam was to be divided into PAVN-controlled areas to be governed by the DRV and French-controlled areas to be governed by the SOV. The idea was that once the areas were delineated, the opposing armies would leave the other's territory and be given 300 days to regroup in friendly zones. Where the partition should be made, along with how to conduct national reunification elections, became the final obstacles to a solution.[50]

Washington made clear it would disassociate itself from the developing agreement on two grounds: its opposition to partition and insistence on free fair elections. None of the other allies were as opposed, and some challenged the American stance as the partition idea had been floating around for months. Even before the Geneva talks began, in March the Soviets had breached to topic of partition to both China and the DRV, and Britain first floated it amongst the Western allies on 25 April. The DRV delegation hinted at partition as a solution on 10 May, the third day of the conference, and continued to be an advocate in subsequent negotiations. After long delays, France wavered a bit and broached the subject to the Americans on 5 June. The road to partition became open, although just barely as witnessed by continued opposition from the State of Vietnam.[51]

By 16 June, the frustrated and increasingly desperate French realized partition was the only path ahead. Two days later, the new French prime minister, Pierre Mendès-France, vowed to resign if an agreement was not reached by 20 July. With that impetus, a ceasefire and partition were adopted with only details remaining. The ceasefire procedure wrapped up on 16 July after a month of private talks between French and PAVN military officials. Partition talks also accelerated following Mendès-France's ultimatum. After an unsuccessful French gambit to create disjointed "leopard skin" zones of control, a north-south partition dominated discussions.[52] The DRV leadership, wrongly fearing American military intervention, moved to quickly resolve the issue, and when the 17th parallel was settled upon, partition became inevitable. The diplomats ironed out an agreement by mid–July—riding roughshod over the SOV's unyielding objections (and Hanoi's private complaints to China and the Soviets that the 17th parallel was too generous). The International Control Commission (ICC) comprised of equal teams from Canada, India, and Poland and answerable to the Soviet-British co-chairs would ensure compliance with the peace accords. It would resolve disputes, violations, and other issues through the Joint Commission chaired by the respective commanders of the PAVN and French Forces.[53]

That left free and fair elections. Having learned its lesson, Washington refused to back vague election language. Earlier on 29 June 1954, President Dwight D. Eisenhower publicly outlined Washington's concerns: "In the case of nations now divided against their will, we shall continue to seek to achieve unity through free elections, supervised by the UN to insure that they are conducted fairly."[54] The DRV delegation realized America's fears when they argued for local commissions to organize and supervise elections (with no mention of outside observers) and that the DRV would exclusively conduct elections in areas it controlled. Conversely, the SOV wanted the process placed under the UN. Aware of the election controversies, the Soviets, Chinese, and DRV were determined to prevent independent oversight. In the end, all the principals except the SOV accepted a 20 July 1956 election with no real safeguards.[55]

With partition settled and no guarantees for free and fair elections, the United States walked away. Similarly, the SOV delegation rejected both DRV locally-controlled elections and partition. In a last-gasp maneuver, on 19 July the SOV delegation fought to remove the entire process from Geneva by proposing that the UN supervise the elections and assume the role of the proposed ICC. The request was ignored, and negotiations were over. The next day the Agreement on the Cessation of Hostilities in Viet-Nam and the related annex were signed between France and the DRV as well as similar agreements with Laos and Cambodia. On the following day, the Final Declaration of the Geneva Conference on the Problem of Restoring Peace in Indo-China was issued. Both the United States and State of Vietnam refused to sign either the agreement or related annex, and the final declaration noted with true diplomatic obfuscation that the SOV and United States "took part" in the conference. It was a troubling beginning.[56]

Washington's action was a surprise to no one. That had been American policy since the planning meetings in April, and the French were so informed in May and re-informed in July after being asked to reconsider. An early June Geneva press conference explained Washington's election-partition rationale, and top negotiator General Walter Bedell Smith backed up words with deed when he left the talks on 16 June and did not return until the closing days in July. Secretary of State John Foster Dulles also put it bluntly in a cable to the U.S. delegation on 16 July, writing that the United States "will not negotiate and sign with the Communist bloc any multilateral declaration on Geneva conference or any agreement issuing therefrom."[57] Smith reiterated that sentiment two days later. There was no ambiguity as to America's intent on the issue.[58]

Before, during, and after the talks, publicly and privately, whether to individual participating states or as a group, Washington conveyed continuously that it reserved its right to refrain from joining any accords reached in Geneva and retained its freedom of action if the ceasefire was violated. To clarify its position, Washington unilaterally announced it would continue to seek free elections in Vietnam supervised by the United Nations. Ignoring the Geneva agreements, it instead stated it would abide by the United Nations Charter's Article II, meaning the United States would not threaten or use force to disturb the peace in the DRV, SOV, Laos, and Cambodia but those restraints would be removed if the region's peace and security were threatened.[59]

Conclusions

The Vietnam Ceasefire Agreement and subsequent Final Declaration achieved the primary objective of ending the War of Resistance. That was a great success.

After that they remained little more than expedients and became problematic. France embraced them but no longer held power in Vietnam. The DRV was guardedly supportive, but the SOV refused to be bound to them either in part or whole, and 20 July came to known as "The Day of National Shame" in the south. Did that matter? The answer was yes but only if the SOV proved viable, and that was by no means certain. By May 1954, one point that the DRV, France, and the United States could agree on was that Bao Dai was inept and his regime teetering.

Bao Dai set a poor example. To the ire and distaste of the French, who had soldiers dying to defend his homeland, the ex-emperor sat safely ensconced in a Riviera villa in Cannes, France. When it came to governance, he failed South Vietnam. Months earlier, Bao Dai's compatriots prodded him to action—not to return to Vietnam—but to at least shake up his cabinet, and still he moved ever so slowly. On 14 May he gained the consent of Ngo Dinh Diem to replace Prince Buu Loc as prime minister. But it was not until 17 June that he made the decision public, and he kept Diem in France until July. Given Bao Dai's indecisiveness, few held out hope that the Saigon regime would long continue.[60]

That pessimism explained why the objections by the SOV's delegation at Geneva were not just ignored by the Soviet-DRV-China delegations but by most of the Allies as well. It seemed unlikely that the State of Vietnam would survive for more than a year at best. In that frame of mind, partition or a UN-supervised election seemed irrelevant. There was little fanfare given to the SOV's refusal to accept the Geneva pronouncements—its delegation considered the outcome "a complete failure"—or that the United States' participation never advanced beyond an advisory role.[61] For many of the other states at Geneva, the unspoken conclusions were that France had been defeated, the DRV had won the war, and without the French, the SOV was doomed. Unlike the rest, as Ho Chi Minh and the VWP took up residence in Hanoi, there was a sense of confidence that reunification soon would be achieved but tempered by a feeling of wariness; complete victory had not been obtained in Geneva, and the struggle not over.[62]

No matter the number of lofty speeches and dramatic press conferences, the 1954 Geneva agreements and declaration had to fail. Both the DRV and SOV independently had decided to ignore the accords from the outset. Technically they were allowed to; the DRV signed an agreement with France, the SOV with no one, and the DRV and SOV governments had never entered into direct bilateral talks with each other. There was no agreement between the two states to break. It became a political game. If compliance advanced national interests or gained international support, especially in the court of public opinion, then the Geneva accords mattered. When they worked to the detriment of the interests of Hanoi or Saigon, they could be ignored.

While all at Geneva welcomed the peace being brought to Indochina, the door to future war had not been closed. The inherent ambiguities contained in the Geneva agreements, along with the conference's unresolved issues and unfinished business over Vietnam and the rest of Indochina, created the dynamics that led to renewed conflict. Further, the life-long revolutionary ardor of Ho Chi Minh, Le Duan, and Vo Nguyen Giap made them readily open to renewed armed struggle.

But the war was not inevitable. The contemporaneous Korean peace negotiations at Geneva also proved an abject failure. There too a path to peaceful national reunification seemed impossible, but war did not follow. Similarly, the 1945 partition of Germany led to a massive military build-up along the dividing line, but no conflict ensued. The reasons why war returned to Vietnam in 1959 were uniquely complex, and the lingering failures of Geneva strongly influenced the deliberations of the VWP when passing Resolution 15. But the deciding final factor was South Vietnam. How did it even survive into 1959? Had things progressed differently, there never would have been a need for war.

2

Fight for Survival
in South Vietnam

The fact that the Democratic Republic of Vietnam had gotten to the point where it felt compelled to wage war on the Republic of Vietnam in 1959 was in itself a surprising turn of events. By all rights, there never should have been a Republic of Vietnam. Even before the ink was dry on the Geneva Accords in July 1954, the situation in the south was dire. South Vietnam should have collapsed years earlier; Central Intelligence Agency (CIA) headquarters in Washington expected Hanoi to gain complete victory by 1956. The feeling was pervasive, and South Vietnam's fight for survival was underway.[1]

Saigon 1954

The first leader of an independent South Vietnam, Ngo Dinh Diem, faced almost insurmountable challenges. At the time of his announcement as prime minister, former Emperor Bao Dai's State of Vietnam was a complete mess, what the French called a basket of crabs (*panier de crabes*). Paul Harwood, the CIA station chief in Saigon, assessed Diem's chances of success: his "task is hopeless but effort must be made."[2] Bao Dai's first loyalty was to himself, and governance at the provincial and national level had been damaged by his absence. Nguyen Huu Tri, a leader of the anti-communist Dai Viet Party and governor of Tonkin, lamented that there was no central government in the SOV. Saigon also suffered from the withdrawal of many French administrators. (Unlike Tonkin and Annam that had been nominally under Bao Dai's control, Cochinchina was ruled directly from France.) He was a fickle ruler as well; since forming the government in late 1949, by 1954 Bao Dai had directed five changes in prime minister, to include a stint where he assumed the job. He shuffled cabinet ministers with equal caprice.[3]

American Ambassador Donald R. Heath added his concerns to those of Harwood over a fledgling country further beset by three private "sect" armies: the Cao Dai and Hoa Hao religious troops and the Binh Xuyen crime organization that effectively controlled Saigon. The soldiers, who originally were supplementary troops fighting under the Inspector General of Cochinchina, had become forces unto themselves. Their alliance with the French led to one of the most iconic phrases associated with counterinsurgencies when Major A.M. Savani, who worked with the sects in 1953, wrote that success was reached when "we conquered all the hearts and 'occupied' all the minds" of the Vietnamese people.[4] Finally, there was General Nguyen Van Hinh, an ardent Francophile who commanded the nation's most powerful force, the Vietnamese National Army (VNA). Hinh held no loyalty for Diem and had begun to make noises about taking over the government, a characteristic his father Nguyen Van Tam, one of Bao Dai's former prime ministers (council president), termed his son's "dictatorial aspirations."[5]

Nguyen Van Hinh started his military career as a bomber pilot in the French Air Force (*Armée de l'Air Française*). He served with distinction in Europe during World War II and was granted French citizenship. Afterwards, as the War of Resistance grew in intensity, the French created the VNA that was in desperate need of experienced officers. With that in mind, then Commandant (Major) Hinh was assigned to the VNA in August 1948. When the VNA Joint General Staff (JGS) was established on 1 May 1952, Hinh became its first chief, and Bao Dai promoted him from lieutenant colonel to major general in one fell swoop that year. By 1953 he was a lieutenant general in charge of the South Vietnamese armed forces. Despite his meteoric rise in the army and a good degree of personal devotion to Bao Dai, Hinh kept his commission in the French Air Force and remained a Francophile.[6]

While Hinh posed the immediate danger to Diem's rule, the three sect armies were no minor threat. Together they commanded over 36,000 soldiers, had some presence in Saigon, and could mass on the capital in days. The Cao Dai sect commanded the largest army, 16,600 strong led by General Nguyen Thanh Phuong. The Cao Dai (Great Palace and short for Dai Dao Tam Ky Pho Do or Third Amnesty of God) followed a creed that combined most of the world's major religions led by the dual political-religious figure Pham Cong Tac residing at Tay Ninh in northwestern Nam Bo. Having been fiercely anti–French, the Japanese Army trained and armed the Cao Dai during their occupation of Indochina, creating an impressive military force. They initially joined with the Viet Minh but were alienated by the Marxism and political purges. They turned to the French in 1948, who rearmed them and ensured their loyalty through monthly payments. Also of note was renegade Colonel Trinh Minh The, who led 2,500 Cao Dai guerrillas called the Lien Minh that were both anti–French and anti-communist.[7]

The Hoa Hao (Phat Giao Hoa Hao) was a Buddhist sect unique to Vietnam. Their strongholds were in the western Mekong Delta and the areas southwest of Saigon abutting Cambodia near the "Parrots' Beak," a part of Cambodia that jutted into South Vietnam. They too broke with Viet Minh after the execution of many followers to include their founder, Huynh Phu So, and joined the French in 1947 with the same "guns and money" model of support. By 1954, the Hoa Hao Army contained 16,000 soldiers. General Tran Van Soai led 7,000 while Colonels Le Quang Vinh, Nguyen Giac Ngo, and Lam Tranh Nguyen each commanded 3,000 soldiers. Le Quang Vinh also was referred to as Ba Cut or Severed Third [Finger], and known as the enfant terrible of the Hoa Hao leaders. Despite their religious bonds, loyalties were flexible when it came to the French or Americans or even Diem, and it was folly to take them for granted.[8]

The leader of the third "sect," the Binh Xuyen, was Bay Vien (Le Van Vien), a shrewd, intelligent, amoral, and ruthless cutthroat. His Binh Xuyen had been formed in the early 20th century as a Vietnamese Tong or Triad criminal society cloaked in secrecy. They descended from the Black Flag pirates who had raided Saigon's commercial trade from their Rung Sat mangrove swamp bases to the south of the city, and the Binh Xuyen still controlled the area. In 1954, its main base of operations was in the ethnic-Chinese dominated town of Cholon to the southwest of downtown Saigon. The "sect" was named after a small hamlet of Binh

General Nguyen Van Hinh, the ambitious VNA commander promotes one of his allies, Hoa Hao military commander Ba Cut, to colonel in 1954. At French urging, both tried and failed to overthrow Diem, ending in exile for Hinh and the guillotine for Ba Cut (CIA).

Xuyen just south of Cholon where Bay Vien first formed the gang. Cholon was ideal for criminal activity as it was close to the city center and bordered the Arroyo Chinois, a waterway off the Saigon River so filled with sampans that it resembled the Hong Kong or Shanghai waterfronts. The gang's headquarters was located in Cholon's Grande Monde, and along with the Cloche d'Or, included the largest and most lucrative casinos in Vietnam (even if they were tawdry establishments). In the exigencies of war, the French concluded, "my enemy's enemy is my friend" and enlisted the support of the Binh Xuyen to eliminate Saigon's Viet Minh guerrillas.[9]

The Binh Xuyen accomplished that task in a bloody but effective manner, and Bay Vien's rewards were many. In addition to keeping control over normal criminal activities (opium, protection rackets and kickbacks, smuggling, gambling, and prostitution with its centerpiece Hall of Mirrors brothel that was described as "spectacular"), the Binh Xuyen controlled "legitimate" monopolies over Saigon's fishing, teamster (collecting "road safety taxes"), and lumber businesses. They also owned Saigon's most upscale department store, the Noveautés Catinat, along with scores of smaller businesses, and held interests in hotels, charcoal distribution, and rubber plantations. Beyond gambling, drugs, and prostitution, if one wanted the best drink, finest food, and poshest shopping, the Binh Xuyen offered it all. They operated side-by-side with Corsican-owned clubs and bars (run by the Unione Corse [the Corsican mafia]) that smuggled Indochinese opium. Bay Vien also endeared himself with colonial authorities. In honor of his war service, the French appointed him a

VNA major general. He commanded 5,5000 troops, with 3,000 in the Saigon-Cholon metropolis comprised of two infantry battalions and a paramilitary shock force wearing distinctive green berets, loosely formed into two "public security" battalions that served as enforcers to include keeping tabs on the National Police.[10]

Bay Vien developed a close working relationship with the Deuxième Bureau, the dated if popular name for the SDECE (France's CIA). Journalist Bernard Fall wrote at the time, "In American terms, it would mean transforming 'Murder, Inc.' into a unit of the National Guard and raising the gang leader to the rank of brigadier-general."[11] Under Bay Vien's sway, Saigon deteriorated from being the "Pearl of the Orient" to "the world's most sinful city."[12] When Diem closed the opium dens and publicly burned the opium in 1954, he was lauded across Saigon. He also made Bay Vien his enemy.[13]

The power of the three groups revealed the absence of civil governance in South Vietnam and the degree to which the illegitimate had been legitimized. Equating the Binh Xuyen to the two religious sects was absurd; it was a state-sanctioned organized crime cartel devoid of religious underpinning. Even the outsized role of the two sects was hard to grasp. Together they constituted perhaps five percent of Vietnam's population and a little over ten percent of the population in South Vietnam. The problem was not that they wanted a political voice. They deserved that. What made their goals intolerable was that they, a small minority, wanted to control South Vietnam and already wielded political clout far beyond what their numbers warranted. Their claim to authority rested on having fought against the communists and the threatening proximity of their armies to Saigon. It was an example of Mao's dictum that political power grows out of the barrel of a gun.[14]

Looming in the distance was the problem of national politics: Vietnam never experienced democracy. To cap it off, the two major parties—the Nationalist Party (Viet Nam Quoc Dan Dang or VNQDD) formed in 1927 that mirrored Chiang Kai-shek's Chinese model, and their one-time allies, the Dai Viet, formed in Hanoi in 1939—believed in one-party rule once they took power. Problems also abounded within the cabinet Diem inherited. In addition to Hinh's raw thirst for power, Minister of Defense Dr. Phan Huy Quat hated Hinh, and the feeling was mutual. Quat had been a respected physician in Hanoi before entering politics as a Dai Viet founder (also known as the Popular Nationalist Party after 1951). When he joined the Bao Dai government in 1953, the defense minister was largely powerless, as the French controlled everything. Geneva changed that, and once Quat had real authority, the friction with General Hinh grew. Quat had a reputation for being honest, hardworking, and anti-communist. He also was an idealist whose democratic vision was unrealistic and perhaps disingenuous, given the Dai Viet's authoritarian tendency, but being pro-democracy endeared him to many Americans. When Bao Dai elected to replace Prince Buu with Diem, Quat became acting prime minster, but high-ranking Dai Viet loyalists like Bui Diem were deeply disappointed. Diem would get no support from the Nationalist or Dai Viet parties.[15]

Diem's job had been made more difficult on 30 April when Bao Dai handed control of the National Police (Sûreté) to Lai Huu Sang (Lai Van Sang), brother of Bay Vien. The 22,000 strong Sûreté mainly consisted of police gendarmes spread across the SOV, but it also had a special branch headquartered in Saigon that handled internal security. To echo Bernard Fall, it was akin to President Eisenhower making a lieutenant of mob Boss Frank Costello director of the CIA and Federal Bureau of Investigation. A jaded American embassy saw it as another example of Bao Dai's divide and rule methods.[16]

Much of this Binh Xuyen mischief was the handiwork of Bao Dai's chief of cabinet, Nguyen De, a shadowy figure who rarely left the ex-emperor's side. De already had worked behind the scenes to remove one prime minister, and his reputation was such that American Chargé Robert McClintock stated he would welcome Bao Dai's return if only he would leave the "evil genius" De in France.[17] Prince Buu had a harsher assessment: "Nguyen De is like a man who can't make love, but doesn't want anyone else to" and blamed him for the intrigues in Saigon.[18] In modern parlance, De was the ex-emperor's "fixer" and not to be underestimated; as senior liaison to the Binh Xuyen and rumored Deuxième Bureau agent, he turned Bay Vien into Bao Dai's supporter. But the gangster's real loyalty was not to Bao Dai; he served France, and France needed him. French war correspondent Lucien Bodard concluded, "Bay Vien and his army were the last support of the French who fought against Ngo Dinh Diem and the Vietnamese army."[19]

During May 1954, political problems continued to mount. McClintock reported that Hinh had sent an ultimatum to Bao Dai demanding that in addition to being VNA chief, he be made both minister of defense and interior, a move that would give him sole control over South Vietnam's national security apparatus. As for Defense Minister Quat, Hinh wanted him moved to minister of the national economy. McClintock noted, "Hinh is heading for dictatorship" and doing so "openly and with such naiveté."[20] Bao Dai took no action in support of Hinh but did nothing to deter him either. Diem said it best himself on 23 July 1954: Overcoming the problems facing the government required an almost superhuman effort.[21]

Bao Dai's decision to replace Prince Buu with Diem caught Washington flat-footed although they were aware of Diem. While several important American progressive politicians had met Diem in 1953, official Washington knew almost nothing about him and did not see him as a potential leader of South Vietnam. Just a few months earlier, in February 1954, Ambassador Heath had suggested some names to Bao Dai to strengthen Prince Buu's cabinet, and Diem was not amongst them. But Diem's stock had been rising amongst the American diplomats in Saigon. Unaware of Bao Dai's 14 May decision, two days later they recommended Diem, not as prime minister, but as one of several candidates to make up a regency council to help Bao Dai rule. The CIA got wind of the potential change in leadership when Diem's brother Ngo Dinh Nhu approached them in Saigon asking what it would take for Washington to support his brother's prime ministership. A short while later Diem's brother Luyen approached the Americans in Geneva.[22]

All the while, Saigon's chattering class tongues wagged that Diem was America's handpicked leader as canards abounded on "Radio Catinat," the rumor mill named after the city's swank boulevard with the best cafés and where the best gossip could be had. Ambassador Eldridge Durbrow, who became the U.S. ambassador in 1957, remarked, "In my 15 to 20 posts after 38 years with the Foreign Service, I never ran into a worse rumor factory than Rue Catinat, Radio Catinat."[23] And Radio Catinat had it wrong.[24]

As both Washington and Paris knew, the French—not the Americans—pushed Bao Dai to choose Diem, and it was time to play catch up in Washington. Colonel Edward G. Lansdale, head of the CIA's Saigon Military Mission (SMM), literally knew nothing of Diem. When the appointment was announced, he hurriedly researched, drafted, and sent a biography to better inform CIA headquarters. He was surprised to find that Diem was "exceptionally well known" in Vietnam and also a political lightening rod: Ngo Dinh Diem was either 100 percent admired or 100 percent disliked.[25]

It was not until 24 May that Ambassador C. Douglas Dillon in Paris was able to meet Diem, who filled Dillon in on the details. Diem stated he had been summoned by Bao Dai on 14 May and asked to return to Vietnam to form a new cabinet. He went on to state that he had met with Prince Buu to arrange transportation and was informed that Quat in Saigon would be acting prime minister until Diem arrived. Diem had carte blanche to run the government. Ambassador Dillon found Diem's sincerity, honesty, and patriotism refreshing. The VWP was concerned. While he was not America's pawn, Washington's positive reaction to his appointment meant it would take a more active role in the fate of South Vietnam—an undesired outcome.[26]

On 7 July 1954, Diem stepped off the plane. Saigon remained one of the most beautiful cities in Southeast Asia if not the world, but it was also a political inferno. He was not without allies or at least neutrals. The three most important were

The erudite, forceful, and polarizing Ngo Dinh Diem shakes hands with President Dwight D. Eisenhower. Beside Eisenhower is John Foster Dulles. The Vietnamese officer on the stairway is General Tran Van Don, May 1957 (National Archives).

American Ambassador Heath, Colonel Lansdale, and General Paul Ely, the French Commissioner General for Vietnam. Heath proved consistently insightful, decisive, and tactful; Washington could not have hoped for a better diplomat. As to be expected, General Ely, who had been replaced as chief of the French General Staff to take command of French forces in Indochina on 9 June 1954, faithfully looked out for the interests of France. That made him overly sympathetic to Hinh and the sects while prejudging Diem as well-meaning but ineffective even before meeting him. Ely tried to be neutral but often was blind to the bias induced by his loyalties.[27]

That left Ed Lansdale from CIA, a talented and endearing maverick who became Diem's confidant and had a disconcerting knack for being at the right place and time with the needed solution in his hip pocket. Like all covert operators, Lansdale had a cover (in this case an important one): He, along with French Colonel Jean Carbonel, ran the Training Relations and Instruction Mission (TRIM) that jointly trained the VNA. His covert assignment focused on keeping the South Vietnamese government afloat, and Lansdale worked on national security issues, which meant counterinsurgency and pacification. That gave his SMM the primary task of supporting Saigon through political-military assistance, civic actions, psychological operations (PSYOPS), and in the north, covert unconventional warfare directed against the DRV. It now also meant helping Diem. The trio soon became deeply involved in General Hinh's political intrigues.[28]

The new prime minister was not unaware of Hinh's maneuverings and stated in June that he would remove the general, who was a "factious Frenchman," but held back at American urging.[29] Diem heeded the American request as he felt South Vietnam's survival now rested with the United States, but to thwart Hinh, he assumed portfolios of both the minister of interior and defense. (Quat stepped aside after Diem arrived.) He later appointed Le Ngoc Chan, a trusted and capable adherent, as defense minister. Hinh's political ambition was not the only pressing concern; Diem informed Ambassador Heath that his chief concern was a growing popular belief that the U.S. would abandon Vietnam because it failed to help their French ally during the Dien Bien Phu battle. He then laid out a detailed request for American help. In addition to military supplies and monies for defense, he needed public assurance of American support, assistance in governance, and aid in bringing in northern refugees.[30]

The Hinh Mutiny (August–November 1954)

All of that became so many dreams and wishes as General Hinh moved to overthrow the weeks-old Diem government before it could find its footing. By August, the coup plot neared completion but the conspirators had been too brazen—Hinh himself told the Americans of his plan to take power through an alliance with the Hoa Hao and Cao Dai sects along with the Binh Xuyen. Repelled by what they heard, the Americans prepared to act. In late August, Ambassador Heath attended a dinner for the newly arrived French diplomat Jacques Raphael-Leygues. Around the table sat the leading conspirators including Hinh. When talk turned to removing

Diem, Heath threatened to end U.S. support and got them to shelve the plan for the moment. Simultaneously, Heath moved to dissuade General Ely from pushing ahead with a different scheme to replace Diem, but Ely abandoned the half-formed plan of his own accord. Dealing with the betrayals, however, did manage to freeze the Diem government into inaction. Everything now revolved around regime survival—the struggle for power with Hinh.[31]

Diem's first approach was reconciliation. He invited General Hinh to a meeting on 31 August. As Hinh's public complaints, often broadcast on the VNA-controlled radio station in Saigon, dwelled on the weakness of Diem's ministers, Diem asked for list of cabinet members who would placate the general and his specific agenda for improving the government. A bit flummoxed, Hinh was at a loss for words and offered nothing of substance in reply. The meeting ended with Diem being both unimpressed and distrustful of the general and the general unchanged in his drive to seize the government. To help neutralize Hinh, Lansdale assigned SMM officer Larry Sharpe to Hinh's radio station. Sharpe managed to put a stop to anti–American and most anti–Diem broadcasts that had been directed by Hinh and written by French SDECE operative Jean Barré.[32]

On 8 September, Defense Minister Chan became aware of renewed plotting and boldly ordered Hinh's chief conspirators, Colonel Tran Dinh Lan (JGS G-6 for Unconventional Warfare and Hinh's liaison to French intelligence) and Captain Giai (of the JGS G-5 PSYOPS that also ran the troublesome radio station), to his office and placed them under arrest. They in turn declared Chan arrested and, as the guards were under Lan's command, Chan's life was in peril. Only the fortuitous arrival of Colonel Lansdale prevented bloodshed. That VNA general staff officers were brazenly insubordinate to civilian authority was disturbing, but the government now knew the danger had not passed. Two days later Diem formally relieved Hinh of his post and appointed VNA Inspector General Nguyen Van Vy, a Bao Dai loyalist, as his successor. To get him out of the way, Diem also ordered Hinh to France for a "study mission."[33]

That created a firestorm of activity and laid bare the confused power structure in South Vietnam. Hinh rebuffed Diem's order on the grounds that Bao Dai appointed him and only the ex-emperor could relieve him, and he tauntingly added that perhaps he would have Diem resign. Hinh not only could be crude but also vulgar. Beyond threatening to oust Diem, he went further by boasting he then would make Madame Nhu, the wife of Diem's bother, his concubine. Further weakening Diem's position, General Ely opposed the relief and insisted that Diem and Hinh find a way to work together. Finally, General Vy balked at taking the job and departed for France to confer with Bao Dai. Diem was forced to name Colonel Ho Thong Minh as acting chief of staff, who was awakened that night by Chan and informed of his new duties. In the morning, Minh declined the offer, and Diem then appointed Chan. Saigon was in a state of political confusion.[34]

But it was not all bad news for Diem. Washington stood behind him and, equally favorable, the VNA General Staff accepted Chan as Hinh's replacement. At Diem's request, Lansdale bolstered the prime minister's position by reaching out to Colonel Trinh Minh The of the Cao Dai, who lived in the remote forests of

Tay Ninh province. It was a hazardous mission. At Lansdale's side was another of the SMM team, U.S. Navy Lieutenant Joseph J. Redick, whose fluent French, dead-eye marksmanship, and steadiness under pressure made him an invaluable asset. He would be needed as Colonel The was a dangerous enigma. On one hand, he had directed a bloody terrorist bombing campaign in 1952 against the French that left a trail of mangled bodies and ruin across Saigon. On the other, he was a selfless anti-communist patriot and champion of the poor. Lansdale won him over, and in mid–September, Colonel The supplied handpicked soldiers to shore up Diem's guard and pledged the support of his guerrillas officially identified as the VNA's 60th Territorial Regiment. It was a major boost for Diem; Major Lucien Conein, another key member of Lansdale's SMM, favorably compared The's soldiers to the PAVN he had seen in Hanoi. It appeared Hinh's support in the army was not as solid as he claimed. If Hinh calculated that he easily could shoot his way into power and assume control over South Vietnam, he now had reason to pause.[35]

In the ebb and flow of the Hinh mutiny, 13 September 1954 was exceptional. By then Ambassador Heath admitted that, against the odds, Diem had "won this round." Heath turned the tables by telling Ely that Hinh was unfit to lead the VNA.[36] Diem then attempted to resolve the crisis with a proposal that he and Hinh issue public statements of mutual support. Hinh would have nothing to do with it as he too had just received a major boost when Bao Dai let it be known that he intended to replace Diem. Heath immediately pushed Washington to put pressure on the former emperor, but Ambassador Dillon in Paris fought back, arguing that such action would be intervening in South Vietnam's internal affairs. A somewhat chagrinned Heath fired back that the United States was not dealing with a constitutional government but an autocratic dictatorship with power invested in "an absolute monarch"—abdication notwithstanding.[37] The day ended incongruously if peacefully with Diem and Hinh attending a state dinner together.[38]

By mid–September, cracks began to appear in French-American unity over South Vietnam. While Washington remained committed to Diem and saw Hinh as a "tool" of the French, General Ely hinted that Paris was working to get Diem removed. Diem's brother Nhu nicely described the interrelations: "We have a friend who understands us very well but who likes to poke sticks into the spokes of our wheels—France—and another very valued friend who give us a great deal of monetary assistance but who understands nothing about Vietnam—the United States."[39]

There were more negotiations between Diem and Hinh. Diem agreed to remove Chan and replace him with the pro–Hinh General Nguyen Van Xuan. Hinh agreed to leave on a trip abroad but would not give up any of duties or position of authority within the VNA. A CIA assessment gave the edge to Diem in the ongoing struggle, concluding that while lacking a "political machine," Diem possessed significant popular support.[40] The report added that Bao Dai's support was declining due to his prolonged stay in France and lack of an active role in ruling the nation. General Ely also recognized Diem's strength, informing the Americans that if a struggle broke out within the VNA ranks, the odds were with Diem. Futile efforts to put together a compromise dragged on as the break between Washington and Paris over Diem and Hinh became almost unbridgeable.[41]

The crisis peaked anew on 19 September when Binh Xuyen leader Bay Vien returned to Saigon with secret instructions from Bao Dai. Whatever the specifics, it energized Hinh, who broke off negotiations with Diem. He then met with Heath, declaring he was not leaving Vietnam and would come out in open opposition to Diem. The general closed his remarks by predicting that the cabinet would collapse (Hinh had been assured that several ministers were to resign) and the sects would come out in one voice against the prime minister the next day. Bao Dai would then call for Diem's resignation. That combination of blows was sure to drive Diem from office, and Monday 20 September lived up to expectations as a day of reckoning in South Vietnam but not as Hinh, Bay Vien, Bao Dai, and the French hoped.[42]

While his opponents had been busy, so had Diem. He had put together a masterful counterstroke. His team, led by his brother Nhu, had been reaching out to the Cao Dai and Hoa Hao sects since at least August, and those labors were about to pay off with Hoa Hao and Cao Dai opposition to Hinh. The price was steep: 4 cabinet posts for each sect with Hoa Hao Colonel Soai as interior minister. But it was apparent that Diem was as adept at executing a "divide and conquer" strategy as Bao Dai.[43] Several days of frantic meetings ensued, centered on where the Americans stood. Once assured of Washington's support, the two sects went over to Diem. Adding to Diem's momentum, on 21 September Madame Nhu orchestrated a mass demonstration in Saigon against Hinh and his Binh Xuyen backers who had been harassing indigent refugees from the north. The French threw in the towel. Bao Dai also blinked and sent a clarifying telegram that merely proposed that if Diem chose to resign, he would accept the decision. Diem sent a polite "no" and regretted that Bao Dai may have been "badly informed regarding the 'complexity of the situation'" in South Vietnam.[44]

On 1 October, Bao Dai stirred the hornet's nest again by urging Diem to reshuffle his cabinet to include bringing in pro–Hinh General Xuan and giving posts to Bay Vien and other Hinh supporters. Diem temporized, and having had enough, Ambassador Heath departed for France for a face-to-face meeting with Bao Dai. The gambit worked, and on 7 October, Bao Dai instructed Hinh and the Binh Xuyen to cooperate with Diem. Hinh threatened another coup, this time on 10 October, but nothing came of it; the General's influence was on the wane. A shameless Bay Vien met with Diem on 11 October and demanded the interior ministry for his gang—a move that would have put South Vietnam on a path to kleptocracy. Diem took no action, and the impasse continued for the next two weeks until the Americans took steps to end the Hinh mutiny once and for all. As President Eisenhower put it, it was time to "get rough with the French."[45]

On 23 October, Heath released a letter from Eisenhower giving Diem his full backing. Then on 1 November, Eisenhower announced that General J. Lawton Collins was going to Vietnam for an indeterminate period as his special representative and would replace Heath. The arrival of Heath's announced replacement, Ambassador Julian F. Harrington, was postponed indefinitely. While the moves left the door open to retaining Hinh, France's goal of replacing Diem was crippled. That Paris was unhappy was made obvious to American diplomats visiting the Quai d'Orsay, as was the fact that Paris had no choice but to accede to Washington's wishes. It was not just the VNA that was dependent on American aid; the Americans also were underwriting the cost of the 150,000 French troops in Indochina, and as Diem realized, the solvency of the South Vietnamese government as well. Hinh planned a last-ditch coup for 26 October, but behind the scenes Lansdale's SMM thwarted the attempt.[46]

The disintegration of Hinh's 26 October mutiny accelerated his eclipse, although the general remained troublesome to the end. The truth was that none of Hinh's backers could risk driving Washington away. Bao Dai understood, which explained his about face with Dillon when, in early November, he promised to give the Diem government his full support. Collins arrived in Saigon on 8 November. Paris did not see him as a welcome addition and to make their intentions known, no one from the French Army, to include Ely, met Collins on his arrival in Saigon. Hurt feelings aside, two days later Bao Dai ordered General Hinh to France. He boarded his flight for Paris on 19 November, never to return to Vietnam, and several of his co-plotters left shortly afterwards. Paris finally admitted to Washington that they had pushed Hinh to overthrow Diem—something General Ely had let slip in September. To his credit, Diem did not purge the army; even loyalists like Hinh's chief of staff, Colonel Tran Van Don, kept his rank and position. Ten days later, Bao Dai relived Hinh of his official duties. General Le Van Ty, another former–career French Army officer but also a selfless Vietnamese nationalist, took over.[47]

In the days before Hinh's departure, Diem began to pivot to the internal communist threat and, in hopes of unifying the nation, made a public address on the issue. Diem also was able to stabilize the army chain of command when Colonel Ho Thong Minh finally became defense minister. Minh was a good compromise candidate recognized for his competence while being a Bao Dai sympathizer. Things in South Vietnam remained relatively calm into December 1954 and through the 1955 Tet New Year celebrations.

The peaceful holidays belied the true state of affairs in Saigon. While Hinh was gone, the sect problem had not disappeared, nor had Bao Dai's unpredictable penchant to undermine his own government. Diem also had to deal with dubious civil servants. Kieu Cong Cung, a former Viet Minh commander who rallied to Saigon, scandalized his fellow bureaucrats by wearing a farmer's ba ba instead of a suit. He was disgusted with what he saw: "They were an arrogant, slow-moving, undisciplined lot of paper pushers, with no political convictions and interested only in their own salaries."[48] Many were ridiculed as "lycée mandarins," and those that had served the French loyally were referred to derisively as "houseboys."[49] Finally, France still played an outsized role as the Expeditionary Corps (CEFEO) overshadowed the VNA and remaining French bureaucrats dominated governmental ministries.[50]

Lansdale described the difficulty. In 1954, the French had decided, "they would move out almost the entire government leadership structure, not only in Saigon but out in the provinces" and that left profound problems within the Vietnamese bureaucracy.[51] With Cochinchina (Nam Bo) ruled directly by France, decision-making authority had rested with the French. Vietnamese officials in Saigon served as subordinates and had to pass muster as French loyalists. Concurrently, Bao Dai's government nominally ruled the rest of Vietnam from Hue with an administration filled with his adherents who, after partition, had departed for Saigon to lead the government. Finally, there were regrouping Vietnamese bureaucrats from Hanoi who judged themselves superior, as France had used Hanoi as Indochina's capital and only the most qualified served there. Those competing loyalties, ambitions, and senses of importance ate away at Diem's authority within the government, and the French exploited the situation.[52]

The year ended with some in Washington ruefully reflecting on its relationship with Paris over Vietnam. Undersecretary of State Robert Murphy confided to Ambassador Tran Van Chuong that the French had acted "to support only puppet governments and sabotage any national government."[53] To a degree Murphy was right, but French motives were not ignoble; they supported loyal sect allies and naturally sided with pro–French factions. Paris and Washington attempted to get along. One temporary casualty was Madame Nhu (Ambassador Chuong's daughter) who, in retaliation for leading the 21 September anti–Hinh protests, was sent to a convent in Hong Kong at French and American urging. If Madame Nhu had been a man, she would have avoided punishment, but she took it in stride, enjoying the company of the nuns and schoolchildren while learning English. She was allowed to return to Saigon in the spring of 1955.[54]

Although it failed, the Hinh mutiny damaged governance in South Vietnam. Murphy addressed the mutiny with Chuong, depressingly noting, "The rebellion of General Hinh, who, encouraged and supported by almost all the French in Indochina, paralyzed the Vietnamese government for nearly three months at one of the most critical periods in its history."[55] Ambassador Heath precisely summed it up that September: the "principle of supremacy of civil authority" had been attacked.[56] The result was tragic, and Hinh's offenses went beyond insubordination. Through faithless and disobedient actions carried out in the public arena and by recruiting active-duty officers into a clandestine conspiracy—the planning of a coup—he corrupted the officer corps at its creation.

In July the Americans had tried to get Hinh to move VNA troops into areas being vacated by the PAVN regroupees. Instead of seizing the opportunity to establish government control over these areas, the general was too consumed with his drive for power to issue the orders. Making matters worse, Hinh and his conspirators, such as Colonel Tranh Dinh Lan, departed for France without being held responsible for their crimes. It was more than a terrible precedent; within weeks of its creation, Hinh cracked South Vietnam's foundation of the civil-military state ruled by law. Had the first VNA chief of staff embraced the loyal subordination of the military to civilian authority and focused on preparing the VNA to fight the communists, the history of South Vietnam might have been very different.[57]

The effects on Diem were nearly as bad. He learned that appointing competent and dedicated ministers made them immediate targets for political destruction, as in the case of Defense Minister Le Ngoc Chan. He found political survival in Saigon to be a twisted Machiavellian sport that did little to advance national unity or social progress. The game with the sects was the perfect example. To foil the September coup, he had to strip away the Cao Dai and Hoa Hao from Hinh and move them into his camp. The price was removing eight capable ministers and replacing them with sect partisans. Although some did become earnest officials who put country before other interests, several proved to be unqualified and inept. Diem also had gone out of his way to offend Bay Vien, putting him on a collision course with the Binh Xuyen. The lesson was that no one in Saigon could be trusted, as all had their own agendas. Perhaps most damaging, Diem soon found himself having to oversee the functions of several of the sect ministries, exacerbating one of his prime weaknesses: the tendency to over-manage and not delegate responsibilities.[58]

The future did not look bright, but there were glimmers of hope. The 900,000 refugees from the north were assimilating, and the war-damaged economy was coming back to life. From a security standpoint, it was clear by December that the U.S. Military Assistance Advisory Group (MAAG) under General John W. O'Daniel (whom Lansdale's SMM purportedly reported to) would assume the VNA training and assistance mission from the French. That meant a significant increase in funding and resources for the SOV's armed forces.

In light of that and following a visit to formerly Viet Minh–held territory in the Mekong Delta, on 31 December 1954 Diem issued his National Security Action [Pacification] Directive. It was South Vietnam's first plan to integrate both military and civic actions aimed at gaining popular support in areas under communist control or pressure. The directive's first priority was to identify "national security" zones where the VWP and stay-behind PAVN cadres exercised considerable control (especially the regroupment areas in the Mekong Delta and Quang Ngai and Binh Dinh provinces in coastal central South Vietnam). They required intervention from the Saigon government and were to remain under martial law until brought under control. Next came the "transition" zones where there was a measurable VWP presence. They ran under joint civil-military authority until fully pacified. Finally there were the secure or "civil" zones that underwent the direct process of returning to peace.[59]

The Sect Rebellion

The early months of 1955 were marked by solid gains for the Saigon government. On 1 January 1955, the French passed to Diem control over sect stipends and flow of military supplies, giving Diem a powerful tool. It was a two-edged sword; he gained greater leverage over the sects but would have to look to the Americans for the money and materials to buy their uneven loyalty. Even that was a short-term solution as the ultimate and more contentious goal was to disarm the groups, leaving the VNA standing as the sole army in South Vietnam. On a positive note, the JGS acted on Diem's National Security Action Directive, and on 8 February the VNA launched its first pacification operation in the VWP stronghold of Ca Mau in the southernmost Mekong Delta.[60]

A few days later, on 14 February, French VNA trainers were out, and General O'Daniel's MAAG assumed sole responsibility for training and equipping the army.

Work on a land reform program and elections for a national assembly also showed signs of progress. All in all, they were small successes but successes nonetheless, and in recognition of his "steady if undramatic progress," Diem earned a vote of confidence from Secretary of State Dulles as the Americans further distanced themselves from Bao Dai. After that, things became dangerously muddled.[61]

Diem's first major thrust in 1955 was going on the political offensive against the Binh Xuyen. On 15 January, Bay Vien's French-approved gambling and other concessions lapsed, and Diem refused to renew them, resulting in the shuttering of the Grande Monde and other casinos. His hard line resonated in South Vietnam, and as the U.S. embassy noted, and the CIA had earlier, Diem's popularity was on the rise. Bey Vien responded by hiring more fighters, and a new Binh Xuyen headquarters went up near the Y Bridge south of Cholon, where the l'Arroyo Chinois and the Canal de Derivation converged (see Map 1). The two waterways served as a dividing line between the city center along with Cholon (the heart of Binh Xuyen controlled areas) and southern Saigon (another Binh Xuyen controlled area). Later, Diem again showed his hand when he demanded that French forces evacuate Saigon and transfer control of the VNA to the government by 15 February. Diem wanted to crush Bay Vien without French interference, but the French Army did not leave.[62]

Concurrently, the Saigon government repeatedly and with some success tried to place the sects under their control by whittling away at their unity; it was a concerted application of the "divide and conquer" methods used to undermine the Hinh mutiny. As in 1954, Diem was unmovable in his opposition to the Binh Xuyen, and this created a two-track policy. While Diem worked with all three groups to get military leaders to peel off, rally to Saigon, and join the VNA (as in the case of Cao Dai General The), when it came to a peace settlement, the government only worked with the Cao Dai and Hoa Hao.

If Prime Minister Ngo Dinh Diem was under any illusions that Bay Vien would knuckle under to the pressure and the tough times were behind him after Hinh's retirement to France, he was disabused of that notion by late February. Rufus Phillips, an Ivy League-educated Army paratrooper and CIA paramilitary officer working for Lansdale, described Binh Xuyen-controlled Saigon as a "snake pit."[63] Diem's aggressive anti–Binh Xuyen policies had brought matters to a head, and a collision with the criminal confederation over control of the city was now unavoidable.

The Battle for Saigon—The Prelude

By early February, Bay Vien began to mass his "shock" public security troops in Saigon. They concentrated around their Sûreté headquarters on Rue Catinat near Saigon's Notre Dame Cathedral and menaced National Police stations still loyal to the government. Soon the Binh Xuyen controlled 21 police stations in Saigon and Cholon. By mid-month, rumors abounded that the sects were forming an alliance. It proved true with the 1 March announcement in Tay Ninh by Cao Dai leader Pham

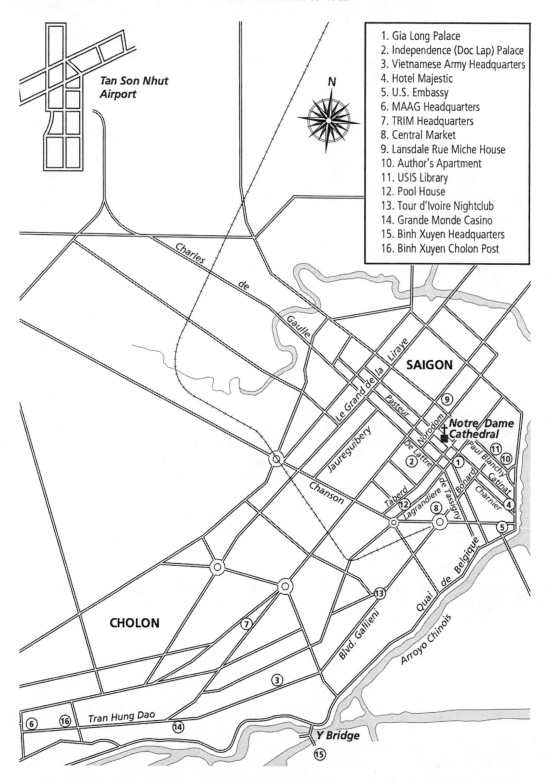

1. Gia Long Palace
2. Independence (Doc Lap) Palace
3. Vietnamese Army Headquarters
4. Hotel Majestic
5. U.S. Embassy
6. MAAG Headquarters
7. TRIM Headquarters
8. Central Market
9. Lansdale Rue Miche House
10. Author's Apartment
11. USIS Library
12. Pool House
13. Tour d'Ivoire Nightclub
14. Grande Monde Casino
15. Binh Xuyen Headquarters
16. Binh Xuyen Cholon Post

Map 1. Saigon, 1955–1956 (not to scale; detail reprinted with permission from Rufus Phillip's *Why Vietnam Matters*, U.S. Naval Institute Press).

Cong Tac that the three sects had formed a "united front" opposing Diem. Later that week, Bay Vien hosted a meeting to plot Diem's overthrow.

Bao Dai was up to his old games. At the meeting was none other than Nguyen De, who had arrived from France unnoticed. Secretly speaking for Bao Dai (Ung An, a member of one of the royal families, was Bao Dai's official representative in Saigon), he encouraged the plotters and promised the ex-emperor's support. Their path to power would begin with an ultimatum demanding that Diem appoint united front adherents to critical ministries while shuffling Diem off into a figurehead position. If he refused, they first would threaten the use of force, and if worse came to worst, force would be used. To accomplish that, they formed a combined sect army under Hoa Hao General Ba Cut, and as an enticement, sect commanders were promised promotions after victory was gained.[64]

March witnessed continuing plotting and political moves and countermoves by the Diem government and the three sects' united front as the security situation in Saigon deteriorated. A good part of the problem was the crooked incompetence of the Sûreté National Police under the Binh Xuyen. It went without saying that Chief Sang was getting rich through corruption; not only was police bribery the rule of the day, but criminals operated without fear as large numbers of their records went missing under Sang's watch. And friction was building between the Binh Xuyen and VNA. Diem went so far as to request a VNA tank unit be sent to the city and deployed paratroopers to backup the loyal police. Then there were the palace intrigues. At the same time the military tensions were growing, Defense Minister Ho Thoung Minh went behind the back of Diem to expand his authority within the cabinet (probably at Bao Dai's urging) while General Le Van Ty—Hinh's replacement—became the object of a rumor campaign claiming that Diem planned to fire him. To help manage the problems, Diem decided to recall Nguyen Ngoc Tho, the ambassador to Japan, who had prior experience with the sects.[65]

Diem continued to fight back. In February he stated he wanted Bao Dai gone as head of state, giving both Collins and Ely a new political headache. He further balked at taking former Defense Minister Phan Huy Quat into his cabinet because he deemed Quat's first loyalty was to his Dai Viet Party, which was fractured, incapable of playing a helpful political role, and opposed Diem (the party had been running an anti–Catholic propaganda campaign against him). The Dai Viet attack displayed decades old anti–Catholic prejudice amongst the nationalists. It also was unfounded. The combined number of Cao Dai and Hoa Hao religionists roughly equaled that of the Catholics in South Vietnam, yet the two sects held eight cabinet seats while Foreign Minister Tran Van Do was the only Catholic besides Diem holding a senior government post.[66]

Diem was not General Collins' only problem as Bao Dai proved even more adept at creating divisions and political chaos. Collins continued to work on Diem's behalf even if that meant crossing General Ely, as happened in late February when Collins pushed Bao Dai to revoke his decree giving Bay Vien control over the Sûreté. He tried to keep the former emperor in check, going so far as to order Ung An to inform Bao Dai that the United States might cutoff aid in the event of a coup. Collins was angered that Bao Dai had altered and then disseminated President Eisenhower's message of support for the Diem government by adding a sentence making it falsely read as a letter of support for the former emperor. By mid-month, Collins was aware of the broad details of the coup that Bao Dai was actively abetting. It was time to act. Collins teamed with Lansdale to convince General Nguyen Thanh Phoung, the Cao Dai military commander, to leave the united front and rally to Diem. It succeeded, and the defection left Cao Dai leader Pham Cong Tac as head of the sect united front but without his army.[67]

Undeterred, front leaders pushed ahead, and on 22 March presented their ultimatum to Diem. He was given five days to capitulate. Collins then met with the front's Binh Xuyen and Hoa Hao military commanders and came away less than impressed, describing them as "alarmingly stupid ... in most instances their accusations are without foundation and arguments without logic."[68] In dealing with the ultimatum, Collins had one overarching concern: preventing violence that General Ely had convinced him would trigger a destructive and possibly fatal civil war.[69]

The ties between Ely and Collins went beyond shared 1944 battle experience in northern France. The two recently had served as general officers with the North Atlantic Treaty Organization (NATO) and shared a weakness of having no prior Vietnam experience (Ely had not served in the 1946–1954 War). Importantly, Collins saw the situation in Saigon not just through a Cold War but a Eurocentric lens where France played a vital role in the defense of Western Europe. Collins would go to great lengths to compromise with Ely and not alienate France. But as Collins' arrival snub indicated, their superiors at home did not share their desire for cooperation when it came to Vietnam.[70]

Paris and Washington were selling incompatible narratives. The French held the sects' united front to be an authentic revolutionary movement that, in alliance with Bao Dai, represented the future for South Vietnam, while Diem was seen as politically isolated and holding no sway within the VNA—which, the French added, did not matter as the sect armies were superior to VNA forces in Saigon. The Americans saw the united front as illegitimate usurpers whose threats of violence were unacceptable and deemed the VNA loyal, in good morale, and superior to the sect forces. The split between France and the United States over South Vietnam was open and getting worse.[71]

Diem too was unyielding when he called for talks with the sect leaders on 25 March. His press secretary announced prior to the meeting, "It is up to the sects to show some humility and take the first step, or we shall destroy them, beginning with that of Bay Vien."[72] The conference went nowhere, and the eight Hoa Hao and Cao Dai cabinet ministers appointed at the height of the 1954 Hinh mutiny resigned en bloc the next day. Diem was unperturbed and escalated the crisis with the Binh Xuyen by proposing to remove Sûreté chief Sang and replace him with one of Diem's allies, Colonel Nguyen Ngoc Le. When Defense Minister Minh heard of the move, and believing the French that the VNA was not behind Diem, he resigned in protest.[73]

Upon hearing of Diem's plans, Vien acted. During the night of 29–30 March, he sent a message by having his public security green berets conduct a series of coordinated attacks on the paratroopers at the Saigon National Police HQ. Later that night, from the Binh Xuyen headquarters at the Y-Bridge south of Cholon, they mortared Norodom Palace. Provocatively named by France for a Cambodian king, it was the French high commissioner's former residence and served as Diem's seat of power. Casualties were light but not insignificant, estimated at ten killed and 50 wounded. The Binh Xuyen additionally assaulted Cholon's 4th District (Arrondissement) police headquarters (also defended by paratroopers) and the VNA JGS Headquarters; another five were killed and 21 wounded.[74]

The route connecting the hot spots was the broad, tree-lined Boulevard Gallieni that joined Saigon's city center with Cholon and paralleled the l'Arroyo Chinois, the Binh Xuyen's waterway for conducting its criminal activities. Diem later renamed Boulevard Gallieni after 13th-century Prince Tran Hung Dao who battled the Mongols. The boulevard and its side streets became the center of action as the JGS Headquarters complex sat on its north side and housed hundreds of soldiers. Less than a kilometer further down the road on the south side stood the closed Grande Monde Casino; the 4th District police station sat in between, making the area all the more volatile.[75]

Senior American opinion in Saigon was divided over how to react. Collins was dismayed, seeing Minh's resignation and the subsequent violence as an example of Diem's inability to compromise, while Lansdale saw Diem as a calm and determined leader in the face of adversity. The Americans also found the united front not that united after all. The other groups were angry with the Binh Xuyen for starting the fighting. The Cao Dai troops had already quit the front while the Hoa Hao accused Bay Vien of forcing them into a war. That the Hoa Hao held when the Cao Dai fragmented could be explained in part by their intertwined illicit bonds with the Binh Xuyen. In Hoa Hao controlled areas, they too ran protection and gambling rackets along with a corrupt monopoly over rice purchasing and milling, and Hoa Hao tax collections were nothing short of extortion. The French alone were united and had one answer to all their problems: Diem. To stop the fighting, French forces moved to occupy key crossroads and city sectors. General Ely argued it was to keep the peace, but some Americans and Vietnamese concluded the actions were designed to protect the Binh Xuyen from VNA reprisals.[76]

The crisis deepened and generally to the united front's advantage, but Bay Vien miscalculated in attacking the VNA. First, while initially caught by surprise, the VNA successfully fought off the assaults. Second, the gang violently besmirched the honor of the army and that created a "blood debt" to be avenged.[77] The March assaults had gained the Binh Xuyen a powerful enemy now eager for battle. VNA Chief of Staff General Ty made his intent clear: The army had been attacked and must respond. He then sent more troops into the city and put artillery units on alert. Washington rallied to Diem. Secretary of State Dulles informed Paris that treating the united front as equal to the official government was unacceptable. Collins informed Dulles that he felt the crisis crippled Diem. The sudden loss of the sect cabinet members had forced him to rely almost entirely on his brothers, what Collins' termed "government by family."[78]

April continued with a gloomy outlook for the Diem government. General Ely declared his full opposition, and General Collins wavered. When Ely proposed a new government, one formed by Bao Dai with Binh Xuyen ministers, Washington made it clear they would have no part of it. On 4 April, Dulles firmly if politely instructed Collins to support Diem. Collins responded, telling Ely that the Binh Xuyen "challenge must be met head on sooner or later and Diem must have freedom of action."[79] Put another way, Collins suggested but did not tell the French to rein in their ally.

A CIA assessment made the same day explained the American position: the sect armies were a French creation "who developed and nurtured them in the course of applying 'divide and rule' policy in Indochina for many years," whereas Diem was trying to "establish the independent character of his government and thus to rally nationalist support."[80] A mid–April VNA-Binh Xuyen skirmish turned ugly, and later disemboweled bodies of captured VNA soldiers were discovered. It was classic Binh Xuyen dirty war, only now the communists were not the targets. The VNA responded. In the intervening weeks, both sides waged a low-level war characterized by drive-by shootings, kidnappings, and assassinations. Dulles saw it as cripplingly destabilizing: "If Diem's authority is defied and immobilized then no government will be able to operate in Vietnam."[81]

To further stir dissension, Bao Dai publicly blamed the VNA for the various attacks, a stunning act of betrayal by their titular commander-in-chief. National leadership splintered, and adding to the pressure, the French remained adamant that Diem must go, while admitting they had no one to take his place. On the lack of successor, the Americans agreed. Collins broached to Diem three candidates not as successors but to share power: Quat, Tran Van Do, and Nguyen Van Thoai. Diem naturally found fault with all. He saw Quat as a weak compromiser, and the sects opposed him for having tried to take away their armies when defense minister. Diem found Do as one who shrank from confrontation and had no plan on how to govern, while Thoai was disinterested and unwilling. After the discussion, Collins informed Dulles, "I see no alterative to the early replacement of Diem."[82] The CIA concurred.[83]

There was, however, some good news for Diem when the top Cao Dao generals reaffirmed their support, but perhaps the most important new factor was a shift in the balance of military power in Diem's favor. Bay Vien still had two public security battalions in Saigon backed up by his main force that had grown to ten battalions in and around Cholon. Bay Vien also counted on four additional battalions led by Binh Xuyen chief of staff Colonel Thai Hoang Minh at Go Cong, 30 kilometers south of the city. While it seemed impressive, the battalions were small and lightly armed; Bay Vien's total forces numbered at most 7,000 troops. As a last reserve, there were four Hoa Hao battalions that could advance on Saigon.[84]

The VNA now had six infantry battalions in Saigon and seven more nearby (most at the Quang Trung Training Center no. 1, located 15 kilometers northwest of Saigon), as well as supporting units to include armored reconnaissance companies and artillery and mortar batteries. The VNA had over 10,000 soldiers at their disposal, some just regrouped from Tonkin (the 154th Regiment). They had one more important advantage: four battalions were combat-hardened soldiers of the Paratroop Group. Diem also held an ace in the hole: Binh Xuyen Colonel Thai Hoang

Minh let it be known that if fighting erupted, he would abandon Bay Vien, rally to Diem, and bring over his four battalions.[85]

The united front remained confident. They and Ely dismissed the VNA's fighting abilities and in any event felt the army would not stand by Diem. The sect united front leadership proceeded with their plans, and by mid–April everything was in place for a second go at a sect-led coup. If what Ely and the united front said was true, then Diem's rule was over as the new plan was better than that of March and would overwhelm the feeble Ngo Dinh Diem regime they assumed they faced.

As in March, the Binh Xuyen would start the fight, and as they advanced, Ba Cut's forces would reinforce if needed, which was not expected. To neutralize if not paralyze Diem, Ely would demand that Diem not call out the army—ideally with Collins' concurrence (who Ely had again convinced to oppose Diem). Politically, Bao Dai would deliver the deathblow with orders of Diem's relief as prime minister and for his immediate departure to France. Finally, Bao Dai's arch-loyalist, General Vy, with two just-arrived battalions of imperial guards from Dalat, would march on the Norodom Palace to take command of both the VNA and government. If it went as planned, it would all be over in one or two days with little or no bloodshed.[86]

Collins' wavering was troublesome. One possible reason was raised by the PAVN's best spy in Saigon, Pham Xuan An, who discovered that a French Deuxième Bureau agent was a Collins confidant and fed him a steady diet of anti–Diem disinformation. Another could be gleaned from Collins' use of the condescending word "experiment" to define the Diem government.[87] French Minister for the Associated States of Cambodia, Laos, and South Vietnam, Guy La Chambre, used the term with General Ely and Ambassador Heath in October 1954 and both subsequently adopted it. So did Bao Dai, who used it to disparage Diem (although the French long referred to his rule as an experiment as well). It was spoken as if engaged in some baccalaureate political science project where leaders such as Diem were tools to be used or discarded at will. Collins cavalierly picked up the quip until Dulles took offense. After a dressing down, the term fell into disuse amongst the Americans. Words had meaning; a ruling government was not an experiment.[88]

Washington was sufficiently unsettled by affairs in Saigon to order General Collins back to Washington for face-to-face consultations, and he departed on 20 April. The general was convinced that a coalition government shaped by General Ely and himself was the solution but they could not agree on a way forward. To Collins, the interests of France were of greater strategic importance than those of a rump nation called the State of Vietnam, but Ely's sect proposal meant the end of any pathway toward representative democracy. And Ely's coalition idea also gave significant governmental power to a criminal organization, one that had no political base and represented a tiny fraction of the South Vietnamese people.[89]

Those proposals did violence to any positive connation of the word coalition. It was beyond realpolitik—just more of Saigon's Machiavellian machinations, and Collins never agreed. In the same frame of mind, Dulles neutered the whole coalition game by putting six pointed questions to Paris about what a post–Diem government would look like. After a delay, the Quai d'Orsay offered in the way of response little more than vague phrases and an unassuring rehash of stale tried-and-failed options. Dulles was unmoved, and the scheme was put off for the moment.[90]

On that Collins and Dulles agreed, but Dulles went further. He was still in the Diem camp; on the same day Collins left for Washington, Dulles informed the embassies in Paris and Saigon, "No one can survive without wholehearted backing," and Washington expected support for Diem.[91] Chargé Randolph A. Kidder, who heeded the admonition, took over from Collins in his absence. Kidder's loyalty would be sorely tested six days later when Diem carried out his March threat and issued a decree relieving Sang as head of the Sûreté. Sang scoffed and declared only Bao Dai exercised authority over him. Diem took no further action, but the tension in Saigon was palpable.[92]

Back in Washington, Collins, after overcoming the opposition of Dulles and others, convinced President Eisenhower to approach Paris to find an effective way to replace Diem. The idea, half-hearted at best, was overcome by events. Nguyen De was back in Paris pushing for Diem's removal and in communication with an unreceptive American embassy that urged all parties to restrain from further violence. De alarmingly replied that Bao Dai concluded the situation was "becoming so desperate that we must take action by tomorrow evening"—late in the evening of 28 April in Saigon.[93]

3

The 1955 Battle for Saigon and Diem Consolidates Power

Bao Dai's estimate was off as the first reports of fighting began circulating around Saigon earlier, at midday on 28 April. Renewed skirmishing began in Cholon near the Petrus Ky School being used as a Binh Xuyen barracks and a short walk around the corner from the JGS Headquarters. By 11:00 a.m. the VNA escalated the fight by directing mortar fire at Binh Xuyen strongholds to include their headquarters near the Y Bridge. As the battle intensified shortly after noon, the shelling wounded several French soldiers guarding the bridge. The Binh Xuyen retaliated by shelling the Norodom Palace at 1:15 p.m. with the objective to kill Diem. Intermittent shelling continued. Diem then ordered the VNA to respond in strength, and fighting raged throughout the afternoon.[1]

The battleground was only slightly expanded from the March skirmishing as it now extended south of Cholon. But in terms of scope and intensity, the Saigon fighting was on an unsurpassed level, even exceeding anything that had happened during the War of Resistance. General Ely had to be credited for allowing the Vietnamese to determine the battle's outcome. With a garrison of 30,000 French troops, he could have intervened on behalf of the sects but did not. Instead, he protected the international population and worked to contain the fighting to parts of the city center to include Diem's headquarters at the Norodom Palace, the Binh Xuyen areas of Cholon, and to its immediate south below the Arroyo Chinois and Canal de Derivation. That did not mean the French Army played no role; rogue elements assisted the sects, soldiers who Bernard Fall considered precursors to the Secret Army Organization that later attempted to overthrow the French government in 1961, but in 1955 they aimed to overthrow Diem. By midafternoon, VNA artillery units joined the fray after setting up their guns in the Tao Dan Gardens just south of the palace. While machine gun fire could be heard nearby, the real fighting took place along Boulevard Gallieni and Cholon.[2]

The boulevard had been built at the turn of the century to provide a needed route to connect Cholon with Saigon. By the 1950s, there was no break between the two cities. The length of the thoroughfare consisted of shaded sidewalks lined with homes, apartments, shops, bistros, bars, and other businesses. The street also was home to Saigon's favorite movie house, the Majestic. Behind the street-front buildings was a dense maze of storage sheds and warehouses. Most common of all were domiciles that on the south side ran right up to Arroyo Chinois, with its fleets of sampans nestled so close together that it was possible to cross the arroyo by walking from gangplank to gangplank to the other bank.

When the fighting erupted on 28 April, those areas became a living hell. Gunfire, grenades, and mortar shells sparked any number of fires, and billowing clouds of black smoke began to fill the city's sky. Jeep and truckloads of VNA soldiers, mainly paratroopers, poured into the battleground to take on the Binh Xuyen soldiers and a short while later were joined by the armored reconnaissance companies. Soon raging fires consumed hundreds of structures as the frightened residents sought to avoid both shot and flame to escape the battle.[3]

A sharp fight broke out at the 4th District police station as the Binh Xuyen attempted to clear Cholon of VNA troops. It was a telling clash. The surrounded police backed up by one company of paratroopers from Do Cao Tri's 6th Paratroop Battalion repelled repeated assaults. Having had enough, the outnumbered paratroopers massed and charged into the Binh Xuyen ranks. Taken by surprise, the Binh Xuyen battalion broke and ran, leaving a trail of green berets on the street. Many did not stop there but stripped off their uniforms and deserted. The superiority of the VNA now was beyond doubt. Similar attempts to knock out the JGS Headquarters failed. The tide of battle turned. By late afternoon, the VNA was on the offensive. Leading the effort were four officers. Overall command was held by Chief of Staff General Ty supported by Colonel Tran Van Don, with the fighting directed by Colonels Duong Van "Big" Minh (Saigon Military District commander) and Tran Van "Little" Minh (commander of Military Region I).[4]

All of this was unknown to the Americans, who were holed up in the embassy, drawing on second hand reports and relying heavily on General Ely's take on events. Predictably, it painted a bleak picture of Diem and the VNA. Rashly, they sent a cable to Washington reflecting those views. Colonel Lansdale, who had been monitoring the fighting in the streets firsthand, arrived bearing contradictory information. He asked and was given permission to send his own cable to Washington. When it arrived, CIA headquarters shot back, directing Lansdale to file a full report by the morning (Washington time) to be presented at a high-level briefing with the president that included his argument to support Diem. Bolstering Lansdale was a similar report by the military attaché who also had ventured out into the fighting. Finally, General O'Daniel, whose MAAG compound was in Cholon, voiced his confidence that the VNA would make short work of the Binh Xuyen. General Ely did not make it easy for the VNA when he refused access to French Army ammunition dumps. To keep up the fight, the VNA had to ship munitions by air from Ban Me Thuot, 350 kilometers away.[5]

The Cholon battling continued into the night, roiling intensely around the Grande Monde Casino. In darkness the Binh Xuyen defense finally broke, and the unseemly landmark brightly burned to the ground, as had the Majestic Theater earlier. With the battle going against the Binh Xuyen, that evening General Ely, with Collins' concurrence, ordered French forces to try to enforce an immediate in-place ceasefire. French tanks blocked additional VNA troops from moving into Cholon, but it did not work. The VNA kept fighting, and by the morning of 29 April, its sweeping attack across Cholon from east to west gained momentum. The soldiers reached the MAAG compound at the town's western end before noon. The great Binh Xuyen stronghold fell into government hands. By this time both sides were exhausted and in need of resupply and rest. Bolstering the VNA, General The's 60th Regiment arrived later that day and entered the battle lines.[6]

On 1 May, the fighting shifted into a two-pronged VNA attack to the south. Along one prong, the paratroopers in Cholon began to force the Arroyo Chinois and Canal de Derivation to reach the Binh Xuyen headquarters near the Y-Bridge. During that fighting, most of the nearby Khanh Hoi district also burned to the ground, but the VNA made little progress. The Khanh Hoi fire was the last major conflagration. Over one square mile of Saigon had been devastated, with any trace of the homes or shops reduced to piles of cinders. The human cost was terrible, leaving several hundred civilians dead, another thousand injured, and 10,000 homeless. A day later, Binh Xuyen Chief of Staff Colonel Thai Hoang Minh rallied to Diem as promised, but his plan had been uncovered. Bay Vien lost his four battalions but most failed to make it to VNA lines, and Colonel Minh and his wife were arrested by the Binh Xuyen and never seen alive again. General Collins returned on 2 May just as the battle peaked.[7]

The next day and four kilometers to the east of the paratroopers, the second VNA prong under General The's battalions pushed south, intent on crossing the arroyo and canal waterways with the Saigon River on their left flank. If that met with success, his battalions could pivot northwest (right) and converge on Bay Vien's Y-Bridge headquarters. The's 60th Regiment quickly crossed the arroyo at its confluence with the Saigon River and reached the canal where the Binh Xuyen resisted fiercely at the Tan Thuan Bridge. Faced with heavy fire and the employment of Binh Xuyen gunboats acquired earlier from the French, The's battalions could not take the bridge. After regrouping and attacking again that evening, The was killed in action (some claimed assassinated by the French). The death of The, who first had stood with Diem when Hinh was most dangerous, deeply affected the prime minister, who openly wept when he heard the news, but the sacrifice was not in vain. Before the sun set the bridge was taken, and the defeated Binh Xuyen began to flee the city. The battle for Saigon had decisively turned toward Diem and the army.[8]

Meanwhile in the government center, a more chaotic if less violent struggle to decide who would rule South Vietnam had been underway for several days. To coincide with the opening battle on 28 April, Bao Dai moved to gain the upper hand in the political struggle by firing Diem. A day later, a hastily-formed pro–Diem congress in Saigon established the National Revolutionary Movement, and at General The's urging, countered by voting to remove Bao Dai from office. As the fight for Saigon raged, an uneasy political stalemate ensued until 2 May when pro–Bao Dai General Vy entered the palace and demanded that Diem step down. Unfortunately for Vy, neither Diem nor the VNA commanders had any interest in his (or Bao Dai's) wants or desires.[9]

Major Huynh Van Cao, commander of the presidential guard, stood steadfastly by Diem. At that point, General The threatened to place Vy under arrest. To defuse the situation, Tri and his paratroopers guaranteed Vy's safe departure from the palace but nothing else. The VNA officers had crossed the Rubicon and were not about to look back. Realizing he had backed a lost cause and faced possible court martial, General Vy quietly slipped from the scene and returned to France. The struggle was over. Diem and the VNA had won the Battle of Saigon, but the Hoa Hao and surviving Bay Vien still stood in opposition elsewhere. For his service, Do Cao Tri was promoted to colonel and given command of the Paratroop Group.[10]

There was one last twist to the rogue French Army officers' intrigues in 1955. During the battle, Americans began to be targeted by bombings, and while no one was hurt, that outcome was more luck than intent. The SMM decided to take action, and Conein uncovered who was behind it: none other than Colonel Carbonel, Landsale's TRIM counterpart. One evening Conein, with help from his fiancée, Elyette Brochot, assembled a number of plastic explosive bombs and then drove around Saigon, throwing them at the residences of the involved French officers to include Carbonel's. It had a happy ending. No one was hurt, the targeting of Americans stopped, and Conein and Brochet married.[11]

Aftermath: The End of the Sect Armies

When the Hoa Hao refused to rally to Diem, they sealed their fate. The conflict was not with the devout Hoa Hao followers—only rebel commanders and their troops. The religionists were decent and hardworking farmers, but that was not the case with the military officers. Lacking the hierarchy of the Cao Dai, the leaders of the Hoa Hao forces acted with great autonomy and become an overlord class in the areas they controlled, to include becoming partners in crime with the Binh Xuyen. The two most notable rebel personalities, newly-promoted Generals Soai (the former interior minister) and Ba Cut, took notably different approaches to the conflict. While Soai was moderate and effective in his rule, Ba Cut was a greedy and corrupt warlord.[12]

Perhaps age was a factor. Soai was in his mid–60s, well past his fighting prime, while Ba Cut was an energetic commander in his early 30s. Those extremes were reflected in the intensity of their rebelliousness; where Soai at least was open to rallying to the government, Ba Cut remained hardheaded and unrepentant. He had a history of acting impulsively and waged his own personal war with the VNA. Even before the battle, he ambushed a VNA infantry company outside Saigon that ended with several soldiers killed and dozens wounded. That created a different blood debt with the army, and during the retaliatory attack, he was badly wounded. The Saigon fighting then took precedence, but how the VNA–Ba Cut feud would play out in the future was anyone's guess. One thing was certain; it did not bode well for reconciliation.[13]

The Hoa Hao avoided the Saigon battle but did take a dramatic step to intensify the crisis. After the May battle, they cut off Mekong Delta rice shipments to Saigon. Although the Hoa Hao were concentrated in poor lands of the western delta, especially in An Giang province, they used the distraction of the Saigon fighting to gain control over most of the delta by taking and holding the Bassac (Hua) River line anchored to the Can Tho rice market (Soai's headquarters) and Long Xuyen (Ba Cut's birthplace) 65 kilometers to the northwest. Across the river from Can Tho astride Route 4, Soai built a fortified position at Cai Vo manned by several thousand soldiers (see Map 2). To break the embargo, the VNA had to quickly retake Can Tho and reopen the road to the delta. During the second week of May, a rushed effort to do just that by imperial guard battalions that had abandoned General Vy and rallied to Diem met with failure. To stiffen the troops, Diem purged the unit of pro–Bao Dai officers. In the meantime, a larger and better-planned attack was needed.[14]

By the end of the month, a 12-battalion VNA-Territorial force (built around the 51st, 52nd, and 154th Infantry Regiments, all from Tonkin) was ready. As a sign of the VNA's growing abilities, one regiment had been airlifted from Da Nang to Saigon to join the attack. The forces were under the command of Duong Van "Big" Minh. Because of his past dealings with Hao Hoa, Ambassador Nguyen Ngoc Tho was named "Big" Minh's political advisor and deputy. Colonel Duong Van Duc led the field operations. Duc was Catholic, attended the Dalat Military Academy, studied at the prestigious Saint-Cyr Military School, and was a ranking Nationalist Party member. Called Operation Dinh Tien Hoang, it began on 23 May and met with immediate success. After the VNA built siege trenches and subjected the Hoa Hao troops at Cai Vo to artillery bombardment, they quit the field. By mid–June through a combination of defections and displays of military might, the VNA broke General Soai's defense along the Bassac.[15]

The Hoa Hao forces retreated westward to their home regions along the Cambodian border to organize a guerrilla resistance. Soai took up positions in the remote areas of Dong Thap province while Ba Cut fell back to his Seven Mountains base in the adjacent An Giang province. To counter that, rallied Cao Dai troops under General Nguyen Thanh Phoung occupied the An Giang provincial capital at Long Xuyen without firing a shot. By the last week of June, rice shipments again flowed freely into Saigon. The VNA regrouped, refitted, and prepared for the next round of battle with the sect armies.[16]

While the VNA had been occupied with Hoa Hao generals Soai and Ba Cut, Vien Bay and about 2,000 of his remaining Binh Xuyen fighters slipped into the Rung Sat mangrove swamp (50 kilometers southeast of Saigon and west of Vung Tau), and he began to rebuild his surviving 5 battalions. The swamp was a traditional safe haven but offered no refuge in 1955. The offensive to destroy them, Operation Hoang-Dieu, began on 21 September and again was under the command of (Big) Minh. Many units that had fought in Saigon were part of the operation: the Paratroop Group, 154th Infantry Regiment, two separate infantry battalions, the reinforced 3rd Artillery Battalion, and supporting troops.[17]

Operation Hoang-Dieu was carried out in three phases. During Phase 1, the Rung Sat swamp was encircled by the VNA with the shoreline patrolled by the navy and marines while the 3rd Artillery Battalion occupied the An Thit high ground in the center of the swamp that offered observed fields of fire over the area. Phase 2 consisted of a VNA sweeping operation under protective artillery fires moving from the northwest to the southeast toward the hamlet of Tac Hoi Bai, the location of Bay Vien's headquarters. Phase 3 was the final assault on Tac Hoi Bai. After several weeks

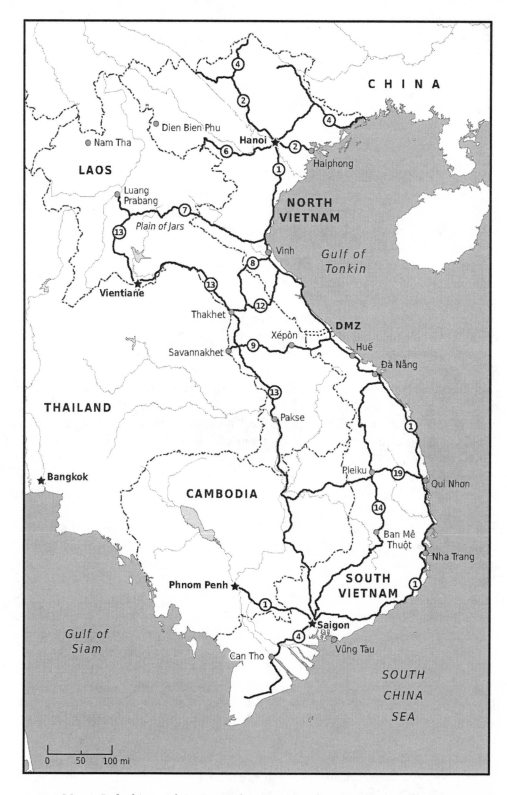

Map 2. Indochina with Major Highways/Routes (Erin Greb Cartography).

of scattered fighting in treacherous terrain, the VNA cleared the swamp, and all five Binh Xuyen battalions had surrendered by 21 October when the operation concluded. "Big" Minh was decorated and promoted to major general while Bay Vien escaped with French SDECE help. He soon made his way to France and spent the rest of his life living in peace and relative luxury. Residual Cao Dai resistance also was squashed that October. Before General Phuong could force his rebellious religious leader Pham Cong Tac into submission, Tac fled into the remote countryside, but the Cao Dai rebellion was over. All that remained of the now badly misnamed "united front" were the last of the Hoa Hao fighters in the far western end of the Mekong Delta.[18]

On 1 January 1956, the final push against the last of the Hoa Hao rebels began: Operation Nguyen Hue named after the famous 18th-century warrior emperor. Elements from four newly formed units, the 4th Field and 13th, 14th, and 15th Light Divisions along with territorial and support troops entered the battle—the VNA's largest operation up to that time. They pursued Soai and his remnants without respite, and within a few weeks the old general knew his band faced imminent destruction. Seeing no out, he opened talks with Ambassador Tho in early February 1956, and on 17 February rallied his troops to the government's side and retired. Pacification efforts were not neglected as 20 mobile Civic Action Groups participated in the operation. That same month, Pham Cong Tac fled to Cambodia. Only Ba Cut refused to surrender. Left commanding a small rabble, he was captured by a Civil Guard patrol on 13 April. Ba Cut was court martialed in June and guillotined on 13 July 1956 in Can Tho. The sect rebellion was over.[19]

At Diem's continued urging, in the wake of the battle for Saigon, the French Expeditionary Force had begun to evacuate the city in May 1955. It was more than symbolic. The sect war ended meaningful French influence in South Vietnam. They had put their stock in Bao Dai, Hinh, and the sects, and all came up short. Diem's government emerged from the war stronger, but damage had been done. The Sûreté was broken, having begun as an arm of the French colonial administration only to be further discredited and corrupted by the influx of Binh Xuyen henchmen. That left Diem bereft of anything resembling a trustworthy or professional intelligence service, and he had to create his own organization. It was a major setback as it meant South Vietnam had little opportunity to develop intelligence sources in the DRV before or during the regrouping period giving Hanoi a major intelligence advantage.[20]

To fill the void, Diem established the Political and Social Studies Service (SEPES), which served as a combined internal and overseas intelligence agency. To lead SEPES, he tapped 30-year-old Doctor Tran Kim Tuyen. Tuyen was a protégé of Ambassador Nguyen Ngoc Tho. Tuyen answered directly to President Diem and his brother Ngo Dinh Nhu, who unofficially acted as the regime's senior intelligence official. The French belatedly helped when the SDECE handed over a number of their stay-behind agents operating in the DRV. They fell under the newly created Liaison Service responsible for covert operations in North Vietnam. Colonel Le Quang Tung headed the service, and the CIA assisted both SEPES and the Liaison Service.[21]

Tuyen was an intriguing if dark character. His duties expanded beyond intelligence to taking on threats either to the regime or himself, and he dealt with then mercilessly. His clandestine death squads were every bit as ruthless as those of the Binh Xuyen and Viet Cong (VC), the name given to Hanoi's remaining loyalists fighting in the south. Both Catholic and fiercely anti-communist, he entered medical school during the War of Resistance, was drafted, and became a VNA officer after graduating from Hanoi's Military Medical College as the war ended in 1954. It was then that Tuyen first worked with the CIA, being active in the SMM propaganda efforts to get as many northerners as possible to resettle in the south. He remained in communication with Lansdale after Lansdale left the RVN and later worked closely with other CIA operatives such as William Colby. His was a risky business, as some saw Tuyen more a subordinate of Washington than Diem.[22]

Like the intelligence services, the cabinet system lay in shambles. Under Bao Dai, ministers came and went with too many never having the least interest in service to nation, instead pursuing aggrandizement, either of self or sect or faction or some combination. The victory over the sects ended the system of gaining cabinet positions by force or blackmail, but nothing could overcome the dearth of skilled, upper-level administrators that had been filled almost exclusively by the French. That was only half the problem, as however many capable government officials there were, next to none sought a posting out in the provinces where the real struggle against the communists was waged. As Lansdale noted, "Some 80% of the civil servants lived and worked in the Saigon metropolitan area and were city folk."[23]

For Washington, the immediate crisis was over, and the outcome was unexpectedly positive. The time for Collins to leave had arrived. Eisenhower did the general no favor when he sent him into the political viper's nest that was Saigon. As Collins recalled, his mission was to be short and simple: "I would go down on a brief mission, make a survey, some recommendations and come back and make a report and that would be that."[24] Instead, he was thrust into a relentless series of military-political crises. Eisenhower rewarded his loyal and trusted subordinate by returning him to his NATO duties. General Collins no doubt left with a sense of relief on 28 May when Ambassador G. Frederick Reinhardt took the helm. While Collins went back to a choice assignment, Diem and South Vietnam entered another perilous stage in the nation's life.[25]

Setting the Stage for War: The 1955–1956 Elections

One of the more controversial events preceding the Vietnam War was the failure to hold the 20 July 1956 reunification elections as directed by the July 1954 Geneva accords. The insurmountable hurdles were that neither the State of Vietnam nor the United States had signed the accords. What slim hope that remained rested with the signatories, especially the French, who were bound by the accords. The French upheld their end, but the influence of Paris was almost nonexistent and its efforts fruitless as the 1954 Geneva framework collapsed well before 20 July 1956.

The commanders-in-chief of the PAVN and French Union Forces signed the Cessation of Hostilities of Agreement in 1954, and it was their job to make it work through the Joint Commission. But Diem removed South Vietnam from the French Union, and the departure of the French Army meant there was no commander-in-chief of French Union Force in Vietnam for Hanoi to work with. It became a dead letter, and the Joint Commission disbanded after General Ely departed on 1 June 1955 without a replacement, an outcome that turned the ICC into an orphan.

So how were elections to proceed? Washington had not altered its opposition to any Vietnam-wide election not controlled and monitored by the United Nations. Making the process more suspect, the Geneva accords gave the ICC no authority to set up the machinery for either a pre-election campaign process or the election itself. The VWP was pessimistic as well but publicly promoted the referendum. After the close of the 1954 Geneva talks, Pham Van Dong told Ho, "You know as well as I do that the elections will never take place."[26] Le Duan went further and characterized the elections an "illusion." He wanted to continue the armed struggle in the south and had gained permission for some PAVN forces to bury their weapons and, along with VWP cadres, remain in the south after 1954. The election impasse became a certainty.[27]

The entire affair became a Cold War propaganda campaign. When the issue first was raised less than a year after Geneva, in March 1955, then-SOV Foreign Minister Tran Van Do reiterated that his country's central objection remained unchanged, citing the justification used for not holding similar reunification elections in divided Korea and Germany: The inability to agree on what constituted free elections. Washington held to the same standard. No guarantee of a free and fair election meant no reunification referendum in Vietnam. The American position was bipartisan. That June, senator and future president John F. Kennedy stated, "Neither the United States nor Free Vietnam is ever going to be a party to an election obviously stacked and subverted in advance."[28]

Washington fretted over the election, not of having one—that was not the goal—but over opening Hanoi-Saigon talks on the referendum. It saw bilateral talks as an opportunity to gain international support in the call for fair elections. They hoped that would paint the DRV as obstructionist and put the onus on Hanoi for any election failure. The stumbling block was Diem. He refused to sit down with Hanoi's representatives. Diem saw danger in vacillating Western Powers who, as they did at Geneva in 1954, would force an election in return for other Cold War concessions that had nothing to do with Vietnam. Pushed by Washington to act, on 16 July 1955 his foreign ministry reiterated that, "though elections constitute one of the bases of true democracy, they can have no justification unless they are genuinely free."[29] Washington changed tack, dropped the push for talks, and again asked for UN supervision. The plea went nowhere.[30]

The most important policy adopted in Saigon over the election controversy was one of fighting fire-with-fire by scheduling elections in South Vietnam ahead of the July 1956 deadline. The policy took form in late spring 1955 and was a modified replay from Korea in 1948, where the UN sanctioned preliminary elections in the south when faced with intransigence in the north. Diem saw two elections: first an up or down vote between Bao Dai and himself to determine the nation's head of state, followed by the election of a national assembly that would then finalize and ratify the draft constitution. But Diem's goal was beyond that attempted in Korea. His intent was not simply to manufacture a propaganda coup to show up Hanoi or even strip away the governing authority granted to Bao Dai by the French and take that authority unto himself. Diem intended to use the elections to mold a national identity for South Vietnam that did not exist.[31]

Washington did not support the first election and was lukewarm to the second. Unfazed, Diem pushed ahead. An election window was set for November 1955. In late June, Diem enunciated four goals regarding the referendum by targeting the 20 July 1956 Reunification Election: (a) Saigon stood for the unification of Vietnam; (b) it was to be achieved by democratic elections; (c) the elections must be free and protected by necessary safeguards; (d) South Vietnam supported elections while still rejecting the Geneva accords. Diem presented those points to the nation during a radio address on 9 August. By September, election dates had been identified. The head of state vote would take place on 23 October followed by a national assembly vote in early 1956. As an added touch, the Diem government launched a nationwide "march north" propaganda campaign pushing peaceful reunification with the DRV through free elections.[32]

The election campaigning only ran three days (16, 22, 23 October 1955). As an indication of their weakness at the time, Viet Cong anti-election activity was not discernable despite Radio Hanoi broadcasts urging an election boycott. Diem's supporters went door-to-door in major cities pushing an anti–Bao Dai and pro–Diem message. It was a one-sided affair. An American embassy official studied a sample of ten posters; six were anti–Bao Dai and four pro–Diem. People were reminded of their duty to vote, and the polls opened from 7:00 a.m.–5:00 p.m. on 23 October. The election employed a simple secret ballot procedure. Voters were given pictures of Diem and Bao-Dai to place in the ballot box. Paying attention to details, Diem enhanced his chances by having his ballots printed with black ink and Bao Dai's in less auspicious green. Given the rate of illiteracy, photo ballots were an appropriate solution. The turnout was impressive, and Diem won by a large margin. The outcome changed Vietnamese history; the Republic of Vietnam came into being on 26 October 1955 with Diem as president and Bao Dai out. Observers from the U.S. embassy noted no voting shenanigans—the election was carried out in accordance with the election laws.[33]

The voting percentages were suspect from the outset. Officially, Diem garnered 97.8 percent of the vote, a figure that rivaled the ill-regarded January 1946 Vietnam election where Ho gained 99 percent of the vote and the February 1955 election of Cambodia's Prince Sihanouk who took 99.8 percent of the vote. As there was no accurate census or a reliable count of eligible voters, precise numbers did not exist, and those that did were questionable. The American embassy wryly noted, "Statistics in Vietnam are notoriously unreliable."[34] That made the 97.8 percent favorable vote touted by Diem not credible but did not change the fact that the vote went his way. Lansdale, who did not buy the 97.8 percent number, nonetheless believed Diem would have received 90 percent of the vote under any circumstance. Analyzing precise percentages was irrelevant. The win had little to do with counting methods or election laws or ballot colors or pro–Diem media bias.[35]

Diem won because it simply was irrational to vote for Bao Dai. During the 1955 battle of Saigon, as his few allies were soundly defeated, Bao Dai fell into disfavor. Rufus Phillips of the SMM departed Vietnam in September and noted that by then, "among Bao Dai's formerly staunch supporters ... not one had a good word to say about him."[36] Even the royal family disowned him and came out in favor of Diem. He also was an absentee leader. Not only had he lived over a third of his life overseas and when not there, often ruled in luxury from his palaces in the resort town of Dalat, he never bothered to run a campaign. Who could put their faith in a leader who not only eschewed living in his homeland but also resided luxuriously in the land of the former colonial masters? It was as if upon regaining independence from Great Britain, Mahatma Gandhi decamped India to establish his government in a country house in Oxfordshire—it was théâtre de l'absurde. Bao Dai was deemed unfit. He was not the ruler of the people, and they rejected him. In Vietnamese custom, Bao Dai lost the mandate of heaven. On a more positive note, in the wake of the election and recognition of his assistance in ending the sect war, Ambassador Nguyen Ngoc Tho was made vice president in December.[37]

On 4 March 1956, the election for the National Assembly was held and, as the Americans concluded earlier, it was a better test of Diem's support as opposition parties were in the race. The election procedures had been revamped since the October referendum when Ordinance 9 went into effect on 23 January. It allocated campaign funds and, to oversee campaigning, created election oversight committees for each assembly district to be comprised of equal members of each party sending up candidates. The campaign season was modestly expanded to 12 days from 20 February to 2 March. Looking to the outcome, observers predicted Diem's candidates would dominate in the voting. Things were tilted due to Diem's control over government media outlets, but by regional standards the election was viewed favorably as to openness, diversity, and honesty. Diem's candidates did not garner 97.8 percent of the vote on this outing. Of the 123 representatives elected, they gathered 47 seats, unaffiliated candidates took 39 seats, the Citizen's Community won 18, Movement for Freedom 11 seats, and small parties filled the remaining eight vacancies. Diem formed a coalition of 90 assembly members, leaving 33 in opposition, and that opened the way to ratification of the constitution.[38]

South Vietnam's 1955 and 1956 elections were far short of expected standards in the "free" developed world. But that was a biased comparison as war-torn South Vietnam was far from a normatively stable society. South Vietnam could only achieve the possible and did well. When looking to the rest of Southeast Asia or even East Asia (excepting Japan), South Vietnam, while dealing with grave internal weaknesses and violent opposition, took a more significant first step toward a democratic future than most of its peers. As far as Southeast Asian elections went, it was a reassuring if modest display of budding democracy. It was not American-style democracy, but it was not the sham elections prevalent in most corners of the world at the time.

In the DRV, the idea of a free and fair election was unwanted if not unnerving.

The VWP wasted no time in transforming the north in its march to socialism and repeatedly in divisive ways. In its entire history, the VWP was never as unpopular as it was in 1956. By then, the party had dismantled the Viet Minh by suppressing all other political parties and opposition voices. It had to be. If the Nationalist and Dai Viet Parties campaigned (whose political bases for decades were in the urban areas of the Red River Delta), a potentially large number of voters likely would have chosen them over the VWP. Making matters worse for the VWP was its crackdown on private businesses, large and small, and attacks on Buddhism, Catholicism, and other religions repelled more.[39]

Most importantly, the extreme and bloody agricultural reforms alienated and stirred resistance across many of North Vietnam's farming masses representing the vast majority of the people. By 1956—the election year—the farmers' revolt was so widespread in some places, such as Nghe An province (Ho's birthplace), that it overwhelmed local security forces and had to be put down by the PAVN. The failed land reforms damaged VWP support amongst the largest population in North Vietnam, and that disillusionment would have been reflected in a free and fair election. Finally, Le Duan's public criticism of the intelligentsia and the drive toward socialism, with its ban on works of art and literature that did not conform to revolutionary *diktats*, divided the educated urban petit bourgeoisie population—even those who had fought with the Viet Minh. During that turbulent summer of 1956, it would have been unlikely that disillusioned segments of northern society would have willingly voted for the VWP government. And things did not improve. A few years later, some diplomats in Hanoi held that the majority of the people living in the countryside were ready to rise up if given the opportunity.[40]

Those problems were in stark contrast to the growing optimism felt in South Vietnam. Diem formed a viable emerging nation state, and South Vietnam had made good progress by July 1956. The countryside and urban areas enjoyed a degree of peace not seen since before World War II, while gains had been made both politically and economically. Diem was reaching the height of his popularity. VWP missteps helped the south. As the north evolved into an authoritarian state, it created an effective political message for its opponents in South Vietnam: To avoid communist rule, we must unite. The Dai Viet and Nationalist Parties had not supported Bao Dai over Diem in the 1955 election. That sentiment, only stronger, would have been reflected in a vote opposing VWP rule in 1956.

There was little likelihood that the VWP would have done as well at the polls in either the RVN or DRV as it claimed. Hanoi recognized the truth and only feebly pushed for the vote. The British embassy there surmised that the VWP ranked the election as a tertiary priority in 1956. Had there been a truly free and fair election, the outcome might well have gone against the communists, and it was possible if not likely that the Vietnam Worker's Party would have found themselves voted out of office. But all that was an abstraction. There never was going to be a fair and free election on 20 July 1956.[41]

A free and fair election never was an option, and the Vietnamese nation would remain divided. Ho and the VWP commanded a powerful military with a unified revolutionary political organization and in the north an effective police apparatus to control any opposition. The VWP would have manufactured as many votes as necessary to win, and the people of Vietnam never were going to freely choose a national government. After partition, reunification only could be decided on the battlefield, and the missed 1956 election simply made reality clearer. Lastly and importantly, bypassing an election crisis by avoiding the referendum while publicly arguing for it served Hanoi's interests. It created an issue to berate both Saigon and Washington—one that resonated both domestically and internationally. It also reassured southern comrades that they had not been forgotten, and years later it provided casus belli to justify restarting the war.[42]

For the South Vietnamese, 7 July 1955 marked Ngo Dinh Diem's first anniversary as prime minster and looking back, a more tumultuous and trying test for the new leader could hardly have been envisioned. Positive steps did follow. With the October 1955 election, Diem finally removed Bao Dai from the political landscape and by extension the meddling French. That in combination with the victorious end to the sect rebellion in 1956 brought immediate stability. But Diem's support was not rock solid. The army did act decisively to save him, but they also acted in their own self-interest as they wanted to be rid of the sect militias as much as Diem. Their actions did not signify unquestioning and enthusiastic loyalty, and what would happen if their mutual interests came into conflict remained to be seen. The great unknown was how or even if the fledgling Republic of Vietnam would continue to progress under Diem's leadership.

And the great enemy still loomed. Hanoi banned the southern VWP comrades from violating the ceasefire, but as the 1955 sect rebellion grew in intensity, the party prepared to take advantage of the unrest. Cadres were sent to infiltrate the sect forces to exploit any opportunities to advance the revolution, and Hanoi authorized the activation of a limited number of PAVN stay behind troops in Nam Bo. They accessed their arms caches and formed a dozen or so squads and platoons dispersed within the old strongholds, and several successfully posed as Cao Dai and Hoa Hao irregulars. Some even engaged the VNA during Operation Nguyen Hue, but the VNA victory ended hope of quick reunification. The guerrillas retreated into remote areas in the Mekong Delta and swamps and forests along the Cambodian border, and in November 1955, there also were reports of communist guerrilla activity in the Central Highland's Kontum province. These forces provided the VWP with a limited military capability tied to political actions such as assassinations. The key was to keep the revolution alive but not trigger a reaction from Saigon that risked annihilation. It was a positive outcome for Hanoi and kept open the path that eventually led to Resolution 15 and future war.[43]

4

South Vietnam Under Ngo Dinh Diem in 1959

On the surface, the Saigon government in 1959 looked like many others. It was a constitutional state with a judiciary, an elected national assembly, and an administrative branch composed of ministries staffed by bureaucrats and led by an elected president. But Ngo Dinh Diem, the RVN president, sought to create an authentic alternative to the DRV and for better or worse largely succeeded. It became what Pulitzer Prize winning *New York Times* correspondent David Halberstam unflatteringly referred to as "a government that had no parallel," and there were three distinct aspects of the government that made it so.[1] The first dealt with how Diem was shaped during his rise to power and the role played by his five brothers and Madame Nhu, the wife of his closest brother. The second was the ideological and organizational underpinnings of the regime that centered on personalism, the Can Lao Party, and the National Revolutionary Movement (NRM), and finally, there was the manner in which Diem governed.

Ngo Dinh Diem and His Rise to Power

That Ngo Dinh Diem came to lead South Vietnam shortly after its inception in 1954 was unsurprising to anyone familiar with Vietnamese affairs. No other non-communist Vietnamese possessed the abilities or had accomplished more as a government official and non-violent resister to French rule. For the bachelor Diem, as with Ho Chi Minh, Vietnam was his life, and the two shared what many saw as the essential traits of a leader: virtue and austerity. Although ten years younger, Diem shared much in common with Ho—both were from Trung Bo, and they attended the same distinguished secondary school. Both fathers were officials who resigned in the early 1900s after the French encroached on the emperor's authority, and both dedicated themselves to Vietnamese independence, laboring to the point of exhaustion. Both also eschewed the material and led simple lives bereft of wealth or most personal possessions. Also like Ho, Diem lived a unique life.[2]

Born into a distinguished mandarin civil service family on 3 January 1901, Diem's father served as a senior official at the Nguyen imperial court in Hue. His family was noted for its dedicated Confucianism and devout Catholicism. In the

1600s Portuguese missionaries converted the Ngo's—generations before the arrival of the French—and in Vietnamese Catholic tradition, at birth Diem was given the additional Christian name Jean Batiste. He never used it, but his faith was unshakable, and his religiosity tempered his life. Inseparable from his religious schooling, Diem was taught to serve selflessly from his earliest years, and despite his family's position, his upbringing was demanding and arduous. He began each morning at church followed by attendance at the rigorous Catholic Bishop Pellerin School in Hue. In time, he became a stoic, devout, hard-working, and brilliant student. Diem later attended the premier Quoc Hoc Academy that his father helped found, and before he entered university, he was fluent in Vietnamese, French, and Latin, and read classical Chinese. Diem's education was capped by attending Hanoi's École Supérieure d'Administration Indochinoise where he graduated first in his class in 1921. Already an ardent nationalist, he declined a scholarship to study in France.[3]

The future looked bright and had France not dominated his country, Diem could have succeeded in any field of his choosing. He opted for the Emperor's civil service, and after a probationary year working at the imperial library in Hue, spent most of the next 11 years in the countryside as a senior government administrator. He had no need to embark on such a hard life. By birthright and education, Ngo Dinh Diem became a highly qualified member of the scholarly class, which in Vietnamese culture made him part of the most revered and highest tier of the social order. Diem could have made an excellent living practicing law in Hanoi, and if so moved, could have comfortably entered politics like his later rival, Dr. Phan Huy Quat. Instead of enjoying the refinements of Vietnam's finest cities, the young and vigorous Diem chose to walk the rice paddies and got to know the struggles, problems, hopes, and joys of Vietnam's farming families.[4]

Diem subsequently ascended the bureaucratic ranks in extraordinary fashion. In 1923, he began as the Thua Thien district chief (which contained Hue) and later served in Quang Tri to the north. In 1929, he became the Ninh Thuan province chief, likely the youngest in Vietnam. It was a momentous time to govern a province. In 1930, rebellion triggered by the Nationalist Party and joined by the communists on May Day (who called it the Uprising of the Nghe Tinh Soviets) erupted above and below Diem's province, and it turned into one of the most violent revolts in modern Vietnamese history. The summer and fall were defined by unspeakable savagery, torture, and bloody retribution as Marxist, Nationalist, and Dai Viet revolutionaries battled the French authorities seeking to suppress them. But the areas under Diem's control remained relatively calm. Diem achieved this through a two-pronged strategy: supporting the farmers (often against French interests) combined with violent repression of the disunited communists who dominated the revolutionaries in his part of Vietnam.[5]

Diem's record of success and earning the respect of local village leaders (his disinterest in material gain made him a model of honest governance) garnered the attention of the imperial leadership in Hue. In May 1932 Emperor Bao Dai chose Diem to head up a civil service reform commission. That presented Diem with the unique opportunity to observe and critique how public governance was conducted in Vietnam both in part and as a whole (save French-ruled Cochinchina).

After accomplishing that task, Diem was appointed by Emperor Bao Dai to the highest civil post available, the minister of interior. (To maintain authority, the French had abolished the position of prime minister.) When the French colonial authorities subsequently rejected Diem's remonstrations for greater autonomy and a national assembly, he resigned in protest. The act made Ngo Dinh Diem a national hero, especially in the ranks of the independence movement.[6]

The 1933 resignation redefined Diem's career. He entered internal exile an unflinching patriot. One leader he joined with was Phan Boi Chau, the country's most admired nationalist and head of the Vietnamese Restoration League, who had lived under house arrest in Hue since 1925. Powerfully outspoken, Chau 25 years earlier had called on the people to awaken and regain their independence. He went on to declare that the French despise and lie to the Vietnamese, hold them in contempt, and "suck the sweat and blood from our people."[7] Diem's father also had esteemed Chau, and Diem too drew close, but it was an unlikely pairing; in 1923 Chau published a vitriolic but popular polemic arguing that France used Catholicism to carry out "a cultural genocide" against the Vietnamese people.[8] Despite the bigotry, Diem shared Chau's philosophy of anti-colonialism, communal Confucianism, and universal public education. The two became allies despite Diem's religion and remained so until Chau's death in 1940. Chau's tract also gave Diem fair warning: the higher he climbed, the more his faith would be used against him.[9]

Diem was open to opposing voices. In 1933, he entered a dialogue with Vo Nguyen Giap. Diem later recalled that the relationship spanned years, and he held Giap in high regard. The feeling was mutual; Giap was quoted as saying, "There are only two true leaders in Vietnam. One is Ho Chi Minh. The other is Ngo Dinh Diem." He then added ominously, "There is no room in the country for both."[10] Giap was a gifted Marxist and despite a shared passion for independence, the two could not reconcile their opposing politics and parted ways. For the rest of the 1930s, Diem lived with his family in Hue, publishing whatever pro-independence tracts he could slip past his French watchers.[11]

When Japan marched into Indochina in 1940 disrupting French rule, Diem took a more active role in national affairs. Like many in the independence movements—especially the non-communist Cao Dai and most Dai Viet followers—Diem looked favorably to Japan, the sole Asian power to evade the imperialist yoke. Even Giap's daughter Luu Trong Lu looked up to the Japanese. Tran Ngoc Chau, a PAVN officer who later went over to the South Vietnamese side, noted that at the time, "we were also somewhat pleased that the Japanese, another Asiatic race, had demonstrated that they were not inferior to the white European race."[12] But when Tokyo continued French control to maintain "peace and order," disillusionment set in.[13]

Then as the Allies began to win the war, the situation changed again. In mid–1944 Diem earned the wrath of Vichy France by forming the pro-independence Association for Restoration of Great Vietnam in Hue and had to escape to Saigon, which was under direct Japanese occupation. Fortunately for Diem, the Vichy regime collapsed in August following the Allied invasion of France. French rule in Vietnam teetered while Japan tightened control. Diem communicated with anti-imperialist Japanese officials but accomplished nothing. When Japan toppled

French rule on 9 March 1945 and granted Vietnam independence (on Tokyo's terms), Japan tried to establish a government. Diem's name came up, but he argued with the pro–Japanese Vietnamese faction under Prince Cuong De. As the French had done before, the Japanese dropped the uncompromising nationalist, opting instead for the pliant Emperor Bao Dai.[14]

Such was Diem's reputation that both sides pursued his services in the emerging independence war. In 1946, Ho Chi Minh sought to recruit him by offering a cabinet position in the united front Viet Minh government. When the French gave partial independence to Vietnam in 1947 under ex-emperor Bao Dai (who abdicated during the 1945 August Revolution and left for Hong Kong), Ngo Dinh Diem had been his first choice for prime minister. Diem turned down both. After meeting with Ho Chi Minh, Diem felt Ho was not forthcoming enough about his plans for Vietnam. The brutal murder by the communists of Diem's eldest brother Khoi and his only son, Ngo Dinh Huan, in late 1945 did nothing to encourage trust between the two. Remarkably, Ho allowed Diem to leave unmolested. Diem's refusal to join with Bao Dai was a replay of 1933. The French were not empowering Bao Dai as an independent head of state. and Diem would not legitimize or waste time as part of such a government.[15]

The murder of Khoi loomed large. Most cannot fathom the familial bonds of the Vietnamese of that era nor that the murder of Khoi and his only son Huan, the future family head, was the worst possible tragedy for the Ngo. It changed Diem and his brothers. Khoi and Huan embodied continuity of the Ngo line, but with father and son dead, the role of patriarch had to be filled. By rights, Ngo Dinh Thuc was next, but since he was a serving Catholic priest, the responsibility fell to the unmarried and heirless Diem. Traditional Confucian balance had been undone. Khoi's death made Diem the center of family fealty that in turn altered and strengthened the bond with his surviving brothers. Ngo Dinh Diem, who dedicated his life to Vietnam, would strongly support his brothers to safeguard the family's future. The responsibility worked both ways. If Diem aimed to lead Vietnam, then the brothers would unquestioningly dedicate themselves to that goal.[16]

Since rejecting Ho and Bao Dai, Diem carefully kept his options open. He never publicly criticized the Viet Minh and helped Bao Dai in his attempt to create a Vietnamese government. Dai's autonomy negotiations with Paris ran from 1947 to 1948 and failed, but Bao Dai and Diem parted amicably. On 16 June 1949, while in Saigon and speaking for many non-communists, Diem published a manifesto arguing for a third way for Vietnam as an alternative to both Bao Dai and the Viet Minh. He argued for three goals: (1) Vietnamese independence on par with that of India or Pakistan, (2) social reforms that would end in the "economic independence of the Vietnamese farmer and laborer," and (3) that the country's rulers should be chosen democratically from those who resisted the French.[17] It was released just as Bao Dai—who lacked resistance credentials—returned to Vietnam, and hobbled his government as many qualified candidates declined to serve; the ex-emperor had to become his own prime minister.[18]

The communists were equally displeased as Diem's actions caused dissent amongst the non-communist Viet Minh. The communists soon sentenced him to death, and he was forced to flee Vietnam in late 1950. It was his first trip abroad. After a short stay in Japan, Diem visited the United States before heading to Europe. Returning to America in early 1951, he spent most of the next two years at the Catholic Maryknoll monastery in New Jersey. It was not all prayer, meditation, and mastering English; by 1953 Diem was on good terms with many of America's most powerful to include leading progressives: Supreme Court Justice William O. Douglas, Senators Mike Mansfield and John F. Kennedy, and Speaker of the House John McCormick—the last three fellow Catholics. In late 1953, as pressure mounted in Paris to end the War of Resistance, Diem left for France to re-enter Vietnamese politics, now with friends in Washington.[19]

At long last in the spring of 1954, with Vietnam about to gain independence, Diem accepted Bao Dai's offer of the prime ministership. That was how Diem viewed foreign influence: He would only serve in a truly free Vietnamese government, and those conditions had not existed before Geneva. Tran Kim Tuyen, a close ally and later enemy, never doubted Diem's patriotism. In 1970, he wrote about Diem's clashes with American officials in the Saigon newspaper *Hoa Binh*: "Everyone close to Diem knew that for him the question of Vietnamese sovereignty was primordial; no question of foreign aid could supersede that."[20] Diem fought foreign meddling, whether from Paris or Tokyo or later, Beijing or Moscow or Washington.[21]

Diem's Five Brothers and Madame Nhu

One of the most influential factors in every facet of Ngo Dinh Diem's rule in South Vietnam was his relationship with his brothers and Madame Nhu, wife of his third and closest brother. Shaped by family ties, Confucian prescripts, and the roiling crucible that enveloped Vietnam during that time, fraternal bonds were paramount, building what historian and CIA veteran of the Vietnam War Thomas Ahern termed the "House of Ngo."[22] Adding to the dynamism, Diem came from a large family with five brothers: Khoi (the eldest by 16 years), Thuc (four years senior), Nhu (nine years junior), Can (ten years junior) and Luyen (13 years younger).

As the eldest, Ngo Dinh Khoi had carried the burden of leading the Ngo family until his murder. He was a faithful son and Vietnamese patriot but never approached either the brilliance or relentless determination displayed by Diem. Khoi was steady, hardworking, capable, and brave, making him an ideal family patriarch. Unlike Diem, Khoi married into a prestigious Hue family also known for service to the imperial family. In Confucian tradition, he followed his father into a career in government, first the army and then the civil service, gradually climbing in rank to become a provincial chief in 1930. He stayed at that rank. It is unknown but likely that Diem's confrontations with the French hurt Khoi's career, but in truth, a provincial chief was one of the most powerful positions a non–Frenchman could attain, a telling example of how France limited capable Vietnamese. While the French held back leaders like Khoi, it was the communists that posed the ultimate threat. When Khoi resisted the communist takeover of his province in 1945, Khoi and his only son were savagely murdered.[23]

The second son, Archbishop Pierre Martin Ngo Dinh Thuc, was an accomplished Catholic priest, and his extreme devotion never allowed him to put loyalty to his brothers, to include Diem, before duty to his flock. After taking primary grades at the Pellerin School, Thuc entered the An Ninh Seminary at the age of 12 and never looked back. He took his orders in 1925 when he was 28. As distinguished a scholar as Diem, he earned three doctorates and briefly taught at the University of Paris. He was elevated to bishop of the Hue diocese on 4 May 1938. A strong advocate of education, Thuc was a driving force behind the creation of the RVN's only private college, Dalat University, in 1957. On 12 April 1961, Ngo Dinh Thuc became the first Vietnamese archbishop and the first Archbishop of Vietnam. He was judged the most willful brother, second only to Diem.[24]

Ngo Dinh Nhu, born on 7 October 1910, was an enigma described almost exclusively in extreme and often-contradictory terms. One thing is beyond dispute: He was one of the most influential figures in South Vietnam's brief history. Handsome and charming, with a commensurate ego, Nhu took a degree at the École Nationale des Chartes, one of France's "grand schools" where he earned a reputation as a skilled archivist. It was in Paris that Nhu studied the philosophy of personalism under Emmanuel Mounier that he later introduced to his brother. Almost all who knew him were impressed with his intelligence. General Collins noted after a 1955 meeting that Nhu was a "pure intellectual who writes Latin and Greek better than he does French."[25]

In 1943, Nhu met his future wife, and they were wed in May in Hanoi. By 1945, Nhu was a senior officer at Hanoi's National Library. The combination of the August Revolution and his brother Khoi's murder led Nhu onto the political stage. He organized anti-communist independence advocates and, in 1948, formed the leftist Workers Party (Travailliste Parti). Of the brothers, he was closest to Diem and a trusted advisor by 1954. In fact, Nhu started building up support for Diem in Vietnam years earlier. He was driven to the point of excess that proved both a source of Nhu's strength and weakness. Living in violent times, Nhu did not shy away from its use to achieve his ends.[26]

Politically, Nhu sought to empower and seek support from the masses to a degree that rivaled his communist adversaries. His first foray into politics, organizing workers in the Travailliste Parti, succeeded to a good degree in the 1950s. After that it was the toiling masses in the fields, and despite his background and education, Ngo Dinh Nhu was the antithesis of an elitist. Brilliant, hardworking, and modest, Ngo Dinh Nhu was a formidable foe and often heartless and merciless.[27]

The second youngest brother, Ngo Dinh Can, held sway over RVN-controlled Trung Bo (to include the Central Highlands) as regional counselor, an unofficial post that belied his authority. Can described himself simply as a "representative of the people," making him the most obscure and Machiavellian of brothers.[28] He never sought public attention, going so far as to cultivate an image of a quiet and frail man—a danger to no one—who chose to work from the shadows and through layers of intermediaries. Adding to his reputation, he lived modestly and cared for his aged mother, the family matriarch, from the family home in Hue not far from the Catholic Phu Cam Cathedral, just across the Perfume River and Hue Citadel.[29]

Ngo Dinh Can was the shrewdest of the brothers in assessing the political dimensions of rule. His strength was obtaining objectives by influencing events—not through the direct application of power. He was so effective that many concluded Can was more powerful than the government head of the region, Delegate Ho Dac Khuong. Can built ties with the Buddhist and Catholic communities and with the Nationalist and other opposition parties. That did not mean Can was a passive counselor; he often stood up to his brother Nhu, and there were many stories of how he brutally suppressed the VWP cadres in his region, to include assassinations. Can firmly believed Vietnam could only be reunited by force, and his hatred for communists knew no bounds.[30]

Luyen, the youngest brother, trained as an engineer—and according to Diem, had the quickest temper. He reserved it, however, for matters inside the family. When in public, Luyen behaved in the most tactful and civil manner. He served initially as Diem's aide-de-camp and accompanied Diem during his trips abroad. Luyen was of significant help in France in 1954, where he sought to gain support for Diem within France's Vietnamese community. He also became his brother's chief liaison with both Bao Dai (the two had attended school together) and French officials in Paris. Luyen spent a considerable time in Switzerland during the various 1954 Geneva meetings, where he cultivated relations with a number of American diplomats. After Diem took power, Luyen returned to Vietnam and performed a similar role by working with French and American officials. Diem formalized and elevated his role, first making him ambassador in 1956 to several Western European countries and in 1959, his ambassador-at-large.[31]

One of the most controversial and famous—if not infamous—members of the Ngo family was Nhu's wife, known universally as Madame Nhu. She was born on 22 August 1924 as Tran Le Xuan into a high-ranking family. (Her mother was a princess of the imperial line.) Naturally intelligent, she received an exceptional education for a Vietnamese female, first being tutored at home and later attending Lycée Albert Sarraut. Perhaps it was in that environment that Madame Nhu developed the force of character to speak to men as equals, heedless of the traditional reticence expected of women. She could be fierce. When General Hinh had made his "concubine" remarks in 1954, she publicly confronted him and stated, "You will never have me because I will claw your throat out first!" Madame Nhu also was highly knowledgeable of national affairs; her father's duties as a high-ranking magistrate exposed her to Vietnamese life from the rural farming communities of the Mekong Delta to the cultured sophistication of Hanoi. She grew into a beautiful woman. At age 19 she married Nhu Dinh Diem but was not destined for an easy future. Three years later she and her family were swept up in the War of Resistance. Having fled to the Ngo family home in Hue, she was arrested along with hundreds of others by the communists. With her baby daughter Le Thuy in her arms, she marched into captivity and survived months of confinement under harsh conditions.[32]

After being released into the custody of a Catholic convent in early 1947, Madame Nhu and her daughter eventually reunited with her husband in the mountain resort of Dalat north of Saigon. As a sign of how small the circle of elites was in Vietnam, the family acquaintanceship with Bao Dai was renewed as Dalat also served as the ex-emperor's safe haven after his return to Vietnam in 1949, and the Nhus lived in the summer home of Tran Van Don's father. Don later became a general under Diem. Dalat offered the Nhus a simple but happy life where they had two sons (Trac in 1949 and Quynh in 1952) and found refuge for the rest of the war. Madame Nhu became the devoted mother as her husband came and went while carrying out his secret political work. The two reunited again in 1954 when she joined her husband and his brother, the new prime minister, in Saigon.[33]

Madame Nhu's 1954 banishment to Hong Kong for anti–Hinh activism again disrupted the marriage, but upon return, she resumed her political life. Her moral conservatism had been shaped by her Confucian upbringing and strengthened by conversion to Catholicism. It also revealed a strong feminist mindset. Elected to the new National Assembly in 1956, she supported repeal of French laws that limited women's legal rights and moved to ban arranged marriages and polygamy. Her greatest achievement was passing the Family Code (Law No. 1/59, 1 January 1959) that encapsulated her reformist agenda. Hers was not an easy road. She was ridiculed for opposing public dancing, but what she attacked were dance halls and bars where women were paid to dance with men, precursors to prostitution. Madame Nhu abhorred the exploitation of women. She later explained that people had asked her to take a public role: "I did not like the life" but "if I did not do those things, nobody would do it."[34] She was a revolutionary; her position on women's equality was indistinguishable from that of the Viet Cong. Ambassador Durbrow later had this take: "She was the original ERA [Equal Rights Amendment] gal in Vietnam … she antagonized all the men in Vietnam naturally for that, so she had quite a few enemies." In a sense she was an incarnation of the fated Vietnamese woman of talent and beauty immortalized in Nguyen Du's epic poem *Kim Van Kieu.*[35]

Le Monde correspondent Jean Lacouture defined her in four words: feminist, Catholic, prude, and anti-communist. She became South Vietnam's most outspoken advocate of women's rights. Adding to her importance, she was de facto first lady for the bachelor Diem. As Lansdale put it, "She knew all the social graces of a hostess in a household of wealth and culture."[36] While Madame Nhu embraced her service in the National Assembly, she did not relish her first lady position; she described it as akin to being a cat grabbed by the scruff of its neck and thrown into the arena

Ngo Dinh Nhu, the gifted and ruthless brother of Diem who keenly understood the rough and tumble world of Vietnamese politics but not the Americans, and his wife, Madame Nhu in happier times (Alamy with permission).

with the lions. By the close of the 1950s, Madame Nhu was at the height of her political power, but her personal life suffered. The separations had taken a toll on the marriage. That both husband and wife pursued political careers in a male-dominated society added to the stress—Nhu wanted her to stay at home and be a housewife. Exacerbating the discord, he took a mistress. They remained married but became estranged. Surprisingly, the Americans never gave Madame Nhu a second thought, but she would change that.[37]

Ngo Dinh Diem's tightly bound relationship with his brothers and Madame Nhu created an irresolvable dilemma. With the exception of Archbishop Thuc, no matter how bad things got, Diem could always count on them, but that overreliance damaged Diem as the nation's leader.

Diem's Governance Framework

The Diem system of governance, the third way, was not the American way, but he was far from alone in rejecting communism and Western liberal democracy, both foreign to Southeast Asia. While his third way eventually took the form of personalism, the Can Lao Party, and the NRM, Diem also looked regionally, and the communists too had a surprisingly strong influence. Diem found communist organizations with their cultivation of loyalty and discipline appealing but rejected their dogma. Communism's militant atheism repelled, him and its political philosophy was antithetical to his Confucian beliefs. He deemed it destructive to the core norms that defined Vietnamese culture.[38]

Most of all, Diem sought to improve upon the ideas fomented by his mentor Phan Boi Chau during his years in political exile. While Diem's opposition to communism was well known, his misgivings about liberal democracy were not. Like Phan Boi Chau, Diem did not believe the Vietnamese people should rush into Western-style democracy that would end in a government trapped in a "chaotic stalemate" between political parties.[39] Even Vietnamese advocates of democracy found it hard to follow in practice; democracy being an alien concept, National Assembly members often fell back on Confucian conformity rather than engage in confrontational public debate over contentious legislation—a trait unfathomable to most Americans. Diem was not opposed to democracy, however. For Diem the first imperative was national development—only then could "true democracy" take hold for the betterment of the people.[40] That was in keeping with the path followed by the Chinese Nationalists that many non-communists of his generation looked to.[41]

Personalism

Diem pushed the ideology known as personalism. European in origin, it derived from a 1930s political school expounded by Mounier, who had been shocked by the 1930s Great Depression and came to oppose Western individualism untethered to social good. Personalism centered on ethical action for the good of society based on free will and belief in God. Nhu introduced it to Diem even though

Mounier's writings were known throughout the French-speaking world of that era to include Vietnam. Diem reinterpreted Mounier's thesis from a Vietnamese perspective and dropped its Christianity component. He aspired to weld his modified version of personalism to Confucian-Taoist traditions of hierarchal loyalty stretching from family to ruler. The personalist "human" was seen as a Confucian ideal recognizing humanity's dual physical and spiritual existence while incorporating the Taoist admonition to live a meaningful life. Ultimately, they hoped it would provide a morally and ethically superior alternative to Marxism.[42]

Embedded in the RVN's 1956 constitution, personalism also captured Diem's economic outlook. Unbridled consumerism concerned Diem, who feared that democracy could degrade into superficial "material happiness."[43] But he defended personal property rights and opposed communist-style nationalization. His brother Nhu described the model as a "mixed economy" that was partly state controlled and partly privately controlled.[44] While embracing free market economics as the foundation for creating national wealth—market economies were as historically ubiquitous in Vietnam as anywhere else on the globe—Diem saw benefit in governmental support for the development and maintenance of economic sectors vital to the nation's health and security.[45]

Finally, personalism was not intended to be a passive belief system. It helped define the citizenry's obligation to the nation—to create a responsible, obedient, and progressive society—and as a theory, pursuing personalism made sense. As a practical matter, it was too foreign to Vietnamese culture and came across as a muddled philosophy. However well intentioned, personalism gained little traction in South Vietnam.[46]

Can Lao Party

To match the communist's organizational discipline, Ngo Dinh Diem formed the Personalist Labor Revolutionary Party (Can Lao Nanh vi Cach Mang Dang) or simply the Can Lao. The name itself, along with the party slogan of "Labor, Revolution, Personalism," reflected Diem's third way. Its founding remains murky, an event cloaked in secrecy, colored by unsubstantiated rumors, and further obscured by the early record that often failed to distinguish between the NRM and Can Lao. Apparently begun in the early 1950s, it was not officially recognized until 8 August 1954. The party covertly exerted control over the nation and especially the government—to include the armed forces—and by 1957, it had infiltrated the national bureaucracy. The Can Lao largely was the handiwork of Nhu, who used his position as party leader to back up Diem. Being the creation of two staunch anti-communists, its similarities to the VWP were disquieting.[47]

Like the VWP, the Can Lao operated opaquely with a secret membership. Yet it was very much in the mainstream of Vietnam's political parties. Both the Nationalist and Dai Viet parties operated as underground organizations, first under the French, and later when they opposed the VWP. Akin to the communists, Can Lao candidates had to be vetted, prove their loyalty before being considered for membership, and admitted only when nominated by party cadres. Also mimicking the VWP and to a degree, criminal organizations such as the Cosa Nostra, joining the Can Lao occurred during a secret ritual ceremony to cement absolute allegiance, perhaps on pain of death. For security purposes and again like other parties, after joining a new member was assigned to a small cell without any knowledge of the members or numbers of other cells. Adding another layer of conspiracy, while Nhu was the titular national party leader, in Trung Bo his brother Ngo Dinh Can and his subordinates controlled both the regional Can Lao and NRM.[48]

As with any party in power, membership brought rewards and with it, resentments. The Can Lao Party was no exception. It engaged in soliciting "voluntary donations" and the like from hapless businesses using tactics identical to the Viet Cong and not all that different from the Binh Xuyen. For those paying, it represented triple taxation, first by the government and then the Viet Cong and Can Lao. Finally, there were credible claims that the party illegally profited from the National Lottery, cinnamon (cassia bark) trade, and other enterprises, again akin to Binh Xuyen practices. Most, with good justification, saw it as a corrupt system to fund the party even if funds were used for political ends and not uncommonly to improve the life of ordinary people. The unsanctioned revenues also did political damage to Diem and Nhu as they led to rumors of the Ngos getting rich by abusing their power. Finally, the party operated as extrajudicial secret police formed into "action groups" to battle the VWP by any means, even murder.[49]

The hidden influence of and "taxation" by the Can Lao, along with the fear brought on by the action groups, alienated those that might otherwise have been regime supporters and further divided a civil service not known for selfless duty. Diem could not see that loyal Vietnamese might eschew the Can Lao and that the uniform obedience he sought wrongly silenced legitimate debate and the ability to present opposing viewpoints. Another warning sign that Diem ignored was Lansdale's opposition. He saw the Can Lao as an obstacle to democracy, and the Can Lao robbed Diem of the moral high ground. How could he condemn secret Dai Viet and Nationalist Party military cells when the Can Lao played the same underhanded and divisive game? Whether the added value gained from Can Lao offset its costs is unknowable, but it was a mixed bag at best.[50]

National Revolutionary Movement

The third pillar of Diem's political society to defeat communism was a mass organization, the National Revolutionary Movement (Phong Trao Cach Mang Quoc Gia). The NRM served as his political party, and its mission was twofold: Gain Diem seats in the National Assembly and serve as an anticommunist bulwark. As with the Can Lao, it was initially the work of Nhu, who used his small Travailliste Parti as the NRM nucleus. In an early step toward building the movement, Nhu organized a labor conference in Saigon during September 1953. Progress was slow and got off to a rocky start when the NRM tried to compete with the established Nationalist and Dai Viet Parties. Nhu later reflected on those early days: "All the sound nationalist elements were already involved in other parties; no talent was left over for the NRM cadres."[51] The party especially struggled to fill the political vacuum at the village level and did not come into its own until General Trinh Minh The chaired the first tumultuous party congress on 29 April 1955 at the height of the battle for Saigon and just days before his death.[52]

After the victory over the sects, the movement grew and developed—after all, everyone wants to join with the winners. By February 1956, the Americans concluded the NRM "looms as the only significant fully overt political grouping remaining."[53] Two years later, NRM ascendancy was complete, and that November, the CIA reported that the movement had "developed in fine fashion."[54] The NRM claimed to have grown from an initial 10,000 members in 1955 to 1,500,000 by 1959. Somewhat troubling, in Saigon a mere 42,000 joined the movement. It became the public face of Diem's political machine with Diem as honorary leader while Nhu controlled NRM operations. The Can Lao also had a major influence on the NRM as its members assumed key NRM leadership and organizational roles, and it became a symbiotic relationship. The Can Lao provided dedicated cadres, and in turn, they looked to the most enthusiastic and advantageously placed NRM members for recruitment into the Can Lao.[55]

The NRM adopted the VWP model of forming various mass associations used to solidify broad support. There were workers and farmer associations, associations for government employees (League of Revolutionary Civil Servants), soldiers, and other professions, along with youth and student groups formed as part of the Republican Youth. Also unusual in Southeast Asia, the NRM formed women's associations, most notably Madame Nhu's Woman's Solidarity Movement (WSM). All this advanced the goal of unifying the country behind Ngo Dinh Diem. The youth and student groups were especially important as they led "get out the vote" efforts during elections, and when the war began in 1959, hundreds of Republican Youths volunteered to go out into the countryside to protect the rural population from the Viet Cong. Later, as the numbers grew into the thousands, they were organized into paramilitary units, the Self-Guard Youth Corps, and clad in distinctive blue uniforms. They stood alongside the Self-Defense Corps (SDC) to protect local villages and communities. Hanoi saw them as rivals to the Viet Cong militia. Important but not directly tied to the NRM, Diem also fostered a nationwide Veterans League to serve as a grassroots anti-communist organization.[56]

Diem's Method of Leadership in Practice

By 1959, Ngo Dinh Diem came to lead a forward-looking constitutional republic anchored to Vietnamese culture while struggling to adhere to Western democratic trends in an underdeveloped corner of Southeast Asia. Diem continuously tried to create a modern Vietnamese identity that still honored and maintained important traditions of the past. Although he called his envisioned transformation of South Vietnam revolutionary, it was more an incremental evolution. Diem pursued that objective on many levels beyond the overarching personalism-Can Lao-NRM architecture.[57]

French influence was replaced with nationalist symbolism and Diem was not above self-promotion. The day he returned to Vietnam, 7 July 1954, became a national holiday known as the "Double Seventh," and his photograph was displayed virtually everywhere across the nation. Following the October 1955 election, he renamed Norodom Palace in Saigon as Doc Lop (Independence) Palace that became the president's offices and residence. Similarly, Rue Catinat, named for a French admiral, became Tu Do (Liberty) Street, Boulevard Gallieni became Tran Hung Dao Boulevard, named after the prince who beat back the Mongols. Chanson Avenue took the name of the famous general Le Van Duyet. Cities were renamed. Cap St. Jacques became Vung Tau while Tourane regained its Vietnamese name, Da Nang. Other heroes, especially those who opposed foreign domination, like Nguyen Trai who fought the Ming Chinese occupation and generals Thoai Ngoc Hau who battled the Cambodians and Truong Tan Buu who fought to reunify Vietnam, became the names of major military operations. That spirited nationalism reflected Diem's deeply held patriotism that Americans often missed.[58]

Ngo Dinh Diem was an imperfect leader. He lacked charm and warmth, being the reserved administrator who shied away from physical contact. Diem had no instinctive popular political savvy and little charisma; beyond malfeasance, worse attributes for a politician were hard to contemplate. Meeting Diem for the first time often left newcomers bewildered as he dominated the conversation and could lecture, albeit intelligently, about Vietnamese affairs for hours at a time. His intellect was a two-edged sword; it made success possible but, when combined with reticence, prevented him from building trusting relationships with his colleagues. Dai Viet Party leader Nguyen Huu Tri saw the flaw and deemed Diem as "intellectually opposed to practical approach."[59] He did well going it alone but never grasped the necessity of forming a broad cohesive team around him. Overreliance on his brothers further affected his ability to work with others as equals, and Saigon's political treachery left him suspicious and stubborn. The upheavals, betrayals, and political and military trials of 1954–1955 aggravated the problem. Afterwards, he instinctively prejudged opposition as an unjustified attack to be repressed.[60]

The same dynamic created in Diem a poor ability to delegate authority, a skill essential to sustained long-term leadership as head of state. Most of the criticism of Diem as being isolated stemmed from this. It was not that he was not out and about—he was—but that he had a small circle of trusted advisors that shrank rather than expanded over time. Similarly, Diem had no gift in working with the National Assembly, where success was built on personal relationships and the give-and-take of the legislative process. Ardent nationalism also affected Diem's ability to govern. His relations with the French often were counterproductive and grew bitter by 1955. Although it could have been better managed (by both parties), it was the right decision. Vietnam gained independence by battling the French, and when Diem stood up to them, the political gain outweighed any loss. The same was not true in his dealings with the Americans where, as leader of a vulnerable and underdeveloped nation, he had to find a way to build relationships through compromise. He struggled with that throughout his presidency. So did the Americans.[61]

Like most Vietnamese, Diem refused to be dictated to by foreigners, even by an ally who controlled his fate. It smacked of imperialism. Equally rankling, a foreign dictate to a head of state was insulting in any culture—but in Vietnam, as for all of East Asia, to submit to such treatment was a crushing loss of face—one that weakened his legitimacy as president. Diem was no fool and realized accommodations with Washington had to be made. His most common technique was to listen to the demands in silence, agree to nothing, and take no immediate action. Later, often through an intermediary, Diem then expressed willingness to accept some or most of the demands and later still, adopted them. A host of American diplomats, journalists, politicians, and military officers rejected his ways as a sign of intransigence if not outright defiance and became foes. Only a handful of Americans discerned his methodology and built constructive relationships.[62]

Diem's relations with the public remained awkward throughout his career. After schooling, he spent most of his early career in rural districts and always kept his affinity for that society. However, he could not connect with other key constituencies. He never identified with the urban middleclass, wanted no part of Saigon high society, and despite his brilliant academic record, eschewed the intelligentsia. The Saigon culture of that era made a bad situation worse. Even Diem's education was a point of friction within the upper crust. Most attended university in France, which was considered the highest attainment. Conversely, Diem turned down the opportunity to study in France out of a sense of patriotism. In a society where status mattered greatly, the French-educated elites considered themselves above him and chafed at the idea of serving under Diem. He in turn viewed them as shallow appeasers and self-centered fonctionaires. His comfort with, even desire for, isolation and lack of social life made him a fish out of water within Saigon's upper class and international community. That was a tragedy, for the few who knew him well noted he always exuded an endearing down-to-earth humanity.[63]

Diem held the bourgeois urbanites in contempt, regarding them as "spoiled middle class, always complaining, not worth anything."[64] That may have been partially true, and they certainly strayed far from his personalism ideals, but the middle class also provided social, economic, and political stability, making them a strong force against communism. Diem missed that fact, much to his detriment—it was a critical mistake. He needed them and failed to make the effort to win them over. During the 1959 National Assembly elections, Diem manipulated the results to deprive the opposition of a political voice. Instead of giving them some power in the Assembly, he cut them out of the national discourse and system of governance. Both sides were at fault, but Diem had to make the first move. He did not, and the nation suffered.[65]

Ngo Dinh Diem's power lay in his energy, intellect, and force of will while even his enemies admired his integrity and patriotism. Diem was a workaholic who, according to one close observer, hardly slept and subsisted on a diet of modest meals, tepid tea, and cigarettes. He lived for Vietnam and sacrificed everything in the performance of his duty as president. That defined his political persona as well. His concern for the Vietnamese nation and ability to communicate with the common people were his greatest assets. Diem's outreach was unconventional by Western standards. He came off as dull before big crowds but excelled amongst a small cluster of villagers. Diem was the only contemporary politician who regularly left Saigon to visit, talk, and listen to the common rice farmers in South Vietnam, especially the northern refugees and resettled Catholic families. Even his enemies admitted that Diem was popular in the rural communities.[66]

He did not hide in the palace. U.S. Ambassador Frederick E. Nolting, who worked with Diem in the early 1960s, found him "an indefatigable traveler."[67] Nolting's predecessor, Ambassador Durbrow, said the same thing. Unlike his detractors' image of an out-of-touch and isolated mandarin, Diem was away from Saigon in the provinces "two-three days out of every week" and visited every province in South Vietnam.[68] Physically brave, Diem's appreciation extended to the foot soldiers who also overwhelmingly came from the countryside. Beyond visits to the troops, starting in 1955 he spent every Christmas sharing the hardships of the infantry, often in a dangerous, isolated outpost. His opponents found fault with that as well; one Vietnamese who was an American favorite dismissed his efforts with the backhanded compliment that Ngo Dinh Diem was "much respected among simple, gullible people in the countryside."[69] It was little wonder that Diem was more comfortable in the company of rural families than with almost anyone in Saigon.[70]

Politically, the pace of democratization under Diem also became the point of friction both in Saigon and Washington. His brother Nhu did not mince words; he saw the combined effect of personalism, the NRM, and Can Lao Party as one of establishing "controlled liberty" in South Vietnam.[71] Diem erred in his attempt to create a one-party state while bringing in democracy advocates without winning them over. That only served to create vocal opposition that undermined his rule. But his opponents erred as well when they sought to overthrow his regime while offering nothing viable to take its place. Soon after Diem became prime minister in 1954, the CIA reported on South Vietnam's centers of power ranging from intellectuals, rich merchants, and landlords to military leaders, a few politicians, and "intriguers."[72] Not mentioned were the people needed to form the backbone of an American-style democracy—the farmers—and the Americans themselves seemed to have little interest in their political voice.

While touting democracy, American diplomats, journalists, and the senior military officers interacted with the Vietnamese who seemingly embraced the plutocracy portrayed in the CIA assessment. They garnered the bulk of their impressions and information from inside Saigon, reading English-language publications such as the *Times of Vietnam* and conversing with the French or English-speaking Vietnamese elites. Ambassador Henry Cabot Lodge, Jr., reflected their sentiment; after being in Vietnam barely a week, he concluded that the only "people who count" were the "educated class."[73] Diem, seemingly alone, never took his eye off the forgotten masses in the countryside.[74]

Despite the long-established Nationalist and Dai Viet Parties, multi-party governance never took root, and Ngo Dinh Diem's concerns over democracy reflected reality. There were political opponents, the CIA's "intriguers," and rival political parties but no loyal opposition in the Western sense. Neither the Nationalists nor Dai Viet held democracy in high repute, as their leaders, with few exceptions, believed in a one-party rule—with themselves on top. Like the VWP, the two parties operated secretly and embraced assassination and other terrorist acts; during the late 1920s and 1930s the execution or imprisonment of Nationalist Party leaders by France was as common as that for the ICP. In the 1940s the Dai Viet and Nationalists united, only to break up over control of the alliance. Some felt that those rivalries during the 1945 August Revolution kept them from taking control of the Viet Minh movement instead of Ho Chi Minh and the ICP. The communists certainly saw the threat and in 1946 bloodily purged both parties.[75]

After partition, many Dai Viet and Nationalist Party adherents settled in and around the urban centers in the northern half of South Vietnam and brought with them their supplementary troops. Their subsequent unwillingness to rally to the VNA led to their forced disarmament in 1955—first with the Dai Viet in Quang Tri province during the Ba Long incident and then a similar rebellion by Nationalist Party supplementaries. The clashes poisoned relations with Diem, and they again went underground, infiltrating the civil service and forming secret cells in the military to work against Diem. It was not that the Dai Viet and Nationalists were not dedicated Vietnamese patriots; they simply were impossible to work with as allies, and both parties boycotted the 1956 assembly elections. Outside the disarming incidents, Diem never used force against them because they had no political base, and, as a French journalist put it, by the late 1950s they "were composed of exhausted and disappointed politicians."[76] The frustrated Americans knew as much but could not sit still; in 1959 they tried to induce Diem to create a loyal opposition, an odd proposition to put to any politician wishing to stay in power. Nothing came of it.[77]

That dynamic created an inherent conflict between the American vision of South Vietnam made in the political image and likeness of the United States and Diem's centralized personalist state. The controversial and oft-astute Madame Nhu described the resulting contradiction: The Diem government was "schizophrenic."[78] That had not been the plan, but it was reality. The unfairness if not invalidity of the American position was made clear early on. In October 1955, State Department official Kenneth T. Young quoted Harvard professor Rupert Emerson in a cable to the U.S. embassy in Saigon: "No one should come to the study of Southeast Asian political institutions with the fixed preconception that they should conform to established Western models."[79] Young added that they needed to find their own balance, a strong central government, and a responsible opposition. The schizophrenia began when Diem's vision had to be reconciled with America's demands for a rapid transition to a multi-party democracy and became debilitating when implemented in the midst of an existential war with the DRV.[80]

Like most of his contemporaries and the opposition parties, Diem held that East Asian states best succeeded under a one-party system led by a powerful leader, a position consistent with Emerson. That explained his focus on personalism, the utilization of the secretive Can Lao Party, and promotion of the NRM. For Diem the way to empower the masses was through political participation in the National Revolutionary Movement—not multiparty democracy. Whether it was a coherent third way was debatable, but Ngo Dinh Diem's vision for South Vietnam was apart from both communist socialism and Western liberal democracy. In opposition to Washington, Diem saw it as the only alternative for a nation that was, as he put it, "under unified, underdeveloped and under attack."[81]

War It Will Be

The competing national goals in Saigon and Hanoi were irreconcilable by 1959. Ngo Dinh Diem would never concede to the DRV. His stance might have been irrelevant when he became prime minister in mid–1954, but by 1959, Diem had organized a viable and increasingly powerful state in South Vietnam. For Diem, once the future of Vietnam was at stake, his moral and ethical code ruled out compromise. While the relationship with Washington proved bumpy, its support allowed Diem to firmly oppose Hanoi. Diem did not start the war but made it clear that he would never allow the DRV to take over the south. The peaceful reunification of Vietnam remained as remote as it had been at Geneva four years earlier. That forced Hanoi's hand and led directly to Resolution 15.

The VWP's decision to go to war in January 1959 was far more dramatic than its limited approval of military force indicated. By design, it was not a mass mobilization-conventional offensive as occurred in Korea in 1950. Instead, it was a new twist on the prolonged struggle experienced during the War of Resistance. In modern military terminology, Resolution 15 initiated two simultaneous military operations. The first, taking place in the RVN, was to stabilize the situation: stop the damage being inflicted on the southern VWP comrades or, in Giap's and Clausewitzian terms, an operation to reestablish the balance of combat power. In Hanoi's terms, the goal was to covertly proselytize, recruit, train, build strength, and eventually counterattack.[82]

The second operation aimed to reinforce the first operation and advance the reunification struggle, the "battle shaping phase" of the military campaign. This effort, characterized by significant mobilization of PAVN resources, aimed to build what became one of the most important logistical networks of 20th-century warfare, the tool that allowed Hanoi to win the war: the Ho Chi Minh Trail. If those two lines of operation attained their goals, the rebuilding of revolutionary movement in the south and the creation of a strategic military line of communication from the north, then a war could be waged to destroy the Republic of Vietnam and reunify the country.

The shortcomings of the 1954 Geneva conference that led to partition paved the way for armed conflict. The war's timing was determined largely by the DRV's growing power and changing political landscape along with the RVN's unexpected survival and success in destroying much of the VWP's military and political infrastructure that remained in the south. How the war would proceed was to be determined to an unusual degree by individual Vietnamese leaders, both north and south of the 17th parallel. The aggressive Le Duan, when put in opposition to the stridently anti-communist Ngo Dinh Diem, created a dynamic that put the two regimes, the Democratic Republic of Vietnam and the Republic of Vietnam, on a collision course that by 1959 could no longer be avoided.

PART II

THE COMBATANTS

Part II: Dramatis Personae

Jean de Lattre de Tassigny—French general who worked tirelessly to make the Vietnamese National Army an effective military in the early 1950s

The South Vietnamese

Le Van Ty—The apolitical general in command of the South Vietnamese military (1954–1962)

Le Van Kim—Pro-Dai Viet ARVN general who, along with Big Minh, led early military operations against the sects and Viet Cong

Tran Chanh Thanh—Former Viet Minh officer who developed Saigon's civil pacification program in the late 1950s

The Vietnamese Workers' Party

Mai Chi Tho—Head of COSVN secret intelligence, the Security Agency, and brother of Le Duc Tho

Nguyen Huu Tho—Clandestine VWP leader who became chairman of the National Liberation Front

Nguyen Van Linh—COSVN Secretary starting in 1961 with the responsibility for directing the war in South Vietnam

The PAVN

Van Tien Dung—PAVN Chief of Staff and Giap loyalist

Tran Van Quang—PAVN general placed in command of the Viet Cong in 1961

Hanoi's Spies

Albert Pham Ngoc Thao—PAVN intelligence operative who infiltrated the ARVN

Pham Xuan An—A natural spy and fluent English speaker, Hanoi's most famous and successful spy of the war

Tran Quoc Huong (Muoi Huong)—Ran Hanoi's spies in South Vietnam until 1962 when replaced by **Tu Cang** (Nguyen Van Tau)

The Americans

William Colby—Experienced CIA chief of station in Saigon who nurtured a positive relationship with Diem and his brother Nhu

Eldridge Durbrow—U.S. ambassador who developed an adversarial relationship with President Diem

John W. O'Daniel—General commanding the U.S. military advisors in Vietnam (1954–1957) who helped form the ARVN

Samuel T. Williams—General who replaced O'Daniel and reformed the ARVN along American lines creating the military that fought the Vietnam War

5

A Comparison
of the Two Vietnams, 1959

The geography, demography, and economies of the two Vietnams shared many common characteristics while exhibiting unique differences. When South Vietnam stood on its own in 1955, they became rivals. In terms of geography, the Mekong and Red River Deltas and lowland coastal plains running almost the entire length of Vietnam broadly defined the heavily populated regions, and in some ways made the nations mirrors of each other. Any movement inland both in the DRV and most of the RVN revealed increasingly hilly landscape until reaching the Annamite Cordillera and the borders of Laos and Cambodia. That naturally divided the country into three regions: Bac Bo (the north), Trung Bo (central Vietnam) and Nam Bo (the south). The French euphemistically called them Tonkin, Annam, and Cochinchina, respectively.

An important geographic distinction was that in Nam Bo, the inland hills and mountains gave way to the vast plain of the Mekong Delta. In most of the region, the elevation averaged a mere one meter above sea level. That 700 kilometer stretch of land, which cut across South Vietnam and Cambodia, consisted of seasonal flat dry lands, flood lands, swamps, and marshes. That matrix of wetlands explained the twisting irregular RVN-Cambodian border that represented about 41 percent of the entire 1,700 km RVN frontier. The remoteness of the ill-defined delta borderlands also provided guerrillas, outcasts, and outlaws with ideal hideouts.[1]

Population figures for the years spanning 1954–1963 often were imprecise in specifics but broadly accurate, and despite the migration of northerners to the south in 1954–1955, the DRV retained the larger population. As for the rival economies, during the early years, both the DRV and RVN grew at roughly the same rates (with an edge to the RVN) and were still in the early stages of development. Finally, both countries were farming societies with the large majority of the population living in the flatland river deltas and coastal regions. Their approach to agricultural reforms, especially land redistribution, highlighted the competition.[2]

In setting the stage for the rivalry and despite a number of positives introduced by France (especially infrastructure and education), the damaging role of French colonialism cannot be overstated. France did not willfully position the newly independent states to fail, but both precariously teetered toward that fate after Geneva. The fuller explanation for their economic fragility—and in the case of South

Vietnam political and military fragility as well—was simple. In addition to dominance, the French assumed they would win the war, and there would be no partition. France took for granted that it would have ample time to assist an independent Vietnam through a mutually beneficial relationship within the French Union. When that dream disappeared, both Vietnams struggled with a challenging, even dangerous present. Paris never envisioned a situation where it would sever virtually all its ties in a matter of months in the north and under two years in the south. Both Vietnams suffered as a consequence. Added was the chief difficulty confronted by any new nation-state: building a better future for its citizens.

The brief window of peace from 1954 through 1959 allowed both countries to develop, and that determined their ability to wage war. To appreciate those conditions, demographics, geography and weather, economy and resources, education, and finally the important issues of agricultural and land reform will be addressed. And as most of the fighting took place in South Vietnam, its challenges will be presented in more detail.

Demographics

When the war began in 1959, the DRV had a growing population nearing 16 million. That made North Vietnam about 15 percent larger than South Vietnam, with a population estimated at just over 14 million that also grew at a robust rate. The high birth rate made for a young population, an asset for countries going to war. The difference would have been greater if not for the estimated 900,000 migrants who left the north for the south during 1954–1955 regroupment period. Both countries were overwhelmingly ethnic Vietnamese with an 85 percent majority in both the DRV and RVN, and as noted, the bulk of the population resided in the coastal and the delta rice growing regions. The key ethnic minorities in South Vietnam were the Chinese (numbering around 900,000 with most settled in the Saigon-Cholon area), Montagnards of the lightly populated Central Highlands composed of some 20 ethnic tribes, and 350,00 ethnic Cambodians (Khmer Krom) who lived in the southwest near the Cambodian border. In the DRV, hill and mountain peoples like the Tai, Hmong, and Nung were the largest ethnic communities.[3]

Geography and Weather

As for size, North Vietnam contained some 159,000 square kilometers, compared to 174,000 for the RVN. In the DRV, the critical region was the Red River Delta that contained Hanoi, the nation's capital and largest city, and the main port of Haiphong. The delta was the central rice-growing region in the north. The RVN had two major urban areas, greater Saigon and Hue. In its north, average temperatures (in Fahrenheit) varied from a low of 65° in January to a high of 95° in July. Nam Bo enjoyed a more temperate climate with an average of 92° in April and 73° in January. In the southern Mekong Delta, normal temperatures ranged between 75° and 90°.

Infrequently the lowlands experienced highs above 100° during the spring while falling to 60° during the summer monsoons. Humidity was always present, averaging 80 percent and often reaching 100 percent. The mountain city of Dalat north of Saigon was the ideal locale with an average temperature of 70°—warmer in the day and cooler at night. Things also were different in South Vietnam's Central Highlands plateau, which averaged 500 meters in altitude and offered a cooler alternative to the coastal lowlands having a year-round temperature averaging around 72° although highs could reach into the 80s in summer. Also, more unique to the high country, the daily swing between afternoon and night could be as much as 20°.[4]

As for precipitation, in North Vietnam the rainy monsoon season ran from April to October when 80 percent of rainfall occurred, while running later in the south, from May to November. Da Nang and Hue were the wettest cities in South Vietnam, where Da Nang received up to 27 inches of rain and Hue 20 inches in October, the height of the rainy season. The Mekong Delta averaged 10–12 inches of rain per month during the monsoon season that ran from late April until early October. Outside the cities, everything revolved around rice farming, and that in turn was determined by the seasons. Like the rest of Southeast Asia, most crops in Vietnam grew during the dry season, and in parts of South Vietnam, it was possible to plant two rice crops a year.[5]

The seasons defined the pace of combat operations. During 1959–1963, the most active period was the spring, with the action picking up again as the monsoons faded in the autumn. Vietnam's traditional seasons did not match those in the West, coming earlier in the year with spring beginning in late February, summer in May, and autumn in late August. Winter began in November. Usually, the lowest level of fighting began in October with rice harvesting followed by pre-drying, threshing, and getting the crop to market—a process that could stretch into January—and another lull occurred during the Tet Holiday. This was not unique to the war in Vietnam; a similar cycle occurred in Laos with peak fighting lasting from February through May (spring) and August through November (autumn).[6]

The ground war was fought in the south, and contrary to the stereotype of Vietnam being a giant jungle, its battlegrounds represented a wide variety of climes and places. By traditional demarcations, South Vietnam consisted of Nam Bo and the southern half of Trung Bo. For military purposes, Nam Bo had three key and distinct regions: (a) The rich expansive rice fields of the Mekong Delta sitting on flood plains and crisscrossed by rivers, streams and canals where half of South Vietnam's population lived; (b) Greater Saigon-Gia Dinh, to include the port of Vung Tau, the nation's governmental and economic center where one in seven South Vietnamese lived; and (c) the Cambodian border region consisting of the Plain of Reeds, swamps along the Cambodian border, and dense forests in northwestern Nam Bo (home to the deadly War Zones C and D). Those remote regions had a small share of the population (six percent) but contained most of Nam Bo's Viet Cong base areas. During the War of Resistance, the French divided the areas around Saigon into four war zones (A–D). During the Vietnam War, references to War Zones A and B fell into disuse but what had been parts of War Zones C and D continued to be enemy base areas, and those roughly defined areas kept their names.[7]

In Trung Bo, the land began with the flat rice growing coastal regions where the majority of the population lived. Inland lay the temperate, sparsely-populated Central Highlands (less than four percent of the population). The northern section of RVN-controlled Trung Bo held the coastal urban centers of Da Nang, Hue, and Dong Ha. Moving inland came the rise of the rugged and heavily forested Annamite Mountains and valleys. In the northernmost region was the DMZ that again began at the coastal plain, headed west along Route 9 (that paralleled the DMZ), and entered the Annamites, then Khe Sanh, and finally the Laotian border.

Economy and Resources

Immediately after the end of the War of Resistance, the two Vietnams underwent phenomenal economic growth—routinely in excess of 40 percent per year. But the high numbers were misleading as much of the growth represented a difficult climb back to pre-war levels. Vietnam had endured over of decade of economic hardship; first during World War II that included the 1940–1945 Japanese Occupation followed by the more economically destructive 1946–1954 War of Resistance. Making matters worse, when the French departed during 1954–1956, they took with them materials, equipment, and even entire factories. On the plus side, Vietnam had become one of the Cold War's most important political battlegrounds by the late 1950s, and both countries benefited from outside aid. They received approximately equal levels of support over a six-year period of nearly a $1 billion each. In the second half of 1959 for example, the Chinese and Soviets provided $87 million in credits and loans to the DRV. That explained why when war started anew in 1959, Vietnam's two gross domestic products (GDPs) were quite small, approximately $800 million for the DRV and a bit under $1.5 billion for the RVN (the 1960 U.S. GDP was $541 billion).[8]

The wars had not hit the two Vietnams evenly and that affected their recovery. That the RVN economically outperformed the DRV was common knowledge by 1957, even within the ranks of socialist states sympathetic to the DRV. The DRV per capita GDP was $51 compared to $105 in South Vietnam. Why the south gained an early lead over the north stemmed from a number of factors. While both states dealt with economic damage upon independence—150,000 Vietnamese working for the French lost their jobs and 60 percent of the roads and the entire railway system had been destroyed in the RVN—most of the fighting during the War of Resistance had taken place in Bac Bo, giving the north the more daunting challenge. The north also had been France's industrial center in Indochina with the large majority of the French-owned factories located in Haiphong and Hanoi, and as noted above, when the French troops left, so did the factory equipment.[9]

Not everything worked to the RVN's advantage. The VWP gave the north a strong stable government, and South Vietnam had to deal with dysfunction. In 1954, not only was the Bao Dai government administratively inept, the state's finances were in disarray with no budgets or controls over spending. It did get better for Saigon. By 1957, Washington was pleased with the RVN's economic progress. Under

Diem the budget was balanced while foreign cash reserves were satisfactory and remained so going into the future. Prices were stable, imports and exports were up,, and rice and rubber production increased. The Diem administration ran a fiscal surplus that year (600 million piasters or $2.3 million) and expected to run a larger one in 1958 (900 million).[10]

Key financial, banking and monetary institutions were formed. In the south, the National Bank of Vietnam came into existence on 1 January 1955, followed by the creation of the Directorate General of the Exchange, to prime the economy, the Credit Commercial Bank of Vietnam was founded on 13 December. But it came at a cost. Before the new piaster currency could be issued, South Vietnam agreed to pay monies owed to the French-run currency institute that provided duan, and not just its share, but because Hanoi refused to pay Paris anything, Saigon assumed 95 percent of the total debt.[11]

The RVN also attracted foreign investment with a very low direct tax rate: ten percent from 1958 to 1962, while every other developing country in Southeast Asia had rates above 20 percent. Indirect taxes gained nearly four times the revenue and accounted for 4.8 percent of GDP in 1960. For a developing nation, the RVN had a healthy import/export ratio—it was worse than Taiwan but better than South Korea. In 1954 the ratio was over 5:1 but dropped favorably to an average of just under 4:1 during the 1955–1963 period before jumping to 6:1 afterwards. North Vietnam also faced high trade imbalances that continually increased during the 1954–1963 period. The imbalances reflected the fact that both Vietnams relied heavily on foreign aid to spur economic growth and development.[12]

Improving the transportation systems in the two Vietnams was defined by divergent results. Throughout the Vietnam War, the DRV's railways system was critical to the war effort, and that priority demanded the commitment of resources and personnel on a large scale to include significant support from China. It remained an important resource. The DRV also made good use of its coastal waters and rebuilt and expanded its road system continuously, using both discharged soldiers and youth labor units that had helped build roads during the war with France.[13]

It was a different story in the south. Viet Cong attacks in the early years of the Vietnam War crippled the RVN rail system; it was closed after the end of 1963, idling 1,374 kilometers of railways along with 102 locomotives, 184 passenger, 718 freight, and 48 tank cars. South Vietnam was forced to turn to alternative means. In addition to its long, easily accessed coastline, the RVN had an efficient waterway system comprised of over 4,600 kilometers of navigable rivers and canals plied by over 3,000 boats of all types with a cargo capacity of 59,000 metric tons. Easing the transportation problem, most industries resided within the Saigon area, and thanks to American aid, if a waterway was not handy then motorized transport was an option. The Saigon region boasted Vietnam's best road system, and a UN highway program begun in 1957 further improved South Vietnam's network. It was at that time that some of the old French routes expanded to become highways; the critical north-south Route 1 grew into Highway 1.[14]

Economically, Diem's RVN rejected the unbridled free-market system and followed his "personalist third-way" model that adopted many of the underlying principles of free-market liberalism with traces of socialist centralized control to include five-year industrialization plans.[15] South Vietnamese policy held that "agriculture must be the basis of our economy" with two objectives: economic independence and raising the standard of living.[16] Growth was fueled by agriculture followed by manufacturing. The "third way" of a mixed government-private sector economy remained unrealized, however. Saigon did nationalize the timber industry as well as the Long Tho cement factory and the RVN's only coal mine at Nong Son (whose production increased by factor of ten by 1959). But Saigon did not exercise the government's right to 51 percent national ownership of critical industries. It had neither the money nor trained personnel to broadly implement state control, and majority ownership never extended beyond a cotton-spinning company and sugar factory. It somehow worked; sugar production increased 26-fold by late 1959.[17]

Major public works projects did get underway in the RVN. By the late 1950s, a 10–20 million piasters infrastructure program in the former Viet Minh–controlled provinces in north-central South Vietnam had begun with nationwide projects equal to 300 million piasters planned for the future. Underlying economic growth were significant gains in the quality of life as people, especially in the countryside, were able to afford and purchase consumer goods at unparalleled levels. Health care also improved; the number of hospitals, clinics, and other health care facilities in the RVN increased dramatically between 1954 and 1959. The DRV made similar gains in health care and quality of life, although it lagged behind in improving the lot of the average farmers and their families. Both countries also made nearly identical progress in electrification and confined it to urban areas and selected facilities. Again, the RVN had an advantage by possessing the new Da Nhim hydroelectric plant built by Japan, while the DRV, with a greater demand for urban electrical power and its industrialization projects, faced brown outs.[18]

Strong support for the private sector in the RVN stood in contrast to government policies in North Vietnam. Ho Chi Minh and other senior leaders were orthodox Marxist-Leninists, and put industrialization first and agricultural collectivization second as economic development priorities. Party Secretary Truong Chinh successfully pushed to fully adopt the Soviet industrialization model in 1955. Elsewhere, they at first went slowly when it came to socializing the economy, perhaps over concern of the hoped for 1956 election, and nationalization of the private sector did not begin with vigor until 1957. It destroyed North Vietnam's small business economy. Anyone who owned a business or held a supervisory position was judged to be a capitalist exploiter and removed; simply having done business overseas was sufficient to be punished as an agent of capitalist imperialism. The entire body of managers and business administrators was eradicated with no capable replacements available and words like "goods" and "markets" forbidden. Only a handful of colonial government bureaucrats were temporarily spared.[19]

In such an environment, the focus on industrialization proved optimistic. After the purges, of the DRV's millions of citizens a mere 30 were industrial experts or engineers, and outside parochial interests, France had done little to promote industrialization in Indochina. Hanoi plunged ahead by adopting a classic communist five-year economic plan (spanning 1956–1961). It focused on heavy industries like cement and mining. The VWP Central Committee funded industrialization over agriculture by a ratio of over 2:1; the DRV devoted 44 percent of its non-defense spending to industrialization and 17 percent on agriculture. In the RVN, 28 percent went toward agriculture and 20 percent to industrialization.[20]

The VWP had little to show for the effort as the gains in the early years were inconsequential, but the party did lay the foundation for future advances. There were areas of growth. North Vietnam benefited from having the majority of Vietnam's mineral resources—especially coal, chromite, and phosphates—and that gave it a marked edge over the RVN. The coal pits at Hon Gai and Hon Quang and mines at Cuc Tho were especially productive. DRV timber production, which stood at 360,000 cubic meters in 1955 and had doubled by 1959. There also were significant iron ore deposits in North Vietnam that spurred the construction of the Thai Nguyen Steel Works in 1959.[21]

In South Vietnam, the Nong Son coal mine was expanded and an iron mine at Hoa My put under development, but both were on a smaller scale than those in the DRV. When it came to overseas commerce, the DRV was the only Marxist country in Southeast Asia and traded solely within the closed circle of fellow communist states, while the RVN did business on a broad international basis dominated by trade with France, the United States, and Japan. When looking at the lackluster DRV progress in the late 1950s, a Canadian diplomat in Hanoi noted that there was no fear of an economic collapse, as there was nothing to collapse. Witticisms aside, the diplomat was right; during the 1954–1959 period, DRV industrialization was a sideshow—a small piece of the economy.[22]

Conversely, RVN industries catered to consumers by focusing on textiles, processed foods, glass, and ceramics, and all did well. The RVN had an advantage by possessing expanding specialized agricultural sectors producing rubber and sugar. Rubber exports matched pre-war levels by 1955 and reached 76,000 metric tons earning $48 million in 1963. The long-term outlook was excellent as many of the trees planted in the late 1950s were due to mature in the late 1960s and early 1970s. In January 1958, a new textile mill was opened, and the Lambretta Motor Scooter Company plant in Saigon thrived. Growth in the RVN continued, although unevenly. Diem's brother Ngo Dinh Can was unconcerned about the pace of development in central RVN. As he saw it, "The economy naturally develops slowly after a long period of economic stagnation and exploitation under the French."[23] As long as things got better, the population was satisfied.[24]

Only the war upset the economic advances. In the south, the rubber plantations were falling into a state of neglect by 1963. Rubber exports from South Vietnam were $84 million in 1960 before going into a steep decline as the war intensified, and the import-export ratio suffered accordingly. The war also fueled inflation; in 1960 $1 purchased 90 piasters. That rose to 110 piasters in 1963, and 160 in 1964—numbers that rivaled the DRV 1955–1956 inflation crisis. During the peace from mid–1954 to mid–1959, the RVN largely outperformed the DRV, and while what might have happened if war had not returned is unknowable, both nations progressed. What is known is that by 1964, the expanding war led to industrial declines in both Vietnams that continued into the 1970s.[25]

Education

At the time of independence in 1954, the education system in Vietnam, both north and south, was sorely lacking. There were two primary causes: the disruption of war and the legacy of the French colonial rule. As a result, the large majority of the population, estimated at 80 percent, was illiterate. Despite gains made by 1959, when war came, both the RVN and DRV had to deal with the challenge that the majority of their military recruits could neither read nor write.[26]

The process of creating a school system for all of French Indochina began in 1906. Prior to that, there were very few schools of any kind and no nationwide education system; only traditional Buddhist seminaries and Confucian exam preparation academies along with a few missionary schools. The arrival of the French changed that. By 1869 in French-controlled Cochinchina, there were 126 primary schools, but they only served 4,700 students. Progress was slow. Even after 1906, a nationwide primary school system had barely scratched the surface even though advocates, such as Phan Boi Chau, began pushing for a universal public education system in 1907. In the same year, Vietnamese reformers established the Tonkin Free School in Hanoi, and the first of several French-Vietnamese schools opened. But as late as 1917, there were only 67 primary schools and one middle school in Tonkin, the most populous region in Indochina. The first major steps were taken during the 1917–1924 period with the passing of the General Regulation of Education by the colonial administration. Progress remained gradual, and only a small fraction of children attended school.[27]

The French concurrently abolished the centuries old mandarin examination system. That system consisted of demanding triennial regional examinations where only the top one percent obtained a second-tier grade with another three percent or so getting a third-tier degree. The rest went home. Those obtaining the second tier could later go to the imperial capital at Hue to test for the top tier. The regional tests ended in 1915 and the top tier examination in 1919. This gradually created a new bureaucratic class where speaking French became prized and attending French schools and especially university studies in France became the apex of achievement. Many Vietnamese, however, resented the new bureaucratic class for its loyalty to the French, earning any number the derisive epithet "rice and meat" bureaucrats, implying they served to serve themselves and were reviled for their graft. Later, Lansdale cynically described their relationship with the French: "The French had trained them … not to run a department but to sit there and be clerks."[28] When the VWP took power in the north, most were purged from the bureaucracy. In South Vietnam, they continued to dominate civil service.[29]

A second era began during 1924–1945 when schools appeared in villages where 85 percent of the population lived and with the implementation of a standard Kindergarten-Primary (grades 1–9) and Secondary (grades 10–12) system. Based on the French model, universal education only was intended up to grade 5; after that, advancement was based upon the fifth-year examination, which had a 60 percent passing rate followed by baccalaureate examinations at the secondary level. Even so, by 1940, less than 20 percent of children were enrolled, with most schools in urban areas. World War II, the 1940–1945 Japanese Occupation, and the War of Resistance did nothing to improve the situation. The DRV made a serious effort to open schools in their base areas—literacy classes began in the early 1940s—but war regularly foiled the efforts. When peace came, Hanoi moved quickly to improve public education. By 1959, 1.4 million students attended First Cycle primary schools, 178,000 were enrolled in Second Cycle middle schools, with 20,000 students attending the Third Cycle classes, a fourfold increase over 1954.[30]

As in the DRV, building a mass education system proved difficult for South Vietnam. The wars not only stopped public school expansion, but the existing system declined due to neglect and disruptions. South Vietnam did possess one advantage; Nam Bo had a tradition of embracing education unlike anywhere else in Vietnam. It was the first to adopt Quoc Ngu, the Vietnamese writing system, and in the later 19th century, there were three modern schools in Nam Bo for every one in Bac Bo. That not only gave it a quantitative advantage in school facilities and teachers, but a pro-education ethic that supported education at the grassroots level. After peace, the number of children attending school in South Vietnam nearly tripled by 1959 and continued to expand rapidly. An American official noted that a province with three schools in 1954 had 40 new ones in 1959. In all over 8,000 new classrooms were built between 1955 and the end of 1959.[31]

Conversely, the DRV held an advantage at the post-secondary level as Hanoi was Vietnam's higher education center. The Université Indochine opened in 1906 and expanded after World War I. By the 1920s, the university boasted schools for law, medicine, administration, veterinary sciences, business, applied sciences, and fine arts. Enrollment was limited, however. As World War II began in 1939, there were only 721 students. After 1954, the university grew steadily as did enrollment. Things were less developed in the south; beyond small branches in Saigon of Hanoi's Schools of Law and Applied Sciences, there were no colleges or universities operating in the RVN in 1954. Saigon moved to close the gap. The State University in Saigon opened in 1955 and a second campus in Hue in 1957. By 1959 there were 10,000 college students enrolled in South Vietnam with another 2,000 studying abroad.[32]

Struggles at Agricultural Reform

The War of Resistance badly damaged rice-producing regions in both Vietnams, and supplying food for the populace became an urgent need. Simply by geography and population, South Vietnam had the advantage when it came to feeding its people. Both countries had approximately the same amount of land under cultivation (13 percent for the DRV and 14 percent for the RVN), but the RVN's larger size meant access to over a million additional acres for rice farming to nourish a smaller population. In 1959 Hanoi had approximately 4.8 million acres dedicated to rice production compared to 6.2 million in South Vietnam—which explains why South Vietnam managed to absorb some 900,000 northerners in 1954 and 1955 while dealing with a growing population.[33]

The legacy of French rule loomed large. The colonial system had been abusive, with 70 percent of land held by five percent of the population, and the landholders retained between 50–80 percent of the harvest grown by landless farmers working their properties. The farmers were further impoverished through usurious loans charging up to 300 percent interest. That is why the VWP slogan "The land to the peasants, finish the reign of the exploiters of the people" resonated within the farming communities, and land reform was a driving issue behind the War of Resistance, second only to the fight for independence.[34] No matter who led Vietnam, that injustice had to be righted. As the vast majority lived in farming communities, much was at stake, and there was a real ideological competition on display with land reform, for as in most things, the DRV and RVN adopted different approaches.[35]

RVN Land and Agricultural Reform

The War of Resistance ravaged southern rice production. It was half the pre-war level with large tracts abandoned; the area under cultivation dropped from 6.1 million to 4.1 million acres. The recovery also was less than ideal as reform efforts began being paralyzed as the government fought for its life, first against General Hinh and then the sects from 1954 into mid–1955. With such a start, the transformation sat unfinished when war again overwhelmed the effort in 1959. The government did its best under the circumstances, and one favorable factor was that the land ownership problem largely was confined to the Mekong Delta. While the rest of Vietnam had long been settled, the delta was contested ground. Its lands had been fought over by Vietnam and Cambodia into the eighteenth century, then the French took direct control in the nineteenth. The tumult created Vietnam's greatest concentrations of wealthy landowners and impoverished peasants—a volatile combination. In the RVN's central coastal rice-growing regions, there was no system of landlord–large farmer dominance, and in many villages, no landless peasants. Divisive land redistribution and excessive crop taking issues did not arise. In those regions the main problem was recovering from extensive war damages.[36]

In the midst the 1954–1955 Hinh-Sect upheavals, Diem took his first step at agricultural reform to reduce excessive takings by landlords. On 8 January 1955, he enacted Ordinance no. 2 that capped rents at between 15–25 percent of the harvest, and required that farm leases be a minimum of five years in length. Landowners also had to report to the government the locations and size of held lands not under cultivation, and it further directed them to find tenants to farm the fields. In another sign of progress, the Dong Cam dam reopened in September, providing irrigation for 19,000 acres in Phu Yen province (south of Qui Nhon) and improving the standard of living for 300,000 people in the region. Saigon sought to further increase areas under tillage by opening areas in the Central Highlands (that disturbed the Montagnards) and reclaiming tracts in the westernmost Mekong Delta's Plain of Reeds. Called land development centers, they formed the core of Diem's resettlement program that came under what eventually was named the General Commission of Pioneer Farming in 1957.[37]

The largest example of the development centers' early efforts was the relocation of 100,000 predominantly Catholic farmers from the north to the Mekong Delta's An Giang province during 1955 and 1956. They were given reclaimed marshlands that became the Cai San settlements. It was painfully ugly and its beginning little more than a string of failures that brought quick and strong resentment toward Saigon and Diem. But the decision proved correct. Despite the obstacles, over time the refugees managed to build thriving farming communities that became anti–Viet Cong strongholds. By 1959, 125,000 "pioneering" Mekong Delta settlers resided in 90 land development centers.[38]

Diem's land reform was not socialist collectivization. Farm ownership remained the law—something the VWP labeled capitalist "appeasement."[39] How to get land to the landless under those constraints captured the problem in South Vietnam. In July 1956, during the visit of Vice President Richard M. Nixon, Vice President Nguyen Ngoc Tho proposed a land reform program to purchase excess holdings that would free up as much as 1.8 million acres. The price tag was massive: $200 million. To leverage the program and make it palatable to the Americans, Saigon asked for $30 to $40 million in up-front monies as a down payment to buy the land from the current the owners, with the balance to be paid by interest-bearing RVN bonds redeemable in 10 to 15 years. Saigon would then sell the land to farmers, who would repay the debt through an interest-free, five-year schedule. The United States also was asked to guarantee the RVN bonds.[40]

There were obvious problems. Beyond the size of the financial request that was certainly inflated, Ambassador Reinhardt pointed out that farmers did not earn enough to meet the repayment schedule. Reinhardt also was less than happy that Tho had made a presentation to Nixon without notifying the embassy in advance. But the U.S. embassy had no counterproposal, and that was an ongoing difficulty when it came to land reform. There was a complete lack of unity, and competing personal rivalries—on the part of both the Americans and Vietnamese—played an unhelpful role in the process.[41]

Tho's proposal was at odds with Ministry of Agriculture—which did not speak well for Diem's leadership—and on the American side alone there were three competing voices all with their own plan: Price Gittinger of the U.S. Operations Mission (USOM), Wolf Ledejinsky, the previous USOM land reform expert and now advisor to Diem; and the Michigan State University Group (MSUG), an experimental partnership between the U.S. Government and a state university, which provided to the RVN expertise in the areas of administration and policing along with limited financial and economic administrative support. Ambassador Reinhardt came out against Tho's plan and further encouraged the Diem regime to maintain the status quo while pushing reform off to 1958. Saigon had to accept that no new U.S. monies were coming, but another long delay was the last thing the South Vietnamese government wanted to hear. Diem pressed ahead.[42]

By the fall of 1956, patience ran thin. For two years both sides had action on land reform, but no one could come up with an acceptable plan. Finally, and at Diem's urging, the National Assembly took action. To reduce large holdings, in October Ordinance 57 was passed that limited farm size to 250 acres—a rule that affected fewer than 3,000 large landlords. Of those, 1,200 had 380,000 acres of land expropriated and were compensated with government bonds. The government purchased the remaining excess, freeing up 1,060,000 acres for resale and redistribution. The power of large landowners had been broken. In 1954, two percent of the farm owners controlled 45 percent of the land. After Ordinance 57 took full effect, they were reduced to holding less than ten percent of RVN farmlands. Inexplicably, Reinhardt and the embassy team still resisted taking decisive action and opposed the ordinance. When the issue was revisited in November, the Americans argued for more studies to be conducted in continued consultation with experts from Japan and the Nationalist Chinese in Taiwan. *Le Monde* journalist Jean Lacouture, however, was impressed with Diem's action, calling the repurchases sensible agrarian reforms.[43]

The ordinance did a great deal of good, as over 650,000 acres of the land had been redistributed to 115,000 families by the end of 1957. But it also became controversial immediately as it created winners and losers—the reform program was unbalanced. The crux of discontent was the return of holdings to absentee landlords that had been redistributed rent-free to poor farmers by the VWP during the war. The return of the landlords meant a return to rent payments, and almost all lacked funds to buy their farms or even come up with the ten percent down payment. As a result, many poor farmers living in lands previously under Viet Minh control suffered a loss in earnings, and some lands were forfeited, instilling fear and distrust of Saigon.[44]

It also ignored the warning made by the Americans. Farmers had virtually no cash. Diem turned to the corvée where a farmer worked for free on a government project both in lieu of taxes and to purchase the farmland. It was a vestige of the colonial era when the French used corvée labor to build public projects like roads. At first it was popular, but over the years when the corvée demands turned excessive, the farmers turned away from Saigon to embrace the VWP "social justice" mantra. Diem undid the VWP wartime land reforms, but the new program inadequately helped the poorest farmers, and the increasing corvée burden alienated many more by the early 1960s. Unrest in Mekong Delta areas continued, and the VWP skillfully exploited it. It was a blunder by Diem.[45]

There were less controversial areas where greater progress was made. Saigon established agricultural improvement stations in the countryside that helped farmers diversify crops, cultivate fruit and nut-trees, build fishponds, and commercially grow mushrooms in simple stacks of rice-straw. The Americans supplied better rice seed strains, and fertilizer use by farmers grew from 79 metric tons in 1956 to 300 metric tons by the early 1960s. Livestock numbers increased with hogs and chickens prized most. There also were improvements in rural water supplies. As a result, rice production grew throughout 1954–1959. Food supplies were sufficient despite the growing population, and the overall diet improved. In 1959, rice production hit a new peak, and the outlook for the next year appeared even brighter. But as war spread, the total area under cultivation stagnated, and the RVN became a net rice importer by the mid–1960s.[46]

Throughout 1954–1959, Diem continued to combine land reform, increased crop production, and resettlement as a security stratagem by populating areas not just to provide farmland but to establish rural anti-communist political centers that, when integrated with the local Self-Defense Corps and Civil Guard, would become barriers against Viet Cong expansion. In 1957, the government provided land to settle 40,000 demobilized soldiers and their families in safe border areas to include the Central Highlands where they were to be both farmers and unpaid defense volunteers. In the highlands, farmers excelled by adopting dry rice and slash-and-burn cultivation of hemp, jute, and other crops, and by 1958, 30,000 had settled there. Even Washington recognized the progress. Dulles noted in March 1958, "Diem is doing a remarkable job with land reform and resettlement programs but will need economic aid for some time to come. U.S. is to be commended for its continuing assistance to free Vietnam."[47]

The restart of war augured by Resolution 15 upset that progress. The increased violence combined with resettlement, the model village concept, and "pioneer" farming eventually led to the Mekong Delta's Agroville Program, inaugurated on 7 July 1959, the Double Seventh, that combined improving agricultural output with security protections against the Viet Cong. It was not a dramatic change but more a modest step back toward pacification. At the basic level, agrovilles regrouped families living on the margins into a protected community situated near a line of communication that offered improved education, health, and civic benefits. There were, however, two types of agrovilles with very different priorities: one for protecting loyal populations and others with the emphasis on relocating populations living in pro–VC areas.[48]

The latter, while subtly nonviolent, was as effective as a military assault on the Viet Cong. By controlling the population, the government denied the VC access to food, recruits, and taxes, as well as current intelligence; it went to the heart of Mao's analogy of guerrillas being the fish that must swim in the sea of the people to survive. The Viet Cong saw the agrovilles as an impediment to expanding or even maintaining control over the rural areas and moved to disrupt the program. The Nam Bo VWP Central Committee reported in 1959 that for the badly pressed Viet Cong, their only active operations were directed against the agrovilles. Many Americans and Vietnamese in Saigon condemned the effort as they wrongly measured it against an ideal—not reality in Vietnam—and the agrovilles did go away but not because the idea was a bad. Agrovilles were not perfect, but they were a check against the Viet Cong.[49]

There was one sinister reason behind some of the American criticism. ARVN Major Albert Pham Ngoc Thao, a senior official overseeing the program, vigorously opposed the segregation of the pro–VC families, claiming that isolation alienated them, and he was widely cited by Americans. How releasing them back into VC controlled areas would be better was left unsaid. But Thao had his own good reason. He was a highly placed PAVN clandestine operative and deliberately sabotaged the program. Ultimately, it failed through a combination of reasons. While Thao's actions hurt, the program was too resource intensive. The funds needed for agroville schools, clinics, and civic centers were beyond reach. As a recourse, cash-strapped Diem doubled down on corvée labor to include requiring relocated families to build their own homes. That alienated friend and foe alike. Finally, the agrovilles were so large that they required an inordinately sized security force for protection (and Thao also was in charge of agroville security).[50]

As significant as the shortcomings were, the Diem agrarian reforms worked well. By the time the war started in 1959, approximately one million acres of land had been redistributed, and the 3.9 million acres that were idle or un-reclaimed in 1954 were under cultivation. Another 100,000 new acres had been opened up in the highlands. The lot of the average South Vietnamese farmer had improved significantly, and a typical farm was 3.3 acres. The truly amazing statistic was the improvement in rice crop yield. By 1959, the annual crop had grown from 2.5 to 5.1 million metric tons. The 1954–1959 years were nearly universally remembered as a period of prosperity in rural South Vietnam. One Mekong Delta farmer recalled, "Even the poorest could make ends meet," and another added that during those years, "people were really living the good life, healthy and happy."[51]

DRV Land and Agricultural Reform

As in the RVN, the DRV was an agricultural nation. Farming provided the livelihood for 85 percent of the families, employed 80 percent of the workforce, and generated about 50 percent of the national income. If South Vietnam with its American allies labored to find the correct approach to land reform, there was no doubt in the minds of Hanoi's leaders as to what was needed—land redistribution, collectivization, and punishing exploiters. And they aggressively pursued those objectives through their Land-to-the-Tiller Program. Reform started innocuously and got underway before the War of Resistance ended. The first major "social justice" program, which was limited to areas under Viet Minh control, began in 1953 and allocated on average one acre of land for a farming family. After partition, the DRV gained a few advantages. Aiding its central planners, the departure of 900,000 people to the south opened up farmlands for landless peasants. Additionally, 123,550 acres owned by French were converted into 16 collective state farms. Finally, exploiters such as landlords had their lands redistributed to landless farmers. Ostensibly, owners of seized lands were to be compensated, but the caveat that they had not committed "crimes against the state" essentially nullified the need for payment.[52]

Those advantages proved of little worth. Under the direction of general secretary Truong Chinh (who along with Vo Nguyen Giap had been a leading VWP voice on the "peasant problem" since the 1930s), the DRV stumbled with its five-phase Agrarian Reform Campaign that began in earnest in May 1954. Chinese Communist Party influence on these events was significant. By 1952 Beijing had steered Hanoi land reform efforts away from winning over landowners to the revolution to making them targets of retribution. The mass mobilization process, "perfected" in 1953 and fully underway by 1955, ran as planned, and its repressive tactics were the problem. First VWP cadres arrived in a village to mobilize the peasants and identify people's enemies. Farmers were divided into five classes through arcane rules propagated in the Population Classification Decree (laborers, poor, middle, and rich farmers, and landlords). Cadres then indoctrinated farmers, and the ardent were given special instructions to identify class enemies, to be "denouncers." Next came the enforcers, PAVN soldiers adhering to the proclamation "To work, to eat, to sleep with the peasants."[53] Lastly, VWP judges arrived on "denunciation day" to convene people's agricultural reform tribunals to try selected class enemies (roughly one per 500 villagers) with the ultimate enemies being landlords—cruel owners—who did not work the land. Landlords were subjected to the severest punishments to include execution.[54]

While the numbers were shocking, it was the process's terror that poisoned the reform efforts. Compounding the problem, the number of enemies was rigidly set at five percent, which exceeded the number of rich farmers and landowners. That created fear in every village and hamlet as the definition of a "class enemy exploiter" devolved into anyone who had lands the VWP needed.[55] Before long, any farmer who owned at least three acres (the average farm size in South Vietnam) was a landlord or rich farmer to be subjected to persecution. Years later it was concluded that well over half of the victims were wrongly punished in order to meet the quotas. That villagers struggled to cope was seen in the selection of many elderly "exploiters," as it led to credible speculation that they volunteered so as to inflict the least hardship on the village.[56]

Once trials began, villagers were called out to witness the proceedings with the accused in bamboo cages bound by leg irons. After being found guilty, prisoners either were sent to Hanoi for confinement—sentences ranged from two to 20 years—or publicly executed. When it came to executions, the VWP did not directly adopt Mao Zedong's quota of one killing per 1,000 citizens. If Mao had been followed, then the total would have exceeded 15,000, but the murders, while numbering in the thousands, likely never exceeded 10,000. To that total were added those who died while imprisoned or after being cast out as non-persons. Being denied work and ration cards, the castouts expired from starvation or suicide or other related causes. The possessions of the guilty were confiscated and distributed amongst the villagers, leaving the weeping family of the accused destitute and confined to a small corner of their former home, which then became state property. It was cruel, unjust, and bloody vengeance but not a holocaust.[57]

Illustrative of the brutality is the story of Nguyen Thi Nam, presented by historian Alex-Thai D. Vo. About 47 years old, Nam became the first victim and demonstrated that even loyal Viet Minh did not escape punishment, as there were no good or innocent landowners. She lived a hard life. Driven into poverty by her profligate husband, Nam worked tirelessly, becoming a thriving entrepreneur and large landholder (over 1,000 acres). In America that would have made her an example of a rags-to-riches story, but in the DRV at that time, success marked her for death. Despite her humane and non-exploitive practices, strong patriotism, and active support of the VWP, she was no longer a person but a doomed symbol. Her May 1953 trial was horrific. The prisoners (her two sons had been arrested as well) were mistreated during pre-trial confinement, and once the trial was underway, farmers watching were encouraged to slap, spit on, and beat the shackled accused. The spectacle ended with cries for execution. Found guilty, she was executed by firing squad on an unknown date in mid–July.[58]

For obvious reasons, as land reform progressed, it proved more disruptive and unpopular than in the south. There were concerns within the VWP. It was feared that rallies where denouncers identified enemies and public trials violated the Geneva accords. More disquieting, they alienated farm families prior to the 1956 reunification election. The cadres were proven correct. Hanoi's rapid and violent drive toward agrarian socialism stirred resentment and resistance across the rural communities. The victims' families—not just of the executed but also the arrested, harassed, and ostracized—almost certainly would have voted against the VWP in a free election, as would many of their frightened neighbors.[59]

The "class enemies" process also chilled north-south trade, as no one wanted to be labeled as friendly with the South Vietnamese, or worse a collaborator. The 1955 trade was valued at over four billion dong but fell to 680 million in 1956. That exacerbated the rice shortage at the most unfavorable moment, as the south traditionally shipped on average 250,000 tons of rice north each year. Cross-border trade soon came to an end.[60]

The road to agrarian socialism in 1956 was far from successful as discontent spread and grew in intensity. A few weeks after Nixon's visit to South Vietnam where he was given Tho's land reform plan, things in the north hit the crisis stage. In August, Ho Chi Minh, who had played an active role in land reform, felt compelled to make a national radio broadcast announcing that the land reform errors would be corrected. By late 1956, the farmers' revolt was so widespread in some places that it overwhelmed the local security forces and had to be put down by the PAVN. That compelled General Giap to apologize publicly for having allowed things to get to the point where the army had to fire on its own people. There was public atonement for persecuting "upright persons," excessive terror, and the normalization of torture.[61] Both the agriculture minister and party secretary Chinh resigned on 29 October. Finally, Ho Chi Minh shut down the agricultural reform tribunals on 8 November.[62]

Agricultural growth during this chaotic period was hard to measure. The official record released at the time showed erratic gains. From 1957 to 1960, the DRV reported a 25 percent growth in rice production, but the numbers contradicted reports of severe shortages into late 1958. Attempts to find alternative food sources struggled as well. In 1959, the amount of corn, yams, and cassava harvested were below their 1956 levels—a combined decrease of 510,000 tons—that was offset by an increase of 22,000 tons of peanuts and 333,000 tons of sugar cane. The reforms did diversify the food supply, creating some stability, but unlike in the south, they did not equate to higher rice yields as they trended downward after implementation of the reforms.[63]

In 1960 DRV rice production estimates again were scaled back and rationing reduced to levels edging on malnourishment. The growing population further strained resources. Grain production in 1960 was dismal, falling 17 percent from 367 kilograms per capita in 1959 to 304 kilograms. A minimal sustained healthy diet required 2,000 calories per day for a woman and 2,500 for a man.[64] In the DRV, the caloric intake, depending on age and gender, was reduced in 1955 to between 1,800 and 2,300 calories per person per day and reduced further in 1960. Throughout 1955–1959 and beyond, food was rationed, and the DRV was a net importer of foodstuffs. Beyond suffering and hardships imposed upon the people, there were serious political ramifications for the failed reform policies. Many in Hanoi's diplomatic corps were downbeat about the DRV's economic future, some going so far as to state that the large majority of the rural population remained unhappy and disillusioned. Things were not going to get better; Chinh's fall from power opened the way for Le Duan to ascend to party leadership and take the DRV into war.[65]

Conclusions

On the eve of war in 1959, Washington did not see trouble ahead in South Vietnam. Its plans for the RVN focused on the economy and the outlook was bright. Rice and rubber production were up (the most important domestic and export crops respectively) and roads, the critical infrastructure requirement, improving. Future projects would continue to focus on infrastructure (the transportation system, power and other utilities, airports, waterways, and ports). After that, the priority was improving rural lives by expanding livestock holdings, the number of fisheries, and farmer credits to buy their land while diversifying crops and increasing rice production. Finally, education and health services would be upgraded. The Viet Cong did not enter into the calculation. When General Collins returned to South Vietnam on a fact-finding mission in February 1959, he saw such little threat to the peace that he recommended cutting the ARVN from 150,000 soldiers to 100,000.[66]

The development of Vietnam between 1954 and 1959 has too often been presented as problems without perspective. When viewed by comparing the DRV and RVN, two questions arise: Could economic mismanagement cause insurgency and could the two Vietnams violently war on each other while relying on their own resources? To address the first question, the economic errors and resulting economic difficulties were felt more acutely in the DRV than in the RVN. If poor economic reform policy helped grow the insurgency, then the north should have been riven by a worse uprising than in the south. But that was not the case. The reason lay not in better economic governance but in Hanoi being a more effective authoritarian state while possessing sizable and destabilizing stay-behind forces in South Vietnam. The same point explains the failed 1956 reunification referendum. The rationale that the DRV would have come out on top in 1956 was not predicated on superior quality of life but that the people in the north had to vote as told by the VWP. The political arguments of the era, that Saigon's incompetence and its violation of the Geneva election requirement laid the foundation for the insurgency in South Vietnam were not rooted in fact. The cause was simpler: Hanoi restarted the war in 1959.

As to the second question, were the two Vietnams capable of waging war? The answer remains complex. Internally, the DRV and RVN were able to wage war because they possessed growing populations, were able to maintain basic levels of food production, and kept essential transportations systems open—again with the aid of their sponsors. However, even with that degree of foreign economic assistance, both lacked both the resources and industrial military base to sustain war, and the fact that they did stemmed solely from the massive military aid received from their Cold War allies.

Both the DRV and RVN faced a myriad of serious economic challenges from the beginning in 1954, and both advanced while meeting alternately with successes and setbacks. South Vietnam clearly made more progress and followed a better trajectory. Vo Nguyen Giap summed the DRV's problems succinctly when he addressed his VWP comrades in 1957, noting that while the errors were temporary, "We are not very good at economic management," and then concluded, "That is why the country still suffers from the problems caused by our management."[67] In 1959, Washington saw South Vietnam as a nation entering an era of peace and prosperity. Meanwhile, Hanoi under the leadership of Le Duan prepared for protracted armed struggle to destroy its enemy to the south.

6

South Vietnam's Military in 1959

On 31 December 1955, the professionalization of the South Vietnamese military took a symbolic step forward with the end of the French-created VNA and the inauguration of the Army of the Republic of Vietnam. That completed the formation of the armed forces under the republic, following the establishment of the Marine Corps (13 October 1954), Air Force (31 January 1955), and Navy (20 August 1955). It had been a long and difficult road with much unaccomplished as the year 1956 was ushered in. Once again the legacy of French colonialism loomed large. What became the ARVN began when the French proclaimed the Bao Dai government in 1947 and recognized the need for a Vietnamese army to serve as a counterweight to the PAVN.[1]

The solution was the Vietnamese National Army established by decree on 23 May 1948. The army took shape in December 1949 and became operational in 1950. While the intention was for the VNA to become an independent service, from its inception France exerted control through both its Land Forces Joint Staff that directed the Indochina war and its Military Mission Standing Committee to oversee VNA operations. The French Army never lost its colonial spirit of commanding the Vietnamese and expected to maintain that influence after the war. Through that vision they staffed, trained, and equipped the VNA. It naturally followed that elite Vietnamese units in the French Expeditionary Corps (CEFEO), such as the paratroopers whose Vietnamese members enlisted in the French Army and were commanded by French officers, received the greatest assistance while VNA units received less assistance and mostly were assigned to secondary missions like occupation duty and stationary defense.[2]

Ostensibly joint French-Vietnamese leadership encouraged the development of high-level Vietnamese leaders, but in practice VNA command and senior staffing was intentionally skewed to the benefit the French. The system was not designed to have a glass ceiling but an impenetrable barrier. At the top, Bao Dai's minister of national defense never had the authority of the counterpart minister in Paris, also the VNA lacked skilled officers to fill high-level billets. It was not failure on the part of the Vietnamese who served. Prior to 1929, no Vietnamese national could serve as a commissioned officer; promotions stopped at the rank of warrant officer. Even after allowing commissions, the French resisted elevating Vietnamese officers to mid-level command until the late 1940s and never to high command. Only a handful of Vietnamese officers were allowed to rise above battalion command or hold senior staff assignments. Most of them were ethnic Vietnamese officers with French citizenship who had served in the regular French military like Generals Hinh and Vy. The French Army prevented the VNA from developing into an independent force that could stand on its own legs.[3]

It was not all bad news. General Jean de Lattre, the French commander in Indochina during 1950–1951, strove to make the VNA a viable fighting force and took steps to support the Vietnamese soldiers. De Lattre was a soldier's soldier and dedicated to making the VNA successful. Materially adding to that effort, in 1950 the U.S. MAAG to Indochina arrived and provided over $350 million in war materiel to the French by 1953. Sadly, de Lattre became ill and died in 1951. His successors did not share his vision or trust in the Vietnamese, with some referring to his policy in the ugliest of terms, describing it as the "yellowfication" of the French forces in Indochina.[4] They saw to it that VNA units remained small with minimal amounts of weapons and authority. Philippine Army Colonel Jose Banzon accompanied the CEFEO on operations in 1953–1954 as an observer. He concluded the VNA had capable soldiers, but they underperformed because the French failed to grant them "real responsibility."[5] De Lattre put the VNA on a better footing, but it remained on an imperfect path.[6]

Another factor that slowed early VNA development was the 1954–1955 regrouping of the 150,000-strong CEFEO to South Vietnam with its largest force situated in and around Saigon. The French believed their army would maintain a major role in South Vietnam's defense and continued to make VNA readiness a low priority. But the troubles in Algeria and Tunisia and the dual failures of the Hinh mutiny and sect rebellion ended that dream. Saigon finally was given control over the VNA on 1 July 1955, and by February 1956 there were only 15,000 French soldiers left in Vietnam. By April, the French Army was gone. That altered the RVN's national security requirements. They now were on their own when facing the PAVN. The Americans became their lifeline.[7]

To a degree, Washington had prepared itself for such an eventuality when on 12 August 1954, President Eisenhower signed National Security Council (NSC) 5429/1 that committed the United States to South Vietnam's defense in the event of invasion. America assumed responsibility, and the implications for the VNA were profound. The lessons of the 1950–1953 Korean War were fresh in American and South Vietnamese minds, and the military strategy to defend South Vietnam focused on defeating a conventional 1950 Korea-style DRV invasion across the 17th parallel DMZ or by an enveloping assault through Laos or both. Also to be dealt with was the guerrilla threat, which Diem feared would be strengthened by North Vietnamese infiltrations from Cambodia, Laos, and the sea. How to address those complexities vexed the Americans and South Vietnamese throughout the remainder of the 1950s.[8]

Mission

From its birth, South Vietnam confronted a powerful if latent enemy in the stay-behind VWP cadres and the PAVN guerrillas capable of unleashing an uprising in the south if Hanoi gave the word. And the DRV was a national security danger in its own right as the regular PAVN was larger and better led, organized, and equipped than the ARVN. Clandestine VWP political power in the RVN, combined with its dual PAVN conventional-guerrilla military threat, defined South Vietnam's security problem before Diem arrived on the scene and remained so afterwards. In Hanoi, Saigon faced an existential threat both from within and without.

Initially, South Vietnam did not have to focus on the external threat, as the 150,000 strong French Expeditionary Corps coupled with American security pledges were powerful deterrents. Internal threats were the priorities. It was during those hectic months of 1954–1955 that Diem had to put down the Hinh mutiny, forcibly disarm the regrouped Nationalist and Dai Viet Party supplementaries, and beat back the even more dangerous sect rebellion. While some action had been taken in early 1955, it was not until after the Battle of Saigon that Diem finally was able to direct the bulk of army to the internal communist threat in accordance with the 31 December 1954 National Security Action Directive designed to establish government authority throughout South Vietnam.[9]

Events did develop favorably. Solid progress was made in gaining control of the countryside, and the withdrawal of CEFEO was well underway. That left dealing with the threat from north of the 17th parallel DMZ. MAAG commander General O'Daniel's solution was to create "two" ARVNs: a conventional force to fight off the PAVN until the Americans arrived, along with a second light mobile force to defeat the internal threat. When General Samuel T. Williams took over from O'Daniel in December 1956, he adopted a markedly different approach to the ARVN mission. Williams saw the PAVN as the primary threat and O'Daniel's two-track internal-external solution as too complicated and inefficient. To Williams, distinct missions requiring manning, training, and equipping the ARVN along two different lines created unnecessary challenges. Further arguing against the approach, Williams saw the ARVN counter-guerrilla force as too weak to fight the PAVN, and that cut its conventional combat power in half. Finally, by relegating a large part of army to internal security, it exposed the ARVN to piecemeal defeat in the face of an all-out PAVN attack. For Williams, that made the concept unacceptable, and he was adamant that the ARVN focus on fighting the PAVN.[10]

In the South Vietnamese Government's assessment, that left the RVN without an adequate internal security force to defeat the communists. Diem's solution was to let the ARVN focus on fighting the PAVN, as Williams wanted, while the newly created and locally formed Self-Defense Corps would serve as the first line of defense against the VWP and its armed cadres waging guerrilla war. To back up the SDC would be the more mobile Civil Guard. The guard was to be trained, armed, and organized as a paramilitary force to take the war to the insurgents and defeat them. Finally, in the event of invasion, the SDC would form a guerrilla force to fight in areas overrun by the PAVN.[11]

During follow-on security discussions with the Americans in May 1956, Diem formalized those goals by pursing three strategic objectives: (1) to deter a PAVN invasion, he asked the United States to publicly declare that it would defend South Vietnam if invaded; (2) to expand the national road network in order to create effective military lines of communication; and (3) expand the Civil Guard to allow the army to concentrate on battling the PAVN. Diem also had never let go of his fear of PAVN attack from Laos into the Central Highlands to cut the RVN in two. He abandoned the old French defensive scheme to defend lower South Vietnam (Cochinchina) along a line that began at Ban Me Thuot and argued instead to move the army back into the Central Highlands and begin the defense there along the Laotian frontier. The Americans had reservations.[12]

By 1956, the Americans wanted the ARVN to focus on blunting a PAVN invasion across the DMZ until reinforcements arrived. It became the basis of the first formal American war plan to defend South Vietnam centering on an enclave strategy of defending RVN port cities to support the landing of U.S. forces. While both the Americans and South Vietnamese accepted that the ARVN's mission was to hold off the PAVN, Washington had no interest in building Diem's anti-guerrilla paramilitary Civil Guard. When it came to counterinsurgency, Williams took a "hands off" approach. In late 1956, he presented Diem with a counter-guerrilla paper and expressed his confidence that insurgents in South Vietnam could be defeated as they had in the Philippines, South Korea, Greece, and elsewhere. General Williams' intent was clear. The RVN insurgency could be contained by existing police, SDC, and Civil Guard without the army. From 1956 to 1959, the ARVN mission was to stop an invading PAVN in conventional battle.[13]

Size and Organization

When the War of Resistance ended, one of the first military challenges facing Diem was reducing the size of the VNA. In May 1950, the VNA consisted of a mere 16,000 troops mostly formed into a dozen or so light infantry battalions with no headquarters or staffs. Four years later, the army was a bloated force of 272,000 to include thousands of poor-quality conscripts and 45,000 supplementary (mainly sect) soldiers. Adding to the urgency, the Americans who were paying the bills proposed to quickly cut the number by 100,000. That proved impossible, but through a combination of desertions following the French defeat at Dien Bien Phu and discharges, by January 1955 over 58,000 soldiers had left the army. The reductions continued, and as 1955 ended, the VNA stood at 145,000 to include a reduced supplementary force of 25,000 soldiers.[14]

While swift, the demobilization had not been universally successful. The best news was the integration into the VNA of the 35,000–40,000 professional Vietnamese soldiers from the French Expeditionary Corps. That also meant the influx of northerners. Under no illusion of what a communist takeover entailed and given first priority for evacuation by the French, some 40,000 northern Vietnamese troops with their families headed south, and the soldiers created a steadying presence. On the flip side, many veterans were summarily discharged, to include 6,000 sub-officers or non-commissioned officers (NCOs)—an outcome that damaged army professionalism—and over 5,000 veterans joined the French Army to fight in Algeria. The

Americans backed off the 100,000 goal, and by 1956 South Vietnam had a competent army of 150,000 soldiers. It stayed at that size through 1959.[15]

How to fill the army going forward became a point of contention. In 1955, the VNA was a volunteer force, and the Americans wanted conscripts. Costs drove the decision, as draftees were to be paid at half the rate of volunteers, but the Americans were divided over how to proceed. General O'Daniel wanted a draft with an 18-month term of service that the JGS opposed. The MAAG goal in April 1955 was to get a conscription system in place by 1 January 1957 to obtain 10,000 recruits. The embassy wanted conscription to begin in 1956. Neither happened. During the 1954–1956 downsizing period, the draft was neither necessary nor feasible. Absent a reliable census with names, ages, and home addresses, induction was not administratively possible. It was also counterproductive, as it would force the discharge of motivated volunteers. Diem finally enacted the conscription law in mid–1957 to take effect on 1 August, although the draft did not begin until 1958. It was limited to 20–21-year-old males for 18 months of service. As the eligibility pool exceeded the need, draft quotas were easily filled, and the law was not vigorously enforced. By 1959, conscripts were to make up 50 percent of the army, but the goal was not reached.[16]

As for ARVN organization, when it came into existence in 1955, it followed traditional lines. Command authority rested with the president and was executed by the Ministry of Defense (established on 26 June 1949). Below it was the Joint General Staff who oversaw the RVN armed forces. General Le Van Ty served as Chief of the JGS throughout the 1955–1959 period. Subordinate to him were the military region (MR) commanders responsible for their areas within the RVN and later the corps commanders. The MR structure began in July 1952 when the French established two MRs that encompassed South Vietnam: Region 1 covered Cochinchina and MR 2 contained Annam. They bore responsibility for defending their part of South Vietnam, and the MRs went through numerous reorganizations.[17]

After partition in 1954, the VNA established three military regions starting with MR 1 in Nam Bo and then moving into central South Vietnam with MR 2 and finally MR 3 in the north with responsibility for defending the DMZ. In 1957, the ARVN was expanded with the military regions redrawn and increased to six. Beyond the Capital Military Region covering the Saigon area, MR 2 started at the DMZ in the north followed by MR 3 and 4 in central RVN. Then came MR 1 for northern Nam Bo and lastly MR 5 that covered the Mekong Delta. The ARVN also established two infantry corps in 1957 with I Corps formed in June and being headquartered in MR 2, followed by II Corps in October that was based in MR 4. III Corps was formed in March 1959. The adoption of the MRs and mobile infantry corps again reflected Saigon's attempt to deal with the dual nature of the threat. The MRs mirrored the French approach to defeat an internal insurgency while the mobile corps addressed American fears of a conventional PAVN invasion.[18]

While the military regions and corps structure evolved, the most difficult ARVN combat formation to perfect was the division. Divisional organization went through a number of transformations between 1954 and 1959 (along with the review of some 200 proposed changes, modifications, and tweaks). One thing was certain, while the South Vietnamese were free to formulate higher command organizations, divisions required equipment that only the Americans could provide and that meant they made the final the decisions. The division problem began when various schemes had been put forth to replace the "static" VNA divisions created by the French in the early 1950s.[19]

The first idea proposed by General O'Daniel in May 1954 was for an army with four light and five medium divisions that supported his concept of the ARVN simultaneously focused on internal and external threats. A year later he adopted a plan for six light divisions (5,500 troops) to deal with internal threats and four medium "field" divisions (8,500 troops) to hold off the PAVN. By mid–1955, the divisions were being formed under MAAG guidance. The four field divisions later were assigned to the two corps in 1957. After his arrival, Williams moved away from O'Daniel's "light-field" model and toward an army centered on seven 10,450-strong infantry divisions. At the end of 1958, the ten-division (six light and four field) structure was gone, replaced by the seven infantry divisions. Those were the divisions that initially fought the Vietnam War.[20]

What happened below the division level was equally important. In 1954, the VNA was basically a collection of battalions with most of limited value. In American military jargon, they could not "shoot, move, and communicate" on the battlefield. There was one exception. In late 1953, the French activated six all-Vietnamese mobile groups (GMs) that had gained combat experience by 1954. GMs were the backbone of the French forces in Indochina. They roughly were equivalent to an enlarged U.S. Army regimental combat team or task force (TF) and contained several infantry battalions along with artillery, engineer, transport, and other support units that allowed them to independently maneuver and fight. After the war, five ARVN divisions were built around the GMs.[21]

Additionally, soldiers from the remaining GM and six French-formed, all-Vietnamese infantry groups (GIs) helped flesh out the divisions. The GIs were larger but less mobile and powerful than the GMs and did not become operational during the war. There also were Montagnard groups (GM 41 and GM 42 that operated in the Central Highlands). To form the divisions, 18 infantry regiments, each with a headquarters and service company and an artillery or heavy mortar battery, had been established in 1955. They came from the GMs and GIs with the regiments renumbered; for example, the 154th Regiment that fought in the sect war became the 12th Regiment and joined the 4th Field Division in November 1955. With the exception of the field divisions, however, the ARVN kept the French expeditionary model for combat operations: form battalions into mobile groups for specific operations with the light division headquarters serving in a supporting role.[22]

Division combat support and service units were lacking as well in 1954. The French had begun forming four-gun VNA artillery batteries in 1950. By 1954 that force had grown to six battalions, which was inadequate for a 150,000 strong army. Similarly, the French only had formed three combat engineer companies by the close of 1951. In July 1952, they were combined into the 3rd Combat Engineer Battalion (CEB) after being augmented by the transfer of two Vietnamese officers and 72 enlisted men from the CEFEO. The battalion and company commanders were all

French, and the total engineer strength was 36 officers, about 100 sub-officers, and 780 enlisted soldiers. In early 1954 a second battalion, the 4th CEB, was set up, but it contained fewer than 100 soldiers. After 1954, the battalions were dissolved and the engineer companies assigned to the divisions.[23]

When first formed, the light divisions only had combat engineer, communications, transportation, and medical companies. The larger field divisions had the same companies along with ordnance and supply companies. As for divisional artillery, O'Daniel intended to provide only a dozen or so artillery pieces or heavy mortars to the field and none to the light divisions. Williams changed that and in 1956 made beefing up the service and support units a priority; he added an ordnance company to each of the light divisions and created one heavy artillery battalion (155 mm) for each of the two corps. Williams saw to it that the seven newly organized infantry divisions were equipped with one 12-gun battalion each of 105 mm howitzers and 4.2-inch heavy mortars. After 1956, a reconnaissance company was added, and the combat engineer company expanded into a battalion. While progress was made, not all seven divisions were ready when war came in 1959.[24]

What about tanks and special forces? General O'Daniel had an easy fix for the mechanized forces: keep the 1954 units. On this Williams agreed. The armored forces dated back to 11 January 1951 when the French transferred many Vietnamese troops to the VNA. By 1954 there were eight armored reconnaissance battalions (companies) that underwent a number of reorganizations. They were formed into four regiments (battalions) shortly after the war. This was the one area where the both the Americans and South Vietnamese assumed the ARVN had an advantage as long as the PAVN honored the Geneva Agreement's Article 17 that prohibited obtaining armored vehicles above 1954 levels. As for special forces, Williams killed a JGS plan to create counter-guerrilla commando companies along the lines used by the French. As VC violence increased, General Ty refused to be put off, and in mid–1959, he started training each battalion's fourth infantry company as a counter-guerrilla "special action" company.[25]

There also was a Women's Army Corps that had been created in 1950 to serve in headquarters staff and the medical corps along with supply, communications, and family service units. It was a volunteer force. Recruits had to be unmarried (but could marry after two years of service), and if under the age of 21, needed family permission to enlist. Women joined for a variety of reasons: out of patriotic duty to support the war effort, as an adventure, and to find a non-traditional career. After 1954, corps strength was set at 600 women. Family Services, whose soldiers were trained at Saigon's Army Social Training School, filled a unique but important role that provided social care for the families of soldiers serving away from home. In 1959, duties were further restricted to two areas: medical and family services. Madame Nhu fought the restriction and advocated expanding the women's role. She made some progress and while still not combat soldiers, nurses and others now were assigned to combat units when necessary.[26]

Finally, there were the sister services. The Navy and Marine Corps were small, and while the Marines grew slowly, the Navy expanded significantly. In 1954, 131 officers and 1,353 enlisted sailors served, most aboard the Navy's 22 vessels comprised of patrol and landing craft. By 1959, the Navy contained 3,600 sailors with 119 ships and boats divided into two operational commands: (1) The Sea Force, which along with numerous patrol craft, held the Navy's five largest vessels, 173-foot submarine chasers (about half the size of a destroyer). It operated along the RVN's coast. And (2) the River Force, consisting of dozens of landing craft and small motor boats formed into River Assault Groups, concentrated in the Mekong Delta. In 1960, a third element, the aptly named Junk Force, was formed that employed both motorized and sail-powered junks to catch coastal smugglers and infiltrators. The Marine Corps formed around one battalion on 1 May 1955 and was largely composed of former Vietnamese members of the French Marine Commando Companies. By 1959 its strength had reached 1,500 marines and fielded three rifle battalions. The headquarters for both the Navy and Marine Corps were located in Saigon with Nha Trang being the primary training center.[27]

The Vietnamese Air Force also was modest. In 1954 it consisted of two squadrons of liaison/observation planes and one squadron of old single-engine fighter-bombers—all of French design. In 1955, it was reequipped with American planes and organized into the 1st and 2nd Liaison Squadrons, the 1st Fighter Squadron, and the 1st Air Transportation Group (with 1st and 2nd Transportation Squadrons). The five squadrons plus one composite squadron, the Special Air Missions Squadron, comprised the whole of the force until April 1958, when the 1st Helicopter Squadron became operational. Those seven squadrons along with a number of T-28 trainers made up the Air Force when war began in 1959. To keep the force flying, the Air Force was authorized a strength of 4,140 servicemen.[28]

In 1955, the VNA held ten "field-light" divisions, one airborne group, four armored reconnaissance regiments, and six artillery battalions, plus supplementary forces that included six light infantry territorial regiments comprised mostly of religious sect troops. There also was one marine battalion. By 1959, the armed forces consisted of seven infantry divisions, four armored cavalry regiments, and in addition to the seven artillery and seven heavy mortar battalions with the divisions, each corps held one heavy artillery battalion. To deal with major threats, the JGS strategic reserve had been created containing the five-battalion strong airborne brigade, three marine battalions, and five separate battalions of artillery. Finally, the ARVN was supported by naval and air forces.[29]

Leadership

There were very few senior officers in the South Vietnamese armed forces. It was one of the army's most unique characteristics as it placed significant power in the hands of a very small and closed group. The 150,000 strong armed forces contained only 17 generals (all from the army) while colonels headed the air force and marines and the chief of naval operations was a captain. Williams had no reservations in deeming ARVN generals as competent by Southeast Asian standards but unqualified by Western professional measures. The system also tended to confuse Western observers who saw low ranks as signs of inexperience as South Vietnamese officers held commands above their rank. In the ARVN, unlike its American counterpart, it was not unusual to see a brigadier general, not a lieutenant general, in charge of a corps or a colonel, instead of a major general, commanding a division. Similarly, the typical battalion commander was a senior captain—unlike the West where a lieutenant colonel held the job.[30]

The top military command was the Joint General Staff. Prior to 1955, senior Vietnamese JGS officers, like army chief Hinh, retained French Army commissions and dominated the staff. One decision by Diem that earned Collins' approval was putting an end to dual commissions. Officers either resigned their French Army commission and renounced French citizenship or left the ARVN. Under the French, Vietnamese officers below the JGS supervised army training and carried out administrative responsibilities but rarely commanded large combat units. During the War of Resistance, the only route to higher command went through the mobile groups. Of those commanders, Le Van Nghiem, Nguyen Huu Co, Nguyen Van Khanh, Nguyen Van Vy, and Ton That Dinh became ARVN general officers. Nonetheless, throughout the war, no Vietnamese led a unit in combat as a general officer, and the French filled senior staff billets.[31]

The problems did not stop. Prior to 1954, the French Military Mission assigned French officers to the top VNA leadership spots. This reflected the French officer corps' inability to rid itself of the desire to remain in charge while retaining hopes of maintaining a presence in Vietnam into the future. In addition to a lack of experienced senior Vietnamese officers, a chronic shortage of middle-rank officers, both for field command and staff duties, plagued the VNA. There was not time to develop these officers as very few qualified Vietnamese chose a military career. As late as 1953, one in three VNA officers were French. Logistical support posed a special problem as Vietnamese had been excluded from many of those jobs. After the French left, Vietnamese officers assumed top logistical positions while having little or no experience. Going forward, finding capable officers in all areas became a tough hurdle to overcome. The Vietnamese did the best they could, and the difficulties were not limited to training and experience.[32]

Organizational issues also affected leadership development. As with GMs and GIs, there were two types of battalions—mobile and static defense—and where officers served imparted uneven strengths and weaknesses. Mobile battalions excelled as combat units but relied on the French for logistical support. Conversely, static battalions had limited combat value, but their officers did interact with French regional service units, not just at the battalion level, but also by supporting supplementary forces in their areas of operation (AOs). That gave those commanders at least a supervisory level of tactical logistical experience. With the rare exception of mid-rank officers who served in both battalion types, the duty left leaders with important gaps in their experience and knowledge.[33]

Finally, there were the political machinations of the Nationalist and Dai Viet parties. In 1946 they had established an officers school at Yen Bai west of Hanoi— scene of the 1929 anti–French mutiny. When the French created the VNA, they incorporated those forces. That created rival cliques within the army from its inception. The Dai Viet influence was more pervasive in the army, but a leading Yen Bai officer and member of the Nationalist Party, Pham Xuan Chieu, rose to become a general in the 1960s. Not all graduates went into the army; senior Dai Viet leader Bui Diem followed a political career and became RVN Ambassador to the United States in 1965. The Nationalists posed less of a problem simply because fewer survived; during the War of Resistance the communists had been brutal in eliminating Nationalist and Dai Viet leaders, but the Nationalists were particularly hard hit. What remained of the party in South Vietnam after partition was divided and disorganized. Exacerbating the problem, the parties retained their clandestine operating methods and followed their own political agendas, an outcome Diem described as digging their "tentacles" into the military.[34]

As it had been in the VNA, loyalty was fungible in the RVN armed forces. The Hinh legacy of politicizing the officer corps never disappeared. By 1959, there were several cliques: Diem loyalists, former Hinh adherents, and always waiting in the wings factions of the Dai Viet-Nationalist Parties. It did not stop with the generals, as lower ranking officers joined the cliques to gain a place of power. Diem unavoidably struggled with officer loyalty and did not make things better. Under his rule, the officer class jokingly referred to ARVN advancement criteria as the "Three D's"— Dao, Du and Dang—meaning promotion came easiest to Catholics or those born in Trung Bo or Can Lao Party members or some combination. Those dynamics and the legacy of General Hinh, along with the ambitions of the Nationalist and Dai Viet parties, ate away at the fabric of the army as the nation's defender and turned the officer corps into a fractured body riven with ambitious officers often seeking political gain over duty.[35]

Logistics and Equipment

The ARVN were almost totally dependent on the Americans for equipping their forces. It had been that way since 1950 when the Americans began to equip the French Expeditionary Corps. The VNA received its equipment from the French, who in turn had received much of that from the United States, to the order of $1.2 billion by 1954. As a result, almost everything used by the VNA dated from World War II. When new American supplies arrived, older French equipment went to the VNA, until by the end of the War of Resistance, the VNA too was equipped with (albeit older) American weapons and other military hardware. The effect was profound. ARVN soldiers went into battle armed with M-1 rifles from 1959 into the mid–1960s. They rode on American trucks, communicated using U.S. radios (Korean War–era AN/PRC-10s), and were supported by fire coming from U.S.-made mortars, artillery pieces, and aircraft.[36]

The RVN armed forces also lacked self-sufficiency. In 1954, the French CEFEO not only had provided key personnel but all essential logistical supplies to the VNA, rendering the American goal for the South Vietnamese to obtain logistical autonomy by January 1956 impossible. As for the American equipment the French possessed, per the 1950 Pentalateral Agreement (Mutual Defense Assistance Program), it was to be returned when the war ended in 1954. The Americans planned to use it to equip the ARVN. The numbers were not insignificant; the U.S. Navy alone transported 68,757 tons of military supplies and 8,135 vehicles from the north to the south in 1954–1955. Due to combat losses, poor records kept by the French, and other problems, the return transfer as envisioned proved unattainable, and the French kept the best equipment for use in the growing war in Algeria. The Americans ultimately received back less than ten percent of what had been given. The rest the French left behind when they departed in 1956.[37]

The result was a logistical nightmare. The ARVN, lacking a robust maintenance capability, was saddled with vast amounts of inoperable and rotting equipment. And most of the combat units were in light battalions formed in 1953 that suffered material shortages in almost everything. As bad as things were, if the rotting equipment could be returned to readiness, then it still would be of great value. Making that a reality became the job of the U.S. Temporary Equipment Recovery Mission (TERM). TERM ran from mid–1956 to 1960 and repaired not just thousands of vehicles and weapons but engineering, communications, and other specialized equipment as well. With limited resources, the "hand-me-down" approach to equip the ARVN never went away. In 1954, the armored force was equipped with five M24 light tanks, 127 M8 and 85 M3 armored scout cars, along with 17 M20 command cars. Those vehicles were kept, but at least the World War II-era M2 halftracks and tracked landing vehicles were retired. Beyond that, what armored vehicles the South Vietnamese had in 1954 were what it had in 1959. The story was much the same in other areas such as artillery, transportation, and communications.[38]

TERM not only repaired equipment, it developed the armed forces' own logistical and maintenance abilities. It began by training the South Vietnamese in every aspect of logistics and maintenance. They turned out to be apt students. Over time, specialists and technicians learned to service almost any piece of equipment, and the problem of having unqualified logistical staff officers disappeared. By 1957, the armed forces' logistical structure had been modernized and expanded to provide support beyond traditional quartermaster, ordnance, and transportation service to medical care, construction, communications, and engineering. Saigon became the logistical hub where the majority of depots, storage, and maintenance facilities were concentrated. When the corps came on line, they also established area of operations logistical facilities to support subordinate divisions. Similarly, as the ARVN increased its mobility, divisions increased their logistical responsibilities, and the old French regional service organizations system disbanded.[39]

Like the army, the air force was remade with American equipment. In early 1955, the MAAG moved to retire the French observation and fighter-bomber aircraft while augmenting the force with C-47s. By year's end, the South Vietnamese received 60 L-19 observation planes, 35 C-47 transports, and 28 aging F-8F fighter-bombers. In April 1958, the 1st Helicopter Squadron received ten Korean War–era Sikorsky H-19s provided by the French. The F-8Fs proved too worn to keep in service. In 1958, the Vietnamese asked for jet aircraft as replacements, but Washington denied the request. Washington tried to uphold the spirit of Geneva that only permitted the replacement of old weapons with new ones of similar characteristics.

Instead, the Americans proposed to send 25 armed versions of the T-28 trainer, but that never materialized. After Hanoi activated its PAVN Air Force Department in 1959, the Americans finally decided to replace the F-8Fs with 25 superior AD-4 Skyraiders in 1960 and another 25 AD-4s plus 6 RT-33A jet photo-reconnaissance aircraft in 1961. The small navy developed along similar lines, having its French vessels and landing craft replaced by used American ships and boats.[40]

The TERM refitting combined with replacement of worn-out equipment marginally expanded RVN military capabilities during the 1954–1959 years. As important as equipment repairs were to the South Vietnamese, it was the TERM training component that made the real difference as it allowed the RVN armed forces to maintain equipment and by extension, logistically sustain the military. TERM trained the ARVN to run logistics, supply, and maintenance branches that supported combat operations. Take away that, and ARVN or Air Force or Navy missions would grind to a halt. That was the critical value of American logistical support.[41]

Training

Training the South Vietnamese military proved challenging as the VNA became the French Army's last priority as soon as it was created. Additionally, the French never granted the Vietnamese full authority to train and lead units above the battalion level. Nonetheless, the French took steps to create a viable training program, and in December 1948 they opened the first basic schools. Again, colonial culture loomed large as officers needed at least a secondary school education, and the schools were located in major cities. As a result, the officer corps came from the middle and upper urban class while soldiers came overwhelmingly from the rural farmer society.[42]

In the war's fifth year, 1951, de Lattre started the reserve officers' course at Dalat. A year earlier Dalat had become home to the Military Academy (which began as a nine-month course at Hue in 1948) and in 1959 it became a four-year, degree-awarding college. De Lattre subsequently opened enlisted and officer schools for infantry, artillery, engineering, communications, and medical services. Enlisted soldiers also received maintenance training there. Other training centers were established in Hanoi and at Thu Duc near Saigon. Initially, the French provided instructors with classes taught in French. Over time Vietnamese officers began to replace the French, but the transfer of responsibilities was far from complete when the war ended. That created an immediate shortage of qualified instructors that plagued the army for years.[43]

At that time, the abilities of the VNA's officers and NCOs varied considerably. At the bottom were leaders of the supplementary forces whose strength was steadfastness in battle but little else. Next were the French-educated officers—until 1955 the best VNA candidates went to France to schools at Saint-Cyr or the Artillery School at Fontainbleau—and they proved to be the most capable staff officers.[44] Finally, there were the officers and NCOs trained in Vietnam and then immediately thrust into combat. The bottom group was gone by the end of the sect wars, while the second group dominated the upper ranks and the combat veteran group formed the fighting backbone of the VNA—especially those from the paratroop units.[45]

Partition, with Saigon as the new capital, created new problems. During the war, the French never allowed the U.S. MAAG mission to expand beyond logistical support. But partition created the need for its involvement in VNA training and led to the formation of the joint Franco-American TRIM group in February 1955, led by Colonels Carbonel and Lansdale respectively. It ran until the MAAG took complete control in April 1956. The Americans also took charge of training the Navy and Air Force in 1957. Additionally, many VNA schools were in the Hanoi region. During regroupment, the schools in the north packed up, as did most schools at Dalat, and relocated to the Saigon area. They also continued to operate under French direction until 1956.[46]

With the French Army rapidly departing South Vietnam beginning in 1955, the Americans feared an immediate attack by the PAVN and focused on crash courses to teach essential staff and operational skills neglected by the French. As that threat diminished, they shifted to more comprehensive training programs. The Americans revamped and expanded training, and soon coursework adhered to U.S. Army doctrine and tactics. Classes were taught by Vietnamese soldiers in Vietnamese. Basic recruit training was carried out in an eight-week program at the Quang Trung Replacement Center, not far from Saigon. Quang Trung also was home to the command and leadership refresher course for active-duty officers and NCOs returning to combat units. The course was highly regarded by both the students and senior ARVN leadership.[47]

By 1959, officers came from two sources. Draftees or volunteers with baccalaureate or college degrees went the reserve officer course at the Thu Duc Inter-Arms School to obtain reserve commissions. They constituted the bulk of the ARVN officers. A smaller and more elite group graduated from the Military Academy. Preparing mid-level officers for higher command was another hurdle. Due to the manner that the French dominated senior VNA military billets until 1954, officers often were unprepared either to lead or assume senior positions in a large unit staff. But the creation of the Command and General Staff College in 1954 and the practice of sending officers to the United States for advanced schooling beginning in 1955 gradually grew a pool of competent leaders. Those going to America prepared at the Army Language School, which opened in June 1956 and focused solely on English. Unfortunately, there was not enough time to complete the job by 1959.[48]

For advanced individual training, Thu Duc contained schools for armor, engineers, artillery, signals and communications, transportation, and quartermasters. Military police were trained in Da Nang. Once soldiers completed their training, they were sent to their units. Advanced infantry schools, to include an NCO academy and a commando-ranger course, were located at Nha Trang. The RVN military did a good job in developing a professional NCO corps. Intelligence training was conducted at Cholon's Fort Cay Mai. Finally, there was an officer preparatory school and medical college in Saigon along with a Political (or psychological) Warfare College that moved to Dalat in 1960.[49]

For military units, standardized 25-week training began in 1955. It followed a building-block approach: eight weeks of small unit training, seven weeks of company training, three weeks each at the battalions and regimental level, culminating in a four-week division-size exercise. The program expanded, first to 32 weeks in 1958 and finally to a year-round training cycle in 1959. Training changes in operations and tactics were most dramatic in the replacement of the French hedgehog strongpoint defense and use of GMs with the American perimeter defense, aggressive patrolling, and large unit foot mobile operations. Importantly, the Americans initially intended to train much of the VNA as an internal security force, then adopted a conventional approach, and by 1956 eschewed specialized counter-guerrilla training. The topic was reduced to a four-hour block of instruction.[50]

The transition from the French to the American military system was difficult at times for the South Vietnamese soldier. The VNA had been trained to reflect French Army traditions, captured in the phrase: "La discipline est la force principale de l'Armée. Les ordes doivent être exécutés sans hésitation, ni mumure [Discipline is the principal force of the Army. Orders must be executed without hesitation, nor murmur]."[51] While the French were rigid in obedience, Americans were rigid in doctrine. It reflected American leadership style. Inherently competitive, Americans were instilled with a will to win even if it meant acting without orders and ended with aggressive officers reined in by a rulebook, if for no other purpose than to provide a baseline to deviate from. As for leadership under fire, the French stressed calmness in battle above all while Americans often were loud, profane, and animated. As a one-two punch, the contradictory French-American martial traditions frequently made for a jarring change.[52]

Despite the difficulties, ARVN training had to be judged a success. The French established a good foundation and integrated Vietnamese instructors early on. The French also worked cooperatively with the Americans under the TRIM program, allowing for a smooth transition. The Americans, with their lack of language skills, necessitated the expanded role of Vietnamese military instructors that only strengthened RVN military professionalism. As for the Vietnamese officers and NCOs who served in the 1950s, to learn their skills from two of the world's leading militaries—despite some difficulties—was an exceptional opportunity for professional growth. Overall, the RVN military was as well trained as any in Southeast Asia in 1959 save the PAVN.[53]

One factor that hurt military readiness in the lead up to war was the cut in U.S. military aid starting in 1958. During the regroupment and transition to full independence, the VNA received an impressive $303 million from the Americans, primarily from the U.S. Military Assistance Program (MAP). Going forward, aid fell to $170 million, but beyond NATO, the RVN remained one of the largest recipients. The American economic recession of 1957–1958, while short-lived, changed that. To fund a domestic U.S. stimulus package, Washington cut the aid to $125 million for 1958—a 26 percent reduction—and kept that level for 1959. The budget cuts arrived at the worst moment as they put Saigon in a difficult position and adversely affected training, operations, equipment purchases, and support for the SDC and Civil Guard. Also, to prepare the influx of draftees that began arriving in 1958, training centers and staffs that needed expansion instead were cut back. The result was a rough start and a less than desirable experience for the recruits.[54]

The Civil Guard and Self-Defense Corps

When it came to internal security, Diem never wavered. Once committed to General Williams' plan to prepare its armed forces to fight the PAVN, Diem moved to strengthen the internal security forces without first obtaining American approval. In April 1955, he established the Civil Guard and in December informed the Americans that the first squads of what became the SDC had been formed in central coastal South Vietnam, even though funding was almost nonexistent and equipment lacking. The SDC was formally established in April 1956. Given the scarcity of resources, the SDC consisted of little more than armed local villagers serving on a part-time basis.[55]

Diem continued to present the SDC as the first line of defense against communist insurgents. The corps was to be supported by a paramilitary Civil Guard organized and equipped along light infantry lines and trained in small unit operations with the ability to work jointly with the ARVN. Under his plan, the ARVN, with MAAG guidance, would answer to the ministry of defense and defend the RVN from external threats. The Civil Guard and SDC would operate under the interior ministry as part of a broader internal security structure that included the Sûreté and Metropolitan Police.[56]

It was another example of Diem formulating his own policy without American direction. His justification for both the Civil Guard and SDC was at odds with the U.S. embassy. The reason was simple: differing assessments of the communist threat. Diem was a provincial chief during the 1930 communist uprising had lived through the communist insurgency from 1945 until he fled for his life in 1950. As such, he recognized the need for robust paramilitary forces. As the U.S. embassy saw it, there was virtually no communist insurgency to speak of in South Vietnam in 1955. Diem further exasperated the Americans when he insisted that arming villagers safeguarded democracy. Washington and its Saigon embassy team did not see the need for such forces; what they saw was a need for more professional police. Nonetheless, the SDC operated on the cheap and thus did not raise strong objections. That was not true for the Civil Guard, as Diem's vision required the commitment of resources that Washington was unwilling to provide. The Americans opposed Diem's Civil Guard concept from the start.[57]

Ignoring Diem, the Americans turned to the Michigan State University Group. To address internal threats, MSUG helped create a Ministry of Interior security force composed of a 4,000–6,000-member National Police and a new 4,000 strong Sûreté. Under the plan, they would be responsible for major crimes, drug enforcement, tax law enforcement, customs and immigration, counterintelligence, and counter-espionage. It was to be backed up by a 25,000-strong Civil Guard with law enforcement, counter-subversion, and limited counterintelligence duties. Unfazed, Diem proceeded with his paramilitary scheme, and as a consequence, neither the

SDC nor Civil Guard received MSUG assistance in paramilitary training or equipment from USOM or MAP.[58]

While the dispute over the Civil Guard divided the South Vietnamese and Americans, the SDC progressed with less friction. In September 1955 Diem pushed the Americans to support a nationwide SDC program and pushed hard again in November. Later that month, Saigon submitted a proposal requesting aid for the formation of ten-man "auto-defense" squads in 6,000 villages and hamlets. Squad members were responsible for defending their village or hamlet and paid a small monthly stipend of 1,000 piasters (about $28) plus free rice from the village. As an added duty, the hamlets were organized into "mutual aid groups" of five families to protect themselves and report on "irregular" activities.[59] They were stationary and only established in pacified areas. The Americans provided limited funds after the first official SDC units were activated in June 1956. While under the ministry of interior in Saigon, leaders at the district, village, and hamlet level exercised a high degree of decision-making authority over the SDC.[60]

In December 1957, the MAAG and U.S. embassy took greater interest in the Self Defense Corps and recommended that additional squads be located in secure hamlets, villages, and towns near the Cambodian and Laotian borders and other remote villages along potential infiltration routes in areas not already under SDC protection. Washington further agreed to support an increase in the size of SDC units depending on the threat; smaller villages would keep the ten-man squad and larger villages (over 1,000 people) would get a 15-man squad. The 639 villages in dangerous areas would be secured by a 25-man SDC platoon. All told, the Americans would assist the SDC in protecting 2,875 villages and hamlets, and the corps would grow to 43,500 defenders.[61]

By 1958, American aid provided SDC squad leader training and paid for 300 piasters of the monthly stipend (about $9), with Saigon paying the rest. The Americans still did not provide arms or equipment. Perhaps unsurprisingly, as the SDC was so minimally supported, most donned the black ba ba also worn by the Viet Cong. Those lucky to have a weapon were armed with old French rifles (two or three per hamlet), and the rest relied on grenades, the odd sidearm, and sharpened farm tools. In September, Diem asked the Americans to support expanding training to individual members. He also altered training to focus on counterinsurgency and intelligence collection while bringing in NRM youth cadres to train the SDC in civic actions. When Hanoi passed Resolution 15 in January 1959, the SDC had modestly grown to 47,000 members. It was a well-earned vote of confidence. That year southern VWP cadres reported to Hanoi that the corps was giving the VWP problems and threatened party organizations.[62]

The Civil Guard followed a less successful road. It descended from a series of French supplementary forces apart from the sect armies that coalesced into the Garde Republicaine in the late 1940s and grew to 13 territorial regiments by 1954 (to include the Garde Montagnarde). As with almost everything connected to the colonial period, they were a mixed blessing. Loyalty was questionable and prior to Geneva, they answered to the chief administrators of Tonkin, Annam, and Cochinchina, with Bao Dai loyalists in charge in Annam, Dai Viet officers in

Tonkin, and the French in Cochinchina. Diem disliked the territorials and instead envisioned two to eight Civil Guard companies assigned to a province and answering to the province chief. To face the insurgency head on, contested "national security" zones would get the most guard companies with a six-battalion reserve established in Saigon to handle any crisis. Simplifying the political infighting, the territorials O'Daniel favored were abolished by Williams in 1956 with the best transferred to the ARVN and the worst demobilized. The rest shifted to the Civil Guard that by default assumed the internal security mission. Over time, Diem hoped that the guard would grow into a force of 68,000 troops.[63]

Due to MSUG resistance backed by Ambassador Eldridge Durbrow and the embassy team, there would be no U.S. support for a Civil Guard paramilitary force. Diem's plan remained unrealized in 1959. Instead, MSUG advisors ensured the guard would be a small force trained as sort of state police in the American style. Even though they were formed into companies, the headquarters were administrative, linked to satellite police stations, and not the tactically cohesive mobile light infantry units Diem had pleaded for. MSUG training got underway in 1955, and its advisory staff made clear their intent in a 1956 report that defined the Civil Guard's mission as enforcing criminal law.[64]

Instead of being trained in both police and infantry tactics and armed with rifles along with light machine guns and mortars, they were issued pistols and shotguns. The revised MSUG Civil Guard training plan concentrated on how to investigate traffic accidents, robberies, and other minor felonies, and to interview witnesses and collect evidence. In response, Diem scrounged up more old French rifles with unreliable ammunition and issued them to the guard, as had been done with SDC. By early 1956, Diem hoped to expand the guard to 55,000–60,000, well above the U.S. approved increase to 40,000 but short of his goal of 68,000. In a compromise, the guard eventually grew to 48,000, which many Americans thought too large. Neither Diem's overt attempts nor private efforts by deputy defense minister Nguyen Dinh Thuan could persuade the Americans to support readying the Civil Guard to assume a counterinsurgency mission.[65]

The year 1957 proved pivotal. Without U.S. support, during February and March the Civil Guard deployed to Viet Cong areas along the frontier, assigning companies to Kontum, Ban Me Thuot, Pleiku, and the Plain of Reeds in the Mekong Delta. As to be expected, by late summer the mission argument between the Americans and Saigon became heated. Diem was relentless but unsuccessful in convincing the Americans that the Civil Guard had to be prepared to fight VC guerrillas. Both USOM and MSUG withheld the entire $3.6 million in aid over his refusal to accept the guard as a "civil police agency."[66] In October he again pleaded with the MSUG to support the paramilitary concept and proposed assigning demobilized ARVN officers to the guard.[67]

Not persuaded, the MSUG insisted that the Civil Guard operate as rural police, walked away from the matter, and focused instead on the Municipal Police and the Bureau of Investigation, the successor to the Sûreté. To add insult to injury, the Civil Guard was not even trained to handle major crimes like homicides, which were placed under the purview of the bureau. While relations with the MSUG ended badly, in a sign of improved relations with sects, in 1957 Diem authorized the formation of Hoa Hao and Cao Dai Civil Guard companies in their strongholds.[68]

Diem was tenacious if nothing else, and the deadlock continued throughout 1958 with Diem making concessions but not backing off the paramilitary demand. Diem's brother Nhu had the Civil Guard's few automatic weapons turned over to the ARVN, a move that surely pleased the Americans. But Durbrow and the MSUG barely gave an inch. They continued to hold back funding, and the one concession in August was to supply M-1 rifles to replace the guard's antiquated French arms. While the security situation remained favorable, there was a growing agreement by some Americans, notably General Williams and the MAAG, to change the policy and better help the Civil Guard. This was urgent as it fought against the VC's Tru Gian (Killing Traitors) assassination campaign that surfaced in late 1956 and reached an average level of 25 killings per month by 1958. While nationally insignificant, the violence was concerning nonetheless.[69]

The rift between Washington and Saigon over the Civil Guard did not improve with the arrival of 1959. Durbrow and the rest of the U.S. embassy team fought to get Diem to significantly scale back his SDC and Civil Guard security objectives to pursue peaceful economic development in its stead. The Americans sought to reduce the combined SDC and Civil Guard to 79,000 members. Things only came to a head when Resolution 15 initiated the armed uprising and, being deployed in VC areas, Civil Guard was on the frontline in an emerging shooting war.[70]

As the 1959 security situation worsened, Washington realized the MSUG-driven "rural police" policy had failed. Ambassador Dillon, now at the State Department, put it coldly if ironically: "The Civil Guard needs to be given equipment as least equal to that of the communists."[71] The Americans scrambled for a new approach. Two positive steps were taken. First, Washington shelved the proposal to cut the Civil Guard to 32,000 members; its strength was kept at 48,000. Second, the USOM Public Security Division took over Civil Guard support from MSUG in July and finally provided the withheld $3.6 million in aid. The progress was minor. By September, beyond gaining some additional equipment, little else changed as USOM continued to train the guard as police.[72]

Starting in 1955, Washington looked askance at Diem, deeming him an out of touch leader who cried wolf about the communist peril. Then, war came. Four years of preparation and development had been squandered. The Guard was unprepared to meet the emerging Viet Cong danger. In May 1960, General Tran Van "Little" Minh opined that the Civil Guard was "worthless" in fighting the VC.[73] The entire process revealed how unwilling Washington had been to face the possibility that Hanoi would restart the insurgency.

Conclusions

The RVN armed forces made great strides between 1954 and 1959. The ARVN was better prepared to face the PAVN; firepower and mobility had been improved, and the paratrooper-marine-artillery strategic reserve was as good as any formed by the French Army. Those serving were well trained, and while their equipment was dated, it was in a higher state of readiness and better maintained than in 1954. Further, the officer and NCO corps had reached new levels of expertise and professionalism. The French legacy still loomed; beyond sect war experience, there was not one VNA officer in 1959 who had commanded a large unit in combat or directed a battle staff. Below that, there was not one officer who had been a senior staff officer, a G-2 or G-3 or G-4, in combat. In that light, the degree to which the ARVN had closed the gap by 1959 was remarkable, but it would take years to fully develop senior officers.

Other obstacles remained. The Americans failed the Civil Guard at almost every level, leaving it unready for war. Additionally, replacing voluntary enlistments with the draft that coincided with sharp military budget cuts adversely affected the quality of lower rank soldiers. Finally, and despite significant gains, the officer corps had been poisoned by political factionalism, in the case of the Nationalist and Dai Viet parties dating back to the 1929 Yen Bai mutiny and for the French-trained elites to the 1954 Hinh mutiny. Then add in Diem's Can Lao. That deprived the military of a sense of unified service to nation and left it lagging in the areas of morale and fighting will.

In that light, the most consequential American decision was to drop the French model of a career army—one whose professional élan and esprit de corps if properly developed ensured cohesion in battle. It was erased to make way for an American-style conscript army only bereft of the patriotic identity that made it effective. But with the improved security situation in early 1959, the Americans did not see a problem. Saigon's authority had been established across the nation, an unequalled achievement, and beyond the VC assassination campaign, the country was at peace and prospering. The future looked promising, and if given time, the problems facing the military could be resolved.[74]

7

The People's Army of Vietnam
and the Entry of the Viet Cong

The Vietnam War's early years were a contest between Hanoi and Saigon, and that put the People's Army of Vietnam front and center. There was never a day or even a moment that VWP leaders in Hanoi did not direct the war or when the PAVN did not exercise overall control of the military struggle. That made what happened in the DRV of critical importance, and as with the ARVN in South Vietnam, great changes took place in the PAVN during the years 1954–1959 with much of it based on the experiences gained during the War of Resistance. However, unlike the RVN military that faced one difficulty after another, the PAVN followed a steadier path of progress under the guidance of the VWP. That left the Viet Cong. While the fate of the Viet Cong also was linked to the wishes and commands of the VWP, they followed the most difficult path of all. Unlike the two conventional militaries, the Viet Cong were under constant assault by the Diem regime and in a struggle for survival throughout the years leading up to war in 1959.

PAVN Size and Organization

The professional North Vietnamese army that the generals in Saigon and Washington worried about in 1959 had advanced an almost unbelievable distance in less than two decades. Established on 22 December 1944, the PAVN's origins dated back years earlier, and from its beginnings in 1930, the ICP had hoped to create a worker-peasant army. The first self-defense units were established briefly in Nghe An and Ha Tinh provinces in coastal central Vietnam in the 1930s, but little progress was made until the 1940 defeat of France followed by the arrival of the Japanese Army. That was when Ho Chi Minh ordered Giap to the rugged and beautiful hill country of Lang Son province abutting the Chinese border to take charge of a handful of mostly Montagnard communist guerrillas. He began to build the PAVN almost from nothing.[1]

In those days, the only thing Giap's troops could accomplish was village defense, and calling them armed was a stretch. Growth was slow if steady, and in late 1943, the French deemed Giap's force serious enough to march against. By then he led a few capable if small 50-soldier infantry companies. The French effort failed, and by early 1945, the PAVN switched to the offense and successfully raided a number of isolated French outposts. Helping the effort, during the summer the PAVN received small but needed quantities of arms, ammunition, and other military supplies from commandos of the American Office of Strategic Services (OSS) to use against the Japanese. The end of World War II halted American aid, but with the arrival of Nationalist Chinese troops, the collapse of the French, and surrender of Japanese forces, weapons became plentiful through any number of methods, from buying contraband to raiding stockpiles. Strengthening Giap further, the onset of the August Revolution made finding eager recruits easier, and the number of volunteers exploded. By 1947, the PAVN contained 60,000 guerrillas in Bac Bo alone. The army continued to expand and mature.[2]

The PAVN adopted a three-tier structure that was maintained by its forces across Vietnam. At the bottom was the people's militia (with hamlet self-defense squads and village platoons). Next came district and provincial guerrillas, and finally main force PAVN units that fought head-to-head with the French. During the war, the militia grew gradually and became a more disciplined and structured fighting force but remained an amalgam of lightly armed units focused on village defense. In 1951 the much-improved regional and provincial guerrillas were reorganized on the basis of one battalion per province/one company per district and began to operate in conjunction with main force PAVN formations. At the end of the war, there were 200,000 serving in the militia as well as between 330,000 and 380,000 troops with the PAVN (to include the guerrillas). Within the ranks were 20,000 officers, with the number of generals and colonels much higher than in the VNA and more in line with the Soviet Red Army or even Western militaries. As with the VNA, demobilization became a pressing problem for the PAVN when the fighting stopped in 1954.[3]

After the war, the VWP determined the long-term goal was to make PAVN main forces a smaller but professionally trained and equipped army. The party followed the Soviet system of centralized multi-year plans, and the PAVN blueprint was laid out in the 1955–1959 Five Year Military Plan. It would transform the PAVN into a regular army (to include air and naval services) by retaining the best while creating an enormous militia as a national reserve. Unlike in the RVN, fit demobilized soldiers were sent to work on infrastructure projects or assigned to local self-defense or territorial militia units. By 1956, the PAVN had been reduced to an estimated strength of 257,000 soldiers. Reductions continued until by 1958, there were approximately 173,000 soldiers serving in the army, a level that was maintained into 1959.[4]

The war taught the PAVN that victory was beyond reach until it could fight the French on an equal footing, and that demanded large units. In 1948, the PAVN fielded 32 combat battalions that grew in number to 117 by 1951. The first regiment stood up in 1947, and divisions began to form in 1949 with the 304th "Capital" Division entering the war in 1951. The PAVN did not adopt a corps structure, having concluded that the division was the key formation. Eventually five divisions were formed in the early 1950s (304th, 308th, 316th, 320th and 325th Infantry Divisions) and due to their distinguished combat record, came to be known as the "Iron" divisions.[5]

The division philosophy extended into the peace as the army reorganized during 1954–1959. The goal was to make a more potent force, and that meant increasing the number of divisions. From September 1954 until June 1955, the newly formed 328th, 332nd and 350th Divisions joined the Iron Divisions. The PAVN also had to deal with its regrouped soldiers. Beginning in January 1955, the 305th and 324th Infantry Divisions along with the 330th Infantry Division (Brigade) were formed from regrouped southern Trung Bo troops. Nam Bo regroupees were organized into the 338th Division in December 1956, and Montagnard regroupees from the Central Highlands formed the 120th Independent Regiment based at Gia Lam near Hanoi. Finally, regrouped ethnic Vietnamese troops from Laos and Cambodia were formed into the 335th Division (Brigade) and 640th Independent Regiment, respectively. The divisions were designated either as "one battlefield" formations prepared to fight anywhere in Indochina or as "locality" units, such as the 335th Division that specially trained for combat in Laos.[6]

In 1955, the infantry division's structure was standardized along lines similar to those used by the ARVN, only smaller in scale; the ARVN division held 10,500 soldiers while the PAVN division contained 8,689. Also similar to the ARVN, the basic structure of the army followed the three-by-three model (also referred to as the triangular model) that was widely and successfully adopted by many militaries after World War I. Units were progressions of three. The foundation began with three soldiers forming a tightly knit cell. Three cells became a squad, three squads a platoon and so on successively for companies, battalions, and regiments, at which point three infantry regiments formed the core of the division.[7]

To further improve combat power, in 1958 the PAVN embarked on the "Train the Troops to Accomplish Feats of Valor" program. This led to gains for infantry regiments and divisional support and service units. Increasing fighting power then expanded to other parts of the PAVN. Mobility was improved with the addition of the 225th and 235th Transportation Regiments, and as more heavy weapons and equipment were procured, three artillery divisions (45th, 359th, 675th) and the 367th Anti-Aircraft (AA) Division joined the 351st Engineer-Artillery (Heavy) Division that had been formed alongside the Iron Divisions in 1951. The engineer department also grew with the addition of the 333rd, 444th, 505th, and 555th Engineer Regiments along with two construction regiments and two bridging regiments. Unbeknownst to both the South Vietnamese and Americans, in October 1959 the PAVN established a tank corps and activated the 202nd Tank Regiment (containing 202 troops) that soon was joined by the 203rd Regiment. Like the ARVN, tank regiments were battalions in size.[8]

Other services, while still part of the PAVN, also received a boost under the "Train the Troops" initiatives when the air and naval services came on line in early 1958. While the first transport planes began flying on 3 March 1955, the Air Force Department was not established until 1 January 1959. To avoid violating the Geneva Agreements, it consisted solely of the 919th Air Transport Regiment, which became operational in May 1959. Concurrently, the Anti-Aircraft Command with its 367th Division grew to 6 AA regiments integrated with two radar regiments. The small navy, called the Coastal Defense Force, consisted of 1,300 sailors serving in two coastal defense groups that contained a combined 28 patrol boats armed with 40 mm and 20 mm guns.[9]

There were additional forces beyond the regular PAVN. Serving as VWP enforcers were two security organizations that targeted political opposition, spies, and other enemies of the state. The largest was the 8,000-strong People's Armed Public Security force that answered to the interior ministry. Their PAVN counterpart was a force composed of ten Security Battalions with a total strength of 4,500 soldiers.[10]

The guerrilla and militia forces followed a separate path from the PAVN after the war. The guerrilla forces in the north and those that regrouped from the south were disbanded and their troops incorporated into the PAVN. The militia was assigned a three-fold mission: (1) Replenish the PAVN, (2) help maintain internal security, and (3) support frontline forces in time of war. After the war, building up the militia became a priority and it became a much larger universal force—greater in size than the PAVN—divided into two groups: the ready reserve and the self-defense units. The first line militia (Category 1 ready reserve) contained 130,000 soldiers and had the primary task of replenishing the army.[11]

To replace the disbanded guerrillas, many reservists were activated and formed into regional regiments and provincial or local force battalions and companies. The units were given approximately six months of basic training with the mission to augment the regular PAVN in combat. They served as territorial troops. The second and much larger part-time militia group consisted of self-defense units in the hamlets, villages, factories, and the like. The unevenly armed units were comprised of both women and men (steadied by the presence of 30,000 discharged soldiers) and provided local security. The passing of Resolution 15 put an added emphasis on the militia. At the same time in 1959 that Washington urged Saigon to reduce its Civil Guard and SDC to 79,000, Hanoi created an equivalent force of village militias and territorial battalions that numbered 780,000—a force nearly ten times as great. In terms of vision and threat analysis, the divergence could not have been more profound.[12]

Two other sources of reinforcement existed in 1959. The first was conscription. During the later years of the 1946–1954 War, the VWP had implemented a draft to increase the supply of recruits, but it ended with the war. Afterwards, a more structured conscription system was studied with a trial program tested in Vinh Puc province in 1957. The results were promising, and the test expanded to several more provinces in the following year. While still not formally established by 1959, a conscription pilot program had been tested across the DRV and was ready for implementation with a targeted goal of 100,000 18-year inductees annually for a three-year term—a requirement that easily could be met given the DRV's demographics.[13]

The second resource the PAVN could tap in 1959 was the Assault (Shock) Youth Group, which despite its martial name had provided manual labor to support the PAVN during the war. Formed in 1950 and with an initial mission of road repair in rear areas, the youth group fulfilled an important role in that and similar logistical support tasks that were essential to the war effort. Brigades consisting of several hundred youths became the standard. They were divided into squads, companies, and units with several units forming the brigade. Containing at least 14,000 youths by 1954, they played a major logistical role during the decisive battle of Dien Bien

Phu. After the war, the brigades were reorganized and redirected toward civil projects, and they remained focused on rebuilding the infrastructure before being disbanded in 1955.[14]

PAVN Command and Leadership

The most important factor in understanding the PAVN was that it existed to serve the VWP, and the goals of the army never deviated from those of the party. That put the VWP's Central Military Party Committee at the top of the PAVN's chain of command. Next in importance in army leadership was one person: Senior General Vo Nguyen Giap. In addition to membership in the Politburo, Central Committee, and CMPC Secretary, Giap was both minister of defense and PAVN commander-in-chief. His positions granted him power over every aspect of the armed forces. To directly lead the army in war or peace, Giap exercised his authority through the "high command," a semi-official body composed of senior officers and supported by the Military Staff that managed day-to-day army operations.[15]

The Ministry of Defense consisted of three major departments (political, training, and rear services), and the ministry controlled the armed forces initially through four military regions (MRs) in the DRV that replaced the interzones used during the 1946–1954 War. At that time, the interzones directed military operations through a system of committees, usually called resistance committees, starting at the village level, then expanded to inter-village, district, provincial, and interzone. The MRs assumed those responsibilities, which was how local PAVN as well as the militia were directed. As part of the 1958 PAVN reforms, MRs 1 through 3 were abolished and replaced with five new ones given geographic names, while MR-4 in the DRV panhandle that abutted the DMZ remained unchanged. To maintain control over stay-behind forces in South Vietnam, Interzone V became MR-5, and the zones in Nam Bo also became MRs 6–9. As another part of the reforms, the training department was placed under the Military Staff and charged with standardizing training across the military. Of all the organizations, the Military Staff was most crucial as it developed war plans and in time of war directed military operations under the guidance of Giap's "high command" that included the PAVN chief of staff and the senior generals in charge of the MRs and defense departments.[16]

Steeling PAVN leadership, during the War of Resistance it institutionalized a merit-based system for developing senior commanders and staffs. Consistent leadership further strengthened the PAVN, as there was great stability in the officer ranks from generals on down that began with the army's founding and carried through into the future. Always at Giap's side stood PAVN chief of staff Senior General Van Tien Dung, along with others who loyally served party and army for many years, but internal friction did exist.

Top commanders were divided roughly into Giap–Le Duan camps. This reflected a geographic split between those who fought with Giap in the north during the War of Resistance and those from south and central Vietnam. The resentment stemmed from the fact that northerners dominated the PAVN's upper echelons.

With Giap stood Dung, Deputy Chief of Staff Hoang Van Thai, and Generals Chu Huy Man and Song Hoa, while Generals Nguyen Chi Thanh, the senior PAVN commissar, Tran Van Tra, and Le Hien Mai backed Le Duan. The beginnings of a non-aligned career military cadre also had begun to emerge, as exemplified by General Voung Thua Vu. Many top generals also served in the CMPC and NRC, and after the war began, PAVN generals from the Le Duan camp were sent south to command the Viet Cong. The greatest source of external disruption amongst the seniors was the Sino-Soviet dispute, with the Giap faction leaning toward the Soviets and the more pro–Chinese generals aligned with Le Duan.[17]

While PAVN leaders were no more exempt from factionalism than their ARVN fellows, it never devolved into the toxic ARVN factionalism, and the overall effect minimal. This was due to one reason: the shared bonds of VWP membership. At least 40 percent of the officers and all the generals were party members. That kept the army powerfully united. Not only did the PAVN possess a cadre of experienced leaders and staff officers, it had established a culture that identified, trained, and promoted officers of potential regardless of faction. When war came, the rivalries were put aside, and the PAVN leaders worked as one toward victory.[18]

Mirroring the senior leaders, the most significant factor affecting PAVN command and leadership at the lower levels revolved around one thing: the centrality of the VWP. The iron will of Party pervaded every level of the army. Units of regimental size and above had a political commissar while a political officer was assigned at the battalion and company level. After the VWP emerged in 1951, every major military unit was co-commanded by a commissar or political officer, and when the war ended in 1954, the PAVN was a disciplined army with its first loyalty to the VWP. Unlike the Soviet system where the commissar often was a much-feared individual, in the PAVN party officers served less as disciplinarians than motivators. They also were responsible for the swift and unquestioning execution of party directives and orders. Finally, the political officer was charged with forming and leading a party organization within each military unit. A squad possessed an activist, the platoon a cell, and the company and battalion a party branch. At the higher echelons, commissars directed a party military committee.[19]

PAVN Military Equipment

Like the ARVN that faced one difficulty after another during the 1954–1959 period, the PAVN followed a difficult path with regard to equipment. The PAVN in 1944 had started with little or nothing in the way of armaments—mostly captured weapons plus a handful of modern weapons provided by the Americans. The end of World War II opened the way to obtaining numbers of weapons from the Nationalist Chinese, surrendering Japanese, and some French weapons seized during the chaotic last months of the war. Weapons were not adequately available until after Mao's Red Army arrived on the Indochina border in 1949. The Chinese provided not only large quantities of infantry weapons but also heavy machine guns and mortars, along with artillery and anti-aircraft guns.[20]

When the war ended in 1954, deliveries from China equipped the majority of PAVN divisions (five infantry and one heavy) to include 116,000 rifles and other small arms along with 4,630 heavier weapons. Most were machine guns, but the total included nearly 700 mortars, 170 recoilless rifles, and over 60 AA and 80 artillery pieces. China also provided ammunition and other munitions and made available over 1,000 trucks, giving the PAVN is first significant motorized capability. Surprisingly, much of it was American, having been captured by the People's Liberation Army (PLA) either from the Nationalist Chinese or in Korea. The PAVN still possessed an eclectic assortment of arms: a mixed bag of French, Nationalist Chinese, American, Japanese, Soviet, and Chinese versions of Soviet weapons, along with the odd weapon produced by the PAVN. As maintaining or even obtaining ammunition for such an array of weapons had proven challenging during the War of Resistance, equipment standardization became a priority after 1954. Fortunately, Hanoi also had a strong ally in Moscow.[21]

By 1955, the Soviets began to send aid directly to the DRV, in part through a $500 million development fund. The effects were profound. The PAVN armored force had begun with an insignificant handful of captured French M24 light tanks. Moscow fixed that deficiency by shipping armored vehicles, and by 1959, the armored force contained over 50 Soviet T-34 tanks and SU-75 self-propelled guns. The Soviets also delivered 39 IL-14 (an improved C-47) and the single-engine AN-2 transport aircraft for the Air Force. Lastly, Moscow provided eight 150 km range P-8 early warning and ground control intercept radars to equip two air defense regiments.[22]

Soviet support coupled with continued Chinese aid helped to solve the PAVN's standardization problem. By 1959, two-thirds of the infantry weapons were modern Soviet or Chinese arms with the SKS carbine the standard infantry weapon. It was not simply a case of replacing older arms. With the new weapons allotted in greater numbers and increases in artillery and mortars, the firepower of an infantry division was more than four times that of a 1954 division. The VWP called strengthening the PAVN by relying on allies "achieving internal unity while gaining external support," and through it much progress was made.[23]

PAVN Training

While similar in most aspects to any military of the era, to include the ARVN, the PAVN's distinguishing training feature was its decentralized focus on division-level schools where each division established its own basic infantry, artillery, and other related schools to train replacements. It was a legacy of the war where divisions had to operate independently and rely on their own resources. The Chinese also shaped PAVN training traditions. The establishment of the People's Republic of China in 1949 presented the Viet Minh with a new ally on Vietnam's northern frontier. That paved the way for the arrival of a Chinese Military Advisory Group in August 1950 (beating out the U.S. MAAG by several weeks), which improved PAVN training at all levels. China provided not just advisory and material support but sanctuaries in Yunnan and Guangxi provinces that expedited the PAVN's shift into the big unit war in 1951. During 1955–1956, Chinese military specialists replaced the Advisory Group and continued to help the professionalization of the PAVN. However, the heart of PAVN training—that of the individual soldier—remained an internal affair, and the DRV never developed large centralized training centers like Thu Duc in South Vietnam.[24]

Enlisted soldiers were trained along traditional lines. After volunteering, each year the military region assigned them to a division that formed a temporary training battalion composed of instructor cadres. Basic training lasted about 60 days, followed by 30 days of training for the infantry, about 13 weeks in all. Following that, the soldiers reported to their units and entered into an advanced training cycle designed to last nine months. Despite the guerrilla warfare mystique, PAVN training throughout the 1954–1959 years centered on conventional weapons employment and infantry tactics as practiced almost everywhere in the world. There was no special jungle warfare training for the average soldier.[25]

The exceptions to the division system were officer and NCO schooling. In the early years, Vietnamese deserting the French Army or trained by the Japanese during the occupation provided a limited cadre of trained small unit leaders, but the majority of officers and NCOs were products of the army itself and promoted due to their performance and loyalty to the party. Officer and NCO schools were located at Son Tay (40 kilometers northwest of Hanoi) and Xuan Mai (30 kilometers southwest of Hanoi). Officers, to include political officers, came up through the ranks, and in time good squad leaders could find themselves lieutenants. The training periods were lengthy. The PAVN officer candidate spent a year in basic training before completing advanced coursework; the infantry officer's course required two follow-on years of schooling.[26]

Basic NCO school lasted six months while advanced NCO schooling was of similar duration for the officers. The commitment to NCO training was a hallmark of the PAVN and made its combat units extraordinarily cohesive—a primary reason why units continued to fight hard after taking heavy casualties. There also was a six-month officer refresher course, and to develop career officers, a senior military academy. The late 1950s "Train the Troops" program led to significant gains for combat, support, and service unit leaders. Like officer and NCO schooling, these specialized programs for communications, logistical services, and armored forces were centrally managed with the schools also located at Son Tay and Xuan Mai. Individual training ran for nine months or more, while the tank crew course lasted ten months for enlisted and 20 months for NCOs and officers. Lastly, coastal training courses for sailors began in April 1955 and were expanded into the Naval Training School in 1959.[27]

Regardless of rank or specialty, ideological instruction was continuous, a defining feature in communist armies. Party cadres underwent their own training program. Potential political officers were chosen from soldiers with demonstrated leadership skills such as squad and platoon leaders. Those selected attended a year-long course at a military region political training school. Socialism was the heart of the training and the unshakable ideological bedrock. Everything done by the political officer was grounded in Marxist theory.[28]

The indoctrination of soldiers was fervent and pervasive in the PAVN. It ran the spectrum from daily talks by political officers to army-wide efforts such as the 1957 "Increasing Socialist Awareness, Opposing Individualism" campaign. Successful indoctrination was achieved through the five "with's." The political officer ate with, lived with, worked with, trained with, and spent their leisure time with their soldiers, a policy borrowed from the Mao's Red Army. Not specifically mentioned in the five "with's" was the political officer's duty to "watch" the soldiers and conduct self-criticism sessions. While the indoctrination was accepted, at times the self-criticism became tiresome and not appreciated, despite idealistic interpretations of its benefits. The troops knew that the officers stressed positive news and suppressed the bad. Nevertheless, on the whole, political officers both were respected and liked. The combination of professional training coupled with political indoctrination created a well-prepared and motivated military ready to face any enemy on the battlefield. By 1959, the PAVN was a formidable foe.[29]

Conclusions on the PAVN

So how did the PAVN compare to the South Vietnamese military? In the ARVN, South Vietnam possessed a balanced, well equipped, and trained force, and even the Viet Cong were impressed. In their assessment, South Vietnam started with small and weak battalions under French control. By 1959 the Diem administration with American assistance had built up a military consisting of regular divisions plus the Civil Guard and the SDC. Further, the VC found Saigon's internal intelligence and counterintelligence agencies very effective. It was high praise, and Saigon also possessed the small but highly capable JGS strategic reserve. It had taken great strides, but the gap with the PAVN had not been closed. In 1959, the ARVN was a jewel in the rough, an unfinished project with great potential and glaring weaknesses.[30]

Hanoi held the edge. Opposing the 150,000-man seven-division strong ARVN in 1959 was the 173,000-strong PAVN, a good 15 percent larger. It was a veteran force that had been growing and expanding its capabilities. At its center were 13 infantry divisions, (six were half-strength and often referred to as brigades) along with one heavy engineer-artillery, one anti-aircraft, and three artillery divisions. The PAVN was better organized for war. Augmenting and supporting the PAVN divisions was everything required of a modern first-rate military: 12 independent infantry regiments and two tank regiments plus a broad range of service and supporting units. It also was true that the small PAVN Navy and Air Force lagged behind their South Vietnamese counterparts, but neither nation possessed a significant offensive naval or air capability.[31]

The PAVN held three further advantages by 1959. First, there was the massive 780,000-strong reserve whose members received basic training and afterwards underwent annual exercises to refresh and add to their skills—a resource the South Vietnamese could not hope to match. Second, the PAVN had an important edge in leadership. During the War of Resistance, PAVN officers had filled every senior command and staff position. Finally, the army embraced the rationale for preparing junior officers for advancement in time of war, a sentiment shared by many armies. After World War I, the U.S. Army realized that when war came, today's lieutenants would be tomorrow's battalion and regimental commanders, with majors and lieutenant colonels being rapidly promoted to division command. Officer preparation was designed to meet that demand. The PAVN followed a similar course. Conversely for the VNA, the French colonial system deliberately prevented Vietnamese officers, no matter how capable, from assuming high command or filling senior staff positions. That gave the PAVN a marked ability to expand in time of war that the ARVN had not been given time to develop.[32]

Unlike the South Vietnamese armed forces that faced one major difficulty after another during the 1954–1959 period, the People's Army of Vietnam was presented with an easier road and took full advantage. The combination of a strong and prepared PAVN plus the DRV's immense militia reserve meant that Hanoi could wage a prolonged war against the RVN for however long it would take to achieve victory. Lastly, the DRV's most valuable asset in the Republic of Vietnam—the Viet Cong—had to be taken into account as the ready-made insurgent force presented Saigon with a tough and challenging internal enemy from the outset.

Enter the Viet Cong and Saigon's Pacification Efforts

When Ngo Dinh Diem arrived in Saigon in July 1954, the French had ceded control over large parts of South Vietnam to the Viet Minh. In addition to the two PAVN regroupment zones, the VWP also held or contested large areas along the Cambodian border in Tay Ninh province, the Plain of Reeds, and central coastal areas stretching north and south of Qui Nhon along with swaths of the Central Highlands (see Map 3). Ideally, SOV officials, backed up by the VNA and other security forces, should have moved into VWP-controlled areas in late 1954 to establish the peace and exert control. The Hinh mutiny and sect war rendered that impossible, and the opening moves to defeat the stay-behind VWP forces did not begin until 1955.[33]

The Americans wanted the MSUG to support the effort in 1955. It was not a viable option. The group members did not start to arrive until May, and the Saigon government could not continue to cede control of the areas to the VWP. The situation in the Mekong Delta was bleak; Assistant Defense Minister Tran Trung Dung stated that the area was "unadministered," or in other words, controlled by the VWP, and that "the French left us nothing."[34] Diem had to act, and the VNA's pacification efforts in the two regroupment zones began after he issued the December 1954 national security directive. The first, Operation Tu Do (Liberty), began in Ca Mau and the western Mekong Delta on 8 February. It was supported by a large VNA force of 12,000 troops led by Colonel Duong Van Duc and headquartered at Soc Trang. Duc later led the fight against the Hoa Hao after they rebelled.[35]

The operation was an attempt at comprehensive civil-military pacification. It included medical teams from the Philippines (Operation Brotherhood) brought in by Lansdale, but the army units arrived at the last minute—too late for sufficient

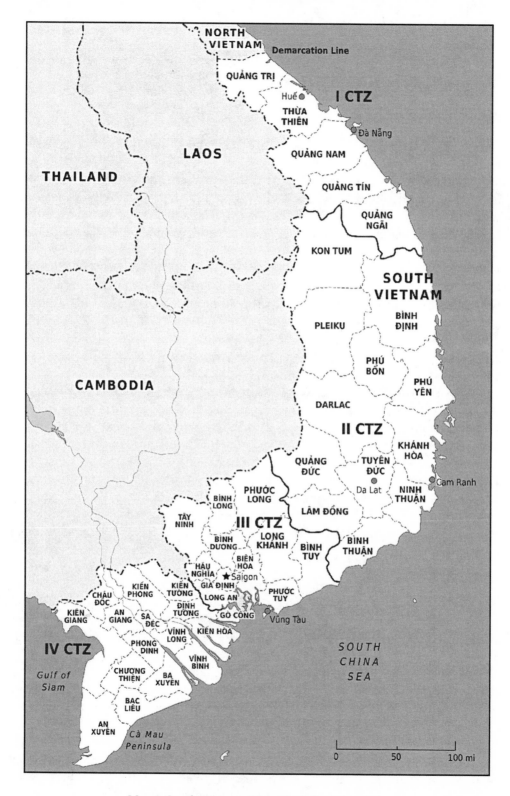

Map 3. South Vietnam (Erin Greb Cartography).

civil affairs training. As a result, the soldiers' rough behavior more alienated than endeared the local people. Saigon learned from that experience, as witnessed in April with Operation Giai Phong (Breaking Slave Shackles) along the coastal provinces of Quang Ngai and Binh Dinh. Monitored by the ICC, it involved Colonel Le Van Kim's reinforced GM 31 (to include the 154th Regiment that went to Saigon in May to battle the Binh Xuyen) and GM 32. The 12,000-strong force also included two Operation Brotherhood teams. Kim was a skilled leader who fought the Germans as a French Army officer in 1940. Serving with the Vichy French, he returned to Vietnam in 1941, joined an artillery unit, and in 1950 transferred to the VNA. The brother-in-law of General Tran Van Don, Kim was neither a Francophile nor apolitical; his sympathies had lain with General Hinh and later the Dai Viet. He ably directed Operation Giai Phong, conducting preliminary human intelligence and psychological warfare operations and ensured his troops received civil affairs training that won over the population. The operation's success was seen when the people willingly revealed the location of a number of hidden PAVN weapons caches and identified secret VWP cadres. The two GMs later became the 2nd Field Division with Kim in command.[36]

The Nam Bo VWP made Diem's efforts easier. Not wishing to reveal the extent of stay-behind party organization and in hope of rapid reunification, the Nam Bo Resistance Central Committee disbanded overt party organs in 1954, went underground, and shifted its efforts to agitation within legal political organizations under party influence. That allowed Saigon to reestablish control without facing organized resistance, although political intimidation, assassinations, and small raids to gain weapons were not uncommon. After Giai Phong, VNA pacification efforts continued, and Operation Brotherhood expanded to ten rural medical centers treating 2,000 patients a day and staffed by 100 Filipino doctors and nurses. Saigon's control in the countryside grew. While losing overt control, the tactic worked as the clandestine party remained intact.[37]

With his power consolidated, on the first anniversary of the day of national shame, 20 July 1955, Diem launched the Chien Dich To Cong (Denunciation of Communist Subversive Activities) or To Cong Campaign. As it gained momentum, the VWP began to lose power—often by the efforts of the campaign's director, former–Viet Minh officer Tran Chanh Thanh. Even modest party actions faced setback. VWP propaganda efforts and attempts to organize leftist student and peace movements were easily suppressed. Similarly, VWP efforts to organize the workers at the important Michelin rubber plantations met with failure. Saigon was successful but less than perfect, however. One notable failure was neglecting to sweep the remote U Minh Forest in the Mekong Delta north of Ca Mau. It soon became the Viet Cong's strongest base and used to train new recruits and launch small-scale raids.[38]

In addition to Thanh, success in expanding government control during 1955 also was due to another rallied Viet Minh leader, Kieu Cong Cung. At Lansdale's urging, on 7 March 1955 Diem made Cung the head of the Special Commissariat for Civic Action. Like Thanh, Cung knew what had worked and failed under the Viet Minh. Unlike Thanh, rather than simply repress the VC, he worked to win them over through persuasion and propaganda. As the Americans were quick to note and despite Diem's support, the effort hit a roadblock. There were too few officials to supervise the countryside. Indicative of the French–Bao Dai legacy, not one Saigon civil servant took up the offer to serve in the provinces. In any case, it is unlikely many would have done well. The villagers were equally contemptuous, deeming the urban bureaucrats "lazy, arrogant turtles."[39] To succeed in the rural villages, volunteers had to be young and fit, dedicated, and instilled with idealism for the mission. That meant that only a handful of cadres were available when over 6,000 were needed. Adding to difficulties, funding was woefully insufficient.[40]

Cung pushed ahead as best he could. There was hope of soon establishing a two-week course on rural affairs at Tan Son Nhut that could handle around 350 students. In the meantime, as a test case, the first Civic Action cadres arrived in Binh Gia province outside Saigon in April, just as Diem's battle with the Binh Xuyen reached its climax. It met with success and expanded into other Nam Bo provinces. Despite their initial reluctance, the Americans began to support the pacification program, and by late 1955, it was functioning in ten provinces with 46 Civic Action teams. To focus the efforts, at the end of 1955, Diem issued Decree 22 that clarified the twofold mission: (1) Raise people's intellectual standards, a direct reference to personalism as an ideology to oppose communism, and (2) improve the people's living conditions or welfare. Regrettably, this led to a divergent emphasis. Diem and Cung focused on the ideological while the Americans wanted to concentrate on welfare improvement. Despite the disagreement, the situation in the countryside improved, and in September, civic action programs under Cung, along with related programs in the ministries of information, education, land reform, and other offices, came under the purview of an inter-ministerial committee to coordinate efforts at the village level. To better unify the anti–VC effort, in 1956 Cung's Commissariat was given the added responsibility to train cadres from other ministries being assigned to the provinces.[41]

That left the village chief problem. Governance at the village level, like everywhere in South Vietnam at the end of the War of Resistance, was broken. Saigon had virtually no control as the majority of the councils and chiefs were either corrupt French holdovers or controlled by the VWP in their areas. In July 1956, Diem abolished the system and appointed chiefs through Cung's Commissariat. These steps were carried out in spite of the Americans; the appropriate agency, USOM, had no interest in Cung's unconventional approaches and wanted democratic elections. The Americans had a point. While the change promised improvements, it ran the risk of dismissing good chiefs. But a hidden truth remained; for generations villagers had locally selected their councils and chiefs. That system was impervious to the Saigon-directed election process envisioned by the Americans. In most cases, villagers continued to pick the chief, with or without election, and Cung took that into account. It was nothing new. A saying going back centuries captured the relationship: "The emperor's edict ends at the village gate."[42]

USOM, MSUG, and other Americans continued to resist Diem, Thanh, Cung, and Lansdale's approach to countering the Viet Cong. It was a matter of experience and perspective. The four recognized that the insurgency in South Vietnam was at best latent and the countryside unsettled. Their fears centered on two ideological problems. First, the VWP either kept or expanded its hold over villages without a government presence. That spurred the drive to act quickly. Second, they knew that VWP political power had not grown by building community projects—the VWP never had the resources—but through proselytizing, indoctrination, and establishing effective local control. That approach had to be countered directly by Saigon. During the 1954–1955 period, many U.S. officials missed both problems as they had gained experience in peaceful nations like India, where the government already was in control. South Vietnam's outward calm hid from them the revolution percolating underneath.[43]

Saigon pushed ahead. In addition to civic actions, it also launched military attacks to batter the Viet Cong that included covert propaganda programs and proselytizing efforts. The Mekong Delta continued to be the center of communist activities—especially Kien Hoa and Vinh Long provinces—and became the focus of the To Cong Campaign. The first major operation there was an expansion of the anti–Hoa Hao Operation Dinh Tien Hoang that ran from 5 June through 28 December 1955. Similar To Cong sweeps in the delta would be repeated in the future. The Viet Cong weathered the onslaught as southern VWP cadres remained under orders from Hanoi not to violate the Geneva ceasefire. They were limited to recruiting in utmost secrecy, and the only acts of violence permitted were defensive and reactionary. How the VC persevered represented the unique local culture in South Vietnam. The bond that often held the VWP together during these difficult times was not as much Marxist dogma but, as in the case of the Ngo, through kinship—by relying on extended familial bonds that proved vital to the survival of the revolution.[44]

Helping Saigon in its 1956 anti–VC operations, a compromise of sorts was reached with the Americans, and slowly, things began to come together. Diem and Cung continued to push pacification efforts to reassert government control over areas lost by the French and Bao Dai, while USOM and MSUG advanced community projects. In April 1956, to address the shortage of civic action cadres, the decision was made to limit village teams to two persons to allow for quicker expansion of the program that reached the Central Highlands for the first time that month. Cung also directed his civic action teams to work with the Americans to improve local infrastructure that had been damaged or neglected during the War of Resistance: houses, schools, roads, ditches, canals, wells, dikes, and abandoned farmland—all effective measures in winning villagers over to Saigon. Joint RVN-American progress was being made. By midyear, there were 1,622 cadres organized into 104 groups operating in 26 provinces. The program continued to grow and benefited from the implementation of popular American community projects.[45]

But the Americans still regarded the VC as weak, and the CIA concluded that remnant Hoa Hao rebels posed a greater danger. Diem was not under such misapprehension and continued to target the VWP. The third major anti–VC sweep, Operation Nguyen Hue, began in January 1956. The VC had been weakened. At the time, the VWP Nam Bo resistance committee controlled 37 poorly-armed, small guerrilla bands, 30 of which operated in the Mekong Delta. To make up for Saigon's earlier lapse, the operation hit VC Mekong Delta strongholds in the U Minh Forest and ran through 31 May. The ARVN gains were not lasting, but they kept at it. In March,

Saigon began a more successful series of anti-communist propaganda and psychological warfare campaigns to strengthen government support and morale within the military and refugee communities. Help came from Cung's Commissariat that had formed 900 of the cadres into mobile groups committed to Operation Thoai Ngoc Hau carried out from 8 May–31 October. It went after Viet Cong forces based along the Cambodian border, a first.[46]

The VWP reacted cautiously to Saigon's 1955–1956 offensives. The Nam Bo Resistance Central Committee reaffirmed the use of assassination against traitorous enemies but declined to authorize renewed armed struggle. Also during 1956, the VWP recruited Hoa Hao and Cao Dai fighters who refused to rally to Saigon. Another hundred or so Binh Xuyen fighters joined with the VWP in eastern Nam Bo as well. That gave the VWP a boost, but its military strength remained meager. Saigon sought to eliminate even that with one more major To Cong sweep, Operation Truong Tan Buu, which ran from 17 July–15 December and focused on eight provinces southeast of Saigon—part of the former VWP base area. It made gains but not decisively so.[47]

The cumulative effect did take a toll on the VWP. By December 1956, the situation had taken a turn for the better for Saigon in almost every meaningful way. The CIA ended both the SMM and Operation Brotherhood that month, and after four successful large-scale operations, the VNA's successor, the ARVN, disengaged from internal security operations in early 1957. Going forward, attacks against the Viet Cong were more counterintelligence, paramilitary, and psychological warfare campaigns than military operations, although local ARVN troops, especially the highly mobile armored cavalry units, did participate.[48]

By the close of 1957, government control extended throughout the country. Even Hanoi admitted that To Cong operations in late 1957-early 1958 had hurt the VC in both Nam Bo and Interzone V. II Corps Commander General Tran Van Don recalled that at the time, he could drive safely from Hue to Dalat in a jeep without guards. But the Nam Bo VWP, while weakened, remained largely intact, and the first VC battalion, Unit 250, was formed that year. Although Unit 250 was a battalion in name only, it signaled that the fight would continue. Nonetheless, U.S. officials in the RVN saw no serious internal security issues, and their deliberations did not dwell on the VC—only building up the conventional ARVN forces. As in the case with the withdrawal of the ARVN from counterinsurgency operations, the improved security situation in 1957 and 1958 finally brought Cung's civic actions into synchronization with the Americans. The focus shifted from counter-Viet Cong programs to community development that increased the people's welfare in the form of agricultural, educational, health, public works, and veterinary projects.[49]

Saigon's internal security and intelligence apparatus continued to improve and kept hammering the communists. Hanoi tried to win a propaganda coup during those difficult days by exploiting the December 1958 Phu Loi incident, where it claimed 1,000 VWP prisoners were poisoned to death. (The British investigated in their official role, noting the deaths were smaller in number and stemmed from incompetence and accidental food poisoning.) Hanoi's ploy did not work, and the incident forgotten. From mid–1958 into early 1959, the Nam Bo VWP began to suffer real losses. Key base areas were broken up and destroyed in Ca Mau, Hau Giang, and Kien Tuong provinces in the Mekong Delta. Only the U Minh Forest and Plain of Reeds remained VC strongholds, and the Nam Bo Resistance Central Committee was forced to admit that Saigon "had real control over the villages and hamlets."[50] They conceded that the Diem regime ran an effective administrative system from the capital down to the villages and hamlets—even family groups—and had established a military presence ranging from ARVN units to the SDC village militia.[51]

But with the passing of Resolution 15, things were about to change. For the VWP in the south, Resolution 15 meant salvation from destruction and the start of the revolutionary march to reunification. The Viet Cong would fight back, and war had returned to Vietnam.[52]

8

Who Were the Viet Cong?
Part 1

For Americans, their opponent was known collectively as the Viet Cong, but who they were was and remains cloudy. It was a shorthand term for Vietnamese communists, Viet Nam cong san, and had been around almost from the end of the War of Resistance. President Diem used it in a 1955 speech, and by 1957 it appeared in South Vietnamese newspapers and American reports. It became a ubiquitous oversimplification, devoid of nuance and ignoring the complexity embodied in that two-word phrase. First and foremost, the Viet Cong did not arise independently; they were the southern VWP and PAVN who had fought and won the 1946–1954 War of Resistance against France and remained during the 1954–1955 regroupment period. Also, many outsiders did not understand that in addition to individual PAVN soldiers and the party rank and file, in 1954 several thousand political cadres and at least three experienced battalions stayed in South Vietnam—although the To Cong campaign decimated them. The appearance of the Viet Cong did not signify the start of an indigenous rebellion in South Vietnam but rather a rebirth or awakening sparked in Hanoi.[1]

Equally important, the Viet Cong evolved, devolved, and transformed in deliberate, unexpected, and often profound ways throughout the conflict. In 1959, when Hanoi renewed war, the conflict was defined by the struggle in South Vietnam where Hanoi provided direction. By 1963, the conflict had expanded, and there was not just a considerable PAVN presence in the RVN but also Cambodia and Laos—although Hanoi never admitted that its army was in the south, let alone Cambodia or Laos. It meant that being in the Viet Cong meant being in the PAVN, and perhaps the war's greatest myth was that the VC were not PAVN. The regular PAVN soldier and the VC village militia member were one in loyalty, motivation, and obligation to the same leadership. The distinction was inter-organizational—different branches of the same military.

For Americans, Viet Cong became a generic term that meant "the enemy" in South Vietnam and was an accurate description. But this does not detract from the fact that the PAVN was their only armed adversary. American soldiers in combat did make a tactical distinction and called them VC unless they wore regular PAVN uniforms (often referring to them as NVA, meaning North Vietnamese Army), but in a broad sense that difference did not matter. From its inception in December 1944, every soldier who fought the French in Vietnam was part of the People's Army, as were the armed southerners who stayed behind in 1954, the PAVN regroupees who returned beginning in 1959, and PAVN regular units that arrived beginning in 1964. Everyone who joined the armed Viet Cong joined the People's Army of Vietnam. That was the army the Americans fought.[2]

The Political Face of the Viet Cong

The answer to "Who were the VC?" begins with the Vietnamese Workers' Party and Resolution 15. As Resolution 15 spelled out, the reunification war was to be waged on three levels where the military effort was subordinated to the political struggle, and international public and diplomatic support were never out of mind. Vital to that was forming a resistance government to rival Saigon, and making that a reality became a priority in September 1960 with the opening of the 3rd VWP Congress. Ho Chi Minh put things in motion when he made an address stating that the DRV had to "step up the national democratic people's revolution in the South."[3] Ho wanted to form another Viet Minh but with a new name and southern face. And like the Viet Minh, it had to appear as an independent movement while in acutality being controlled by the party. The groundwork had been laid earlier in 1958 when VWP operatives began contacting sympathetic southern politicians who established a "mobilization committee" that sent representatives (all VWP members) to Hanoi that year and again in 1959 to create what became the National Liberation Front (NLF). After gaining Hanoi's approval, on 20 December 1960, the NLF came to life with Nguyen Huu Tho as chairman. (Tho had been a clandestine communist party member since 1949.)[4]

The NLF presented as a united front of both communist and non-communist opposition to the Saigon regime and controlled through a combination of overt and secret VWP members. In addition to Tho, the other four senior NLF leaders all were VWP members: Vo Van Khiet, Phung Van Cung, Nguyen Van Hieu, and Huynh Tan Phat. This was the lesson learned during the War of Resistance: the indispensability of secret party members in dominating a united front movement. To provide an organizational structure for the resistance government and show its independence from Saigon, Hanoi replaced the 44-province RVN map with one that contained 38 provinces, often with new names. In each province, a shadow government that reached down to the district and village level was created under a central committee answering to the NLF.[5]

To provide ideological structure, in December the NLF issued a political manifesto. Despite claims to the contrary, it was the work of Hanoi; according to one NLF founder, Truong Nhu Tang, it was marked with "the delicate fingerprints of Ho Chi Minh."[6] While the manifesto itself was a moderately Marxist statement of opposition to the Diem government, the VWP intended to enforce a strict Marxist-Leninist dogma consistent with the Resolution 15 implementation instructions of a year earlier. The NLF was to place its primary reliance on the urban proletariat while the rural masses were placed next in importance; this followed the socialist tenet that defined people by their relationship to the means of production. It ignored the fact that South Vietnam's urban proletariat was almost nonexistent and politically powerless. In a nod to Mao's enlarged set of political class divisions, the NLF also appealed to the religious sects and bourgeois nationalists while aiming to subvert rival leftist organizations. Concerned VWP members were tactfully reassured that the bourgeoisie and other questionable NLF members were only there so the party could "utilize their abilities and their prestige in order to push forward the revolution," but it was "not going to entrust these classes with heavy responsibilities."[7]

In the early 1960s, the relative dormancy of the southern cadres worked to Hanoi's advantage, for when the guerrilla war expanded, the announced formation of the NLF gave the appearance that the NLF-VC represented an independent revolutionary opposition that arose of its own accord in reaction to Saigon's oppression. That story had great value as it weakened the credibility of the RVN government while legitimizing the NLF war effort in the eyes of audiences both at home and abroad. NLF leader Tho never would have garnered the same international acclaim had his VWP membership been made public. It also gave North Vietnam excellent cover to plausibly deny its aggression against South Vietnam. The notion of an indigenous and authentic NLF-VC movement taking up arms in response to Diem's misrule was powerful propaganda.[8]

The NLF would remain the face of the Viet Cong for the rest of the war within Vietnam and abroad, or as Hanoi put it, with the "justice-loving and peace-loving people of the world."[9] As in so many things, Hanoi acted as the chess master, playing multiple pieces while looking moves ahead. Internationally, the NLF was not simply intended to gain support amongst Western leftists, especially in America. It also was integral to the DRV's strategy for navigating the Sino-Soviet split within the socialist camp. Making the NLF the symbol of the struggle in the south meant Hanoi had not violated Moscow's peaceful coexistence urgings. Nor did it aggravate relations with Beijing, which feared embroilment in a ground war with the United States if the DRV was identified as the aggressor, triggering an American military invasion. This was one area where Ho Chi Minh was of great value. His revolutionary achievements and past Comintern service made him respected in both Beijing and Moscow.[10]

The VWP placed high value on its international socialist duties and couched its war of reunification in those terms, stressing how, as part of the world socialist revolution, it confronted in South Vietnam the great evil, the Yankee imperialists. For that reason, the Sino-Soviet split created problems for Hanoi as it fought to reunify Vietnam. Prior to World War II, the communist movement was monolithic with Josef Stalin in command. In the VWP, the feeling was that Stalin had been infallible. That changed after 1945 as cracks appeared, most notably in Yugoslavia, but from a Cold War standpoint, they were not critical. It was Mao's unification of China in 1949 that created a major communist rival, triggering what came to be called the Sino-Soviet split and threatening Soviet leadership of the socialist revolution, a position it had held since 1919. The fissure became pronounced after Stalin died in 1953, followed by the rise of the hot-tempered Soviet Premier Nikita S. Khrushchev and his moderate policy of peaceful coexistence with the West. While Mao sought global victory through Marxist-oriented wars of national liberation, the Soviets looked to avoid a nuclear war and were confident they could win the Cold War by economically outperforming free-market democracies.[11]

From the moment the VWP opted to restart the war in 1959, the split had to be taken into account. Fortunately, Beijing was distracted that year. The Great Leap Forward economic plan was faltering, military tensions with Taiwan and India were high, and the army was putting down an uprising in Tibet. For its part, Moscow sought to improve relations not just with the DRV but other nations in South Asia, to include India. That aggravated the rivalry, as Stalin had given Mao a free hand in the region. Further vexing Beijing, Khrushchev reneged on the agreement to share nuclear weapon technology. In that tense environment, Hanoi took a risk by acting unilaterally in 1959, something it had done before when Stalin reprimanded Ho after Ho suspended the ICP in 1946 to shore up united front unity. There would be no reprimand in 1959, however. When Resolution 15 became known, Moscow was not overly concerned and agreed to assist the DRV. Beijing cautioned Hanoi not to get into a war with America but deemed Resolution 15 a "reasonable idea" and pledged help. Once Ho gained support from Moscow and Beijing, they stood by Hanoi for the rest of the war. The war of reunification moved forward.[12]

Having successfully navigated the Sino-Soviet issue, Hanoi broadened its political focus. While the creation of the NLF was a major step in advancing the revolution, it was not enough. To bolster the appearance of independence from the DRV and reassure non-communists both in the south and internationally, Hanoi publicly declared the NLF regime a "special case" that would possess its own distinctive economy, pluralistic government, and neutralist foreign policy with the objective of gaining reunification through "national concord and reconciliation" with the DRV. Over time, the NLF also adopted platforms on civil rights, land reform, and social welfare. It even established a Foreign Relations Commission in February 1962 when the 1st NLF Congress convened.[13]

Embedding covert VWP leadership and direction within the NLF proved a brilliant tactic. Hanoi controlled the revolution at every stage while the NLF won followers and supporters, not just in the RVN but across the globe, often people that otherwise never would have supported a communist movement. It was impressive as even non-communist NLF members truly believed in the front. They should have. The VWP carefully acted to ensure that only essential party policies were adopted and carried out by the front. Otherwise, ideas and policies put forth by non-communist members were listened to and routinely acted on. Even vital issues were handled delicately. The ideal was to have the key issues raised openly by non–communists (to include clandestine VWP members) before being acted on; only as a last recourse and in the face of opposition would overt party members push through the adoption of the party line.

The "concord and reconciliation" line was exceptionally convincing. Many NLF revolutionaries, even some southern VWP members, believed Hanoi supported a two-state DRV-NLF solution. They also believed they would be treated as equals during post-war reunification talks. NLF leader Nguyen Van Tien stated in the mid–1960s that the front spoke for southern Vietnam—not Hanoi—and reunification would take "10 to 20 years of negotiations."[14] In the actual event in 1975, it took the VWP just six days to dictate terms to the NLF before abolishing it. A founding NLF leader was VWP member Dr. Duong Quynh Hao. After discovering Hanoi's control over the southern revolution, she reflected bitterly, "They [the DRV] never worked for national concord" and "They behave as if they conquered us."[15] A non-communist NLF founder, Nguyen Van Khanh, sheepishly remarked they were naïve in assuming the VWP would find "a place for us in a new government of reconciliation."[16] Speaking in more blunt terms, Truong Nhu Tang described the whole NLF effort as "breathtaking pretense."[17] It did not matter. Hundreds of thousands both in and outside the RVN accepted the notion of an independent NLF, but the VWP always was in charge.[18]

Hanoi pressed ahead. With the NLF up and running, the next step was to create a Marxist political organization. On 1 January 1962, the People's Revolutionary Party (PRP) was formed and its existence revealed by Radio Hanoi on 18 January. The name was not particularly original; Cambodian communists belonged to the Khmer People's Revolutionary Party (KPRP) founded in 1949. Overtly, the PRP was distinct from the VWP only sharing "fraternal ties of communism."[19] In reality, VWP members formed the PRP core. After the PRP's creation, the NLF came under its authority during the 1st NLF Congress as selected PRP members dominated NLF central committees from the regional to village levels. Adding to the subterfuge, overt PRP candidates in the NLF committees did not exceed 40 percent of the total; it was the secret cadres that ensured a majority. It took a while for some old Viet Minh members to discover that the VWP ran the show. When the truth became known, southern comrades deemed VWP membership superior to that of the PRP, and over time promising PRP members quietly entered the VWP.[20]

The PRP operated as a subordinate wing of the VWP. It had a good foundation to build upon. During the War of Resistance, the VWP organized militia units and farmer associations that carried on in areas under party control after partition in 1954. And party membership meant gaining a position of leadership, as it continued to be restricted to only the most promising candidates. As such, VWP and later PRP membership was limited; in a village of 2,000 people, only 15 or so would be party members (along with a handful of secret members), but they led the village, the militia, and the various mass associations along with the finance-economy and security committees. Even in areas dominated by the VC, no more than five percent of the population were party members.[21]

With the passing of Resolution 15, party reach needed to be expanded, leading to the creation of sub-organizations such as the Women's and Youth Liberation Associations founded 1961. They mirrored the VWP's Ho Chi Minh Labor Youth Union and Women's Union in the DRV, and Woman's Union regroupees returned south to take over the leadership. The Women's Association made important contributions. They provided cadres for provincial and district associations and assumed roles ranging from supporting political and military committees to participating in armed propaganda units. Because of their reliability, they also carried out intelligence tasks and acted as clandestine couriers. These were dangerous duties; any woman identified as an association leader faced arrest, imprisonment, or worse. The most distinguished leader was Nguyen Thi Dinh, a career PAVN officer and party member since 1938 who remained in the south after 1954. She was a founding NLF member and led the anti–Agroville campaign in Kien Hoa province. She also headed the all-female "Long-Haired Army" who carried out anti–Saigon protests and steadily rose in the NLF ranks.[22]

The VWP, imbued with fresh PRP blood, continued to run the revolution in the south. While NLF central committees nominally were independent and non-communist, behind the scenes the VWP/PRP current affairs committees made the decisions. To unify the political and military campaigns, as a rule the provincial party secretary served as the political commissar while the VC military commander served as deputy party secretary. An American intelligence officer who debriefed and interrogated hundreds of defectors and prisoners summed up the difference between the NLF and the communist party succinctly. Regarding the NLF, "they knew nothing." To gain information, intelligence officers went after communist party members; that "was the name of the game."[23]

Directing the new organizations that formed a maze of committees overwhelmed the VWP's Nam Bo Resistance Central Committee in 1960. To lead both the political struggle and war in South Vietnam, the Central Office for South Vietnam—Le Duan's old War of Resistance command—was re-established by the VWP Central Committee in Hanoi on 23 January 1961. It subsumed the Nam Bo committee and reported to Hanoi's NRC overseen by Le Duc Tho. Additionally, because of the importance of South Vietnam's capital region, earlier in 1960 Hanoi had established the Saigon-Gia Dinh Special Zone. It fell under the supervision of COSVN in 1961.[24]

Decision-making authority rested with the COSVN Central Committee led by the secretary, while the Central Committee's Current Affairs Committee carried out COSVN's day-to-day operations. The Politburo in Hanoi selected Nguyen Van Linh to be the first COSVN secretary, and he took office in October 1961. Linh, a VWP Central Committee member, was born in Hanoi and had joined the communists in his youth when his abilities attracted the attention of Ho Chi Minh; during the War of Resistance, he served under Le Duan in Nam Bo. The NLF leadership reported to Linh. To ensure VWP guidance was being adhered to, a NLF leadership meeting was held on 31 January 1962 under the direction of Vo Van Khiet. Khiet was not simply a secret VWP member; he was simultaneously the VWP Party Chairman for the Saigon-Gia Dinh Special Zone and member of the COSVN Central Committee.[25]

It was critical for Hanoi to exert firm control both politically and militarily in the south. Before the reinstitution of COSVN, the Nam Bo Resistance Committee cited weak discipline and control as a problem. It was not a new complaint. Not only were non-party NLF members a cause for concern, but Diem's To Cong campaign damaged and even eradicated party control in numerous villages and hamlets. That caused the northerners to look upon southern VWP and PRP members with some suspicion. Left to their own devices, southern cadres routinely flouted party directives and acted unilaterally. It also was known that many had independent streaks and did not take naturally to Hanoi's orders. Even in the armed Viet Cong, a number of PAVN regroupees complained of a lack of obedience; General Nguyen Chi Thanh diplomatically called it "their own special nature and character."[26] To ensure there would be no deviation from the party line, in 1961 Hanoi sent a contingent of 500 VWP and military leaders known as the Orient Group to South Vietnam. These party-faithful fleshed out the COSVN staff and filled important positions in the regional and provincial central committees.[27]

Friction within the revolutionary ranks continued. The combination of northern-southern differences, the unbalanced VWP-PRP relationship, and the perception by some southern revolutionaries that the orientation group and other northerners saw themselves as "older brothers" in the hierarchical Confucian sense led to resentment.[28] A similar rift developed between northern and southern soldiers. With the war escalating by the day, such discord was unacceptable, and stern measures were taken. To re-instill discipline, COSVN issued Directive 137 in 1961 that initiated a purge of many old VWP cadres with an emphasis on the cause of "liberation" reflected in the new mass association. As they were replaced with young and enthusiastic members, the internal squabbling dissipated, and Hanoi's control over the war in the south was assured. Nonetheless, the distrust between northern and southern comrades never entirely disappeared.[29]

The Americans struggled to make sense of it all; a few weeks after the February 1962 PRP Congress, a CIA report stated that Hanoi might still hope for a peaceful reunification through a nationwide election or possibly attempt to establish a rival government. It suggested the announcement of the NLF—that had occurred over a year earlier—merely showed Hanoi was "preparing for such a move."[30] The report then concluded, "in the short run, we believe that there will be no significant change in the pattern of Viet Cong activity."[31] The CIA could not have been more wrong. The reunification war had begun three years earlier, the pace of events accelerating, and the NLF functioning exactly as planned. VC leaders followed Hanoi's orders with the front organizations, the NLF and PRP, fully subordinated to the Vietnamese Workers' Party.[32]

The Viet Cong Military Command

The power of the Vietnamese Workers' Party was every bit as strong within the Viet Cong military forces as in the PRP and NLF, if not more so—in all key army units the party commissar was the equal of the military commander. In keeping with the political face of the Viet Cong, the VWP role remained hidden, and as with the creation of the NFL and PRP, on 1 January 1961 the CMPC sent secret instructions to formalize the VC military arm as the People's Liberation Armed Forces (PLAF). Overtly for propaganda purposes, it was distinct from the PAVN. But the CMPC order made clear the forces were subordinate to PAVN command. In 1975, with the need for wartime propaganda over, the term disappeared. Even in the north, the actual chain of command was not revealed. Officially, the DRV premier served as the PAVN supreme commander who was advised by the national defense council. In reality, authority rested with the Politburo and its Subcommittee on Military Affairs (SCMA) with Le Duan and Giap serving as senior members. The SCMA was the most powerful military body in the nation.[33]

The CMPC, assisted by the PAVN Military Staff, continued to carry out the day-to-day tasks directed by the Politburo and SCMA. That completed the long military chain of command from the VWP Politburo to the SCMA to CMPC to COSVN and on to the regional and provincial military committees in South Vietnam. To strengthen command communications, in April 1962 VC radio procedures were aligned with those of the PAVN (the changing frequencies and call signs, transmission schedules, and message formats). Even worse for the Americans, in the same year the PAVN adopted new encryption technologies for communications with COSVN and high-level commands in South Vietnam, Laos, and Cambodia, part of its "one battlefield" concept. The changes provided greater security that set back ARVN and American signals intelligence (SIGINT) operations targeting the VC. The Americans did not break the system until 1967, depriving Washington of critical intelligence during the intervening years.[34]

Mirroring Hanoi's command arrangements, COSVN set up a Military Affairs Committee (akin to the CMPC and headed by PAVN general Tran Van Quang) that was supported by the COSVN Military Staff. To mask Hanoi's role, Quang's PAVN rank was hidden, and he officially led the PLAF front organization. Nguyen Thi Dinh held the figurehead position of PLAF vice commander. After the war, she became the PAVN's first woman general. Her story highlighted a difference over how women were treated. In the ARVN, women overwhelmingly were enlisted with the rest of the junior officers. In the VWP and PAVN, to include the VC, women climbed much higher in rank, but there was a ceiling. A few women joined the Central Committee, but none entered the Politburo or the Secretariat, and none held high position in senior VWP or PAVN staffs and committees.[35]

At the operational level during the years 1959–1963, COSVN directed the war in South Vietnam through the existing PAVN Military Regions 5 through 9. MR-5 covered all of South Vietnam from the DMZ south to Dalat. MR-6 encompassed northern Nam Bo and the provinces to the immediate north, while MR-7 covered eastern Nam Bo, MR-8 central Nam Bo (and adjacent bases in Cambodia), and MR-9 western Nam Bo. There were some modifications to the command structure; most notably MR-8 and MR-9 were renumbered MR-2 and MR-3 respectively in 1961. The Central Highlands did not become a semi-autonomous front under MR-5 until 1964.[36]

The COSVN Military Staff carried out the functions seen in any Western military organization and was responsible for overseeing military operations and drafting war plans. In the early years, local conditions dictated the pace of operations, and that required centralized planning but decentralized execution at the MR, provincial, and district levels. To accomplish this, military affairs committees or sections were created at each level and command staffs assigned to each regional committee while the COSVN Military Staff tasked its Combat Operations Section to coordinate efforts of subordinate committees and sections. To protect the command and control structure, COSVN and MR command headquarters were located in strongly defended secret zones within base areas.[37]

Conclusions

Every political and military organization needed to wage war was in place by 1 January 1962. First came the National Liberation Front to politically challenge the Saigon regime. Next came the reactivation of COSVN to ensure Hanoi's control over the war effort—both politically and militarily—and on its heels came the establishment of the People's Liberation Armed Forces. Ten months later, the creation of the People's Revolutionary Party completed the process. Even though the NLF, PLAF, and PRP were transitory front organizations—when the war was won, Vietnam continued to be ruled by the VWP and defended by the PAVN—it was an impressive feat. And there was no time to waste. As soon as they were up and running, the organizations turned to waging war. Despite hopes and rhetoric, that meant a fight on the battlefield, not simply a political struggle. To win the war, Hanoi would rely on the Viet Cong to defeat South Vietnam and its American ally.

Viet Cong Recruiting

There could be no war without soldiers, and that meant effective recruitment. Viet Cong recruitment was a dual track political-military affair and the major burden fell on proselytizing committees at the village and district levels, usually with separate military and people's sections. Proselytizing was inseparable from propaganda during the early years of the war in South Vietnam. They were considered the most powerful political tools at the Viet Cong's disposal, and women proved to be exceptionally effective. Methods included individual contact, village indoctrination meetings, and even dissemination of propaganda through travelling dancing troupes and singers—a highly successful recruiting method. As a sign of their importance, later in the war when personnel shortages became acute and other non-combat VC organizations were reduced in size, proselytizing teams remained fully staffed. There also was a rich array of propaganda materials employed, varying from public letters, leaflets, and posters to handkerchiefs bearing slogans and "peace" boats adorned with revolutionary messages. In addition to recruitment and persuasion purposes, these acts demonstrated Viet Cong power that strengthened the morale of individual VC and their supporters.[38]

The proselytizers' objectives spanned the full range of support for the revolution. At the bottom, the goal was to neutralize or discourage pro-government supporters; for this group, apathy equaled victory. The next desired outcome was to convince people to be open to VC political and military objectives. From there, proselytizers sought to gain sympathizers formed into the liberation associations who obeyed orders, willingly paid taxes, engaged in labor projects, and acted as informants. The ultimate objective was to gain members, especially soldiers. Although positive persuasion dominated proselytizing efforts at least through 1963, it was not all winning hearts and minds.[39]

If positive incentives proved insufficient to control the masses, then coercion was applied. The Viet Cong 1960–1961 Destruction of Oppression Campaign was characterized by assassinations and terrorist attacks designed to shift the "balance of fear" to the VC and away from Saigon.[40] It also captured the change from before Resolution 15: Afterwards the primary goal was to expand control by eliminating Saigon officials and replacing them with VWP cells. Intimidation in contested areas was raised to a new level. The widespread and coldly effective armed propaganda method was to assemble villagers, instruct them to obey the VC, and close by executing a bound prisoner or prisoners—usually the village chief or police officers. Beheadings or even crudely hacking victims to death by machete proved effective, and cutting off arms and castration also worked. They were darkly creative; the assassin of a War Zone D district chief took the extra step to place the victim's head in the headquarters' toilet. The most savage was death by disembowelment, not just of say a village chief, but the wife and children as well. While the measures succeeded in cowing people into submission and shifting the balance of terror toward the VC, they seldom worked as a recruitment tool.[41]

Recruiting Soldiers

For fit adherents, military service was always the top priority. In the early years, the Viet Cong had little trouble recruiting soldiers from liberated areas. Enlistees were restricted to males with no significant ties to the RVN government and if married, without many children. Members of the Cao Dai and Hoa Hao were banned. To grow the pool, in 1960 the Assault Youth Brigades, an organization temporarily formed during the War of Resistance, began anew for boys aged 15 and 16. They served in village militia units, and like their DRV counterparts, provided manual labor and logistical support for guerrilla and Main Force units. In Vinh Dinh province, average in size for Nam Bo's 28 provinces, the military recruitment quota was 45 soldiers per month, a goal easily met through volunteers. At the time, joining brought prestige, and reflecting that status, they were not called soldiers but revolutionary fighters. As the war escalated into the big unit conflict in 1962, demand overwhelmed the volunteer system, and it transitioned into a volunteer-recruiting system where proselytizers played a central role.[42]

Even those steps were not good enough to meet the growing need for recruits. A military draft had to be imposed in December 1963. At that time, recruitment of women for service in logistics units began, and bans on religious sect membership or those with prior ties to the South Vietnamese government could be waived. The draft also extended to contested areas despite concerns over an inductee's lack of a clean background. The VC evolved from an all-volunteer force during 1959–1962 to a volunteer-recruited military from late 1962 into 1963 to one that came to be dominated by involuntary drafts after December 1963.[43]

The Duties of the People

The broad nature of the War of Reunification demanded mobilization of the entire population. That made gaining politically motivated followers in contested or VC-controlled villages almost as vital to the military struggle as recruiting soldiers.

In the early years, proselytizing efforts made gains, and liberated areas expanded. In conjunction with the militia, villagers made important contributions to the war effort. First, the rice tax—the crop portion given to the party—fed the VC war machine. Second, people served as porters to carry supplies and munitions. Third, they built bunkers, tunnels, military camps, and the like. Finally, they assembled and placed thousands of booby traps in homemade "bomb factories." That proved to be one of the most dangerous threats faced by South Vietnamese soldiers and magnified the militia threat far beyond what their limited training and third-rate weapons suggested.[44]

Proselytizing in government-controlled regions, especially urban areas, was exceptionally challenging. As party membership was a crime, the efforts were covert by necessity. An ongoing goal was to recruit followers who secretly would advance the party agenda from within South Vietnamese organizations. The main targets were the military and security forces, government employees, and influential civilian groups. Ideally, the goal was to win over the masses, leading to the internal collapse of the Saigon regime. Proselytizers sought to undermine the ARVN by getting soldiers to desert (ideally to join the VC), obtain military supplies, and pass along information of value. They accomplished this by contacting ARVN soldiers or Civil Guard or SDC during their off hours in public places or by convincing families, friends, and other loved ones to write letters urging soldiers to desert. Even if they failed, the constant pressure on ARVN soldiers to not fight or desert undermined morale.[45]

Beyond the military, proselytizers recruited "secret" or "illegal" VC who resided either contested or under government control. Again, the chief goal was to win over the masses from within to foment an uprising against the Saigon government. The proselytizers also "talent spotted" for the security and intelligence services when they induced promising supporters with important access in either the RVN military or civilian sectors. Once on the hook, the sympathizer was handed over to a senior proselytizer for further direction or passed on for recruitment into espionage units. Their clandestine activities included gathering and passing intelligence, conducting sabotage attacks, targeting corrupt officials, and secretly supporting logistical operations by procuring otherwise unattainable supplies. While these secret activities proved the most expansive of proselytizing operations, they arguably were the least effective. They did well in specialized tasks like intelligence but failed in their primary mission; efforts to reach and win over the urban masses fizzled.[46]

Viet Cong Training

Perhaps no other area better demonstrates the changing nature of the Vietnam War than the training methods for Viet Cong soldiers. In 1959, the process of training volunteers was informal and began at the local village as part of their service with the militia. Few in number and poorly armed, they were taught only the rudiments. Over time, the militia provided soldiers for the provincial militia and regional Main Force VC units where they received more training, frequently under the guidance of PAVN regroupees, and evolved into professionals.

Training During the Early Years

Given the small number of Viet Cong soldiers at the war's outset in the late 1950s and into 1960—a few thousand at best—training by the PAVN stay-behind soldiers was based on local conditions, making it uneven and haphazard. Adding another layer of complexity, there were multiple levels of soldiering, and each required its own training program: part-time village and hamlet militia, full-time provincial guerrillas, and regional Main Forces. In the early years, the village militia was comprised almost exclusively of fit, military age males who possessed some ability to move and fight. Because they were unpaid soldiers, their training was limited and focused more on political indoctrination than military skills. Schooling at that time stressed the need to continuously propagandize and rally the people to the revolution, be self-sufficient, and take action. One misunderstood aspect of the village militia was that if the enemy approached, then its primary mission was not to defend the village but buy time for party cadres to make good their escape.[47]

In those years, training was simple as militia units were no larger than squads and weapons so scarce that the goal was to provide at least two per squad. The hamlet militia often had no firearms and were lucky to have hand grenades; the weapons shortage extended into the early 1960s. The Viet Cong augmented their arms with knives, halberds, crossbows, spears, scythes, and anything else useful. To maintain some level of readiness, mandated daily training emphasized squad tactics, close combat skills, and weapons practice, but as ammunition was harder to come by than weapons, marksmanship training almost always was a simulated "dry-fire" drill.[48]

Even with the arrival of a significant number of PAVN regroupees in 1960–1961, training for guerrilla or Main Force units was primitive and not much better than the militia. A typical daily schedule for the VC in the Central Highlands consisted of morning sessions dedicated to physical fitness and political indoctrination, followed by an afternoon session in hand-to-hand combat and small unit tactics. Guerrillas operated in platoons, some of which made pretenses to be companies, and the Main Forces were usually formed into small companies, although they routinely only conducted platoon-size attacks. There were virtually no crew-served weapons (mortars and machine guns) so instilling basic rifle and pistol skills—again, often without actual shooting—was the drill.[49]

There were positives. When Assault Youth members in the militia who had gained rudimentary training and often some combat experience reached age 17, they went to provincial guerrilla units and eventually on to Main Force units. Along the way, they received additional training and combat experience. In the early and mid–1960s, the typical militia soldier needed eight days of intense training before joining the provincial guerrillas and required four months of additional training to be ready for duty in a Main Force unit. This made for an ingenious and exceptionally robust "upgrading" pipeline filled with combat-tested and well-trained soldiers that gave Main Force Viet Cong units a high degree of resilience no matter how severe their battle losses.[50]

Things took another step forward on 15 February 1961 when regular, local, and militia Viet Cong were all placed under the direction of COSVN, a move that led to uniform training and more weapons and munitions. As in the regular PAVN, three was an important number. Three soldiers formed a team, three teams a squad, three squads a platoon, and so on. Provincial guerrillas executed "triangular formation" training where units were broken down into three groups and two would take turns training in guerrilla tactics against each other while the third evaluated their performance. Other subjects centered on Mao's principles of guerrilla warfare, studying local conditions, and post-battle analysis, as well as more mundane duties such as cleaning weapons. Military training was mandated not just for guerrilla and militia units, but for party cadres as well. Political studies focused on Resolution 15 political-military guidance for waging revolutionary war and amplifying instructions provided in a 31 January 1961 VWP Politburo directive. Even then, combat objectives were limited as guerrilla forces remained at platoon or company strength. Main Forces also did not operate beyond the company level and trained accordingly. It was slow progress but progress nonetheless.[51]

Training for the Big Unit War

To fight Le Duan's big unit war required concentrating troops for training (large VC formations were sometimes called concentrated units) and was risky business in the early 1960s. Big units made a big target. In 1962, the Viet Cong in the Mekong Delta province of Dinh Tuong suffered a heavy blow when the training base for its 514th Provincial Battalion was discovered and attacked by the ARVN with 82 out of 106 Viet Cong soldiers killed. Similarly, the adjacent Long An province was forced to send recruits to be trained in its remote and almost uninhabitable Plain of Reeds along the Cambodian border. One solution was to keep units moving. In 1963, the An Xuan provincial military committee in the southernmost Mekong Delta established a mobile school for the infantry with 30 students per class and four instructors who never stayed in one fixed location. After Viet Cong advances in the wake of Diem's death in November 1963, more schools were established in the Mekong Delta, but to permanently alleviate the ARVN threat, in 1964 training camps shifted to Cambodian sanctuaries that never had gone away after 1954.[52]

As more and larger weapons arrived from the DRV, to flesh out big units, the Viet Cong had to create courses to meet the growing need for officers and NCOs along with a number of schools for special skills. Using the VC base area in Dinh Tuong province as an example, training on crew-served weapons like mortars, machine guns, and recoilless rifles lasted four months, communications school lasted five months, while sniper training took up to nine months, and a radio maintenance course lasted a full year. There also were schools for quartermasters and armorers, and medical support was not neglected. While doctors were recruited, the VC created schools for medics, nurses, and even an 18-month program to train physician assistants. Cadres in Dinh Truong could train over 1,000 soldiers in advanced courses per year by the mid–1960s.[53]

The most unique specialists were the sappers. The sapper-reconnaissance concept originated during the years 1961–1963 when the PAVN in North Vietnam formed three Mobile Sapper Training Battalions to be sent to South Vietnam. The goal was to have a sapper platoon for every Main Force battalion. The sapper, a combination of combat engineer and shock assault soldier, completed a three-month basic course and then was assigned to independently operating squads, platoons, and companies that trained together for periods of three to six months before becoming combat ready.[54]

Over time, Viet Cong training made great strides, from starting as little more than small bands of rag-tag infantry in 1959 to forming fully armed and equipped Main Force companies and battalions by 1963.

Intelligence Operations

One of the most underappreciated of the Viet Cong's strengths was the ability to conduct full spectrum of intelligence operations at a very high level of professionalism. These areas included traditional military combat intelligence (to include ground reconnaissance tasks) as well as communications intelligence and a wide array of espionage activities.

Combat Intelligence

In combat units, PAVN and Main Force VC intelligence sections were similar to those used by most of the world's militaries. There were the "collectors" who conducted reconnaissance, observation, and surveillance missions and "analysts" who used collected intelligence to support military planning and execution. Where VC and PAVN combat intelligence differed from the Western model was the outsized role played by ground reconnaissance. The battalion reconnaissance platoon carried out the lion's share of the work but was augmented by other assets starting at the highest military echelons. The senior intelligence center was the Military Intelligence Department of the COSVN Military Staff which also possessed a strategic reconnaissance force, first of one and later two ground reconnaissance (GR) battalions. Finally, there was an elite sapper reconnaissance company that conducted special missions to analyze key defenses and bases for attack and obtain information on specialized subjects such as the enemy's military organization and types and numbers of critical enemy weapons and equipment.[55]

Detachments from the GR battalions often were forward deployed to headquarters such as that at Cu Chi to support major operations. Located about 35 kilometers northwest of Saigon, Cu Chi was a Viet Cong stronghold. With its extensive tunnel systems, proved ideal for conducting high-level VC intelligence activities. Typically, the first step was to dispatch a reconnaissance team, often as small as three soldiers, in advance of an operation to develop in-depth information ranging from the

geography to the political situation to enemy military habits and any other requirement as directed. As the soldiers were alone in enemy territory, as a precaution they
carried ARVN PSYOPS leaflets granting VC good treatment if they surrendered. In
the event of capture, they presented the leaflet and claimed they were surrendering.
That both provided a cover story as to why they were there and might later present
an opportunity to escape if believed and left unguarded. Viet Cong ground reconnaissance was a redundant affair, and the first mission invariably was followed by
an additional mission to check, recheck, and crosscheck information accompanied
by last-minute missions to uncover the unexpected. A more thorough methodology
was hard to imagine.[56]

During the 1959–1963 period, this unique one-two punch of traditional military
intelligence coupled with expansive ground reconnaissance proved more than adequate for fighting in sparsely populated jungle and mountain regions. To battle in
inhabited areas where the VC held ideological sway, VC Main Force and provincial
guerrilla formations also could task local VC at the district, village, and hamlet level
to carry out information gathering. Known as the "people's intelligence system," this
was a marked advantage. As compared to their limited combat value, the local VC
cells, combined with input from sympathizers and the secret VC, performed invaluable service. They became the eyes and ears of the VC provincial and Main Force
units and worked with the reconnaissance teams. It was a deadly force multiplier
and made the VC far more effective than their numbers and firepower would otherwise have permitted.[57]

Signals Intelligence (SIGINT)

Augmenting the pervasive tactical intelligence network, one of the VC's strongest capabilities—and one often least appreciated by the Americans—was the
comprehensive and sophisticated PAVN SIGINT arm, referred to as technical reconnaissance. DRV security services SIGINT dated back to 1955, when the Soviets provided initial equipment and training. Soviet support grew significantly between 1959
and 1961, and what happened in the south stemmed directly from those beginnings
in the north. Starting in 1961, Hanoi conducted its own SIGINT and electronic eaves-
dropping missions that penetrated South Vietnamese and foreign countries' embassies, facilities, and communication networks under the highly secretive B12,MM
Operation. As for the military, while the Soviets did not directly advise PAVN personnel, they did provide modern radio intercept equipment that in turn was introduced by the PAVN into South Vietnam.[58]

In the early years of the Vietnam War, Viet Cong SIGINT operations were ad
hoc and amateurish but often effective as in the January 1963 battle at Ap Bac where
the VC monitored the operation in real time allowing for decisive tactical countermoves. Perhaps based on the Ap Bac success, later in 1963, COSVN centralized operations with the creation of Technical Reconnaissance Units (TRUs) assigned to the
PAVN 47th Technical Reconnaissance Battalion. The TRUs then began operating
against the ARVN and later the Americans, carrying out intercept, traffic analysis,
jamming, and imitative deception missions. Passive intercept and traffic analysis

provided timely tactical information while active measures like jamming and imitative deception intrusion into ARVN and American radio nets were timed to create confusion at critical moments such as helicopter landings or airstrikes or artillery missions; a common deception tactic was to transmit "cease fire" calls, often with claims of friendly fire. Both the ARVN and Americans failed to react to this threat, and throughout the 1959–1963 period, they continued to communicate without encrypting their radio transmissions.[59]

Counter-Espionage and Espionage

Viet Cong counter-espionage and espionage differed from most other militaries in that they included counterintelligence (CI) and human intelligence (HUMINT) operations combined with special tasks such as assassinations and terrorist attacks. In another notable difference, while combat and signals intelligence fell under the Military Intelligence Department of COSVN's Military Staff, counter-espionage and espionage were handled differently. They were carried out under a variety of organizations with shifting authority. The DRV's efforts got off to a good start when the Japanese left unattended the Sûreté archives in Hanoi after they surrendered in 1945. The VWP quickly exploited them, gaining not just information but key insights into how to conduct counter-espionage and espionage operations that were carried out by the Security Service.

Staffed by political officers, the Security Service worked under the Ministry of Public Security, and by the end of the War of Resistance, counterintelligence efforts were well developed. The ministry was led by the formidable Tran Quoc Hoan (referred to as the DRV's Beria, Stalin's infamous security henchman). Its officers were the equivalent of and as ruthless as the Soviet secret police. The PAVN had their own secret police in the Military Security Service. Both operated together in the south before partition and continued afterwards. In 1961, direction of the CI operations transferred to the COSVN Security Agency staffed by Military Security Service political officers. It was headed by Le Duc Tho's brother, Mai Chi Tho. Tho also served as COSVN chief political commissar. Ultimate CI authority within the RVN rested with Phan Van Dang, COSVN deputy secretary for security.[60]

The COSVN Security Agency blanketed South Vietnam and expanded as the war grew. Political officers generally came from the ranks of reliable low-level VC platoon leaders and underwent a six-month course run by the agency. They then attended a seven-month school where they were taught investigative and surveillance skills and how to set up and operate a province-level security office. Secret police assigned to security offices answered to the agency's Internal Section for areas contested or under VC control (to include base areas in Cambodia), while the External Section oversaw operations in regions controlled by the Saigon government.[61]

Mai Chi Tho's authority was centralized through MR security offices overseeing their provinces and the Saigon Gia-Dinh Special Zone. The provinces and special zone were divided into sectors, each with a secret police headquarters that reported to the provincial or special zone headquarters, as in the case of Saigon's Binh Tanh district where the secret police security sector designation was A.23 with the headquarters identified as A.536. Tho's secret police exercised a great deal of independence and worked with, but not under, the direction of various party current affairs committees that reached into every level of South Vietnam down to individual villages. As the secret police had the responsibility to instill party discipline and ferret out traitors, spies, and saboteurs, they ran a vast network of informants to include party members, and at the village level they could deputize the self-defense militia if needed.[62]

The espionage counterpart to the Security Service was the Military Intelligence Service (MIS), which provided the spies. The service was a veteran and competent organization. During the War of Resistance, highly effective MIS HUMINT missions spanned all of Vietnam and were directed by the Liaison Directorate. After 1954 things began to change. To enhance espionage efforts, in 1957 Hanoi created its equivalent of the CIA, the Central Research Agency (CRA). Placed discreetly within the Defense Ministry, it provided strategic intelligence analysis for the Politburo and Central Committee. The CRA stood apart as it, like the CIA, assigned clandestine intelligence officers from its Collections Division to overseas postings. The division was divided into a number of geographically defined subdivisions focused on Cambodia, Laos, and other targeted countries. Finally, MIS and Liaison Directorate operations merged with the CRA Collections Division to better coordinate strategic-level espionage operations.[63]

Then came 1959's Resolution 15 which ushered in renewed war in the RVN, and things changed anew. The reason was that HUMINT operations directed against South Vietnam preceded Resolution 15 as MIS espionage networks remained in place after partition and never stopped working. During the 1954–1955 regroupment, MIS made a concerted effort to use PAVN clandestine intelligence operatives to infiltrate every part of the Saigon government and military. It would have been both counterproductive and dangerous to disturb well-established and sensitive intelligence operations that already were fraught with risk. In 1959, the Politburo and Central Committee initially decided that the MIS headed by General Huong Minh Dao would continue to direct espionage missions in South Vietnam while Hanoi built up its political-military organizations in the south. But as the war picked up in the early 1960s, they shifted operations to Tho's COSVN Security Agency, although many HUMINT operatives continued to come from the MIS in Hanoi.[64]

By the mid–1960s VC CI, HUMINT, and the security apparatus were highly trained and well organized. That allowed for a unified espionage-counterintelligence effort in the south at the COSVN, MR, regional, and provincial levels. Each secret police headquarters or provincial security office ran its own espionage group, normally designated subsection B.3, such as Major Tran B who directed MR-2's espionage operations in the Mekong Delta. Subsection B.3 was divided into three branches: A.1—human intelligence officers, couriers, and support personnel; A.2—investigators who created "blacklists" for assassinations, kidnappings, terrorism, and to enforce discipline; and A.3—selected "security cadres" formed into three-person cells that executed blacklist tasks.[65]

Blacklist tasks were not carried out without reason. Kidnappings, assassinations, and other acts of terrorism were deliberately executed and the goals complex, but they almost always sent an underlying psychological warfare message. In VC areas, targeted attacks primarily served to maintain party authority while in contested or government-controlled areas; they targeted corrupt or cruel oppressors to gain popular support, and in the case of well-functioning government organizations and competent individuals, to fracture Saigon's authority. Assassinations targeted hated government figures and individuals or conversely, highly effective officials such as local leaders, doctors, nurses, and teachers.

Traitors were dealt with harshly. After a VC guerrilla leader rallied to Saigon, his infant child was shot through the head and the wife savagely beaten and left for dead. Given the importance Vietnamese culture placed on family, killing children along with spouses and grandparents was an effective terror tactic. However, while it often cowed a community, in many instances it created a fierce will to fight the VC. For similar reasons, random acts of terror only were used in contested or government-controlled areas for psychological ends, to intimidate the people into submission. The rules were different in VC-controlled areas. In VC-controlled villages, troublesome and recalcitrant villagers were harangued, intimidated, and shamed, but physical violence rarely occurred.[66]

North Vietnamese HUMINT accomplishments were amazingly impressive. By April of 1963, the CIA concluded, "The Viet Cong evidently have been able to maintain intelligence coverage of virtually every level in the South Vietnamese military and civil establishment."[67] It was an understatement. When the Buddhist Uprising began in Hue the next month, one reason that the civil disturbances spun out of control was the fact that Hue's police chief was a long-serving PAVN clandestine operative. And that revealed just a small piece of the puzzle.[68]

The Saigon Gai-Dinh Special Zone was the ultimate intelligence prize as it was the center for strategic HUMINT operations. As such, Saigon subsection B.3 operations were closely monitored by H Section (HUMINT) led by Tran Quoc Huong until 1962, then Tu Cang (Nguyen Van Tau). Mai Chi Tho in turn supervised H Section. The Saigon operatives scored a number of noteworthy successes. One of the earliest stars was Vu Ngoc Nha (agent A.22), leader of the A.22 network charged with penetrating the Saigon civil government. Vu Ngoc Nha began his career by developing Catholic spies in Trung Bo during both the Resistance War and Diem era. He was arrested in December 1958, but there was not enough evidence to obtain a conviction. He was detained until mid–1961 when he gained the trust of Ngo Dinh Can, Diem's powerful brother, who revived his career. After Can's death, Nha became a supporter of General Nguyen Van Thieu, allowing him to place agents and penetrate the highest levels of the Saigon government after Thieu seized power in 1965.[69]

A key member of Nha's A.22 network was Le Huu Thuy (agent A.25). Thuy began as a colonial police intelligence officer in Tonkin with the French, and he secretly joined the Viet Minh in 1949, inaugurating his career as a clandestine operative. One of the MIS operatives sent south after partition, he joined Diem's Ministry of Interior's security branch and in 1958 joined the ARVN CI service as a lieutenant; he was discovered and arrested in 1960. Released after Diem's death, he became a journalist, joined the Ministry of Information in 1967, and continued his clandestine work.[70]

The most illustrious and highest placed member of Nha's A.22 network was Huynh Van Trong. He served as interior minister in 1955 and plotted with the French to remove Diem, which ended his public career. Through Nha's efforts, Huynh Van Trong revived his governmental career in 1967 to become President Thieu's special assistant for political affairs, a position that gave him almost unlimited access to major governmental decisions. In July 1969, General Nguyen Ngoc Loan's National Police rolled up the A.22 network leading to 42 arrests including Nha, Thuy, and Trong. Trong's arrest, due to his high social status, sent shock waves through the Saigon elites and made international headlines. For Hanoi, it was a crippling blow to high-level intelligence operations within the Thieu administration. Both Vu Ngoc Nha and Huynh Van Trong gained release in 1973 as part of the prisoner exchange accord in the Paris Peace Agreement.[71]

The most flamboyant of the H Section operatives was Albert Pham Ngoc Thao, who served as an ARVN Lieutenant Colonel while holding a similar rank in the PAVN. A former Viet Minh officer who converted to Catholicism and posed as an anti-communist, Thao gained the trust of Ngo Dinh Nhu and became the Kien Hoa province chief. Kien Hoa quickly became one of the most peaceful provinces in the Mekong Delta, further burnishing Thao's reputation. However, he was successful because Thao turned Kien Hoa into a protected VC rear area, and to avoid ARVN operations, the VC did not launch attacks there. In 1961, CIA officer William Colby met Thao at Kien Hoa and was impressed to see that the colonel needed no bodyguards when traveling throughout the province; Thao must have relished the moment. Later, when the agroville program threatened VC control in some Mekong Delta areas, Thao (who by then was in charge of agroville security) wrote a highly critical analysis that helped derail the program.[72]

In a move that must have delighted his Hanoi superiors, Thao was appointed inspector general of the new Strategic Hamlet Program by Nhu for his agroville work. COSVN saw the program as a major threat, and in his capacity, Thao was able to help sabotage it from its inception. He then played his most important role: destabilizing the Saigon government through his participation in the 1963 military coup d'état. He continued to be an active coup plotter after 1963, but his luck ran out. He was arrested in July 1965 and executed; his body was never found. Another of Huong's achievements was the H.67 Subsection that infiltrated government agencies to include the placement of Dang Tran Duc (Ba Quac) as the staff assistant to the director of the Domestic Intelligence Department of the Central Intelligence Office (CIO), the South Vietnamese CIA. Hanoi had a "mole" in the bowels of the RVN's most important intelligence service.[73]

The greatest agent was Pham Xuan An of H.63 Subsection. An was a journalist who worked for a number of international news outlets. He began his spying career when he joined the VNA in the mid–1950s, being assigned to G-5 PSYOPS where he met important Americans like CIA operatives Lansdale and Rufus Phillips. Having learned English from American missionaries, through a stint with the Saigon office of the American CalTex Oil Company (a Chevron subsidiary), and two years of study in the United States, he worked first with *Reuters* and after 1964, *TIME* magazine. With his journalist cover and credentials, An proved invaluable in penetrating the highest levels of not just the South Vietnamese but American hierarchy, from other journalists to diplomats to senior military officers, passing on to COSVN important intelligence for years. An also played a role in undoing the Strategic Hamlet Program and saliently warned Hanoi that Diem's overthrow did not mean the Americans would quit South Vietnam as hoped in the DRV. Perhaps his greatest value, however, was in shaping the anti-war opinions of American journalists throughout the Vietnam War, especially in subtly promoting negative press coverage of both the 1963 battle of Ap Bac and the 1968 Tet Offensive. Pham Xuan An retired as a highly decorated PAVN major general in 1990.[74]

Conducting B.3 espionage training and operations was demanding and secrecy paramount. The Cu Chi area became the COSVN forward operations center in the south and the home for B.3 schools. Additionally, strategic HUMINT operations for the Saigon Gai-Dinh Special Zone were handled at Cu Chi by a subsection of Huong's H Section. Also at Cu Chi, CRA and MIS professionals schooled A.1 officers in the full range of spy tradecraft to include living under an alias, photography, writing with invisible inks, disguises, counter-surveillance measures, meeting with couriers, and transferring materials through dead drops and brush passes. Courier work was especially perilous; Pham Xuan An saw 23 of his 47 couriers captured, but none gave him up. For A.3 operatives, Cu Chi hosted a highly classified four-week sabotage course where students were segregated, their identities kept from each other, and the instructors sometimes hidden from the students during lectures. While there, they trained in the art of bomb making using various detonators, plastic explosives, and TNT, along with field expedients utilizing hand grenades, B-40 antitank rockets, and other materials and devices.[75]

Extensive security precautions were not limited to H or B.3 operatives but extended to senior VWP officers as well. To operate behind the lines, false identity papers were essential, and the VC excelled in forging identity cards and other documents that carried on down to the cell level. Their reach was so pervasive that often forging was not necessary, as clandestine operators penetrated Saigon's central identification card issuing office to obtain hundreds of real cards, even for government agencies such as the National Police, making them undetectable. Another of their effective security measures to protect cadres and secret operatives was the adoption of a myriad of aliases, although some techniques, such as adding a number to the first name, proved ineffective.[76]

As a testament to the security measures, the CIA team assigned to identify and locate key VC, called CT-4, constantly struggled. CT-4 had obtained thousands of names but had limited success in matching them to the thousands of captured photographs, resulting in very few "true name" identifications. Other difficulties in catching behind-the-lines Viet Cong were self-inflicted. Although fingerprints were taken routinely, the South Vietnamese Bureau of Investigation continued to use the antiquated French systems and had no central file system to match fingerprints, a problem that dated back to the days when the Binh Xuyen ran the national police. Fingerprints obtained as evidence or taken off a prisoner could not be used to uncover their identities in a timely manner. In combination, the security measures allowed Viet Cong espionage operations, despite setbacks, to operate with good success throughout the war.[77]

In its entirety, Viet Cong intelligence operations represented some of the most remarkable and successful achievements of the Vietnam War, and the danger they posed was consistently underestimated by senior Americans both in and out of uniform.

9

Who Were the Viet Cong?
Part 2

Having good organization, recruiting, and training capabilities, along with highly skilled intelligence services, left one more critical area to be addressed: acquiring weapons, equipment, and supplies. That proved a constant challenge for the Viet Cong. When the war began anew in 1959, they fell back on the weapons cached in 1954, an assorted collection of captured French and American arms. The stocks proved inadequate, as during Diem's To Cong operations, many if not most had been captured or destroyed; 307 arms caches were seized between 1955 and 1960. Nonetheless, 1960 began promisingly with a surprise raid that netted several hundred weapons. But it was a success not repeated over the next few years.[1]

The meager number of small arms captured from Saigon's Civil Guard, SDC, and other security forces did little to improve the situation; by the close of 1960, the VC in the Mekong Delta had captured a mere 197 rifles, and ammunition supplies were chronically short. If the goal merely had been to keep the resistance alive through a small and lightly armed militia, then that might have sufficed. But to even come close to the objective of waging General Giap's mobile conventional counteroffensive with Le Duan's "big unit" battalions, regiments, and divisions, an entirely new and more dynamic logistical system had to be put in place. Its backbone became the Ho Chi Minh Trail.[2]

The acquisition of weapons, supplies, and munitions by the DRV for transfer down the trail was equally important, and for that Hanoi turned abroad. To wage big unit protracted war against South Vietnam, both the PAVN and Viet Cong depended on their allies, with China being the closest and most important. While arsenals to store and repair weapons were present, the DRV had virtually no armaments industries. The French built neither weapons nor munitions works, and what little arsenal equipment they brought left when the French Army withdrew. Giap learned during the War of Resistance that trying to manufacture weapons without quality materials and specialized machinery was impossible. Similarly in 1959, the VC only had one effective capability: the manufacture of improvised explosive devices. They included homemade mines, grenades, and booby traps. Supplementing them were the ever-present non-explosive booby traps, such as the much-feared punji sticks. But despite the fear factor, punji stick pits mostly served as a handy substitute for barbed wire—a nonlethal barrier. Both exploding and non-exploding devices were effective defensive measures, but the war had to be won through offensive action, and that required small, medium, and heavy arms. The DRV, and by extension the VC, had to look elsewhere for modern weaponry.[3]

To fight the war against South Vietnam, China had to come to the DRV's aid, and fortunately the timing was ideal. China had followed the Soviet Union's lead of standardizing infantry weapons, and this led to the fielding of an entire series of weapons in 1956. For the soldier, either a Type 56 carbine, modeled on the Soviet SKS, or Type 56 assault rifle, modeled on the AK-47, were issued. For heavier fire support, there were Type 56 light machineguns (Soviet RPD) and Type 56 rocket propelled grenade launchers (Soviet RPG-2). There were also French, American, and Chinese 60 mm light mortars that could fire the same rounds. Not long afterwards, the superior Type 59 RPG(Soviet RPG-7) replaced the Type 56 RPG. Making the standardization all the more efficient, the carbines, assault rifles, and light machine guns used the exact same 7.62 mm ammunition. Duplicating this system became the goal for arming both PAVN regulars and VC very early on, and China did everything it could to realize that vision.[4]

China's support evolved to meet the demands of the war. During January 1961 talks, Beijing pledged $507 million in long-term, multi-year loans. In the summer of 1962, as the conflict heated up, Ho Chi Minh again went to Beijing to request additional military aid in the form of 90,000 weapons, which was granted. That was followed up by a Chinese military delegation visit to Hanoi in March 1963. Hanoi knew it could count on the strong support of Beijing for as long as the war lasted.

Viet Cong Military Tactics

In many regards, Viet Cong tactics were similar to those used by any army. The U.S. Marines quickly noted that basic Viet Cong and PAVN tactics were nothing new. That was to be expected. The first half of the 20th century witnessed war on an unprecedented scale, a crucible that honed infantry skills to a high degree across the globe, and the combatants in Indochina had fought with or against many of these militaries. By the time the Vietnam War erupted, every army shared common core tactics. Yet there was a uniqueness to the way the Viet Cong battled that brought it singular success. Equally to the Viet Cong's credit, their tactics were aligned to the war's strategy and adapted both to local conditions and the changing military situation in South Vietnam.[5]

Hanoi set the strategic imperatives. There was no doubt that the War of Resistance had been won by fighting on offense, and it stood to reason that the war of reunification had to be fought in the same manner. In accordance with one of General Giap's people's war tenets, the VC were to remain on the offensive and fight everywhere. He further explained that only by "developing to the utmost the offensive spirit of the army" could a decisive victory be attained.[6] That sentiment was the embodiment of Giap's strategic duality of a mobile conventional war "strongly marked by guerrilla warfare."[7] The VC had the demanding task of preparing large main forces for mobile war while simultaneously waging unabated guerrilla war. It was a long hard relentless struggle.[8]

Hanoi's related imperative was to rapidly transition to Le Duan's big unit war. Tactics were adjusted accordingly, but in 1959, the big unit war was more a concept than a possibility; as in 1946, the war began as an insurgency. Giap and Duan's aims were not the only factors driving tactics. Increasing American aid in the early 1960s altered almost everything, and as the conflict wore on and out of necessity, the VC developed a variety of tactics distinctive to the Vietnam War.[9]

The Offensive

The PAVN had reached a high level of offensive acumen by 1954. There were three major campaigns during the War of Resistance where they had defeated large French forces. The first victory came during the 1950 battle over Route Coloniale 4 along the Chinese border. The second was the great 1954 battle at Dien Bien Phu. Both of those took place in Bac Bo, the north. The last, the lesser-known destruction of GM 100, took place in Trung Bo, in the Central Highlands, where the 803rd, 108th, and 96th PAVN regiments along with the 30th Independent Battalion took turns cutting GM 100 into small bloody pieces during June 1954. Those battles ultimately proved decisive and explained why Giap insisted that victory could only be obtained through offensive mobile war.[10]

But it was easier said than done. In 1959, the Viet Cong could not even combine three companies in their Mekong Delta strongholds and would be lucky to group three platoons together in the Central Highlands. Under those conditions, Giap's mobile warfare had to be put off for the future. During the opening years of the war, the VC focused on inflicting the most casualties possible on the enemy in small clashes. With no chance of launching conventional offensive operations, assassinations and other forms of terrorism dominated Viet Cong operations. Up through 1960, there had been over 1,700 assassinations, and the widespread use of booby traps and harassment sniping added to Saigon's losses, but effective unit-on-unit attacks had been negligible.[11]

As arms, munitions, and most of all experienced PAVN regroupees began to arrive, slightly larger operations became possible, and by 1961 ambushes began to supplant assassinations as the primary means of attack. As a measure of the Viet Cong's weakness and the risks involved, major offensive operations had to be approved by the provincial, regional, and COSVN military affairs committees. It was a prudent step for it allowed the Viet Cong forces to train and grow their forces while they successfully carried out limited offensive operations with few significant setbacks.[12]

The Ambush

The ambush dominated Viet Cong offensive tactics from the beginning, and they became its unparalleled masters. During 1960–1963, the dominant idea when engaging ARVN or other security forces was "fight small to achieve great victory," and the ambush met that goal by massing the otherwise weaker VC to attack isolated detachments and then quickly retreat.[13] An early favorite when the war was a true insurgency was the baiting-attack ambush sequenced to first attack an outpost and then ambush the reaction force sent to its aid, a method developed during the War of Resistance. They aimed to drive out government forces from populated areas and expand the VC base area. Four criteria had to be met: (1) assembly of a superior force, (2) local popular support gained, (3) fixed objective and enemy's reaction force location identified, and (4) predictable reaction force routes identified.[14]

As the Viet Cong grew in power and numbers, more varied types of ambushes became routine. Eventually, in addition to the general baiting-attack, they developed techniques for specific types of ambushes: those targeted at patrols, small units, isolated mopping up units, and vehicle convoys, and those launched from underground positions and at river crossings. River crossing ambushes even expanded to include targeting navy watercraft on the rivers and canals.[15]

As with all VC tactical operations, advanced intelligence gathering and planning with attention to detail were keys to success. Ideal terrain would create uncertainty in the enemy and constrict, channelize, and separate the force while allowing for an encircling attack after the ambush was triggered. Ambush sites were to be unpredictable, and patterns avoided entirely. If needed, a safe harbor was occupied away from the actual ambush site to reduce the chance of early detection. Similarly, ambush timelines were not rigid. If required, sites were occupied 48 hours in advance or longer or occupied at the last possible moment. Terrain, enemy activity, and other factors determined timing. A selected ambush site would maximize concealment (augmented by camouflage) and employ automatic weapons not just in the kill zone but also through all phases of the ambush. Finally, the site permitted emplacing concealed observation posts to alert the ambush force and facilitated undetected infiltration and exfiltration.[16]

Preparatory and execution actions were critical, as ambushes were not simply hit-and-run raids. Conducting rehearsals for all phases of the ambush was mandatory. Assault firing positions could be linear or "L" or "Y" or "X" shaped, where the latter two created multiple kill zones or even a "U" or "Horseshoe" ambush that required a large area and took a sizable force but maximized enemy casualties. During the assault, fire discipline was paramount to ensure violent lethal point-blank fires—from as close as five meters. In some cases, overhead foliage was carefully removed to allow mortar fire to impact the kill zone. They also placed mines, booby traps, or other obstacles along enemy escape routes out of the kill zone. Beyond the assault team, other soldiers took up security positions to prevent the ambushers from being ambushed. These were important tasks, and up to one third of the force could be assigned to observation posts, security duty, and obstacle preparation. As added safety measures, noise and light discipline were strictly enforced, and the force remained at a high state of readiness throughout. Ambushes rightfully defined Viet Cong sophistication and effectiveness.[17]

The Raid

Much of what was considered an attack during the early years of the war was in fact a raid. The Western distinction between the two was the presence of a withdrawal plan during a raid, but that always did not hold true in Vietnam. Similarly,

Western attacks were couched in terms of "attack and seize" to gain and hold terrain. No Viet Cong assault sought such a goal. Even after Hanoi's big unit war took hold, attackers had no interest in terrain; they waged a war of attrition to inflict casualties. Also making the holding any piece of dirt cost prohibitive was deadly ARVN and American firepower.[18]

There were two characteristics that separated VC raids from deliberate attacks: the duration of the operation and the objective. The raid was a short violent assault carried out by a well-prepared unit followed by an equally rapid withdrawal, what General Vo Van Dan called "Fight fast and withdraw fast."[19] Like ambushes, raids were directed at vulnerable and isolated military outposts, police stations, and government buildings. Conversely, deliberate attacks involved larger forces and were of sufficient length to potentially annihilate the enemy force before withdrawing. In the early 1960s, the VC seldom had the might to launch deliberate attacks. Raids were the best alternative.[20]

Raids of this era also revealed one of the most effective ways the Viet Cong blended the military and political struggles: by driving out South Vietnamese government officials and security forces. The job was to make them abandon their posts, not to replace them but to create a security void. If the VC had sought a conventional solution (for example to capture and hold a district seat with cadres and soldiers) then they would have faced certain defeat. Capturing and holding a police station or village chief's office was not the objective. Raids could create a power vacuum that allowed secret and semi-covert VC to gain control over a region without being seen, and that was the real goal. It was a subtle process; the presence of government outposts or facilities did not assure control of nearby villages but abandonment signified defeat for the South Vietnamese.[21]

There were two raid types. The first was the "overt" or "superior strength" raid where a combined 10:1 ratio of soldiers and firepower would overwhelm any defender—a brute force attack. The second was the "covert" or "secret and surprise" raid, which used a much smaller force that relied on stealth, surprise, and speed. Regardless of the type, advance reconnaissance was critical, and often the objective was placed under observation for two or more weeks. Rehearsals and detailed briefings using a "sand table" mock-up of the objective took place before the raid. At the battalion level, the identity of the objective was only passed on to squad leaders and those in higher positions. There were other commonalities of all raids. Perimeter penetration was directed at a single point, they were launched in darkness, and they used four specialized elements for execution: command-communications, sapper, assault, and fire support.[22]

Each element had its own tasks. Command-communications directed the raid to include the employment of local forces used for security, intelligence, and logistical support. In most cases, success rested with the elite sappers who cleared breach lanes and cut communication lines prior to the attack by the assault element. The priority targets were enemy command and communications (C2) centers, followed by crew-served weapon emplacements and munitions bunkers. In an overt raid, explosives and Bangalore torpedoes opened the lanes. To offset the surprise lost through the blasts, the overt assault sought to spread chaos and confusion through the "one point-two faces" breach comprised of one breaching attack combined with two diversionary attacks. In the case of a covert raid, sappers silently and painstakingly cleared the lanes by neutralizing mines and cutting through the barbed wire barriers by hand. Ideally the enemy would not be aware a covert raid was underway until after the VC were inside the perimeter.[23]

As the raid's success often hinged on cutting communications and destroying the command post, different tactics for taking out the C2 centers were developed. In an overt raid where the centers were visible, the fire support element used mortars, RPGs, or recoilless rifles to destroy them immediately prior to the assault. If they could not be eliminated by fire, the first troops through the breach (often sappers) were responsible for destroying them. In a covert raid with no preparatory fires to preserve surprise, the support element's fire on the centers would be the raid's opening volley. Finally, in a vitally important raid, ready-to-die teams were employed to carry out suicidal attacks against the C2 centers.[24]

Depending on the size of the raid force, the assault element would be split into two sub-elements, dividing the raid's objectives between them. The job of the first assault element was to eliminate the C2 centers if not already destroyed. Casualties and difficulties were to be expected. With two sub-elements, the second followed the first and assumed its mission if the first faltered. If not then the second unit carried out its assigned tasks as planned. If the initial assault succeeded, the now-leaderless and isolated ARVN defenders were to be annihilated in a series of secondary assaults. This scheme was called the "blossoming flower" and had been perfected during the War of Resistance. Finally, the command element supervised the removal of captured equipment, materials, and the dead and wounded before directing the withdrawal of the raid force.[25]

The Defense

The Viet Cong eschewed defense. This was due to the emphasis placed on vigorous and continuous offensive action and driven by the situation on the battlefield. Operationally, the driving imperative was to expand base areas, and that could never be accomplished while on defense. Even the ability to make a defensive stand changed over time. In 1959, the Viet Cong did not have the weapons and experience to stand and fight the South Vietnamese security forces. It was only during the period running from the close of 1962 up into 1963, when the arrival of large numbers of PAVN regroupees and arms shipments gave the VC an advantage, they could stand and fight.

In most circumstances, the defense for small combat units only was a transitional tactic, something to adopt while halted during a movement, in camp, a rear area, or in harbor near an ambush site. When adopted, defensive terrain was selected to optimize fields of fire, dense overhead vegetation to prevent detection from the air, and high-speed routes of withdrawal. In populated areas, defenses were built near hamlets within a village boundary, and the position also served as a temporary camp. The defense was built around security and spadework. Security was a twofold affair: camouflage served to both prevent detection and create surprise if battle was forced, while observation posts and lookouts served to prevent surprise. Spade-work centered on building trenches and bunkers. The most common defense was built in an "L" shape to allow defenders to avoid being outflanked and to deliver fires if attacked from different points of approach. In addition to the "L" shaped defensive position, "U" shaped defensive lines were also common. For larger units, a circular perimeter defense was employed.[26]

There were distinctive attributes to the Viet Cong defense. Even hasty defenses routinely included a second line of defensive works emplaced several hundred meters from the first. This reflected the ingrained Viet Cong desire to remain mobile—even when in a fixed location. Similarly, every VC defensive plan included an enveloping counterattack once the ARVN force was pinned in place. If the VC enjoyed size superiority, they planned maneuvers to encircle and destroy the attacking enemy.[27]

Improving positions never stopped, and when time permitted, dummy positions also were prepared. If available, landline communication circuits were set up. When radios were used, antennas were placed far away from the operators and transmission power set as low as possible to avoid radio communications detection. Messages also were encoded. Finally, every defense included a withdrawal plan for the entire unit or, if necessary, the breaking up and movement of the unit into sub-groups that ended at a pre-designated, known assembly point within their area of operation. If necessary, subunits launched diversionary attacks to protect the main body withdrawal. To ensure success when battle was joined, all phases of the defense, to include counterattacks and withdrawals, were briefed and rehearsed.[28]

Tactical Movement

How Viet Cong units travelled the battlefield followed the course of the war and was determined largely by three factors: the number, type and size of Viet Cong formations, the effectiveness of the South Vietnamese security forces—especially air power—and improved ARVN mobility after the introduction of M113 armored personnel carriers (APCs) and U.S. Army helicopters in 1962. In the early years, there were no large Viet Cong units, and local forces never ventured much beyond their villages. Guerrilla and Main Force platoons and companies mostly confined their tactical operations to the home province. Tactical movements reflected traditional methods with an emphasis on surprise. As Viet Cong units grew into battalions, greater security precautions were adopted. It was the growing ARVN and American threat from the air, however, that made movement tactics essential to survival, creating what came to be called the "evasion strategy."[29]

By the mid–1960s, Viet Cong units were forced to remain on the move as a matter of survival. The story of two Viet Cong battalions in the Mekong Delta demonstrates the extent of the measures taken to keep from being caught. After 1962, Viet Cong formations in the delta could no longer linger in areas for weeks or even months as they had before. The need to move also was driven by population and terrain. In highly populated areas networked by roads and waterways, frequent movement was critical for survival, but some camps in hard to access remote areas, like the Plain of Reeds, still could safely be occupied for weeks or months.[30]

When the ARVN began to conduct sweeps by multiple battalions, special movement dispersion tactics (a process called "reintegrating nature") were adopted. To avoid battling a superior foe, a VC battalion would break down into consecutively smaller groups, to companies and even platoons, while fanning out into an ever-larger area. Small units would engage in harassing fires and conduct ambushes with varied timing and directions to confuse the ARVN as to the actual size and location of the VC. As the Viet Cong grew familiar with ARVN tactics, they gained a sense of the enemy's area of operations size and learned to reach safety by hiding at a fortified campsite or move beyond the area of operation's limits. One of the simplest survival lessons learned was that the dreaded helicopters often were not flying to seek them out but on assigned missions along set routes; after quick concealment, the VC realized the helicopters soon passed and were not the omnipotent threat initially believed.[31]

As daytime movement became too dangerous, the night became the realm of the Viet Cong. Night movements started from a base area to a predetermined objective, and Viet Cong battalions and other large units moved, not through the underbrush, but on existing trails and roads and along canals and dikes to maximize speed and avoid creating a fresh trail that would reveal their presence. Whenever halting, they immediately assumed a defensive stance to include digging in; these positions were preserved for use on the return to the base area if they were being followed, as the pursuing enemy would not expect to run into prepared defensive works and would suffer needless casualties. It was an effective tool in delaying and disrupting the enemy during movement.[32]

Formations were determined with three objectives in mind: speed to limit exposure, security to avoid being surprised by the enemy, and dispersion to limit casualties from air attack or artillery fire. At the head of the VC battalion formation were scouts from the reconnaissance unit who were sent out at a considerable distance ahead of the main body. After the scouts came the rest of the intelligence-reconnaissance unit, acting as the advance guard that also provided flank protection and liaised with hamlet and village VC for intelligence and security purposes. Messengers were used for communications. The advance guard was followed by an infantry company reinforced with machine guns and mortars, then a second company with the command group, and finally the third company with an infantry squad acting as a rear guard. The companies travelled in a column formation. Troops were spaced widely apart with the usual distance between soldiers at two meters, but distances varied due to terrain and weather. No movement took place if aircraft were present, and camouflage was used to cross open areas. Viet Cong companies approximately mimicked this system at a smaller scale.[33]

In another example of how thoroughly the VC analyzed problems, they deliberately used the areas along South Vietnam's administrative-military boundaries as bases and lines of communication. It was a clever move. For South Vietnamese forces, movement near or across boundaries had to be coordinated with commanders on both sides of the boundary, if only to prevent friendly fire casualties. That complicated and slowed things down for the ARVN; in the case of artillery support or airstrikes, it doubled the response time. That extra pause often gave the VC the needed time to escape and avoid casualties. As a result, boundary areas were the least likely to be routinely patrolled and searched in any given region, province, or district. The VC knew it and exploited the weakness.[34]

The Viet Cong adapted and changed their movement techniques as the war unfolded during the 1959–1963 period and beyond, eventually settling on complex methods that provided a high degree of safety for the Viet Cong soldiers. Their evasion strategy passed the ultimate combat test. It worked.

Anti-Armored Personnel Carrier and Anti-Helicopter Assault Tactics

One of the turning points for Viet Cong tactics was its reaction in 1962 to the dramatic shift in ARVN mobility that began with the widespread introduction of U.S. Army helicopters, both as troop transports and gunships. At nearly the same time came the introduction of the M113 APCs, but the VC had learned how to defeat lightly armored vehicles in fighting the French; what they lacked was the means. After the initial shock wore off and as expected, the APCs proved at least vulnerable to heavy machine guns and recoilless rifles that arrived in increasing numbers from the north. In the meantime, the use of hand grenades, Molotov cocktails, and rifle fire directed at exposed crew members—especially the gunners atop the APC— were reliable stopgaps. As long as the number of M113s was small, the VC had a short-term solution and arrived at a long-term fix in 1965 with the "Attack on the M113 APC" manual. The arrival of the helicopter was different.[35]

Up to that point in the war, South Vietnamese forces were either foot mobile or relied on road-bound vehicles, and the Viet Cong, when massed, were capable of fighting these forces on equal terms. The only comparable strike capability possessed by the ARVN before the helicopter was the handful of airborne battalions that were too few to change the course of the war. The helicopter upset that balance. The first American squadron arrived at the close of 1961, and by 1962 helicopters were changing the face of the battlefield to the Viet Cong's disadvantage. At the heart of the insurgency in the Mekong Delta, a Dinh Tuong province first secretary lamented, "At that time [mid–1962] we really began to encounter difficulties and were in disarray."[36] The speed, surprise, and flexibility of helicopter-borne forces posed a serious danger.[37]

As discussed above, ARVN helicopter assaults had an immediate effect on large unit maneuver by forcing VC units to break down into smaller groups and operate in close proximity so they could provide mutual support if struck by an ARVN helicopter assault. But more was needed. Counter tactics aimed at helicopter landing zones (LZs) quickly developed. The most important dealt with techniques and procedures to anticipate LZ locations to focus the countermoves. An easy but inadequate countermeasure was placing tall bamboo spikes in potential LZs to damage helicopter rotor blades, but the VC knew they could not set up spikes everywhere. As a solution, they identified LZs that posed the greatest danger. The goal became to try to deny access to the helicopter assault forces. Emplacing mines (especially captured, command-detonated claymore mines) in the LZs was effective, but they were in short supply during the 1961–1963 era, and letting them lie idly in or near an empty LZ was wasteful. A better solution was pre-aiming mortars and rockets to hit likely LZs, but the optimal solution, as they became available, was deploying AA guns that successfully deterred landings entirely.[38]

Learning to defeat the helicopter assault force took time and hard experience, but sometimes other sources helped. In 1962, the VC got a break when ace spy Pham Xuan An was able to pass on current American tactical and operational plans. In the words of spymaster Mai Chi Tho, "That allowed us to develop on the tactical scale a way to fight the new war."[39] It led to success in October 1962 when a Viet Cong unit in My Tho, Dinh Tuong province, stood and fought an ARVN ranger company in the helicopter LZ, inflicting many casualties.[40]

With these and other battle experiences, the VC also learned to exploit the helicopter's key weakness: its engines could be knocked out even with small arms, and soldiers were trained in offset sighting techniques to improve accuracy. The helicopter would remain an invaluable US-ARVN weapon for the rest of the war and beyond, but the days of its seeming invincibility were over after early 1963. The Viet Cong had met a new and lethal threat, adjusted their tactics, and rebalanced the battlefield.[41]

Harassment, Mines, and Booby Traps

Fighting Giap's dual-natured war required the Viet Cong to wear down the enemy continuously by using simple, low-risk methods that required minimal resources. One was harassing fires and the other mines and booby-traps. These were secondary or supporting actions designed to inflict casualties, delay operations, and psychologically exhaust the enemy. While not decisive, they achieved the goal of degrading ARVN combat power as well as favorably shaping the battlefield.

Harassing attacks took many forms and principally were directed at either fixed positions or foot units. The mortar attack on permanent enemy camps and bases was a highly favored method. One technique was to place simple mortar tubes into well-camouflaged, angled holes pre-aligned at the target, making them virtually undetectable. This allowed the Viet Cong to remove the camouflage, quickly fire a short barrage, replace the camouflage, and withdraw before the South Vietnamese could strike back. Another technique used to harass bases or camps was to fire mortars when ARVN mortars fired. The aim was to inflict casualties and cause destruction while creating confusion with the appearance of friendly fire. When done in tandem with imitative deception radio attack, the effects were powerful. Augmenting harassing fires on bases and camps, the VC placed mines and booby traps where troops or vehicles entered or exited the bases and along routes and paths used to conduct defensive perimeter patrols.[42]

Harassing fires on ARVN foot patrols and sweeps generally took the form of sporadic rifle fire, and when available, by snipers. Snipers prioritized targets: first radio operators (to cut off mortar, artillery, bomber, and helicopter support) followed by others using radios, holding maps, or directing activities (to eliminate unit leaders). In addition to inflicting casualties, the ARVN sometimes were subjected to harassing fires in conjunction with the emplacement of mines and booby traps as a delaying tactic to ensure the enemy arrived at the right time at an ambush site. There were risks involved for the VC. When operating in populated areas, the fires had to be carefully executed, or they could prove counterproductive. If VC harassing fire from a village or hamlet resulted in repeated artillery or air strikes—a form of reverse harassment—the people were more likely to blame the Viet Cong, and many subsequently would flee to the relative safety of government-controlled urban areas.[43]

More dangerous for the ARVN than harassing fires were booby traps and mines. They were used constantly by units ranging from village militia squads to Main Force units. The VC did not employ conventional defensive minefields, focusing instead on maximizing casualties. As a rule, VC Main Force units used mines, either captured or provided by the Chinese or Soviet Bloc, while the VC militia and their supporters employed booby traps. Most preferred by the Main Forces were captured U.S. or Chicom claymore-type mines, but a wide variety of Soviet and other Chinese mines, from anti-personnel to anti-tank, found their way into the RVN, only not in large numbers. Referred to as the invisible enemy, they did extraordinary damage, accounting for most ARVN casualties as well being as the primary cause for lost ARVN vehicles.[44]

The Viet Cong militia were masters of the booby trap, both non-explosive and explosive, and when creating a trap or placing a mine, camouflage was paramount. Non-explosive booby traps came in a dizzying array of forms and shapes. The most basic included boards with nails, wooden arrows, barbed metal, or bamboo stakes and spikes, bamboo whips (called Malayan whips by many Americans), swinging clubs (some barbed), and punji stick pits. Even stinging insects, scorpions, and snakes were used. Explosive devices were manufactured in crude workshops or homemade "bomb factories" at the provincial or district level, with an average output of about 135 explosive devices per month.[45]

Improvised explosive devices could be encountered anywhere. The most common locations were where natural terrain restricted movement, whether hills or dense vegetation or other obstacles such as waterway crossing points. Restrictive man-made features included rice paddies, dikes, trails, fences, and gates. Devices could be located in the ground, flanking grasses and bushes, or even in overhead foliage. One simple expedient used in watery rice farming areas was to bury a board with nails in the mud on a trail. Another method was to place a stake, spike trap, or mine underwater or in mud below a footbridge, rigged to break when crossed. Additionally, military terrain likely to be searched by the ARVN was targeted, such as potential campsites, dominating high ground, and sources of fresh water. Dead bodies or abandoned equipment also were routinely booby-trapped. If South Vietnamese soldiers reused trails, devices were placed after they passed to kill or maim during the return movement.[46]

There were restrictions. The Viet Cong did not lay mines or booby traps inside villages or hamlets or at burial mounds or tombs without consulting with hamlet or village cadres. If approved, the preferred locations were near gates or entrances, away from heavily trafficked areas. Mine and booby-trap locations also were secretly marked so villagers knew their locations. When feasible, mines and booby traps were placed or armed only when the enemy neared and then otherwise made safe or removed. Similarly, in the countryside, the bomb factories were placed well away from populated areas. Taken in their entirety, harassing fires, mines, and booby traps were some of the Viet Cong's most effective weapons.[47]

Underground Warfare

The Vietnamese long used the underground to shield their forces. Earliest PAVN diggings dated back to World War II, and caves, tunnels, and bunkers were used during the War of Resistance. The most extensive were at Cu Chi base area in Binh Duong province, where some 50 kilometers of tunnels had been dug by 1954. With the passing of Resolution 15 and the increasing expansion of ARVN and U.S. air operations in the early 1960s, underground operations went into overdrive. Everything possible was built underground. It was more than mere survival; underground works were there to support the offensive war.[48]

This led the Viet Cong to embark on a nationwide effort to improve caves and dig anything from small crude underground bunkers capable of hiding and protecting a few soldiers to large underground tunnel systems, virtual underground communities. Amazingly, in most cases the tools were simple: hand spades, hoes and picks, reed baskets for removing earth, and bamboo tripods with ropes to lift the baskets. Numerous diagonally dug vents ensured a fresh air supply, and to hide the digging, soils were dumped at night into rivers, used to construct dikes and banks, or combined with soils routinely removed from cultivated fields. Protection of earthworks was greatly enhanced by one outstanding characteristic: superb camouflage. By scrupulously avoiding detection, the VC not only enhanced the survival of the occupants, safeguarded supplies, and provided safe spaces for planning and directing operations, they created the advantage of surprise. If an unprepared enemy stumbled upon them, Viet Cong attackers would suddenly appear delivering deadly fire. When the Viet Cong retreated, the underground works provided a covert refuge via secret trapdoors, where they seemingly disappeared into the countryside.[49]

In addition to camouflage, secrecy and security were major Viet Cong strengths in underground warfare. A favorite technique was constructing tunnels that could only be entered from underwater along river or canal or dike banks. Entrances aboveground were kept small to reduce detection, usually a little over two feet in diameter. To defeat any enemy willing to enter, entrances were booby-trapped with explosive devices, punji stick pits, and the like; partially flooded tunnels also served as a deterrent.[50]

A clever air raid warning technique was to build underground, conical rooms whose shape magnified sounds, alerting the VC to approaching aircraft. On the down side, they magnified the noise of the bomb blasts, creating a terrorizing experience for the occupants. If attacked by ground forces, the VC occupants were shielded by firewalls protecting them from explosions and shrapnel. These often were not actual walls, but cockeyed tunnels descending to safer lower levels. U-shaped "water bend" dips were built along the tunnel's path at set intervals to prevent flooding but also proved effective in defeating smoke grenade or tear gas attacks. Finally, multiple trapdoors eased escape.[51]

Geography determined the location of the subterranean facilities. Belowground bunkers could be and were built almost anywhere Natural caves could be exploited through improvement and expansion, but they were few in number. Tunnels were a solution, but they too had limits. The rocky Central Highlands often were less than ideal, while coastal lowlands were suitable but constrained by unstable soils and high water tables. Some regions were ideal, like the clay soil lands northeast of Saigon heading toward Cambodia with Hau Nghia Province and its capital, Cu Chi, at the center.[52]

When the order went out in 1960 to return Cu Chi to a base area, a massive effort began. Such were the soils around Cu Chi that a fully resourced, bomb proof hospital was constructed 60 feet underground near the Saigon River. But large, complex tunnel systems like those employed at Cu Chi had a serious drawback. If detected they drew a strong ARVN response, and the safe haven quickly became a deathtrap offering those Viet Cong hiding underground little or no chance of escape.[53]

The use of subterranean structures varied widely. Underground holds were used as ammunition and supply dumps, headquarters, communication centers, troop berths, classrooms, aid stations, kitchens and even latrines. Another important use was the "bomb factory." Camouflaged bunkers were used to create fortified villages from which various strongpoints were linked by narrow communication tunnels, on average around three feet wide and a bit over four feet high. They made for a formidable defense. No opportunity was wasted. In one of the five Marble Mountains on the coast just south of Da Nang, there was a well-known Buddhist shrine located in the Am Phu (Hell) cave replicating visions of the religious underworld. Less known was that behind the cave's shrines, a Viet Cong hospital had been carefully carved out.[54]

Myriad floor plans were employed in the underground war. In the case of village bunkers, often the first chamber was an air raid shelter. Behind or below it, depending on conditions, other chambers were dug to serve as sleeping quarters or supply caches. Bunker complexes also contained additional chambers used for any number of purposes. Some offered an additional layer of protection with a hidden room built at a lower level. The hidden room was occupied during searches, as the discovery of the outer chamber did not reveal it existence. The placement of underground structures was carried out in creative fashion. In the hamlets, tunnels and bunkers were regularly built beneath the homes with entrances routinely located in cooking areas, especially beneath large communal pots. Pigsties were another favorite spot for hidden entrances. Where the village well's water level was sufficiently low, a tunnel complex was dug between the surface and water table with camouflaged entrances built into the well's sides.[55]

The Viet Cong created one of the most effective underground systems in the world. It was, as one Viet Cong officer reflected, "something very Vietnamese," a manifestation of the inextricable bond between the Vietnamese farmer and the land.[56] The ceaseless efforts in waging an underground war saved many lives during the war. Most of all, the unground war gave the Viet Cong a powerful tool that sty-mied and often defeated the best efforts of its enemies on the battlefield.

Conclusions

During the 1959–1963 period, the Viet Cong often were in a state of flux, but they progressed nonetheless. Material improvements exemplified that progress, and Colonel Bui Tin, a PAVN Military Staff officer and veteran of Dien Bien Phu, stated that the "outstanding characteristic" of the Vietnam War was that the PAVN possessed "modern weaponry."[57] Politically, the VC remained under the direction of the VWP, but in the early 1960s, with the creation of the NLF and PRP, it con-vincingly portrayed the image—both at home and internationally—of an indige-nous and authentic rival political movement equal to the Saigon regime. That was a significant geopolitical victory. Its military command structure also evolved into a dynamic warfighting organization. By 1963, COSVN, which directed the military and political campaign in the south, was superior to that of its 1949–1954 predeces-sor. For its purpose, it was as capable as many of the Allied or Axis theater com-mands during World War II and certainly more unified and expert than the North Korean–Chinese command during the 1950–1953 Korean War.

Who made up the Viet Cong military also changed dramatically over time. The year 1959 began with the VC fighting in small units—squads and platoons—com-prised of local recruits and PAVN stay-behinds. As with the changes in recruiting and training, Viet Cong weapons, equipment, and the quantities and quality of sup-plies improved but only at a measured pace that largely was a result of increased Chi-nese military aid. Finally, there were formidable VC intelligence capabilities, which made the military all the more effective in combat.

During the years spanning 1959–1963, the Viet Cong became a highly skilled force—to a degree its enemies and even friends would not admit. As good as they were, they were not perfect, and they were not invincible. Idealized training and tactics goals did not always measure up in practice. Terror tactics often were coun-terproductive. Their enemies, the South Vietnamese and Americans, were equally adept at learning and improving inside the crucible of war, so standing still meant falling behind. Battle losses and illness degraded leadership and readiness. The qual-ity of equipment continuously improved but started at a miserable level in 1959. Despite the challenges, the VC were a determined, relentless, and intractable foe that learned to fight any enemy, either on the battlefield or in the hearts and minds of the South Vietnamese people or in the arena of world opinion. The Viet Cong relished exploiting those who misunderstood or underestimated them and were utterly com-mitted to final victory.

PART III

WHAT ABOUT LAOS?

Part III: Dramatis Personae

The Laotians

Kaysone Phomvihane—Unassuming leader of the Pathet Lao communists and obedient ally of Hanoi

Kong Le—Paratroop commander, nationalist, and champion of Laotian neutrality who led the December 1959 coup to restore Prince Souvanna Phouma

Phoui Sananikone—Foreign Minister at Geneva 1954, anti-communist nationalist, prime minister from 1950 to 1951 and 1958–59

Phoumi Nosavan—Pro-Western general who became first FAR chief of staff in 1955 and minister of defense; served as unofficial ruler variously during 1959, 1961–62 and alienated the chief U.S. diplomat, W. Averell Harriman

Vang Pao—Hmong military leader who led the CIA-directed secret war against the PAVN in eastern Laos

The Three Princes

Boun Oum—Hardline anti-communist and pro–Western prime minister from 1948 to 1950 and 1960–62

Souphanouvong—Half-brother to Phouma and known as the "**Red Prince**" for his leadership role in the communist Pathet Lao

Souvanna Phouma—Left-leaning neutralist prince who served as prime minister from 1951 to 1954, 1956–58, 1960, and 1962–75

The North Vietnamese

Chu Huy Man—Highly capable PAVN general who directed Hanoi's military operations in Laos beginning in the mid–1950s and continuing into the 1960s

Tran Van Tra—General who proposed sending PAVN regroupees to South Vietnam to lead the war of reunification

Vo Bam—PAVN colonel put in command of Group 559 to build the Ho Chi Minh Trail

The Americans

W. Averell Harriman—Kennedy's energetic and irascible ambassador-at-large who led the diplomatic effort in Geneva to resolve the Laotian crisis, later assistant secretary of state for Far Eastern affairs

Roger Hilsman—Harriman's loyal subordinate who dismissed the importance of the Ho Chi Minh Trail in 1962

William H. Sullivan—Harriman's deputy at Geneva and later U.S. ambassador to Laos

Others

Marek Thee—Polish communist member of the ICC who almost singlehandedly destroyed the commission's ability to enforce the 1962 Geneva agreement to neutralize Laos

10

The Agony of Laos

Why Laos? During the years spanning the 1954 Geneva accords to 1963, what happened in Laos was held to be key to the Vietnam War effort by many American leaders at different times and for various reasons. As important as that may have been, the argument to make Laos central to American political and military strategy in South Vietnam never gained critical traction. That failure, arguably, was the most significant of the war, for the fates of Laos and South Vietnam were inextricably intertwined. To comprehend that, we need to look at what happened in Laos and how those events shaped the Vietnam War. That begins with a study of the conflict in Laos, starting with the years 1946 to 1958, followed by events occurring between 1959 and 1963.

Background (1946–1954)

Few places figured less into the military-political calculations of the world's major powers than the Kingdom of Laos. That changed in 1953 when General Giap moved to take control of the nation. Even as the War of Resistance raged in neighboring Vietnam, Laos had remained a quiet backwater. The Kingdom encompassed a landlocked region of 238,000 square kilometers with a population of perhaps two million, as compared to Vietnam with a population in excess of 25 million living in an area of 331,000 square kilometers. It was a tranquil land led by King Sisavang Vong, the titular ruler reigning at the royal capital of Luang Prabang (Luangphabang) in Upper Laos, and governed by a civil administration residing at Vientiane (340 kilometers to the south).

Its complex, multiethnic population was built around Lao people, principally wet-rice farming families that lived in the Mekong River lowlands. The Lao were just barely a majority. The hill country contained tribal federations where some 15 percent of the population was comprised of Khmuic speakers (Khmu) concentrated in the north, the Tai (Phutai), who accounted for another 13 percent, while the mountain Hmong people constituted an additional ten percent, followed by numerous minor hill and mountain tribes making up five to six percent of the population. There also was a small but influential ethnic Vietnamese minority. The Kingdom of Laos succeeded as a decentralized nation that lived in peace by having a light-handed system of governance—a social balance that did not survive the whirlwinds of the War of Resistance.[1]

The events leading up to Giap's 1953 invasion of Laos dated back nearly a decade. Like the Vietnamese, the Laotians had moved for independence as soon as World War II ended. The movement of the mid–1940s, the Lao Issara (Free Laos), had been divided between those who looked to Thailand for guidance, given their shared cultural and linguistic ties (Bangkok had referred to the Lao as Northeastern Thai since the 18th century), and those led by ICP comrades Kaysone Phomvihane and Nouhak Phomsavanh.[2] As the drive for independence grew in late 1946 and after the French Army made short work of the Lao Issara fighters, Ho and his comrades moved to shore up their Laotian brethren by sending 500–700 Vietnamese political and military advisors. This began an effort to control the Laotian revolution, but it did not succeed. Divisions within the independence movement widened when many nationalists accepted France's offer of limited independence on 26 November 1947 and orchestrated the admission of the Kingdom into the French Union. By 1949 the combination of political differences and the escalating war with France split the movement.[3]

The majority of the non-communists in the now defunct Lao Issara rallied to conservative nationalists willing to work with France, to include King Sisavang who returned from Thailand that year (he had fled from the French in 1946). Their two most important leaders were Prince Souvanna Phouma and former anti–Japanese resistance leader Prince Boun Oum. The communists and other leftists continued to look to Vietnamese communists and opposed close relations with France. They established the Pathet Lao (Lao Nation) resistance in 1950 to further their aims and were represented by Souvanna's half-brother, Prince Souphanouvong (the pro–Vietnamese "Red Prince"). Collectively, they were known as the "Three Princes" due to the central role they played in post-war politics. The Pathet Lao also formed a political party called Neo Lao Issara (Free Laos Movement), and the Red Prince became the party's public face. Afterwards, as the nationalists gained the upper hand, the Pathet Lao fled to the sparsely populated Sam Neua (Xam Neua) border area with Vietnam in Laos's northeastern Houa Phan (Houaphan) province. The political split was non-violent; there was no civil war in Laos.[4]

While Pathet Lao adherents were few and never gained much support during the War of Resistance, the number of communists was smaller still. In the early 1950s, there were an estimated 60,000 VWP members in Nam Bo alone, and of the 2,000 secret ICP members in Laos in 1951 when the Pathet Lao was formed, only 31 were ethnic Laotians—the rest were Vietnamese. That the Laotian communists were a minority within the Pathet Lao led many to believe, to include Prince Souvanna, that the Lao communists did not control the party, and for the most part they were correct. The lack of Laotian members was so severe that the VWP retained control over the Pathet Lao through its Central Lao Party Affairs Committee until 1955. The Pathet Lao remained subordinated to the VWP afterwards.[5]

The Pathet Lao military was just as needy. There were between 500 and 700 ICP political and PAVN military advisors in Laos by early 1947 and fewer than 100 trained and equipped Pathet Lao main force fighters. Progress was painfully slow. In 1949, the Pathet Lao only fielded two companies of fighters, and keeping the Pathet Lao in check at that time proved no problem for the government in Vientiane. The

17 infantry companies of the Royal Lao Army (Armée Nationale du Laos or ANL) formed that year proved more than adequate in handling them. (As a comparison, the French had 62 battalions struggling against the PAVN in Vietnam.) Things were so calm that informal truces were in place between Pathet Lao and ANL soldiers. The former only would attack French troops, and the ANL was equally glad not to harm their countrymen, as one Pathet Lao officer reflected, "If Lao met Lao, we would not do anything."[6] The VWP was determined to end such complacency.[7]

To the VWP, the struggle against France was waged on "one battlefield" that spanned Indochina. That included Laos, and the VWP was determined to bring Laos into the war, even if the process began slowly and discreetly. Efforts to gain control over what became the Lower Lao Zone began in 1947. By the close of 1950, the number of PAVN soldiers in Laos, called Vietnamese People's Volunteers, skyrocketed to 8,000. Most were still concentrated in the Lower Zone that was used as a rear or transit area to get from one area of Vietnam to another—a precursor to the Ho Chi Minh Trail. The ANL attempted to adjust; its companies formed into 650-soldier strong battalions beginning in 1950 and joined eight Lao 680 strong Lao light hunter (chasseur) battalions transferred from the French Expeditionary Corps. Later, a well-trained paratroop battalion and one artillery battery were formed. The battery was equipped with eight barely functioning 105 mm howitzers representative of the poor quality of ANL arms. It received hand-me-down equipment from the French, which often had been hand-me-down equipment from the Americans. That sufficed when facing the Pathet Lao, but the ANL was ill prepared to fight Giap's battle-hardened troops.[8]

The 1953 Spring Northwestern Front Offensive

General Giap was an avid student of Napoleon's wars of maneuver and decisive battle. In that frame of mind and in light of the PAVN's new prowess with the addition of the iron divisions, in 1953 Giap decided that Laos provided the ideal battlefield. In April he launched his Northwestern Front campaign from base areas in and around the small Vietnamese village of Dien Bien Phu. The invasion force was split into two columns. The northern column, comprised of the PAVN 312th Division and 148th Independent Regiment, entered into Phong Saly (Phongsali) province while the southern column, made up of the PAVN's 308th and 316th Divisions, crossed into Houa Phan province, the Pathet Lao stronghold (see Map 2). The total number of "People's Volunteers" now reached over 30,000. The Pathet Lao main forces were so few in number, perhaps a few hundred soldiers, that they were used as scouts, guides, interpreters, and propagandists for the PAVN—an auxiliary force. As one PAVN soldier put it, because of the backwardness of the Laotian revolutionary struggle, "The Vietnamese, as their older brothers, must bear the brunt of the fighting, must organize and lead."[9] This was Giap's battle from the start.[10]

Caught off guard by the magnitude of the PAVN invasion, the French scrambled. On 3 April, the 6th Laotian Chasseur Battalion in Phong Saly was ordered to make a desperate last stand at Muong Khoua (Muang Khua) on the Nam Ou River, southwest of Dien Bien Phu, against the northern PAVN column that overran the nearby border post at Sop-Nao. They were told to hold for two weeks to buy time for the French and ANL forces to organize a defense of the royal capital at Luang Prabang. The 148th PAVN Regiment battered the surrounded ANL garrison at Muong Khoua while the 312th bypassed the town, captured Muong Sai (Muang Xai) located about halfway between Muong Khoua and Luang Prabang, then pressed on to the royal capital.[11]

A dozen other isolated garrisons—mostly only a company or platoon in strength—received similar "last stand" orders. It seemed to make little difference. Except at Muong Khoua, the PAVN advanced with little difficulty. The 1,750-strong ANL garrison at the provincial capital of Sam Neua in Houa Phan was nearly wiped out as it fled the assault of the 316th Division. During the retreat, the 5th and 8th Laotian Chasseur Battalions fell apart under continuous attacks. Only the 1st Laotian Paratroop Battalion fought effectively, although fewer than 300 of the soldiers survived the ordeal.[12]

Those sacrifices, however, and the unforgiving terrain did slow down the PAVN advance just enough for the French to a build fortified "hedgehog defense" base aéro-terrestre (air-land base) at the Plain of Jars, a crucial junction with the royal palace at Luang Prabang to the northwest and Vientiane to the southwest. A second base aéro-terrestre was established to guard the northern approaches to Luang Prabang. The air-land base was a new French tactic used successfully at Na San (150 kilometers east of Dien Bien Phu) in 1952 and revolved around a system of mutually supporting strongpoints (hedgehogs) centered on an airfield and supported by air power. Offensive in nature, they were to be safe havens for forces to launch attacks, raids, and ambushes on the PAVN. But if needed, they could put up a formidable defense, as happened at Na San where the PAVN suffered heavy casualties during failed assaults against the fortifications.[13]

The military airhead at the Plain of Jars soon was manned by ten battalions, including paratroopers from the French strategic reserve, who beat off an attack on 26 April 1953 by the 308th and 316th Divisions. A similar attack that month by the 312th Division failed to penetrate the northern Lao-French defenses before Luang Prabang, which also had been reinforced by French and Laotian paratroopers. In less than four weeks, the PAVN offensive had reached its culminating point and halted.[14]

As Lao-French forces began to build up in mid–May, and the rainy season loomed, the PAVN withdrew back to northwestern Vietnam, but not before annihilating the 6th Laotian Chasseur Battalion at Muong Khoua, which had managed to hold out for 36 days—only four soldiers survived. The offensive was over, and lessons had been learned. The steep hills and mountains that covered an almost impenetrable jungle proved a greater impediment to PAVN conquest than the meager ANL companies and battalions. Given the frontier's length, both sides now knew how vulnerable Laos was to invasion. Vientiane tried to adjust as soldiers filled ANL ranks following a national mobilization order on 14 May 1953; soon ANL battalions expanded from three to four infantry companies, but the improvements were not enough to offset the strength of the oncoming PAVN.[15]

The French also realigned their strategy, opting to create a number of air–land bases—fortified islands in the sea of mountain jungle—to maintain control of Laos.

The two existing bases at Luang Prabang and on the Plain of Jars were expanded and reinforced, while Muong Sai was reoccupied, fortified, and the airfield enlarged. Additionally, the airbase at Seno (Xeno) adjacent to Savannakhet in Middle Laos became a full-fledged base aéro-terrestre. Vietnam was not neglected. The small air-land base at Lai Chau was modestly improved with two new bases created: one at Pleiku in the Central Highlands and the other at Dien Bien Phu (200 kilometers to the northeast of Muong Sai and 200 kilometers south of Lai Chau), which was seized from the PAVN by paratroopers on 20 November 1953.[16]

The French concluded that Dien Bien Phu was the key logistical hub supporting Giap's Upper Laos operations. As explained that day by General Henri Navarre, the commander in Indochina, the air-land base there aimed to cut PAVN attack routes toward Luang Prabang and protect the Tai tribes in the region who opposed the communists. Logistics was deemed the PAVN's Achilles heel in the Tai highlands and Upper Laos and explained French confidence in seizing the place. If held, then PAVN assaults against the local Tai and in nearby upper Laos would be crimped as PAVN Main Force units could only operate in the remote area for no more than a week or two before supplies ran out. A short time later, the paratroopers at Dien Bien Phu (save the Foreign Legionnaires) were airlifted back to Haiphong, being replaced by GMs 6 and 9. It was all for the good as far as General Giap was concerned. Laos and the rugged western highlands of Vietnam had become a major theater of the war, and he held the strategic initiative.[17]

The 1953–1954 Winter-Spring Campaign

Even as his divisions in Laos fell back during May 1953, General Giap knew he commanded his most capable army yet, and he knew what needed to be done. When the weather cleared, his army would launch the most ambitious offensive Indochina had witnessed in centuries. This was to be the largest PAVN campaign of the war, with Laos as the first objective, followed by the Central Highlands of Vietnam, and ending with the capture of Dien Bien Phu in the far north. He would use five lines of advance from Vietnam into Laos. All but one ended at Route 13, the north-south road that tied the Kingdom together like a spine. The exception was the rugged overland track southwest from Dien Bien Phu toward Muong Khoua and Muong Sai. The five-front offensive (Lower, Middle and Upper Laos along with Vietnam's Central Highlands and Dien Bien Phu) would be executed in two phases (from December 1953 to March 1954 and March 1954 until the rainy season). But first the situation in Laos needed to be tilted further in the PAVN's favor.[18]

The road system, primitive as it was, was key to the Laos offensive. The Route 13 backbone began by running roughly parallel to the Mekong River from the Cambodian border to Pakse (Pakxe) in Lower Laos to Savannakhet in Middle Laos then north to Vientiane, where it cut inland to Luang Prabang in Upper Laos. The four roughly east-west roads Giap would use to invade Laos were, from north to south, Routes 6 and 7 in Upper Laos, along with Routes 12, and 9 in Middle Laos, all ending at Route 13. From Vietnam's Moc Chau district, Route 6 entered Laos reaching Sam Neua and on to Muong Khan where it merged with Route 7. Route 7 originated in Vietnam's Nghe An province, entered Xiang Khouang province in Laos, and then extended on to Muong Khan, the Plain of Jars, and Vang Vieng where it met Route 13 between the two Laotian capitals. Route 12 entered Laos through the Mu Gia Pass at Ban Na Phao then headed west, where it merged with Route 8 at Ban Phou Keng and then to Thakhet on the Mekong and Route 13. Route 9 followed the 17th parallel from Dong Ha near the South China Sea to Tchpone (Xepon), and finally to Route 13 and Savannakhet on the Mekong.

The first step was taken that summer when the PAVN advanced down Route 6 and captured Sam Neua in Huoa Phan province, again threating the Lao-French forces in the Plain of Jars. The second took place in Phong Saly, where the Muong Sai air-land base was cut off, making it reliant on aerial resupply after 20 November. The French further aided Giap when they decided to abandon the air-land base at Lai Chau. A lucky 300 troops were flown to safety on 10 December; the remaining 2,100 soldiers, almost entirely lightly armed Tai tribesman, were left to walk south to Dien Bien Phu. Over the next several days, they were cut to pieces by the PAVN 316th Division; none of the Tai light infantry companies survived intact, and only some 100 stragglers made it to Dien Bien Phu. Giap now had both the 308th and 316th Divisions, along with elements of the 351st Heavy Division, lurking around Dien Bien Phu with more PAVN units on the way. Soon the French were surrounded. For General Giap, the time to strike had come. During the third week of December, he issued an order of the day urging his troops to "smash the French attempt to regain the initiative," and attacks along the Middle Laos Front began the next week.[19]

On 22 December 1953, several thousand People's Volunteers (the 66th and 101st PAVN Regiments) accompanied by Pathet Lao guides crossed into Laos and beat back the French-Laotian border garrison (built around a Moroccan infantry battalion) at Ban Na Phao on Route 12 that led toward Thakhek on the Mekong River, 65 kilometers to the west. By 25 December, the regiments had reached Thakhek, which fell two days later. The PAVN then began a 120 kilometer advance south along Route 13 toward Savannakhet and the nearby air-land base at Seno. Also on 22 December and farther south, the 18th PAVN Regiment departed Vietnam and drove deep into in Middle Laos along Route 9. Since the PAVN had destroyed three key bridges behind them as they advanced, the road-bound French reaction force from Hue, Mobile Group 2, was unable to prevent the 18th Regiment's advance. By late December, all three PAVN regiments were converging on Seno and Savannakhet. Giap had cut Indochina in two and captured large swath of Middle Laos.[20]

The French had not been idle since the PAVN onslaught began. Beginning on 25 December, they began a major build-up of forces at Seno, starting with paratroopers from the strategic reserve at Haiphong. Other forces were tapped as well. There had been another Moroccan-Laotian battle group like the one at Ban Na Phao, located to the north and guarding Route 8 at Lak So (a possible sixth invasion route Giap chose not to use). Having been bypassed, the combat group was airlifted into Seno on 26 December. By month's end, a strong French force built around five paratroop battalions supported by artillery defended Seno.[21]

Recognizing the strength at Seno, Giap directed the 66th and 101st Regiments to avoid the airhead and plunge into Lower Laos. They soon reached the Bolaven

Plateau, 350 kilometers to the south, and in late December, pushed out the Lao battalion defending Attapeu, just 40 kilometers from the Cambodian border. The loss hurt as Attapeu served as the main base for the Composite Airborne Commando Group (GCMA) in Lower Laso. Run by the secretive SDECE, the GCMA deployed special operations teams who parachuted behind PAVN lines to organize guerrillas, in this case pro–French guerrilla units in the Laotian panhandle. The French countered by reinforcing the garrison at the important city of Pakse on the Mekong about 80 kilometers to the west, preventing its fall to the PAVN. To the east in Vietnam's Central Highlands, the 803rd, 108th, and 96th PAVN regiments advanced into Kontum province, and elements of that force crossed into Lower Laos to link up with the 101st Regiment on 31 December. It was the invasion's high-water mark.[22]

The three PAVN regiments from Vietnam soon returned and completed the conquest of Kontum province that February while the 66th Regiment reached Seno, but there was little fighting. The largest engagement there ran from 5–9 January 1954 when the 3rd Vietnamese Paratroop Battalion beat back a strong PAVN probing attack directed at the village of Hine Siu near the airport. A short time later, two mobile groups (GM 1 and GM 51) replaced the paratrooper battalions, and on 24 January, the 66th Regiment bloodied GM 51 as it went to the relief of a Laotian outpost. That skirmish effectively ended the PAVN offensive in Middle and Lower Laos. The PAVN withdrew, the French reoccupied the Laotian territory, and the battle shifted north.[23]

The Upper Laos offensive began in January with the PAVN liberation of Muong Khoua and the investment of the air-land base at Muong Sai in Phong Saly, followed by an advance that again threatened the royal capital of Luang Prabang in February. It was the work of the reinforced 308th Division that had slipped away from the siege at Dien Bien Phu on 27 January to sally into Laos. It was unexpected, as Giap originally intended to attack Dien Bien Phu that day but opted instead to start the Upper Laos operation to further distract the French. Its mission was to tie up French troops who might otherwise aid Dien Bien Phu—Giap's real target. The stratagem succeeded when the powerful GM 7 began its airlift into Luang Prabang on 13 February. With its task complete, the 308th Division left a force behind to freeze in place the French garrison at Muong Sai and quickly returned to the Dien Bien Phu battlefield. PAVN offensive operations in Laos were over; it was time to concentrate on Dien Bien Phu.[24]

Initially, the French welcomed Giap's Dien Bien Phu focus. Taking the village back in November helped end the 1953 PAVN offensives in Laos, and Navarre was confident his forces there would grind down the PAVN as had happened at Na San in November–December 1952. He was badly mistaken, and having never sought decisive battle (his focus was on central coastal Vietnam), did not realize the danger until it was too late. What the French did not anticipate was Chinese aid that came in two decisive forms during the Dien Bien Phu battle. The first was the construction of a road capable of carrying trucks from Chinese supply depots across the border to near the battle area. Additionally, thousands of Tai abandoned by the French in December were pressed into service as porters to carry supplies to Dien Bien Phu. That immediately shifted the advantage in the logistics war toward the PAVN. The second was the delivery of over fifty 37 mm anti-aircraft guns that allowed the PAVN to commit an entire AA regiment to the battle in early 1954.[25]

When General Giap launched Phase 2 of his offensive on 13 March 1954, he had massed a dozen infantry regiments backed by combat engineers and powerful artillery and anti-aircraft units in the hills surrounding Dien Bien Phu. That revealed the Achilles heels for the bases aéro-terrestre: the airfields. In late March, PAVN mortar and artillery fire closed both of Dien Bien Phu's airfields and making the situation untenable, the arrival of the 37 mm AA guns made air deliveries below 2,000 meters too dangerous. With the increased altitude, the percentage of drops missing the garrison skyrocketed. The base was doomed. From that point forward, the fortified stronghold became a trap for French troops. Their losses could not be made good, and supplies ran critically low. After an overwhelming attack on 7 May 1954, the defenders surrendered.[26]

The War of Resistance had been decided. The PAVN had won, and Laos had played an important rol. Absent the 1953–1954 PAVN campaigns in Laos, especially in Upper Laos, Dien Bien Phu would have remained a virtually unknown border town of little or no interest to anyone. More importantly, General Giap had perfected his military strategy for victory in future wars. In 1960 he wrote, "The Dien Bien Phu campaign and Winter-Spring 1953–1954 campaign were most successful models of coordination between mobile warfare and guerrilla warfare" where mobile war was carried out on the main battlefield supported by guerrilla operations in the enemy's rear.[27]

Laos and the 1954 Geneva Conference

During the subsequent Geneva negotiations, reestablishing peace in Laos became one of the conference's most challenging problems. During 1953 and 1954, the PAVN expended great effort at no insignificant cost to make its claim (in the name of the Pathet Lao) for Laos. The DRV was not about to give it up. The claim was boosted by the relative military weakness of the ANL. To the PAVN, they could take any part of Laos at will. From its perspective, the DRV was negotiating from a position of strength, and it was not surprising that their Geneva delegation wanted a major—even controlling—say in the Kingdom's future. Alternately, the Laotians focused on the political and military weakness of the Pathet Lao. As they saw it, the only threat to their peace and security was the invading PAVN; if the Vietnamese simply would go home, then everything would return to as it had been before 1953. Neither side would compromise.[28]

For the DRV, it was not simply might makes right; Laos held strategic value. When preparing for the talks in March 1954, the U.S. State Department concluded the PAVN would not quit Laos as it was an "inexpugnable base" ideally situated to put pressure on Central Vietnam, Cambodia, and even Thailand. The CIA reached a similar conclusion in May shortly after the fall of Dien Bien Phu.[29] Laos also played the role of a buffer state in defending the DRV. With Laos subordinate to the DRV, Hanoi's security problems became more manageable. It was unsurprising that when the DRV delegation came out with its opening demands on 10 May, they included international recognition of the Pathet Lao, the withdrawal of all "foreign troops," a coalition government, and national elections overseen by "local commissions." It was a blueprint for Hanoi to dominate its neighbor as the terms "foreign troops" and "local commissions" were loaded with hidden meaning. By "foreign troops," the DRV delegation meant French forces as the PAVN in Laos was made up of "people's volunteers" and therefore not foreign, while "local commissions" meant elections controlled by the Pathet Lao backed up by the PAVN.[30]

The outraged Laotians came back with equally inflexible demands. On 13 May, Crown Prince Savang Vatthana let it be known that they refused to accept any role for the Pathet Lao, seeing it as nothing more than an "infiltration" strategy to allow the DRV or China to take over Laos, a view also reflected by Laotian delegation leader, Phoui Sananikone, the foreign minister and anti-communist nationalist. As far as he was concerned, the solution was twofold: immediate withdrawal of the PAVN invaders and an end to their support of the Pathet Lao. As to proposed elections, he avowed that they were an internal Laotian affair, already addressed in the nation's constitution and of no concern to the DRV. The Western powers backed the Laotian delegation. The only hint of a possible agreement appeared when China came out in support of partition for all of Indochina, but no progress was made for the rest of May and well into June.[31]

A breakthrough of sorts occurred on 17 June when Zhou Enlai, the head of the Chinese delegation, stated that Beijing had no interests in Laos and wanted Laos to become an independent state like India or Burma. The next day, Zhou announced that China was prepareåd to recognize the royal government—not the Pathet Lao—as the legitimate government of Laos. At the same time, the communist bloc withdrew its request to seat the Pathet Lao delegation. To put a fine point on the issue, on 22 June Zhou further informed the DRV delegation that they would have to withdraw their forces from Laos. The change in China's position was significant. The DRV saw it as betrayal and a sign that China was trying to gain influence in Indochina at the DRV's expense. China certainly did not want a military threat on its southern flank and vigorously sought to keep U.S. forces out of Laos, but that concern also included its centuries old disputes with Vietnam. That China also proposed keeping the French Army in Laos, an abhorrent idea to the DRV, revealed the PRC's desire to create a neutral Laos.[32]

Resolution of the Laos issue ran right up to the last day, with frantic back and forth that ended with a peace agreement, the "Agreement on the Cessation of Hostilities in Laos," ready for signing on 20 July. As in Vietnam, the Canadian-Indian-Polish ICC would supervise the regrouping, ceasefire, and national election. America's regional security concerns were addressed; the final declaration permitted foreign aid to include war materials, military personnel, and instructors to be introduced into Laos "for the purpose of the effective defense" of the Kingdom, a clause the United States later would cite to mute objections to its military assistance to the ANL. It was agreed that the Pathet Lao would be given two regroupment zones; Houa Phan and Phong Saly provinces represented 13 percent of Laotian territory and 11 percent of the population. Dominance over the two provinces was justified not by the Pathet Lao's paltry military strength and limited political influence but by PAVN power and might. The DRV was disappointed in not gaining control of the SOV-Laotian border through a third regroupment area in Middle Laos, an area it had intended to use in an armed struggle against South Vietnam, but resignedly signed the document.[33]

A primary reason for obtaining peace was that the DRV had decided to ignore the agreement before its representatives put pen and ink to paper. In it they pledged to transfer all troops out of Laos (Article 13) and not to introduce troops or war materials or establish new bases (Articles 6, 7 and 9). On 18 July, two days before the DRV delegation accepted the agreement, VWP leaders put in motion four objectives for Laos: (1) establish a revolutionary party, (2) strengthen and expand Pathet Lao control in Laos, (3) build up Pathet Lao military forces, and (4) train political cadres—objectives that violated the articles and joint declaration. Weeks earlier, on 28 June, the VWP Central Committee already had decided to secretly deploy an advisory unit to Laos and join a detachment of PAVN soldiers already there. It was an ominous beginning.[34]

Laos, 1954–1958: Peace at Last?

To the outside world and indeed to most of the peoples of Indochina, the 20 July 1954 Geneva accords meant peace. For the people of the Kingdom of Laos, it was not to be. As in the War of Resistance, the Pathet Lao's future would be decided by the VWP. Hanoi's army did withdraw from Laos by the 16 October deadline, but over 300 PAVN advisors remain behind with its headquarters located across the border in the DRV. Activated in August under the command of General Chu Huy Man and known as Group 100, it was formed in secret to evade Geneva accord prohibitions against keeping PAVN forces in Laos. In addition to Group 100, hundreds of secret VWP cadres were ordered to remain behind and were soon augmented by another 100 VWP political cadres.[35]

Group 100's mission to facilitate the Pathet Lao's political and military objectives was made clearer by the VWP Politburo in October: build the Pathet Lao Army and advance the revolution throughout Laos by first concentrating on the contested provinces just evacuated after Geneva. The Group 100 headquarters soon moved into Laos, bringing the total North Vietnamese presence in the Kingdom to over 800 PAVN troops and VWP cadres. No matter how disappointed Hanoi may have been over Geneva, it had to be satisfied with the outcome. It remained a force in Laos, and control over Houa Phan and Phong Saly regroupment provinces gave the PAVN jumping off points for a future conflict while creating ideal base areas to expand Pathet Lao control over Laos.[36]

The VWP members continued to work closely with Pathet Lao political cadres, and on 22 March 1955, the communist Lao's People's Party was formed in Houa Phan. It began with a membership of 343 dedicated activists that rapidly grew to nearly 3,000 members before year's end. It is hard to overstate the VWP role in organizing the Laotian communists; they were instrumental in forming not just the political apparatus but police forces, socialist economic structures, and tax systems. So as not to disturb the tenuous domestic political tightrope walked by the People's Party, not just membership but the very existence of the party was kept secret.[37]

The PAVN members of Group 100 also trained and advised the estimated 2,500 Pathet Lao Main Force and guerrilla soldiers, with another 3,600 militia who had regrouped. Instilled with ardor through political indoctrination, they were given first-rate training. As an added incentive for the many illiterate recruits, a basic elementary education supplemented their military schooling. The Pathet Lao's armed forces grew steadily and soon possessed a 7,000-strong army built around nine battalions, although only two were worthy of the name. It was enough to upset the 1954 ceasefire. With their newfound clout, by early 1956, Pathet Lao skirmishes with the ANL in the regroupment provinces became common.[38]

To end the nascent fighting, in July Princes Souvanna Phouma and Souphanou-vong opened reconciliation talks. On 5 August the two princes signed a neutralization agreement, and a new ceasefire took hold on 30 October 1956. The talks proved difficult, although China played a helpful role by telling Hanoi it opposed Pathet Lao provocations. It was not until the fall of 1957 that an agreement was reached that would return the two regroupment provinces to government control by 18 November, followed by the integration of the two main force Pathet Lao battalions into the ANL. By December the provinces were back under Vientiane's control, while the 1st Pathet Lao Battalion arrived at the air-land base near Luang Prabang, and the 2nd Battalion reported to the ANL near the air-land base on the Plain of Jars. Souvanna vowed to follow "vigilant neutrality" in Laotian foreign relations.[39] Soon many Pathet Lao demobilized, and the size of its military arm decreased significantly. The agreement between the princes effectively ended the presence of Group 100 in Laos, but Hanoi had no intention of remaining neutral. Renamed Group 800, in the future, its Laos operations would be run from the DRV.[40]

While the Pathet Lao had improved through the efforts of Group 100, the ANL had fallen into decay. Its battalions had contained a sizable contingent of French regular officers and NCOs, up to 10–15 percent in the case of the chasseurs, and when the war ended in 1954, eight of 12 ANL battalions had a French officer in command. An ANL NCO school had not opened until 1952, while basic officer and sergeant schools were not set up until 1953. Adding to the problem, the ANL senior staff had come entirely from the French Military Mission. They left after Geneva, effectively removing the ANL's senior leadership. There were not enough capable Lao officers and NCOs to replace them. As a stopgap, a number of promising NCOs and officers were given a few months training and promoted up to command level. The first army chief of staff appointed in late 1954, Nosavan Phoumi, had been a lieutenant in 1950.[41]

Things did not improve going forward. Articles 6 and 8 in the 1954 Geneva Agreement on Laos gave the French Army the lead in developing the ANL, and they were allowed to keep up to 5,000 troops in the Kingdom (3,500 combat troops and 1,500 advisors for the ANL), but France's commitment hinged on maintaining a major military presence in South Vietnam. That hope died in April 1956 when the last French soldier left the RVN, and with it the French Army lost any real interest in the ANL; by 1957 fewer than 2,000 disinterested French troops remained. That outcome, when combined with the poor quality of its equipment and lack of funds, left the ANL unprepared to defend Laos from any meaningful threat and certainly not the Pathet Lao backed up by the PAVN. The Americans did step in to supply military equipment, but that alone could not correct the shortcomings. The Americans could not go into the field with the ANL, and the U.S. equipment fell into disrepair as soon as it left Vientiane. (They were not able to arrange the first field survey of the gear until November 1958.)[42]

The 1957 negotiations breakthrough by the princes did nothing for the ANL and failed to deter PAVN efforts to expand the Pathet Lao as training shifted to the DRV. Up to 400 Pathet Lao guerrillas at a time were sent to Son Tay near Hanoi to attend a comprehensive six-month program while officer training took place at Dien Bien Phu. In the wake of the 1957 agreement, PAVN instructors told the Pathet Lao students in North Vietnam that the war was not over: "It is only a temporary ceasefire—but the struggle continues."[43] The words were followed by actions. To offset the proposed integration of the two Pathet Lao battalions into the ANL, Pathet Lao recruits training in the DRV were assigned to two newly formed battalions. To aid in that process, the best of the two existing battalions' arms and equipment was sent to the DRV in late 1957 to help outfit the new battalions. The Vientiane government and Pathet Lao ended 1957 with little real progress to show for their peace efforts.[44]

The year of 1958 looked to be a year of conciliation and reunification with the scheduling of the national election required by the Geneva accords, but there was little political unity. The 4 May elections to enlarge the national assembly proved to be a fascinating example of miscalculation and unintended consequences. The non–Communist parties should have won handily as they constituted a popular majority. To strengthen that support, the CIA funneled $500,000 into civic "political impact" projects (Project Booster Shot) to build and repair schools, irrigation dams, and roads, and the U.S. Air Force delivered aid to remote locations. But the two largest parties, the National Progressive and Independence Parties, were riven by petty differences and refused to draft a united candidate slate. That ensured their nationwide vote would be split, and making matters worse, for the first time the military, led by ANL chief-of-staff Phoumi Nosavan, assumed a political role.[45]

Conversely, the Pathet Lao ran a focused and clever campaign. They did not run as Pathet Lao communists but as the Lao Patriotic Front. And unlike the opposition, they created a joint slate with the leftist Peace Party, pushing a platform that stressed national unity and anti-corruption, two appealing policies. When the votes were tallied, the Patriotic Front-Peace Party garnered an impressive 33 percent of the vote. With the split non-communist vote, that gained them 13 of 21 open seats (9 Patriotic Front, 4 Peace Party) which, when combined with the existing left-wing bloc, gave the Patriotic Front influence over 21 of the 59 assembly seats. Overnight they had become a national political force.[46]

Shocked by the outcome, Prime Minister Prince Souvanna declined to form a government with the Patriotic Front. He also demanded that the disliked ICC leave Laos, which it did that July (evoking complaints from both the DRV and China).

Souvanna also unsuccessfully dealt with the upstart anti-corruption "Young Turks" in the Committee for the Defense of National Interests (CDNI), which had been formed on 15 June with CIA assistance. With Washington and specifically the CIA and Pentagon belatedly entering the game with Hanoi (most of the CIA's previous efforts focused on "hearts-and-minds" civic actions like Project Ricedrop in 1955 and Booster Shot), Laos became an active Cold War battleground. The political situation in Laos remained uncertain. When the CDNI refused to join his cabinet, Souvanna had no way forward to obtain the needed votes and resigned on 23 July. The country slid into confusion until mid–August when—over Patriotic Front opposition—the assembly voted in pro–Western Foreign Minister Phuoi Sananikone (29 to 21 with eight abstentions and one not present).[47]

Sananikone was no stranger to the political arena, being a member of a wealthy aristocratic family, a former prime minister (1950–1951), and the leader of the Laotian delegation at Geneva in 1954. ANL Colonel Oudone Sananikone was a close relative. To broaden his support, he moved to the right by allying himself with the "Young Turks" in the American-backed CDNI and refused to admit communists into his cabinet. It was a solution, but what the "Young Turks" and military, who had no particular loyalty to the prime minister, would do remained to be seen. The same could be said for the Pathet Lao and disenfranchised left. The political infighting also divided the Americans with the State Department backing Sananikone and the CIA backing the CDNI.[48]

Phoui Sananikone hung on somehow. Relations with his DRV neighbor deteriorated, as November and December witnessed ANL-PAVN skirmishing north of Tchepone on the Laotian side of the border. Called the Houng Lap incident, it was viewed as a national crisis, and the Laotian people ended the year with dimmed hopes for peace. Washington was concerned but optimistic, and unlike Hanoi, continued to enjoy good relations with the Kingdom. In February 1959, Crown Prince Sisavang Vatthana looked to the West when he asked for a U.S.-led Southeast Asia Treaty Organization (SEATO) or a direct U.S. guarantee to protect its DRV border. Although sympathetic, Washington judged the proposal a violation of the 1954 Geneva Agreement Laos had signed and no action was taken. The situation did not improve with the anti-communist Laotian government divided by factionalism and its army in disarray while the Pathet Lao, with DRV backing, steadily grew in power both politically and militarily.[49]

War Renewed 1959–1962

War returned to Laos on 3 June 1959 during a meeting between Pathet Lao and VWP leaders in North Vietnam where it was decided that, as with South Vietnam, the Laotian revolutionary tide would shift to armed struggle. It became almost foreordained when Hanoi passed Resolution 15 in January; there was no escaping the VWP's one battlefield way of war in Indochina, and Hanoi judged support of the Pathet Lao as "vital in aiding the liberation struggle" in South Vietnam.[50] Laos was to play a central role in the Vietnam War, and Pathet Lao integration into the ANL proposed in 1958 was the catalyst to open the fighting, as the obstacles had become almost insurmountable.[51]

While Phoui Sananikone's government defined integration as individual Pathet Lao enlisting into the ANL, the Pathet Lao insisted on keeping their two battalions intact and apart from the ANL. A second roadblock dealt with the officer corps. The ANL expected to join about 20 Pathet Lao officers (a standard ANL battalion had ten junior officers), while the Pathet Lao demanded twice the number and at higher ranks. The ANL saw this as an attempt to infiltrate communist officers throughout the army.[52]

After a year of difficult negotiations, a compromise was reached in early 1959 with Colonel Oudone Sananikone representing the ANL. The Pathet Lao battalions could stay together and the higher number of officers accepted if they could pass a literacy test, but future troop assignments into and out of the battalions would be controlled by the ANL. ANL leaders did not know what of make of the hyper-indoctrinated Pathet Lao; during an earlier meeting with the ANL general staff in Vientiane, one Pathet Lao officer repeatedly attempted to put his knife through a tank and searched vainly for "American" drivers. He had been taught that the tanks were paper fakes to trick the Pathet Lao and that U.S. imperialist soldiers drove ANL vehicles. Despite the distrust and misperceptions, integration appeared on the verge of going ahead by May, and then suddenly it was not.[53]

The first blow came on 11 May, Independence Day, when Pathet Lao leader Prince Souphanouvong, representing the Patriotic Front in Vientiane, ordered a boycott of the ANL commissioning ceremony for the Pathet Lao officers. Adding injury to insult, Pathet Lao soldiers removed the ANL officer presiding over the ceremony at gunpoint. Not one to take such an affront in stride, Prime Minister Sananikone informed the Pathet Lao soldiers on 14 May that they had 24 hours to effect integration into the ANL or face forced disarmament and the dissolution of the two battalions. Prince Souphanouvong directed the battalions not to comply.[54]

The sudden turn of event toward confrontation was not a surprise to either the Pathet Lao leaders or Hanoi. The impasse provoked by Prince Souphanouvong created an opportunity to end the negotiation's charade, as both Hanoi and the Pathet Lao held Vientiane's position as unacceptable; neither wanted to passively watch the Pathet Lao battalions dissolve over time within a hostile and suspicious ANL. What was unexpected was the suddenness of Phoui Sananikone's ultimatum and the short compliance timeline. Hanoi fired off a sharp rebuke to Vientiane over the mistreatment of the Pathet Lao battalions and again blamed Laos for the 1958 border clashes.[55]

Phoui Sananikone, despite having rule-by-decree power since January (in response to the PAVN-ANL border fighting), was in no way as prepared or decisive. When the 15 May deadline passed, the ANL took middling steps; ANL commanders had no stomach for stern measures and simply moved to cut off supplies to the Pathet Lao troops or if necessary, use tear gas—not live ammunition—to control the situation. After several days of inaction, on the foggy night of 18–19 May, Thao Tou Yang's 2nd Pathet Lao Battalion slipped away from the Plain of Jars and moved toward the DRV frontier.[56]

That was the situation in Hanoi on the eve of the 3 June decision to restart the war in Laos. From that point forward, there was nothing the Laotians could do to formulate a peaceful solution between its various factions. A military clash was inevitable and like the 1953–1954 period, it would be waged in conventional battle; there never was a meaningful revolutionary guerrilla aspect to the Pathet Lao–PAVN fighting in Laos. After follow-on VWP Politburo and Central Committee meetings in early July, the graver step was taken to send the PAVN back into Laos to help the Pathet Lao. More action was coming. On 6 July the Central Committee formed a special committee for Laos with General Giap as senior military advisor. It would report to the Politburo (through the top secret CP38 Committee, which also oversaw operations in Cambodia). On 15 July the Central Committee took the additional step of creating a team of VWP-PAVN Laos veterans to guide senior Pathet Lao leaders. Finally, and in secrecy, Giap alerted PAVN units near the Laotian border. Soon the 316th Division, which had such success in the Laotian province of Houa Phan in 1953, along with the 120th and 270th Independent Regiments and others, began preparing for battle.[57]

There was little Phoui Sananikone could do. In June 1959 the British military attaché in Vientiane deemed the ANL so riddled with problems, ranging from poor training to inadequate weapons, that it was incapable of defending the nation without foreign advisors. Now free from their encampment, first shots by the 2nd Pathet Lao Battalion were not long in coming, and raids on isolated outposts in Phong Saly and Houa Phan became routine. Perhaps symbolically, the Sop-Nao border station, the same outpost overrun during the bloody 1953 battle at Muong Khoua, again became a battleground in July when several ANL soldiers were killed, including the platoon leader.[58]

The attacks continued over the following weeks. By then Paris, who per the Geneva Accord controlled foreign military training, grudgingly allowed a combined French-US mission to begin (Project Disallow). Comprised of 12 Operational Detachment A's or ODAs (155 soldiers) from the U.S. 77th Special Forces Group (SFG), it was run by the CIA under the name Project Hotfoot. The mission was to covertly train the ANL while CIA-operated transport planes resupplied remote ANL outposts. Clad in civilian attire, the U.S. soldiers reported to the senior American officer in Laos, Brigadier General John A. Heintges of the U.S. military aid Programs Evaluation Office (POE).[59]

Unaware why war again had come to Laos, Phoui Sananikone and his American backers became increasingly bewildered as the situation deteriorated throughout the rest of 1959. In early August, the 1st Pathet Lao Battalion outside Luang Prabang split apart. With many troops rejecting integration, they followed in the path of the 2nd Battalion and headed for the hills and then on to North Vietnam. The few "loyal" remnants joined the ANL as the 26th Battalion. Later that month, troops from the two Pathet Lao battalions were ensconced in the DRV's Nghe An province (southeast of Houa Phan), being refitted with Soviet weapons and put on a war footing. As the tensions rose, the quarreling between the State Department and CIA increased, as did the political bickering amongst Phoui Sananikone, the Crown Prince, the army, and CDNI. They were incapable of uniting to battle their real foe, the Pathet Lao–PAVN forces. An angry Sananikone, who had placed "Red Prince" Souphanouvong and the rest of the Patriotic Front leadership under house arrest in July, now put them in prison.[60]

The breach was complete. On 4 August, a state of emergency was declared in Phong Saly, Houa Phon, and three other provinces bordering North Vietnam. The PAVN-supported Pathet Lao offensive lasted into the fall. By September, they had recaptured parts of Phong Saly and Houa Phon, threatened the royal capital of Luang Prabang, and penetrated into Houa Khong in the extreme northwest. In its first major move to affect the war in South Vietnam, the PAVN entered Laos to chase away ANL detachments along the RVN border. It might have been a minor operation, but gaining control over the Laotian-RVN border was a key strategic objective for Hanoi. And going almost unnoticed at the time, the PLA in Yunnan began training and providing equipment to the Pathet Lao. The stage was for set for escalation by all parties.[61]

Phoui Sananikone tried to respond by taking diplomatic action. As the Pathet Lao–PAVN offensive wound down, he appealed to the United Nations on 4 September, protesting what he described as a North Vietnamese invasion. With no objective observers on the ground, it was an impossible case to make and did little to help his embattled premiership; the DRV went to great lengths to conceal PAVN involvement. Next came Phoui Sananikone's political enemies. The inability of the ANL (who had suffered over 300 casualties by October) to defeat the Pathet Lao damaged him politically, and his opponents were quick to strike.[62]

In mid–December and in the face of CDNI and military opposition, Sananikone tried to move closer to the neutralists and purged the obstructionist CDNI "Young Turks" from his cabinet. That political turmoil, combined with Pathet Lao fighting, led the king to take action. When the Assembly's term expired on 25 December, he ordered military rule until the April 1960 elections, and by threat of a coup (led by the Defense Minister Colonel Phoumi Nosavan), the army forced Sananikone to resign six days later. The non-descript Kou Abhay, president of the King's Council, became caretaker prime minister. In the meantime, power rested with Nosavan. The quasi-rightist coup united the neutralists and Patriotic Front, and Laos, a nation wracked by a growing war, began to break apart.[63]

While watching the events in Vientiane, Hanoi decided that September to form Group 959, the successor to Groups 100 and 800. The Politburo spelled out two main tasks for the group: provide direction to the Pathet Lao central committee and coordinate DRV aid. Led by General Le Choung, initially there were just 88 members to include the July veteran team, but they were some of the DRV's best Laos experts. Group 959, in coordination with the Pathet Lao, took charge of logistical support and worked to plan and guide political and military operations against the Royal Laotian Government. Another priority, training the Pathet Lao in the DRV, remained fast-paced with nearly 700 troops arriving in late 1959. Prime Minister Kuo Abhay and Colonel Nosavan in Vientiane had no clear understanding of the growing military threat they faced.[64]

Politically, Laos remained fragile. Seeking to change that, in the early months of 1960, Colonel Nosavan sought to consolidate his control, only to suffer several setbacks. The looming April elections brought concerns amongst the Americans that he would impose military rule akin to Marshal Sarit Thanarat in neighboring Thailand. But an outcome just as bad was realized during the vote overseen by Nosavan's loyalists. Some of it was clever if dirty politics. The government instituted a reasonable-sounding basic education requirement for candidates, but given rampant illiteracy in Laos, it disqualified five of the nine Patriotic Front delegates. In the end, the vote was so rigged as to be discredited. Not one Patriotic Front candidate was elected, and the neutralists were marginalized.[65]

The error was more egregious than in 1958, as Nosavan's anti-communists would have won without corrupting the process. Civil disturbances, protests, and international condemnation followed. He had alienated everyone but his strongest followers. Adding to now-General Nosavan's dismay, in darkness and during a raging tropical storm on 24 May, Prince Souphanouvong and his compatriots snuck out of jail and joined their Pathet Lao comrades in northwestern Laos. Militarily, things were a bit better. With notable U.S. assistance, the ANL had made some gains against the Pathet Lao. The rainy season brought its usual reprieve, but the crisis could only increase in intensity as the weather cleared with the passing of summer.

The Kong Le Coup

The respite ended with the explosive events of 9 August 1960. While the Phoumi Nosavan cabinet was in Luang Prabang attending to King Sisavang Vong's official state funeral (the king had died on 29 October 1959), Captain Kong Le, the uncompromising acting commander of the 2nd ANL Paratroop Battalion, seized control in Vientiane. Although claiming itself to be the High Command of the Revolution, Kong Le orchestrated a mild-mannered coup stressing continuity and neutrality, not revolution. Nonetheless, the king was disturbed and ordered Nosavan to form a new government on 13 August. That was easier said than done. On 17 August Kong Le declared the return to power of Prince Souvanna, and his government leaned toward the Pathet Lao, DRV, and China. The opposition began to gel, and a third-rate civil war ensued befitting the political leadership. In late August, General Nosavan, along with Boun Oum, another of the Three Princes who initially joined with Souvanna, and allied members of the National Assembly formed a rival government, the Revolutionary Committee, at Savannakhet. By September most of the ANL had rallied to them with the backing of the Americans. Bangkok also redoubled its support, seeing Kong Le's closeness to its enemies as a new and imminent threat to Thailand's security. And Kong Le was a serious opponent.[66]

On 21 September, the first clash with Kong Le's troops took place at Paksane (Pakxan), 150 kilometers southeast of Vientiane along the Mekong River. In a well-executed night attack, Kong Le's soldiers emerged victorious. To the north, the Pathet Lao exploited the uncertainty created by Le's coup to capture Houa Phan's provincial capital of Sam Neua on 26 September. The fighting by all parties, however, did not expand, and things muddled along into October with Kong Le striding down the middle by refusing to obey Phoumi Nosavan while protesting Souvanna's diplomatic recognition of the Soviet Union. A frustrated United States cut off aid to

Vientiane on 1 October, then discreetly began sending military aid to Phoumi Nosavan's forces a week later. But the Americans were at a loss. How could the Pathet Lao do well against the ANL?[67]

Things remained chaotic. On 10 November 1960, Major Bountheng of the 3rd ANL Battalion staged an abortive coup in Luang Prabang against Souvanna and Kong Le, and to add confusion to chaos, ousted Prime Minister Phoui Sananikone reappeared and tried to assume a leading role. He was ignored by all parties. On 18 November, Princes Souvanna and Souphanouvong met at Sam Neua, the de facto Pathet Lao capital, and agreed to form a coalition government but provocatively banned Phoumi Nosavan and Prince Boun Oum from serving as ministers. Events continued on a downward spiral for the pro–Western faction.[68]

Three days later, Kong Le's army, now called the Neutralist Army Forces (FAN), combined with the Pathet Lao to march onto the Plain of Jars. In early December, FAN units advanced from Paksane 65 kilometers south along Route 13 to the junction with Route 8 and threatened the ANL stronghold at Savannakhet. But the ANL did not quit. GMs 1 and 15 along with the paratroopers rallied at Savannakhet, and GM 11 (3rd and 21st Infantry Battalions) guarded Luang Prabang. The 10th Battalion also held firm at Muong Khoun to the east of the Plain of Jars. The next week GM 1 (4th and 5th Battalions) counterattacked north toward Paksane with success and then toward Vientiane, spearheaded by an airborne assault by the 1st and 3rd Paratroop Battalions. GM 11 also advanced on Vientiane from the north. A pro–Novasan colonel attempted a coup in Vientiane on 8 December that soon fizzled but threw the capital into further disarray. The next day as the battle for Vientiane took shape, Prince Souvanna fled to Cambodia.[69]

Hanoi too prepared to escalate the war in Laos. During the September plenum of the 3rd VWP Congress, the party passed the new five-year military plan that addressed the Laos situation and directed the CMPC to order the PAVN to assist the Pathet Lao and send forces into Laos to "fight alongside the troops of our allies."[70] Group 959 sprang into action. On 7 December 1960, Major General Chu Huy Man (the former PAVN Group 100 commander) took charge of Vientiane's defenses, and PAVN advisors arrived in the capital. Strong elements of the PAVN 120th Regiment, largely composed of Montagnards along with two border guard battalions, crossed into northeastern Laos along Route 7 and captured the border post at Nong Het (Nonghet). By December they had reached the intersection with Route 6 near the eastern end of the Plain of Jars.[71]

To disguise the invasion, troops did not wear PAVN uniforms and were given Laotian aliases and identification cards. Impossible to detect were 335th PAVN Division (Brigade) soldiers—ethnic Vietnamese Laotians specially trained to operate in Laos. As in 1953–1954, PAVN "volunteers" again carried out combat operations in the Kingdom. There was new source of aid as well. Using aircraft based in Hanoi, an overt Soviet supply airlift began that assisted Kong Le, the Pathet Lao, and the PAVN forces in Laos. December witnessed the start of large-scale Soviet and DRV weapons transfers, supervised by Group 959. Over the next six months, Kong Le received over 4,000 weapons while the Pathet Lao took possession of 7,000—most delivered by DRV-based Soviet aircraft. Soviet Deputy Foreign Minister Georgy M. Pushkin boasted to the Americans that the Soviet air operations were the largest since World War II.[72]

As the battle for Vientiane intensified, the PAVN sent a battery of 105 mm howitzers with a battery of 120 mm mortars (again flown in by Soviet aircraft). And as the Pathet Lao had never handled large weapons, PAVN soldiers manned the guns. Despite the help, on 13 December the ANL pushed into the city, and mutual artillery duels destroyed whole sections of the capital, killing and wounding hundreds of civilians but few soldiers. The next day the battle reached the city's heart. It was chaotic and destructive as squads of soldiers switched sides at will, and fire from their high-powered rifles tore through the city's thin-walled houses and stores. The heaviest fighting occurred around the Defense Ministry and nearby strongpoint at the Immigration Office, which fell to ANL but not before destroying the ambassador's residence at the U.S. embassy. By 15 December, General Man realized the battle was lost, and on the next day he and Kong Le withdrew to the northeast and the city's airfield. Having gained majority support from the Assembly three days earlier, the king came out for the Revolutionary Committee, and they triumphantly arrived at Vientiane.[73]

Kong Le's retreat continued. Vang Vieng and its airfield (160 kilometers north of Vientiane) were abandoned, but not before a Soviet plane spirited Le out on 31 December. Pushing him on, GM 11 in Luang Prabang advanced south to join Nosavan's GM 15 at Vang Vieng. FAN troops finally regrouped at the old Plain of Jars air-land base, where they received needed aid again delivered by Soviet aircraft. Prince Souvanna, who refused to resign, returned from Cambodia and reestablished his government at Khang Khay in the northern Plain of Jars. Kong Le and his FAN also had to keep their guard up as ANL Major Vang Pao's Hmong irregulars, members of the largest confederation of mountain peoples in Laos, held key nearby hills. The war now entered a more destructive and deadlier phase.[74]

The 1961 Winter-Spring Offensive

On 1 January 1961, Pathet Lao–PAVN forces advancing from Sam Neua reached the Plain of Jars and joined Kong Le. It was time to launch a counteroffensive against the forces of General Nosavan and Prince Boun Oum. To support the operations, Group 959 grew to over 3,000 advisors over the coming months. The 120th PAVN Regiment continued its advance along Route 7; by 4 January they had taken Muong Kham, just 55 kilometers east of the Plain of Jars. Simultaneously, PAVN–Pathet Lao forces consolidated control over Phong Saly province by taking Phong Saly town and Nam Bak on the Mekong River in northeastern Luang Prabang province. Soon elements of the 120th Regiment arrived on the Plain of Jars, and to the south, the villages of Muong Khoun and Tha Tom fell to their forces, nearly completing the occupation of Xiang Khoung (Xieng Kouang) province. To the north in Houa Phan province, ANL outposts at Pa Thi and Muong Hiam fell by month's end. Northeastern Laos had been conquered.[75]

The major battlefield sat between the two capitals. The arrival of mortar and machine gun companies from the 120th regiment and other PAVN units in January allowed the lightly armed Pathet Lao–FAN battalions at the Plain of Jars to attack west and seize a stretch of Route 13 between Vientiane and Luang Prabang, cutting off the two capitals from each other. An ANL counterattack on 6 February made little headway. The CMPC escalated the war by committing more regular PAVN units to the fighting in Upper Laos, but the ANL battled back. The Route 13 struggle stretched into March as the combined forces of the PAVN–Pathet Lao and Kong Le's FAN found the fighting hard and progress slow. During this period, the town of Vang Vieng traded hands four times before the PAVN–Pathet Lao–FAN force took it for good on 23 April. But afterwards they only advanced 10 kilometers closer to Luang Prabang and made no effort toward Vientiane.[76]

In light of the aggression, on 9 March 1961 newly elected President John F. Kennedy approved National Security Action Memorandum 29 (NSAM 29) that authorized a number of changes to include increasing the number of U.S. advisors in Laos (U.S. Army ODAs surged from 12 to 21), expanding military aid, and gaining Thailand's agreement to increase military support for Laotian operations. Kennedy lifted the covert shroud over Project Hotfoot, making it an overt assistance program, and the U.S. Special Forces soldiers donned their uniforms. The new effort became Operation White Star. Additionally, MAAG-Laos was created in April, subsuming the PEO, and General Andrew J. Boyle replaced Heintges to become its first commander. Boyle was further directed to work with General Nosavan to improve the Laotian Army, and Boyle helped reorganize the ANL along with the small air force and paramilitary units that were unified into the Royal Armed Forces (Forces Armées du Royaume or FAR). GM 15 was redesignated GM 12, and the paratroopers formed into GM 15(A). Colonel Oudone Sananikone was promoted to general and became the FAR chief of staff.[77]

The PAVN remained just as active as the Americans. Hanoi never took its eye off the real priority: the reunification war in South Vietnam. As in 1953–1954, Giap realized that victory in Vietnam remained linked to events in Laos, and the objective was to control the Laotian-RVN border region to allow the PAVN to outflank the ARVN DMZ defenses and enter the Central Highlands. Dubbed the Ta Khong Offensive, it was a scaled down version of Giap's December 1953 Middle Laos campaign. Calling it an offensive was a bit of a misnomer as there were no significant FAR units to battle. It was more an occupation.[78]

After brief border excursions in March to obtain assembly areas and gain intelligence on FAR defenses (to include the same areas involved in the 1958 Phu Loi incident), the operation kicked off on 11 April 1961. The FAR proved as feeble as expected. The PAVN's 19th Border Guard and 927th Local Force Battalions rapidly advanced along Route 8 and soon threatened Thakhet. Picking up on the increased North Vietnamese activity, on 1 May the Pentagon reported that there were perhaps 4,100 PAVN soldiers with the Pathet Lao. That would increase dramatically in the next few weeks after large elements of the PAVN's 325th Division and 271st Regiment covertly entered the Laotian battlefield as part of Operation Ta Khong.[79]

By mid–May, the 325th Division's 101st Regiment had seized the Middle Laos market hub of Tchepone and Muong Phin, both sitting astride Route 9. Again, there was little or no fighting; the ANL outpost at Tchepone had been abandoned back in 1960. From there, along with the 271st Regiment, they advanced south, sweeping everything before them until halting in eastern Savannakhet province. The RVN border was now fully exposed to PAVN infiltration from Laos. To consolidate their conquests, the remainder of the PAVN 325th Division marched into Laos in late May. At its height, over 20,000 PAVN soldiers had entered Laos in 1961. As in the War of Resistance, PAVN troops easily outnumbered the Pathet Lao. Bernard Fall noted at the time, "The Laotian problem had not changed one iota since 1953."[80]

11

Geneva, the Battle of Nam Tha,
and Hanoi's Logistics War

The intense fighting in Laos had a sobering effect on all parties—to include the Soviet Union and United States—and forced a halt to hostilities before it became the next hot war in the Cold War. It was time for negotiations. The idea to reconvene the Geneva Conference on Laos, the International Conference on the Settlement of the Laotian Question, originated externally with Cambodia's ruler, Prince Norodom Sihanouk, a strong advocate of regional neutralism, and within Laos by Kong Le, who pushed for both a ceasefire and peace conference. The pleas were received sympathetically in Moscow and London, the two chairs of the 1954 Geneva talks on Laos. On 24 April 1961, they contacted the three Laotian factions urging a summit in Geneva, while simultaneously inviting 13 other participants to attend and additionally reaching out to India, Canada, and the Polish People's Republic with a request to re-establish the ICC in Laos that had gone dormant in 1958. A short while later, representatives from the Three Princes met at the remote villages of Hin Hop and then Na Mon. After a fitful start, on 3 May a rough ceasefire was settled on that barely held.[1]

The Three Princes then consented to go to Switzerland to renew peace talks. Those talks soon bore fruit as they quickly agreed to the reentry of the ICC teams to supervise the ceasefire. Getting in the ICC teams proved simple; they returned to Laos on 11 May 1961. What would be their duties and with what authority remained unresolved. The success was significant nonetheless, as Washington then tabled direct military intervention into Laos. In a further breakthrough, on 22 June the Three Princes issued a communiqué in Zurich announcing the formation of a coalition government led by Souvanna and containing ministers loyal to Princes Boun Oum and Souphanouvong. It established a framework to advance the peace process: neutralization of Laotian foreign policy, restoration of civil rights to include the electoral laws, and formation of a coalition government. Beyond those steps, the negotiations went nowhere.[2]

Unlike the private talks between the Three Princes, the 1961 Geneva deliberations began badly. There was an initial delay over which delegation represented Laos until it was agreed that all three sides would participate. There were 16 seats at the table, making for what William H. Sullivan, a senior member of the U.S. delegation, politely described as "something of a circus."[3] The show then crashed on 7 June after

PAVN–Pathet Lao forces seized the Hmong's Padong (Ban Pa Dong) stronghold. It was a troubling development, as it not only violated the ceasefire but also showed the ICC to be less than effective. From that point forward, the remaining obstacle revolved around two related sticking points: Washington's insistence on guarantees from Moscow that Laos not be used for infiltration into South Vietnam and that the ICC have robust authority to investigate reported violations based on a majority vote of the three participating states (India, Canada, and Poland).[4]

As the Kingdom was wracked by civil war, the ICC legacy did not instill confidence, and the split over ICC responsibilities was obvious. The Soviet-Chinese-DRV side wanted a symbolic commission that could not investigate violations—effectively securing PAVN conquests in Middle Laos. The Americans, under the leadership of Ambassador-at-Large W. Averell Harriman, wanted a robust ICC able to seek out and force the withdrawal of PAVN forces. Harriman was a successful industrialist, scion of one of America's wealthiest families, during World War II chief negotiator for lend-lease aid, and later ambassador to Moscow. He was arguably the war's most important ambassadorial assignment. Although 70 years old, making him an American political éminence grise, Harriman was both energetic and ambitious, letting it be known he intended to climb to the top of the State Department. A ruthless master of bureaucratic wars, he became the driving force behind Southeast Asian policy. As he started his work with the Laotians, it was clear they were as badly divided as the superpowers over the ICC role, with the factions supporting either the American or DRV position or neutralization. The Laotians only were united in wanting a good degree of authority over the ICC operating in their country.[5]

The infiltration point of contention also roiled the negotiations. Harriman's expressed concerns over PAVN infiltration into the RVN through Laos became a major roadblock to agreement in Geneva. The final area of friction dealt with process, due to the tendency on the part of the United States and Soviet Union superpowers to view negotiations largely as their exclusive domain with all other parties, to include the Laotians, assuming a subordinate role. While the 1954 Geneva talks lasted three months, the new parlays fruitlessly droned on throughout the rest of 1961 and into 1962.[6]

President John F. Kennedy with the remarkable and acerbic Undersecretary of State W. Averill Harriman, the man who drove American policy not just in South Vietnam but Laos as well. Harriman took a deep disliking to Diem and led the charge for his overthrow in 1963 (John F. Kennedy Presidential Library).

Gradually progress

was made after Secretary of State Dean Rusk and Harriman met a number of times with Soviet Foreign Minister Andrei Gromyko and his deputy, Pushkin, who headed up the Russian delegation at Geneva. While the neutralization issue neared consensus, the Soviet-DRV-China side still resisted a strong independent ICC, and agreement amongst the Laotians on the ICC stayed out of reach as well. In September the parties accepted the Laotian neutrality proposal made earlier by the Three Princes. With neutralization finally addressed, in October Pushkin verbally agreed to a majority ICC vote to initiate investigations. Washington, however, still sought assurances that Moscow would rein in the DRV and Pathet Lao if either or both violated the protocols. Without it, the search for a final solution remained elusive, and the talks stalled again.[7]

The official sticking points in December 1961 were the role of SEATO and the old issue of integrating Pathet Lao forces into the FAR. They were distractions. SEATO would have no role, and the Pathet Lao would never integrate into the FAR. The real issues were where to draw the ceasefire lines, and for Washington, reassurances from Moscow that the agreements would be enforced. The action then shifted from Geneva as Hanoi turned to the battlefield in Laos convinced that, as a North Vietnamese official put it at the time, "only a demonstration of military supremacy could break the deadlock."[8]

The Battle of Nam Tha

In late 1961, General Choung of Group 959 approached the VWP Politburo with a plan for a decisive offensive in northwestern Laos centered on the capture of the FAR air-land base at Nam Tha (Luang Namtha) north of Luang Prabang. At the conclusion of the 1961 campaigns, PAVN–Pathet Lao–held territory extended into northern Laos to include the Plain of Jars air-land base. That made Nam Tha the FAR center of authority in the northwest, and Choung intended to destroy it. The base sat adjacent to the small town of Nam Tha, which served as the Houa Khong provincial capital. Just over a day's walk from China and a few days from Burma, it sat in an isolated valley eerily reminiscent of Dien Bien Phu. Tied to the Nam Tha anchor were two satellite FAR bases, one at the old French aéro-terrestre base at Muong Sai (110 kilometers northwest) and the other at Muong Sing (60 kilometers to the northeast and also near the Chinese border). Muong Sing had gained fame as home to Dr. Tom Dooley's medical center. The FAR maintained control over the region through the three bases and a combination of outposts, patrols, and sweeps.[9]

Hanoi was receptive to the Nam Tha offensive, but things were to be done differently from 1961. First, General Giap would play a major role in his capacity as a Politburo and CMPC member and senior military advisor to the CP38 special committee. Second, the campaign would follow the 1954 model—especially the Dien Bien Phu operation—where FAR bases would be isolated by shutting down airfields and roads, followed by the seizure of the satellite strongpoints, and culminating in an all-out assault on Nam Tha. Lastly, the PAVN had learned its lesson in 1961; no amount of support could make the Pathet Lao victorious. The PAVN would fight in the vanguard and seven battalions (a reinforced regiment from the PAVN's 316th Division, the 330th Brigade's 3rd Battalion, and the 2nd and 4th Battalions of the 335th Brigade) along with supporting units would join several Pathet Lao battalions in the Nam Tha–Muong Sing region. To keep them in supply, the PAVN 919th Air Regiment joined the campaign. Among the communist allies, there was no pretense of a Pathet Lao operation, as the official PAVN history stated, "After eight years of army building under peacetime conditions, our army would launch its first offensive campaign."[10]

In March 1962 there was a high-level meeting in Hanoi to discuss the offensive. Chaired by the VWP, there were representatives from the Pathet Lao, Moscow, and Beijing. The political goal was stressed. The offensive was to put the Pathet Lao in a position of military superiority before agreeing to a coalition government. The senior Polish ICC official, Marek Thee, was to ensure the commission would not interfere in the PAVN–Pathet Lao attacks. (The Pathet Lao had been using the ICC Poles as a secure communications conduit with the DRV since 1958.) Until the offensive ran its course, there would be no movement in the Geneva negotiations.[11]

The Chinese delegates agreed to provide support. They had been concerned about nearness of the Nam Tha troops to their border since 1959, and the arrival of American advisors heightened concerns. They further were outraged that FAR forces held the 22nd Volunteer and the 111th Special Battalions containing former Nationalist Chinese soldiers. PLA units with the Kunming Military Region were already present near the border, and for the Nam Tha campaign, Beijing directed them to assist logistically the PAVN. This was vital. As it stood, the PAVN forces massing near Nam Tha were at the end of their longest and most tenuous logistical route in Laos. With Chinese support, that problem disappeared as supplies now could arrive from China in a day, a disaster for the FAR whose appreciation of Nam Tha's remoteness lulled them into a false sense of security. The Soviets took a different tack to the offensive and distanced themselves from the plan, in no small part to preserve their relationship with the Americans. They informed Hanoi that the DRV, China, and Pathet Lao should decide what to do without them. Final preparations began immediately and in secrecy.[12]

Washington and Vientiane strove to stay alert but realized neither Hanoi's determination nor the scope of the PAVN effort. It was not complacency but belief that the 1961 ceasefire would be honored, and there was no indication of if, let alone where, a blow might fall. Warning signs emerged as U.S. reconnaissance flights detected a build-up of Pathet Lao–FAN military supplies in Upper Laos during November. The Americans also noted that PAVN troop strength in Laos had increased in January 1962, but nothing pointed to the isolated base at Nam Tha.

The Americans used the ceasefire to strengthen and reorganize the FAR while making good its 1961 losses. Within the FAR, the French Army's groupement system gained new life. In government-controlled areas, "first line defense" soldiers and other security units were organized into light infantry Tactical Groups (GTs).[13] To support them, the GMs were restructured, beefed up, and assigned to threatened areas. GM 11 with three infantry battalions was assigned to Nam Tha in support of the region's GT 2 (which contained the former Nationalist Chinese and several volunteer battalions). Finally, a strategic reserve was created, consisting of a few infantry battalions and Field Artillery Group 1 (GAC 1) in Vientiane along with the paratroopers of GM 15(A) at Seno. Under Operation White Star, U.S. equipment, arms, and munitions fleshed out the formations that were also stiffened by assigning one ODA to each combat battalion. However important the improvements, MAAG-Laos commander General Boyle concluded that the increase in North Vietnamese forces had shifted the advantage to the PAVN.[14]

The Battle

The action in Upper Laos began in December at Muong Sai when GT 2 and GM 11 elements came under attack while trying to keep the road open between Nam Tha and the Muong Sai garrison (GM 11's 1st Infantry Battalion). There were related trouble spots. Muong Sai, long an object of contention, had been lost and then recaptured by the FAR in mid–1961. This time PAVN–Pathet Lao pressure became too great. First the Ban Na Mo outpost fell, then the Muong Sai garrison withdrew to Nam Tha in early January. The PAVN stepped up the pace by isolating Muong Sing on 21 January after overrunning two intermediary outposts that connected it to the Nam Tha.[15]

The first direct sign of trouble for Nam Tha came four days later on 25 January with an intense mortar barrage of the air-land base from hills to the southeast. Simultaneously, PAVN troops overran two FAR outposts about 20 kilometers distant. Objecting to the ceasefire violations, Prince Boun Oum halted talks with Prince Souvanna. To bolster GT 2's four weak Volunteer Battalions defending Nam Tha, days later General Phoumi Nosavan committed four GAC 1 batteries along with the 30th Infantry Battalion from the strategic reserve. The American commander-in-chief in the Pacific (CINCPAC), Admiral Harry D. Felt, was concerned as the fresh FAR troops sent to Nam Tha left Vientiane with no significant reserve and had done nothing to improve the situation. He stated flatly, "Nam Tha could be taken at the enemy's choosing."[16]

Souvanna's attempts to restrain the PAVN–Pathet Lao had no effect. On 1 February, that year's start of Vietnam's Tet holidays, another heavy mortar attack on the Nam Tha airfield forced its aircraft to depart for Luang Prabang. Washington reacted on 3 February when the U.S. ambassador in Moscow, Llewellyn Thompson, complained to the Kremlin. Three days later, Harriman was directed to reapply pressure on Souvanna to restore the peace. Harriman, known by the acerbic nickname "the old crocodile," blamed General Nosavan and sent the general a blunt order to grant more concessions to Prince Souvanna in Geneva. He then purged the State Department of Nosavan supporters and arranged to have pro–Nosavan CIA officers at the embassy sent out of Laos. When the general stubbornly opposed further compromise, Harriman held him responsible for the Kingdom's continued problems. The communists continued to escalate tensions.[17]

As if to embarrass Washington, on 9 February the ceasefire was again violated with the heavy mortaring of Nam Tha, only this time the town took the brunt of the fires where dozens of homes were destroyed. General Nosavan moved to send in the elite 1st Paratroop Battalion, but General Boyle warned him that Nam Tha was a trap and refused to allow American aircraft to fly the mission. Rather than making the combat jump, on 12 February Phoumi had them ferried to Nam Tha on Laotian military planes. By that date, the PAVN–Pathet Lao siege trenches were four kilometers from Nam Tha's defensive perimeter. Things settled down for several weeks then picked up again. In March, two battalions from the PAVN's 316th Division arrived on heights overlooking Nam Tha, and PAVN artillery augmented Pathet Lao mortars, dramatically increasing the bombardment's lethality.[18]

In response, Nosavan sent in the 55th Paratroop Battalion on 27 March, and the two paratrooper battalions drove the PAVN artillery off the hills, restabilizing the situation. Feeling satisfied with that success, in early April he then withdrew GM 11 into the reserve at Vientiane but sent in the fresh 28th Infantry Battalion to offset the loss. The PAVN countered by systematically eliminating Nam Tha's supporting outposts and recaptured the hills. Nosavan responded by dropping in the bulk of the 11th Paratroop Battalion on 16 April and ordered it to interdict PAVN–Pathet Lao supply lines, but they failed. A short while later, the rest of the battalion jumped into Nam Tha. The entire GM 15(A) had been committed. Due to Nosavan's continued intransigence, at Harriman's urging the U.S. Special Forces teams pulled out of Nam Tha, leaving Major Patrick Marr, the senior American advisor, and one other officer behind. Battle soon would be joined.[19]

The PAVN offensive in May developed rapidly. PAVN–Pathet Lao attacked and seized Muong Sing and its garrison on 2 May. On the same day, the Nam Tha perimeter was probed and the base heavily shelled as PAVN guns had returned to the hills. Unaware of the danger, on 3 May the 1st Paratroop Battalion advanced from Nam Tha to reopen the road to Muong Sing. They ran head on into the much larger advancing PAVN–Pathet Lao force; badly bloodied, they beat a hasty retreat but managed to briefly upset the timeline for the Nam Tha assault. It made no difference. The last remaining Nam Tha outpost, only two kilometers away, fell the following day. The base was completely isolated.[20]

Throughout 5 May, the defenders at Nam Tha endured sporadic artillery and mortar attacks. In the darkness at 3:00 a.m. on the following day, the PAVN attacked in strength, smashing its northwest sector. (Earlier PAVN probing had succeeded, as that was the weakest spot.) In a rapid series of follow-on assaults, the PAVN–Pathet Lao battalions attacked from the east, northeast, and southeast. By late morning, the FAR defenses broke. Abandoning their heavy equipment, a pell-mell retreat ensued with only the paratroopers conducting a fighting withdrawal. That allowed the PAVN to enjoy a brief celebration the next day, 7 May, to mark the eighth anniversary of the great triumph at Dien Bien Phu. With victory in hand, the PAVN pursuit of the retreating FAR units halted on 12 May.[21]

The FAR defeat was devastating and the retreat shameful, but some Americans gave the soldiers grudging credit. Major Marr argued that the FAR "gave a better account of themselves than during any previous engagements in the face of a Pathet Lao/North Vietnamese attack, which was well-planned, fully-coordinated, and skillfully executed."[22] The May 1962 Battle of Nam Tha in its own way was as significant as Dien Bien Phu, and the similarities were noted at the time. An overeager

General Nosavan had sent his best units—the paratroopers and artillery—into a geographically remote battleground, and as in 1954, everything climaxed in a PAVN victory that led to an agreement at Geneva.[23]

In the aftermath, the Americans were surprised to find that the FAR did not blame General Nosavan for the defeat, but the North Vietnamese. A Pathet Lao guerrilla and veteran of the fighting agreed stating years later, "After two or three big battles [at Nam Tha], the Vietnamese finally swept out the remaining Yao [the term for FAR volunteer troops]."[24] They were right. Had the battle been against the Pathet Lao, the FAR almost certainly would have prevailed. In 1961, Hanoi rated the Pathet Lao as too weak to achieve victory in Laos. The Americans drew the same conclusion; earlier on 26 November, U.S. advisors reported that FAR could deal with a purely Lao enemy. Averell Harriman expressed the same thought when reflecting on the battle in 1965.[25]

That might have been what General Nosavan was thinking when he sent his best forces into Nam Tha: He could beat the Pathet Lao while discounting the PAVN threat. In a similar misjudgment, he refused to accept what General Boyle described as the FAR's "almost pathological fear of the Vietnamese" who added that the FAR had "no stomach" for fighting them. Boyle was mostly right, and General Phoumi Nosavan mostly wrong. American advisors reported that from the start of the Nam Tha campaign in January, FAR troops routinely retreated at the first sign of khaki-clad PAVN regulars.[26]

The May 1962 Battle of Nam Tha, a manifestation of Hanoi's one battlefield philosophy, effectively ended its war in Laos that began in 1959. As hoped, the PAVN victory tilted the scales in the DRV's favor in Geneva. The real consequence of the war in Laos and PAVN success at Nam Tha, however, dealt with the war in South Vietnam. Having achieved its military objectives during the 1961 Ta Khong Offensive and at Nam Tha in 1962, the Politburo in Hanoi understood the significance of the gains, and they were going to fight to preserve them in Geneva. If successful there, then Hanoi could focus without distraction on the primary objective: victory over Saigon.[27]

By 1962, Hanoi was keen on accelerating the war in South Vietnam to the point where victory could be reached within several years. To do that, the DRV had to use the areas captured during the Ta Khong Offensive in eastern Middle and Lower Laos as a logistical pipeline to infiltrate troops and supplies into the RVN's open flank. And it had to solidify those gains at the negotiations table in Geneva. The Vietnam War was about to enter a critical phase still defined by Laos and centered on logistics and diplomacy.

Hanoi's Logistics War

To fulfill the objectives of Resolution 15, Hanoi had to take the dominant role in the reunification struggle in the south. Part of that mission became the DRV's logistics campaign, which began shortly before the conflict in Laos. And 1959 was not 1954, as the Democratic Republic had both greater resources and ambitions. Hanoi was confident it could fight on multiple fronts, and like Group 959 in Laos, the logistical efforts were dominated by two special units created that year. On 19 May, Ho Chi Minh's birthday, a team of PAVN soldiers that would become Group 559 was charged with carrying out overland infiltration, and in July, another team of soldiers who later formed the core of Group 759 was given responsibility for maritime infiltration into South Vietnam.[28]

It would take time to train and equip the maritime force, so overland infiltration adopted an aggressive timeline. To get it started, Colonel Vo Bam, an experienced logistician with experience in the DRV-RVN border region during the War of Resistance, was chosen for command. While not Resolution 15's most profound consequence—that was going to war—the decision to form Groups 559 and 759 in 1959 was one of its most amazing and successful outcomes. As with all facets of the new conflict, how the two groups fought their campaign—the logistical war—changed dramatically over time. Those changes, however, never detracted from its importance, and it was not by chance that Hanoi referred to the line of communication as "our strategic transportation route."[29]

Colonel Bam's first infiltration route of what became known as the Ho Chi Minh Trail—known endearingly by veterans as the "Old Man Trail"—had a modest start.[30] The only PAVN unit under Bam's control was the 308-soldier strong 301st Transportation Battalion drawn from the 305th Division. To get the project off the ground, the division also provided laborers who hewed out a rough path by hand in the far west of the DMZ near Khe Sanh. The trail began as a single pathway consisting of nine clandestine connecting stations running roughly parallel to Vietnam's western border with Laos along the Annamite Cordillera. By 20 August, the group had finished the first primitive stations that began in the DRV, crossed the DMZ, and then headed south some 70 kilometers into South Vietnam ending at Station 9 in the A Shau Valley, Thua Thien province. To maintain secrecy, when the bearers crossed South Vietnam's Highway 9, they walked on gunnysacks on the road so as to leave "no trace of their passage."[31] In those days, as Colonel Bui Tin related, "It was just a jungle trail for transporting goods on people's backs in deep baskets."[32]

Colonel Bam's command was formally expanded into Transportation Group 559 on 12 September 1959. The numerical designator signified its importance: May 1959. May was auspicious as it not only coincided with Ho's birthday, but also was the anniversary month of the victory over the French at Dien Bien Phu. The group initially headquartered near the port city of Vinh but later moved closer to the DMZ battlefront south of Dong Hoi by the Ben Hai River that separated the DRV from the RVN. It was seen as a sacred mission. The assigned PAVN soldiers would go on to build and operate an indestructible military line of communication between north and south. In the years to come, the trail spread out like a spider web to cover every possible route into South Vietnam and became one of the most versatile logistics systems in modern warfare.[33]

The trail was not a new concept; a nationwide logistics system had been created during the War of Resistance, and part of that system, the "Indochina Trail" begun in 1950, formed the model for the Ho Chi Minh Trail. At that time, a crude network of camps, roads, and pathways covering the western highlands of South Vietnam along the Annamite Cordillera, as well as eastern Laos and Cambodia, was established. The strategy of using Middle and Lower Laos as a base to allow attacks in the Central Highlands remained in effect. After PAVN soldiers chased out isolated FAR garrisons along the border with South Vietnam, Group 559 began running limited infiltration operations in Laos through a detachment from the 301st Battalion.[34]

At this stage, group operations were covert by necessity, as military movement through the DMZ and Laos violated the 1954 Accords. To disguise their presence, Group 559 soldiers wore civilian clothes and carried RVN identification cards. At this time, weapons sent south were either French or American captured during the War of Resistance or provided by China. That was done to give the appearance of having been captured in the south. To avoid discovery, widening or improving the trail was forbidden and motorized vehicles ruled out. As the trail could only support foot and bicycle traffic, the flow of supplies was limited and mirrored methods used earlier. During the War of Resistance, a human porter carried at most 55 pounds, to include his own equipment and supplies. They averaged a distance of 24 kilometers at day, less at night, with a bicyclist moving a farther distance. Adding to the limitations, porters consumed each week two and a half pounds of uncooked rice plus supplements for sustenance. Going south in 1959 initially proved difficult. The distances often did not exceed ten kilometers per day, and of the eight successful trips, only 2,000 weapons and 200 pounds of explosives plus other supplies were infiltrated.[35]

As events moved into 1960, the greater Ho Chi Minh Trail began to take shape. Simultaneous to the trail being built by Group 559, Nam Bo and MR-5 were moving north to connect their own networks to the trail; by October, it stretched from the DRV to the Mekong Delta. Control over the trail at that time came to be defined by these relationships: Group 559 ran operations in the DRV, northern RVN, and Laos, but once personnel or supplies reached the designated final station in either Nam Bo or MR-5, regional commanders took over further transshipments and distributions. Regardless of who was in charge, it was a perilously long journey as it could take six months to complete a passage to Nam Bo with some lost to injury or illness or death. In keeping with Resolution 15 and in light of the recent successes to include growing the trail, the VWP Central Committee directed southern comrades "to elevate the Southern Revolution to a new, higher stage."[36] By the end of 1960, the Ho Chi Minh Trail had been used to infiltrate 2,617 soldiers and cadres into South Vietnam, and an additional 1,174 weapons were delivered to the Viet Cong. The war became more lethal.[37]

The Return of the Regroupees

The name "regroupee" dated from the 1954 Geneva agreement that directed warring parties to regroup their forces to areas under their control, which after partition meant North Vietnam for the PAVN. The stay of southern regroupees was supposed to be short-lived with reunification expected by 1956, so many stayed behind despite Geneva. The Mekong Delta proved particularly problematic as of the 4,500 soldiers and VWP cadres in My Tho province, only 1,500 went north. But the Geneva admonition was not disregarded; the French estimated that 40,000 PAVN soldiers in South Vietnam headed north to be regrouped. There things stood until after the passing of Resolution 15 when it was decided to send the majority of the regroupees south to form the backbone for the Viet Cong. An added benefit of using regroupees was their ability to re-assimilate into the south, negating the need to be sustained by the fledgling Group 559.[38]

The idea for the return originated with General Tran Van Tra, a regroupee himself, who heard reports of Viet Cong fighting bravely but suffering due to poor training. He convinced Le Duan to send PAVN southerners to the RVN to provide needed training and leadership to make the VC more effective in battle. General Tra picked 25 soldiers (without Politburo authority) who left in mid–1959 for Nam Bo. It was a success, and VWP approval followed. Before he was sent to Laos, General Nguyen Chi Thanh then took over and sent the first official contingent of 542 small unit leaders, normally platoon and company commanders, along with NCOs. They trained during May and infiltrated in June, starting at Vinh Linh before crossing the Ben Hai River along the DMZ. By August they were back in the Central Highlands organizing VC units. A third group left in 1959 as well, a small detachment of 30 PAVN Montagnard regroupees that also infiltrated into the Central Highlands. The trip took about two months. The southerners referred to them as the "autumn cadres" as most had left the south in the autumn of 1954.[39]

To facilitate training, the 338th Division was dissolved and its troops divided between those sent back south and those assigned to Group 338, who trained the troops going to South Vietnam. As in the first groups, subsequent PAVN regroupees selected to go south were primarily officers and NCOs who would serve as leaders and staff officers of provincial guerrilla and Main Force units (from battalion commanders on down), trainers, sappers, and other specialists. Their preparatory training in the DRV was tailored to those duties. Being veteran soldiers, regroupees normally required only a month of specialized instruction with a heavy emphasis on political indoctrination, and upon graduation, were promoted in rank. In those early years, that included weapons training on the French and American arms. Forced marches with heavy field packs also became a training staple. On the trail, they had neither money nor weapons that were not issued until arrival at their final destination. Until 1964, regroupees additionally were reequipped with non–PAVN military gear, and their southern dialects disguised their origin.[40]

Operations accelerated, and by mid–1961 multiple groups were departing each month. Also by that time, the north was sending heavier crew-served weapons down the trail to the Central Highlands. And that year, the first "framework" contingent, the Nam Phong Group, was sent south. It was organized into several 200-soldier detachments, each of which provided the leaders and specialists needed to form a 2,000-soldier regiment. All that was needed were basic soldiers and arms. Absent the regroupees, it would have taken the VC years to develop the needed senior company, battalion, and regimental leaders, staff, and specialists.[41]

The regroupees and handpicked VWP cadres ensured Hanoi's control over the revolution, especially in Nam Bo. After departing in May, on 28 July 1961 the 500-strong Orient Group led by General Tran Van Quang, who became deputy COSVN military affairs committee chair, arrived in Binh Long province near

Cambodia (about 100 kilometers north of Saigon). The name "orient" reflected both Hanoi's revolutionary aspirations and the hardships then faced in traversing the Ho Chi Minh Trail; the group left just after the Soviets launched the first manned space-ship, Orient 1 (Vostok 1), with Cosmonaut Yuri Gagarin onboard. Like the historic space mission, the Orient Group embarked on a long dangerous journey into the unknown to advance the socialist revolution. A second 400-strong special group under Colonel Le Quoc San reached Nam Bo in September. Colonel San then took command of MR-8 in the Mekong Delta. Together, these senior and mid-level cadres and PAVN officers filled out the COSVN, regional and provincial party central and military affairs committees, and were an important part of the total of 5,000 regrou-pees and cadres that arrived in the RVN in 1961.[42]

Regroupees were not just veterans used to stiffen the Viet Cong or become the "framework" of a new unit. On occasion in the early years, they formed the bulk of VC Main Force units where only foot soldiers were needed to fill out the forma-tion. One group became the 70th VC Battalion in Quang Tin province. Another was the 271st PAVN Regiment. In early 1961, a number of regroupees from the 324th Division were reassigned to the regiment at Vinh that was training for the 1961 Ta Khong Offensive in Laos. Once there, they received additional training for fight-ing with the Viet Cong in South Vietnam. At the conclusion of the operation, most of the soldiers then pushed on into South Vietnam and in July became the 761th VC Regiment in Tay Ninh province, although it was a little larger than a battalion in size. It became a two-battalion regiment in 1962 and renamed the 1st Nam Bo Reg-iment in late 1963.[43]

During the first four years of the war, regroupees were the large majority of the infiltrators. In 1963, that dropped to 30 percent with the rest being PAVN regu-lars. At that time, PAVN groups deployed as platoons and companies to form larger VC units. Going forward, every PAVN soldier heading south was a northerner. By then, Hanoi had sent over 40,000 PAVN soldiers south, and an estimated 27,000 were regroupees. But again, it was not just the numbers but where they went. Regrou-pees were not sent to the VC militia; they went to the big units, the nascent provin-cial guerrilla and Main Force battalions. According to the official PAVN war history, by the close of 1963, PAVN infiltrators comprised half of the VC Main Force units and 80 percent of the cadres, staff officers, and technical experts. That was their real value. In comparison, there were 16,000 U.S. advisors in the RVN in 1963, and while the American role was restricted, PAVN soldiers carried out full-spectrum combat duties.[44]

Finally, the propaganda war over infiltration was not forgotten. Despite the massive influx of northern soldiers, Hanoi continued to deny that any PAVN sol-diers were fighting in the south; it similarly denied the existence of the Ho Chi Minh Trail. Hanoi even had the confidence and audacity to complain publicly about the increased number of U.S. advisors. The story went that the VC threat stemmed from a home-grown insurgency that did not need support from the north, and it was the Americans who were wrongly escalating the war. The lie worked in many quarters around the world.[45]

Maritime Infiltration

Concurrent with the overland infiltration and to expand support to the armed Viet Cong, Hanoi initiated parallel seaborne infiltration operations in 1959. Like Group 559, what became Group 759, the unit responsible for seaborne operations, was headquartered near Vinh and had a humble beginning: the lone 603rd Special Battalion with 107 soldiers. A year later, it was fully staffed and busily conducting small-scale operations that snuck couriers, weapons, other military supplies into the RVN via junks and sampans. Because seaborne infiltration was more difficult than movement by foot, operations began slowly. An early try in late 1959 by a small group of couriers failed three times due to rough weather at sea, and they were captured during a fourth attempt in January 1960. Ironically, the arrests led the South Vietnamese and Americans to believe that the maritime operations were militarily inconsequential. The Americans began supporting the RVN Navy's Junk Patrol Force in March 1961 and considered infiltration from the sea blocked by early 1962. Going forward, they opted not to devote significant additional resources to counter PAVN maritime infiltration efforts.[46]

The bumpy start did not reveal its significance. As vital as the trail became, what happened at sea in the early years of the war often was as, if not more, important. Unlike the trail where personnel movement was central, maritime operations aimed to deliver weapons and munitions, and with the arrival of Chinese and Soviet arms, there were over 100,000 older French and U.S. weapons available to ship south. Given Viet Cong weakness, the weapons and their munitions often were more valuable than experienced PAVN soldiers, and the hope was that maritime infiltration would open a fast infiltration route all the way to Nam Bo. It was dangerous work with secrecy paramount. To covertly operate, the "fishing boats" needed to originate in the RVN with South Vietnamese crews and papers and from southern ports. Furthermore, clandestine landing sites had to be developed within VC controlled areas in the south with access to pro–VC local laborers who could rapidly and discreetly unload the vessels, ideally at night.[47]

Faced with those challenges, Group 759 did not become operational until June 1961, but steady progress was made. By early 1962, covert VC from four Nam Bo provinces sailed six motorized junks to the DRV for training and to begin the infiltrations. By April, various craft had completed 21 trips to Nam Bo delivering 60 tons of weapons and munitions without being detected by South Vietnamese security forces. That month, the first Mekong Delta landing site opened in southernmost Ca Mau province. A second, also in Ca Mau, became operational in October. Ocean Transport Group 962 (formed in the delta during September 1962) carried out the unloading and distribution operations.[48]

As the war in the Mekong Delta was an insurgency, Group 962 used everything from porters and oxcarts to cyclos, cars, and trucks to secretly disperse the arms, munitions, and other supplies. Concurrently, more boats and crews were recruited and trained for duty with Group 759. Junks and small ships—some with 20–30 ton holds—soon sailed up the coast from the delta to the DRV, uploaded, and then returned home to disperse their hidden cargo. Those advances gradually improved the combat power of the Viet Cong forces by delivering hundreds of tons of arms, munitions, and explosives. And the ships also continued to ferry couriers, important cadres, and intelligence operatives.[49]

In January 1963, as part of a general PAVN reorganization in preparation for expanding the war, Group 759 was renamed Naval Group 125, and its duties and responsibilities were transferred to the Coastal Defense Force. With the Ca Mau landing sites up and running, crew-served heavy weapons were arriving in impressive numbers in Nam Bo and were shifting the balance of battlefield combat power in the VC's favor. Shipments steadily increased. In all, Group 125 executed 25 round trip shipments by year's end that delivered 1,430 tons of weapons, munitions, explosives, and other critical military supplies including precious heavy machine guns, medium mortars, and recoilless rifles. It had become clear that Viet Cong success in battle in Nam Bo often depended on DRV material support delivered from the sea by Naval Group 125.[50]

The Ho Chi Minh Trail Expands

While 1961 marked the beginning of maritime infiltration, it also proved to be a transformative moment for the Ho Chi Minh Trail, with the PAVN's Ta Khong offensive being the catalyst. Its success allowed Hanoi to redirect strategic supplies to the western Annamite Mountain chain—to "flip" the main trail from the RVN to Laos. The mission took on added urgency on 29 March 1961, when the ARVN discovered and destroyed the Calu trail station. Captured documents revealed that the station assisted in guiding an estimated 1,840 regroupees during the October 1960–March 1961 period, over 300 per month on average. This alerted ARVN units along the DMZ who initiated aggressive efforts to stop the infiltration and drove Group 559 to further develop the overland routes in Laos. Despite the setback, the victories in Laos so encouraged Hanoi that in late-1961, the Politburo opted to send an additional 25,000 PAVN soldiers into the RVN by 1963.[51]

As soon as the critical parts of Middle Laos were captured in 1961, PAVN engineers went to work improving the trail's new Laos-based main branch. The ban on vehicular traffic was lifted, and the CMPC directed Group 559 to "develop capacity for mechanized transport over new routes still deeper into Laos."[52] Given its new orders, overcoming the border terrain presented advantages and challenges. Virtually all of it, aside from rare crop fields in the sparsely populated region, consisted of rolling or rough hills covered with multiple-canopy forest that were difficult but easier to traverse than the trail in the RVN. Given the lack of population and overhead vegetation that prevented detection by aircraft, they could improve the speed and magnitude of infiltration while operating in secrecy. Hanoi saw it as a superior solution. Leaders in Washington drew the opposite conclusion. In the words of Roger Hilsman, director of the State Department's Bureau of Intelligence and Research (INR), the Americans did not believe the trail could "be used as a major source of supplies and equipment."[53] The CIA concurred.[54]

It arguably was the largest PAVN wartime engineering effort until then. In addition to the 325th Division's engineers who improved the French airfield at Tchepone, the 25th and 26th Engineer Battalions arrived and were followed by the 98th Engineer Regiment from the strategic reserve. Before returning to the DRV, they turned Tchepone and the surrounding region into one of East Asia's largest military logistics bases and built a 130 kilometer road to connect Routes 9 and 12 (aptly named Route 912) that allowed supplies and troops to be sent by truck from the DRV to the RVN border. Despite rainy season hardships and formidable terrain, the road opened in December. The importance of having flipped the Ho Chi Minh Trail to Laos was already evident by late 1961 and explained how the VC sped up the advance to Giap's Phase 3 mobile conventional war.[55]

After completion of the road, General Rear Services Department (GRSD) trucks began delivering soldiers and supplies to Tchepone, which became known as Base Area (BA) 604, the most important logistics center of the war. Operations centered on the weather. The fall rainy season reduced vehicular traffic, so war materials were accumulated in secret DRV base areas near the passes. Once the monsoons subsided, primary operations shifted to Laos with a maximum effort made during the winter-spring dry season. Simultaneous with the arrival of the trucks, which now had the responsibility to deliver supplies and troops from the DRV to BA 604, Group 559's 301st Transportation Battalion was expanded into the 70th Transportation Regiment and assumed duties of transporting military supplies and troops from the Tchepone base area to MR-5 and Nam Bo, although most troops still marched by foot.[56]

The regiment operated along rugged trails that, as in the old RVN track, entered the RVN's A Shau Valley and extensions that inched toward the Central Highlands and Cambodia. While the GRSD used trucks to get its supplies through, the 70th Regiment relied on bicycles, porters, and horses, and as Laos was once known as the "Kingdom of a Million Elephants," a number of pachyderms were put to work as well. By operating in the safety of Laos, their bicycles were able to receive an upgrade to reinforced-frames—a favorite was the Chinese-made Phoenix model—nicknamed "steel horses." They were moved by two-porter teams and could transport up to 550 pounds of supplies with marches set at an average of ten kilometers a day.[57] The trails from BA 604 opened in July, and new waves of PAVN regroupees arrived in the Central Highlands by August 1962.[58]

For protection, the 325C PAVN Division stood guard in MR-4 near the Laotian stretch of the trail, while the 25th and newly arrived 27th Engineer Battalions maintained the roads. Additionally, the Tchepone airfield became a destination for the 919th Air Transportation Regiment, the unit of the Battle of Nam Tha fame, and it began delivering mortars, recoilless rifles, and light artillery. By the end of 1961, Group 559 had grown to nearly 3,000 soldiers and several times that size by late 1962. Hanoi avowed its actions in Laos were taken to stem American imperialist ambition, but as far as Middle Laos was concerned, this was territory needed for the Ho Chi Minh Trail. Without it, enlarging and sustaining the war of reunification with the south was not possible. As in 1954, the DRV had achieved Giap's goal of making Laos the base for attacks into central Vietnam.

The 1961–1962 PAVN offensives had allowed the Ho Chi Minh Trail to switch over to Laos, to the great benefit of Hanoi. The regroupees and supplies sent down the trail began to transform the war of reunification, and the efforts proved indispensable to the war effort. Once again, Hanoi gambled and won on a daring large-scale and covert operation that brought the DRV closer to victory. But nothing was secure. The international reaction to the battle of Nam Tha threatened everything that had been gained by jumpstarting negotiations in Geneva aimed at forcing foreign forces out of Laos.[59]

12

End of the Laos Crisis:
A Solution that Doomed the Peace

The PAVN victory at Nam Tha achieved much of what Hanoi had hoped for. In the immediate aftermath, General Nosavan was thoroughly discredited and for a time lost much if not all of his influence with the Americans. Prince Souvanna became even more dedicated to Laotian neutralization, as did leaders in the Soviet Union and United Kingdom, the two co-chairs of the peace talks. That created a new impetus in Geneva to resolve the Laotian crisis, but PAVN military success did not mean Hanoi had a free hand diplomatically. It simply meant its position was stronger, and any agreement had to be one that satisfied the competing goals and objectives of the United States and the Democratic Republic of Vietnam.

American Perspectives

Washington approached the Laotian crisis foremost as one battlefront in the global Cold War that was heating up. The start of the 1961 PAVN Offensive in Laos coincided with the Bay of Pigs fiasco in Cuba, that was followed by the Berlin Crisis in June. Crisis management took on new meaning. From that vantage, Washington followed the Europe First strategy adopted during World War II. President Kennedy did not want a two-front conflict in both Europe and Southeast Asia. The challenges did not stop there. During an April 1961 meeting with former Vice President Richard Nixon, President Kennedy told him, "I don't see how we can make any move in Laos, which is thousands of miles away, if we don't make a move in Cuba, which is only 90 miles away." Berlin and Cuba were of greater importance than a small land-locked nation in Southeast Asia.[1]

Events changed priorities. Laos no longer held the position of the "key to Southeast Asia" given to it by President Eisenhower. The growing war in South Vietnam had supplanted the importance of Laos in the minds of many Americans, and as Dean Rusk saw it, the Laotians were not in a bitter civil war. In a 1961 incident, local FAR and Pathet Lao troops quit the battlefield to jointly celebrate a water festival. He considered them gentle, civilized people who had no interest in killing each other. Kennedy also did not see the use of U.S. military force as a solution and wanted to turn Laos into a land-locked buffer state to reduce the risk of conflict in the region.[2]

Even within Southeast Asia, Thailand remained centermost in American regional security strategy, followed by South Vietnam and then Laos. Both Eisenhower and Kennedy realized that Laos had to be split into informal spheres of influence or partitioned, where the United States sought to keep communist forces off the Laotian frontiers of Thailand and South Vietnam, while recognizing that having hostile anti-communist Laotian forces backed by the United States on the borders with China and North Vietnam did not serve anyone's interests. There also was a tendency in Washington to see Laos as a discrete problem apart from the war in South Vietnam and a conviction that it could be handled sequentially first before addressing South Vietnam. The thinking went that in a worse-case scenario, if pressure were applied to America on too many fronts in the Cold War, Laos would be of a tertiary concern, and its strategic value might not rise above that of a bargaining chip.[3]

Finally, many Americans still saw the communist bloc as a monolithic entity under Moscow's ultimate control. This was especially true with senior leaders, beginning with Rusk and Secretary of Defense Robert S. McNamara. Had it been a decade or so earlier, the two would have been correct, but the death of Stalin in 1953 followed by the Sino-Soviet rift a few years later ended Moscow's supremacy. Unfortunately, the Americans had yet to fully grasp that reality. Nothing revealed the fallacy of monolithic communism better than Resolution 15—Hanoi's unilateral 1959 decision to start the war—but due to its secrecy, the Americans had no clear understanding of the resolution.[4]

Harriman, who also believed in Moscow's dominant role, was put in charge of Washington's efforts in Geneva and by extension, Southeast Asia. When he arrived in Indochina on 2 May 1961, Diem was one of the first leaders he met in his new duties, and Diem strongly warned that if Laos fell, then South Vietnam would not survive. He held that the loss of Laos would "open all doors to mass infiltration or invasion" by North Vietnam.[5] Diem was right about the danger. The DMZ between North and South Vietnam stretched 75 kilometers, which was long but defensible if the ARVN was committed there in force. The border with Laos ran for over 400 kilometers, and it was impossible for the ARVN to defend both.[6]

If the Ho Chi Minh Trail expanded into Cambodia, as the old Viet Minh Indochina Trail had done in the early 1950s, then border defense became a meaningless term. When the two met, Harriman shared Diem's concern but did not take to Diem's argument that a neutral Laotian coalition government under Prince Souvanna would ensure PAVN infiltration. Having heard enough, Harriman—who detested long meetings—insultingly turned off his hearing aid and dozed as Diem droned on. The two parted on a sour note even though Harriman henceforth worked to diplomatically deny the DRV infiltration routes from Laos into the RVN.[7]

To achieve that goal, the Americans placed great faith in the ICC. If two security objectives could be obtained in Geneva—a Soviet guarantee of a PAVN withdrawal from Laos backed up by ICC enforcement action on the ground—then a political solution seemed more than possible, as the White House fully supported the neutralization of Laos. Similar opinions were held in Congress, where the influential Senator Mike Mansfield advocated the ICC-backed neutralization solution that followed the approach used along the Pakistan-Indian border. As Rusk put it,

"The US does not oppose a neutral policy for Laos, so long as the Lao government desires it and it can in fact be maintained."[8]

The DRV's Perspective

Hanoi faced a different but no less complex set of foreign policy challenges well before the 1962 Battle of Nam Tha. In 1961, General Giap wrote that the United States' goal in Laos was "aimed at turning it into a colony and military base for a new war of aggression."[9] He was wrong, but revolutionary rhetoric provided cover to mask Hanoi's primary aim to use Laos to defeat South Vietnam. Its next major objective was to get the U.S. military mission out of Laos, as Laos also was perceived by Hanoi as an essential buffer between the DRV and America's Thai allies. Finally, the goal of incorporating Laos into a VWP-led socialist federation never went away. The DRV's vision was never a neutral Laos as discussed in Geneva; that would cripple its ability to wage war in South Vietnam and expose it to potential attack along its border. Neutralization for Hanoi meant a kingdom forgotten by the powers combined with the expansion of the Ho Chi Minh Trail and establishment of base areas across from the RVN border. While the negotiations were underway in 1961, Hanoi issued those exact orders to the PAVN: expand the trail and build base areas. As in 1954, Hanoi had mapped out its Laos strategy that either ignored or contradicted what its diplomats were agreeing to in Geneva.[10]

While the DRV had no global security commitments beyond political support of international communist socialist struggles, their return support, especially in the case of the Soviet Union and China, was vital to winning the war of reunification. That made the ongoing Sino-Soviet split a diplomatic minefield that Hanoi had to successfully navigate if it hoped to defeat South Vietnam. Adding to the sensitivity, as Hanoi had done with Resolution 15, it failed to inform Beijing or Moscow of its intent to intervene in Laos in 1959. Moscow used it to their advantage in the confrontation with Beijing. While Soviet Chairman Nikita S. Khrushchev opposed Hanoi expanding the war in South Vietnam, he wanted a neutral Laos that benefited the DRV. Afterwards Moscow used military aid to Hanoi, especially that going to Laos, both to help Hanoi and as a message to Beijing that it had interests in the region that had to be respected. The Sino-Soviet split had reared its ugly head again, and Hanoi had the difficult task of keeping both powers on its side.[11]

Diplomatically, China was more supportive of Hanoi's aggressive position, but it was a tricky proposition. Like Khrushchev, Mao wanted a neutral Laos, but unlike the Soviets, he supported Hanoi's expanding war against Saigon. And as in 1954, while Beijing opposed a Western military presence near its border, it did make clear to Hanoi that it did not want the DRV to dominate Laos. To stress the point, China began to provide direct aid to Laos that previously had been coordinated with the DRV. Hanoi in turn gained Beijing's favor by calling for the withdrawal of American forces in Laos and not obstructing Beijing's overtures to Prince Souvanna that increased China's influence. The DRV did not, however, relinquish its dominant position in Laos, which years later did lead to friction with China. When it came to the central issue, choosing China or the Soviets, Hanoi was circumspect. The DRV sided with Beijing in private but never publicly crossed Moscow during the crisis in Laos. Other differences remained.[12]

Hanoi and Beijing argued over what Laotian terrain had to be controlled as the ceasefire lines were being finalized in Geneva. In August 1961, China, seeking a friendly buffer, supported a north-south partition of Laos giving the Pathet Lao Upper Laos and the pro–Western Laotians Lower and much of Middle Laos. The DRV strongly objected, as such a demarcation would sever the Ho Chi Minh Trail. During a 23 October meeting, the DRV not only opposed demarcation but also turned against other tentative agreements over cease-fire lines favored by China, as they would adversely affect the war in South Vietnam. Hanoi wanted Laos informally divided along east-west lines. By November, Beijing came around. It now reasoned that a land bridge joining anti-communist RVN, pro–Western Laotian factions, and Thailand would create a unified bloc hostile to China. Beijing would support Hanoi's east-west position.[13]

That left Moscow to be won over, and it proved difficult. Encouragingly, the Soviets were willing to meet their allies halfway. In November 1960, the international convention of 81 communist and worker parties in Moscow adopted a platform to support revolutionary struggles. That helped reassure Beijing and Hanoi that Moscow was not rigidly following Khrushchev's peaceful coexistence policy. But socialist solidarity did not hold during the Laos crisis once the Americans assumed a major role. For Moscow, aiding wars of liberation in Africa was different from forcing confrontation between the world's two nuclear-armed superpowers. To avoid that, during their private 1961 consultations, Moscow stated it was willing to cut support to the Pathet Lao and comply with neutralization to reach a settlement.[14]

The Soviets, like the Americans, did not see Laos as a primary security issue, and Khrushchev continued to throw his support behind neutrality. While troubling, Hanoi was not alarmed; Moscow never exerted much pressure to restrain the DRV's actions in Indochina. As in the 1954 Geneva talks, its disinterest worked to Hanoi's favor as absent a vital interest in Laos, Moscow acceded to the DRV's positions as long as neutralization was achieved. More disturbingly for the DRV, the Soviets continued to oppose military escalation in South Vietnam (it cut off airlifts to Tchepone in December 1961 after discovering the Pathet Lao arms shipments were being diverted to the RVN), and Hanoi had to thread the needle. When the diplomats met in Geneva in late 1961, both China and the Soviet Union backed Hanoi's goals and objectives, but Moscow soon lost interest both in the events in Laos and South Vietnam as well. That was fine with Hanoi, having gotten what it needed from Moscow and Beijing. All that was left was to put real pressure on the Americans, and that was when the plan for the Nam Tha offensive had first come to life.[15]

American Efforts in 1962

As Hanoi anticipated, the Nam Tha battle moved the United States to act. When ramifications of the disaster reverberated across Washington, the White House sent a message that the aggression would not go unanswered. McNamara, who was in Saigon with Joint Chiefs of Staff (JCS) Chairman General Lyman L. Lemnitzer and Admiral Felt, discussed the defeat. They did not reach consensus for strong action but agreed to prepare. On 10 May, President Kennedy authorized the buildup of forces in Thailand for possible intervention in Laos. Strong elements of the U.S. 7th Fleet were ordered to the Gulf of Siam, and dozens of U.S. Air Force and Marine aircraft began to arrive in Thailand. They were joined by contingents from Britain, Australia, and New Zealand.[16]

On the ground, a U.S. Army combat group built around the 17th Infantry Regiment joined Thai Army units preparing to move to the Laotian border, and U.S. Marine Battalion Landing Team (BLT) 3/9 came ashore. Combined Joint Task Force 116 headquarters, formed in late 1959 when the Laos crisis first arose, arrived from Japan to take command of the U.S. forces. That month the U.S. Army 9th Logistics Command also deployed to Thailand to prepare lines of communication to support a military campaign if it proved necessary. Finally, the Joint U.S. Military Advisory Group-Thailand was activated on 15 May. The seriousness of the situation was not lost in Geneva.[17]

The PAVN's Nam Tha victory changed the political dynamics against Washington, but even before the battle, the Americans had their hands full with their Laotians allies who rightly feared that protecting Laos was not the priority in Geneva. When negotiations stalled over PAVN withdrawal guarantees and ICC authority, the Americans pressured the Phoumi Nosavan–Prince Boun Oum delegation to soften their objections. By this time Harriman had become frustrated with the lack of progress. He had thrown in the towel on a robust ICC. As he saw it, if the Pathet Lao wanted to keep the ICC out of certain places, then that was that, regardless of the Geneva provisions. The bad feelings between Nosavan and Harriman also had come to a head earlier in March when the general balked at attending a meeting with Harriman, after which the general became "public enemy No. 1" within Harriman's circle.[18] INR Director Roger Hilsman, a close Harriman ally, later reflected on the difficulties: "A small and supposedly weak ally can be powerful in stubbornness," and that was how Harriman and Hilsman saw Phoumi Nosavan.[19]

What Hilsman omitted was that powers often put weak allies in a bind. Powers resist committing blood and treasure and therefore pressure a weak ally to negotiate "realistically," as it was put in the case of Laos.[20] In the same breath, the power's desire for settlement often leads to a willingness to accommodate demands by the other side that endanger the weak ally, making it all the more wary and hesitant. The underlying premise, that the power would come to the aid of the weak ally, was a risk vulnerable weak states found perilous if not acceptable. For the weak ally, its fate would be decided by how quickly the power recognized the danger and acted. When Harriman told Phoumi Nosavan that the Soviets guaranteed PAVN withdrawal from Laos, a Nosavan advisor who did not take Harriman seriously responded, "You have played your [Cold War] game. For us it is a matter of life and death."[21] Such concerns, deeply shared by Saigon, were not recognized in Washington.

Unaware that the PAVN's Nam Tha offensive had been planned months in advance, the State Department was clear in pinning responsibility for the crisis on

General Nosavan. The British reached the same conclusion. Harriman declared that the general was "a soldier out of step" and went to work on knocking him into line.[22] The British and French also were fed up with the general, but when Harriman argued for his ouster, they opposed the move, seeing nothing to be gained. Admiral Felt at CINCPAC spotted the disconnect and was troubled enough to ask why the Western Allies were not applying as much pressure on the communist side as on Nosavan. The White House also had misgivings, and on 22 May President Kennedy let it be known he wanted Harriman to ease up. Progress was being made.[23]

On 11 June 1962, the Three Princes reconfirmed their commitment to a coalition government and took the further step of reaffirming Prince Souvanna as leader. The next day, General Nosavan and Prince Boun Oum met with Souvanna and agreed to another ceasefire, while Boun Oum gave up his claim to the prime ministership. The Western Allies were delighted. With the road to a solution over the Laos crisis open, the consensus was that Nosavan "behaved more or less like a little soldier," and the general was once again in Washington's good graces.[24] The Laotian crisis entered a new phase.[25]

Having made a show of force and gotten its Laotian allies in line, the Americans gave ground in Geneva on both the infiltration and ICC issues but not without serious internal debate that extended into June 1962. Intense argument surrounded any changes to the hard anti-infiltration position. Harriman overcame the opposition, principally the military to include MAAG-Vietnam commander General Lionel C. McGarr, by arguing that the Ho Chi Minh Trail did not pose a serious threat to South Vietnam. A Hilsman report cited by Undersecretary of State Robert H. Johnson in an influential 9 June memorandum stated that the trail was "used principally to bring in cadre and probably some organized units" plus "limited quantities of specialized supplies" that were "not decisive considering total Viet Cong needs."[26] As the memorandum sadly revealed, the Americans had no insight into the extensive activities of PAVN Groups 559 and 759.[27]

The debate, as it had between Hanoi and Beijing, then shifted to the unofficial partition of Laos with the same two choices: either a north-south partition again along the 17th parallel to close the Ho Chi Minh Trail (a solution Diem pushed) or an east-west partition. There was not really a choice. The demarcation of the fighting forces put in place by the ceasefire followed an east-west pattern, and an east-west partition created a defensive buffer for Thailand, Washington's top security priority in Southeast Asia. It also gave the pro–Western Laotian side control of both its capitals as well as the important Mekong River lowlands all connected by the strategic Route 13. To fully overcome the opposition, Harriman continued to stress that the trail did not pose a major risk to the security of South Vietnam. Most in Washington optimistically believed that a Geneva neutrality agreement could work with formal partition avoided.[28]

To further bolster the argument of dismissing the Ho Chi Minh Trail, a new RAND study showed that the trail in the Annamite Mountains was primitive, of limited logistical use, and virtually worthless during the rainy season. The vital logistical passage remained Route 13. As Hilsman later recounted, "The State Department made the most," of the RAND study.[29] When it came to bureaucratic infighting, Hilsman often was a pit bull, and that was true during the debates over the trail. He heatedly argued that even "a wall fifty miles high along the infiltration routes" would fail. It was a "straw man" argument that actually made his opponents' point: No army could defend the RVN's long border with Laos making the trail a great threat.[30]

Hilsman also had misrepresented the RAND findings. They addressed the current situation and did not offer a strategic assessment of the Ho Chi Minh Trail's potentialities or capabilities. (It only projected out 40 days from the outbreak of a hypothetical limited war in 1962.) Rufus Phillips noted this trait in Hilsman during a contemporaneous visit by Hilsman to South Vietnam, stating that he "was not a good listener unless what he heard matched his preconceived ideas."[31] Harriman and Hilsman simply refused to entertain the possibility that Hanoi would expand the trail. Writing in 1964, Hilsman outlined their assumptions in 1962; the PAVN would not make a significant effort to improve the trail, and their presence would be "small and inconspicuous."[32] Harriman and Hilsman could not have been more mistaken as they addressed what the trail could become or the long-term danger it posed. The two convinced their opponents that holding Route 13 while ceding the Ho Chi Minh Trail terrain to the enemy was an advantageous compromise.[33]

Assistant Secretary of State for Far Eastern Affairs Roger Hilsman in 1963. A decorated officer who fought behind Japanese lines with the OSS in World War II, Hilsman was driven and combative. He became convinced that Diem was the obstacle to winning the war in South Vietnam and played a crucial role in the coup plotting to topple Diem in 1963 (John F. Kennedy Presidential Library).

To further reassure his critics, Harriman also had been working with the Soviets, and earlier on 15 May he obtained affirmation from Ambassador Anatoly Dobrynin in Washington that Moscow wanted a free and neutral Laos. This reconfirmed for Harriman the earlier pledge by Pushkin that Moscow's guarantee of neutrality was so rock solid that the ICC would have nothing to do. On the same day, Ambassador Thompson in Moscow warned that the Soviets were having less success in controlling Hanoi than Washington had with Nosavan. Soviet promises were not rock solid.[34]

Thompson's concerns aside and based on the assurances of Pushkin and Dobrynin and the State Department's reassuring assessment of the Ho Chi Minh Trail, Washington decided to drop the demand for verifiable guarantees of PAVN withdrawal with the caveat that future action through "continuous political pressure on the Soviets" could stop infiltration.[35] A similar compromise was made regarding the ICC. Harriman, still imbued with confidence in Soviet primacy, obtained a promise from Moscow that the ICC would operate as required. Given earlier Soviet promises to keep Hanoi under control, the optimism in Washington swelled on 23 June when Souvanna became prime minister.[36]

Washington's last task was overcoming Diem's resistance to the Geneva agreement based on a lack of guarantees to close the Ho Chi Minh Trail. He had been raising the issue since he first met Harriman in May 1961 and reiterated his concern when the details of the Pathet Lao–controlled areas along the RVN border were presented that September. He was still trying to work through the system to keep the PAVN and Pathet Lao away from the RVN's Laotian border. In May 1962, he sent a formal letter to the Commission asking for a "system of ICC controls" to prevent infiltration along the Laotian-RVN border and the DMZ.[37] No action was taken.[38]

It did not help Harriman that American Ambassador Nolting in Saigon agreed with Diem, stating that as far as halting infiltration from Laos was concerned, "all of the safeguards had been removed."[39] Harriman's arguments, pleas, and threats had no effect, and as late as 6 July, Diem still balked at signing the Geneva accord. At Harriman's request, President Diem received a private letter of assurance from President Kennedy on 10 July that finally gained South Vietnam's support. With the last hurdle behind them, a consensus in Geneva was obtained and the protocol signed on 23 July.[40]

The 1962 Geneva Settlement

The settlement was actually two documents. The first was "The Declaration on the Neutrality of Laos" presented by the Royal Laotian Government that had been accepted in Geneva on 9 July 1962. It was unchanged from the 22 June 1961 joint communiqué issued by the Three Princes. All parties accepted the fiction of a unified government and held a credible ceasefire feasible. The most troubling aspects were vows in Declaration 4 not to allow "any country to use Laotian territory for military purposes of interfering in the internal affairs of other countries" and Declaration 6 to "require the withdrawal from Laos of all foreign troops and military personnel, and not allow any foreign troops or military personnel to be introduced Laos."[41] The Laotian government had no means or will to enforce either declaration. The United States pinned its hopes on the ICC combined with separate Soviet assurances obtained by Harriman to rein in the DRV.[42]

The second document, the multiparty "Protocol to the Declaration on the Neutrality of Laos," also contained its share of problematic clauses all centered on Washington's two greatest concerns: (1) withdrawal of the PAVN (Article 2) and the ban on future entry into Laos of the PAVN and (2) war materials to be used against South Vietnam (Articles 4 and 6). To accomplish this, Washington adopted a full compliance posture that not only pulled out U.S. military personnel by the October deadline, but also CIA paramilitary officers along with allied Filipino military and paramilitary personnel. Similarly, Moscow halted its assistance, and Red Air Force aircrews returned to the Soviet Union (with their aircraft turned over to the PAVN).

The Americans hoped that DRV aggression in Laos could be curtailed by a good faith effort on their part that would gain ICC and Royal Laotian Government support in enforcing the protocol. By abiding by the letter and spirit of the protocol, Washington upheld its end of the neutralization bargain made with Moscow, and the Americans remained confident that the Soviets could stop DRV violations.[43]

Geneva Aftermath: Violations for All

Days after the protocol was signed in Geneva, Prince Souvanna visited the White House and met with President Kennedy and other senior administration officials. There was still a glow of optimism and, in the case of the Souvanna, what appeared to be a stunning display of naiveté. The Americans at every level pressed Souvanna over PAVN infiltration from Laos into South Vietnam. Souvanna reassured them by stating that he had talked to the DRV's prime minister, Pham Van Dong, who denied that any PAVN soldiers had entered the RVN—through Laos or by any other means—only cadres. President Kennedy held that was a distinction without a difference and infiltration a serious problem. The prince incongruously countered with a hypothetical untouched by fact that the PAVN would not use Laos for infiltration because it would "be easy to control this."[44] How was left unsaid. The sole point of agreement was a shared belief that the ICC would prevent infiltration or other protocol violations.[45]

American positive thinking persevered as all waited to see what would happen after the 7 October foreign troop withdrawal deadline. Trust in the ICC and the Soviets still ran strong. Dobrynin sent the first warning sign that something was amiss during an August lunch with Harriman. While all the right things were said, the Russian was uneasily vague about what the DRV was up to and whether it would abide by the protocol. As August and September passed, the PAVN took no observable action in Laos; while there had been over ten thousand PAVN troops in Laos in May, the ICC reported less than 50 "technicians" had departed the Kingdom through their checkpoints by the October deadline. It was a prearranged charade, and the timing for Hanoi ideal. Washington was fully occupied by the Cuban Missile Crisis that began on 17 October and said nothing.[46]

What the Americans did not know at the time was that during the Geneva negotiations, Prince Souvanna secretly reached an agreement with the DRV that permitted them to use Laos as an infiltration route into South Vietnam. The prince would not allow the ICC either to inspect the Ho Chi Minh Trail area or use the Geneva protocol to call out Hanoi for violating Laotian neutrality. What the prince got in return is not known. For Hanoi it was sweet victory; control over the Laotian–South Vietnamese border was a goal it had pursued in vain since the 1954 Geneva talks.[47]

Washington had been conned, but being in the dark, continued to believe the Soviets would enforce the agreements. As PAVN withdrawal looked more and more suspect that October, both Hilsman at the State Department and Michael V. Forrestal, the senior NSC official for Vietnam, evoked the name of Khrushchev as a sort of curative. As no further assurances were forthcoming from the Russians, the Americans reexamined at the Sino-Soviet split but could not see how to exploit it to their favor. Meetings with Dobrynin and First Deputy Chairman Anastas I. Mikoyan went nowhere in November. The Soviets wanted to talk about Cuba and closed off discussions on Laos with the response that they honored their commitments, which they had. Left unspoken was what Hanoi was up to, and Pushkin died in early 1963, removing the Soviet's strongest advocate for enforcing the agreements. Washington would get no meaningful help from Moscow but continued to try. Finally, over year after enactment, Rusk made one last direct appeal to Khrushchev on 9 August 1963. The chairman repeated that Moscow honored its commitments and had no further interest in Laos: "The USSR was not going to do anything."[48]

This poor turn of events between Washington and Moscow had to been seen within the larger context of the Cold War, where Laos was of no importance. While the Geneva talks were underway, the 1961 Berlin Crisis ended peacefully by mutual de-escalation: first by Western Allied restraint when confronted by the erection of the Berlin Wall in August and then by the Soviets when their deadline of forcing the Western Allies out of Berlin by December passed without incident. That ended the last major East-West confrontation in Europe. Building on that degree of mutual trust also allowed the United States and Soviet Union to edge away from the brink of nuclear war during the Cuban Missile Crisis, even while dealing with the notoriously quick-fused Khrushchev. Washington had made headway in reducing tension with Moscow and would not risk that success in a diplomatic spat over Laos.

On an equally vital front, President Kennedy and Chairman Khrushchev exchanged nine letters in 1962, beginning on 10 March, that led to the breakthrough on banning nuclear weapon tests. On 10 June 1963, Kennedy publicly announced the start of high-level talks with the Soviet Union on the ban. They began on 14 July and by 25 July, an agreement was reached. On 5 August 1963, the Limited Nuclear Test Ban Treaty was signed by the Soviet Union, the United Kingdom, and the United States. The head American negotiator was Averell Harriman. It is unarguably true that the neutralization of Laos was a failure for the United States, but Harriman had been wise in working forthrightly with the Soviets and that significantly benefited the United States.

One of the tragedies of the Vietnam War was placing Harriman in charge of Southeast Asian foreign policy. As his 1962 successes in Geneva and the 1963 test ban negotiations reiterated, his strength was Europe and his expertise with the Soviets unparalleled. Harriman knew nothing of Indochina. And he could not stop himself from applying his corrosive "crocodile" attack methods to Southeast Asian leaders where it worked against America's interests. Unfortunately, it was inevitable. Dean Rusk led European policy, and there was no room on his team for a formidable rival like Harriman. Washington pushed forwards against the headwinds.

If frustration had been found in Moscow when it came to Laos, American dealings with the ICC reached a level of pure exasperation. All the assumptions had proved wrong. To prevent renewed fighting on the Plain of Jars in the spring 1963, Prince Souvanna and the three ICC commissioners, along with the British and Soviet ambassadors, representing the Geneva protocol co-chairs, flew to the plain. When Souvanna and the ambassadors proposed to send ICC teams to both sides to create a peace buffer, true to form the Polish representative Marek Thee vetoed it. The powerlessness of the ICC framework was laid bare when the PAVN-backed Pathet Lao offensive went off as scheduled. Later even the patience of Prince Souvanna had been worn away, and he declared that the communist Poles would do nothing to keep the peace and only force could halt PAVN–Pathet Lao aggression. The ICC could not be taken seriously.[49]

With the protocol in tatters, Washington sat at a crossroads with three poor options. It could force a third Geneva conference to fix the first two—an unappealing venture into nearly certain failure. To try to force compliance, it could make a case to the international community through the United Nations and by other diplomatic means, but given Kennedy's reluctance to intervene militarily, it was a feeble option at best. Lastly, the United States could join the club: violate the protocol by covertly restarting Laotian operations in conjunction with other Southeast Asian allies. The Americans settled on the third option. In an Orwellian twist all too common in the Cold War, the opposing sides battled while both denied such a thing happened. That created one more problem for Washington: what to do about their local Laotian allies—most of all the Hmong.

The Americans, the Hmong, and Fighting the PAVN in the Shadows of Laos

The Hmong people had lived in the remote hills and mountains of southern China for centuries, but beginning in the late 17th and into 18th centuries, Chinese migration drove them out of their native homeland and into Laos. A second wave of remaining Hmong immigration began during the 1927–1949 Chinese Civil War and stretched into the 1950s. While the Upper Laotian lowlands were filled with Lao and the hills with various other indigenous people, the mountains remained unsettled. There the Hmong found their new home. Their alliance with the Americans was surprising at first glance, for as late as August 1959, the U.S. embassy in Vientiane reported that the Hmong were hostile to the Royal Lao Government and aided the Pathet Lao. But very few things in Laos either were simple or easily understood, and Hmong support for the Pathet Lao always was tenuous. That opened the door, but Washington knew little about the Hmong, and many outsiders ignorantly called them the Meo, an insulting word used by their enemies. Even the number of Hmong out there in the misty jungle covered hills and mountains was unknown as an accurate census had never been conducted, but they numbered in the 100,000s.[50]

Also troubling to the relationship, the Hmong's main source of cash came from opium, and scandalous to the prim Americans, cultivating, possessing, selling, and using opium was legal in the Kingdom (and what the Americans would have done had they known of the Indochinese-Corsican Mafia opium-heroin network can only be imagined). Who was in charge also was unclear; the Hmong had a king but locally were led by headmen or chiefs who did not adhere to a hierarchal scheme. That stemmed from the fact that the clans lived in isolated mountain areas that spanned a large part of eastern Upper and Middle Laos, and after farming in one location for a number of years, they moved to new soil-rich spots. That allowed the croplands to recover but also meant there were few permanent unifying settlements. While the Hmong identified themselves as a single people and shared common cause, they eschewed centralized control.[51]

Bonds between the Hmong and Americans formed in the mid–1950s. The foundation was laid by the good works of American Christian missionaries and aid workers, like the International Voluntary Service, who arrived in 1954 to help the Hmong. They remained until escalating fighting in 1960 forced them to evacuate. The U.S. Government further cemented good relations. During the 1955 famine, the CIA's humanitarian Operation Ricedrop provided badly needed food to the Hmong. Also in 1955, as it had in South Vietnam, Washington was instrumental in expanding medical care through the Filipino-sponsored Operation Brotherhood. The efforts continued. In 1961, the U.S. Agency for International Development (USAID) workers arrived in numbers, as did CARE and Catholic Relief. From that point forward, USAID played a central role in helping the United States gain and keep the support of Lao, Hmong, and other ethnic groups in the Kingdom.[52]

The idea for the CIA to assist the Hmong militarily came up in late 1960, as the Hmong had built up a reputation as hard soldiers. It was well earned. They had been fighting off and on since World War II, first as part of the Lao Issara resistance battling the Japanese Army, and as with the rest of the Lao Issara, the Hmong fighters split when the French returned. While some joined the Viet Minh, the French gave the Hmong a good deal of autonomy, so most sided with France. Hmong fighters did not join the French Army but were recruited by the SDECE and joined GCMA special operations teams. By the early 1950s, the Hmong comprised the bulk of GCMA Groups Malo and Servan. They were demobilized in 1954, and some then joined the ANL's local volunteer forces.[53]

In 1956, the ANL reorganized the volunteers into self or auto-defense companies of 80–100 soldiers to fight the Pathet Lao. As the fighting grew in intensity, they were given better weapons and retrained to become Assault (Shock) Defense Companies (ADC's). This brought American military advisors into contact with the Hmong as they readied the ADCs. That, combined with reconciliation between Hmong king Touby Lyfoung (Ly Touby) and the new King of Laos, Sisavang Vatthana, allowed the Americans to reach out to the Hmong without alienating Vientiane when war erupted in 1959.[54]

By 1960, much of the fate of the American efforts with the Hmong lay in the hands of one man: ANL Major Vang Pao, the leader of the Hmong guerrillas. (He would be promoted to colonel in 1961.) An ethnic Hmong, Vang Pao began his military career after selection for officer training with the GCMA. In 1954, he found himself a lieutenant with a GCMA unit in the Laotian hills not far from Dien Bien Phu, preparing to rescue any French forces that might escape the siege. After the war, he was given an ANL commission and command of a Hmong volunteer battalion containing many GCMA veterans. He continued to excel at forming irregular forces used to fight the Pathet Lao and PAVN after they returned in 1959. It was then that Vang Pao became acquainted with the CIA through operative Stuart Methven. The relationship blossomed over time.[55]

One reason that the Hmong rose to such importance during the Vietnam War was simple geography; their lands abutted the strategically located Plain of Jars, the Pathet Lao stronghold at Sam Neua, and the DRV passes where the Ho Chi Minh Trail entered Laos, as well as the important border province of Xiang Khoang. The Pathet Lao tried to win them, over but it proved impossible. First, the Pathet Lao relied heavily on the DRV, whom the Hmong viewed as an enemy, and second, the Pathet Lao insisted on disarming forces loyal to Touby and Vang Pao. That pushed the Hmong toward the Americans, who welcomed their support. Combining the Hmong's strategic location and fighting skills with their mountain enclaves that were difficult to attack (although more susceptible to siege and blockade), both Washington and Vientiane saw them as near ideal allies. The last stumbling block to alliance—the distrust between General Phoumi Nosavan and Vang Pao—was overcome when the two reconciled in 1960. From that point forward, the Hmong became staunch allies.[56]

The CIA built on Methven's contact, with relations cemented after a meeting between fellow CIA officer William "Bill" Lair and Vang Pao that had been facilitated by Thai Colonel Pranet the Ritileuchai. The three would remain key figures throughout the secret war in Laos. The first CIA airdrop of arms for Hmong fighters occurred in December 1960 during the close of the Eisenhower administration and in the immediate wake of the battle for Vientiane. Named Project Momentum, it got underway in earnest during January 1961. Vang Pao led 1,500 guerrillas but stated he could quickly have 7,000 if equipped and supported by the Americans. Washington agreed and increased support to the Hmong was included in Kennedy's NSAM 29.[57]

As mentioned above, the appearance of a new Hmong force on the battlefield, which at the time only conducted small unit ambush patrols, triggered a sharp response by the PAVN and Pathet Lao despite the May ceasefire. On 28 June, they launched a major assault on the Hmong mountain stronghold at Padong near the Plain of Jars just as the Geneva conference began. When Padong fell in July, the ceasefire violation caused a cessation of the talks. The defeat also caused the CIA to rethink the light infantry ADC concept and develop a greater conventional capability to counter the PAVN. The Hmong ADCs near the Plain of Jars were reorganized into battalions, given heavy weapons, formed into Mobile Group-B (GM-B), and placed under Vang Pao's command. The PAVN made no further penetrations into the Hmong homeland in 1961.[58]

The CIA continued to build up Vang Pao's forces with General Lansdale assisting from the Pentagon. By July, Project Momentum supported 9,000 Hmong soldiers, and to secure their loyalty, Lansdale also pushed the CIA to provide humanitarian aid to the Hmong population. Their areas were organized into nine zones where dozens of camps were set up and supported by a network of rough landing strips called Lima Sites. To sharpen their fighting skills, Vang Pao's troops received training from CIA paramilitary officers under Bill Lair's direction. This was nothing new to Lair, as he had worked with Ritileuchai to create the elite counterinsurgency Thai Police Aerial Reinforcement Units (PARUs) in the 1950s. They moved to assist the CIA in Laos.[59]

By mid–1961, there were 13 Thai PARU Teams totaling 99 officers operating side-by-side with Laird's CIA paramilitary officers in Laos. The covert operations were run out of Thailand's Udorn Royal Air Base at Headquarters 333 for the PARUs and Building AB-1 for the CIA. The reason for the support was simple. Thailand was on the frontline—making any regional conflict not just dangerous but potentially an existential threat to Bangkok—and while the RVN shared a border with Laos of over 400 kilometers, the twisting border with Thailand stretched for over 1,700 kilometers. Nothing of substance that happened in Laos could be ignored by Bangkok, and the Vietnamese were an old enemy. During the late 18th and early 19th centuries, Vietnam and Thailand fought a series of wars over Laos, with Bangkok ultimately prevailing. It required active measures to keep the PAVN away from its border, and that was the basis of the CIA-PARU alliance.[60]

The two countries complemented each other in helping their Lao allies, and the support of Headquarters 333 proved indispensable. They provided facilities near the battlefields, language skills, cultural knowledge, and military trainers and advisors. The United States augmented the support of the Lao, especially the Hmong, with highly trained officers, weapons, munitions, other military supplies and equipment, along with air support. And again, at Lansdale's urging, the CIA provided Lao fighters' families with monies, food, and medicines. Thing progressed accordingly, and on 29 August 1961, President Kennedy approved plans to further grow the Hmong Army to 11,000 troops.[61]

American operations were not limited to fighting the Pathet Lao and PAVN in Upper Laos. The CIA and U.S. Special Forces also had teams in Middle and Lower Laos. Missions in Middle Laos tried to keep track of activities along the Ho Chi Minh Trail. Washington wanted to keep an eye on things, and the Thais and Hmong had watched Route 8 coming out of Nape Pass in North Vietnam since December 1960. In 1961, the CIA sent in Michael Duell to join with PARU Team C to focus the trail efforts in what became Project Hardnose. But when the PAVN went on the offensive in February 1962, the trail watchers were forced to abandon the mission. With the Geneva agreements, Hardnose went dormant in October. It was also during this period in 1962 that the British Royal Air Force covertly inserted a New Zealand Special Air Service team to look at the Ho Chi Minh Trail. The New Zealanders left a few weeks after the October deadline.[62]

In Lower Laos, U.S. Special Forces carried out Operation Pincushion, which began in December 1961. Pincushion organized self-defense guerrilla units among the Lao Theong ethnic minority that dominated the Bolaven Plateau, much as the French had done with the GCMA. The operation also mirrored in many ways Project Momentum, and by early 1962, 12 guerrilla companies had been organized, equipped, and trained. Like support to the Hmong, as the Geneva deadline approached, Operation Pincushion shut down, and the Lao Theong units disbanded. It was a setback for the Americans and their allies. The southern Mekong River lowlands population represented Prince Boun Oum's political base, and with the joining of the Lao Theong in the highlands, control over Lower Laos rested securely in pro–American hands.[63]

Like Project Hardnose and Operation Pincushion, Project Momentum drew down in accordance with the Geneva Protocol. Hmong weapons shipments ended on 27 June and munitions resupply on 21 July; only Air America humanitarian support continued. The exceptions were munitions resupply runs during the July–October regroupment period but only when PAVN or Pathet Lao forces attacked Hmong territory. All 666 American military advisors, along with a similar number of support troops and CIA paramilitary officers, were gone by the 7 October deadline. Two CIA officers stayed with Vang Pao for intelligence and liaison duties—not to conduct paramilitary operations. The Thais also pulled back. Only four of 13 PARU teams (about 28 Thai border police) remained in Laos after the deadline. Hanoi did not follow suit. The CIA put the number of PAVN in Laos at 9,000 just before the protocol was signed and 6,000 afterwards, with the large majority working the trail. When Hardnose and Pincushion ended, the Americans and Thais abandoned eastern Lower Laos. The PAVN quickly filled the vacuum.[64]

In hopes of mitigating the loss of information gathering, in September 1962 the CIA put a team in Thailand across from Thakhek to keep an eye on the Laotian panhandle. They were joined by the PARUs. As paramilitary operations were banned, their mission was to recruit Laotian agents to gain intelligence on Pathet Lao and PAVN activities and possible violations of the Geneva Protocol. Seeing the need to do more, CIA officers moved to restart Project Hardnose, only limited to surveilling the Ho Chi Minh Trail. That was given a boost in the fall of 1962 when CIA case officer Richard Holm, who had prior experience with the Hmong, joined Duell. But as Holm soon discovered, of his seven watcher teams, none were positioned to look at the trail, and what they collected from the rest of Middle Laos was done sporadically and of little value.[65]

So poor was the quality of information about the trail that in late 1962, the Americans only knew of rumors about PAVN road construction between Routes 9 and 12 when it had been completed in December 1961. Holm moved to redirect operations toward the trail and soon found half his team members unwilling to take on the new and risky mission. After weeding out the unfit, he forged an effective field force of trail watchers that, when combined with PARU Team W radio operators, were ready for deep reconnaissance missions along the trail. The emphasis was on PAVN activities along the Nape Pass, Route 8, the Mu Gia Pass, and Route 12. Too late to influence the Geneva negotiations, some Americans were beginning to see the trail for the threat that it was.[66]

The Fall of Kong Le and Renewed War

One of the best measures of the consequences stemming from PAVN and Pathet Lao violations of the Geneva Protocol was the reaction of Kong Le. From 1960 until 1962, Kong Le just had not just opposed General Phoumi Nosavan and Prince Boun Oum, he also was openly sympathetic to Red Prince Soupanouvong and the Pathet Lao. In November 1960, Kong Le in his dress ANL uniform met with Pathet Lao leaders at their Sam Neua headquarters, made public appearances, and forged a FAN-Pathet-Lao military alliance. He was not a communist. Kong Le was unique in his loyalty to Prince Souvanna, loathed the idea of Lao killing Lao, and believed neutralism was the only path to a peaceful unified Laos. Over time, the Pathet Lao relationship deteriorated with rumors of a rift arising in July 1962. His frustrations were troubling but not critical: the withholding of some supplies from the FAN and too much communist propagandizing by PAVN military advisors. It was not until after the Geneva Protocol that distrust took root. As he watched the American military advisors leave and the FAR honor the accords, Kong Le saw a very different stance taken by the PAVN and Pathet Lao.[67]

After the 7 October 1962 deadline for the withdrawal of foreign troops passed with sizable PAVN forces still in Middle Laos, the Kong Le–Pathet Lao–PAVN relationship deteriorated further. By then Kong Le and Prince Souvanna had reached out to the Americans to provide non-military supplies to FAN troops in the Plain of Jars. Tensions grew. By late November, the Pathet Lao launched a propaganda campaign to discredit Prince Souvanna and undermine his government. The political attacks on Souvanna stretched into early 1963. Infuriating Washington and widening Kong Le's breech with the Pathet Lao, on 28 November 1962 pro–Pathet Lao soldiers shot down an Air America mission approved by Souvanna delivering food and clothing to Kong Le's troops. Pro–Pathet Lao FAN Colonel Deuane Sunnalath was implicated in both the shoot-down and the subsequent assassination of his commander, one of Kong Le's trusted lieutenants. With those outrages, Kong Le became so distrustful of the Pathet Lao and PAVN that he asked for direct American military aid and began cooperating with Van Pao and his Hmong irregulars. The breaking point had been reached.[68]

As civil war loomed again in February 1963, Forrestal sent a request to President Kennedy to provide Kong Le with weapons and munitions since the PAVN and Pathet Lao had begun to threaten Le's Plain of Jars bases. Ominously in early April, Red Prince Souphanouvong and his officials secretly departed Vientiane for Pathet Lao areas. By that time, Prince Souvanna had learned how the Pathet Lao worked. Souphanouvong was a figurehead, and Kaysone Phomvihane and other People's Party leaders were in charge, while the Lao Patriotic Front was little more than a tool of Hanoi. That made the breakup of the coalition government disappointing but expected as Kong Le now shared those views. By early spring 1963, the FAN stood side by side with the FAR for the first time since the August 1960 coup, and a joint FAR-FAN command was formed. Prince Souvanna returned to Vientiane to lead the new coalition government.[69]

Tensions on the Plain of Jars continued to build. The next month, Kong Le purged his forces of Pathet Lao supporters, and sporadic clashes broke out in the Plain of Jars. Casualties were about even, but Kong Le additionally had to deal with several hundred deserters. The PAVN-backed Pathet Lao responded with their 1963 Spring Offensive in April, the fighting that the ICC failed to prevent and which so infuriated Washington. The FAR and Hmong came to the aid of the FAN as six FAR battalions were airlifted to the battlefield. The Hmong were especially effective. They counterattacked and recaptured Padong and cut Routes 4 and 7. After the Pathet Lao offensive waned and then halted after a few weeks, the FAR and FAN with Hmong assistance launched a counteroffensive over the same 1961 battleground at Route 13 to the west of the Plain of Jars. It ended in victory. Begun in mid–July, by month's end when the operation ceased, several Pathet Lao battalions had been badly mauled and a number of prisoners captured along with a dozen trucks, six armored cars, six 85 mm guns and four 105 mm howitzers.[70]

In the wake of the PAVN-backed 1963 Pathet Lao spring offensive and Marek Thee's sabotage of the ICC peace efforts, President Kennedy had enough. It was as if the Geneva talks had never taken place. On 25 June 1963, he approved NSAM 249. It provided a comprehensive outline of actions to address the situation in Laos and immediately approved Phase I of its three phases that authorized funds and military aid to support the FAR (to include armed T-28 aircraft) and Kong Le's FAN, restarted Air America's military resupply of the Hmong, and expanded intelligence gathering operations in Laos in coordination with Thailand and South Vietnam.[71]

The NSAM further directed the appropriate agencies to complete planning for Phase II that addressed a long and comprehensive range of options: (a) the start of U.S. reconnaissance flights over Laos and possibly the DRV, (b) the return of U.S. military advisors, (c) basing U.S. air-land combat forces in Thailand and naval forces in the South China Sea, (d) a further expansion of support to the Hmong, (e) increased cross-border ARVN operations directed at the Ho Chi Minh Trail, (f) an expansion of the CIA secret war in DRV, (g) preparations to implement CINCPAC Operations Plan (OPLAN) 33-63 that addressed the military's role in the secret war, and (h) preparations to deploy SEATO forces to Laos. Finally, NSAM 249 directed that Phase III undergo review and refinement. It proposed diplomatic action to include reconvening the Geneva conference and a push for the partition of Laos to cut off panhandle infiltration into the RVN.[72]

In Laos and Thailand, orders came down that the United States would overtly adhere to the protocol, but the CIA was given latitude to conduct covert paramilitary operations against the Pathet Lao–PAVN forces to include the Ho Chi Minh Trail. Bill Lair continued to skillfully run the CIA show from Vientiane, and directed his officers to return to Laos. The secret war was on. That summer Duell expanded Hard-nose missions into the former Operation Pincushion area of Lower Laos to cover the southernmost trail section. To boost Duell's mission, Thailand sent back into Laos PARU Teams T and W to make things happen on the ground. Team T went to the area around Tchepone and Route 9, and Team W watched the trail to the north where it entered Laos along Route 8 at Nape Pass. In early 1964, Duell and Holm were assigned another CIA officer, and the pace of missions increased. To expand the anti-trail projects, Lair sent Roy Moffitt to Pakse to assist Duell's work with the Theong Lao tribes. In early 1964, the Hardnose missions grew from reconnaissance and intelligence gathering to include covert raids against the Ho Chi Minh Trail. By May Hardnose officers with PARU assistance supervised 20 trail-watching teams. In November the project expanded again.[73]

The fallout from the 1963 offensive was not limited to Lower and Middle Laos. As elsewhere in Laos, American support for the Hmong ended in October 1962, creating what some in Washington called the "unstable equilibrium."[74] During that time, Vang Pao had to rely on FAR support that proved adequate for his forces to defend their lands and little else. Even Washington's most ardent supporters of the Geneva agreements were uneasy. The Hmong had proven loyal, effective, and deserving of American support.[75]

Now that the violations had reached the breaking point and with NSAM 249 approved, Air America again supplied and transported Vang Pao's troops to deal with the Pathet Lao, and getting them into the fight against the PAVN took on urgency. The CIA also reached out to the Upper Laos Yao hill people in Houa Khong province near Nam Tha. Going forward, the Hmong and others like the Yao tied up thousands of PAVN troops for the rest of the war. For the Hmong, it was a cyclic conflict where the PAVN attempted to dislodge them from their mountain strongholds during the dry season followed by the Hmong harassing the Ho Chi Minh Trail when the rains came.[76]

Faced with the American response, Hanoi's decision to approve the April 1963 offensive proved disastrous. Not only did Hanoi learn that its Pathet Lao allies were not able to win without PAVN troops, they triggered the secret war. Given the limited American and Thai resources committed to sustain the fight against the PAVN, as compared to the cost of supporting equivalent-sized U.S. or ARVN forces, for Washington it was one of the war's most resource-effective efforts. But in retrospect, it was a great tragedy. For the FAR and Hmong, the fighting also meant that Laos never freed itself from the unstable equilibrium. The brutal secret war would rage on with no end in sight.

Closing Acts

The aftermath of the Battle of Nam Tha that led to the 1962 Geneva neutrality declaration and protocol was one of the few achievements that the VWP hierarchy unanimously rejoiced over as the DRV got everything it wanted. Minister of Foreign Affairs and Central Committee member Ung Van Khiem, representing the Giap faction, termed it a "big victory," and Le Duan similarly categorized it as a "big achievement."[77] That did not mean Hanoi would honor the agreements. As with the 1954 Geneva accords, the protocol was respected but only when it served Hanoi's aims. Group 559 troops along the Ho Chi Minh Trail in Laos continued to increase, and while Group 959 fell from over 3,000 soldiers and cadres to 49 advisors by the October deadline, it did not go away. In early 1963, it became Group 463 to assist the ill-fated Pathet Lao offensive.[78]

Hanoi's enthusiasm over the Geneva negotiations led it to seek the neutralization of South Vietnam. Duan explained the strategy to COSVN in a 19 July 1962 communiqué. Neutralization along the Laos lines would preclude the conflict in the south from becoming a big war with American intervention. RVN neutralization meant victory and reunification, and that was when the value of the NLF came into play, as Hanoi wanted to keep its fingerprints off any neutralization proposals. Beginning that month, the NLF led the neutralization drive, but it was not alone. Only weeks after the Geneva settlement, Hanoi convinced Cambodia's Prince Sihanouk to call for a conference to neutralize the RVN on 1 August. It all was for naught. The fickle prince soon changed his mind and called instead for a conference to neutralize Cambodia. Further attempts in 1962–1963 failed. South Vietnam, unlike Laos, was not divided into multiple armed factions, and Diem rejected a neutralist coalition government seeing it as nothing other than surrender, a view shared in Washington. Hanoi's efforts, however, did present Diem's brother Nhu with an opportunity to engage in political mischief.[79]

Ngo Dinh Nhu always was open to meet and listen to almost anyone, but as to why often was not as clear. What his neutralization motivations were remain a mystery, but Hanoi was so eager and Washington so wary that in 1963 he opted to distract them both by responding to the feelers. Madame Nhu argued that he felt the RVN was winning the war against the Viet Cong, that they approached Saigon first with the intent of deescalating the war, and Diem told Nhu to handle the talks. In May Nhu let the U.S. Embassy in Saigon know that he had been in communication with the VC but made no reference to neutralization. That same month, he stirred the pot in Hanoi by reaching out to the new head of the Polish ICC delegation, Mieczyslaw Maneli, with an offer to establish diplomatic relations with the DRV. Later in September, when the Americans threatened to suspend U.S. aid, Nhu again played the Hanoi card.[80]

In response, Ho Chi Minh conducted an interview published in Moscow that reiterated the neutralist party line by pushing for a ceasefire between Saigon and the NLF. In the end, Nhu's neutralization games never went anywhere. Although some, like influential journalist Joe Alsop, expressed grave fears, most senior Americans never took Nhu seriously. Hilsman judged the whole affair "irrelevant."[81] The DRV was only slightly more disturbed; neutralization was a possibility worth exploring, and when it failed, it was minor setback outweighed by the successes already obtained in Geneva. The American military mission left Laos, and powerful PAVN forces remained along the Ho Chi Minh Trail. Hanoi saw the war progressing positively on all fronts.[82]

In the aftermath of Geneva in 1962, there was no joy on the American side—only relief that the crisis appeared over. The protocol got the administration out of the Laotian mess but at a cost. The agreement meant de facto partition of Laos into roughly east-west halves. Ambassador Harriman characterized it as a "good bad deal."[83] It turned out to be much less with the launching of the 1963 Pathet Lao–PAVN offensive. The response, NSAM 249, was a success. It laid down a political-military plan that if carried through, offered the Americans and their allies a pathway to reshape the "good bad deal" into a good deal. Subsequent covert operations rebalanced the situation for the short term, and the return to informal partition protected Thailand. Conversely, the RVN's border defense became hopelessly outflanked. Nonetheless, making the defense of Thailand marginally better combined with the unrealistically rosy assessment of the threat posed by the Ho Chi Minh Trail explained why Washington accepted the 1962 Geneva deal and was satisfied with its 1963 NSAM 249 countermove.

Washington did not succeed fully in Geneva but not from a lack of strategic vision; it was certainly on the top of its Cold War game in 1962. It accomplished its aims for Laos and Thailand. Where it tripped up was over South Vietnam, specifically, an inability to see Hanoi as Indochina's dominant power that operated with a high degree of freedom and relentlessly sought reunification. That in large part stemmed from misreading Moscow's authority. Harriman and others believed that the Soviet ambassador in Hanoi accompanied by a few deputies could visit the VWP Politburo and tell them to quit Laos or end the war with the south. Things no longer worked that way. The absolute power of Moscow within the communist bloc was gone. What been true before and mostly true in 1954 was no longer true by 1962. Moscow went to lengths to ensure the West did not find out the extent of its fall from power and succeeded—to America's loss.[84]

The Ho Chi Minh Trail remained the real problem for the Americans as the flow of PAVN soldiers and war materials entered the RVN in increasing numbers. Although there was no consensus as to degree amongst the Americans, all agreed success in the war in South Vietnam was linked to the trail. Deservedly it earned a new nickname in Washington: "The Averell Harriman Highway."[85] Hilsman later described the trail situation in equally cynical terms; the Geneva clauses banning PAVN infiltration were of no use "except as a propaganda points."[86] Harriman saw the error. He later remarked that the DRV "broke the '62 agreements before the ink was dry," and tried to correct it.[87]

That was when the American position unraveled. Enforcement of Laotian neutrality policy was built on two pillars that collapsed under the least of pressures: a robust ICC to minimize PAVN presence in Laos and Moscow's good offices. As for the first pillar, Marek Thee sabotaged the ICC. The issue with the Soviets was subtler. Harriman's assessment that Moscow acted in good faith was correct, and trusting Khrushchev was the right thing. Where the Americans went wrong again went back to assuming Russia could control the DRV and China. The American failure was not brought on by egregious Russian duplicity—the Soviets acted forthrightly throughout the negotiations—rather the United States asked for something beyond the power of the Soviets to give.

The DRV was the big winner. Hanoi emerged greatly strengthened. Its military campaigns in Laos ended in victory, and switching the Ho Chi Minh Trail to Laos with its subsequent growth allowed North Vietnam to escalate the war in the south at will. Hanoi held the initiative on the battlefield in South Vietnam and had no intention of relinquishing it. By the close of 1962, the strategic components Hanoi needed to win the Vietnam War were in place, and that put Saigon at a marked disadvantage. It had no control or even a real say over the course of events but had to live with the consequences. For the RVN, the Geneva agreement represented a defeat of the first order. Diplomacy had failed Saigon. The options had narrowed, and the road to greater war broadened.

PART IV

HOW THE WAR WENT AND THE FALL OF DIEM (1959–1963)

Part IV: Dramatis Personae

In Washington

McGeorge Bundy—Former World War II intelligence officer, foreign policy expert, and Harvard College dean who served as Kennedy's National Security Advisor

Lyndon B. Johnson—Vice president who supported Diem and opposed his overthrow

John F. Kennedy—Elected president in 1961 and greatly expanded America's role in Vietnam

Robert S. McNamara—Kennedy's highly capable and forceful secretary of defense who made the war in Vietnam a focus of his attention

Walt W. Rostow—World War II OSS officer and brilliant academic who formulated Vietnam War policy in the State Department

Maxwell D. Taylor—Decorated World War II paratrooper who became special military assistant to President Kennedy and then chairman of the Joint Chiefs of Staff in 1962

The Harriman Team

W. Averell Harriman—Undersecretary of State given a free hand to execute Vietnam policy

Roger Hilsman—Replaced Harriman as Assistant Secretary of State for Far Eastern Affairs

Michael Forrestal—Point man on Vietnam within the National Security Council

William Trueheart—Headed the U.S. Embassy in the late summer of 1963 in Nolting's absence

Henry Cabot Lodge, Jr.—Senior statesman who replaced Ambassador Nolting in August 1963

The Buddhists

Thich Tri Quang—Charismatic and idiosyncratic leader of the radical Buddhists

Thich Quang Duc—Buddhist monk whose 1963 self-immolation stunned the world and shook the Diem regime to its foundations

Thich Tinh Khiet—Passive senior Buddhist leader manipulated by Quang

The Saigon Country Team

Frederick E. Nolting—Ambassador in Saigon who supported Diem in 1963

Paul D. Harkins—The first MACV commander who led the initial American military effort to assist the ARVN in defeating the Viet Cong

William Colby—Former OSS officer who fought behind German lines in World War II, head of the CIA's Far East Division and station chief in Saigon

John Paul Vann—U.S. Army colonel who advised the ARVN during 1962–1963

The Coup Leaders

Duong Van Big Minh—General and military advisor to the president who fell out with Diem after Diem removed him from command

Nguyen Van Khanh—General in charge of II CTZ located to the immediate north of Saigon

Tran Van Don—General who planned the overthrow of Diem through a military coup d'état

Others

Robert Grainer Ker Thompson—British counterinsurgency expert who advised Diem

13

The Vietnam War in 1959–1961 and the CIA's Secret Wars

The war in 1959 evolved gradually. While not fully satisfying, by the spring the work done in Hanoi on Resolution 15's guidelines and directives was comprehensive enough to order the southern VWP comrades to relaunch the struggle. Resolution 15 defined the use of force for "armed propaganda" as permitting two types of military operations: self-defense, which included assassinations and kidnappings, and more offensively minded armed proselytizing in the villages where cadres accompanied by soldiers sought to persuade the masses to come over to their side. That guidance ensured a strong start, but finding the correct pace for the revolution remained elusive. The guidelines and directives had to be revisited repeatedly in the years that followed.[1]

Making the task more challenging, the party in South Vietnam was not what it had been in 1954. Hanoi could not simply pass Resolution 15 and expect the war of reunification to light up across the RVN like flipping a switch. Party weakness was real, and a chief reason for the difficultly lay with Diem's To Cong campaign. Its effect could be seen easily. In 1954, there were 30,000 VWP members in the Mekong Delta, and by 1959 only 3,000 remained. The Nam Bo Resistance Central Committee summed it up: "The enemy succeeded in implementing most of his basic policies … and caused our Party and the people heavy losses."[2] A VWP cadre considered the period the "darkest in their lives."[3] An impressive 80–90 percent of the Viet Cong base areas had been destroyed.[4]

The southern VWP had been so badly damaged that Hanoi no longer tightly controlled the revolution in the south—a problem that took several years to fix. Even what Hanoi did tightly control was feeble; the Ho Chi Minh Trail was little more than a jungle footpath, and maritime infiltration consisted of nothing more than smuggling small quantities of military supplies and a handful of VWP couriers. There was no way to sustain a major uprising in 1959, but that was fine for the time being.[5]

Unaware of Hanoi's decision, Washington was so pleased with the situation in the RVN that the efforts for 1959 focused almost exclusively on the economy. A U.S. Senate report noted that governmental authority extended to all of the RVN's major cities, and it was safe to travel by road and rail almost anywhere. The Americans opined that simply by improving coordination between the Civil Guard and ARVN, the Viet Cong problem could be contained. On 8 January 1959, the U.S. embassy told Washington that Diem was complaining about the lack of increase in U.S. military aid. His concern was brushed aside, and when he raised the issue again at the end of March, Durbrow dismissed it as a political ploy to get more money. The ambassador informed Washington that the U.S. should cut military support further and redirect it to economic aid.[6]

But the effects of the Resolution 15 were being felt. Although Civil Guardsmen were being killed regularly and even some ARVN troops came under fire, the most obvious sign of the new danger was the increased number of Viet Cong "self-defense" assassinations, as over 30 government officials were being murdered a month and a larger number kidnapped. General Williams and the MAAG detected the change. The increased VC activity required greater ARVN involvement, and Williams requested expansion of the role of American advisors. Admiral Felt at CINCPAC gave him limited approval for greater involvement in planning ARVN counterinsurgency operations and sending advisors down to the regimental level, but they were not to go into combat.[7]

Vice President Tho and others in Diem's cabinet also saw the growing danger and took a more nuanced approach to try to alert the Americans. They argued the application of military force was necessary despite American misgivings, but to win them over, they pushed for aid to support psychological and civic actions rather than more economic or military assistance. Diem went a step further by requesting U.S. Army anti-guerrilla experts. In the same vein, the CIA's Colonel Lansdale urged the deployment of U.S. Special Forces officers or others trained in counterinsurgency tactics to Vietnam, as conventionally trained U.S. Army officers were not up to snuff.[8]

By mid–1959, it was clear to even the doubters that the insurgency had come alive. Durbrow backed off demands to cut military funding, and as the often brutal and savage VC assassinations and other attacks increased, Diem doubled down on repression. His reaction to the bloodletting brought on by Resolution 15 was more arrests and Law 10/59 enacted in May. It expanded prosecution of accused communists through trials conducted by three special military tribunals. The law was draconian as it permitted only two punishments: death or life in prison, although later the law was changed to allow the tribunals to issue lesser sentences. Justice was speedy; hearings lasted no more than three days with no appeal, and death sentences were carried out quickly—usually in public by guillotine.[9]

The 10/59 law coincided with the implementation of the agroville program and its attendant increase in the use of corvée labor. Taken in combination, people in areas where fighting took place believed they had no choice but to fight back. Even those less supportive of the Viet Cong had to reach some form of accommodation to survive. Like the DRV's 1955–1956 land reform, the two policies were misguided; thousands were arrested with many killed and farmers had to work longer for no gain. That alienated whole communities. Many saw the road to reconciliation closed, as anyone who had even the slightest connection to the communists lived in fear—a number that reached the hundreds of thousands. Ngo Dinh Diem and his brother Nhu discarded forgiveness to embrace a counterproductive and bloody policy of social purification. In doing so, the president began to lose the people's hearts and minds in areas with a VC presence.[10]

As tragic as Diem's missteps were, they should not have mattered, as the VC were on the brink of defeat and Saigon on the road to victory as 1959 opened. That should have remained true even after committing errors like Law 10/59 and an excessive application of corvée labor.

But one factor changed that calculation in its entirety: the power of the Viet Cong's superiors to the north. Once the DRV with all its resources entered the fray, the struggle was transformed. Indicative of the change, the United States crossed a threshold on 8 July when the first American soldiers were killed in a terrorist attack at the Bien Hoa MAAG compound. More was to come. The first unambiguous signal that real war had arrived was the inauguration of the Viet Cong's 20 July 1959 Concerted Uprising Campaign, the first offensive since 1954 and begun on the anniversary of the Geneva Accords. (A spike in VC military operations starting on the anniversary became a norm throughout the war.) Despite the symbolism of 20 July, there was not a lot to show for the effort in 1959, but that worked to Hanoi's advantage. As the mobilization of old and new PAVN cadres got underway along with recruiting efforts, military activity in South Vietnam increased to a point not seen since the 1955–1956 sect war.[11]

In late 1959, the U.S. embassy in Saigon informed Washington that guerrilla attacks had steadily intensified, and Saigon estimated the number of VC fighters had increased from about 2,000 to 9,800 to include 3,500 Main Force soldiers and guerrillas. But even that number was not terribly alarming, and the war remained limited to the Mekong Delta and Nam Bo's western border reaches with Cambodia. Combatting the guerrillas remained the job of the poorly armed SDC and wrongly trained Civil Guard. The bulk of the ARVN continued to prepare for a conventional war against the PAVN. It was hoped that following the advice of Williams, Lansdale, Durbrow, and Tho would right the ship.[12]

One casualty of the reversal of fortunes was General Duong Van "Big" Minh. In January 1959, "Big" Minh remained Diem's favorite and was given command of all of Nam Bo (MRs 1 and 5 as well as the Saigon MR). After the situation steadily deteriorated, in January 1960 Diem removed "Big" Minh and gave authority back to the three MR commanders. Even though "Big" Minh later was assigned as the JGS head of operations, the bond between the two was never the same.

Saigon and Washington did not fully understand the how or why the security situation deteriorated over 1959 and distressingly, where to find the answers. Both were at a loss and looked for something or someone or even each other to blame. For the Americans and the Diem regime, 1959 began as a hope-filled year ushering in an era of peace and prosperity, but as the consequences of Resolution 15 took effect, Washington and Saigon realized they faced an unprecedented threat.

The War in 1960

The events of 1960 altered everyone's perceptions as political convulsions rocked East Asia, and almost had as great an effect on Saigon as the nation's growing internal security problem. The initial focus was on Indonesia when its ruler,

Sukarno, strengthened his authoritarian rule by abolishing the national legislature. Tensions heightened. On 9 March an Indonesian Air Force jet flown by a rebellious pilot strafed the presidential palace in Djakarta. More shocks followed elsewhere. On 26 April, the long-serving strongman of South Korea, Syngman Rhee, was forced to resign following a rigged 15 March reelection vote that led to widespread rioting and massive protests. Closer to home, Prince Sihanouk in Cambodia, who opposed Western-style democracy, used strong-arm tactics to suppress the press, arrest protesters, and eliminate opposition political parties. Then came paratroop commander Kong Le's coup in Laos on 9 August. It was a time of regional unrest, and South Vietnam was not spared.[13]

In April, a group of 18 opposition politicians and leaders met at Saigon's newest and most stylish accommodation, the Caravelle Hotel, to draft a manifesto against the Diem government. Although many were from factions that had long opposed Diem (old Bao Dai loyalists, Dai Viet and Nationalist Party leaders, and representatives from the Cao Dai and Hoa Hao), there also were apolitical leaders of goodwill, such as Tran Van Huong, who had served as the Prefect of Saigon-Cholon under Diem in 1955, and the political elder Tran Le Chat. In truth, the group only was united in their dislike of Diem. Given the disjointed political agendas of the signatories, the document was self-serving—essentially a call for the return to power of those defeated by Diem—and an unrealistic proposal to reform national governance, the military, economy, and political system.

It was a quixotic adventure, and to this day the Caravelle Manifesto remains an empty document. For the people of Vietnam, its demands were unrealizable and to use the words of the manifesto, it jumped "from promise to promise, until finally hope ended in bitter disillusion."[14] The tragedy was that too many Americans both in government, like Ambassador Durbrow, and the press took it seriously. They, like the Saigon elites, could not come to grips with the threat from the north. They judged Diem against an idealization, not the political reality reflected in East Asia and certainly not the alternative: VWP rule from Hanoi.[15]

The few years of peace blinded them to the peril, and they were incapable of unifying to meet it. Years later in 1968, Lansdale returned to Saigon and found nothing changed. The Caravelle factions remained divided yet espoused closely aligned hopes for the future. Lansdale admonished them, "The trouble with you is you never talk to each other enough to discover that you share a great deal in common" and warned, "For God's sake learn to work with each other or you're going to lose your country."[16] Diem, the target of their ire, was not under such an illusion as to the true enemy and made the case in July when Saigon published *Violations of the Geneva Agreement by the Viet-Minh Communists, From July 1959 to June 1960.*[17]

Things grew worse; a number of the Caravelle leaders were soon in contact with Colonel Nguyen Chanh Thi, the Paratroop Brigade commander who had fought to save Diem during the Battle of Saigon in 1955 and now saw himself as the next Kong Le. Before dawn on 11 November, Thi acted on his plan to take power. It followed Kong Le's takeover of Vientiane to the letter; his paratroopers seized Saigon's national police headquarters, army headquarters, airport, telephone exchange, and radio station. His troops then closed in on the presidential palace. The moment he heard of it, Ambassador Durbrow informed Washington, "paratroopers (apparently about one battalion) mounted a coup attempt as they had done in Laos."[18] There was a difference. When Kong Le acted, government leaders were away, while Diem stood in a defended palace.[19]

When the two sides met, a fierce gun-battle erupted. The paratroopers almost succeeded by luck as heavy machine gun fire just missed killing Diem, but after he moved to safety, the paratroopers could not overcome the presidential guard. Madame Nhu played a prominent role throughout in organizing the resistance, and her cool resolve brought her to the attention of the Americans for the first time as a force to be reckoned with. By late morning, a standoff ensued. As the rebels demanded surrender, Diem played for time and ordered in loyal troops to restore order. As soon as they arrived, the coup collapsed. The paratroopers fell back having failed to take the palace. It had lasted barely 30 hours.[20]

Nguyen Chanh Thi and other rebel officers fled to Cambodia where Prince Sihanouk granted them asylum. Less fortunate, the Caravelle group members allied with Chi reaped the whirlwind as Diem's security services jailed them. The coup reinforced in Diem a lesson learned in 1955: political survival in Saigon depended on personally loyal troops. That reality the Americans not only refused to accept but also condemned. Rufus Phillips, who had served in Lansdale's SMM and was back in South Vietnam, took it a step further, arguing that vocal anti–Diem animus espoused by Americans like Durbrow encouraged coup plotters. Phillips was right to a point. What senior Americans said publicly did matter. Durbrow had been vocal in his criticism, but he and Diem respected each other and found ways to work together.[21]

The coup was too brief for the VWP to exploit, but with Resolution 15 fully implemented, the party and armed VC were finding their way; "defensive" measures now included attacks on military targets. The year began with an exciting success. Taking advantage of the Tet Holidays with most of the soldiers away on leave, a surprise 26 January raid on the 32nd Regiment's base in Tay Ninh province netted some 600 weapons to include two mortars and two machine guns. While the feat was not repeated, momentum continued to build, and this period witnessed the beginning of the cycle where the government ruled by day and the increasingly more powerful VC by night. The fighting did have a downside in winning hearts and minds of the masses as it terrorized people in contested areas. Villagers felt they had "one neck bound by two nooses and did whatever they were told by both sides."[22]

Their lot would not get better, for the war grew both in the number of combatants and casualties. In January, 180 armed clashes were reported; in September the monthly total was 545. The years 1958–1960 witnessed over 1,700 assassinations with most occurring in 1960. The VC were building base areas and winning the intimidation campaign. In the delta, the extent of VC power was hidden from Saigon, and some VC units were disguised as Cao Dai militia while others posed as Binh Xuyen gangs. The ARVN estimated that the number of Main Force and guerrilla Viet Cong grew to nearly 10,000 (the actual number was 12,500). What they did not fully realize was that total included the arrival of some 2,000 PAVN regroupees and VWP cadres from the north.[23]

Saigon reacted strongly to the increased violence and expansion of VC controlled areas. On 24 March, Diem declared all-out war on the Viet Cong. Critically, the ARVN expanded. The 9th Infantry Division was activated that month in Binh Dinh province, followed in July by the formation of the 25th Infantry Division at Quang Ngai, bringing the total number of divisions to nine. To complete the transition away from feebly armed light divisions, also during 1960 the 15th and 16th Light were combined, becoming the 23rd Infantry Division based at Ban Me Thuot in the Central Highlands. March also marked the opening of the ranger school to conduct six-week counterinsurgency courses for 65 ARVN infantry companies. Within the ARVN every fourth rifle company (one per battalion) became a ranger company, while the rest of the rangers were assigned to provincial chiefs as a rapid strike force. In June, a number of ranger companies were used to form four ranger battalions that in time became an MR-level mobile reserve.[24]

June witnessed the end of the Concerted Uprising Campaign. Based on its successes, during a July meeting the Nam Bo Resistance Committee recommended increasing the tempo of the revolution, and the Destruction of Oppression Campaign was launched on 20 July 1960. By this time, the VWP had made progress in reestablishing party discipline, and it showed. The campaign, more effective than in 1959, continued as a political effort signified by armed propaganda and other proselytizing efforts along with protests and civil disturbances. By any measure, the war in Nam Bo developed favorably for the Viet Cong.[25]

As part of the Destruction of Oppression Campaign, on 23 September, the anniversary of the start of the 1945 Nam Bo uprising, the Viet Cong initiated a series of wide-scale attacks and political demonstrations. It was not universally successful. In the Central Highlands, there was significant small-unit VC activity along Routes 19 and 14 in Kontum province, but nothing lasting was gained, and the casualties were heavy. It was then that the Nam Bo Resistance Central Committee decided the military priority was not in fighting but building up base areas. That led to greater efforts to organize armed village militias and form local revolutionary associations.[26]

For Saigon, it brought to the fore the difficulties faced by frontline Civic Action Teams and the Civil Guard. In addition to being targeted by the VC, the civic action program was weakened when its leader, Kieu Cong Cung, fell ill that summer and died in October. There was no one of equal caliber to replace him. Ngo Trong Hieu took over and did his best. On the plus side, Durbrow and the MSUG recognized their error over the Guard. In December, they blessed Diem's decision to move it to the defense ministry, and the MAAG agreed to train it for counterinsurgency operations. The first class of 330 guards reported in January 1961. Of greater concern to Hanoi, 12 ARVN regiments now were assigned to counterinsurgency operations, primarily in Nam Bo, while those in the north moved to close off the DMZ from infiltration.[27]

Before 1960 ended, Hanoi knew progress had been made and that it had entered a demanding conflict in the south (and Laos as well). During the September session of the 3rd VWP Congress, the leadership approved a new five-year military plan. In addition to increasing the quality of military training and acquiring new equipment, the PAVN was to grow from 173,000 to 260,000 by 1965 and the militia to expand to 1.4 million with a ready reserve of 180,000 soldiers. It would take time, and the political struggle in the south remained the focus in the meantime. To advance the cause, on 20 December Hanoi announced the formation of the NLF that provided non-communist cover while allowing COSVN along with VWP regional and provincial central committees to execute Politburo policy. That generated some frustration in Hanoi. The war remained centered in Nam Bo, and Hanoi prodded COSVN to get things going in MR-5, especially the Central Highlands. It worked. A limited offensive from 21 October to 11 November succeeded in overrunning a number of isolated Civil Guard posts, and many villages began to receive regular visits from VC armed propaganda teams. The efforts to spread the revolution in the highlands became known as the Mountain Cong System and proved effective.[28]

The War in 1961

The year 1961 was one of the most pivotal of the war, but the consequences rolled out so gradually that their effect was not realized until later, sometimes years later. On the political front, the presidential election of 9 April was little changed from 1955; Diem organized a grassroots nationwide campaign. He won about 80 percent of the eligible vote (ten percent voted for other candidates, and the rest did not vote) and the U.S. embassy in Saigon concluded there was no sign of blatant fraud. Also encouraging, Viet Cong attempts to disrupt the election failed. It did reveal a troubling political reality, however. When it came to metropolitan Saigon-Cholon, Diem only garnered 48 percent of the possible votes. His opposition was concentrated in Saigon, and his support amongst the educated class was weak. That would make his relationship with Washington more difficult as Saigon was where the overwhelming majority of Americans formed their opinions about Diem's rule.[29]

Militarily, the increased Civil Guard–ARVN anti-infiltration patrols along the DMZ paid off. In March they discovered and destroyed the Calu trail station that forced Hanoi to switch the Ho Chi Minh Trail from the RVN to Laos. But the most significant consequence had to be entrance of the Kennedy administration that took office in January, and it did not take long for it to take action. A major step forward in America's involvement was made on 11 May 1961 when President Kennedy approved NSAM 52. It was the first of three memoranda issued between 1961 and 1963 that importantly shaped the Vietnam War (the others being NSAMs 104 and 273). A broad ranging document, the memorandum (1) created a special interagency Vietnam Task Force in Washington that answered to the president, (2) allocated additional economic resources to the RVN, (3) authorized an increase in the number American military advisors, (4) directed the task force to assess further expanding the ARVN, and (5) began joint US-RVN covert operations that targeted the DRV.[30]

Vice President Lyndon Johnson was sent to Saigon both to offer a strong public statement of endorsement for South Vietnam and to cement agreement with Diem. This was a major shift in policy, not just in terms of commitment, but also approach. A few days earlier, Durbrow, with his hard-nosed approach toward Diem, was replaced. Nolting, his successor, was a rising star in the State Department and directed to make real Kennedy's message of cooperation. Lansdale, by then a general, also was sent back to Saigon to help gain Diem's buy-in to the new program. He reported that Diem opposed the introduction of U.S. ground forces into South Vietnam, an idea under discussion, but agreed with increased American military support to include more U.S. military advisory personnel. Diem forwarded those opinions in a personal letter to Kennedy in June.[31] The Americans were ramping up their efforts.

From Hanoi's perspective, the war in the south advanced favorably in 1961. Coordinated military actions began when COSVN was reactivated in January, and Hanoi was eager to keep up the pace of operations. Although the political struggle remained dominant, in February Le Duan ordered COSVN to form big VC units, 12 Main Force or provincial guerrilla battalions, with six to be formed in Nam Bo augmented by a seventh PAVN regroupee Main Force battalion and the rest in MR-5. The transition toward Phase 3 moved forward. In recognition of increased VC activity, in the spring the JGS transferred the well-regarded 7th Infantry Division from the secure MR II to MR V in the Mekong Delta. The move worked to a degree. By the summer, the Viet Cong's campaign had run its course The Civil Guard reinforced by ARVN units in the delta stabilized the situation, but the Viet Cong had made significant gains, and their morale soared.[32]

In late spring, President Kennedy approved the recommendation of the Vietnam Task Force to send teams of economic and military experts to Saigon to study the problem firsthand, then craft a framework for success in South Vietnam. The first part dealt with programs to improve the RVN's economy and standard of living and stabilize government finances that were being drained to pay for the war against the Viet Cong. To address that, the Special Financial Group led by Stanford University professor Eugene A. Staley was organized. In June, the Staley group arrived in South Vietnam, did their work, and submitted their initial report to Presidents Kennedy and Diem on 14 July. The heart of the program was a realignment of the RVN's budget to focus overwhelmingly on defeating the Viet Cong, while the United States would augment the effort with substantial monetary and other forms of aid. The next key area for a country whose economy depended on rice production was the agroville program begun in 1959. Deemed too costly, too ambitious, and designed to fight the low-intensity insurgency of the late 1950s, it quietly ended in 1961 with only 23 agrovilles established. Staley's group found value in the concept but recognized its weaknesses. That spurred support for its successor, the Rural Construction Program.[33]

The security challenges did not go away. During March and April, Diem mobilized the reserves, and in May the MAAG approved a Civil Guard expansion and paramilitary retraining program. It did not begin until late 1961, and progress was slow. Of the 372 Civil Guard companies, only 32 finished the required training by year's end, and there was no battalion-level program. As for weapons, the Guard was never as heavily armed as their VC Main Force opponents, and the firepower gap only grew as modern Chinese and Soviet Bloc weapons arrived in numbers. Nonetheless, the implementation of the December 1960 decisions to increase the guard's size, place it firmly under control of the Defense Ministry, and belatedly properly train and arm it for the counterinsurgency were positive steps. Madame Nhu entered the fray in November after Diem approved the recruitment of women for the SDC. She led the program that graduated 1,200 women in the first class that adopted the slogan "Determined to Win."[34] The women were trained in the use of small arms, hand-to-hand combat, and civic action PSYOPS. It was a groundbreaking step. For the first time pro–Republic of Vietnam women assumed an armed combat role.[35]

At the same time, the flow of PAVN troops and equipment down the Ho Chi Minh Trail through Laos gained momentum. The two VWP-PAVN senior leadership groups along with thousands of regroupees had arrived in the RVN by late summer as Hanoi took full control over the revolution in the south. That tilt in the balance of forces finally allowed the Central Highlands to become an active front on an ongoing basis. When the first PAVN regroupees and VWP cadres arrived in the summer of 1959, they recognized how weak the revolutionary forces were and concluded Resolution 15 allowed them the use of "armed self-defense" in a broad sense to support the political struggle.[36] They slowly built up strength, and after augmentation by several thousand PAVN regroupees by the fall, the Viet Cong offensive in the Central Highlands peaked (with modest gains made in rural Kontum, Pleiku, and even previously quiet Darlac provinces). Again, it was not an unmitigated success. The highland operations were capped by an attack on a Civil Guard camp at Dak Ha north of Kontum on Route 14. The camp was overrun and the garrison destroyed, but an ARVN reaction force from the 22nd Division's 41st and 42nd Regiments inflicted heavy casualties on the VC. To the south, the grizzly 1961 highlight in Nam Bo occurred in late September when the Viet Cong raided the Phuoc Thanh provincial capital of Phuoc Vinh (90 kilometers northwest of Saigon) and publicly beheaded the province chief along with a number of captured ARVN soldiers.[37]

Alarmed by the worsening situation, in October Kennedy sent General Maxwell D. Taylor (special military assistant to the president), Lansdale, and Walt W. Rostow (head of the State Department's Policy Planning Council) to assess the military situation. Taylor wrote a comprehensive plan and submitted it to Kennedy on 3 November. Amongst the counterinsurgency recommendations, three stood out. The first was the introduction of a U.S. combat brigade TF. The second addressed the need to improve ARVN battlefield mobility, and the third, the infiltration problem. Taylor's report became the military counterpart to Staley's economic effort, and together they addressed the economic and military issues raised by NSAM 52. After the details were fleshed out, it was approved. Implementation got underway at the close of the year, but the full effect would not be felt until 1962. Known as the Staley-Taylor Plan, it made military and security issues the priority to be followed by RVN economic development and was the first comprehensive American effort to provide enough support to enable South Vietnam to win the war.[38]

Under the plan, the South Vietnamese military would receive greater aid across the board that allowed it to expand to 200,000 troops. The recommendation to improve ARVN mobility went forward, as did the concept for Taylor's anti-infiltration Northwest Frontier Force made up of light mobile infantry companies to attack the Ho Chi Minh Trail but not under U.S. military direction.

December saw the new American policy in action with the arrival of 400 U.S. Army personnel. Part of the contingent addressed Taylor's urge to improve ARVN mobility and took the form of something still relatively new to warfare: the U.S. Army 8th and 57th Helicopter Companies. Also arriving with the U.S. troops and helicopters were over 20 M113 armored personnel carriers.[39]

The JGS adjusted to the changing battlefield by shifting another division in December, this time the 21st Infantry Division, from Tay Ninh to the Viet Cong's Mekong Delta stronghold. In January 1961, the number of American military personnel in the RVN totaled 685 and by year's end 4,000. Not everything Taylor recommended was granted. His request for the U.S. Army brigade hit a roadblock. In his November letter to President Kennedy, Diem requested more assistance to include U.S. military personnel, however Diem still opposed introducing U.S. ground troops, and Admiral Felt, who oversaw U.S. military support in the RVN, concurred. Taylor's plan for a ground combat force was tabled. American involvement grew at a significant but measured pace.[40]

Some later held that U.S. military support begun in 1961 violated its commitment to the 1954 Geneva agreements. That was false. In 1954, Washington told the world that it would not disturb the peace, but those restraints would be removed if the region's peace and security were threatened. Hanoi's relentless infiltration of soldiers, VWP cadres, and war materials into South Vietnam did exactly that. And it never signed the Geneva Agreement and Final Declaration; instead it invoked the UN Charter's Article II.[41]

During a September address to the UN General Assembly, President Kennedy warned of the danger to the peace in Southeast Asia. In November Washington reached out to London to see if they could get Moscow to put pressure on Hanoi to stop the infiltration into South Vietnam. The effort failed, and two weeks later Dean Rusk made a direct appeal to the ICC. As in Laos, nothing happened. In December the Kennedy administration publicly denounced and documented the DRV's violations in a report whose title began with the words enunciated in 1954: *A Threat to the Peace: North Viet-Nam's Effort to Conquer South Viet-Nam*. It built on arguments presented earlier in the RVN's *Violations of the Geneva Agreement*. There was no violation by the United States. It acted in accordance with its commitments.

For the DRV, the actions by the Kennedy administration in 1961 were grave. It was a marked expansion of what the VWP termed the special war or My-Diem struggle that was directed the US-RVN alliance where Washington supported every facet of the RVN's war effort. Hanoi still held the upper hand, however. Its gains in the south were significant and tangible. The Americans only had a plan, albeit one backed by comparatively unlimited resources.

While the violence escalated in the RVN, neither Hanoi nor Washington had made the war in Vietnam its overriding focus in 1961. Both had concentrated on Laos, the DRV on securing and opening its strategic logistical entryway into the RVN and the Ho Chi Minh Trail, and the United States on containing what it saw as a broader attempt to spread communism across Southeast Asia. In the case of both countries, however, the Laos actions were temporary measures that more shaped than ignored the real struggle: the war in South Vietnam.[42]

What Were the Secret Wars?

In its efforts in Vietnam, the new Kennedy administration did not limit itself to the RVN and Laos. It also sought to destabilize North Vietnam the way Hanoi had destabilized South Vietnam. In May, just months after taking office, President Kennedy approved a broad range of CIA covert operations in support of South Vietnam initially directed in NSAM 52 (Annex 6). It was intended to realize the president's desire to have "guerrillas operate in the North."[43] The CIA's clandestine and covert roles in thwarting Hanoi dated back to 1954 with the activities of the CIA's Saigon station and Lansdale's SMM. Added to that were CIA missions in Laos begun during the late 1950s in what became a low-intensity surrogate war between the U.S. and DRV. By 1961, the effort in Laos involved the FAR and Hmong, and when the Ho Chi Minh Trail switched over from the RVN, CIA operations grew in Middle and Lower Laos. But the Kennedy administration intended to go beyond what had occurred in the past: to wage a concerted secret war directly targeting the DRV inside North Vietnam. To kick things off, during mid–1961, the CIA met with its South Vietnamese counterparts in Saigon to plan the way ahead.[44]

Washington opted to fight fire with fire, and the President's NSAM 52 directive proposed both retaliatory guerrilla actions in the north and targeting Hanoi's infiltration routes into the south. The guerrilla operations would follow three lines of operation: (1) develop agent networks inside the DRV; (2) harass the DRV through covert paratroop and amphibious underwater demolition and sabotage raids; and (3) execute a variety of psychological operations. While called operations, the military term, the CIA usually called them projects, and soon a number were underway. In other quirks of terminology, the military assigned missions or tasks while the CIA sent requirements. And the CIA routinely used the word "paramilitary" in lieu of "covert military" to define missions.

Covert projects, unlike CIA clandestine espionage, were subjected to greater oversight, and this was accomplished through a group of senior officials in Washington. Established in 1955, the 5412 Committee (also known as the Special Group or 303 Committee) was charged with directing overseas covert operations. The number 5412 came from the 15 March 1954 document authorizing and supervising the secret missions, NSC 5412, Covert Operations. The number 303 referred to the committee's meeting place, Room 303 in the Old Executive (now the Eisenhower) Office Building in Washington. The committee answered to the president, was headed by the president's national security advisor, and included senior representatives from the Defense and State Departments, CIA, JCS, and others as directed by the president. Selected members of the NSC staff supported the committee. From 1961 through 1966, National Security Advisor McGeorge Bundy chaired the committee and oversaw the secret wars in Indochina. During the Vietnam War, the military had two layers of oversight for its proposed covert operations in addition to the committee: the assistant secretary of defense for special operations and the JCS special assistant for counterinsurgency and special activities.[45]

To appreciate what Bundy supervised, understanding the distinction between clandestine and covert actions was important. In a successful clandestine operation, no one outside the operators and top seniors knew anything happened; the mission was invisible to the eyes of both friend and foe. That was why they were so often linked to espionage. Differently, the effects of a successful covert operation could not be hidden but did ensure there was no direct trail of evidence that led back to the operators. During the secret wars in Indochina, if covert operators blew up a bridge at midnight in the DRV, then the fact that something happened could not remain hidden, but its covert nature could provide plausible deniability. The suspects might have been the Americans or South Vietnamese or both or ideally, anti-communist North Vietnamese guerrillas, but nothing irrefutably pointed in one direction—and if accused, the explosion could be attributed to a cover story, like a PAVN munitions truck mishap.

The military's role in covert operations rose to national prominence during the Vietnam War. The reason was simple. The CIA had dropped the ball in Cuba with the 1961 Bay of Pigs fiasco. In its wake on 26 June 1961, President Kennedy signed NSAM 57 that gave the military the lead in major covert operations and delegated the CIA to a supporting role. In October Walt Rostow in the White House, through McNamara and General Taylor, tasked CINCPAC to develop a covert retaliatory cause-and-effect plan to deal with North Vietnam that would do everything the CIA planned to do, only on a larger scale. On 6 June 1962 it became an appendix of OPLAN 32 that dealt with a possible war in Indochina.[46]

The transfer evolved gradually. At that time, only the CIA knew how to conduct wide-ranging covert operations, and the OPLAN 32 appendix was just a paper plan. The military had to play catch-up, but McNamara embraced the opportunity and with new lines of authority drawn, the transfer of CIA paramilitary operations to the Defense Department got underway—only slowly. The military had resources but limited experience and no purpose-built organizations in place: joint unconventional warfare task forces (JUWTFs).[47]

While the Defense Department built up its capabilities, the CIA carried on in Indochina. In addition to CIA operatives, the proposed combined force was to consist of U.S. military personnel, hand-picked members of the 400-soldier strong RVN Airborne Special Forces (LLBD), and selected northern regroupees living in South Vietnam. NSAM 57

The analytical and supremely confident Secretary of Defense Robert S. McNamara (National Archives).

had given the power over covert operations to the military, but as an institution, it was uneasy with unconventional warfare, and the Bay of Pigs legacy loomed large as well. No one in the Pentagon wanted to be responsible for another failed covert operation. General Taylor, who was comfortable with the CIA's secret war abilities, opposed having the military jump in too quickly. When he became JCS Chairman (CJCS) on 1 October 1962, he saw to it that things continued to go slowly.[48]

The CIA Acts

After Kennedy's NSAM 52 order, the CIA got to work under command of its Far East Division Director in Saigon, William Colby. Fortunately, Colby did not have to start from scratch; a CIA paramilitary section already existed within the Saigon station, and there was a covert operations capability in the DRV. It began in 1954 with Conein of Lansdale's SMM. Lansdale had given him a team that included a Harvard-educated Marine who had worked behind enemy lines in Korea, Arthur "Nick" Arundel, and sent them to Hanoi to set up operations. The CIA also procured a variety of weapons, special equipment, and C-3 plastic explosives. Conein's requirements included psychological operations to motivate Vietnamese, especially Catholics, to regroup south and establish and equip both intelligence and paramilitary resistance and sabotage networks made up of anti-communist northerners. They were skills Conein mastered during World War II in the OSS when he worked first with the Maquis in occupied France, and more importantly after France was liberated, in Vietnam where he met both Ho and Giap in 1945.[49]

In 1954, Conein set up two clandestine paramilitary groups: Hao Detachment comprised of Nationalist Party volunteers and the Binh Detachment made up of Dai Viet recruits, with many selected by party leader Bui Diem. In October, Conein was forced to evacuate Hanoi but

National Security Advisor McGeorge Bundy in Vietnam with unidentified U.S. soldiers. Another World War II OSS officer who later became a Harvard academic of exceptional renown, Bundy served as Kennedy's closest and most trusted subordinate when it came to executing Vietnam policy (National Archives).

The CIA's veteran point man on Vietnam, William Colby (right) speaking with Vice President Nelson Rockefeller (left) and USAF Lieutenant General Brent Scowcroft in April 1975 (National Archives).

continued to build networks until the regroupment window closed in 1955. The Binh Detachment was located in the Red River Delta with cells in Hanoi and Haiphong. It was broken and mostly rolled up by VWP's security services in 1956. The last of the detachment was captured in November 1958, publicly tried in 1959, and its Hanoi commander executed by firing squad after a one-day trial. The Hao Detachment, which operated in the same area, remained dormant and undetected in 1961.[50]

There was more. In the late 1950s, the CIA station in Saigon began sending a handful of Vietnamese agents from the RVN into the DRV by sea (Pacific missions) and across the DMZ (Atlantic missions). The CIA station also worked with Diem's Liaison Service's Office-45 to build up low-level clandestine agent networks. The results were bland; they did provide "atmospherics," insights into average life in North Vietnam, but rarely anything of political or military importance. A second low-level network in southern DRV run by Diem's brother Ngo Dinh Can in Hue augmented the effort. The CIA now had to expand operations and move away from intelligence gathering toward supporting a guerrilla war in the north, and low-level networks proved to be of no use.[51]

Helping that effort, the CIA's Saigon station also had been instrumental in creating the South Vietnamese Special Forces in 1955 who would be needed to implement NSAM 52. The LLBD soldiers originally came from two sources. One contingent came from Conein's northern Vietnamese recruits who still were undergoing CIA training when overt access to North Vietnam ended. The second contingent came from Vietnamese veterans of the French GCMA that had operated behind enemy lines during the War of Resistance. Together they formed the nucleus of the RVN's Special Forces, the 1st Observation Group (1st OG), which entered service in February 1956 under the direction of Colonel Le Quang Tung's Liaison Service.[52]

In 1957, the 1st OG grew when U.S. Special Forces trained a group of 58 soldiers at their Nha Trang base, followed by a second group of 50 in October 1959. They were designed to operate in small teams. When the war began, there were about 300 South Vietnamese Special Forces soldiers formed into several separate companies. By then a 1st OG company was in the thick of it hunting for PAVN infiltrators from a forward operating base at Khe Sanh-Lang Vei (strategically nestled close to both Laos and the DMZ). As the NSAM 52 covert projects had been envisioned as a South Vietnamese effort, in 1961 Colby called on Tung and his 1st OG (renamed the 77th LLDB Group in November) to get the secret war off the ground.[53]

Operations Against North Vietnam

To run covert operations targeting the DRV, Colby formed a cover organization, the Combined Studies Division (CSD), and placed it under the direction of the experienced Colonel Gilbert B. Layton. Concurrently, Colonel Tung stood up a corresponding section, the Topographical Exploitation Service (TES), to work with the CSD in waging the secret wars. To staff the TES, the Liaison Service recruited and vetted northern regroupees for duty in covert units, and the JGS G-5 directorate provided PSYOPS personnel. With the organizations in place, the next job was to get people into the field and start operations.[54]

For the CIA, the guerrilla war effort was a sideshow carried out by missions from the sea and by air. Both missions helped to organize a resistance network of guerrillas and spies in North Vietnam and conduct supporting PSYOPS. Beyond PSYOPS, the primary means of initiating the guerrilla war in North Vietnam was through the insertion of both single agents to set up clandestine intelligence gathering operations and paramilitary agent teams to conduct covert operations. The paramilitary agent teams' tasks mirrored the original mission of the U.S. Special Forces when they formed in the 1950s: insurgency. In mid–1962, that mission was expanded into sabotage and raids akin to the OSS and British Special Operations Executive missions in World War II.[55]

As the DRV was a "denied area" police state, getting in was a risky undertaking from the outset. It required a dangerous "black entry" insertion that meant getting in both illegally and clandestinely. The teams had it a little easier as they operated in remote areas, wore non-national clothes (often old French camouflage uniforms), and were heavily armed, but they also had to master deep reconnaissance and surveillance skills where detection meant almost certain capture and often death. Doubling the risk and unlike the DRV's infiltrators entering the RVN, most agents went in "blind," meaning there was no friendly "welcoming party" on the ground to get them established. While Hanoi had cadres across South Vietnam, the French never allowed a national non-communist political movement to develop, and the mass movement of the regroupees south further reduced the anti-communist population; the Americans and South Vietnamese had no supportive base areas to tap into in the DRV and no safe havens.[56]

If the covert teams had a tough time, trying to give the clandestine agents a decent chance of survival was an even taller order. The CIA made the effort. To avoid capture, an agent would arrive in North Vietnam and immediately have to blend in so as to be invisible to the DRV's expansive security apparatus. That required nearly perfectly forged current identity papers and passes. And everything worn from head to toe and all belongings, to include incidental personal "pocket litter," had to match exactly with those of everyday North Vietnamese. To try to reduce the risk, the areas where the agents were sent were where anti-communists had been strongest: Dai Viet and Nationalist Party strongholds in the Red River Delta and places like Yen Bai and Son La or predominantly Catholic areas or amongst the northwestern hill and mountain peoples where the French GCMA had built a guerrilla army of thousands during the War of Resistance.[57]

Also, to improve the chances of survival, whenever possible, northern regroupee volunteers returned to their home regions. To help them assimilate, northern infiltrators who had recently rallied to Saigon taught a course focused on DRV "survival skills" needed in daily life. Instruction covered everything from food rationing to public transportation, and even though agents fluently spoke the northern dialect, they needed updates in post–1954 vocabulary and slang. The CIA's chief weakness was not agent preparation. It was a failure to prevent penetration of the projects by the robust DRV intelligence services operating in South Vietnam. In 1961, the CIA had no active counterintelligence program vetting the agents. It relied entirely on Office-45.[58]

Maritime Operations (MAROPS)

Beginning in 1961, the MAROPS project consisted of surveilling the DRV's coastal waters, raiding PAVN coastal targets, PSYOPS, and "black entry" agent insertion by motorized junks. The boats were procured by the TES and operated under the cover of the Coastal Security Service. CIA officer Tucker Gougleman, a Marine World War II veteran who had run similar CIA operations during the Korean War, headed up MAROPS. The project had a humble beginning. It operated out of Da Nang, and the naval force consisted of one motorized junk named *Nautilus I*. In the way of personnel, there were Office-45 agents and Chinese Nationalist crews along with CIA officers. The first mission was a success when *Nautilus I* inserted a clandestine agent code-named ARES in April 1961. Things then went downhill. The junk was lured into a trap to resupply ARES, sunk, and the crew captured. *Nautilus II* was not ready until early 1962.[59]

In the spring of 1962, MAROPS expanded into across-the-beach raids and sabotage missions conducted by junks and a pair of Korean War–era PT boats. It also was possible to task the Navy's special operations diesel submarine USS *Catfish* for missions to surveil PAVN patrol boats. Using information obtained by the *Catfish*, in June 1962, *Nautilus II* carried out the first sabotage raid on the PAVN *Swatow* motor torpedo boat base at Quang Khe (near Dong Hoi, 50 kilometers north of the DMZ). The *Nautilus II* arrived near the base, and 1st OG frogmen moved in to attach limpet mines on the torpedo boats. The mission was exposed when a mine detonated prematurely. While trying to escape, *Nautilus II* was sunk and most of the frogmen and crew killed or captured.[60]

In all, the CIA procured seven junks (the first three named *Nautilus I, II,*

III), augmented in late 1962 by three Patrol Craft Fast swift boats and then superior "Nasty" patrol boats in 1963. The junks and boats carried underwater demolition commando teams, also recruited by Office-45, who passed them on to TES, and beginning in 1963 for training by the newly-formed U.S. Navy Sea Air and Land (SEAL) Teams assigned to the CIA (created in January 1962). By late 1963, the SEALs had trained four naval commando teams, informally referred to as RVN SEALs. MAROPS employed 45 Vietnamese personnel along with foreign nationals to pilot the boats, and the missions ran until January 1964.[61]

AIR OPERATIONS

The aerial portion of the covert operation scheme was more extensive and ambitious than MAROPS. Beyond a few clandestine agent drops, the covert airborne missions over the DRV inserted agent teams to conduct intelligence, paramilitary sabotage operations, PSYOPS, and later resupply and reinforcement airdrops. Again, Office-45 and TES obtained the personnel who joined one of two cover organizations: Group 11 and Group 68. The results were more than discouraging. In June 1961, a C-47 carrying a team was shot down, and of the five completed drops in 1961, four teams were rapidly captured, and three of those were turned by DRV security services (became "dirty" or "were doubled"), while one managed to survive for two years before capture. The year of 1962 was no better; one team was captured, turned, and then fed bad information to the CIA; one jumped into a trap set up by a dirty team; another survived for two years; and only one became a long-term asset. The year 1963 was an unmitigated disaster as 14 of 16 insertion teams were captured, and the two that survived were reinforcement drops to existing teams.[62]

From a technical standpoint, things were difficult for the air operations as beginning in 1960, improved PAVN radar coverage tracked incoming aircraft throughout their routes. Hanoi also shifted to a sophisticated radio encryption system for its security services that ended the American's ability to listen in, a capability that would have revealed that the team's aircraft often were being tracked and ground forces alerted before they even jumped. Even more effective were the DRV's Ministry of State Security radio counterintelligence-SIGINT units that intercepted covert communications. When added to the skills of the security officers on the ground, the risks became prohibitive. During the entire 1961–1963 run of the CIA project, a total of 29 covert teams and eight clandestine agents were inserted, with the overwhelming majority captured or killed. By 1963, Colby recognized that the DRV was impenetrably hostile and changed the mission so that the CIA only dropped teams into remote areas. He further recommended that by 1965, the existing teams be exfiltrated and the entire project shut down.[63]

PSYCHOLOGICAL OPERATIONS

PSYOPS were to help foment the resistance and were the easiest and safest missions. They consisted of special projects and propaganda operations headed by veteran CIA officer Herbert Weisshart. Special projects included forging currency as a form of economic warfare and false official documents to spread disinformation designed to undermine support for the VWP, as well as sending faked letters and messages that compromised VWP leaders. DVR officials who travelled abroad were especially vulnerable as the letters and such could be sent from overseas, adding to their credibility and eliminating the need to clandestinely get them into the DRV. The chief PSYOPS special project was creating the illusion of a resistance movement in the DRV, a nonexistent VWP splinter group called the Sacred Sword of the Patriots League. The league was given an extensive backstory or legend, served as cover for sabotage attacks, and could falsely take credit for any act in the DRV that discredited the regime.[64]

Propaganda operations targeted the North Vietnamese people, not to cause an uprising or directly threaten VWP rule, but to increase apathy, discontent, and ideally create a permissive environment that would permit agents to grow the resistance. The CIA employed two types of propaganda against the DRV: black and grey. Black could be partially or totally false with its origins appearing legitimate and to have come from DRV sources. Grey propaganda aimed to shift public sentiment toward the resistance. It had no apparent source of origin and used false or attributed information that was carefully selected and edited to damage the VWP. There also was white propaganda that aimed to get the people of South Vietnam to support Saigon but was not used by the CIA.[65]

A number of methods were employed. There were three radio stations. For black propaganda, a fake *Radio Hanoi* broadcasted at nearly the same frequency as the real *Radio Hanoi* (called snuggling) but with altered damaging messages, while the others appeared to come from the DRV's internal resistance such as the Voice of the Sacred Sword of the Patriots League. Augmenting the broadcasts were grey propaganda leaflets delivered by air or shot from mortars and cannon on MAROPS boats onto the shore. Finally, there were "gift operations" that combined gifts with a propaganda message. Gifts consisted of inexpensive transistor radios preset to the propaganda stations and packages of popular everyday items—especially those hard to get in North Vietnam. They were delivered by airdrop or left on beaches during MAROPS. By 1962, PSYOPS became a mainstay of the CIA operations directed against the DRV.[66]

ANTI-INFILTRATION OPERATIONS

Within South Vietnam, anti–DRV infiltration actions dominated the CIA's covert war, but the initial plan to defeat infiltration was not a covert operation at all—its focus was counterinsurgency. In 1961, Colonel Conein returned to Saigon to take up his old paramilitary duties, this time as advisor to Minister of Interior Bui Van Luong. One of his first tasks was to help make a reality of the brainchild of CSD chief Layton and CIA officer David A. Nuttle: develop a Montagnard force to beat back the VC in the highlands. After a successful experiment in the Rhade village of Buon Enao in Darlac province during mid–1961, the CIA organized the Citizens Irregular Defense Group (CIDG) later that year. It concentrated on winning over and protecting the Montagnard population, becoming the Village Defense Program (VDP) in October. With the cooperation of the Diem government, over 90 CIA officers augmented by U.S. military personnel were sent to Vietnam to work under Layton and Conein. Two U.S. Army ODAs arrived in November to support the CIDG, and eight more were sent in May 1962. They fell under U.S. Special Forces–Vietnam (Provisional) (SF-V [Prov]) that worked hand-in-hand with Layton's CSD in Saigon. The CIDG became the heart of the CIA's efforts in the RVN and was a great success. Despite concerted VC efforts to crush the VDP, the majority of the Montagnards rallied to Saigon despite the long history of distrust of the Vietnamese. In war over hearts and minds in Central Highlands, the VDP proved superior to the VC's competing Mountain Song System.[67]

There was another lesser-known CIA-Montagnard project. Where the VDP used the trompe d'oeil method to expand support among the Rhade, the CIA station's political operations section worked with Diem's brother Can in Hue to create offensive strike forces to improve security across the 16 highland provinces: the Mountain Scouts under maverick ARVN Captain Ngo Van Hung. Formed into 15-man heavily armed teams of Montagnards, they were used to hunt down and kill Viet Cong guerrillas and cadres. After gaining approval first from the CIA substation in Hue then Saigon and finally Washington, the CIA sent a team headed up by Ralph Johnson and Stewart Methven (who previously worked with the Lao CDNI and helped win over the Hmong in 1960) to get the Mountain Scout project off the ground. It went operational on 26 October 1961 and proved successful. One year later, there were 1,100 Mountain Scouts with the project scheduled to expand by 1,500 more. The CIA also began to discreetly organize and arm Cao Dai, Hoa Hao, and Catholic "sea swallow" paramilitary forces in Nam Bo. The gains, especially in the highlands, finally led to efforts to try to stop PAVN infiltration through cross-border raids into Laos targeting the Ho Chi Minh Trail.[68]

As with the agent operations in the DRV, efforts to watch the Ho Chi Minh Trail in Laos predated NSAM 52 as witnessed by the 1st OG activities at Khe Sanh-Lang Vei. But the PAVN's 1961 Ta Khong Offensive allowed Hanoi to control the critical crossroads at Tchepone. Also taken was the Laotian stretch of Route 9 from Tchepone to the RVN border where the only allied force, the inexperienced FAR's 33rd Volunteer Battalion, was holed up in its camp and of no use. That posed a new danger to South Vietnam, and the pressure to do more increased. Under CIA guidance, additional 1st OG teams arrived and were paired with Montagnards to conduct reconnaissance missions targeting PAVN infiltration through Laos. This became the Border Surveillance Program (BSP).[69]

As the CIA stepped up its support, BSP OG-Montagnard forces were expanded and organized into squads, platoons, and small light infantry companies. Begun on 12 May 1961, patrols and raids on the trail in Laos increased in size and frequency. Saigon called it Operation Lei-Yu (Thunder Shower in Mandarin). In early 1962, U.S. Special Forces under the CIA expanded Thunder Shower to include long-range patrols operating out of two CIDG bases near the border: at Dak Pek in the northern end of the Central Highlands and farther north at Khe Sanh-Lang Vei. The missions focused on three areas: the Laotian border along the Central Highlands, Route 9 in Laos, and the DMZ.[70]

None of the efforts significantly degraded PAVN infiltration nor did intelligence obtained fully reveal the expansion of the trail. During this period, beyond traversing the main trail itself, the PAVN did not infiltrate soldiers into the Khe Sanh area or to its immediate south. There was no one for the BSP patrols to detect; the action was in the highlands and northern Nam Bo. But BSP missions did trigger a PAVN reaction. They mined and booby-trapped routes leading from South Vietnam into Laos and reassigned infantry units to patrol the trail. That was the only real success: tying down PAVN troops and resources better used elsewhere. BSP cross-border missions continued until the Geneva agreements went into effect in October 1962. That led to orders from Washington implementing both a ban on U.S. military personnel entering Laos and a halt to deep missions—but not short-range penetrations. By then nearly 50 deep patrols had been completed.[71]

Covert Air Support

The covert war could not be waged without aircraft—all kinds of aircraft from fixed to rotary winged, both armed and unarmed—and that part of the war was fought by three organizations: Air America, the Vietnamese Air Transport (VIAT) Company augmented by the RVN Air Force, and USAF special operations units (along with selected U.S. Army helicopter squadrons). The most famous was Air America with its impressively accurate motto, "Anything, Anywhere, Anytime," but all three played important roles. Air America began life in 1947 as Civil Air Transport (CAT), a commercial airline in China headed by the famed Flying Tigers commander, Claire Chennault. After Mao's victory over the Nationalist in late 1949, CAT was nearly bankrupt and had lost its key market: Mainland China. On 10 July 1950 the CIA stepped in, paid $1 million for the business, and took over the company. For most of the next decade, CAT operated as both a legitimate air transportation company and a covert operator for CIA missions. In February 1959, it was renamed Air America. During the Vietnam War, Air America flew commercial flights covering South Vietnam, Laos, and Thailand while the bulk of its covert operations focused on Laos.[72]

The CIA also used Air America to form VIAT in early 1961 to support covert and clandestine agent team insertion, supply, and PSYOPS missions over North Vietnam. Despite its name, VIAT was mostly staffed with former Nationalist Chinese air force personnel. RVN Air Force's 1st Transportation Squadron led by Colonel Nguyen Cao Ky provided additional crews and aircraft for VIAT. VIAT barely survived as its only aircraft flying covert missions, a C-47, was shot down over North Vietnam in July. While VIAT's DRV mission team regrouped, the focus shifted to South Vietnam, and two C-46s were acquired along with Piper Comanches and six light and versatile Helio Courier propeller planes (ideal for handling on short crude airstrips). They became workhorses for VIAT support of the CIA's VDP in the Central Highlands as well as other missions required by the Saigon station.[73]

The U.S. Air Force's role began with the 1045th Operations, Evaluation, and Training Group, a joint Air Force–CIA formation that supported covert air operations globally. To restart the DRV mission, they provided VIAT (via Air America) with a superior C-54 in late 1961 that became the primary aircraft for agent drop and resupply missions. When it crashed, the 1045th Group obtained three additional C-54s and continued to support Ky's 1st Transportation Squadron. Laos was not forgotten. As part of NSAM 29's Laos support tasks, Air America began a major build-up of aircraft in Laos and Thailand to include 16 additional CH-34 helicopters to augment the four already in service, one C-47, three DC-3s, four new C-130 transports, and eight B-26 bombers along with the requisite crews. While flown by Air America aircrews, in Udorn Thailand the U.S. Marines maintained the helicopters as part of Operation Millpond, and the Air Force took care of the rest. The aircraft divided their efforts between assisting the FAR and Hmong irregulars.[74]

The USAF mission continued to grow. On 13 October 1961, President Kennedy ordered the 4400th Combat Crew Training Squadron to South Vietnam. This joint air effort with the South Vietnamese became Operation Farm Gate. Its primary task was to train RVN Air Force personnel in close air support, much of it for CIDG units. Conducted under authority granted in NSAM 104 for Southeast Asia, the squadron began carrying out combat missions on 13 January 1962. The 4400th used aging aircraft with RVN Air Force markings: eight armed T-28 trainers, four SC-47s for dropping PSYOPS leaflets, and four RB-26 medium bombers for reconnaissance missions.[75]

The USAF 2nd Air Division arrived at Tan Son Nhut on 20 November 1961 and assumed control over USAF operations in the RVN until 8 October 1962. Afterwards, Farm Gate mission planning and execution fell under the 2nd Advanced Echelon of the 13th U.S. Air Force. Farm Gate only was authorized to conduct limited air support for the South Vietnamese, and the restrictions were severe. Its aircraft only could fly within RVN airspace on missions the RVN Air Force could not support, and combat sorties by all-American crews were prohibited. In December, Farm Gate picked up an additional task to provide combat transportation of ARVN units using C-123 aircraft from the USAF 346th Troop Carrier Squadron. Its missions came to be known as Operation Mule Train. In March 1962, the 4400th was expanded and in mid–1963 redesignated the 1st Air Commando Group. By then, with the exception of some air commando missions, the U.S. Air Force was operating overtly.[76]

Air America support of the CIA rolled on. When a VIAT C-54 was lost in early 1962, the RVN Air Force pilots were replaced with Nationalist Chinese crews who received advanced training from Air America. In March, Air America also provided a helicopter to insert an agent team close to the DRV-Laotian border, a first. As American involvement grew, the need for improved transportation capability became clear; for DRV operations, Taiwan provided VIAT with four more capable C-123Bs. Aircrews underwent CIA-sponsored training late 1962, and by mid–1963 they became operational. The rate of agent team insertions into North Vietnam increased accordingly.[77]

Assessment of the CIA's Secret War

After more than two years of activities, an assessment of the covert battle with the DRV revealed much. For the Americans and South Vietnamese at the tactical and operational level, they were a failure, with the costs far outweighing the gains. Nor did the secret war achieve its strategic purpose to create a guerrilla force within

North Vietnam, but the covert operations did achieve one unstated strategic outcome. The VWP was seriously concerned and reacted accordingly. PAVN coastal and air defense forces did little other than focus on uncovering and foiling CIA-1st OG MAROPS and air insertion missions. Additionally, thousands of security troops and police were tied up trying to locate and capture agents.[78]

Nonetheless, Hanoi was winning the secret infiltration war. The reason why tied in to the different approaches taken by two combatants in their respective secret wars. The DRV used infiltration for vital strategic purposes in its war and the Americans and South Vietnamese did not. One statistic captured reality. From 1961–1963, 143 South Vietnamese operatives went into North Vietnam while the DRV infiltrated 36,264 soldiers and cadres into the RVN, a ratio of roughly 1:250. For success, the Americans and South Vietnamese would have to search elsewhere, and they did not have to look far. With the Staley-Taylor plan in place and resources flowing into the RVN, there was cause for optimism on the ground in South Vietnam as the Vietnam War entered 1962.[79]

14

The Vietnam War in 1962–1963 and the Battle of Ap Bac

The year 1962 did not begin much better for Washington and Saigon than 1961 had ended. During the opening months, the VC initiated an average of 188 engagements per week, putting the ARVN on defense while PAVN regroupees made good progress in forming Main Force units. Gradually the influx of American advisors and new equipment began to be felt, and eventually advisors served at every level from division headquarters down to five-soldier teams with the battalions. Making the ARVN more lethal, divisions received additional artillery batteries, and the number of ranger companies grew from 65 to 86, while the Viet Cong faced a new and deadly threat in the Mekong Delta: the 7th and 21st Mechanized Infantry Companies each equipped with 15 M113 APCs assigned to the ARVN 7th and 21st Infantry Divisions respectively. It took time; the ARVN still were mastering the new APCs as well as the conduct of helicopter operations throughout 1962, but the effort began to pay off.[1]

February was a dramatic month for both sides. COSVN outlined its two military objectives: (1) attack ARVN units, with an emphasis on rangers and JGS reserves, and (2) hit military bases, especially aircraft at airbases. On 2 February in Washington, Roger Hilsman at the State Department submitted his strategy paper on the Vietnam War that saw the war as an internal insurgency, and the next day in Saigon, Diem approved the Strategic Hamlet Program concept—although it took months to get the program off the ground. The concept, an improved version of the agrovilles, had been percolating for months. Sir Robert Grainer Ker Thompson, the English counterinsurgency expert leading the British Advisory Mission in Saigon (formed in September 1961), first outlined the strategic hamlet idea. It aligned nicely with Saigon's New Line civic action concept to deal with the insurgency, and after it passed a trial test overseen by the Rural Construction Program, Diem adopted it.[2]

Next on 8 February, the MAAG was subsumed by the Military Assistance Command, Vietnam (MACV), the largest new military headquarters created since the Korean War, and on 13 February General Paul D. Harkins became its first commanding general. Harkins had been the deputy commander, U.S. Army Forces Pacific, in Hawaii. During World War II, he served under General George S. Patton and under Maxwell Taylor during the Korean War. In 1961, Harkins had been appointed SEATO Field-Force-Center commander based in Bangkok, where his job was to prepare for possible military intervention into Laos (Field Force Plan SFF 5/61) while concurrently leading the U.S. military advisory group in Thailand. He was a well-qualified candidate.[3]

Despite the impressive pace of VC attacks, ARVN field operations began to show positive results. The 21st Infantry Division arrived in the Mekong Delta in December 1961 and in early 1962 began a series of aggressive missions in the southern delta to include the dangerous U Minh Forest. By the end of February, the division had crushed both VC guerrilla battalions operating there (the 1st and 10th). More successes followed.[4]

On 22 March, the ARVN went on offense and launched Operation Binh Dinh (Sunrise), its first major pacification campaign of the year as dozens of battalions from the 7th and 21st Divisions conducted cascading sweeps of VC controlled areas in the Mekong Delta and provinces surrounding Saigon. The 7th Division began in Binh Duong province north of Saigon (in MR-8 or War Zone D, a major VC stronghold centered about 50 kilometers northwest of Saigon) while the 21st Division focused on An Xuyen, Dinh Vinh, and Phong Dinh provinces (see Map 3 for province locations). Control over the Cao Dai's Tay Ninh stronghold also improved when Diem backed Province Chief Nhuan, who replaced all the district and village chiefs with Cao Dai administrators. And a new tactic was introduced: clear and hold. It mirrored the "province rehabilitation" program used in Malaya by Thompson.[5] The ARVN troops would first "clear" the area of Viet Cong. On their heels, the Civil Guard and SDC "holding" forces arrived to established outposts and fortified camps and then patrol and engage in other small unit actions to keep the VC at bay. Finally, civic action, medical, and governance support teams cemented the gains by establishing strong and effective civil authority.[6]

The initial operations were followed up by similar "clear and hold" missions by the two ARVN divisions during April in the Mekong Delta's Can Tho province and then in Gia Dinh with its Rung Sat swamp to Saigon's south. May witnessed the ambush of elements of the 261st Main Force Battalion by the 7th Division in Kien Tuong province. When the 261st Battalion decided to fight it out again during July, it suffered a second defeat. Not all the action was in the Mekong Delta. The other old VWP regroupment area in coastal central South Vietnam remained a problem that needed addressing. In April, improved popular support for Saigon in contested Quang Ngai province led to Royal Phoenix conducted by the ARVN's 51st Infantry Regiment, where an intelligence tip allowed the ARVN to crush a major Viet Cong attack. That was followed up by the 22nd Infantry Division's "clear and hold" Operations Hai Yen (Sea Swallow) I and II in Phu Yen province (south of Quang Ngai) that began in May.[7]

By the time the summer rains brought a halt to most operations, Viet Cong momentum had been stymied. Both the Americans and South Vietnamese found the VC more vulnerable than expected in 1962, and one reason was the helicopter that allowed the ARVN to land in their rear without warning. The versatility of the helicopter continued to be felt as the number of units increased. In April, Operation Shufly began when a self-sustaining U.S. Marine Corps helicopter squadron (HMM-362) arrived, and by the summer the U.S. Army had a battalion headquarters directing the operations of five army transport helicopter companies and one helicopter gunship company. The two M113 companies became equally invaluable.[8]

When the monsoons waned, a new wave of "clear and hold" ARVN pacification operations began, and the now highly mobile ARVN pressed their advantage. Phase I began in August, followed by Phase II that ran from September to October. They met with success. In August, the ARVN hit the Viet Cong's MR-9 in western Nam Bo, and the 514th Provincial Battalion suffered severely when its training base at My Phuoc Tay (also in Kien Tuong province) came under assault. The battalion took over 150 casualties with one company being nearly wiped out, losing 82 killed out of 106 soldiers. In September the 7th Mechanized Company almost single-handedly wiped out the 504th Provincial Battalion that left well over 100 VC dead on the battlefield.[9]

The JGS followed with "clear and hold" operations by the 25th Infantry Division in Tay Ninh and Long An provinces in October, and in November the division conducted another major operation against Nam Bo's MR-8. While not every operation succeeded—the gains in Binh Duong province were mixed at best, and those that did succeed often failed to live up to the ideal—the ARVN's 1962 campaign was good enough to threaten and even roll back VC control in a number of areas. As Hanoi's official history of the war put it, "areas where the masses had seized control shrank" and "guerrillas from a number of villages and hamlets were forced to move to other areas or flee to our base areas."[10]

It was not all good news for the Viet Cong's enemies. Distressing to Washington and Saigon and in an imitation of an incident in Indonesia two years earlier, on 27 February a handful of Nationalist Party radicals in the air force bombed the presidential palace. One of the two jet aircraft was shot down, and although the damage was significant, the casualties were light; only two people reportedly suffered wounds, and Diem, who was in the palace, emerged unharmed. The surviving conspirators fled to Cambodia, whereas in the failed 1960 paratroop coup, Prince Sihanouk granted them asylum, an act that further soured Cambodian-RVN relations. While the attempted assassination failed, the strike was politically damaging and unsettling. The most alarming outcome came during meetings between Conein and several senior ARVN generals. They made clear they did not support the attack on Diem but had grown frustrated because he would not let them honestly report on the war—it had to be good news, as anything else met with unconstructive dressing downs by Diem.[11]

Setting aside Saigon's political intrigues, the Staley-Taylor plan became reality and met with good results. One of its most distinctive characteristics was the erection of strategic hamlets that began with the "hold" phase of Operation Binh Dinh and expanded from there. The program was formally inaugurated on 17 April as the National Policy of Strategic Hamlets and the CIDG village defenders were integrated to a degree into the process. One key initiative was the creation of Rural Rehabilitation Teams to implement the program in the field. They were comprised of personnel from multiple ministries to include the Civic Action Teams. Diem put his brother Nhu in charge by naming him chair of the Inter-Ministerial Committee for Strategic Hamlets. General Nguyen Ngoc Thang, director of Revolutionary Development, oversaw the program's operation.[12]

Thompson helped guide Nhu and Thang by falling back on his Malayan experiences where he had implemented a similar "New Life" village program. There were important differences. In Malaya the villages were built with the aim of winning over landless ethnic Chinese farmers. The Chinese had been a discriminated-against minority, and in rural areas this centered on landlords denying them land; they wanted laborers, not Chinese farming communities. Addressing that was where the program made inroads against the insurgency. It created a one-two punch that emancipated 360,000 rural Chinese by giving them farms and a stake in a peaceful future while separating communist guerrillas from the population. In Mao's terms, the over 300 New Life villages cut off the guerrilla "fish" from the vital "sea" of potentially sympathetic people.[13]

But South Vietnam was not Malaya. Vietnamese villagers wanted security, but the Strategic Hamlet Program was not the one-size-fits-all model of success its proponents presented. In pro-government areas (green zones), the program was popular and often minimally intrusive, amounting to added security forces combined with improved defensive barriers and strongpoints. For the hundreds of thousands of Vietnamese who had fled the north and just had been given new farmlands, the Strategic Hamlet Program proved ideal as it paralleled the Chinese situation in Malaya. The program's added security also had some appeal to villagers living in violently contested areas (yellow zones). But for hundreds of thousands of Vietnamese hamlet dwellers uprooted from their ancestral homes in VC controlled areas (red zones), a strategic hamlet was not their first choice and for many, never a choice they willingly accepted. In those circumstances, it only worked to the degree that the villages served as quasi detention camps that cut VC fighters off from the support of a friendly population.[14]

Thompson convinced Diem, but to obtain the resources needed to make the Strategic Hamlet Program work, a South Vietnamese-American alliance had to be formed. Fortunately, USOM and the CIA were eager to help. After Lou Conein finished his VDP work, he supported Cung's civic action initiatives during Operation Sea Swallow in Phu Yen. That coincided with start of the Strategic Hamlet Program, and soon Conein and other CIA officers like Thomas Ahern, a veteran of Project Momentum in Laos, were working on strategic hamlets; as in Laos, they also were aided by the International Voluntary Service. In July, USOM established the Office of Rural Affairs (carefully avoiding the word counterinsurgency) to work with General Thanh on the Strategic Hamlet Program and unify American support.[15]

Providing security for the farming families was the heart of the program, but it was much more than erecting defensive barriers, establishing tactical radio links to local Civil Guard or ARVN units, and adding SDC squads. The program was a modified version of the French oil spot method with forces over time spreading into red zones, turning them yellow and ultimately green. It aimed to comprehensively address the insurgency. In practical terms, that meant improving farming methods and providing clean water, health care, and education, while proselytizing and adopting good village governance to win over the population. The initial effort, carried out by provincial rehabilitation offices, covered seven provinces in the Mekong Delta just south of Saigon. Colonel Huang Lac, USOM's Rufus Phillips, and CIA officers like Ahern led the effort. It was not perfect. The startup required a large logistical operation as well as trained "establishment teams," and there was corruption to battle, bureaucratic red tape and, for the Americans, political meddling from Saigon. Despite the obstacles, the program slowly emerged as a success.[16]

Operation Sunrise—Binh Dinh—was a turning point. It was the first broad pacification operation since 1955's Operations Tu Do and Giai Phong and far broader in scope. Operation Sunrise represented the concerted effort to combine the three critical lines of operation essential in defeating an insurgency: security, economics, and governance. While there were many shortcomings along all three lines, under the aegis of the Strategic Hamlet Program for the first time since the war began in 1959, South Vietnam's counterinsurgency struggle was moving in the right direction.

Efforts continued in central RVN where the ARVN launched a series of clear and hold operations, where again "hold" meant erecting strategic villages. Building on May's Operation Hai Yen, the ARVN launched Operation Dong Tien in Binh Dinh province in October and Operation Nhau Hao in Phu Bon province in November. Things continued to look up for Saigon. In the Central Highlands during 1962 (and unlike 1960 and 1961), the VC did not succeed in destroying a single military camp and only overran a few villages. The ARVN attacks peaked in November and early December with Operation An Lac, when the 23rd Division's reinforced 44th Infantry Regiment rolled though the Viet Cong base area in a remote highland area where the three provinces of Darlac, Quang Duc, and Tuyen Duc met. To show they were not defeated, a few days later the VC regrouped, massed (to include a new unit, the VC's 200th Artillery Battalion), and launched an attack on the 44th Infantry's Dam Rong camp west of Dalat City. It was easily beaten off but made clear that the VC, while on their heels in some places, were alive and still fighting.[17]

From its inception, the Viet Cong saw the Strategic Hamlet Program as a danger and violently resisted (COSVN quickly added it to its military objectives list). It was described as a "poisonous American and puppet scheme combining political, economic and social tactics," and COSVN directed the provincial committees to review the problem and come up with solutions.[18] Militarily, they concluded that to survive, the strategic hamlets had to be attacked. Targeting hamlets for Viet Cong raids and assaults became a priority. Politically, the VC encouraged people to refuse to enter the hamlets, and they sought to infiltrate their supporters into the hamlets to undermine Saigon's control.[19]

One of the cleverest efforts dealt with destroying the program from within through two top North Vietnamese espionage agents, Pham Xuan An and ARVN Major Albert Pham Ngoc Thao. Fortuitously for Hanoi, Thao became one of Nhu's trusted lieutenants, and helped sabotage the program by issuing counterproductive or dragging-his-feet orders and, in parallel with An, helped turn American officials and journalists against the program. Thao's actions had an added benefit for the Viet Cong; being seen as Nhu's agent, strategic hamlet missteps made Nhu even more unpopular and undermined support for the Diem regime. The strategic hamlets evolved in uneven fits and starts, but the program took root nonetheless, as turning the two coastal provinces east of Saigon, Binh Tuy and Binh Thuan, from "yellow" to "green" was nearly completed by late 1962.[20]

There was another somewhat new tactic to defeat the insurgency: chemical defoliation. Ground-spraying defoliation had been used in Vietnam in the past, but in Malaya a wider aerial spraying program had hurt the enemy and that inspired Diem. While the RVN had no capability, the U.S. Air Force had mastered the skill in the mid–1950s. Diem asked the Americans for help and to accommodate, in August 1961, President Kennedy approved two test missions of air-delivered spraying, one by helicopter on a crop field in the Central Highlands followed by a C-47 mission along a portion of the RVN's Route 13. Both worked. Washington then approved aerial spraying, and six specially outfitted U.S. Air Force C-123 aircraft were assigned to Farm Gate. This became Project Ranch Hand that began flying missions in January 1962.[21]

The defoliation job was limited but important: remove obstructively dangerous vegetation to improve perimeter security at major airbases and along lines of communication (200 meters on each side of critical stretches of highways, main roads, railways, and canals). In May 1962, as the Nam Tha Battle raged in Laos, the mission was completed, and all but two of the C-123s were reassigned as Operation Mule Train combat transports. The broader idea of stripping away jungles was discussed but deemed infeasible. A more contentious but viable option considered at the time aimed at crops in VC held areas. It gained only tepid support. Crop destruction was opposed on the grounds that it both could provide an international propaganda win for the Viet Cong and make more enemies than friends amongst rural populations. Proponents persisted, and in November 1962, Washington approved a target in Phuoc Long province in the Mekong Delta, three more in War Zone D, and then ended the operation.[22]

Despite the range of challenges that the Americans and South Vietnamese threw at it, Hanoi was not about to throw in the towel. There was no argument that the strategic hamlet program was progressing and increased American military support had raised the ARVN's performance to unequalled levels, but no battlefield or war remained static; Vietnam was no exception. The Viet Cong learned how to deal with the new dangers. To their advantage, the Staley-Taylor Plan was compromised when in early 1962, a copy literally was handed to Pham Xuan An by the head of the SEPES intelligence bureau, Dr. Tran Kim Tuyen. Tuyen was not reckless, he considered An—who worked for the international press and had lived in America—above suspicion, and because of those experiences and his mastery of English, he wanted An's input.[23]

Hanoi also could take comfort in the fact that no matter how many ARVN sweeps, important parts of Nam Bo and MR-5 remained under VC control. It was so obvious that many areas were demarked by real if unofficial boundaries recognized by both sides. South Vietnamese villagers knew which roads and hamlets were safe and who controlled them. The VC cadres in the delta remained confident as politically, their hold over the people they still controlled grew in strength. Even in MR-5 there were positive signs. In Phu Yen province, VC ambushes along Highway 1 and the paralleling railroad became a problem for Saigon for the first time since 1954. That had triggered Operations Hai Yen I and II. The Viet Cong also began the process of forming MR-5 Main Force battalions and regiments, although the battalions were mere companies and regiments not combat formations but static sub-regional military headquarters.[24]

Importantly, the Viet Cong developed tactics to confront the new helicopter attacks. In October, the VC 514th Battalion gained a measure of revenge. It inflicted a number of casualties on a 7th Division ranger company when the VC stayed and fought in their trenches during an assault helicopter landing in My Tho province. That success encouraged COSVN. Later that month, it ordered Main Force companies to engage the ARVN if they landed next to their entrenched positions. Some, like 7th ARVN Division senior advisor Colonel John Paul Vann, noted the stiffened Viet Cong defensive stance, but it would take more than one small fight to bring home the importance of the new tactic—even for talented officers like Vann.[25]

To keep pressure on the Viet Cong, in November Saigon initiated the Chieu Hoi (Open Arms) program, the idea of Minister for Civic Action Ngo Trong Hieu. Chieu Hoi was a psychological warfare-propaganda project that urged Viet Cong to rally to Saigon. As opposed to the treatment for deserters or prisoners, they were "re-indoctrinated" and debriefed for intelligence information once they agreed to support Saigon and were vetted by the government. They then were reintegrated into society. It began on a test basis that extended nationally on 17 April 1963. From relatively few VC prisoners prior to that, it quickly rose to 3,200 per month before stabilizing at an average of 1,600 per month in the latter part of 1963. It remained an effective program for years to come.[26]

To better manage the war, the ARVN also overhauled its national command and control structure. By December 1962, the old military region and army corps system was abolished. It was replaced with four Corps Tactical Zones (CTZs) with I CTZ starting along the DMZ and progressing southward, II CTZ that included the Central Highlands, III CTZ north of Saigon, and IV CTZ to Saigon's south covering the Mekong Delta (see Map 3). Each corps zone was further divided into division tactical areas (DTAs) with numerical designations such as 11th and 12th DTAs for I CTZ and 41st, 42nd, 43rd and 44th DTAs for IV CTZ. Each DTA consisted of a number of provinces. Saigon and the surrounding area continued as a separate command. Additionally, two new provinces were created: Hau Nghia in IV CTZ, a VC stronghold, and quieter Phu Bon in II CTZ.[27]

As 1962 ended, it appeared the Kennedy team had hit upon an effective counterinsurgency strategy. Beyond battlefield successes and the unexpected gains made through the use of helicopters and APCs, over 2,000 strategic hamlets had been established in Nam Bo alone, and of the 372 Civil Guard companies, all but 19 completed the counterinsurgency course. The training was urgently needed. Despite the growing ARVN role, the bulk of the fighting and dying in 1962 still fell on the backs of the Civil Guard and SDC. Yet there were no claims of victory in Washington or Saigon. Diem deplored the casualties and let his commanders know it. CINCPAC in Hawaii reported that expectations were for a "protracted and difficult war" and that RVN forces "failed to inflict serious defeat upon the Communist inspired and supported Viet Cong."[28]

The effectiveness of the Staley-Taylor plan was inescapable, nonetheless. Viet Cong attacks dropped by more than half, to 92 per week for last six months of 1962, and while the ARVN and Civil Guard still showed many weaknesses, the ratios of VC to GVN casualties moved in its favor. The number of Viet Cong casualties rose significantly. Despite having spent most of the year on offense, ARVN fatalities only grew from 4,004 in 1961 to 4,457 in 1962—an outcome Diem appreciated. Hanoi despaired of the fact that nothing had been gained in 1962; they were no closer to victory than in 1961. Frank G. Hooton, the Canadian ICC Delegate in Saigon, concluded that during the second half of 1962, the consensus over the war's outlook had gone from qualified optimism to optimism. For the American and South Vietnamese, victory was not close at hand, but things appeared to be on the right track.[29]

Perspective was everything. While guardedly positive, many Americans were frustrated. The Viet Cong battalions the ARVN mauled during 1962 had been reconstituted and were back on the battlefield. It seemed no matter how successful an operation was, no lasting progress had been made. COSVN too was frustrated. Instead of growing the number of Main Force and guerrilla battalions and expanding the base areas, all their resources were committed to holding on to what they held and rebuilding units chewed up by the ARVN.[30]

The future could not be seen. The war in 1963 was not a continuation of 1962. It became the year when American impatience with the protracted conflict took a sharp turn away from concentrating on Hanoi and the Viet Cong and instead toward criticism of and disagreement with their South Vietnamese allies. The reason was simple. Washington really knew very little about the DRV or the Viet Cong but each and every shortcoming, error, and misstep by their ally was there for all to see. Many Americans focused on what they knew while ignoring the counterbalancing effect of the largely unknown enemy. Blaming Saigon became almost an obsession. That divisive process began from the outset in 1963 and progressively worsened into tragedy.

The War in 1963: The Battle of Ap Bac

What became the battle of Ap Bac (Bac hamlet) evolved innocuously but became the most important military clash of the Vietnam War up to that point. In December 1962, a top secret, joint ARVN-US radio direction-finding unit located and analyzed signals from a VC radio transmitter near two small adjacent hamlets of the larger Tan Phu village in the Mekong Delta province of Dinh Tuong: Ap Tan Thoi and to its south Ap Bac (75 kilometers west-southwest of Saigon). The information indicated the presence of a VC company with an estimated strength of 120 soldiers. The hamlets sat in IV CTZ's 41st DTA that covered five provinces and garrisoned by the 7th Division. With that, the JGS ordered the 7th Division to capture the radio site. The targeted hamlets had never been the scene of a major operation, so they would be fighting on unfamiliar ground. Making things even more risky, they sat in a Viet Cong "liberated" base area—enemy territory.[31]

American advisors with the 7th Division planned the attack, Operation Duc Thang I (Righteous Victory I), that would begin with air strikes to soften up the target area. Afterwards, on 1 January 1963, the 7th Division's 330-man strong 2nd Battalion, 11th Infantry Regiment (2/11 Infantry) in helicopters would land north of Ap Tan Thoi at 7:00 a.m. It would advance south across the Tong Doc Loc Canal to attack and seize the hamlet. To reinforce the battalion and take advantage of the network of canals, the 21st River Assault Group with the 352nd Ranger Company in landing craft would sail up from My Tho to assume a blocking position along the canals north of Tan Thoi (see Map 4).[32]

To handle the advance from the south to Ap Bac were two Civil Guard groups (Task Force A under Captain Tri and B under Lieutenant Thi) with about 300 troops each. TF A contained the 174th, 842nd, and 892nd Companies while B held the 171st, 172nd, and 839th Companies. The groups often were referred to as battalions but actually were ad hoc tactical formations. They were not formally organized, trained, nor equipped to fight as battalions. They would advance north toward Ap Bac to block the Viet Cong's retreat as 2/11 Infantry attacked to the south—the classic "hammer and anvil" maneuver. Both groups were under the province chief, 31-year-old Major Lam Quang Tho. Although Tho had been a ARVN battalion commander (2nd Armored Cavalry Regiment), as province chief he had a lot to handle with no regimental battle staff.[33]

Coordinating the forces converging on Ap Bac was complicated beyond just dealing with the infantry, rangers, and Civil Guard. Because the Civil Guard had to travel north several kilometers on foot after being dropped off from trucks on Highway 4, they would begin their foot march toward Ap Bac first, at 6:30 a.m.

Additionally, the division's 7th Mechanized Company (with 13 of its 15 M113 armored personnel carriers) under Captain Ly Tong Ba was positioned by one of the many canals to the southwest so it could hit either the Viet Cong's west flank or reinforce as needed. The company had been renamed the 4th Squadron, 2nd Armored Cavalry Regiment in 1962, but the old name stuck. The outfit, one the first M113 units in Vietnam, had a good reputation—it was the same unit that crushed a VC battalion in 1962.[34]

Heavy 4.2-inch mortars and 105 mm howitzers from the division's 7th Artillery Battalions along with fighter-bombers, medium bombers, and helicopter gunships would provide fire support. Colonel Vann, in an unarmed observation plane, intended to fly over the battlefield to provide command and control advice to the ARVN units fighting on the ground. If help was needed, the 7th Division alerted two 1/11 Infantry companies near a dirt airstrip and LZ at Tan Hiep (10 kilometers east of Ap Bac) to be ready to fly into the battle area. Finally, the 8th Paratroop Battalion in Saigon was held in strategic reserve by the JGS. The American advisors and ARVN commanders were confident the hamlets would be secured and the Viet Cong defeated, but it was a complex operation.[35]

Although few knew it, the going would not be easy. Ap Bac sat in a flood plain with the paddies and irrigation dikes half full, the canals at high water, and the mud deep. The Viet Cong called the soaked ground "spongy," meaning that a rapid advance or maneuver on foot by the ARVN soldiers would be impossible.[36] Nonetheless and as they had been doing for months, the American and ARVN officers expected the Viet Cong to cut and run once they realized the size of their force. Then came the first major change to the plan, made by the 7th Division's chief of staff, Colonel Bui Dinh Dam: the launch date. Since the Americans would be celebrating New

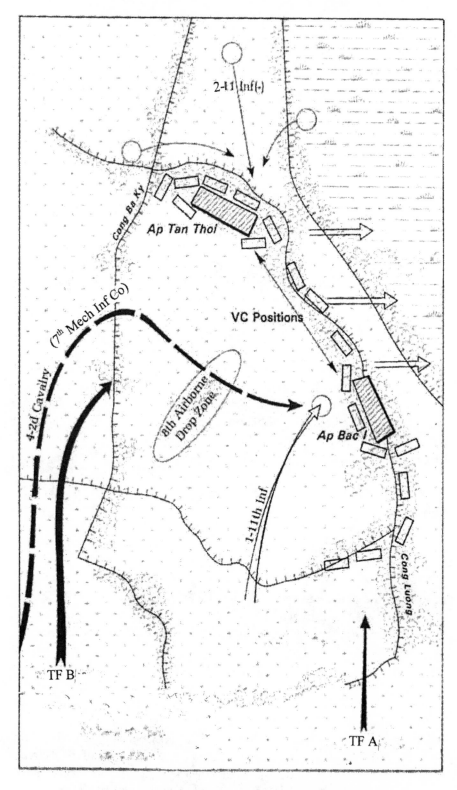

Map 4. Battle of Ap Bac (U.S. Army Center of Military History).

Year's Eve until early on 1 January, he deemed starting the operation at 4:00 a.m. unwise. It now would begin at 4:00 a.m. on 2 January.[37]

The objective would not be the typical lightly defended enemy camp that the ARVN and Americans advisors had come to expect during sweep operations. Unknown to the ARVN and Americans, Ap Bac and Ap Tan Thoi formed a single fortified position consisting of a series of bunkers and trench lines located atop dikes that were overgrown with trees and bushes providing protection, camouflage concealing them from the ground and air, and clear fields of fire into the surrounding paddies. A tree-lined irrigation ditch connected the settlements, allowing rapid covered and concealed movement between the two hamlet strongpoints. They were textbook defensive works. Manning the trenches near Ap Tan Thoi was the understrength 514th Provincial Battalion (having not fully recovered from its 1962 losses) and a reinforced company from the 261st Main Force Battalion dug in around Ap Bac. A platoon of district militia and a squad or two of local village militia augmented the two small VC battalions.[38]

The Viet Cong had not massed at Ap Bac with the intent to fight a battle, as they were preparing for assaults on strategic hamlets—COSVN's strategic objective for 1963. But the ARVN were coming, and they readied themselves. The 261st Battalion being closest to Route 4 was expected to do the bulk of the fighting. It was well armed and considered by many to be the best in South Vietnam. Virtually all its leaders and senior cadres, from battalion commander Hai Huang on down, were PAVN regroupees, although the second in command, Tu Khue—a northern-born PAVN officer—was a rarity at the time. They welcomed the attack. The 514th Battalion, unlike the 261st, was a local force unit with few regroupees led by Thanh Hai, one of the PAVN officers who had remained behind in 1954 and had been with the battalion (when it only had 40 soldiers) since that time. It was a veteran unit having fought in the province in one form or another since the late 1940s, and they too were ready for action.[39] Hai Huang was in overall command and confident in his troops' combat abilities.

In total, there were about 350 Viet Cong soldiers—nearly three times the estimate—and in addition to small arms, they possessed grenades, automatic rifles, medium machineguns, RPGs, and one mortar. Adding to the Viet Cong's advantage, the Americans and South Vietnamese had been lulled by their successes, and their operational security was lousy. In particular, the press learned in advance of the operation, and that meant Pham Xuan An was able to alert the Viet Cong at Ap Bac. When they learned of the looming attack, they immediately devoted their full efforts to improving and expanding the defenses, and because the attack had been pushed off to 2 January, they now had an additional day to prepare. Not surprisingly, Ap Bac radio transmissions ceased.[40]

Neither the ARVN leaders nor their American advisors had any real notion of what they were facing. Ap Bac was not even the top mission that day. The center of attention was a larger operation being conducted by III CTZ's 21st Division. Named Operation Burning Arrow, it targeted the COSVN headquarters in War Zone C. That led to the second and third major changes to the plan: the diversion of the preliminary airstrikes on Ap Bac to War Zone C and replacement of the assigned helicopter unit with the understrength 93rd Transportation Company. The Ap Bac defenses would not be softened up before the attack, and instead of being able to airlift the 2/11 Infantry in two lifts, the reduced number of helicopters necessitated three.[41]

The German General Helmuth von Moltke famously said that no battle plan survived the first clash. For the South Vietnamese, the battle of Ap Bac proved that dictum true to the extreme. Once the operation got underway, difficulties arose. After the first lift dropped off the soldiers of 2nd Company 2/11 Infantry north of Ap Tan Thoi at 7:03 a.m., ground fog set in, making it impossible to complete the airlift on schedule—a literal example of Clausewitz's "fog of war" creating friction on the battlefield. The lone ARVN infantry company soon came under small arms fire and dug in. The ARVN battalion that was to lead the attack sat out the start of the fight. There would be little fighting at Ap Tan Thoi as the action shifted south to Ap Bac and the two Civil Guard groups.

Even veteran Civil Guard officers and sergeants were not prepared for what was coming. At American insistence, from 1954 into 1961, they trained, served, and were promoted based on their policing skills related to traffic accidents, burglaries, and the like. Unlike an infantry soldier where experience led to the mastery of a wide range of combat skills, Civil Guard officers and NCOs often were veteran police officers and little more experienced in large combat operations than the privates. Making the deficiency critical, unlike privates, these guard members were about to lead their units into battle against a VC Main Force unit. Major Tho's Civil Guard companies, the least capable units in the ARVN, were now leading the attack against the largest and best-defended VC strongpoint encountered since the War of Resistance. Their day of reckoning had come.[42]

Viet Cong scouts who had moved out in darkness at 4:00 a.m. alerted the VC main body to the movements of both the company from the 2/11 Infantry, landing craft to the north, and Civil Guard to the south. Helping paint the ARVN movement for the VC commander, a SIGINT team monitored the American and ARVN tactical communications using captured American military radios. Hai Huang could not have been more pleased. He now knew that instead of being attacked from two directions, he could concentrate his power on the approaching Civil Guard with its every move monitored. All he had to do was bide his time and wait for the perfect moment to strike.

It was not long in coming. Having marched toward Ap Bac for the better part of an hour, the two Civil Guard groups made uneven progress. To the west of the hamlets, Lieutenant Thi's TF B encountered no opposition, reached its first two objectives, and searched for VC. TF A to the east advanced directly on Ap Bac and sensed the danger as it approached the hamlet's outlying tree lines and dikes. At about 7:40 a.m. Captain Tri held up along a dike short of the hamlet and sent the 842nd Company to scout ahead. Lying in ambush was a platoon from the 261st Battalion.

Once in the kill zone, they engulfed the guards in a fusillade of fire, killing the company commander and assistant commander. Battle was joined. At the opening volley, Captain Tri was taken by surprise and failed to give adequate support to his ambushed men, who beat a retreat back to the dike after losing several more soldiers.

Eventually Tri gathered his wits and made number of attempts to advance toward Ap Bac by enveloping maneuvers, but they were beaten back. During an attack at about 9:45 a.m. Tri was wounded in the leg at the head of his troops. By then TF A had suffered 22 casualties, and halted their attacks on Ap Bac.[43]

If Captain Tri was initially unnerved, his superior Major Tho was in over his head. He had never encountered anything like the Ap Bac fight and proved unable to direct the battle. Task Force A was on its own. The only savior for Tri's pinned down soldiers was artillery and air support, most of it directed by Colonel Vann in the observation plane that fearlessly flew at low level over the battlefield. That revealed another problem; the Viet Cong were so well camouflaged that no one in the air could see where they were. Vann directed fires and air strikes, but they were less than effective. The VC held their ground and kept up a stout defense. The morning could not have started better for the Viet Cong defenders at Ap Bac and Ap Tan Thoi. The action then shifted to the north.[44]

The fog cleared by 9:30 a.m. The helicopter lifts of the rest of the ARVN 2/11 Infantry were finally completed, but they made little headway attacking south against the fully alerted, dug-in, and nearly invisible fighters of the 514th VC Battalion. With both the northern and southern attacks stalled, it was time to call in the reserves. Soon one of the 1/11 Infantry companies stationed at Tan Hiep was in the air flying toward Ap Bac. No one had a clear picture of what the Viet Cong were doing, either as to exact location or strength. Vann took charge, consulted with the American helicopter pilots by radio, and decided to land the ARVN soldiers in a flooded rice paddy to the west of Ap Bac so they could hit the Viet Cong from the flank.[45] What happened next turned a tough fight for the ARVN and Americans into a disaster.

Like the rest of their compatriots, the American pilots expected the Viet Cong to flee as soon as they neared, as the VC had done routinely since the helicopter companies first arrived in force in 1962. Experience had taught them that the best chance to get the enemy was to land in an LZ as close as possible to give the ARVN soldiers a decent chance to close with the Viet Cong before they broke up, slipped away, and disappeared into the countryside. Unfortunately for them, this fight would be very different. The VC SIGINT team picked up the landing and alerted the Ap Bac defenders. They were hidden in the tree-lined dikes to the west and north, forming an L-shaped ambush around the LZ. The troops of the 261st VC Battalion were at the ready, and on this day the American aircrews encountered what became routine in the future: the "hot" LZ.[46]

At 10:20 a.m. the helicopters began landing in the paddies to the front of the concealed 261st Battalion. Sitting in plain sight with no protection, it became a "turkey shoot" for the VC. The U.S. helicopters began taking hits before they even landed, and the ARVN's 1/11 Infantry entered a hailstorm of fire. First one then another helicopter was out of action. A gunship tried to rescue the crews, but it too was shot down, while a damaged fourth helicopter made a forced landing a safe distance away. Around noon one more helicopter tried to land to evacuate casualties. It was hit so many times that it abandoned its mission and only managed to make it to Ba's 7th Mechanized Company, where it too made a forced landing. Of the 15 helicopters, five had been downed in less than two hours, and all but one of the others suffered damage. The off-loading infantry suffered greater losses—over half of the 102-man company were killed or wounded. It was a massacre. Now desperate to save the American and ARVN troops trapped in the rice paddy kill zone, Colonel Vann ordered in the 7th Mechanized Company.[47]

Once again things did not go according to plan. Captain Ba's M113s had not operated in the area before. They found the spongy ground tricky going but made good initial progress over the dikes and one canal. Ba kept the company in a column for speed and to minimize the damage to the farmer's rice crops. They roughly followed the route taken by the Civil Guard TF B until they hit what the locals called the Orchid Canal (Cong Ba Ky) some two kilometers west of the hamlets and realized it could not be forded at their location. Crossing paddies and most irrigation dikes was one thing, but a canal was different; it was really a fast-moving boggy stream. In an earlier operation, the company had tried to force their way under similar conditions and spent the day recovering M113s stuck in the "bottomless" mud.[48] If an armored vehicle sinks down to the hull, a vacuum can form. It literally can become stuck to the bottom and unable to free itself. A rapid search for a crossing site began, while over the radio, Vann frantically swore, threatened, and demanded an immediate advance on Ap Bac. Vann was an infantry officer and did not understand the M113's mobility limitations. Captain Ba had enough. He sourly thanked the shouting Vann and ended the conversation.[49]

The 7th Company was forced to continue looking for a usable ford, a search that took until noon. Ba managed to get his vehicle across, but the tracks churned up the bottom mud. Each following M113 had to be rigged by tow cable to his M113 on the other bank and pulled across. Several M113s reached friendly forces at Ap Bac by a little after 1:00 p.m. The 1/11 company commander briefed Ba on the situation, and he ordered the only available unit, Lieutenant Nguyen Van Nho's platoon, to attack the VC on the left flank of the beleaguered helicopter force. On the way, they passed by the wrecked helicopters and rescued some of the crews along with badly wounded American and ARVN soldiers. As the VC fire increased in intensity, a weakness of the ARVN M113s became apparent. Officers, vehicle commanders, and the .50-caliber heavy machine gunners had no protection, no gun shields; they fought exposed from the waist up while the Viet Cong fired from covered and concealed positions. Lt. Nho and company Sergeant Major Nguyen Van Hao both were killed during the advance. The M113 attack failed.[50]

A short while later, another two M113s crossed, and by 2:00 p.m., Ba had most of the company across. He pulled them together for a second assault on the Viet Cong lines. VC fire remained deadly. It killed a warrant officer positioned near Captain Ba in the command M113, and before the assault was over, six more of Ba's soldiers died with another seven wounded, most of them leaders and gunners. Things continued to go wrong as the flamethrower M113 could not get the weapon to work. The assault failed to take the dike line, but the armored assault signaled the beginning of the end of the battle. By that time, Thi's Task Force B had arrived, but Major Tho, who had taken charge, denied Thi permission to attack Ap Bac. He first wanted more airstrikes on the dug-in VC. By late afternoon, the 7th Company's APCs assaulted again and took the trench line. The Viet Cong prepared to withdraw in the coming darkness.[51]

Too late to matter, at dusk two 8th Paratroop Battalion companies jumped into the battlefield. As with the helicopter company, their arrival was no surprise as again the VC SIGINT team intercepted the communications. Compounding the error, the paratroopers jumped late, and many drifted over the Viet Cong positions and were killed. The paratroopers suffered 52 needless casualties. After the fighting ended, the casualty toll highlighted the extent of the Viet Cong victory. The ARVN, to include the Civil Guard, suffered 66 killed and 109 wounded. The majority (over 70 percent) came from three engagements: the 1/11 Infantry helicopter landing, the paratroop drop, and the armored assaults. The ARVN casualties were stunning. In 1962, the army averaged 12 soldiers killed in action per day for the entire country. In one day at one small cluster of two hamlets, 66 soldiers were killed. The Americans lost three soldiers with six wounded. The ARVN took 36 prisoners and found 18 VC bodies. How many wounded and dead soldiers the Viet Cong hid or evacuated will never be known.[52]

Those setbacks were not systemic problems, but tactical weaknesses easily remedied. The LZ disaster proved the old soldier's maxim that complacency kills. The aircrews were veterans of dozens of similar missions and flew into Ap Bac assuming that it would be like the others. After the battle, Vann publicly stated the helicopter losses were unavoidable, while in his official report, he blamed the pilots for not landing 300 meters from the tree lines as he ordered. Both conclusions were wrong. A distance of 150 meters or 300 meters made no difference as the VC's medium machineguns and assault rifles were effective at a range of 1,000 meters, and the captured M-1 rifles could accurately shoot to 450 meters. The fault lay in the tactic of landing close to the enemy in open terrain.[53]

A return to the old procedure of landing troops in LZs out of the range of direct fire weapons whenever possible minimized future occurrences of what happened at Ap Bac. The same was true for the unneeded paratroop jump where winds and reduced visibility could play havoc, and the arrival of helicopters in numbers made most paratroop jumps obsolete. As for M113s, to protect the exposed soldiers, the vehicles were retrofitted with gun shields. The canal mire problem remained but was alleviated by field expedients until a mechanical bridging solution for the M113s was obtained in mid-1965. That was why there were no more "Ap Bac fiascos" going forward. The only deep-seated problem dealt with Civil Guard readiness, and that required heavier weapons and time to reorganize and train. But the lack of Civil Guard combat readiness rested squarely with the American embassy in Saigon during the late 1950s and into 1960—not the ARVN.[54]

None of that detracted from the importance of the Viet Cong victory. In a single battle, they proved that both helicopter and M113 assaults—the ARVN's two most successful battle maneuvers— could be defeated. The integrated use of human intelligence and SIGINT, along with aggressive scouting and surveillance, went far in offsetting ARVN advantages in numbers and firepower. Similarly, the emphasis on camouflaged and protected defensive positions allowed the VC to withstand the strongest ARVN assaults. At Ap Bac the Viet Cong stepped up their performance, and after the hard times of 1962, their morale climbed. The victory at Ap Bac resonated across Vietnam and beyond. Its psychological value vastly outweighed its military significance.[55]

The Americans roundly condemned the ARVN for the defeat. Much of the blame falls on Colonel Vann and his briefing to the American press just after the battle. General Bruce Palmer previously served as Vann's commanding officer and knew him well enough to listen to what he had to say about the situation in South Vietnam when he later reported to the Pentagon. However, he also knew Vann to have a "short-fused temper," a sentiment shared by other advisors who served with Vann. Vann was not infallible and was too quick to criticize the ARVN; following a 2 September 1962 sweep in My Tho, Vann complained about what he saw as futile chasing by the ARVN. He was wrong as it reflected a Viet Cong morale problem— they no longer wanted to fight.[56]

The problem with the press reporting on Ap Bac was that Vann lost his temper, and in such a state, his criticism was poorly informed, especially remarks directed at Colonel Cao. Colonel Tran Ngoc Chau, a friend of both officers, was saddened and disappointed that Vann had not worked out his differences with Cao in private, as that was the Vietnamese way, and Vann's public comments benefited no one. Cementing the negative coverage, spy Pham Xuan An subtly encouraged the journalists' anti–Saigon and anti–ARVN conclusions. Vann's rant was presented to the American people in unfiltered form as both measured and accurate. It was neither. His description of events with the M113 company was particularly flawed, and later Vann was big enough to apologize to the company commander, Ly Tong Ba. The 7th Company had fought competently and bravely before, during, and long after the battle. But the damage had been done.[57]

Colonel Vann was a capable, courageous, and energetic combat leader but he missed the mark at Ap Bac. He wanted things done his way and fast. That impatience was the product of his "can do" attitude so characteristic of his generation of Americans and the urgency brought on by a one-year Vietnam tour. But it was not a one-year war. It was going to be, as Giap predicted, a long war that was in its fourth year when Vann arrived in March 1962. As Vann saw it, to get the war over with, the ARVN had to be aggressive, even if it meant taking higher casualties; it was a maximum-effort sprint to the finish. When they hesitated, he saw weakness. For his ARVN counterparts, there was no rotation date, and lives were to be risked when the gains obvious. To the ARVN, Vann and the Americans were "milers" while they were in a marathon, and to follow them was to lose the race.[58]

In the battle's telling, distinction between fact and fiction, myth and reality was lost at the outset. Harkins declared victory because the ARVN captured the ground. It was nonsense. The VC never intended to hold Ap Bac—nor did the ARVN—and no one dared mention the whereabouts of the radio whose intended capture triggered the whole mess. Similarly, Cao feared reporting casualties (which reflected poorly on Diem), but as told by journalists Neil Sheehan and David Halberstam, the victory revealed glaring ARVN weaknesses and called into question the war effort. It was unfounded even if Ap Bac was the most important VC victory since the war began. That was the real legacy of Ap Bac: the psychological damage done by

Vann, Halberstam, and others in the battle's aftermath. That exaggerated and unbridled criticism was splashed across newspapers and marked a turning point in public opinion of the war. It began an erosion of American support and sowed opposition toward Saigon and its leader, Ngo Dinh Diem.[59]

In the wake of Ap Bac, the VC became more adept at fighting helicopter and M113 assaults. Even then the change was subtle. Company-sized attacks increased to new levels, and as 1963 progressed, the Viet Cong expanded its Main Forces. The boost came from Group 125's seaborne delivery of modern Chinese and Soviet-bloc heavy weapons and munitions. For the first time, the VC had the firepower to engage U.S. helicopters in the air and ARVN armored vehicles on the ground. It was no secret; in early 1964 U.S. pilots noted the "a serious increase in the quantity and effectiveness of VC ground fire" in the Mekong Delta. Nonetheless, in April 1963 Washington correctly concluded that "VC progress had been blunted," but there was "no quick and easy way to end the war."[60]

The fighting that remained was a far cry from Duan's big unit war, for Saigon adjusted as well, and the Americans sent more helicopters and M113s that continued to bedevil the VC. Additionally, more ranger battalions were formed and grouped to provide each CTZ with its own mobile reserve, while the number of JGS strategic reserve paratroop and Marine battalions increased. The ARVN became more dangerous by the month. Ultimately, who would prevail remained undecided. The Viet Cong's annual 20 July offensive began and again became a back-and-forth struggle over strategic hamlets from the Central Highlands to the Mekong Delta, with the edge going to the VC but only slightly. By then, the war had taken a backseat to an internal South Vietnamese political struggle of immense consequences that started a few months earlier.[61]

15

What Was
the 1963 Buddhist Crisis?

In April 1963 during a trip to Hue, Vietnam's scenic ancient imperial capital, Ellen Hammer—arguably America's foremost historian on Vietnam at that time—happened to ask a local doctor about the current comings and goings. To her surprise, he made no mention of the war. Instead, he told her, "Something important: The Buddhist Youth are organizing."[1] How important few people could have realized, but in a few weeks a seemingly minor incident in Hue would change Vietnam's history. The catalyst would be the Buddhist youths and their leader, the monk Thich Tri Quang.

The Spark

On 6 May 1963, the Diem regime issued a circular reviving Decree 10, which directed that only the national flag could be flown on all occasions; when religious flags were flown, advance permission had to be obtained. It also stipulated that the national flag was to be given superior position. Decree 10 was an obscure rule enacted by Emperor Bao Dai in 1950 shortly after he had become head of state and intended to visually reinforce the fledgling government's authority. It had been reissued as Decree 189 in 1958 but not enforced. In keeping with former French colonial rules, exceptions were made for flags of Catholic, Protestant, and Chinese congregations. There was no exception for Buddhist flags, and that distinction helped ignite the crisis.[2]

If any place was ripe for confrontation, it was Hue, a city that was the center of Vietnamese traditionalism and filled with Catholic and Buddhist activists and embittered survivors of failed Dai Viet and Nationalist conspiracies. William Colby described Hue's political climate as "Byzantine" and filled with "competing ambitions and convictions."[3] With those underlying tensions, troubles began after Hue's Buddhist province chief, Colonel Nguyen Van Dang, implemented Decree 10 by directing the police to remove religious flags on 7 May. The burden, however, fell entirely on the Buddhist community, as 8 May was the Buddha's birthday (Vesak Day), and their flags were on full display.[4]

Making the situation more volatile, just three days earlier Catholic Papal flags had flown unmolested, even extravagantly, to celebrate the 25th anniversary of the consecration as bishop of President Diem's elder brother, Archbishop of Hue Ngo Dinh Thuc. For Catholics it was a particularly significant event as it represented the Vatican's decision to recognize the Vietnamese Catholic church as independent of the French church. By some accounts, the flag ban had been triggered by the excesses of Bishop Thuc's celebration—not unlikely for an outspoken, hardline defender of the faith. If true, then the ban's timing could not have been more impolitic or irresponsible. Thuc single-mindedly concerned himself with his stewardship of the Catholics under his charge and turned a deaf ear to the concerns of the region's Buddhists. In turn, monks like Thich Tri Quang reciprocated with equally narrow-minded religious bias. Catholic-Buddhist tensions in Hue reached levels not seen in decades.[5]

As police carried out the flag removals, outcries and complaints from the Buddhist community quickly followed. Regardless of aim or legality, the result was that within a matter of days, Hue officials had permitted Catholic flags to be flown in great numbers while Buddhist flags were pulled down. It rightly was seen as discrimination. That evening Province Chief Dang and Interior Minister Bui Van Luong, who by good fortune was in Hue, met to discuss the flag issue and decided to rescind the removal order. They then met with Bonzes Thich Tinh Khiet, the senior Buddhist monk in Hue, and his closest aide and leader of the 80,000 strong Buddhist Youth, Thich Tri Quang, to explain that the Buddhist flags could be flown on Vesak Day and no further police action would be taken. A reassured Bonze Khiet agreed to spread the word and calm his followers while Luong returned to Saigon, assuming the problem to be resolved.[6]

Whatever Khiet's intent, on the next morning Thich Tri Quang stepped before a crowd of several hundred followers gathered at the Tu Dam pagoda, the most important Buddhist site in Hue, and proceeded to give a fiery anti-government speech to his youthful adherents that railed against Diem's preferential treatment toward Catholics and discrimination against Buddhists. He closed by declaring, "Now is the time to fight."[7] Quang saw the flag dispute as the chance of a lifetime, an opportunity that might never be repeated, and he would use it in every way possible to advance his cause. His followers defiantly carried banners calling for religious equality, sacrifice for the Buddhist cause, and opposition to taking down Buddhist flags.[8]

That night, Quang led a crowd of followers, other protestors, and onlookers to the Hue radio station to demand that the recording of his anti-government address be broadcast instead of the scheduled religious program honoring the Buddha's birthday. A standoff ensued after the radio station manager, backed by the police, denied Quang entrance. The crowd refused to disperse even after the fire department employed water hoses. Reinforcements led by Deputy Provincial Chief Major Dang Sy arrived, and soon there were over a hundred police and Civil Guard along with police armored cars at the entrance to the radio station. Further orders to disperse went unheeded even after the Guard fired into the air on Sy's order. The situation remained extremely tense.[9]

Eventually Sy agreed to talk with both Quang and the manager inside the station, but at that moment some of Sy's Civil Guard threw concussion grenades into the crowd. It is unclear if the guardsmen understood that concussion grenades could not just stun but kill. Unlike a fragmentation grenade that maximized casualties, the World War I era U.S. Mark 3 concussion grenades were designed for use in confined areas such as trenches or bunkers, and to protect the user, they only had a casualty range of two meters (compared to 15 meters for a fragmentation grenade). They did not expel shrapnel, and if thrown onto an empty street, the result was a frighteningly loud noise accompanied by a cloud of smoke but nothing else, leading some to wrongly describe it as a stun grenade. When they were thrown into the dense crowd outside the radio station, the concussion grenades wreaked deadly damage. Although the reported numbers of fatalities vary, most sources concluded that nine unarmed protesters were killed; all were Buddhists except for one Catholic. More were wounded to include women and children and the fact that Major Dang Sy was Catholic only made matters worse. The flag dispute had turned into a national tragedy.[10]

As the news of the deaths, unintended or not, spread to Saigon and Washington and from there across the United States, the political conflict between Diem and Quang's followers continued to grow. The Buddhist crisis had begun, and Thich Tri Quang would stay at the fore every step of the way. While Quang deliberately unraveled the agreement reached between Bonze Thich Tinh Khiet and Interior Minister Bui Van Luong on the night of 7 May, there is no evidence that Quang (or Sy for that matter) went to the radio station with mortal intent: to create martyrs for the cause. But it is clear that Quang wanted to precipitate a crisis. It would not be the last time in the weeks and months that followed that he would sabotage attempts to resolve the dispute in order to escalate tensions. To try to comprehend his motives, it is necessary to have an understanding of religion in South Vietnam and the underpinnings of the Buddhism that Thich Tri Quang practiced at that time.

The Role of Religion in Vietnam

While Quang was keenly aware of the religious situation in Vietnam and acted accordingly, not one American leader, either in Washington or Saigon, had an accurate grasp of religious practices in Vietnam or how they played out in the lives of its citizens even though, as the crisis grew, it drove America's Vietnam policy during much of 1963. Perhaps it was just too hard, for if one word described Vietnamese religious beliefs, that word would be complexity. But for foreign journalists populating Saigon and American leaders, it was a subject not worth mastering. *New York Times* correspondent David Halberstam summed up the attitude: "Like other Americans in Vietnam, we were concerned with the war. After eight months there, I knew no Buddhist priests, knew little about Vietnamese Buddhism and had never been to a pagoda."[11] The NSC's Michael Forrestal said much the same about the Buddhist movement: "We didn't have their names or the faintest idea of what their organization was all about."[12] Instead of critically studying the situation, they opted for a descriptor that had the advantages of being simple and understandable—a one-dimensional platitude: Vietnam was an overwhelmingly Buddhist country.

If South Vietnam was strictly a Buddhist country, why was that not already obvious to American observers like Halberstam? Any visitor to the United States in 1963 who ventured out on a Sunday morning would have been confronted by obvious manifestations of American Christianity. If South Vietnam was so devoutly and pervasively Buddhist, why the ignorance? Even odder, none of the veteran French writers and journalists, like Bernard Fall, Gérald Tongas, Jean Lacouture, and A.M. Savani, made the claim that Vietnam was predominantly Buddhist. It was an erroneous American assumption, and adding to the misconceptions, many if not most Americans naively assumed that Buddhism was a nonviolent religion, making the deaths in Hue seem all the more outrageous. In truth, East Asian history, to include Vietnam, was replete with examples of warrior monks and Buddhist-inspired armed conflicts. Buddhism was and remains to this day the creed for tens of thousands of soldiers.[13]

Not everyone accepted the story. Another Pulitzer Prize winning journalist, Marguerite Higgins, refuted the Buddhist majority claim, as did former Ambassador Durbrow, but theirs remained lonely voices. When the crisis erupted, it was cast as religious discrimination orchestrated by President Ngo Dinh Diem, creating a storyline "peg" that was political dynamite: the Buddhist majority in South Vietnam was united in opposition to a Catholic despot wrongly persecuting them. The problem was that was never the truth. If one belief system did transcend every sector of Vietnamese cultural life, it was ancestor worship—from animistic Montagnards in the highlands to most Catholics and even the Westernized urbanites in Saigon.[14]

Upon that foundation came a religion that did encompass most Vietnamese: the Tam Giao (Three Teachings), which during the Nguyen Dynasty (1802–1945) had been the state religion. It originated in China, arrived in Vietnam in the 11th century, and remained deeply ingrained in the culture. In Vietnam, the Three Teachings was a syncretic faith that blended ancestor worship with an eclectic combination of Buddhism, Confucianism, and Taoism, and it was not unheard of to see a statue of or quotation by Confucius at a pagoda or Taoist temple. As A.M. Savani noted in the 1950s, the teachings were "entangled in very material forms."[15] In practical terms, the Three Teachings was simple to adopt, as there were no monks or priests or rigid body of tenets. It proved reassuring, harmonious, and with a bit of self-interest, a way to keep on the good side of all the gods. And nothing captured the Three Teachings like the nation's most important celebration, the Tet lunar new year holidays, which usually began in Confucian tradition with ceremonies to honor family ancestors, followed by visits to Buddhist pagodas, and on to Tao shrines dedicated to the Jade Emperor. Another example and second only to Tet for many Vietnamese was the Mid–Autumn Festival, celebrated on the night of the full moon to honor the Taoist moon goddess deity. It was enjoyed by watching the full moon while savoring a special delicacy, the aptly named mooncake.[16]

That inclusion of Buddhism in the Three Teachings, nonetheless, created the loophole Americans used to define Vietnam as a Buddhist majority nation. After all,

Buddhism easily fit into the Western definition of religion, and no one could blame Vietnamese champions of Buddhism if they wanted to claim the largest number of followers possible. But the place of Buddhism within South Vietnamese society was more nuanced and might be described best as a laissez faire relationship. People revered Buddha and respected monks just as long as they did not try to run their lives. When someone said they were Buddhist, it was almost certain that they also were Taoist and Confucian to some degree. In the case of Confucianism, the same was true of Catholics.[17]

By that logic it could have been stated with equal veracity that Vietnam was predominantly Confucian. After all, virtually all Vietnamese had been exposed to Confucianism, but that too was misleading. As a primary belief, Confucianism chiefly held sway within the elder educated class—of Diem's 19 cabinet members, five were practicing Confucians (the majority were Buddhist or nominally Buddhist to include the vice president and interior minister). Outside the context of the Three Teachings, the importance of Confucianism was in decline as the educated younger generation sought their degrees at Western universities and colleges and adopted Western philosophical and political theories. That did not detract from the truth that Confucianism formed Vietnam's moral and ethical underpinnings. Taoism similarly retained broad cultural influences. Most Vietnamese, especially in the countryside, believed in the Jade Emperor in Heaven and his emissaries, the hearth spirits—central figures in the Taoist pantheon—but the number of practitioners was waning. Vietnam was a land truly inhabited by a people who revered and worshipped their ancestors, and the Three Teachings reached into every corner of the nation. After that, generalities became fuzzy.[18]

For the Americans, cultural understanding was poor across the board and not limited to Buddhism. In the mid–1950s, a former senior Vietnamese official tried to explain how pure democracy would harm a proposed national assembly. As Vietnam had no history of democracy, he put forth a singularly un–American argument that 45 percent of the members should be elected with 55 percent chosen by the head of state. Where Americans saw democracy perverted, the Vietnamese saw effective government. Why? Too many inferior candidates would run. In the Confucian tradition, the best and brightest eschewed self-promotion, making it impossible to publicly run for office. They were to sit modestly on the sideline and wait to be asked to join the government, at which point they would be morally compelled to honorably serve the nation. In a decade or two, it might have been possible to convince Vietnam's most qualified candidates to run, but Americans wanted things done right then and there. It was a formula for missteps.[19]

Aside from near universal ancestor worship, assigning percentages to the faiths was difficult in the absence of a contemporary national census, but reasonable estimates could be made. Approximately half the people adhered to the Three Teachings to one degree or another; perhaps as many as three million (22 percent) devoutly followed Buddhism as it was practiced elsewhere in East and South Asia; another five to six percent belonged to the Hoa Hao; and a bit over ten percent were Catholic. Rounding out the religious groups were the Cao Dai, another distinctly Vietnamese religion that sprang up in the 1920s and combined the Three Teachings with

Christianity and even Hinduism. It made up a bit over four percent of the population (although its followers claimed ten percent). Finally, Central Highland peoples mostly were animistic, but many Cham practiced Islam and together represented another five percent. South Vietnam was a land covered by a rich tapestry of religions and beliefs.[20]

Making matters worse, both Americans and other South Vietnamese, especially Thich Tri Quang and his followers, basely stereotyped Vietnamese Catholics. Because of their faith, they often were viewed as disloyal, monolithic, and unthinking adherents of Diem. The first charge stemmed from Vietnam's colonial masters, the French, who were overwhelmingly Catholic and reflected crude prejudice. Catholics also were far from monolithic. Regroupment proved deeply disruptive, and in most areas northern Catholics soon outnumbered southern Catholics, an outcome that badly strained the church. Even where that situation did not exist, resettled northern Catholics often were transplanted as whole farming communities into the countryside, reinforcing the outsider image. Finally, while many Catholics looked to Diem with hope, they were quick to criticize him, especially southern Catholics who, unlike northerners, did not feel indebted to Diem for saving them from a harsh fate. They were not blindly loyal.[21]

Also contrary to stereotype, South Vietnam was not a majority Buddhist nation by any objective measurement. At no time did monks like Thich Tri Quang—whose actions soon influenced deliberations in the halls of Washington and captured the front pages of major American papers—speak with authority for the majority of the people. Nominal Buddhists were put off by religious conflict and had no time for firebrands. The feeling was mutual; prior to May 1963, the Hue radio broadcasts by devout Buddhists had shown disdain for nominal Buddhists, mostly followers of the Three Teachings, although they eagerly claimed to be their leaders once the crisis began. Further weakening the "radical monks" claims, true Buddhist believers, like the Catholics, did not constitute a monolithic political force. Those who faithfully practiced Buddhism saw their congregations divided along ethnic lines (Vietnamese, Cambodian, and Chinese) as well by followers of the Mahayana (the majority in Vietnam), whose monks usually wore purple robes, and Theravada schools (the majorities in Cambodia and Thailand) with monks normally dressed in saffron. Finally, there was the Hoa Hao sect who adhered to a puritanical form of Buddhism viewed as heretical by both the Mahayana and Theravada.[22]

Who led the radical monks also was difficult for Americans to discern. Although Buddhism traditionally eschewed formal hierarchies, Vietnamese Buddhist clergy did have a system of titles, but they did not designate rank. Once ordained they became a bonze or monk, and for those who reached an exceptional state of enlightenment, the title "venerable" was given that conferred more a sense of reverence than superior rank. Additionally, when novitiates began their religious life, a new name was assigned. By leaving home, they left their past behind and joined the Buddha's family, the Shakya clan, signified in Vietnam by the new surname of "Thich." (Some incorrectly used Thich and bonze interchangeably.) The closest thing to rank was seniority, as it normally brought added responsibilities and duties, such as those of an abbot, but even that designation was not permanent and did not impart a formal sense of superiority. When leaders were needed, they often were selected democratically and served on a temporary basis.

Why the Buddhist uprising was possible in those circumstances went back to the internal dynamics within the dominant sect in Vietnam, the Mahayana. And the proximate cause was the fact that they had achieved significant cohesion by the early 1960s. This was a new phenomenon in Vietnam that had its origins in teachings at the Buddhist schools and monasteries during in the decade before World War II. It was called the Buddhist (or neo–Buddhist) movement, and many associated Mahayana organizations were established near the end of French rule. The Buddhist movement was a theological-ideological force that had come to dominate the thinking of Vietnam's Mahayana clerics, and arguably everything that happened during the Buddhist crisis could be traced back to the movement's influence on Thich Tri Quang and his fellow monks and nuns. Those motivations allowed them to act in 1963.[23]

Thirty-nine years old in 1963, Thich Tri Quang had entered religious life as a novitiate in 1937 at age 13, a time when the Buddhist movement in Vietnam had entered a dynamic period. The French introduced far-reaching and wide-ranging new ideas, and by the 1930s, deep theological and philosophical debates raged within the ranks of the Mahayana Buddhist clergy (as well as the Theravada in Cambodia). The conservatives argued to stay the course and ignore French influence. It was not an unrealistic position; when the French took power, Buddhism had been practiced in Indochina for nearly 17 centuries, and the conservatives held that it could certainly withstand French dominion, which as it turned out, only lasted seven decades.[24]

Many, however, concluded that these new ideas merited serious study. The Buddhist movement's adherents explored many questions. Christianity's focus on an eternal soul raised issues regarding Karma and did that have implications for Nirvana and Paradise? Could Buddhism be reconciled with modern science? Was Buddhism a religion or philosophy or pantheistic theology? And then there were Marxist-nationalists castigating Buddhists for focusing on an afterlife that prevented them from playing a role in gaining independence from France.

All those debates shaped the mind of the young bonze who later would be described as an intelligent, courageous, and strong-willed individual possessing very considerable leadership powers. There was a dark side to the brilliant young cleric as well. During his studies, Thich Tri Quang had come to deeply resent France's preferential treatment of Catholics. This became a driving emotion over time, and at some point, Quang accepted that the French used Catholics to "exterminate Buddhists" in Vietnam, a sentiment commonly held by Vietnamese nationalists since the writings of Phan Boi Chau in the 1920s.[25] His pent-up rage was almost palpable in 1963.[26]

After he completed his formal religious studies in 1944, Thich Tri Quang dedicated his life to advancing the Buddhist movement and worked tirelessly to make Vietnam a nation guided by Buddhist principles to include its government, a return to what the clerics considered Buddhism's "golden age" in Vietnam under the Ly and Tran Dynasties (1009–1400) when the clergy enjoyed the emperor's patronage and even advised the court. His goals incorporated a strongly anti–Catholic prejudice that eventually evolved into a desire to exclude Catholics from public office. Tri

Quang also was swept up in the independence struggle. He witnessed the August Revolution firsthand while preaching in Hanoi and was in Hue when the 1946 War of Resistance against France began.[27]

Powerfully opposed to French rule, Quang briefly was jailed in 1947, marking his first major foray into the political arena, but advancing the Buddhist movement made him as unpopular with the communists as the French. World War II followed by the War of Resistance had suppressed and retarded the advance of the Buddhist movement. After partition in 1954, the movement regained momentum in the south, and Thich Tri Quang rose in influence at the movement's epicenter in Hue. Its greatest achievement during the following years—and one that gave Quang and his followers great legitimacy—was the establishment of the General Buddhist Association of Vietnam in 1956.[28]

It was the culmination of an eight-year struggle. In 1948, senior bonzes of Hanoi organized the clergy and laity into a unified sangha, or association, for all of Tonkin. The idea spread. In 1950 the Association for Buddhist Studies was created in Saigon to unify the followers in Cochinchina, followed by a similar organization in Hue for all of Annam. In 1951, a nationwide congress convened at the Du Tam pagoda in Hue and voted to merge the three sanghas and join the World Buddhist Federation. This secured Hue's position as the center of the Buddhist movement.[29]

Following partition and the creation of two states in 1954, the national structure was reorganized, leading to the General Buddhist Association composed of the three communities: The Association of Buddhist Studies in South Vietnam in Saigon, the Buddhist Association of Central Vietnam headquartered in Hue, and the Vietnamese Buddhist Association in Hanoi. To guide the associations, boards made up primarily of bonzes, were created that followed a model of democratic deliberations, and in a break with tradition, the General Association created the position of president. Thich Tinh Khiet of Hue was elected to the post, the same bonze who reached the peaceful settlement to the 8 May flag dispute with Interior Minister Luong.[30]

By 1963, the association claimed three million members along with 3,000 bonzes and 600 nuns from across Vietnam, both north and south. Even Diem had gotten into the act by sponsoring the Co Son Mon (Ancient Mountain Gate) Buddhist Association in the Mekong Delta. As a sign of the Buddhist revival in South Vietnam, in March 1963, just weeks before the Hue incident, 25,000 of the faithful attended the opening of a new pagoda at the port of Vung Tau. Sacred relics from across South Vietnam were brought, and the ceremony was headed by the Venerable Narada, a distinguished monk from Sri Lanka, the original home to the World Buddhist Federation.[31]

Things were very different in the DRV. Partition allowed religions to grow freely in the Diem-led south, but followers paid a heavy price in the north. As soon as the VWP took power in Hanoi, temples, churches, and pagodas were taken over by the government; many were closed, and some destroyed. That stood in stark contrast with South Vietnam. Diem had not shut down but helped expand the number of upper schools for bonzes from four to ten. There had been 2,206 Buddhist pagodas in 1954; the number rose to 4,766 under Diem's presidency, and the government directed nine million piasters toward renovations that helped most of the existing pagodas. This was deliberate policy as the Diem regime held that the practice of religion in South Vietnam undermined communism, whether Buddhism or Christianity or Islam or Cao Dai-ism.[32]

In the north, the VWP labeled public adoration at places like Hanoi's Taoist Princess Lieu Hanh Shrine as religious oppression and forbade it. The VWP even wasted three years (1955–1957) in a futile attempt to suppress the Tet Holiday period by making 1 January the official New Year's Day. Party cadres declared Tet "an old feudal custom carefully maintained by French colonists, desirous of keeping the people oppressed in obscurantism in order to better to enslave them."[33] Hanoi's goal was clear: to cleanse the population of anything the party deemed as superstition. That presented another reason that Hanoi never pushed hard for 1956 reunification elections; the VWP had completely alienated devout religious communities in North Vietnam.[34]

While a good degree of unity was reached within the Mahayana community in South Vietnam through the General Association, the scheme proved unworkable in the DRV despite the association's claim of broad membership. The Vietnamese Buddhist Association recognized in the RVN was suppressed in Hanoi, and in its stead the VWP created the Vietnamese United Buddhist Association in 1958. It too was headquartered in Hanoi, but unlike in South Vietnam, it was subordinated to the government. Regardless of the June 1955 Decree on the Religious Question protections, in the DRV religious practice in any form was discouraged, and Buddhist followers and their monks either submitted to the will of the party or faced persecution or arrest. That was the opposite of how Diem's government treated Buddhists, as witnessed by the celebration of the new Buddhist pagoda at Vung Tau in early 1963. North of the 17th parallel, the Buddhist movement was dead, but in the south, Thich Tri Quang was about to spur it forward to incredible heights under his militantly political vision of theocratic nationalist Buddhism.[35]

The Emerging Buddhist Crisis

The Buddhist flag incident that Thich Tri Quang exploited was a deliberate attempt to energize the Buddhist movement. Their influence belied their numbers, for while the Mahayana were a minority, they were united. Adding to their political power, they were concentrated in the urban centers in and around Hue and Saigon with hundreds of monks and nuns poised to act. So empowered, Quang and his adherents never hesitated to speak for all Buddhists in Vietnam. In an amazingly brief period of weeks, this small handful of activist monks were soon referred to by most diplomats and the international press as "the Buddhists," as if they alone embodied the will of millions of people. What Quang brilliantly manipulated was not the power of Mahayana Buddhism but the Three Teachings, which created a wellspring of sympathy for Buddhism across South Vietnam.

It was heady stuff, and in the months that followed, Quang would find his path tortured and difficult; he obtained unbelievable powers and later, seemingly lost his way. But one thing was beyond doubt. Tri Quang was in command and would drive events even if high-ranking officials in Saigon or Washington or the American press thought otherwise. What Diem would come to call the "Buddhist Revolt" was underway.[36]

In the immediate aftermath of the Hue killings, there appeared a willingness to find a peaceful solution to resolve the problem. The following morning the radio station found some 800 of the Buddhist Youth assembled outside its doors. They were addressed by province chief Dang, himself a Buddhist, who expressed deep regret for the loss of life, pledged to personally use all his power to address their concerns, and pled for calm. While tensions remained high and despite some ugly "down with Catholicism" chants that morning, there were no more acts of violence either by the protestors or security forces. An uneasy return to normalcy took hold. A funeral march of 6,000 Buddhists led by Quang on 10 May also was peaceful. To court the Americans, the protest banners were written in both Vietnamese and English.[37]

On that day, monks at Tu Dam pagoda published a manifesto with five demands: (1) permanently rescind the flag ban, (2) give Buddhists equal exceptions granted to Catholics in Decree 10, (3) stop government arrests and terrorization of Buddhists, (4) grant full freedom of religion for Buddhist monks and followers, (5) compensate the victims of the Hue killings and punish the guilty (with most fingers pointing at Major Sy). It was signed by five leading bonzes including Tri Quang and the current General Buddhist Association president Thich Tuong Van. Quang also telegraphed President Diem and the Honorable U Chan Htoon in Rangoon, Burma (Yangon, Myanmar), the president of the World Buddhist Federation, and called for Buddhist meetings in all of South Vietnam's provinces. Three days later in Hue, a representative of Diem met for the first time with the Buddhist leaders, but no progress was made, and the government's unconvincing and counterproductive claim that the grenades were thrown by a VC terrorist satisfied no one. On May 15, a delegation of monks and lay Buddhist leaders from Saigon's Xa Loi pagoda, the most influential in the capital, delivered the five demands to Diem at the Gai Long Palace (see Map 1).[38]

After two days of silence, Diem took the first positive step to build on Province Chief Dang's conciliatory work over a week earlier. That day a series of high-level meetings in Saigon were conducted with the Xa Loi delegation. The delegation met first with Vice President Nguyen Ngoc Tho and then attended a second meeting with Diem, Tho, and a number of cabinet ministers. Diem proved to be a hard but flexible negotiator. Rather than rescind Decree 10, he insisted that the national flag must always take precedence but agreed that restrictions would apply equally for all religious flags, and claims of special treatments under the decree would be investigated.

Diem went on to affirm that the government would not issue blanket arrest bans in Hue for fear of abuse by subversives. He did reaffirm the constitutional right to freedom of religion and stated that acts of mistreatment needed to be reported to authorities. Muddying the waters, the two sides could not agree on the facts of what happened at the Hue radio station on the night of 8 May. Diem adamantly would not admit to any guilt on the part of the government but agreed to compensate the murdered victims' families and those injured. The Xa Loi delegation also raised a peculiar complaint over the Japanese film *Sakya* on the life of Buddha that they found offensive (released as *Shaka* in Japan and under the title *Buddha* in America).

Diem assured them that permission to show the film in South Vietnam would not be granted.

Diem also directed Interior Minister Bui Van Luong, who obviously was well acquainted with the Hue events, and Minister of Civic Action Ngo Trong Hieu to ensure the safety of the delegation during their proposed visits to the victims' families. Finally, he approved small-scale memorial services for the victims to be held on 21 May at pagodas across South Vietnam. It was a productive session but far from a submissive acquiescence to the five demands—and that distinction, coupled with Diem's low-key slow-pace approach, greatly annoyed the Department of State in Washington.[39]

Things remained calm over the next two weeks, despite protests in Saigon and tensions in Hue, and the 21 May funeral ceremonies went off without violence or incident. To highlight the confusion caused by lack of a formal Buddhist hierarchy, on 29 May (three weeks after the murders in Hue), Diem met with one "leadership" group in the morning only to be presented with a different group later in the day, both claiming to be the "real" Buddhist leaders. Confusion aside, President Diem took a major step forward when he finally made a public declaration that clearly reaffirmed religious freedom and vouched for strong measures against religious discrimination. The National Assembly confirmed his declaration four days later.[40]

Diem was confident he was making the right moves, and Washington was convinced that he was wrong. Diem handled the Xa Loi delegation effectively but erred in assuming the matter resolved, as no one in the delegation walked away believing the issues settled. Critically, Thich Tri Quang was in Hue with the city still near the boiling point. Seeking a way forward, Washington believed that a reasonable settlement was possible if Diem just followed their guidance, but the State Department completely misread Quang and his goals. They correctly assessed that the crisis had not passed, but neither Washington nor Diem had yet to understand what they were confronting. Diem could be excused to a degree as his political opponents had been playing the "Catholic card" against him since 1955 and nothing had come of it. He did not realize this time would be different.[41]

A hint of what was in store was revealed on 1 June when Thich Tri Quang, in a show of strength, held a rally for 10,000 supporters outside the Tu Dam pagoda in Hue. Two days later, a false story swept through the city that Quang, who had been on a two-day hunger strike, had died. That incited approximately 1,500 members of his Buddhist Youth to take to the streets. They were met with a large contingent of soldiers who moved in and forcibly ended the protest. Although there were no fatalities, 67 youths were hospitalized, a number from exposure to tear gas.[42]

What occurred next revealed how emotions had begun to get the better of judgment on the part of some at the State Department. Because several victims had burns, a wild rumor circulated that ARVN soldiers had used mustard gas on civilians. Stunningly, this story gained traction in Washington and led to a series of condemnations by State Department officials before the facts and cooler heads led by Dean Rusk put an end to the affair. That neither France nor America had ever considered, let alone provided, chemical weapons like mustard gas to South

Vietnam should have immediately discredited the rumors; that it had not was a sad commentary.[43]

Rumors that harmed Diem, like the chemical attack and false story that ARVN M113s crushed to death two children at the Hue radio station on 8 May, were all to the good for Thich Tri Quang as he stoked unrest. Back in Saigon, the U.S. embassy began to see the danger, describing Quang as "among the staunchest of militants" and reportedly stated that rapprochement with Diem had moved "beyond compromise."[44] The disconnection between perceptions that held sway with State Department officials in Washington, who placed blame for the troubles squarely on Diem, and those in Saigon, who raised concerns about Quang's motives, widened.[45]

On 4 June Diem took another step forward, albeit after strong American urging, with the creation of a high-level joint commission made up of representatives from the government and the Xa Loi Buddhist leadership to resolve their outstanding differences. Vice President Tho and Secretary of State for Defense Nguyen Dinh Thuan led the government's delegation. To try to calm the restive Hue-Da Nang area, Diem ordered Colonel Tran Ngoc Chau—perhaps the ablest province chief in South Vietnam—to replace the ineffective mayor of Da Nang, and the Hue security forces were given orders to use only "peaceful action" in controlling protests.[46] Chau asked why he was chosen, and Diem answered that he wanted a Buddhist officer to settle the crisis there.[47]

In Saigon, the situation at the Xa Loi pagoda settled into a routine of protests and demonstrations that no longer seemed to matter. American *AP* journalist Malcolm Browne concluded that the efforts of the monks and nuns "were having no impact," and the international press corps had "lost interest completely" in the Buddhist protests.[48] Remarkably, there had been no further fatalities since the 8 May incident at the Hue radio station. Equally disconcerting to Thich Tri Quang, the majority of people in Hue did not support his Buddhist movement.[49]

The Self-Immolation of Thich Quang Duc and the 16 June Settlement

With the announcement of the joint commission, Thich Tri Quang realized his control over the struggle was slipping from his hands and only dramatic action could correct the slide toward a peaceful resolution, an outcome that likely would doom his goal of toppling Diem. Khiet and Quang arranged to have a loyalist, Thich Thien Minh, assigned to the commission to represent their interests during the talks. Minh hurriedly departed Hue and arrived in Saigon late on 4 June, the day Diem announced the creation of the commission. Before the first meeting, Thich Thien Minh entered into discussions with Defense Secretary Thuan. Remarkably, common ground was found, much progress was made, and the session ended in a tentative agreement. The next morning Thuan met with Diem, who accepted the accord. Thuan then informed Minh that there was a "good chance" the government would adopt their agreement and that it could take effect immediately. In the meantime, there also would be a truce where both sides agreed to stop street confrontations and cease their mutual propaganda wars.

All five of the 10 May demands were addressed: (1) there was mutual agreement on flag displays, (2) the government would disclaim Decree 10 and gain its abolition in the National Assembly, (3) the government would take prompt corrective action on complaints of infringement of freedom of religion, (4) the government would investigate claims of harassment and cease arbitrary arrests of Buddhists, (5) compensation for victims and their families would be completed. The government would take the agreement immediately to the joint commission and then to Diem for formal acceptance. Thich Thien Minh made it clear to Thuan that he only represented the central Vietnam Buddhist associations, but Thuan was sure that the southern associations would accept. Minh closed by stating that he had to return to Hue that day to obtain approval from the leaders at the Tu Dam pagoda but he was persuaded to remain for a meeting the next day, 5 June, with the representatives of the southern associations to gain their concurrence.[50]

The next day the meeting took place, and Thich Thien Hao, representing the southern Buddhists associations, also accepted. The joint commission ratified it a short time later. As Thich Thien Minh departed for Hue, it seemed that all parties had peacefully resolved the crisis. As soon as approval from Hue was obtained, the agreement would go to President Diem for signature and implementation. Earlier, a hopeful acting-ambassador William Trueheart in Saigon cabled to Washington, "I am keeping my fingers crossed."[51] Everyone had underestimated Thich Tri Quang.[52]

What exactly transpired when Minh met with Khiet and Quang upon his return to Hue with the 5 June tentative agreement in hand is not known, but based on subsequent events, a number of things can be asserted. First, as he did after the Khiet-Luong accord on 7 May, Tri Quang sabotaged the agreement—there would be no reply to an anxious Defense Secretary Thuan in Saigon. Second, Thich Tri Quang was unalterably committed to his path: there would be no reconciliation, no agreements, and no peace until the Diem government was destroyed. Third, Quang was in a power struggle with Khiet that Quang was determined to win. Finally, the decision was made to approve Thich Quang Duc's request for self-immolation in Saigon.[53]

Thich Tam Chau would see to the details. Chau, two years younger than Quang and a close lieutenant, had been sent from Hue to the Xa Loi pagoda earlier to form and head up the Inter-Sect Committee for the Defense of Buddhism. Chau later stated that there were seven volunteers for self-immolation, but Thich Quang Duc was selected due to the intensity of his feelings over the martyrs in Hue and that "he requested that the Great Truth [of suffering] be supported by him."[54] Duc's fiery death would set the stage for Tri Quang's arrival in Saigon to take personal command of the uprising.

It was not unheard of in Vietnam for a Buddhist monk to die for his faith. It was permitted as an ultimate offering to the Buddha or an act driven by the purest motivation or compassion for others, although it usually resulted from a protest hunger fast. Self-immolation also was acceptable, and during their studies clerics had been schooled on the mythical tale of Bonze Dam Hoang's self-immolation in the year 445. He did so as to be reborn in the world of Supreme Happiness. Such an act was not buried in the distant past; during the pre-war decades that witnessed the birth of the Vietnamese Buddhist movement, a number of self-immolations had taken place, and a bonze had died after he set himself afire in Bac Bo in 1950. It was, nonetheless, extremely rare and, being unknown in the West, shocking to the sensibilities—even for a generation that had lived through the savagery of World War II.[55]

That was the effect when Thich Quang Duc, a stern-looking monk in his mid-60s, entered one of Saigon's busiest thoroughfares on the afternoon of 11 June 1963. The intersection of Le Van Duyet (Chanson) Avenue and Phan Dinh Phung Street was in the heart of downtown Saigon, not more than 300 meters southeast of the Xa Loi pagoda and perhaps twice that distance to the west of the lush parks of the Tao Dan Gardens and presidential palace grounds (see Map 1). A small British Austin automobile carried Duc with a procession of hundreds of monks and nuns in tow, to include Thich Tam Chau. It made its way from the Xa Loi pagoda to the intersection. Once there, the clerics proceeded to block the traffic. One placed a cushion in the center of the intersection for the bonze to sit on. As he assumed the lotus position, another monk thoroughly doused Quang Duc in a flammable mixture of gasoline and diesel.[56]

Thich Quang Duc then lit the match; as he was consumed in flame, the monks and nuns wept. A robed bonze yelled in English into a portable loudspeaker, "A Buddhist priest burns himself to death. A Buddhist priest becomes a martyr."[57] Browne, one of several journalists who had been tipped off by the Xa Loi monks to get to the intersection to see "something dramatic," took in the spectacle and snapped a rapid sequence of photographs of the horror that changed the world's opinion of South Vietnam and its leader, Ngo Dinh Diem.[58]

Thich Tri Quang succeeded beyond his wildest dreams. As Browne's photos made their way onto the front page of newspapers and magazines around the globe, a seemingly unimportant religious-political struggle in an often-unnoticed country became an international sensation. It also was a diplomatic and political hammer blow to the Diem regime. At the Saigon embassy, Public Affairs Counselor John Mecklin concluded that the photograph "had a shock effect of incalculable value to the Buddhist cause becoming a symbol of the thing in Vietnam."[59] President Kennedy realized the domestic American and international ramifications immediately, crying out "Jesus Christ!" upon seeing it for the first time; he later concluded, "No news picture in history has generated so much emotion around the world as that one."[60]

In the days leading up to Duc's self-immolation, relations between Diem and the State Department had worsened, and Madame Nhu started the fight. After two days with no reply from the Hue monks, on 7 June, Madame Nhu's Women's Solidarity Movement issued a proclamation that began harmlessly enough with "an expression of respect for Buddhist philosophy and veneration for the Buddha" but degraded into an attack on Thich Tri Quang and his allied bonzes, irresponsibly claiming they were "exploited and controlled by communism and oriented to sowing disorder and neutralism."[61] Everything but the claim that they were sowing disorder was false. It is hard to overstate the vitriol most American diplomats and journalists had for Madame Nhu by then, but Halberstam captured it best when he aired his resentment of her "delving into men's politics with sharp and ill-concealed arrogance."[62] They gave her a new name: The Dragon Lady.

Her resolution then took a swipe at the Americans, pressing for the immediate expulsion of "foreign agitators" and urging vigilance against "those inclined to take Vietnam for a satellite of a foreign power."[63] Everyone was on edge. Quang so rattled Diem's government, as well as Quang's American detractors, that many accepted Madame Nhu's argument that the communists were behind the Buddhist uprising. They were wrong; knowing well the fate of Buddhists in the DRV, Quang was ardently anti-communist. When Madame Nhu's missive reached Washington, it pleased no one. The State Department fired back a complaint overseen by Roger Hilsman, who replaced Harriman as Assistant Secretary of State for Far Eastern Affairs, instructing Trueheart to meet with Diem and "urgently request" a repeal of Decree 10 (which already had been agreed to) and discover if the WSM resolution had been approved by the government. As if to prove Madame Nhu's "satellite" comment correct, another message cleared by Hilsman that day laid out a laundry list of micromanaging "actions" for Diem to obey.[64]

Washington *was* treating Saigon like a satellite government. The demands pried into every corner of Diem's government, from muting the political theme of the Can Lao Party to appointing Buddhist chaplains for the Air Force to ensuring more Buddhist monks won election to the National Assembly in August to creating either a ministry of religious affairs or a national religious council. It was meddling in the internal affairs of an ally, and if not intended to incite Diem's belief in Vietnamese independence, then it represented a profound misreading of how to influence South Vietnam's president. That might have been a manageable diplomatic rift if not for the horrible death of Thich Quang Duc. That tragedy magnified disagreements between Washington and Saigon, further polarizing an already strained relationship.

The timing of Quang Duc's death remains intriguing. A tentative agreement had been reached six days earlier, and all expected a positive reply from the leaders in Hue. Instead, a traumatic self-immolation took place. Why? Was Thich Quang Duc aware that agreement sat in the offing? It seems implausible that such an extreme act was done for bargaining leverage. Was it done to dramatically signal a rejection of the agreement? Perhaps. There already were reports that Buddhist hardliners were "talking about bringing about the overthrow" of the Diem regime.[65] That goal was certainly important enough to justify such a terrible and spectacular gesture. And it was certainly consistent with Thich Tri Quang's holy war against Diem and his government.

That evening Diem gave a radio broadcast to the nation. He urged calm, stressed the ongoing negotiations, and closed by affirming to all that they could rely on the constitution to protect religious freedoms and he would be its guardian. The next day, Thich Tinh Khiet and Tri Quang arrived in Saigon and took residence at the Xa Loi pagoda. The Americans focused on Tri Quang, described as the "spark plug" behind the Buddhists' actions who displayed "considerable flair as a demagogue."[66] A request by Vice President Tho for a quick resumption of talks was declined on the grounds that Khiet was weak from fasting and exhausted by the air flight; Tho was told to wait.[67]

On 14 June, meetings were held between the joint commission under Defense

Minister Thuan and the Buddhist delegation led by Thich Thien Minh. As before, quick agreement was reached to include the flag issue, supposedly the last major sticking point. Later that day, Bonze Thich Tinh Khiet sent out a national message for all to "avoid manifestations and incidents, in view of the favorable progress." Concurrently, the police removed barricades from in front of the pagodas. Two days later, on 16 June, a joint press conference was scheduled and the drafting of a joint communiqué completed. It would be the last time Khiet assumed the leadership role during the Buddhist crisis.

That Thich Quang Duc's death was tied to a goal larger than achieving the five demands of 8 May became clear on 16 June. That morning, while the joint communiqué was broadcast across the nation, a crowd of some 2,000 including over 200 students erupted into violence at the site of Duc's immolation. U.S. Embassy observers stated the crowd initiated the riot—not the police—and it was followed by a major demonstration with rock throwing at police outside the Xa Loi Pagoda. The reason for the protesters' fierce rejection of the peace accord was not hard to understand. Prominently absent from the earlier negotiations was Thich Tri Quang. The American embassy considered his absence "puzzling and conceivably ominous."[68] How ominous they now knew.

The fierce protests revealed both how quickly Thich Tinh Khiet's calls for peace were ignored and that the raw political power of Thich Tri Quang was at its peak. It also revealed that, Saigon reporting to the contrary, the Buddhists had not united—not under Khiet or Quang or anyone else. Some Buddhists felt that with the agreement over the five demands, a return to normalcy was best. Thich Thien Hoa, one of the most revered Buddhist teachers in Vietnam, rejected Quang's methods and opposed him, as did Thich Nhat Hanh, editor of the General Buddhist Association's official publication, *Vietnamese Buddhism,* and a guest lecturer on Buddhism at Columbia University in New York City.[69]

Many Buddhists also found self-immolation repulsive, offensive to their beliefs, and walked away from Quang. They saw it in conflict with Buddhism's peaceful tenets and held that suicide violated the First Precept against killing, while martyrdom was antithetical to Buddhism. Without seeing into the martyr's heart, no one could judge the correctness of self-immolation, but it was not met with universal approval. There were other divisions within the movement. Once the action shifted to Saigon, other anti–Diem groups there joined with Quang, such as some student groups and members of the Caravelle faction, but all with the goal of advancing their own political agendas—none of which envisioned Thich Tri Quang's goal of a Buddhist-guided government in South Vietnam. Even within his own ranks, Quang was no longer the sole voice; Thichs Tam Chau and Thien Minh also had risen in prominence and began to cultivate their own followings.[70]

Despite the far-reaching effects of Thich Quang Duc's self-immolation, Quang again was losing control over events. After a CIA colleague asked for a briefing on South Vietnam's Buddhists by the agency's most experienced analyst, Molly Kreimer, he left, describing the situation in terms of "a mosaic of splits within the Buddhist hierarchy, schisms between and disputes within the pagodas, and monks who were fervent followers of one faction or another or undecided or anything in between."[71] Molly Kreimer had it right. That was the situation in South Vietnam during the hot, rainy summer of 1963.

Spiraling into Chaos

If Thich Tri Quang struggled to keep his movement together, then Diem was in worse shape, and opposing Diem would be enough to keep unity amongst most bonzes. Quang held the upper hand for the moment. It also appeared that Quang had a new ally. That Diem was on infirm ground with the State Department had been revealed in a highly publicized 15 June article in the *New York Times* that stated Washington would "publicly condemn" Diem if he did not meet the Buddhist's demands.[72] It was a marked shift in American policy. Prior to the uprising, the Kennedy administration had pursued, in William Colby's words, "steadfast" support for Diem.[73] The State Department now pursued a new "tough American line" that Diem implement the department's demands to resolve the Buddhist dispute or face sanction.[74]

The acceptance of Diem's bias by many Americans was surprising. Ambassador Durbrow, who never shied away from criticizing Diem, stated, "He was the most tolerant devout Catholic I've ever known about other religions."[75] Others expressed similar feelings, and how did senior State officials not know the majority of both Saigon's civil and military leaders were not Catholic—in the ARVN just three of 17 generals? Yet Hilsman implied the opposite when he told Kennedy the war effort soon would suffer under Diem because Catholic officers dominated Buddhist soldiers. McNamara knew it to be untrue, objected, and demanded proof. It was not forthcoming. Weeks later, Hilsman pushed a report of a spike in VC attacks in July and blamed Diem. That too was disingenuous. The VC always launched a July offensive; it was nothing new. But he was in full bureaucratic "pit bull" mode. As he put it, he was not afraid to "step on toes," "fight," "kick," and "make some enemies."[76] McNamara was right to call him out, but misrepresentations hurt Diem and were not limited to Hilsman. Harriman backed him, and Forrestal wrongly referred to the Diem regime as a Catholic government into 1964.[77]

Not helping matters, Diem was having little success in controlling Madame Nhu and her Women's Solidarity Movement who announced on 16 June that they stood by their confrontational 7 June resolution condemning Buddhist leaders. By early July, she was in an open and heated confrontation with Diem over the 16 June agreement, self-fulfilling her schizophrenic description of the government. Having opened a line of communication with the CIA, Tri Quang now was positioned to exploit the growing splits, both internally between Diem's officials and advisors and externally with the Americans.[78]

The 16 June agreement itself provided a tool for Quang to attack Diem as it had a number of weaknesses, and to build pressure, there was an implied implementation deadline at the end of June. Another point of attack was the committee established to address Buddhist complaints over arrests and detentions. On its face, it seemed reasonable. But when closely looking at the agreement, it became clear that many terms and conditions addressing arrests and detentions were open to subjective interpretation if not manipulation. If a committee decision went against a Buddhist, then Quang and his followers could argue that the agreement had been violated.[79]

There were more political booby traps. The 8 May Incident inquiries that did not satisfy Quang could be touted as a cover-up. Even more convoluted was the right to "normal and purely religious activities" at the pagodas and General Association headquarters. By Quang's standards, the protest marches, self-immolations, and violent confrontations with police were purely religious activities. By the government's standards, such activities had nothing to do with religion. Again, divergent views created the perception that Diem was not abiding by the agreement. Aside from the clear-cut determination on flags, it was almost impossible for Saigon to prove compliance.

Finally, if accusations of noncompliance were not enough, then Quang reverted to disinformation. Stories of abuses directed at Buddhists continued to excite Saigon as rumors abounded on "Radio Catinat." Tales of pagoda burnings, monks being tortured, forced conversions to Christianity, and executions of the faithful were rife and politically explosive. The details always were fuzzy and seemingly occurred in remote locations. Vagueness was essential so that the atrocities could not be verified. When reporters like Higgins ventured into the hinterlands, they refuted the rumors. On her first visit to the Xa Loi pagoda, a monk related a grisly tale where Quang Ngai Catholics forced Buddhists to convert, and those that refused were burned alive. Higgins decided to go to the city and found no outward signs of religious tensions. Probing deeper, Higgins visited the main Buddhist temple where the monks thought her crazy for repeating such outlandish tales and stated that all the religions got along peacefully. But for many, facts no longer mattered. After the death of Thich Quang Duc, the jury was in, and Catholic Diem was guilty.[80]

As if on cue, on 28 June, a letter from Thich Tinh Khiet arrived warning of renewed demonstrations, possible bloodshed, and more as the end of the month grew near. Thich Tinh Khiet had never used threatening language before, and it is not known if he even wrote the letter. A short time later, Quang revealed to the CIA that he was in charge of the movement and was both writing and signing the public declarations issued under Khiet's name. Many Americans mistakenly assumed that the 16 June agreement had created a path to resolution, but Quang's war on the Diem regime was far from over.[81]

Trueheart in Saigon and Hilsman and others in Washington suspected but did not believe that the radical monk's objective was to overthrow Diem. Yet they did not reject the idea. When Quang ensured that the 16 June agreement fell apart, Harriman and others in the State Department blamed Diem. Harriman had taken a disliking to him during the Laos negotiation that began in 1961. It continued through the signing of the 1962 Geneva pact and beyond. Harriman saw Diem as a wrongheaded, stubborn, and poor ally.[82]

For Washington, a hard line against Saigon was to be taken and changes made. On 20 June, Diem was informed that Nolting was to be replaced by Henry Cabot Lodge, Jr., and the official public announcement was made a week later. Diem was under no illusion that the move was a routine reassignment or that American policy remained unchanged. Nolting embraced Lansdale's path of conciliation with Diem. Overt political niceties aside, that was to end as conciliation was not in Lodge's marching orders. The new policy followed the old adage: If you take the King's shilling then you do the King's bidding—only this time it was dollars from Washington. Diem saw through it and on 25 June told Thuan that Lodge's posting was an effort to make him "do our [Washington's] bidding or unseat him" and "they can send ten Lodges but I will not permit myself or my country to be humiliated."[83] Thich Tri Quang and his followers and senior State Department officials independently converged on the same objective: Get rid of Diem.[84]

16

How About a Coup?

The drive to replace Diem within the State Department had gained steam when a 23 May report from Ambassador Nolting titled "Eventual Change in Government in Viet-Nam" arrived on Hilsman's desk. Hilsman found the report a godsend, for while it was not what the ambassador intended, it provided a template to replace Diem. What must have been especially appealing was Nolting's conclusion that the only options to succeed Diem were either a military government or a constitutional succession backed by the military. It also was timely as Nolting left Vietnam that day for an overdue and extended vacation, and the Buddhist crisis was peaking. Further, now-Undersecretary of State Harriman and his team were at the height of their power. The team, which Hilsman called "an informal set of working relations," first jelled during the 1961 Laos crisis. It included Hilsman, Sullivan, Forrestal (a family friend who served under Harriman in Moscow in 1946), and Trueheart in Saigon. It was tight group; Forrestal remarked that Harriman and Hilsman thought so alike on Vietnam that you did not need both at a meeting. Others called Forrestal and Sullivan the "gold dust twins" because of the favor they incurred from Harriman. The team also had the support of Undersecretary of State George W. Ball.[1]

Hilsman keyed in on Nolting's comment that the Americans needed to maintain current relations with "persons likely to play important roles in a change in government."[2] Back in January, Hilsman asked Harriman to end the policy dating back to the Eisenhower administration forbidding U.S. officials (except CIA) from maintaining contacts with anti–Diem leaders. Nolting's report provided an ideal justification for adopting Hilsman's recommendation. The standing policy was not a minor matter over information gathering. Since partition in 1954, where there was opposition, there were coup plotters from Hinh onwards, and opening lines of communication with the U.S. Government was the only impetus needed to stir them to action. To discourage it, a firewall had been erected as early as 1958: no official contact with the opposition. Inciting plotters may not have been Hilsman's intent in January when he headed up the INR and before the Buddhist crisis, but he now ran Far Eastern affairs. He saw developing options to replace Diem as critical, and since the ARVN had to be involved, it was time to talk to the generals. The old policy was out.[3]

The first major step toward removing Diem was taken at the State Department on 1 July, the Monday before the long 4th of July weekend. It was not a typically quiet summer Monday. With Nolting away, Trueheart was in charge in Saigon while President Kennedy, Secretary of State Rusk, and National Security Advisor

Bundy were overseas in Rome. That left George Ball in charge at State backed up by Harriman and Hilsman, along with Forrestal on duty with the NSC. Never before had the anti–Diem team been presented with such an opportunity to put their plans into motion.

The four met that morning and outlined a strongly worded démarche to Diem demanding that he (1) cut ties with Nhu and his wife and send them out of the country and (2) make a dramatic and sincere public move to dispel the belief of Buddhist persecution by his regime. They then prepared and dispatched a cable that instructed Trueheart to present the message to Diem and recommended that he also bring up the demands made on 8 June in the wake of Madame Nhu's anti–Thich Tri Quang and thinly veiled anti–American polemic. Trueheart was to go into battle against Diem and promptly went to the presidential palace.[4]

After discussing the cable with Thuan, even compliant Trueheart realized the démarche went too far and hesitated Not only would Diem perceive the terms as an affront to South Vietnam's national sovereignty, it was the worst possible approach. As a young man, Diem had given up a successful—even stellar—career in public service because he would not subordinate his drive for Vietnamese independence to the will of the French colonial administration, and two decades later, he was sentenced to death in absentia for opposing the communists. It was a given he would reject dictation from Washington. It also had to be remembered that Diem had not forgotten the murder of his older brother, Ngo Dinh Khoi, by Ho Chi Minh's agents, and telling Diem to abandon and exile his brother Nhu would only intensify his resistance to the Americans.

A sobered Trueheart returned to the embassy and contacted Washington about the overreach issues. With that feedback, on 2 July the Harriman team backed down. A rewritten cable toned down the language, withdrew the exile demand, and moved toward conciliation with Diem. It now stated that if Diem made a public declaration "designed to bridge the gap of understanding" with Quang and the Buddhists, then the United States would publicly defend Diem in the event of a future Buddhist incident.[5] Trueheart presented the new message to Diem, who agreed to consider it but made no commitment.

Later that week, Nolting, who had arrived in Washington, met with Ball, Harriman, and Hilsman. (Rusk was still in Europe.) Nolting tried to address Diem's resistance, explaining "that when Diem gave his word, he followed through although sometimes it was handled in his own way" adding, "as to tactics, the more Diem was prodded the slower he went."[6] His opinions were not well received. He found Harriman "testy and uncommunicative" and concluded the reason he had not been kept up to date on the deteriorating Washington-Saigon relationship during his absence was because the Harriman team did not want him to return to Vietnam. By then the Harriman team saw Nolting as Diem's apologist and wanted him out. Nolting concluded they wanted the crisis "to come to a head, to make a change in government in Saigon inevitable."[7] Nolting was pessimistic for good reason; while the 1 July cable called for his return to Saigon, Lodge was waiting in the wings.[8]

The Harriman team got a boost on July 4 after Conein cabled Washington informing them that after joining with several ARVN generals that day at the

Caravelle Hotel bar, he discovered they were contemplating a plan to oust Diem. The Harriman team did not see Diem's overthrow as a problem. They saw an opening. Ball and the Harriman team met with President Kennedy later on the 4th of July. Hilsman spoke of the coup—raising that ugly possibility with the president for the first time. Also raised was the subject of Thich Tri Quang, who too sought Diem's removal, and none proposed taking steps to rein in Quang's extremism. Hilsman downplayed any ill effects from a coup and was untroubled by Quang. He nonchalantly conceded there was "an element of truth in Diem's view that the Buddhists might push their demands so far as to make his fall inevitable."[9] The coup talk went nowhere, as Kennedy was not interested.[10]

Coup momentum in both Washington and Saigon built nonetheless. On 8 July, the CIA's Saigon station expanded Conein's information when it sent Washington a detailed report on coup activities. It confirmed Hilsman's conclusion that, "Buddhist strategy is polarizing around the views of Thich Tri Quang ... who has openly stated his intention not to cease agitation until the Diem government falls."[11] The CIA then outlined the activities of three interrelated coup groups. Ousted SEPES head Tran Kim Tuyen led the most significant group. The other two were less credible but importantly, Colonel Pham Ngoc Thao (Hanoi's operative) led one trying to join with Tuyen. That meant Hanoi knew of the plotters' activities with an ideally placed agent of influence. Tuyen was key as he worked with military advisor to the president, General Duong Van "Big" Minh, and III CTZ commander, Ton That Dinh—among the officers Conein met at the Caravelle. The summary chillingly closed by stating that the generals aimed at "the assassination of Ngo Dinh Nhu and his wife and the 'elimination' of the President by less forcible means if possible, but by assassination if necessary."[12] Despite the shocking nature of the information, no one in Washington moved to dissuade the plotters from murder.[13]

After meeting with Harriman and Hilsman on 9 July, McGeorge Bundy left, uneasy after the two stressed that a coup was likely and more ominously, that they had concluded Diem was no longer essential to American success in South Vietnam. The two argued that American interests in South Vietnam were no longer aligned with Diem, and they should not confuse themselves by believing otherwise. Harriman and Hilsman were leaning toward a complete break with the regime. The White House still was having none of it. By then Nolting had met with the president, who directed him to quickly return to Vietnam and restore confidence and trust between Saigon and Washington. In the meantime, Diem would get no public support from the Americans.[14]

Nolting was back in Saigon by 10 July, and in keeping with Kennedy's order, relations with Diem began to improve throughout the month. Even before Nolting arrived, on 9 July, Trueheart was made aware that Vice President Tho was sending conciliatory messages to Quang and his followers, and the cabinet ministers were reviewing Diem's long hoped for national address on the Buddhist crisis. Diem was not acting as badly as expected, and Trueheart briefly wavered; he was confused over Diem's mixture of opposing American demands on the one hand while taking constructive steps to enact them on the other. To continue to meet American demands, on 11 July, Diem announced the appointment of the nation's inspector general to address Buddhist concerns. Six days later, Diem also agreed to stop relying solely on his province chiefs for information on local Buddhist complaints.[15]

Things took another step against the coup on 18 July when President Diem made the national address that the Harriman team had so strongly urged in the 1 July démarche. Diem issued instructions (1) to extend Decree 10 flag privileges to the General Association of Buddhists, (2) to form an Inter-ministerial Committee in cooperation with the Buddhist delegation to consider, inquire into, and settle together all complaints related to the Joint Communiqué, and (3) that the public and private sectors actively contribute to the implementation of the Joint Communiqué.[16] His message ended by expressing his "hope that all of you, my compatriots, will take note of the utmost desire of conciliation of the government in settling the Buddhist problem." He asked his listeners to "judge the facts objectively and to adopt an attitude and a behavior which will permit no one to impede the march forward of our people in its mission of crushing communists for the salvation of the nation."[17] On the following day, Diem ordered the removal of police and other security forces' barricades surrounding pagodas, and that bonzes be permitted to return, while banning public assemblies at the Xa Loi pagoda. It all was for naught.[18]

Having made considerable headway with Diem, Nolting immediately cabled Washington asking it to honor its 2 July pledge to make a public declaration in defense of Diem, as Diem had met the speech demand. The State Department balked, and on 23 July, Hilsman drafted a cable directing Nolting not to publicly support Diem. He added, do not run the "risk of putting us in position of having backed a loser" and "alternatives to Diem seem to be emerging, it is not yet clear who and what they are." Just to make sure Nolting understood, Hilsman repeated himself in a second cable two days later. The Harriman team had reached the point of no return—Diem had to go—and again there would be no pressure on Quang or his followers to either work constructively with Diem or moderate their radicalism. Meanwhile the coup plotting advanced apace.[19]

For the next several weeks, the situation in Saigon drifted toward another confrontation with Thich Tri Quang. Under no pressure to change his ways and either ignoring or sabotaging the steps Diem had taken, Quang continued his attacks on the Saigon regime without let-up. As the month closed, Diem made further conciliatory moves. He ordered Interior Minister Bui Van Luong not to use force against the Buddhist protests, and not knowing that Thich Tinh Khiet had been shunted aside by Quang, President Diem made a futile effort to arrange a meeting between the two. Vice President Tho's outreach to Quang similarly was ignored.[20]

Fed up with the protests and State Department inaction, on 28 July Nolting commented to the *UPI*, "I myself, I say this very frankly, after almost two and one half years here, have never seen any evidence of religious persecution, in fact I have the feeling that there is a great deal of religious toleration among Vietnamese people at all levels."[21] Quang was livid. On 31 July, his Inter-Sect Committee for the Defense of Buddhism complained bitterly and condemned Nolting in an open letter issued under Thich Tinh Khiet's name (but as the CIA learned, was actually Quang's handiwork). Harriman and Hilsman were equally incensed and resolved to remove Nolting as quickly as possible and replace him with Lodge, who had joined the team.[22]

Diem's repeated positive acts had done little to retard coup machinations. Although even Hilsman had to admit during a 6 August meeting with Ball that the combination of Diem's speech, removal of barricades, release of prisoners, and restraint from using force at protests "have pointed to an amelioration of the situation," he was undeterred in his goal of removing Diem.[23] Hilsman had never backed off the 1 July demand of removing the Nhus—which meant removing Diem as well—and highlighted the Nhus extreme opposition to Quang's movement as justification.

Madame Nhu certainly aided Hilsman. A few days earlier, during a 1 August interview on *CBS News*, she correctly stated that the Buddhist leaders were trying to topple the government, crudely and outrageously disparaged the self-immolation of Thich Quang Duc as a bonze "barbecue," and refused to walk back the comment. She forcefully spoke to men as equals and used their language. Madame Nhu could not understand why Americans were upset with the word "barbeque" to describe the self-immolation, as it had originated with American press photographers. Why there was an important difference between nearly identical utterances of hardened war photographers and a woman closely associated with the president of the Republic of Vietnam was lost on her. She certainly saw it as double-standard sexism and was not alone. USOM officer Harvey Neese met Madame Nhu in December 1962, ironically at a barbecue. He later wrote that her "off-the-cuff remark overshadowed all the positive things Madame Nhu had done for women's rights in South Vietnam, which were considerable."[24] Halberstam got it right; the men would see to it that she would not survive if she continued to delve into their politics. Rightly or wrongly, the Nhus were proving to be of no help to Diem.[25]

During the same 6 August meeting, Hilsman admitted that Quang had the objective of overthrowing Diem and would not stop. The truth was out, but not only did the Harriman team not care, they liked Quang's radicalism. They saw Thich Tri Quang as a tool, a means to their ends, and the notion that pressure should be applied to moderate Quang counterproductive. With that in mind, Hilsman outlined how his staff was using Nolting's 23 May "change in government" plan to throw American influence behind Diem's replacement. He added they were "urgently seeking further but discreet contact with oppositionist elements … to give us a better chance to manipulate the outcome of a coup attempt."[26] As to what would happen after? Hilsman merely echoed without amplification the vague "Vice President Tho–military" or "military junta" options of Nolting's report. That revealed the flaw with the Harriman team's deliberations. They focused on removing Diem—not the successor government. Colby described it as "an almost total absence of consideration and evaluation of the personalities who might succeed Diem."[27] By early August, the State Department was committed to a coup, and the Harriman team marched forward without a clear vision for the future.[28]

Thich Tri Quang also was not a man to be put off. On 3 August, there was second self-immolation at the small coastal town of Phan Thiet, a third near Hue on 13 August, and another by a nun near the port city of Nha Trang. None, except the death in the movement's stronghold of Hue, drew much of a reaction, but a second Hue self-immolation by an elderly bonze on 16 August at the Tu Dam pagoda tipped the city into near riot. Hue remained a tinderbox of tension as rumors gripped its inhabitants. Quang's "flag" rumors had roiled the city in May, but now in August, they became both absurd and frightening. The most divisive purported that Diem's brother, Archbishop Thuc, schemed to round up the city's Buddhists and force conversion to Catholicism, presumably on pain of death or some other violent coercion. That such wild stories held sway indicated the extent of hysteria in Hue.[29]

Things were not much better in Saigon. Madame Nhu continued to stir things up. In an interview with *Time* published on 8 August, she criticized Diem's approach as futile appeasement, chastising him for being naïve: "He would like to conciliate as the Americans desire, smooth, no bloodshed, everyone shaking hands."[30] She thought it nothing more than wishful thinking. Quang also escalated tensions. Flouting Diem's 19 July order, the bonze returned the Xa Loi pagoda to the center of unrest. A crowd estimated at 15,000 gathered on Sunday 18 August, and even a strong rainstorm could not deter them as the bonzes addressed the masses to fan the fires of protest. Halberstam wrote of the event, "The Buddhists were 'playing a fast and dangerous game.'"[31] They waved banners that no longer even pretended to relate to the 8 May demands; instead, they called for the overthrow of the Diem government. Thich Tri Quang's movement had finally forced the South Vietnamese government to act.[32]

The 21 August Pagoda Raids

That evening on 18 August, ten of the country's 17 generals representing all four CTZs and the major commands in and around Saigon asked for an urgent meeting with President Diem. While the day's demonstration proved to be the catalyst, the underlying reasons that the generals chose to act were several and variously overlapping. Some, Diem's enemies, deemed their move as an essential step in the coup process, that taking action would put them on the political stage and the path to ruling South Vietnam. Others more warily saw the hand of Nhu, whom they believed sought to use the army to end Quang's drive to oust his brother. A more hawkish viewpoint concluded Quang had begun to target the military, and due to Diem's "indecisiveness," they had to prevent mob rule that threatened the government and the integrity of the armed forces.[33]

Remarks about the threat to the government and armed forces were not idle rhetoric. For several weeks General Do Cao Tri, the commander in I CTZ (that included Hue and Da Nang), had been pushing for a crackdown. As with many others, Tri concluded that the radical Buddhists' real intent was to overthrow the government. Adding fuel to the fire, earlier that day, a group of Buddhists militants assaulted an army captain in Da Nang. That act of violence resembled the 1955 Binh Xuan provocations, which created a "blood debt" that demanded a response by the army. Regardless of the reason or reasons, the crisis was at a head, and it was clear the generals had contemplated action for some time, for they arrived with a plan in hand.[34]

After hearing out the generals that steamy Sunday evening, Diem approved the nationwide suppression of Quang's Buddhist movement by force, to include the removal of several hundred bonzes from Saigon to be returned to their home provinces, and the imposition of martial law. The generals specifically urged a raid on the Xa Loi pagoda. Operations tentatively were to begin in darkness either late Tuesday or after midnight. Afterwards, Nhu was informed of the deliberations and must have been delighted by what he heard. He avidly endorsed the raids and scheduled a Tuesday meeting to finalize the plans with South Vietnam's top seven generals headed by acting JGS Chief Major General Tran Van Don, who was no supporter of Diem. During the second meeting, Nhu moved to have Duong Van Hieu's special police, supported by Colonel Tung's Saigon Special Forces units, lead the assault on Saigon's Xa Loi pagoda. According to General Don, when the final plan was presented, Diem pleaded with the generals to ensure that no Buddhists would be injured.[35]

At 12:30 a.m., Wednesday, 21 August, in cities across the nation, the police, other security forces, and ARVN troops—especially the combat police—began raiding some two dozen or more pagodas used by Thich Tri Quang's followers. At Quang's Buddhist Youth stronghold in Hue, police were augmented by troops from General Do Cao Tri's 1st Division. In the ensuing fighting, a number were killed and dozens wounded. In Saigon, the army played a secondary role as Hieu's special police and Tung's LLDB troops forced their way into the Xa Loi pagoda. Elsewhere in the country, local security forces—backed up by ARVN units under command of the generals—detained offending monks. About two hours later, the operations had been completed, and while there had been dozens injured nationwide, the only fatalities occurred in Hue.[36]

By morning, over 1,400 monks and nuns had been placed into custody. The completeness of raids impressed the American embassy in Saigon. They cabled Washington, noting the "expertness, speed, and coordination with which operations carried out against Buddhists in widely separated cities indicate that careful and detailed prior planning must have been carried out on contingency basis before final decision to move taken."[37] And what of Thich Tri Quang? Halberstam wrote that the monks at Xa Loi stood their ground because, as Thich Quang Do put it, "We had done nothing wrong; therefore we could not flee. If we had, it would have been an admission that we were guilty."[38] That statement either was a brazen lie or a stunning admission of guilt, given that Thich Tri Quang and his top lieutenants fled Xa Loi at the first signs of trouble and eventually took refuge in the U.S. embassy.[39]

During the evening of 22 August, General Don was more than content with himself; the raids had gone off like clockwork, and Saigon was quieter than it had been for many weeks. More boisterously, III CTZ commander Major General Ton That Dinh let it be known to the American press that "I, Dinh, am a great national hero. I have defeated the American Cabot Lodge. He was on his way here to pull a coup d'état but I, Dinh, the hero, have foiled him."[40] He then left for a meeting with the president.

Diem was more sedate and continued to seek a peaceful resolution. Late on Thursday, Generals Don, Dinh, and Tran Thien Khiem went to see Nhu about the activist students and recommended that Saigon's schools be closed. Nhu agreed, and they went to seek Diem's approval. According to General Don, Diem said, "No. The young people must have means of expressing themselves."[41] All were disappointed when student protests turned violent the next day, and over one thousand were arrested. Fortunately, it was the last major street protest. In the days and weeks that followed, a sometimes tense calm returned to Saigon and the other troubled cities in South Vietnam. Things in Washington, however, were heating up, and a coup remained on the Americans' agenda.

The Harriman Team Strikes

As they had on 1 July, the Harriman team took advantage of the absence of key leaders. On this summer Saturday, 24 August 1963, President Kennedy was in Hyannis Port and McGeorge Bundy out of town. Dean Rusk was in New York, and McNamara was on holiday in Wyoming, while CIA Director John A. McCone vacationed in California. The situation in Saigon was equally favorable. Nolting had departed Vietnam on 15 August, and Lodge, who arrived on 22 August, was working in tandem with Trueheart.

In Washington, Harriman, Hilsman, and Forrestal got to work on a cable that would change history. Their labors would not be a replay of 1 July. This time there would be no half measures or looking back or allowing any possibility of the Diem regime surviving.[42]

The mortal blows to the Diem regime were contained in three lines of the cable. The first directed Lodge to tell key South Vietnamese military leaders that if the Nhus remained part of the government, then the United States would cut military aid. This was decisive; getting rid of Nhu meant getting rid of Diem, and just as important, without U.S. military aid, the war was lost. Colonel Thieu, the 5th Division commander at Bien Hoa in 1963, recalled, "The Americans created the conditions for the army to revolt.... American military aid was a constant sword of

John A. McCone talks with President Kennedy during the ceremony swearing him in as Director of Central Intelligence, 29 January 1961. In the background (from left) are Senator Henry M. "Scoop" Jackson, Atomic Energy Commission Chairman Glenn T. Seaborg, and Supreme Court Chief Justice Earl Warren (John F. Kennedy Presidential Library).

Damocles over our head."[43] General "Big" Minh put it more directly: if military aid stopped, "It would have been the end of everything."[44] The difference was that while Diem refused to admit it, Minh and the other generals knew South Vietnam had no future if it did not obey Washington.

The second key line directed Lodge to inform "appropriate" South Vietnamese generals that Washington would support them if the Diem government were to "breakdown."[45] Who was to instigate the "breakdown" was left unsaid. Finally, Lodge was to figure to out "how we might bring about Diem's replacement"— in other words, foment regime change in South Vietnam.[46] This was not simply a departure from long-standing American policy toward South Vietnam. It was a radical course of action. Rufus Phillips, the former CIA SMM operative now working with USOM, stated that the embassy interpreted the cable to mean they were to "inspire" a coup.[47] That was exactly how General Tran Van Don saw the situation. The Americans had come far since 1954 when Ambassador Heath in Saigon wrote critically of the French, "A strong foreign occupying army can protect a country, but it can also dominate, paralyze its government and even favor a 'coup d'état' by its opponents."[48] How the worm had turned.[49]

The next job for the Harriman team was to get the cable approved. It would be a brilliant display of Washington bureaucratic legerdemain. Ball was on board, assuring State Department approval. Similarly, Forrestal was on watch at the NSC, so his "yes" was a foregone conclusion. Richard Helms, the CIA's no. 2, did not deem it an intelligence matter and concurred without informing either McCone or Colby. As for the military, they would be cut out of the process. It was decided, "that it [the cable] was not something on which Defense clearance was desired."[50] There would be no attempt to gain either McNamara or Taylor's consent. But someone had to be informed. Shopping for a receptive ear and breaking the chain of command, Hilsman contacted Admiral Felt in Hawaii and obtained a favorable response. Forrestal half-heartedly attempted to reach McNamara's deputy, Roswell L. Gilpatric, that afternoon without success. None of the leaders in the military or at Defense would see the top-secret cable until after it was sent.[51]

With their bases covered, it was time to contact President Kennedy. Earlier in the day, Forrestal sent an informal feeler to the president in Hyannis Port, stating incorrectly, "It is now quite certain that Brother Nhu is the mastermind behind the whole operation against the Buddhists and is calling the shots." He added, "Averell and Roger now agree that we must move before the situation in Saigon freezes." Forrestal followed up by sending a draft of the cable to the president and closed by writing, "Please let me know if you wish to comment or hold up action."[52] President Kennedy assented later that day. Gilpatric was finally reached early in the evening by telephone and "was in accord with" the cable's intent, but it was unthinkable that he would do otherwise since the president had already given his approval. At 9:39 p.m. Saturday night, the cable was sent under Ball's name to Lodge for action. It was a duplicitous sequence of events, and to make things more distasteful, the target was not an enemy but ally of the United States.

The Harriman team now shifted to making a coup work. Since the ARVN generals were key to everything, they had to be made to look like the "good guys" both at home and abroad. The 21 August pagoda raids potentially threatened that image. To ensure the right message got out, the storyline had to be rewritten in essence to claim (a) Nhu alone orchestrated the 21 August raids—not the senior generals—and if revealed, their 18 and 21 August meetings were to be disavowed (with General Dinh's public boast conveniently forgotten), (b) the army played no real role, and (c) whatever role they did play either resulted from being duped by Nhu or were acts of above-board patriotism. References to nationwide raids were recast to focus solely on the raid at Saigon's Xa Loi pagoda that was portrayed as Nhu using Colonel Tung's Special Forces to savagely attack innocent followers of Thich Tri Quang. This suited the ARVN generals as it absolved them of responsibility and kept them in Washington's good graces. In the 1980s, General Don still repeated the story that the army had no role in the raids even though he had been a central participant. To back up the story, Diem's cabinet chief and ardent Nhu opponent, Vo Van Hai, provided Hilsman with a perfect stew of less than truthful propaganda that placed the blame for the 21 August raids squarely on Nhu and falsely implicated Madame Nhu for good measure.[53]

Hilsman pushed the same tale but made a tactical error when he hastily drafted a related story, passed it to *UPI* reporter Stewart Hensley, and instructed *Voice of America* to broadcast it in Vietnam on 26 August. It stated, "High Americans blame police, headed by President Diem's brother, Ngo Dinh Nhu, for anti–Buddhist actions" and "Vietnam military leaders are not, repeat, not responsible for last week's attacks against the pagodas and the mass arrest of monks and students."[54] It went on to again threaten to cut off aid to South Vietnam. The story backfired, as Ambassador Lodge strongly objected. He wanted the final word on U.S. aid and felt it presented a public "kiss of death" to Nhu that tipped him off to the U.S.-backed coup.[55]

Despite their successful manipulations, support for the Harriman team's gambit quickly unraveled. That evening Marine General Victor Krulak was able to read the cable and was alarmed enough to bring it to General Taylor at his home. Taylor read it and quipped, "It reflects the well-known compulsion of Hilsman and Forrestal to depose Diem."[56] Taylor was more correct than he knew; Hilsman apparently also had misled Harriman into believing that Taylor approved of their cable. Instead, Taylor loudly complained about the suspect staffing process and argued that had McGeorge Bundy, instead of Forrestal, been present at the White House, the cable never would have been released. When Colby at the CIA finally saw a copy on Sunday, he immediately contacted Director McCone. McCone was sufficiently concerned that he directed Colby to fly immediately to California with the top-secret cable in hand. After reviewing it, McCone decided to return the next day to Washington with Colby.[57]

The Coup Becomes Irreversible

On Monday, 26 August, everyone of importance was summoned to the White House to assess what had happened on Saturday, and the meeting ended with a badly divided cabinet. Rusk had misgivings and also was uneasy, but the Harriman team held firm, while McNamara and McCone concluded the cable had been done in haste. The president leaned toward staying the course with Diem. He then took a swipe at Halberstam's pagoda raid reporting, stating, "When we move to eliminate this government, it should not be a result of *New York Times* pressure."[58] It was decided they would meet again in two days to hammer out what was to be done.[59]

The situation in Saigon was more straightforward. Ambassador Lodge acted with alacrity. In public, Lodge was the proper diplomat, saying all the right things. Behind the scenes it was another story. His first order of business was to call in the CIA's Lucien Conein. Conein immediately understood that Lodge's arrival signified a "very dramatic change" in policy.[60] Lodge swept away the old prohibition against working with coup plotters, and when it came to American coup-shaping, he was in charge. He directed that the "American official hand" should not be visible, that Conein was to handle everything and answer only to him.[61] The relationship worked; Lodge later stated Conein punctiliously and explicitly carried out his orders. Getting to work, Conein met again with Generals Don and Nguyen Van Khanh (commander of II CTZ) and "Big" Minh to test, per the cable, if they were "appropriate" officers to carry out the coup. They passed, and in the decisive step, Conein let them know that the Americans would support a coup.[62]

Things were not so cut and dried in Washington. When a 28 August meeting got underway at the White House, President Kennedy defined his understanding of the fluid situation with the remark, "If the coup is not in the cards then we could unload."[63] He was telling everyone that they were in control, and if a successful coup was not likely, then they could stop it. Bundy also was concerned about "gaining operational control of a coup."[64] George Ball tried to make clear to the president that the cable had pushed things "beyond the point of no return" and insisted that it made no sense to go back. Diem had to be removed, and he insisted, "The question is how do we make this coup effort successful."[65] Hilsman and Harriman offered full agreement. Hilsman bluntly stated that Diem had to be overthrown if the United States wanted to win the war. Harriman argued that they could not give Lodge "any idea we are wobbling on our course" and brooked no opposition.[66] When Ambassador Nolting objected to the coup, Harriman shut him up by calling him a "god-damned fool."[67] Calming the waters, the president countered, "We must not let the field feel that we are in any way heavy-handed, or obliging them to take actions which, are not, in their good judgment, sound."[68] McNamara, Taylor, and McCone supported the president, and McNamara wanted no part of a plot to remove an ally. The lines could not have been drawn more sharply.[69]

Harriman also crossed a line with the president when he stated that MACV's General Harkins supported the coup. Harkins only saw the 24 August cable after the president had approved, and Harkins stated he would accept and obey the president's order—a position Rusk also claimed, stating that Kennedy's approval "restricted my freedom of action."[70] Harkins had not, however, been asked if he supported the plan, which he did not. When caught by Kennedy, Harriman was asked to stay after the meeting to address the discrepancy. He extricated himself by mumbling something about being puzzled by Harkins' reply. After he left the room, the president chuckled and noted, "Averell Harriman is one sharp cookie."[71] Whether Kennedy appreciated it or not, the sharp cookie and his team were pressing ahead with the coup, come what may. The events at the White House were a watershed in many ways, but the most crucial was that participants left with very different understandings of what the president wanted.

Fortunately, or unfortunately, depending on perspective, the coup fell apart before it began. The disunity revealed in the ARVN generals' mixed motives that led to the 18 August meeting with Diem remained, and even those who previously appeared receptive got cold feet with one exception: "Big" Minh. Adding to the morass, they had no plan as to how to stage the coup or form a coherent follow-on government. Colonel Thao (Hanoi's spy), who had fallen out of the generals' grace, passed to Conein one telling fact on 30 August that "Big" Minh also passed on to the CIA Station and Lodge: "The first step is to kill Diem."[72] The CIA and State, to include the Harriman team, knew Minh's plan broached in July—to assassinate Diem—remained the goal. With things going nowhere, the plotting died. Harkins reported that most ARVN units remained loyal to Diem, and Nhu had done a fair job in keeping the support of Khiem and other generals. To close out the sordid affair, on 31 August, the CIA declared, "This particular coup is finished."[73]

During early September, President Kennedy sought to stabilize the relationship with Diem. The CIA assessed that the contest between the U.S. and Diem to gain the generals' support had been a draw and Washington's relationship with Diem only minimally damaged. After seeing a proposed cable drafted by Hilsman to reinvigorate plotting in Saigon, Kennedy changed the ground rules on 3 September. In the future, the Americans would not initiate any contact with coup plotters. The plotters would have to come to them, and any change in aid to South Vietnam would be decided in the White House—not at the State Department or by Ambassador Lodge. The president's orders had little effect.[74]

Convinced they were on the right path, the Harriman team was having none of it. Back on 29 August, Lodge echoed Ball: "We are launched on a course from which there is no respectable turning back: the overthrow of the Diem government."[75] Further poisoning Lodge's mind, he had taken on one of Quang's acolytes, Thich Quang Lien, as an advisor on the Buddhist situation. At best, Lodge overtly would work with Diem in the near term and as a hedge in the event Diem somehow survived, but behind the scenes, he worked on his overthrow. On 15 September, INR issued a scathing condemnation of Ngo Dinh Nhu, and the next day the State Department hosted a high-level meeting in Washington. In attendance were Rusk, Harriman's Washington team, McGeorge Bundy, McNamara, and McCone. During the top-secret Vietnam briefing, it was reiterated that some generals still intended to go through with a coup and to kill Diem and Nhu at the outset.[76]

Lodge's position about removing Diem was consistent. He had been with the Harriman team since his briefings at State in early August. He also had met with President Kennedy on 15 August, who opened the door to replacing Diem. Kennedy's take was more nuanced, however. He instructed Lodge to get Diem on board; if not that was not possible, then he should look for a replacement. He told Lodge, "We've gotta just have to try to do something about Diem," and added about finding a replacement, "I think we have to leave it almost completely in your hands and your judgment. I don't know if we'd be better off—whether the alternative would be better. Maybe it will be. If so, then we have to move in that direction."[77] It was a significant disconnect. For the president, the door to keeping Diem remained open. For the Harriman team, it was shut; Diem had to be removed.

Unhappy with the continued divisions within the leadership, Hilsman fell back on his OSS training and compartmentalized coup planning; going forward, the NSC, Defense, and MACV would be cut out of the loop to the greatest extent possible. And with both McCone and Colby opposed, Lodge ensured, as he had with Conein, that CIA officers in Saigon took their orders from him. As Conein already had contacted the generals, Lodge could comply with the president's order by keeping those relations intact while not initiating "new" contacts. Also, to obey the president, Lodge modified Hilsman's goal to halt military aid by threatening suspension instead. He also tried to force the Nhus into exile and coerce Diem. Ironically, Washington condemned Madame Nhu that September for her "anti–American" comment that the U.S. was trying to destroy the Diem regime. She was spot on, as that was exactly what the Harriman team aimed to do. The Harriman team was encouraged further, for Vietnam now was headline news in America. In May when the Buddhist crisis began, *Time* published one article; in September they published ten, and media coverage was overwhelmingly anti–Diem.[78]

By this time, Lodge was frustrated with CIA resistance to the coup and moved to replace John Richardson, the CIA station chief, who opposed the coup. Lodge justified the change so he could "carry out a new policy now."[79] Lodge even floated the idea of bringing back Lansdale. When Director McCone refused (he abhorred Lansdale), Richardson's clandestine status was leaked to Richard Scarnes of the *Washington Daily News*, who published a story with the sensational title "The CIA Mess in South Vietnam—Arrogant CIA Disobeys Orders." Richardson was ordered home. The entire affair smacked of the Harriman team exploiting the media to advance their agenda, but Saigon was not their only point of trouble. They continued to face obstacles in Washington.[80]

With the protests gone after the 21 August raids, Diem lifted martial law and ended censorship in mid–September, while the repairs to the Xa Loi pagoda neared completion. All sides also drew a sigh of relief when Madame Nhu departed on 9 September for Belgrade, Yugoslavia (Serbia), beginning a prolonged overseas trip as South Vietnam's representative to the Inter-parliamentary Union. Significantly, Diem had cut out the heart of the August coup faction by appointing one of its leaders, Tran Kim Tuyen, as ambassador to Egypt; he left the country on 12 September. McCone noted that Diem was strengthening his position and reducing the possibility of a coup.[81]

Like most things associated with South Vietnam, how the war actually fared by the fall of 1963 remained complex. The Buddhist crisis in itself minimally affected the effort. Strategic hamlets were under unprecedented attack, but that was the logical Viet Cong reaction to their effectiveness—not the Buddhist uprising. The key factor was the ARVN. When asked by the Americans what effect the Buddhist unrest was having on the army, General Lu Lan, 25th Division commander in IV CTZ, stated there was no Buddhist-Catholic friction either in the army or among the population. The ARVN's problem was not Thich Tri Quang but the coup plotting by the generals. That was when ARVN units in and around Saigon froze, especially those in the critical III and IV CTZs. Both Diem and the generals were to blame as they maneuvered to keep loyal troops free to move in the event of a coup while trying to neutralize potentially hostile units. That did damage the war effort—a truth the "blame-Diem" advocates did not want to hear.[82]

At the same time, McNamara became a thorn in the side of the Harriman team. He urged for a return to the policy of working constructively with Diem that was in place before the 24 August cable, stressing, "We have no alternatives" to Diem.[83] Harriman vigorously countered. Backing up Harriman, Hilsman argued that the only solution was the removal of Diem. A week later, he moved to undo Diem's gains when he proposed a pressure-persuasion reconciliation policy that was suicidal for Diem. He would be directed to rapidly create a liberal democracy, free the militant monks, and allow Quang to resume his activities without interference from the South Vietnamese government.[84]

Hilsman's scheme required Diem to simultaneously betray his loyal generals and return the country to Quang's brand of destructive chaos. Hilsman's demands reflected a cynical view of events. He later wrote that by launching the 21 August pagoda raids, Diem "had violated our deepest sense of decency and fair play."[85] The only South Vietnamese of consequence guilty of that charge was Thich Tri Quang, and Hilsman's own actions were more than a bit dubious. He knew better; on 10 September the Saigon CIA Station which had dug into the causes of the Buddhist uprising reported that Quang's political objective was to upend the Diem government and had been adopted before the 8 May Hue incident. It added that the Saigon government realized Quang was abusing Diem's reconciliation policy, and Quang's followers sowed disorder to turn international public opinion, especially in the United States, against Diem.[86]

Equally duplicitous was Hilsman's demand for South Vietnam to aggressively move toward a broad-based democracy. It was a theory also put forward by his assistant, Joseph Mendenhall, after his visit to Saigon. In September 1963, Malaysia was just coming into being, the DVR was a communist dictatorship while Burma and Thailand were ruled by military juntas, Laos had ceased to exist as a functioning state after Geneva, and Cambodia was ruled by a one-party dictatorship under Prince Sihanouk. That South Vietnam, a country in the midst of a bloody and escalating war with the DRV, could achieve what no other Southeast Asian country found possible was setting a goal that only could end in failure. Even the newly-arrived Ambassador Lodge realized the RVN was not ready for liberal democracy. Diem never took the Hilsman demands seriously, but his enemies in Washington used Diem's inaction to undermine support for his regime and pushed through the suspension of non-military economic aid to South Vietnam in retaliation.[87]

Those developments moved Bundy closer to McNamara's position, which brought the divisions within the cabinet to a head again. Forrestal urged Bundy to ask the president to intervene and resolve coup policy differences between State and Defense. Forrestal, working in the NSC and a Harriman team member, was ideally placed to see the gulf between the actions of the two sides. Bundy declined. He wanted the White House to keep its options open by both working with Diem as McNamara, General Taylor, McCone, and others argued while maintaining oversight over the coup machinations. Giving him confidence in his course of action, he developed a strong skepticism over the ARVN generals' ability to successfully execute a coup after their August failure. Kennedy contacted Lodge telling him to retain control of events, and McGeorge Bundy still believed the White House could rein in Saigon's coup plotters.[88]

On 27 September, elections for the RVN National Assembly took place and, with the possible exception of Malaysia, were the freest in Southeast Asia with what an American observer termed a "massive voter turnout."[89] Of the 123 seats for the National Assembly, Diem's coalition won 96 seats (including 50 National Revolutionary Movement and 19 female candidates from the Women's Solidarity Movement). Fifteen of Diem's candidates were defeated, and there was a fair amount of turnover as only 60 of the 85 incumbents who ran were reelected. Two ethnic-Chinese candidates won election from Cholon (a first), and Viet Cong attempts to disrupt the election failed. Lodge was mostly silent on the whole matter and the Diem regime received no credit for the effort in the State Department. The American press treated it as a non-event.[90]

Five days later, on 3 October, the split between the Defense and State Departments resurfaced when McNamara and Taylor sent President Kennedy a report that stated if there were to be a coup, an authoritative regime would arise and "after an initial period of euphoria" following the end of the Diem regime, "a resumption of the repression at least of Diem" and "the corruption of the Vietnamese Establishment before Diem" would ensue "with at least an equivalent degree of xenophobic nationalism."[91] That raised again the Harriman team's critical weakness. No one had come up with a credible alternative to Diem. McNamara and Taylor concluded that as for a coup, "We believe this course of action should not be undertaken at the present time."[92]

Fateful Days: 5 and 9 October 1963

The 5th of October witnessed a calamitous nexus of activities. That morning in the White House, President Kennedy chaired a high-level meeting to discuss how to work better with Diem and best apply economic pressure to get him to accept American guidance. McCone later recalled that by this time, Kennedy was aware that the generals had discussed killing Diem, and he wanted no American role. After the specifics were worked out, Lodge was directed to inform Diem that U.S. aid and loan cuts were to be conditionally restored. Reconciliation dominated the discussion with not a word devoted to coup plots—it no longer was an issue. It also was a busy morning in Saigon. The CIA's John Richardson departed, removing the last senior civilian official in Saigon trying to stop the coup; from then on CIA operatives took their orders from Lodge and the State Department, while Director McCone and Colby in Washington were shut out.[93]

Events continued to unfold that day. Conein met with "Big" Minh, who discussed the coup and made clear that it was not possible without assurances that the United States (1) would not thwart the coup and (2) economic and military aid would continue following Diem's overthrow. Minh also became cagey about assassinations, stating the intent was to kill Diem's brothers Nhu and Can while it was "easiest" to keep Diem in power.[94] After being briefed by Conein, Lodge, who believed that Diem had to be removed to win the war, cabled Washington seeking approval for "Big" Minh's assurances. That led to another high-level White House meeting. Afterwards Bundy bluntly told Lodge that the president would not give assurances, and "no initiative should now be taken to give any active covert encouragement to a coup."[95] The president made his position clear. The next day, McCone took the only direct step to prevent murder. He cabled the Saigon station, instructing them to tell Lodge that the CIA could not condone the assassination of Diem. The active American role in coup plotting was over—or so it seemed.[96]

Four days later on 9 October, Lodge received an unsigned cable via the CIA's top secret "Saigon 20 series" communications from Washington addressing "Big" Minh's assurances that walked back the president's 5 October order. While it came from CIA, the State and Defense Departments, NSC, and White House also used the system to send sensitive messages. Who authored it was unclear; it stated that the message's "general thoughts" had been discussed with the president and "cleared" by "high officials" in State, Defense, and CIA. It was a masterful work of vagueness that created an ideal environment for mischief and mayhem. And in keeping with such undertakings, it directed Lodge to closely hold its contents, in part for plausible deniability purposes.[97]

The cable's language was not directive but a compilation of "general guidance" that led to considerations, wishes, and desires. The critical sentence danced along: "While we do not wish to stimulate a coup, we also do not wish to leave the impression that U.S. would thwart a change in government or deny economic and military assistance to a new regime."[98] It also addressed Minh specifically; Conein was to tell Minh that he would not forward the "assurances" request until the general presented a completed plan that offered "a high prospect of success," an argument often made by McGeorge Bundy.[99] Minh was not given a "No" reply but instead admonished to get to work. While that encouraged the general, it did nothing to unify policymakers in Washington.

For those not briefed on the cable in the Defense Department and military, their understanding remained unchanged. They would obey the president's 5 October order. In the White House, the intent of the 9 October cable again aimed to keep options open and control events. As a practical matter, the cable implied the White House's understanding that if a plot was deemed unlikely to succeed, then Washington could veto it; put another way, the final decision to carry out a coup rested with the White House. The goal remained working with Diem, but if that failed and viable alternative leadership presented itself, then at that point the president could make his decision.

For the Harriman team, the 9 October cable was a bright green light to push ahead. There was not a keen awareness in the White House of how determined the Harriman team was. It may very well have been that neither President Kennedy nor McGeorge Bundy could believe that the Harriman team was carrying out a single-track coup policy. The reason may have been that such a degree of misguided loyalty was unthinkable. Regardless of the disparate understandings, rationales, and motivations, after 9 October affairs plunged inevitably toward a final confrontation.

17

The Murder of Diem
and Its Consequences

As October 1963 progressed, President Kennedy had to feel confident that the coup situation was under control, and for the next several weeks events seemed to bear it out. Behind the scenes, the Harriman team also saw positive results. On 18 October, Colonel Tung lost command over almost all of Saigon's special forces troops, greatly reducing the number of soldiers loyal to Diem in the capital, and General Minh's coup planning proceeded favorably. It was not all smooth sailing for Harriman. At the same time, Hilsman became frustrated with McCone's continued opposition to the coup after McCone again went after its great flaw: "that an alternative government acceptable and useful to us is unlikely to arise." He further opined that the United States should abandon Hilsman's coercive "pressure and persuade policy" and instead normalize relations with Diem. Ironically, Diem himself raised the issue with American reporter Marguerite Higgins that October. He held it would be "folly" to let the generals run South Vietnam: "I am afraid there are no George Washingtons among our military."[1]

To rebut McCone's claims, the Harriman team argued that "Big" Minh could get the job done, as he was not just popular and acceptable to the other generals but the most respected officer in the army and had no political ambitions. That contradicted General Harkins, who had let it be known in September that as far as he was concerned, Minh was a chronic critic, earning Minh the sobriquet of "general bellyache," and "has contributed nothing to the war effort or as an advisor to the President."[2] Harkins' misgivings were not new. Two years earlier, Secretary of Defense Thuan told the McNamara-Taylor mission that "Big" Minh was "always complaining, and doesn't take action when he has the opportunity; his plans never seem to be complete"—and Minh was the JGS chief of operations directing the war at that time. With General Don in charge of coup planning, maybe Minh would be ready this time.[3]

Things again heated up in Washington. The final policy battle began on 22 October when General Don informed Harkins that "Big" Minh was leading a major coup effort. Abiding by President Kennedy's 5 October order, Harkins flatly told Don that it was the wrong time for a coup. That must have come as a shock as Don was the brains behind the effort. How far things had gone was revealed that day by "Big" Minh's aide, Colonel Nguyen Khuong, who told Colonel Jones, the U.S.

military attaché in Saigon, that they "can assassinate Diem almost at will."[4] But the Harkins problem did not go away. An unnerved General Don went to Conein to ask if Harkins had stated official American policy, and Conein informed him that Harkins erred. Conein's response was inadequate. The encounter shook the ARVN generals, and Don wanted to hear from Ambassador Lodge that assurances remained in place. The difficulty over how to resolve the competing Harkins-Conein messages soon made its way to Washington, with Lodge advocating that everyone get behind the 9 October cable.[5]

McGeorge Bundy was not pleased by the flap and contacted Lodge and Harkins on 24 October to restate that the president's 5 October order stood: There was to be no active encouragement of a coup. He was equally disturbed that General Don referred to a presidential directive supporting the coup, a reference to the 9 October cable, and requested Lodge to return to Washington to discuss the matter. Bundy had to wonder what had happened to plausible deniability. He told Lodge that there was no basis for him meeting with Don and that he and Harkins had to remove themselves from any coup discussions with the generals. In reaction, Lodge opted to exclude the troublesome Harkins from further coup deliberations within the embassy, while Harkins again met with Don and reiterated that he was having nothing to do with a coup. Harkins then cabled Washington to alert them that a coup would not stop at one but would set off amongst the generals "a continuous effort to upset whoever gains control."[6] His warning was ignored or marginalized by senior pro-coup American officials.

That night, a busy Don then met with Conein, who reiterated that no assurances for a coup could be given before the generals' plans were studied in detail. Reassured that the Americans were not saying "no," Don replied that for security reasons, the plans were not available, and the coup would take place no later than 2 November. It must have evoked the sweet scent of revenge. General Don had been General Hinh's most able lieutenant, and after Hinh's ruin following his failed 1954 mutiny, Don became Diem's foe. That same day, the sidelined Lansdale bleakly described the hopelessness of the situation: "We essentially are pointing a gun at Diem's head and asking him to commit suicide."[7]

Things calmed down for a few days—the Saturday Independence Day ceremonies led by Diem went off without incident—only to resurface with a vengeance on Tuesday. That was when the various American misunderstandings and wrong assumptions about the coup came to light, and deadly reality was at least glimpsed if not fully grasped. At the State Department, Hilsman presented a glowing paper to the Harriman team about a vibrant civilian government replacing Diem following a successful coup under the leadership of "Big" Minh, whom he fatuously described as the "most respected and popular of all military officers."[8] Apart from the coup, little of it was true. It was hope-filled speculations and guesses, as the generals' plans had never arrived to be reviewed. At the Pentagon, McNamara and Taylor discovered that since Harkins had stuck to the president's 5 October order in his talks with General Don, he had been removed from coup deliberations in Saigon, and they concluded that he needed to reestablish close communications with Lodge immediately.[9]

In the meantime, focus shifted to the scheduled White House meeting with the president on Vietnam that aimed to formulate and send additional guidance to Lodge in Saigon. The Harriman team developed talking papers, as did McNamara, Taylor, and McCone. McGeorge Bundy, still unconvinced of the wisdom of backing a coup, presented Kennedy with an advance memorandum that finally echoed Forrestal's earlier misgivings by emphasizing the need to eliminate contradictory interpretations of the president's wishes. Bundy drafted instructions to be cabled to Saigon accordingly.[10]

At 4:00 p.m. 29 October, the White House meeting opened with an update briefing by Colby then directly went into a coup discussion. The Americans' internal divisions and intrigues were on full display. Rusk revealed that he was not fully aware of the Harriman team's coup activities when he wrongly told Kennedy that Lodge was obeying the restrictive 5 October order. Rusk was out of touch, having assumed coup plotting within State had ended weeks earlier. In fact, Lodge had been following the unsigned top secret 9 October cable since it arrived three weeks earlier, and the Harriman team encouraged him. But Rusk was not against the coup; he went on to argue that if the United States backed away, the ARVN generals would lose heart and the war effort suffer.[11]

Attorney General Robert Kennedy, a member of the Vietnam Task Force and the president's brother, came out against the coup. He went to heart of the problem about sending another cable asking for more information. By engaging the generals, "it will appear that we are in favor of a coup," which was not what President Kennedy wanted.[12] General Taylor backed Robert Kennedy and did not feel the war effort would be damaged if the coup was cancelled. McNamara had never wanted the United States involved in overthrowing Diem. (A few days earlier in the White House, he told the president, "I hate being associated with this effort" and went on to complain about Lodge and Conein.)[13] CIA Director McCone also opposed. Speaking of Diem, McCone stated, "Mr. President, if I was manager of a baseball team, and I had one pitcher, I'd keep him in the box whether he was a good pitcher or not."[14] McCone also recommended to the president a hands-off approach regarding the assassination of Diem. The decision was made to rewrite Bundy's draft cable and then reconvene.[15]

At 6:00 p.m. the White House meeting resumed. There would be a joint Lodge-Harkins team to handle the coup issue in Saigon, and Harkins was to be fully briefed on the plotting. The big question was whether or not the generals could win a quick victory over troops loyal to Diem and avoid a civil war or stalemate. The task of answering that was assigned to Lodge. The president closed by directing Lodge to "tell the Generals that they must prove they can pull off a successful coup or, in our opinion, it would be a mistake to proceed. If we miscalculated, we could lose our entire position in Southeast Asia overnight."[16] With that, Bundy arranged for the cable to be sent.[17]

The gravest misconception, one held by almost everyone in Washington, was that they had final authority over launching the coup. As the cable to Lodge stated, the senior leaders in Washington "believe our attitude to coup group can still have decisive effect on its decisions" and that a coup could be stopped.[18] They were mistaken. Washington's repeated demand to the generals that assurances would not be given until the Americans approved their plan had been discounted by Minh, Don, and other generals. While Washington's demand seemed to carry weight, the generals correctly concluded that the Americans could not back out if their coup succeeded. General Harkins had warned Washington about that possibility from the start, stating in the wake of the Harriman team's 24 August cable that once the CIA met with the ARVN generals, "the die is cast."[19] The ARVN generals knew that if they carried out a successful coup, then the all-important economic and military aid would flow—the lack of prior American approval notwithstanding.[20]

It was Lodge who tipped Washington off to that reality the following day, Wednesday, 30 October, when he responded to Bundy's cable by stating he did "not think that we have the power to delay or discourage a coup." He added a painful truth; the only way to stop the coup was to tip off Diem, which would result in the removal—if not deaths—of the ARVN generals, an outcome that likely would devastate the war effort. That response hit Bundy like a slap in the face, and he cabled back, "We do not accept as a basis for U.S. policy that we have no power to delay or discourage a coup," and then rejected Lodge's argument that only betrayal could end the coup.[21]

Bundy directed that Trueheart take over when Lodge departed for Washington before the coup, but that Harkins, a strong coup opponent, would be consulted immediately before and be present when any instructions were given to Conein to pass on to the generals. If Harkins and Trueheart disagreed, then they were to contact Washington for resolution. These steps were not intended to stop the coup but to reestablish Washington's control over events. Bundy made that clear; if a coup led by the generals gets underway, "it is in the interests of the U.S. Government that it succeed."[22]

The second major misconception in Washington was that they had time to affect the situation in Saigon. This again stemmed from the compartmented flow of information, and different actors still following conflicting interpretations of what the White House wanted. That assumption also was destroyed on 30 October. Per the Bundy cable, Harkins finally learned how much had happened in the last few days and was shocked: "When I said last week I was out of the coup business I did not realize I was going to be kept out of touch." He had been removed from access to the "Saigon 20 series" messages.[23] After reading them, Harkins informed Taylor that the execution of General Don's coup plan was "imminent."[24]

Confusing the Americans over the timing of the coup may have been part of Don's plan. Lodge later claimed as much, stating the coup plotters "deluged" Saigon with rumors.[25] After all, reported coup dates seemed to float along unfulfilled. In mid–October, Conein vaguely thought it might occur in the next several weeks. Supposedly it first had been set for Independence Day on 26 October, then 30 or 31 October, or sometime on or before 2 November. Further, the generals promised to provide the plan for review and give advance warning, neither of which had occurred, and there remained the precedent of the stillborn August coup. Minh and Don did have their hands full. At the last minute, General Tran Thien Khiem wavered. He wanted to abort the coup and reconcile with Diem. He was shoved back into line, and the generals succeeded in keeping their activities to themselves. That distracted the White House leadership to the point where they were unaware the clock was at midnight.[26]

That raised concerns over the timing of Lodge's return to Washington. How imminent was the coup? Lodge knew Don had been adamant about the ambassador being available during the coup, and Don saw his looming departure as a problem. It was resolved after Don talked it through with Conein. The crafty Don realized a sudden change in travel plans might alert Diem or the equally crafty Nhu that something was amiss. President Kennedy expressed his own concern over moving Lodge's departure date, as it could "tip off our foreknowledge of the coup."[27] Lodge would leave as scheduled. But that showed the generals were committed to a coup timeline of their choosing—not of Washington's—and that revelation never was fully appreciated by the White House. The ARVN generals were in charge. There no longer was time to alter the course of events, and the Americans no longer could stop the coup even if they wanted.[28]

At 1:45 a.m., 1 November 1963, Washington time (1:45 p.m. in Saigon), the coup began. It was a bloody affair from the start but well planned and executed, which no doubt reduced the number of casualties. Both the barracks for the presidential guard and Special Forces were surrounded in the first 45 minutes. The trapped soldiers put up a fight but surrendered within hours. Diem lost the use of the majority of his troops at the outset. To make up for their loss, Diem tried diligently to get loyal troops to Saigon. He failed. The coup continued to advance as key leaders loyal to Diem also were neutralized.[29]

Several of Diem's loyal officers paid a heavy price. The Chief of Naval Operations, Captain Ho Tan Quyen, was shot out of hand, while Liaison Service director and Special Forces commander, Colonel Tung, and his younger brother, Major Le Quang Trieu, were detained. "Big" Minh called the Presidential Palace while it still was fighting off the coup troops and had Tung, with a gun at his head, speak to Nhu in an attempt to force surrender. It failed. Later that day, Tung and Trieu were summarily executed. Trieu's body was never found. Others, to include the airborne troops' commander, Colonel Cao Van Vien, Marine commander Colonel Le Nguyen Khang, Air Force chief Colonel Huynh Huu Hien, Special Police director Duong Van Hieu, and Ngo Trong Hieu, the minister of civic action and Chieu Hoi program creator, were placed under guard. Civil Guard commander Duong Ngoc Lam switched sides and agreed to help with the capture of Diem and Nhu. The coup leaders effectively cut the head off of the Diem regime.[30]

The focus of the action shifted to the Presidential Palace where the fighting was heavy. It lasted well into the evening, and despite repeated demands to surrender, Diem refused. Four hours into the coup, a CIA officer located near the palace reported "heavy fighting, including armor, small arms and possibly some light artillery."[31] None other than Hanoi's agent, Colonel Thao, was with the tanks attacking the palace. Diem called Lodge for support and was not given any. Just before the coup began, Diem spoke to Lodge as he prepared to leave for Washington. Diem told him he expected a coup but did not know the specifics, and then he relayed a personal message for President Kennedy: "I am a good and frank ally, that I would rather be frank and settle questions now than talk about them after we have lost everything. Tell President Kennedy that I take all his suggestions very seriously and wish to carry them out but it is a question of timing."[32]

Several hours later in the midst of the fighting, Diem spoke to Lodge for the last time. Lodge told him, "I admire your courage and your great contributions to your country. No one can take away from you the credit for all you have done." Diem closed by declaring, "I am trying to re-establish order."[33] Lodge was sincere; later when the narrative painted Diem as an isolated and cold leader, Lodge humanized him. He refuted claims of Diem's heartlessness to counter that, "Diem was an attractive man. He had a nice personality and had a kindly side." He was not a villain. At some point, Diem and Nhu escaped the embattled palace and made it safely to the Cha Tam Catholic church in Cholon not far from the MAAG HQ, but their cause was lost. The next day, Friday 2 November, they agreed to surrender. As soon as the two were in ARVN custody and on General "Big" Minh's orders, they were bound, placed inside a wheeled armored car, each shot in the back of the head, and then stabbed. "Big" Minh's chief bodyguard, Captain Nguyen Van Nhung, oversaw the executions. For his actions, Nhung was made a major. The generals announced the two had committed suicide, and the coup was over.[34]

The Consequences of Diem's Downfall

It is hard to overstate the significance of Diem's assassination. In Hanoi, it gave Le Duan the justification needed to greatly escalate the war. In Saigon, it created nothing of lasting benefit, as it ended with an even sharper decline in effective national governance and left Thich Tri Quang thirsting for more power. In Washington, Diem's murder led to a crisis in confidence and unity over the American mission in South Vietnam.

Hanoi Acts

NLF leader Nguyen Huu Tho considered Diem's murder a "Gift from Heaven," an odd turn of phrase for an atheistic Marxist.[35] Ho Chi Minh was more direct, declaring, "I can scarcely believe that the Americans would be so stupid."[36] If Tho looked upward in gratitude and Ho reflected on the assassination's ramifications, then Le Duan saw opportunity. He smelled blood and went in for the kill as Diem's demise, as he saw it, changed the dynamics of the war; victory was at hand. In 1959 he had to compromise, settling for Resolution 15 that directed a two-track solution splitting the DRV's limited resources between developing the socialist economy of the north and waging a war of reunification in the south. In the intervening years, he had subdued the opposition led by General Giap, and party leaders now took their cue from Duan. After the death of Diem, Hanoi saw no viable civil government in Saigon and that left only one obstacle to reunification: the South Vietnamese military. If it could be broken, then the war was over—either through the intermediate step of neutralism or outright military victory. Now that no one effectively ruled Saigon, half measures no longer were acceptable.[37]

Beginning on 23 November, just a day after President Kennedy's assassination and weeks after Diem's assassination and at Le Duan's urging, the Politburo and Central Committee convened the 3rd Party Congress' 9th Plenum and began work on a new war policy. By December the job was complete and embodied in Resolution 9, passed in January 1964. On the surface, it appeared only moderately more ambitious than Resolution 15, vaguely stressing a greater role for the DRV in the South's revolution, along with the importance of the political struggle, and addressing the North First objective to strengthen the DRV.[38]

That was misleading. Like Resolution 15, Resolution 9 had a secret amendment with the aggressive title "Strive to Struggle, Rush Forward to Win New Victories in the South." In it Duan had what he so long had fought for—reunification to be achieved through a General Offensive and General Uprising (GO-GU)—and he believed it could be fulfilled by the end of 1964. Also of great moment and unknown to the Americans, Le Duan used his platform before the Party Congress to criticize Ho Chi Minh and remove him from the dominant position of power he had held for over three decades. While Ho retained a leadership position, played a key diplomatic role, and remained the face of Vietnam's revolution, the message was clear; no one could stand in the way of Duan's war policy.[39]

As Le Duan envisioned it, the conflict would enter into General Giap's final Phase 3 of revolutionary war. As a unifying compromise, Giap's cautions were addressed in language about "protracted war" and "gradual advance."[40] But the emphasis was on quickly obtaining victories through big unit mobile war. There also was a shift in the emphasis of the political versus military aspects of the revolution. In the Mekong Delta and other parts of Nam Bo, the political struggle still would dominate, with VC attacks focused on destroying strategic hamlets and "seizing the opportunity" operations, while in the mountains of the Central Highlands and in the jungles, the decisive conventional big unit counteroffensive would begin with two objectives unchanged since 1954: cut southern Vietnam in two by attacking from the Central Highlands to the coast and destroy the enemy's strategic reserve forces. As General Giap saw it, "To seize and control the Highlands is to solve the whole problem of South Vietnam."[41]

Military success would allow VWP cadres to lead uprisings of the masses in the cities. The key was Plan X for the Saigon–Gia Dinh Special Zone, a comprehensive proselytizing-propaganda effort that immediately brought to mind successes of Thich Tri Quang's ongoing Buddhist protests. It aimed to incite members of the ARVN, government workers, and the local population to rise up. As Plan X took hold, the Saigon regime would collapse under the combined weight of the GO-GU campaign.[42]

Four further acts revealed Resolution 9 meant a "rush forward" over "protracted war." First, to direct the war effort, one of the PAVN's best, General Thanh, was appointed COSVN secretary and ordered south. Second was mobilizing and putting the PAVN on a wartime footing. In stunning secrecy, reservists were called up, and additional drafts brought the army to full combat readiness. During the 15 days after mobilization began, the PAVN grew from 173,000 to 260,000 soldiers. Third, Resolution 9 directed the PAVN to reach the strength of 300,000 soldiers by the end of 1964. Finally, to sustain the GO-GU, Group 559 with its strategic Ho Chi Minh Trail and Naval Group 125 were directed to increase the 1963 logistical transportation capacity by four-fold in 1964.[43]

There were other important indicators as to Hanoi's intent, as timing was everything to the GO-GU. Victory had to be obtained before full-scale military intervention by the Americans could occur as had happened in Korea. To prevent the special war from becoming a Korea-style limited war, regular PAVN formations would enter into South Vietnam only as a last resort and even then, disguised as Viet Cong. Steps were taken to accelerate the number of PAVN military and leadership groups heading south and significantly increase the flow of weapons, munitions, and other war supplies. For the first time, a major PAVN formation, the 325th Infantry Division, was ordered to prepare to march south.[44]

Winning the reunification war demanded the imposition of iron discipline in all aspects of the war effort. To make that happen, the Two Le's—Le Duan and Le Duc Tho—moved to turn the DRV into a tightly controlled police state. Resolution 9 addressed that in a key section, "Intensifying the Struggle against Counterrevolutionary Forces following the coup against Diem and Nhu," that gave the Two Le's nearly unlimited policing powers. The crackdown was not limited to the north; two of the targeted threats to victory were those in the south who adhered to Mao's guerrilla tactics over the big unit war strategy and disobedient southern party cadres. If there had been any lingering doubts before, after Diem's death it was clear that the direction of the Vietnam War would be determined in Hanoi and nowhere else.[45]

The Saigon Government Plunges into Disarray

After Diem's assassination, the new government, termed the Second Republic, was thrown into confusion. There was no constitutional succession with Vice President Tho assuming the presidency to be followed by his appointment of a broad-based coalition of able officials. Instead, there was the Revolutionary Military Council filled with ambitious generals eager to gain as much power and influence as possible. As a sop to the Americans, they later made Tho a figurehead prime minister heading a nearly powerless cabinet. After meeting the council in December 1963, a demoralized Tho realized the generals were incapable of running a functioning government. Other Diem power centers were eliminated. The Republican Youth, National Revolutionary, and Women's Solidarity Movements were dissolved and the Can Lao Party banned. The opposition made gains as the Dai Viet staged a comeback. But as before, it only was interested in one-party rule and focused on gaining more followers in the military and in a change in policy, within an increasingly fearful and endangered Catholic minority. At the same time, the Hoa Hao and Cao Dai religious factions reformed their private militias and reestablished semi-autonomous states. Civilian rule in any substantive sense ceased.[46]

Similarly, the pre-coup American admonitions to avoid purges proved meaningless. A few months after the coup, McNamara informed President Johnson that government authority from Saigon to the hamlets disappeared following Diem's assassination, noting, "The faith of the peasants has been shaken by the disruptions in experienced leadership and the loss of physical security."[47] The initial reports that only a handful of provincial chiefs had been replaced turned into a mass purge of 31 of 41 chiefs (nine provinces had three province chiefs in three months; one province had four) and continued into mid–1964. The purges soon extended into the ranks of the district chiefs as well, a destabilizing outcome that even disturbed Hilsman. When Taylor realized the extent of the purges, he concluded the Saigon government would have "a short life expectancy."[48] The dreamy pre–November predictions that there would be a minimal disruption and even a marked improvement in civil governance went up in smoke. What the South Vietnamese and Americans got instead was a mess eerily similar to the teetering state of early 1954.[49]

Militarily, things deteriorated for Saigon. While the revolving chairs in provincial-district leadership badly disrupted counterinsurgency efforts, Hanoi was unified and turned its full attention toward reunification. The Viet Cong went on the attack as the Strategic Hamlet Program fell apart and large-scale ARVN sweep operations in the Mekong Delta ended entirely in the weeks after the coup. To appreciate the magnitude of events, in I CTZ's four northernmost provinces, there had been a total of six VC incidents in June. After Diem's murder in November, there were 87. One Viet Cong soldier reflected on the period following Diem's assassination: "At no other time were members of the Front so enthusiastic."[50] As the VC advanced, Saigon's intelligence services also stumbled. Not only was SEPES dissolved, but MACV HQ noted that the National Police counterintelligence operations targeting the VC "disintegrated," and JGS J-2 fared only a little better. All the predictions by the Harriman team that Diem's removal meant putting the war back onto the right tack proved to be empty words. Yet there were signs of hope. Despite the turmoil, the ARVN continued to battle as the full weight of Hanoi's General Offensive pummeled it without respite. Somehow South Vietnam's military held on.[51]

Diem was finally recognized for the leader he had been. "Big" Minh had a cynical if telling take on why he ordered the assassinations: "We had no alternative. Diem could not be allowed to live because he was too much respected among simple, gullible people in the countryside."[52] A defecting VC guerrilla leader and PRP member in I CTZ had a similar take; he concluded that Diem was a "true nationalist" and conceded that many rural people in Quang Nam province had respected him.[53] Tran Van Huong, the former Saigon mayor who became another powerless prime minister a year after Diem's death, later admitted, "The top generals who decided to murder Diem and his brother were scared to death. The generals knew very well that having no talent, no moral virtues, no political support whatsoever, they could not prevent a spectacular comeback of the president and Mr. Nhu if they were alive."[54]

Too late the error was recognized. PAVN Military Staff officer Colonel Bui Tin wrote after the war, "One thing is certain, the murder of Diem and Nhu brought about a period of instability that lasted until the day of the final collapse of South Vietnam."[55] General Khanh, reflecting on the whole affair in 1994, summed up his thoughts this way: "Most of the Buddhist he knew were in full support of the coup— and even of the subsequent killing of the man—changed their minds in the intervening decades and came to regard his murder as a mistake of unparalleled proportions for South Vietnam."[56]

The Fall of Thich Tri Quang and the Buddhist Movement

Thich Tri Quang's decline and that of his movement began with the death of Diem. While destroying the Diem regime was spectacular, every step he took afterwards revealed more and more a confused and destructive vision for South Vietnam. The road became much harder as well. Going forward, his unchecked freedom to manipulate if not manufacture facts to attack his enemies came under scrutiny. His deep anti–Catholic bias also came to be understood. Finally, his intractable battling with successor governments alienated both friends and foes. In combination, these behaviors divided, exhausted, and finally ended his movement and witnessed his departure from the political stage.

The chain of events leading up to the assassination of Diem hinged on the false narrative communicated by Quang that the Diem regime persecuted Buddhists because of their religion. There was one last chapter to that drama. Nearly two months before the coup, on 4 September, a number of United Nations member-states led by Ceylon (Sri Lanka) and Cambodia lodged a complaint, claiming Diem's government led a "systematic campaign to repress" the religious rights of Buddhists in South Vietnam.[57] To address the charges, a discussion of the complaint was placed on the General Assembly agenda. South Vietnamese Ambassador to the United States Buu Hoi let it be known on 2 October that Saigon favored a UN investigation, as "such a visit would have an ameliorating effect on the concerns about the Buddhist crisis at the United Nations."[58]

On 4 October, at the request of the South Vietnamese government, the United Nations agreed to send a seven-member fact-finding mission to study the relations between Diem and the Buddhists. The mission arrived in Saigon on 24 October, and during its investigation, spoke to President Diem, Nhu, and six other government officials, as well as 51 witnesses that included monks, nuns, students, and prisoners. The UN mission also accepted and reviewed over one hundred written statements. Ambassador Lodge in Saigon informed Washington that the Diem government "appears to be off to a good start with the U.N. mission. So far they have allowed them to meet everyone, including imprisoned Buddhists."[59] In the wake of Diem's assassination, the mission abruptly ended its investigation and departed Saigon on 3 November.[60]

Too late to serve a meaningful purpose, the mission's report was completed on 7 December 1963, and with crisis deemed over, the UN never published the findings. It was revealed, however, that the conclusions were not nearly as unfavorable to the Diem regime as anticipated. The member from Costa Rica concluded that the 4 September complaints heard in the UN General Assembly were not sustained in fact, and the Diem-Buddhist dispute was political—not religious—in nature. The member went on to add that the evidence did not support claims of religious discrimination or persecution or encroachment of Buddhist religious freedoms in South Vietnam. Diem had been exonerated in death. Madame Nhu later described the UN investigation into the charges of religious persecution as having "pricked the Buddhist balloon flat."[61]

In another meaningless post-mortem revelation, Marguerite Higgins reported that both the State Department and CIA found "no evidence of any corruption" by the Ngo family. If further proof was needed, Madame Nhu and her children struggled financially from November 1963 onwards.[62] Durbrow noted the same. When in France a few years later, he discovered that Madame Nhu with her two children and her brother-in-law Ngo Dinh Luyen's family with eleven children lived crammed into one Paris apartment. Malicious rumors of stolen secret wealth again had won the day in Saigon and Washington.[63]

In the aftermath of the November coup, Thich Tri Quang was free to leave the sanctuary of the American embassy, and he immediately resumed his zealotry with vigor. More disturbingly, it seemed as if Diem's death liberated Quang from rational restraint, and it was during this period that Quang revealed the extent of his anti–Catholicism and hatred for Diem and his followers. There had been earlier signs as in September 1963 when he told the Americans he had been planning to go all out against the Diem regime, and the flag ban provided him the pretext to start his crusade, his "social revolution." Quang saw the Buddhist crisis as a binary religious battle between Buddhism and Catholicism.[64]

It was clear that his hatred for Diem did not stem solely from a conclusion that Diem was bad but that Diem was unfit because all Vietnamese Catholics were suspect, or in his words, "even 'good Catholics' have two strikes against them."[65] As he imagined it, the oppression of Buddhists could not end simply by the removal of Diem. Thich Tri Quang wanted a government free of all pro–Diem officials, Catholics, and members of the "evil" Can Lao Party.[66] That created a new political headache for the Americans. After the November coup, there were thousands of badly needed government workers and military officers who had served Diem loyally or were Catholic or both, and Quang wanted them purged with further repressive steps to follow. To be expected, there was an upsurge in Buddhist-Catholic violence in the major cities. By September 1964, fellow radical Buddhists in Thich Tri Quang's home base of Hue organized what amounted to an anti–Catholic pogrom as the city teetered on the brink of religious war.[67]

Quang's extremism disturbed many Buddhists, who wanted no part of a religious war. Thich Tam Chau took the opposite approach by condemning violence while reaching out to Catholics. When the Unified Buddhist Church was formed in January 1964, Thich Quang Do and moderate Thich Huyen Quang became its leaders. Lines were drawn as Quang lost appeal but gained more intense support from his followers. His attempt at social revolution to create a nationalist Buddhist state extended beyond what that term implied; it was a formula for societal anarchy. French journalist Jean Lacouture met with Quang in 1964 and compared his movement, in a chillingly prescient analogy decades before its time, to the Muslim Brotherhood [Frères musselmans] who in the name of "religious compassion—unleashed terror."[68] The cracks apparent during 1963 grew deeper and wider in the years that followed as the Buddhist movement fragmented. Within the Unified Church, the venerable Thich Tinh Khiet regained his footing as an elder leader, Thich Tam Chau became Quang's equal amongst the bonzes in Saigon, and the moderate Thich Thien Minh spoke for the majority of Buddhists in Nam Bo.[69]

Unfazed and filled with a sense of empowerment after Diem's murder, Quang assumed the role of kingmaker, or more accurately, a political boss. Only weeks into "Big" Minh's rule, Quang joined with the neo-Hinh army faction and came out against Minh. Minh was gone by the end of January 1964. His successor, General Khanh, fared no better with Quang, but Quang's opposition only led to a return of "Big" Minh, leaving the monk frustrated anew. As these machinations showed, Thich Tri Quang seemed an unguided missile at times, and the Americans finally lost patience. In August when he presented another list of demands, Ambassador Maxwell Taylor told Khanh (who again was in power) "not to give in to pressure from a minority group."[70] The Americans observed that Quang gave little or no systematic thought to the problems of leadership, and he neither fully understood the forces he set in motion nor accepted that they could change things for the worse. The zealous monk seemed unable to master his emotions as the pattern was repeated over and over again throughout 1964 and 1965 and into 1966. Each time, Quang's movement emerged more drained and divided.[71]

Reports from Saigon captured the shifting American opinion of Quang. In October 1963, a few days before the Diem coup, Lodge cabled the White House recommending Thich Tri Quang for a high position in the new government. By May 1964, Lodge still supported Quang but saw him as a potential troublemaker and was concerned that he appeared to be more anti–Catholic than anticommunist. The relationship continued to deteriorate. During August, when Quang paralyzed the Khanh regime to the point of collapse, Taylor, who replaced Lodge on 7 July, called him a demagogue. By April 1965, the same State Department that had sided with Quang against Diem in the summer of 1963 now focused on destroying him as a political force.[72]

The end came in 1966 when once again a Roman Catholic, General Nguyen Van Thieu, came to rule South Vietnam. As far as Tri Quang was concerned, that was as unacceptable in 1966 as it had been in 1963, and Thieu had to go. Once again Quang used a pretext to try to force an overthrow of the Saigon government: Thieu's removal of the pro–Quang I CTZ commander General Nguyen Chanh Thi (who led the 1960 paratroop coup). When Thi refused to go, Buddhist protests supporting the general erupted in Saigon and Hue, but despite a declaration that they would fight "to the last drop of blood, to the last breath," the old unity and energy were missing.[73] Unlike 1963, Saigon and Washington now were under no illusions as to the monk's aims and acted in unison. The Americans advocated using force to maintain order, and this time they called for pagoda raids if used as sanctuaries by Quang's lieutenants. Further, the radical bonzes would not be given refuge in the embassy, and Washington would publicly support the arrest and trial of Buddhist activists who broke the law, to include Thich Tri Quang. Things had come full circle—Washington adopted Diem's 1963 policies.[74]

Quang's Saigon movement capitulated first, being split into factions led by various radical monks, while moderate Buddhists quit his movement and turned to Thich Tam Chau. The radicals ignored Chau's demands for nonviolence and instead boycotted the 14 April opening of the new Congress that had been formed to replace the disbanded National Assembly. They then called for a mass demonstration, but the entire project fizzled. The era of Buddhist militancy in Saigon was over.[75]

That left Thich Tri Quang and his followers in Hue. With General Thi's support, Quang virtually ruled the city, and in an attempt to revitalize the movement, he went on a hunger strike in early June. As his strike entered its second week, Saigon acted. On 10 June, National Police commander Colonel Nguyen Ngoc Loan with 400 Field Force Police (an anti-riot National Police branch formed in 1965) arrived and assumed command of the Hue police. The police chief who had done little to rein in Quang was fired and a number of officers relieved of duty. Five days later the first of two ARVN paratroop and two Vietnamese Marine battalions arrived. They moved to retake the city and had complete control of Hue by 19 June 1966. Quang's movement died in the same city where it began just over three years earlier on 8 May 1963. For having played a lead role in another failed uprising, General Thi once again fled South Vietnam, this time for a life of exile in the United States. Lodge declared on 22 June that Thich Tri Quang's "rabble rousing activities ... have been effectively stopped."[76]

The actions of 1966 cast a long shadow on what had come before. In 1963, at the most critical moment of America's involvement in Vietnam to that point, Washington put its trust in the words and actions of the charismatic and deeply flawed Thich Tri Quang. It was one of the United States' greatest foreign policy failures of the Cold War era and ended badly both for the United States and the young dynamic monk. After 1966, Thich Tri Quang would remain in Hue under house arrest until the fall of the Republic of Vietnam in 1975. After the establishment of the Socialist Republic of Vietnam, Quang was subjected to severe reeducation regimens before returning to house arrest, this time for life. His beloved Buddhist movement was eradicated and the number of practicing Buddhists in Vietnam fell into sharp decline.

The American Failure

The Vietnam War was the first time Washington had to develop a constructive relationship with an ally fighting a very difficult conflict without first committing large American air, naval, and ground forces. In the war's early years, the United States had limited itself to a vital supporting and advisory role in South Vietnam, and the Americans wrestled with it; they never found the necessary balance between advice and direction. By 1963, the Kennedy administration was divided over how to proceed. The Departments of State and Defense held strongly divergent positions. While Harriman, Ball, and Hilsman saw Diem's continued rule as the chief problem facing the RVN, McNamara and Taylor were accepting of Diem and saw the Viet Cong as the most dangerous threat. That imbalance led to decisions that created a path that ended in the overthrow of an allied government and the assassination of its elected head of state, the consequences of which tossed that nation into political turmoil and onto the road to defeat.[77]

The repercussions were lasting. When Thieu became South Vietnam's leader in 1965, he never stopped looking over his shoulder. He was convinced that if he stood up to the Americans, then they would kill him. The effects in Asia were more far reaching. Pakistan's President Ayub Khan drove home the point: "I cannot say— perhaps you should never have supported Diem. But you did support him for a long time, and everyone in Asia knew it ... and then suddenly you didn't support him anymore—and Diem was dead." Khan concluded, "Diem's murder meant three things to many Asian leaders: that it is dangerous to be a friend of the United States; that it pays to be neutral; and sometimes it helps to be an enemy! Trust is like a thin thread. When it is broken it is very hard to put together again."[78] A worse outcome was hard to contemplate.[79]

Compounding the catastrophe, President Kennedy neither ordered nor approved the 1 November coup—not through public statement or private discussions or even backchannel CIA communications. But the president was not without blame. While he never sought a coup to overthrow and assassinate Diem, he knew both were being planned and never forcefully tried to stop either. That stemmed from the wrongheaded belief that the White House had operational control over the coup and could prevent the assassination. President Kennedy made the final judgment on 4 November 1963: "We must bear a good deal of responsibility for it beginning with our [24 August] cable ... in which we suggested the coup ... that wire was badly drafted, it should never have been sent on a Saturday. I should not have given my consent."[80]

The real blame lay at the feet of Averell Harriman and Roger Hilsman, along with Henry Cabot Lodge and William Trueheart in Saigon, while George Ball and NSC staffer Michael Forrestal earned less-than honorable mentions. Regardless of devotion—all were totally committed to President Kennedy—the Harriman team played the driving role in Diem's murder, and that arguably brought the State Department to the lowest point in its history. For that, Secretary of State Dean Rusk also shared the blame for letting them get out of control. McNamara later wrote that during the coup period, Rusk "utterly failed to manage the State Department and supervise Lodge," a sentiment shared by Ambassador Nolting.[81] Nolting recalled that Rusk never took an interest in Vietnam in 1963 and when pressed, Rusk dismissed him with the comment, "Averell's handling this."[82]

And Harriman aimed to bring down Diem. It was unprecedented. Washington never forced reforms on Sigmund Rhee during the Korean War, but first the Eisenhower and then the Kennedy administration did so with Diem. By the early 1960s, Thompson advised Diem to create an emergency government, what he termed the Super State War Executive Committee, as had been implemented successfully in Malaya, one that combined extraordinary policing authority with broad powers under extended martial law. Thompson argued for a strong government focused on winning the war—everything else could wait. Washington pushed the opposite: no martial law, no broad executive powers, dismantling the Can Lao Party, allowing for opposition parties, and rapid progress toward democratic reforms. In 1969, former–Vice President Tho reflected on the hopeless situation Diem faced with the "crushing and contradictory demands of the Americans that he win the war and at the same time turn South Vietnam into an American-style democracy."[83]

It all ended terribly. The Harriman team ran the American policy on Vietnam almost in its entirety and mucked it up. Even dismissing the failure to firmly identify a viable successor to Diem as excessive overconfidence, nothing demonstrated their narrow vision better than the fact that none of them ever held a single serious meeting to discuss what would be the DRV's reaction to Diem's removal. They never coldly and objectively assessed the consequences their actions would have on the war being waged by Hanoi. It was as if they faced no real opponent, and that was recklessness writ large. President Kennedy granted extraordinary special trust and confidence to his key subordinates, and in the case of the Harriman team, they failed him. The trajectory of the war was altered for the worse. Senate Majority Leader Mike Mansfield later admitted, "I lost all hope after Diem was assassinated," and later he went on to help lead the anti–Vietnam War movement in Congress.[84]

When it came to winning the war, Washington and Saigon now had two strikes against them—the failure to neutralize Laos and the murder of Diem—but Mansfield had become too pessimistic. The war had turned for the worse but it was not lost. The leaders in Hanoi certainly knew that and rededicated themselves to victory but they also knew that the ARVN was still fighting hard and the Americans had applied only a small fraction of their might against them. As the year 1964 got underway, what the future would hold was anyone's guess.

Chapter Notes

Preface

1. There is not even a consensus on either the war's name or duration. This book and most Americans call it the Vietnam War. Some argue it should be called the American War or Indochina War or that there were two Indochina wars. Hanoi prefers two wars, both called wars of resistance, one against the French and the second against the Americans. Even the years are in dispute: Is it 1965–1975 or 1961–1975 or 1946–1975 or 1941–1989 or some other span of time?

Chapter 1

1. Communist Party of Vietnam, *Communist Party Documents* (Hanoi: National Publishing House, 2002), 20, 82.

2. King C. Chen, "Hanoi's Three Decisions and the Escalation of the Vietnam War," *Political Science Quarterly*, 90, no. 2 (Summer, 1975), 246.

3. Bui Tin, *From Enemy to Friend: A North Vietnamese Perspective on the War* (Annapolis: Naval Institute Press, 2002), 46; Ang Cheng Guan, *Vietnamese Communist's Relations with China and the Second Indochina Conflict, 1956–1962* (Jefferson NC: McFarland, 2012), 98.

4. National Security Council Memorandum (NSCM) "Communist Problems in South Vietnam During the 1954–1959 'Cease-fire,'" 28 May 1971. 1; Pierre Asselin, *Hanoi's Road to the Vietnam War, 1954–1965* (Berkeley: University of California Press, 2013), 49; Chen, "Hanoi's Three Decisions," 244; Merle L. Prebbenow, *Victory in Vietnam: The Official History of the People's Army of Vietnam, 1954–1975* (Lawrence KS: University Press of Kansas, 2002), 15.

5. Lien-Hang T. Nguyen, *Hanoi's War: An International History of the War for Peace in Vietnam* (Chapel Hill: University of North Carolina Press, 2012), 30; David W.P. Elliott, *The Vietnamese War: Revolution and Social Change in the Mekong Delta, 1930–1975*, concise edition (New York: M.E. Sharpe, 2007), 85; Prebbenow, *Victory in Vietnam*, 15.

6. Michael H. Hunt, *A Vietnam War Reader: A Documentary History from American and Vietnamese Perspectives* (Chapel Hill, NC: University of North Carolina Press, 2010), 39; Asselin, *Hanoi's Road to the Vietnam War*, 53–4, 58; Robert K. Bringham, *Guerrilla Diplomacy: The NLF's Foreign Relations and the Vietnam War* (Ithaca NY: Cornel University Press, 1999), 10.

7. A note on Vietnamese names: As in most of East Asia, the surname comes first but it is traditional to call people by their given name which comes last; thus Le Duan would be referred to as First Secretary Duan. The exception is Ho Chi Minh who was called Ho.

8. Lien-Hang T. Nguyen, *Hanoi's War*, 52; Guan, *Vietnamese Communist's Relations with China*, 98; Asselin, *Hanoi's Road*, 51, 53–4; Bui Tin, *From Enemy to Friend*, 44. Central committee plenum sessions were numbered sequentially after the convening of a VWP Congress. The 2nd Congress was held in February 1951 and the 3rd Congress met in September 1960.

9. Lien-Hang T. Nguyen, *Hanoi's War*, 52.

10. Lien-Hang T. Nguyen, *Hanoi's War*, 24.

11. Bui Tin, *Following Ho Chi Minh: Memoirs of a North Vietnamese Colonel* (Honolulu: University of Hawaii Press, 1995), 41; Lien-Hang T. Nguyen, *Hanoi's War*, 60; Asselin, *Hanoi's Road*, 48; Max Hastings, *Vietnam: An Epic Tragedy, 1945–1975* (New York: Harper Collins, 2018), 119.

12. Asselin, *Hanoi's Road*, 40; William J. Duiker, *Ho Chi Minh: A Life* (New York: Hyperion, 2000), 499; Pierre Asselin, "Le Duan, the American War, and the Creation of an Independent Vietnamese State." *Journal of American-East Asian Relations*, 10, no. 1/2 (Spring–Summer 2001), 12. Truong Chinh had been "general secretary" and when Le Duan took the post, it was retitled "first secretary."

13. Bui Tin, *Following Ho Chi Minh*, 32; Hastings, *Vietnam: An Epic Tragedy*, 118; Lien-Hang T. Nguyen, *Hanoi's War*, 17, 24, 34; Bringham, *Guerrilla Diplomacy*, 8; Guan, *Vietnamese Communist's Relations with China*, 48.

14. Lien-Hang T. Nguyen, *Hanoi's War*, 35; Bui Tin, *From Enemy to Friend*, 69; Foreign Relations of the United States (FRUS), Vietnam, 1964–1968, I, document 392. The NRC also was known as the Central Reunification Department and Unification Commissariat.

15. Asselin, *Hanoi's Road*, 64, 115, 149.

16. Hunt, *A Vietnam War Reader*, 39; Duiker, *Ho Chi Minh: A Life*, 296; Foreign Broadcast Information Service (FBIS), "Translation of 'The Anti-U.S. Resistance War for National Salvation, 1954–1975: Military Events'" (Arlington, VA: Joint Publication Research Service, 1982), 28–30; Pribbenow, *Victory in Vietnam*, 50; Guan, *Vietnamese Communist's Relations with China*, 98.

17. FBIS, "The Anti-U.S. Resistance War," 30; Tuong Vu. *Vietnam's Communist Revolution: The Powers and Limits of Ideology.* (New York: Cambridge University Press, 2016), 20, 68, 134, 145; Asselin, *Hanoi's Road*, 54; Lien-Hang T. Nguyen, *Hanoi's War*, 33; Duiker, *Ho Chi Minh: A Life*, 493; Bui Tin, *From Enemy to Friend*, 11; Hastings, *Vietnam*, 119; Guan, *Vietnamese Communist's Relations with China*, 47, 97; Asselin, "Le Duan, the American War, and the Creation of an Independent Vietnamese State," 7.

18. Andrea Matles Savada and Donald Whitaker. *Laos: A Country Study* (Washington, DC: Federal Research Division, Library of Congress, 1994), 32; Guan, *Vietnamese Communists' Relations with China*, 195.

19. Gareth Porter, *Perils of Dominance: Imbalance of Power and the Road to War in Vietnam* (Berkeley: University of California Press, 2006), 113–4.

20. Hoang Ngoc Lung, *Strategy and Tactics* (Washington: U.S. Army Center of Military History, 1983), 3–4; FBIS, "Anti-U.S. Resistance War," 30; Guan, *Vietnamese Communist's Relations with China*, 101; Vo Nguyen Giap, *People's War, People's Army* (Hanoi, Foreign Language Publishing House, 1961), 12; Oscar Salemink, "The Regional Centrality of Vietnam's Central Highlands," *Oxford Research Encyclopedia, Asian History*, 2018 (asianhistory.oxforde.com), 12.

21. Asselin, *Hanoi's Road*, 53.

22. Douglas Pike, *The PAVN: People's Army of Vietnam* (Novato, CA: Presidio Press, 1984), 43.

23. Hoang Ngoc Lung, *Strategy and Tactics*, 3–4; FBIS, "Anti-U.S. Resistance War," 30. "My" is the sound for the Chinese character meaning rice and in East Asia refers to America—the land of plentiful food.

24. FBIS, "Anti-U.S. Resistance War," 28–30; Pierre Asselin, *Vietnam's American War: A History* (New York: Cambridge University Press, 2018), 98.

25. George W. Allen, *None So Blind: A Personal Account of the Intelligence Failure in Vietnam* (Chicago: Ivan R. Dee, 2001), 23.

26. Sophia Quinn-Judge, *Ho Chi Minh: The Missing Years, 1919–1941* (Berkeley, University of California Press, 2001), 11–2, 36; Duiker, *Ho Chi Minh, A Life*, 92–3.

27. Duiker, *Ho Chi Minh, A Life*, 105–6; Quinn-Judge, *Ho Chi Minh*, 2–6, 9.

28. Ellen J. Hammer, *The Struggle for Indochina, 1950–1955* (Stanford: Stanford University Press, 1987), 81; Quinn-Judge, *Ho Chi Minh*, 126–7, 151–2, 154; Duiker, *Ho Chi Minh, A Life*, 166–67; Oliver Tappe, "Thailand und Laos—eine historiche Hassliebe [Thailand and Laos—A Historical Love-Hatred]" in Orapim Bernart and Holger Warnk, eds. *Thailand—Facetten einer südostasiatischen Kultur [Thailand—Facets of a Southeast Asian Culture]* (Munich: East Asia Publishing Company, 2013), 10.

29. Edward Miller, *Misalliance: Ngo Dinh Diem, the United States and the Fate of South Vietnam* (Boston: Harvard University Press, 2013), 189–190; Quinn-Judge, *Ho Chi Minh*, 2–6, 157–58, 160, 195, 198; Duiker, *Ho Chi Minh, A Life*, 179, 191; Vu. *Vietnam's Communist Revolution*, 67.

30. Duiker, *Ho Chi Minh, A Life*, 227; Quinn-Judge, *Ho Chi Minh*, 206, 213–4, 216, 224, 227.

31. Porter, *Perils of Dominance*, 33; Robert Conquest, *The Great Terror: A Reassessment* (New York: Oxford University Press, 1991), 440.

32. Duiker, *Ho Chi Minh, A Life*, 231, 235–6; Pike, *PAVN*, 22; Quinn-Judge, *Ho Chi Minh*, 229, 238.

33. Duiker, *Ho Chi Minh, A Life*, 240; Quinn-Judge, *Ho Chi Minh*, 239; Vu. *Vietnam's Communist Revolution*, 91–2. Two years later, in May 1943, Stalin dissolved the Comintern.

34. Duiker, *Ho Chi Minh, A Life*, 240–1; Cecil B. Currey, *Victory at Any Price: The Genius of Viet Nam's General Vo Nguyen Giap* (Washington: Potomac Books, 2005), 26, 27, 34 37, 51. Ming Thai was also referred to as Quang Thai.

35. Duiker, *Ho Chi Minh, A Life*, 244–5; Currey, *Victory at Any Cost*, 37, 43–4, 53.

36. Vu. *Vietnam's Communist Revolution*, 104.

37. Duiker, *Ho Chi Minh, A Life*, 492; Bringham, *Guerrilla Diplomacy*, 8; Quinn-Judge, *Ho Chi Minh*, 245; Harvey Neese and John O'Donnell, ed., *Prelude to Tragedy: Vietnam 1960–1965* (Annapolis: Naval Institute Press, 2001), 181; Asselin, "Le Duan, the American War, and the Creation of an Independent Vietnamese State," 2–3; Asselin, *Vietnam's American War*, 89.

38. Quinn-Judge, *Ho Chi Minh*, 245; Lien-Hang T. Nguyen, *Hanoi's War*, 24, 35.

39. FRUS, 1952–1954, Geneva Convention, XVI, documents 23, 102, 233, 241; Mark Moyar, *Triumph Forsaken: The Vietnam War, 1954–1965* (New York: Cambridge University Press, 2006), 58.

40. Adam B. Ulam, *Expansion and Coexistence: Soviet Foreign Policy, 1917–1973* (New York: Praeger, 1977), 385–6, 393.

41. Boris Bazhanov, *Vospominaniia Byvshego Sekretaria Stalina [Memoirs of the Former Secretary of Stalin]* (Moscow: III Tysiacheletie, 2002). See: (http://lib.ru/MEMUARY/BAZHANOW/stalin.txt); "Poland: Free Election," *Time*, 13 January 1947.

42. Ulam, *Expansion and Coexistence*, 421–2; Allen Millett, *The War for Korea, 1945–1950: A House Burning*, vol. 1 (Lawrence KS: University Press of Kansas, 2005), 13, 150–1; Department of State *Bulletin*, 12 April 1954, 539–2; James Cartnal, "Dispelling a Myth: The Soviet Note of March 1952," *The History Journal Ex Poste Facto*, 8 (1999) (https://history.sfsu.edu/sites/default/files/EPF/1999_James%20Cartnal-ilovepdf-

compressed.pdf), 77–8; FRUS, 1952–1954, Germany and Austria, VII, document 67.

43. FRUS, 1952–1954, Geneva Convention, XVI, document 420.

44. FRUS, 1952–1954, Geneva Convention, XVI, documents 283, 420.

45. Pierre Asselin, "The Democratic Republic of Vietnam and the 1954 Geneva Conference: A revisionist critique" *Cold War History,* 11, no. 2 (May 2011), 165.

46. Duiker, *Ho Chi Minh,* 456; FRUS, 1952–1954, Geneva Convention, XVI, document 487.

47. FRUS, 1952–1954, Geneva Convention, XVI, documents 473, 487, 667; Porter, *Perils of Dominance,* 37–8; Asselin, "Democratic Republic of Vietnam and the 1954 Geneva Conference," 167; Arthur J. Dommen, *Conflict in Laos: The Politics of Neutralism* (New York: Frederick A. Praeger, 1964), 52.

48. Vietnam Central Information Service, *Manifesto and Platform of the Vietnam Lao Dong Party,* April 1952.

49. FRUS, 1952–1954, Geneva Convention, XVI, document 473, 485, 667; Asselin, "The Democratic Republic of Vietnam and the 1954 Geneva Conference," 169.

50. Asselin, *Hanoi's Road,* 13; Geneva Convention, XVI, documents 607, 982, 1000.

51. Duiker, *Ho Chi Minh,* 457; Porter, *Perils of Dominance,* 35; FRUS, 1952–1954, Geneva Convention, XVI, documents 352, 491, 687; Moyar, *Triumph Forsaken,* 30.

52. FRUS, 1952–1954, Geneva Convention, XVI, documents 761, 765, 956.

53. Asselin, "Democratic Republic of Vietnam and the 1954 Geneva Conference, 173; FRUS, 1952–1954, Geneva Convention, XVI, documents 758, 947, 1012.

54. FRUS, 1952–1954, Geneva Convention, XVI, documents 487, 982.

55. FRUS, 1952–1954, Geneva Convention, XVI, documents 506, 1000.

56. FRUS, 1952–1954, Geneva Convention, XVI, documents 1000, 1038. For the agreements and declaration text see: http://avalon.law.yale.edu/20th_century/inch005.asp.

57. FRUS, 1952–1954, Geneva Convention, XVI, document 946.

58. FRUS, 1952–1954, Geneva Convention, XVI, documents 318, 412, 667, 765, 902, 969, 972.

59. FRUS, 1952–1954, Geneva Convention, XVI, documents 777, 1009, 1039.

60. David L. Anderson, *Trapped by Success: The Eisenhower Administration and Vietnam, 1953–61* (New York: Columbia University Press, 1993), 57; FRUS, 1952–1954, Geneva Convention, XVI, documents 628, 649, 687, 688, 736, 737.

61. Bernard B. Fall, *The Two Viet-Nams: A Political and Military Analysis* (New York: Praeger, 1967), 233.

62. Duiker, *Ho Chi Minh,* 459, 461; Leslie H. Gelb and Richard K. Betts. *The Irony of Vietnam: The System Worked* (Washington: Brookings Institute Press, 1979), 62; Fall, *Two Viet-Nams,* 232.

Chapter 2

1. Thomas L. Ahern, Jr. *Vietnam Declassified: The CIA and Counterinsurgency* (Lexington KY: The University Press of Kentucky, 2010), 7; Rufus Phillips, *Why Vietnam Matters: An Eye Witness Account of Lessons Not Learned* (Annapolis: Naval Institute Press, 2008), 15.

2. Ahern, *Vietnam Declassified,* 7.

3. Cao Van Vien, *Leadership* (Washington: Department of the Army, 1978), 20, 21; Moyar, *Triumph Forsaken,* 33; Anderson, *Trapped by Success,* 45; FRUS, Indochina, 1952–1954, XIII, Part 2, document 834; Phillips, *Why Vietnam Matters,* 5.

4. Elliott, *Vietnamese War,* 73.

5. FRUS, Indochina, 1952–1954, XIII Part 2, documents 873, 1082; Anderson, *Trapped by Success,* 45; Miller, *Misalliance,* 90; Bernard B. Fall, "The Political-Religious Sects of Viet-Nam," 26, no. 3, *Pacific Affairs* (September 1955), 24; Elliott, *Vietnamese War,* 73.

6. Ha Mai Viet, *Steel and Blood: South Vietnamese Armor and the War for Southeast Asia* (Annapolis MD: Naval Institute Press, 2008), 274; Miller, *Misalliance,* 90.

7. A.M. Savani, *Visage et Images du Sud Viet-Nam* (Saigon: Imprimerie Francaise d'Outre-Mer, 1955), 77–8; Lam Quang Thi, *The Twenty-five Year Century: A South Vietnamese General Remembers the Indochina War to the Fall of Saigon* (Denton TX: University of North Texas Press, 2001), 68; Elliott, *Vietnamese War,* 73; Edward Geary Lansdale, *Midst of Wars: An American's Mission to Southeast Asia,* (New York: Fordham University Press, 1991), 187, 188; FRUS, Vietnam, 1955–1957, II, documents 19, 32n2, 105n2, 242; Hammer, *Struggle for Indochina,* 211. At its peak, the Cao Dai had 30,000 soldiers under arms. Trinh Minh The is also cited as Trinh Minh Tay.

8. Savani, *Visage et Images,* 88, 90 and also see photo caption on page facing 85; Elliott, *Vietnamese War,* 73–4; Seth Jacobs, *Cold War Mandarin: Ngo Dinh Diem and the Origin of America's War in Vietnam, 1950–1963* (Lanham MD: Rowman and Littlefield, 2006), 61; Miller, *Misalliance,* 91, 111; Hammer, *Struggle for Indochina,* 210–1; Lansdale, *Midst of Wars,* 195; Fall, "Political-Religious Sects," 247–8; *Pentagon Papers* (Gravel Edition), I, document 95; FRUS, Indochina, 1952–1954, XIII Part 2, document 1150 and Vietnam, 1955–1957, II, documents 105n2, 200, 242.

9. Robert J. Antony, "Turbulent Waters: Sea Raiding in Early Modern South East Asia—Abstract" (https://www.tandfonline.com/doi/full/10.1080/00253359.2013.766996); *Pentagon Papers* (Gravel Edition), Volume I, Chapter 5, Section 2, Subsection 1 (I.5.2.1); FRUS, Indochina, 1952–1954, XIII Part 2, document 847. The Arroyo Chinois was dug in 1820 to connect Saigon-Cholon and the Saigon River to the My Tho rice center.

10. Cao Van Vien, *Leadership,* 41; Moyar, *Triumph Forsaken,* 41; Lansdale, *Midst of Wars,* 176; Fall, "Political-Religious Sects," 250; Monique

Brinson Demery, *Finding the Dragon Lady: The Mystery of Vietnam's Madame Nhu* (New York: Public Affairs, 2103), 88; *Pentagon Papers* (Gravel Edition), I.5.2.1.; FRUS, Vietnam, 1955–1957, II, documents 37, 60, 105n2, 242, 246; Phillips, *Why Vietnam Matters*, 20–1; Scott Anderson, *The Quiet Americans: Four CIA Spies at the Dawn of the Cold War—A Tragedy in Three Acts* (New York: Doubleday, 2020), 374; Brendan Kelly, "Edward Lansdale and the Saigon Military Mission: Nation Building and Counterinsurgency in South Vietnam, 1954–1956," MA thesis, National University of Ireland Maynooth, 2014, 16.

11. Fall, "Political-Religious Sects," 250.

12. Seth Jacobs, *America's Miracle Man in Vietnam: Ngo Dinh Diem, Religion, Race, and U.S. Intervention in Southeast Asia* (Durham NC: Duke University Press, 2006), 175–6.

13. Mai Elliott, *The Sacred Willow: Four Generation in the Life of a Vietnamese Family* (New York: Oxford University Press, 2017), 229; Fall, "Political-Religious Sects," 250. The Deuxième Bureau was replaced by the Service de Documentation Extérieure et de Contre-Espionnage (SDECE), but the old name stuck.

14. Fall, "Political-Religious Sects," 242. To appreciate how small the sects were, when Bao Dai held a Congress in 1953 of non-communist nationalists, the Cao Dai sect had the largest bloc of seats—a mere 17 of 203.

15. Jacobs, *Cold War Mandarin*, 61; FRUS, Indochina, 1952–1954, XIII, Part 2, document 827; Bui Diem, *In the Jaws of History* (Boston: Houghton Mifflin, 1987), 88; Kelly, "Edward Lansdale and the Saigon Military Mission," 39.

16. Tuong Vu and Sean Fear, eds. *The Republic of Vietnam, 1955–1975: Vietnamese Perspectives on Nation Building* (Ithaca NY: Cornell University Press, 2020), 72; Anderson, *Trapped by Success*, 45; FRUS, Indochina, 1952–1954, XIII, Part 2, document 1127; FRUS, Vietnam, 1955–1957, I, document 59 and Indochina, 1952–1954, XIII, Part 2, document 827; Ronald H. Spector, *Advice and Support: The Early Years, 1941–1960* (Washington: U.S. Army Center of Military History, 1985), 244; "Vietnam: A Television History; Interview with Lucien Bodard" (Open Vault, WGBH, http://openvault.wgbh.org/catalog/vietnam), hereafter: (WGBH Media Library & Archives). Lai Huu Sang was also known as Lai Huu Tai. Rumor had it that Bao Dai issued the police decree in return for Bay Vien erasing his gambling debts.

17. FRUS, Indochina, 1952–1954, XIII, Part 2, document 834. Hammer, *Struggle for Indochina*, 286.

18. FRUS, Indochina, 1952–1954, XIII, Part 2, document 981.

19. Anderson, *Trapped by Success*, 45; FRUS, Indochina, 1952–1954, XIII, Part 2, document 1127; FRUS, Vietnam, 1955–1957, I, document 59 and Indochina, 1952–1954, XIII, Part 2, document 827; Ronald H. Spector, *Advice and Support: The Early Years, 1941–1960* (Washington: U.S. Army Center of Military History, 1985), 244; "Interview with Lucien Bodard" (WGBH Media Library & Archives).

20. FRUS, Indochina, 1952–1954, XIII Part 2, document 885.

21. FRUS, Indochina, 1952–1954, XIII, Part 2, document 1082.

22. FRUS, Indochina, 1952–1954, XIII Part 2, documents 896, 916n1; Thomas L. Ahern, *CIA and the House of Ngo: Covert Action in South Vietnam, 1954–63.* (Washington: Center for the Study of Intelligence, 2000), 16; Neil Sheehan, *A Bright Shining Lie: John Paul Vann and America in Vietnam* (New York: Vintage Books, 1989), 353; Miller, *Misalliance*, 50, 52.

23. "Vietnam: A Television History, Interview with Eldridge Durbrow, Part 2 of 2" 1 February 1979 (WGBH Media Library & Archives).

24. FRUS, Indochina, 1952–1954, XIII Part 2, document 981; Miller, *Misalliance*, 50, 52; William Colby, *Lost Victory: The Firsthand Account of America's Sixteen-Year Involvement in Vietnam* (Chicago: Contemporary Books, 1989), 71.

25. Nguyen Ngoc Chau. "The potential competitor to Ngo Dinh Diem in 1954" in *Việt Nam—L'histoire Politique des deux guerres—Guerre d'indépendance (1858–1954) et guerre idéologique ou Nord Sud (1945–1975)* Editions Nombre 7, France, 2019, 11.1; Vietnam, 1955–1957, II, document 128, 270; Lansdale, *Midst of Wars*, 155; Stanley Karnow, "Vietnam: A Television History; America's Mandarin (1954–1963); Interview with Edward Geary Lansdale, 1979, Part 1 of 5," (WGBH Media Library & Archives); "Vietnam: A Television History; Interview with Lucien Bodard, 1981," 18 February 1981 (WGBH Media Library & Archives).

26. FRUS, Indochina, 1952–1954, XIII Part 2, documents 896, 916, 891; Thomas L. Ahern, *CIA and the House of Ngo*, 16; Sheehan, *A Bright Shining Lie*, 353; Miller, *Misalliance*, 50, 52; Colby, *Lost Victory*, 71; Asselin, "The Democratic Republic of Vietnam and the 1954 Geneva Conference," 168.

27. Pentagon Papers (Gravel Edition), I, document 95; Tucker, *Encyclopedia of the Vietnam War*, 1726; FRUS, Indochina, 1952–1954, XIII Part 2, document 975; David L. Anderson, *The Vietnam War* (New York: Palgrave, 2005), 24.

28. Phillips, *Why Vietnam Matters*, 38, 60. Pentagon Papers (Gravel Edition), I, document 95; FRUS, Indochina, 1952–1954, XIII Part 2, document 975; Lansdale, *Midst of Wars*, 137, 161, 181, 217; David L. Anderson, *The Vietnam War* (New York: Palgrave, 2005), 24; Karnow, "Interview with Edward Geary Lansdale, 1979, Part 1 of 5."

29. FRUS, Indochina, 1952–1954, XIII Part 2, document 921.

30. FRUS, Indochina, 1952–1954, XIII Part 2, document 846.

31. Miller, *Misalliance*, 102–03; Moyar, *Triumph Forsaken*, 45; FRUS, Indochina, 1952–1954, XIII Part 2, documents 1152, 1157.

32. FRUS, Indochina, 1952–1954, XIII Part 2, document 1159; Phillips, *Why Vietnam Matters*, 31.

33. FRUS, Indochina, 1952–1954, XIII Part 2,

document 1173; Tran Van Don, *Our Endless War: Inside Vietnam* (San Rafael CA: Presidio Press, 1978), 121; Lansdale, *Midst of Wars*, 173; Cao Van Vien, *Leadership*, 44.

34. Cao Van Vien, *Leadership*, 22; FRUS, Indochina, 1952–1954, XIII Part 2, documents 1171, 1173; Demery, *Dragon Lady*, 83; John Prados, *Vietnam: The Unwinnable War, 1945–1975* (Lawrence KS: University Press of Kansas, 2008), 43.

35. Pentagon Papers (Gravel Edition), I, document 95; Max Boot, *The Road Not Taken: Edward Lansdale and the American Tragedy in Vietnam* (New York: Liveright, 2018), 255–6; Lansdale, *Midst of Wars*, 185, 192. Cao Van Vien, *Leadership*, 22; Phillips, *Why Vietnam Matters*, 52. The French High Commissioner for Cochinchina governed out of the Norodom Palace.

36. FRUS, Indochina, 1952–1954, XIII Part 2, document 1176.

37. FRUS, Indochina, 1952–1954, XIII Part 2, document 1177.

38. FRUS, Indochina, 1952–1954, XIII Part 2, document 1176.

39. Moyar, *Triumph Forsaken*, 34; FRUS, Indochina, 1952–1954, XIII Part 2, document 1179.

40. FRUS, Indochina, 1952–1954, XIII Part 2, document 1181 (SNIE 63-6-54).

41. FRUS, Indochina, 1952–1954, XIII Part 2, documents 1179, 1180, 1185, 1210.

42. FRUS, Indochina, 1952–1954, XIII Part 2, document 1188.

43. Miller, *Misalliance*, 101; FRUS, Indochina, 1952–1954, XIII, Part 2, documents 1119, 1154, 1181, 1191

44. FRUS, Indochina, 1952–1954, XIII Part 2, document 1195; Fall, "Political-Religious Sects," 251; Miller, *Misalliance*, 102, 105–6; Demery, *Dragon Lady*, 86–7.

45. Miller, *Misalliance*, 104; FRUS, Indochina, 1952–1954, XIII Part 2, documents 1247, 1264; Karnow, "Interview with Edward Geary Lansdale, 1979, Part 2 of 5."

46. Pentagon Papers (Gravel Edition), I, document 95; FRUS, Indochina, 1952–1954, XIII Part 2, documents 1271, 1292, 1306; Miller, *Misalliance*, 105; Phillips, *Why Vietnam Matters*, 32.

47. "General Hinh Loses Post," *Sydney Morning Herald*, Tuesday 30 November 1956; Tran Van Don, *Our Endless War*, 43; FRUS, Indochina, 1952–1954, XIII Part 2, documents 1179, 1301, 1316, 1345 and Vietnam, 1955–1957, II, document 28; Pentagon Papers (Gravel Edition), I, document 95.

48. Lansdale, *Midst of Wars*, 208.

49. Neese and O'Donnell, *Prelude to Tragedy*, 100; Elliott, *The Sacred Willow*, 30.

50. Lansdale, *Midst of Wars*, 182, 257. FRUS, Indochina, 1952–1954, XIII Part 2, document 1316n3, 1377 and Vietnam, 1955–1957, II, document 14; Stewart, *Vietnam's Lost Revolution*, 25–6. CEFEO stood for Corps Expéditionnaire Français en Extrême-Orient or French Expeditionary Corps in the Far East.

51. Karnow, "Interview with Edward Geary Lansdale, 1979, Part 1 of 5."

52. Phillips, *Why Vietnam Matters*, 4.

53. FRUS, Indochina, 1952–1954, XIII.2, document 1375.

54. Demery, *Dragon Lady*, 91, 93.

55. FRUS, Indochina, 1952–1954, XIII.2, document 1375.

56. FRUS, Indochina, 1952–1954, XIII, Part 2, document 1182.

57. Lansdale, *Midst of Wars*, 171.

58. Lansdale, *Midst of Wars*, 177, 259n; Moyar, *Triumph Forsaken*, 34; FRUS, Indochina, 1952–1954, XIII Part 2, document 1364.

59. Pentagon Papers (Gravel Edition), I, document 95; Edward G. Lansdale, "Memorandum for the Record: 'Pacification' in Vietnam'" (Washington: Office of the Secretary of Defense, Special Operations, 1958), 3; Lansdale, *Midst of Wars*, 229, 230–1; Edward G. Lansdale, "Civic Activities of the Military, Southeast Asia," (Washington: Anderson-Southeast Asia Subcommittee for the Draper Committee, 13 March 1959), 5; Spector, *Advise and Support*, 242; Phillips, *Why Vietnam Matters*, 33.

60. Fall, "Political-Religious Sects," 251; Miller, *Misalliance*, 111–2; Lansdale, *Midst of Wars*, 171; FRUS, Vietnam, 1955–1957, II, documents 8, 19; Lansdale, "Memorandum for the Record: 'Pacification in Vietnam,'" 4; FRUS, Vietnam, 1955–1957, II, document 32n4.

61. Miller, *Misalliance*, 109; FRUS, Vietnam, 1955–1957, II, documents 16, 28.

62. Lansdale, *Midst of Wars*, 271; FRUS, Vietnam, 1955–1957, II, documents 6, 34, 37, 156.

63. Neese and O'Donnell, *Prelude to Tragedy*, 9.

64. FRUS, Vietnam, 1955–1957, II, documents 37, 58, 59n3; Lansdale, *Midst of Wars*, 245, 246, 247; Cao Van Vien, *Leadership*, 42; Miller, *Misalliance*, 114.

65. John Ernst, *Forging a Fateful Alliance: Michigan State University and the Vietnam War* (East Lansing MI: Michigan State University Press, 1998), 64, 70; FRUS, Vietnam, 1955–1957, II, documents 58, 61, 64, 68.

66. Tran Van Don, *Our Endless War*, 128–129; FRUS, Indochina, 1952–1954, XIII Part 2, document 1057 and Vietnam, 1955–1957, II, documents 44, 45.

67. FRUS, Vietnam, 1955–1957, II, documents 57, 58; Lansdale, *Midst of Wars*, 244–5.

68. FRUS, Vietnam, 1955–1957, II, document 70.

69. Lansdale, *Midst of Wars*, 252, 255. FRUS, Vietnam, 1955–1957, II, document 69; FRUS, Vietnam, 1955–1957, II, document 68, 82.

70. Lansdale, *Midst of Wars*, 252, 255. FRUS, Vietnam, 1955–1957, II, document 69; FRUS, Vietnam, 1955–1957, II, document 68, 82; Phillips, *Why Vietnam Matters*, 33; "Vietnam: A Television History; Interview with Lawton Collins," 29 April 1981. (WGBH Media Library & Archives); Allen, *None So Blind*, 26.

71. FRUS, Vietnam, 1955–1957, II, documents 71, 73, 75, 76.

72. Fall, "Political-Religious Sects," 252.

73. Fall, "Political-Religious Sects," 252; Lansdale, *Midst of Wars*, 256; Miller, *Misalliance*, 115; FRUS, Vietnam, 1955–1957, II, document 79.

74. Cao Van Vien, *Leadership*, 43; FRUS, Vietnam, 1955–1957, II, documents 81, 156; Miller, *Misalliance*, 115; Lansdale, *Midst of Wars*, 177, 261–2; Phillips, *Why Vietnam Matters*, 56–7.

75. FRUS, Vietnam, 1955–1957, II, documents 81, 156; Miller, *Misalliance*, 115.

76. Thomas L. Ahern, Jr., "The CIA and the Government of Ngo Dinh Diem: Power Struggles in Saigon," (https://www.cia.gov/library/center-for-the-study-of-intelligence/csi-publications/books-and-monographs/Anthology-CIA-and-the-Wars-in-Southeast-Asia/pdfs/ahern-cia-ngo-in-dinh-diem.pdf), (Hereafter CIA Library) 44; Lansdale, *Midst of Wars*, 260, 268, 314; Fall, "Political-Religious Sects," 249, 252; Louis J. Walinsky, ed. *Agrarian Reform as Unfinished Business: The Selected Papers of Wolf Ladejinsky* (Oxford: Oxford University Press, 1977), 230.

77. The Vietnamese term for blood debt is han tu.

78. FRUS, Vietnam, 1955–1957, II, documents 82, 83, 84; Cao Van Vien, *Leadership*, 43.

79. FRUS, Vietnam, 1955–1957, II, document 97.

80. FRUS, Vietnam, 1955–1957, II, document 98.

81. FRUS, Vietnam, 1955–1957, II, documents 90, 97, 103, 143; Anderson, *Trapped by Success*, 111; Cao Van Vien, *Leadership*, 44; Miller, *Misalliance*, 119–20; Republic of Vietnam, *The Victory of Rung Sat* (Saigon: Government of the Republic of Vietnam, 1955), 6; Spector, *Advice and Support*, 247; Lansdale, *Midst of Wars*, 270–1, 275, 281, 287; Jacobs, *Miracle Man*, 204; FRUS, Vietnam, 1955–1957, II, documents 90, 97, 103.

82. FRUS, Vietnam, 1955–1957, II, documents 127, 143; Anderson, *Trapped by Success*, 111; Cao Van Vien, *Leadership*, 44; Miller, *Misalliance*, 119–20; Republic of Vietnam, *Victory of Rung Sat*, 6; Spector, *Advice and Support*, 247; Lansdale, *Midst of Wars*, 270–1, 275, 281, 287; Jacobs, *Miracle Man*, 204.

83. FRUS, Vietnam, 1955–1957, II, documents 84, 88, 98, 127, 148; Miller, *Misalliance*, 110.

84. Miller, *Misalliance*, 116; Lansdale, *Midst of Wars*, 268, 284; Cao Van Vien, *Leadership*, 42.

85. Cao Van Vien, *Leadership*, 45, 245; Ha Mai Viet, *Steel and Blood*, 291; Spector, *Advice and Support*, 246; Lansdale, *Midst of Wars*, 273–4; FRUS, Vietnam, 1955–1957, II, document 99; Gordon Rottman, *Vietnam Airborne* (London: Osprey, 1990), 24. The Group consisted of the 1st, 3rd, 5th, and 6th Paratroop Battalions plus support units.

86. FRUS, Vietnam, 1955–1957, II, documents 106, 116.

87. Miller, *Misalliance*, 86.

88. Larry Berman, *Perfect Spy: The Incredible Double Life of Pham Xuan An* (Washington: Smithsonian Books, 2008), 78; FRUS, Indochina, 1952–1954, XIII Part 2, documents 1274, 1322 and

Vietnam, 1955–1957, II, documents 93n5, 105, 128; Hammer, *Struggle for Indochina*, 304.

89. FRUS, Vietnam, 1955–1957, II, documents 117–8, 122.

90. FRUS, Vietnam, 1955–1957, II, documents 117–8, 122.

91. FRUS, Vietnam, 1955–1957, II, document 128.

92. Lansdale, *Midst of Wars*, 280; FRUS, Vietnam, 1955–1957, II, documents 136, 138, 148; Ahern, "Power Struggles in Saigon," 44; Miller, *Misalliance*, 119; Jacobs, *Miracle Man*, 205–6.

93. FRUS, Vietnam, 1955–1957, II, documents 138, 148; Ahern, "Power Struggles in Saigon," 44; Miller, *Misalliance*, 119; Jacobs, *Miracle Man*, 205–6.

Chapter 3

1. FRUS, Vietnam, 1955–1957, II, document 143; Anderson, *Trapped by Success,* 111; Cao Van Vien, *Leadership*, 44; Miller, *Misalliance*, 119–20; Republic of Vietnam, *The Victory of Rung Sat*, 6; Spector, *Advice and Support*, 247; Lansdale, *Midst of Wars*, 270–1, 275, 281, 287; Jacobs, *Miracle Man*, 204; Karnow, "Interview with Edward Geary Lansdale, 1979, Part 2 of 5."

2. Spector, *Advice and Support*, 247; Fall, *Two Viet-Nams*, 256; Lansdale, *Midst of Wars*, 283; Phillips, *Why Vietnam Matters*, 56. OAS stood for Organisation Armée Secrète.

3. Cao Van Vien, *Leadership*, 45; Republic of Vietnam, *Victory of Rung Sat*, 7, 10. For a short newsreel of the Saigon fighting see: https://www.britishpathe.com/video/saigon-revolt.

4. Lansdale, *Midst of Wars*, 269–70, 285–6, 306; Phillips, *Why Vietnam Matters*, 66; Prados, *Vietnam: The Unwinnable War*, 45–6.

5. FRUS, Vietnam, 1955–1957, II, document 145; Lansdale, *Midst of Wars*, 288, 295; Dong Van Khuyen, *RVNAF Logistics* (Washington: U.S. Army Center for Military History, 1984), 33.

6. Miller, *Misalliance*, 121; Anderson, *The Quiet Americans*, 411; Lansdale, *Midst of Wars*, 292, 294; Karnow, "Interview with Edward Geary Lansdale, 1979, Part 2 of 5."

7. Fall, "Political-Religious Sects," 252; Elliott, *The Sacred Willow*, 231; Lansdale, *Midst of Wars*, 289, 298; Republic of Vietnam, *The Victory of Rung Sat*, 6.

8. Cao Van Vien, *Leadership*, 45; FRUS, Vietnam, 1955–1957, II, documents 170, 172; Tran Van Don, *Our Endless War*, 61; Lansdale, *Midst of Wars*, 305–6, 309–10.

9. Lansdale, *Midst of Wars*, 296, 300, 303, 304; Cao Van Vien, *Leadership*, 44; Miller, *Misalliance*, 129; FRUS, Vietnam, 1955–1957, II, documents 152, 157, 159, 176, 200.

10. Phillips, *Why Vietnam Matters*, 141; Lansdale, *Midst of Wars*, 296, 300, 303, 304; Cao Van Vien, *Leadership*, 44; Miller, *Misalliance*, 129; FRUS, Vietnam, 1955–1957, II, documents 152, 157, 159, 176, 200.

11. Phillips, *Why Vietnam Matters*, 77–8; Anderson, *The Quiet Americans*, 419–20.

12. Fall, "Political-Religious Sects," 249.

13. FRUS, Vietnam, 1955–1957, II, document 32; Miller, *Misalliance*, 114.

14. Fall, "Political-Religious Sects," 252; Lansdale, *Midst of Wars*, 313; Director, Special Operations Research Office, "Ethnographic Study Series: Selected Groups in the Republic of Vietnam, The Binh Xuyen" (Washington: The American University, 1966), 8; FRUS, Vietnam, 1955–1957, II, document 173; Miller, *Misalliance*, 92, 129; Lansdale, *Midst of Wars*, 314–5; Neese and O'Donnell, *Prelude to Tragedy*, 101; Phillips, *Why Vietnam Matters*, 72.

15. Dong Van Khuyen, *RVNAF Logistics*, 33; Cao Van Vien, *Leadership*, 50; Fall, "Political-Religious Sects," 253; Lansdale, *Midst of Wars*, 320–1.

16. Cao Van Vien, *Leadership*, 50.

17. Lansdale, *Midst of Wars*, 310; Cao Van Vien, *Leadership*, 45, 47; Republic of Vietnam, *Victory of Rung Sat*, 6, 12, 14. The area later became the Rung Sat Special Zone and now is the Can Gio Mangrove Forest.

18. Republic of Vietnam, *Victory of Rung Sat*, 16, 18, 29, 36, 43; Cao Van Vien, *Leadership*, 45–6, 48, 49; Ha Mai Viet, *Steel and Blood*, 291; Lansdale, *Midst of Wars*, 311; Jessica M. Chapman, *Cauldron of Resistance: Ngo Dinh Diem, the United States, and the 1950s Southern Vietnam* (Ithaca NY: Cornell University Press), 126–7.

19. Tucker, *Encyclopedia of the Vietnam War*, 1709–10; Chapman, *Cauldron*, 126–7; Miller, *Misalliance*, 126; Cao Van Vien, *Leadership*, 50, 51, 52; Stewart, *Vietnam's Lost Revolution*, 82. For the next several years, Pham Cong Tac's many loyalists pleaded in vain for his return until his death finally settled the matter in 1959.

20. Lansdale, *Midst of Wars*, 270, 319.

21. Sedgewick Tourison, *Secret Army, Secret War: Washington's Tragic Spy Operations in North Vietnam* (Annapolis MD: Naval Institute Press, 1995), 30; Lansdale, *Midst of Wars*, 270; Shelby L. Stanton, *Green Berets at War: U.S. Army Special Forces in Southeast Asia, 1956–1975* (Novato, CA: Presidio Press, 1985), 36. SEPES also was known as "Room 4" and the Liaison Service as "Room 6," references to the location of their headquarters at the Doc Lap Palace.

22. Berman, *Perfect Spy*, 83–4. Perhaps the best indicator of Tuyen's close relationship with the CIA is that his name never appeared in the published accounts of either Colby or Lansdale.

23. Lansdale, *Midst of Wars*, 208; Frederick Nolting, *From Trust to Tragedy: The Political Memoirs of Fredrick Nolting, Kennedy's Ambassador to Diem's Vietnam* (New York: Praeger, 1988), 31, 61.

24. Spector, *Advice and Support*, 232.

25. French General Paul Ely departed South Vietnam to resume his post as Chief of the General Staff in Paris a few days after Collins, on 1 June 1955.

26. Marc Jason Gilbert, ed. *Why the North Won the Vietnam War* (New York: Palgrave, 2002), 56.

27. Bui Tin, *Following Ho Chi Minh*, 43; Miller, *Misalliance*, 97; FRUS, Vietnam, 1955–1957, I, document 5, 229; Asselin, *Hanoi's Road*, 13, 28.

28. Remarks of Senator John F. Kennedy at the Conference on Vietnam Luncheon in the Hotel Willard, Washington, D.C., June 1, 1956 (https://www.jfklibrary.org/Research/Research-Aids/JFK-Speeches/Vietnam-Conference-Washington-DC_19560601.aspx); FRUS, Vietnam, 1955–1957, I, documents 55, 196.

29. FRUS, Vietnam, 1955–1957, I, document 230.

30. FRUS, Vietnam, 1955–1957, I, documents 199, 203, 229, 230, 255.

31. Millett, *The War for Korea, 1945–1950*, 150–1; Jessica M. Chapman, "Staging Democracy, South Vietnam's 1955 Referendum to Depose Bao Dai," *Diplomatic History*, 30, no. 4 (September 2006), 681.

32. FRUS, Vietnam, 1955–1957, I, documents 202, 217, 240n5, 261n2; United States Forces, Vietnam, "The Situation in Nam Bo since the Restoration of Peace to Date [1961]" (translation of incomplete document captured in Phuoc Long province, RVN, on 28 April 1969), (Vietnam Center and Archive, Texas Tech University, hereafter TTU), 8, 16.

33. Chapman, *Cauldron*, 154; Fall, *Two Viet-Nams*, 209; FRUS, Vietnam, 1955–1957, I, document 268; Miller, *Misalliance*, 141; Oguzhan Yilmaz, ed. *History of Vietnam and the Socialist Republic of Vietnam* (Konya, Turkey: University of Selkuc, 2019), 112; Karnow, "Interview with Edward Geary Lansdale, 1979, Part 3 of 5."

34. FRUS, Vietnam, 1955–1957, I, document 278.

35. Tran Van Don, *Our Endless War*, 26; FRUS, Vietnam, 1955–1957, I, document 278; Karnow, "Interview with Edward Geary Lansdale, 1979, Part 3 of 5."

36. Phillips, *Why Vietnam Matters*, 81.

37. Edward Garvey Miller, "Grand Designs: Vision, Power and Nation Building in America's Alliance with Ngo Dinh Diem, 1954–1960" (Ph.D. diss., Harvard University, 2004), 208; FRUS, Vietnam, 1955–1957, I, document 165 (SNIE 63. 1-2/1-55); Tran Van Don, *Our Endless War*, 40; Chapman, "Staging Democracy," 678; Elliott, *The Sacred Willow*, 232.

38. FRUS, Vietnam, 1955–1957, I, documents 278, 301, 308, 361.

39. Lien-Hang T. Nguyen, *Hanoi's War*, 34.

40. Fall, *Two Viet-Nams*, 188–9; Truong Nhu Tang, *A Viet Cong Memoir: An Inside Account of the Vietnam War and its Aftermath* (New York: Vintage, 1986), 300; Gérald Tongas. *J'ai vécu dans L'enfer Communiste au Nord Viet-Nam [I lived in the Communist Inferno of North Vietnam]* (Paris: Nouvelles Editions Debresse, 1960), 222–3, 426–7; Nguyen, *Hanoi's War*, 35–7, 319–20n60; Asselin, *Hanoi's Road*, 38, 83; Tuan Hoang, "Ideology in

Urban South Vietnam," 170; Asselin, *Vietnam's American War*, 87–8.

41. Asselin, *Hanoi's Road*, 39.

42. John Dumbrell, *Rethinking Vietnam* (New York: Palgrave McMillan, 2012), 29; Guan, *Vietnamese Communist's Relations with China*, 12–3.

43. U.S. Forces, Vietnam, "The Situation in Nam Bo," 30–1; Elliott, *The Vietnamese War*, 114; Cao Van Vien, *Leadership*, 51; FRUS, Vietnam, 1955–1957, II, document 276.

Chapter 4

1. Ellen J. Hammer, *A Death in November: America in Vietnam, 1963* (New York: E.P. Dutton, 1987), 76.

2. Hammer, *Death in November*, 47; Miller, *Misalliance*, 25; Fall, *Two Viet-Nams*, 235.

3. Jacobs, *Cold War Mandarin*, 18–9; Fall, *Two Viet-Nams*, 239; Miller, *Misalliance*, 19, 24–5. A Jesuit missionary developed the Vietnamese alphabet, Chu Quoc Ngu, during the same era.

4. Fall, *Two Viet Nam's*, 239; Geoffrey Shaw, *The Lost Mandate of Heaven* (San Francisco: Ignatius Press, 2015), 29; FRUS, Indochina, 1952–1954, XIII Part 2, document 1316n3; Office of Current Intelligence, "Cast of Characters in South Vietnam, 28 August 1963," (Washington: Central Intelligence Agency, 1963), 12.

5. Fall, *Two Viet-Nams*, 86, 239; Miller, *Misalliance*, 24, 189–90; Demery, *Dragon Lady*, 73; Currey, *Victory at Any Cost*, 23; Stewart, *Vietnam's Lost Revolution*, 16. Some sources say Diem also was governor of Phan Thiet province north of Saigon. As a comparison, at the time of Diem's appointment, his eldest brother Khoi (16 years his senior) became the head of Quang Nam province.

6. Fall, *Two Viet-Nams*, 239; Shaw, *Lost Mandate*, 32; Jacobs, *Cold War Mandarin*, 20; Miller, *Misalliance*, 25, 35, 101–2; Hammer, *Struggle for Indochina*, 86–7.

7. Hunt, *A Vietnam War Reader*, 6.

8. William J. Duiker, "Phan Boi Chau: Asian Revolutionary in a Changing World," *The Journal of Asian Studies* 31, no. 1 (November 1971), 86; Fall, *Two Viet-Nams*, 235. The paper was titled "Oh Heaven, Oh God!" (Thien Ho De Ho).

9. Miller, *Misalliance*, 28, 138; Shaw, *Lost Mandate*, 33; Tran Thi Phuong Hoa, "Franco-Vietnamese Schools and the Transition from Confucian to a New Kind of Intellectual in the Colonial Context of Tonkin" (Boston: Harvard-Yenching Institute Working Paper Series, 2009), 6; Duiker, "Phan Boi Chau," 86–7; FRUS, Vietnam, 1961–1963, II, document 23; Tuan Hoang, "Ideology in Urban South Vietnam," 107.

10. Phillips, *Why Vietnam Matters*, 17.

11. Miller, *Misalliance*, 28, 138; Shaw, *Lost Mandate*, 33; Tran Thi Phuong Hoa, "Franco-Vietnamese Schools," 6; Duiker, "Phan Boi Chau," 86–7; FRUS, Vietnam, 1961–1963, II, document 23; Bui Diem, *Jaws of History*, 18, 41; Tuan Hoang, "Ideology in Urban South Vietnam," 74; Kiyoko

Kurusu Nitz, "Japanese Military Policy Towards French Indochina during the Second World War: The Road to the 'Meigo Sakusen' (9 March 1945)," *Journal of Southeast Asian Studies* 14, no. 2 (1983), 333.

12. Neese and O'Donnell, ed., *Prelude to Tragedy*, 181.

13. Miller, *Misalliance*, 28, 138; Shaw, *Lost Mandate*, 33; Tran Thi Phuong Hoa, "Franco-Vietnamese Schools," 6; Duiker, "Phan Boi Chau," 86–7; FRUS, Vietnam, 1961–1963, II, document 23; Bui Diem, *Jaws of History*, 18, 41; Tuan Hoang, "Ideology in Urban South Vietnam," 74; Kiyoko Kurusu Nitz, "Japanese Military Policy Towards French Indochina," 333.

14. Miller, *Misalliance*, 30–31; Jacobs, *Cold War Mandarin*, 21–2; Demery, *Dragon Lady*, 75; Duiker, "Phan Boi Chau," 79; Hammer, *Struggle for Indochina*, 44, 48; John King Fairbank, *The Great Chinese Revolution, 1800–1985* (New York: Harper & Row, 1986), 150, 152; Currey, *Victory at Any Cost*, 86; Shaw, *Lost Mandate*, 33–4; Nitz, "Japanese Military Policy Towards French Indochina," 343, 345; Ralph B. Smith, "The Japanese Period in Indochina and the Coup of 9 March 1945" *Journal of Southeast Asian Studies*, 9, no. 2 (September 1978), 274; Stewart, *Vietnam's Lost Revolution*, 16.

15. Anderson, *Trapped by Success*, 45; Hammer, *Struggle for Indochina*, 101, 149–50; Shaw, *Lost Mandate*, 31; Tran Van Don, *Our Endless War*, 18; 101; Jacobs, *Cold War Mandarin*, 22.

16. Sedgewick D. Tourison, Jr., *Talking with Victor Charlie: An Interrogator's Story* (New York: Ivy Books, 1991), 66–7.

17. Ngo Dinh Diem, *Major Policy Speeches*, 41.

18. Hammer, *Struggle for Indochina*, 218–9, 227–8, 245, 247; Miller, *Misalliance*, 32.

19. Jacobs, *Cold War Mandarin*, 25, 27–29, 31; Diem, *Major Policy Speeches*, 44; Hammer, *Struggle for Indochina*, 286; Robert Mann, *A Grand Delusion: America's Descent into Vietnam* (New York: Basic Books, 2001), 180; Anderson, *Trapped by Success*, 47.

20. Shaw, *Lost Mandate*, 239–40.

21. Hammer, *Death in November*, 51–2.

22. Ahern, *House of Ngo*, cover.

23. Miller, *Misalliance*, 24; 31 January 1979 interview of Ngo Dinh Luyen (WGBH Media Library & Archives).

24. Archbishop Ngo Dinh Thuc, "Declaration of Archbishop Ngo-Dinh Thuc," (http://www.cmri.org/thucletter.html); Directory of the Vinh Long School, "Biography of Bishop Pierre Martin Ngo Dinh Thuc" (http://giaophanvinhlong.net/Duc-Cha-Phero-Ngo-Dinh-Thuc.html); Edward Miller, "Vision, Power and Agency: The Ascent of Ngo Dinh Diem, 1945–54," *Journal of Southeast Asian Studies*, 35, no. 3 (Oct., 2004), 448; Miller, *Misalliance*, 27; Lansdale, *Midst of Wars*, 160. In 1982, Thuc rebelled against the Pope for what he saw as the Catholic Church's adoption of decadent modernism and was excommunicated.

25. FRUS, Vietnam, 1955–1957, I, document 56; Shaw, *Lost Mandate*, 69; Jean Lacouture, *Vietnam*

Between Two Truces, Konrad Kellen and Joel Carmichael, trans. (New York: Random House, 1966), 88; Lansdale, *Midst of Wars*, 160; Miller, *Misalliance*, 43; Miller, "Vision, Power and Agency," 447–8, 449; Karnow, "Interview with Edward Geary Lansdale, 1979, Part 2 of 5."

26. Shaw, *Lost Mandate*, 69; Lacouture, *Vietnam Between Two Truces*, 88; Lansdale, *Midst of Wars*, 160; Miller, *Misalliance*, 43; Miller, "Vision, Power and Agency," 447–8, 449.

27. Miller, *Misalliance*, 129–30; Anderson, *Trapped by Success*, 48.

28. FRUS, Vietnam, 1958–1960, I, document 94; Miller, *Misalliance*, 42.

29. FRUS, Vietnam, 1958–1960, I, document 94.

30. Miller, *Misalliance*, 264; FRUS, Vietnam, 1955–1957, II, documents 56, 60, 72 and 1958–1960, I, documents 94, 213; Lacouture, *Vietnam: Between Two Truces*, 21; Hammer, *A Death in November*, 110; Gerald Cannon Hickey, *Free in the Forest: Ethnohistory of the Vietnamese Central Highlands, 1954–1976*. New Haven: Yale University Press, 1982), 8. Under Diem, the South Vietnamese part of Annam was divided into two administrative regions headed by a Delegate. Ho Dac Khuong in Hue was responsible for the Central Midlands while Ton That Hoi in Dalat was the Delegate for the Central Highlands.

31. Lansdale, *Midst of Wars*, 160; Miller, *Misalliance*, 42, 102; Shaw, *Lost Mandate*, 37; FRUS, Vietnam, 1955–1957, II, documents 56, 79; Fall, *Two Viet-Nams*, 253. Bao Dai was several months older than Luyen.

32. Lansdale, *Midst of Wars*, 160; Demery, *Dragon Lady*, 27, 29, 33, 54, 83.

33. Don, *Our Endless War*, 51; Demery, *Dragon Lady*, 57, 60, 61, 65.

34. "Vietnam: A Television History; Interview with Madame Ngo Dinh Nhu," 11 February 1982. (WGBH Media Library & Archives).

35. Demery, *Dragon Lady*, 102, 104; Lacouture, *Vietnam Between Two Truces*, 80; Julie Annette Riggs Osborn, "War, Women, Vietnam: The Mobilization of Female Images, 1954–1978," doctoral dissertation, University of Washington, 2013, 94, 101–2; Wendy N. Duong, "Gender Equality and Women's issues in Vietnam: The Vietnamese Woman—Warrior and Poet," *Pacific Rim Law and Policy Journal*, 10, no. 2 (Summer 2001), 277; David Hunt, *Vietnam's Southern Revolution: From Peasant Insurrection to Total War* (Amherst MA: University of Massachusetts Press, 2008), 90; "Vietnam: A Television History; Interview with Eldridge Durbrow, Part 2 of 2."

36. Karnow, "Interview with Edward Geary Lansdale, 1979, Part 2 of 5."

37. Julie Annette Riggs Osborn, "War, Women, Vietnam: The Mobilization of Female Images, 1954–1978," doctoral dissertation, University of Washington, 2013, 94, 101–2; Wendy N. Duong, "Gender Equality and Women's issues in Vietnam: The Vietnamese Woman—Warrior and Poet," *Pacific Rim Law and Policy Journal*, 10, no.

2 (Summer 2001), 277; "Vietnam: A Television History; Interview with Madame Ngo Dinh Nhu."

38. Miller, "Vision, Power and Agency," 449; FRUS, Vietnam, 1958–1960, I, document 3; Tuan Hoang, "Ideology in Urban South Vietnam," 104–5.

39. Nguyen Ngoc Tan, "New Road, Path of Progress," *Vietnamese National Association*, Special Issue 2007, 132–160. (http://hon-viet.co.uk/TsNguyenNgocTan_ChuNghiaNhanViConDuong MoiConDuongCua TienBo.htm).

40. Duiker, "Phan Boi Chau," 81.

41. Duiker, "Phan Boi Chau," 77, 87–8; Diem, *Major Policy Speeches*, 26; Miller, *Misalliance*, 27–8; Hammer, *Struggle for Indochina*, 86; Nolting, *From Trust to Tragedy*, 59–60.

42. FRUS, Vietnam, 1958–1960, I, documents 45, 56; Mitchell Tan, "Spiritual Fraternities: The Transnational Networks of Ngo Dinh Diem's Personalist Revolution and the Republic of Vietnam, 1955–1963" *Journal of Vietnamese Studies*, 14, no. 2 (Spring 2019), 1Fall, *Two Viet-Nams*, 246; Thomas D. Williams and Jan Olof Bengtsson, "Personalism," The Stanford Encyclopedia of Philosophy (Summer 2018 Edition), Edward N. Zalta (ed.), (https://plato.stanford.edu/archives/sum2018/entries/personalism/); Tuan Hoang, "Ideology in Urban South Vietnam," 107; Miller, "Vision, Power and Agency," 449; Nguyen Ngoc Tan, "New Road, Path of Progress."

43. Diem, *Major Policy Speeches*, 27.

44. FRUS, Vietnam, 1958–1960, I, document 3.

45. Tan, "Spiritual Fraternities: Ngo Dinh Diem's Personalist Revolution," 1, 5; Diem, *Major Policy Speeches*, 14, 24; Stewart, *Vietnam's Lost Revolution*, 95–6.

46. Pentagon Papers (Gravel Edition), I, 5, 2; FRUS, Vietnam, 1958–1960, I, documents 36, 45, 56; Tuan Hoang, "Ideology in Urban South Vietnam," 109; Stewart, *Vietnam's Lost Revolution*, 47.

47. Shaw, *Lost Mandate*, 68; Tran Van Don, *Our Endless War*, 51–2; Miller, "Vision, Power and Agency," 450; Spector, *Advice and Support*, 279; Ahern, *House of Ngo*, 115; Thomas L. Ahern, *Vietnam Declassified: The CIA and Counterinsurgency* (Lexington KY: The University Press of Kentucky, 2010), 24.

48. Lansdale, *Midst of Wars*, 145; Fall, *Two Viet-Nams*, 250; Miller, *Misalliance*, 47, 48; FRUS, Vietnam, 1958–1960, I, documents 36, 56; Miller, "Vision, Power and Agency," 450; Ahern, *House of Ngo*, 106; Bui Diem, *Jaws of History*, 17, 23.

49. Gregory Palmer, *The McNamara Strategy and the Vietnam War: Program Budgeting in the Pentagon, 1960–1968* (Westport, CT: Greenwood Press, 1978), 90; Spector, *Advice and Support*, 281; FRUS, Vietnam, 1958–1960, I, document 56; Don, *Our Endless War*, 55–6; FRUS, Vietnam, 1958–1960, I, documents 36, 56.

50. Demery, *Dragon Lady*, 215; Fall, *Two Viet-Nams*, 250; Neese and O'Donnell, *Prelude to Tragedy*, 18; FRUS, Vietnam, 1955–1957, I, document 409n4; Nolting, *From Trust to Tragedy*, 30, 61.

51. Ahern, *House of Ngo*, 107.

52. Hammer, *Struggle for Indochina*, 305; Miller, *Misalliance*, 130–1; Ahern, *House of Ngo*, 12, 107.

53. Ahern, *House of Ngo*, 124.

54. Ahern, *House of Ngo*, 128.

55. *Pentagon Papers* (Gravel Edition), I.5.2.4; Shaw, *Lost Mandate*, 70; Ahern, *Vietnam Declassified*, 31; Ahern, *House of Ngo*, 32; Tuan Hoang, "Ideology in Urban South Vietnam," 125.

56. Tran Van Don, *Our Endless War*, 54–5; FRUS, Vietnam, 1955–1957, I, documents 409 and 1958–1960, I, documents 89, 112, 185, 201; Ahern, *Vietnam Declassified*, 28; Porter, *Perils of Dominance*, 125.

57. Miller, *Misalliance*, 129–30.

58. Lansdale, *Midst of Wars*, 174; Tuan Hoang, "Ideology in Urban South Vietnam." 335.

59. Chapman, *Cauldron*," 72–3.

60. Marguerite Higgins, *Our Vietnam Nightmare* (New York: Harper and Row, 1965), 165; Nolting, *From Trust to Tragedy*, 2–3; Karnow, "Interview with Edward Geary Lansdale, 1979, Part 1 of 5.

61. FRUS, Vietnam, 1955–1957, I, document 357; Nolting, *From Trust to Tragedy*, 60; Phillips, *Why Vietnam Matters*, 119.

62. Nolting, *From Trust to Tragedy*, 98.

63. Higgins, *Nightmare*, 162; Shaw, *Lost Mandate*, 27; Nolting, *From Trust to Tragedy*, 59–60; Stewart, *Vietnam's Lost Revolution*, 13, 21; Karnow, "Interview with Edward Geary Lansdale, 1979, Part 1 of 5."

64. Hammer, *A Death in November*, 77.

65. Colby, *Lost Victory*, 65; Karnow, "Interview with Edward Geary Lansdale, 1979, Part 4 of 5."

66. Fall, *Two Viet-Nams*, 235; Demery, *Dragon Lady*, 97; Higgins, *Nightmare*, 161–2; FRUS, Vietnam, 1955–1957, I, document 40 and 1958–1960, I, document 33; Shaw, *Lost Mandate*, 268; Tran Van Don, *Our Endless War*, 63.

67. Nolting, *From Trust to Tragedy*, 27; Higgins, *Nightmare*, 161–2.

68. Nolting, *From Trust to Tragedy*, 27; Higgins, *Nightmare*, 161–2.

69. Robert S. McNamara, *In Retrospect: The Tragedy and Lessons of Vietnam* (New York: Times Books, 1995), 84; Higgins, *Nightmare*, 162.

70. FRUS, Vietnam, 1955–1957, II, document 284; Higgins, *Nightmare*, 162; Karnow, "Interview with Edward Geary Lansdale, 1979, Part 1 of 5"; "Vietnam: A Television History; Interview with Eldridge Durbrow, Part 2 of 2."

71. Ahern, *Vietnam Declassified*, 31.

72. FRUS, Indochina, 1952–1954, XIII, Part 2, document 1342 (SNIE 63-7-54).

73. FRUS, Vietnam, 1961–1963, IV, document 12.

74. Colby, *Lost Victory*, 30.

75. Tobias Rettig, "French military policies in the aftermath of the Yen Bay mutiny, 1930: Old security dilemmas return to surface" *South East Asia Research*, 10, no. 3 (September 2002); 316, 317; Tran Van Don, *Our Endless War*, 22, 27; Pike, *PAVN*, 149; Bui Diem, *Jaws of History*, 47; Phillips, *Why Vietnam Matters*, 23.

76. Lacouture, *Vietnam: Between Two Truces*, 99.

77. Hammer, *A Death in November*, 79; U.S. Forces, Vietnam, "The Situation in Nam Bo," 7; Lam Quang Thi, *Twenty-Five Year Century*, 119, 127, 203; FRUS, Vietnam, 1955–1957, I, document 400; Hammer, *A Death in November*, 141; FRUS, Vietnam, 1958–1960, I, document 55; Phillips, *Why Vietnam Matters*, 87.

78. FRUS 1961–1963, III, documents 196, 198.

79. FRUS, Vietnam, 1955–1957, II, document 262.

80. Nolting, *From Trust to Tragedy*, 138.

81. Nolting, *From Trust to Tragedy*, 2; Miller, *Misalliance*, 140.

82. Carl Von Clausewitz, *On War*, Michael Howard and Peter Paret, trans. (Princeton; Princeton University Press, 1984), 271, 469.

Chapter 5

1. T.T. Connors, M.G. Weiner and J.A. Wilson, *The Land Border of South Vietnam: Some Physical and Cultural Characteristics* (Washington DC: Advanced Research Projects Agency, January 1970), 2; Khuyen, *RVNAF Logistics*, 5; Office of Research and Reports, "A Comparison of the Economies of North and South Vietnam" (Washington DC: Central Intelligence Agency, 1961), 1, 15. Hereafter: ORR, "Comparison of Economies."

2. Connors, Weiner and Wilson, *The Land Border of South Vietnam*, 2; Khuyen, *RVNAF Logistics*, 5; ORR, "Comparison of Economies," 1, 15.

3. ORR, "Comparison of Economies," 8; Savani, *Face and Images*, 117, 127; Dong Van Khuyen, *Logistics*, 5; Salemink, "Regional Centrality of Vietnam's Central Highlands," 14; Fall, *Two Viet-Nams*, 151. See Table 1.

4. ORR, "Comparison of Economies," 10; Dong Van Khuyen, *RVNAF Logistics*, 5.

5. Marion R. Larsen, "Agricultural Economy of North Vietnam" (Washington DC: Department of Agriculture, 1965), 15–6; USAID, *Vietnam: Grain Storage and Marketing System Economic and Engineering Study* (Toledo OH: Wildman Agricultural Research, March 1970), 9; ORR, "Comparison of Economies," 107.

6. Bui Tin, *From Enemy to Friend*, 44; Michael Lee Lanning and Dan Cragg, *Inside the VC and the NVA: The Real Story of North Vietnam's Armed Forces* (College Station TX: Texas A&M University Press, 2008), 189.

7. Guan, *Vietnamese Communists' Relations with China*, 87; Warren Wilkins, *Grab Their Belts to Fight Them: The Viet Cong's Big Unit War Against the U.S., 1965–1966* (Annapolis: Naval Institute Press, 2011), 98–9.

8. Vuong Quan Hoang, "The Vietnam's Transition Economy and Its Fledgling Financial Markets, 1986-2003" *Centre Emile Bernhiem*, Working Paper no. 04/032 (January 2004), 5, see Figure 1; Robert A. Mann, *A Grand Delusion: America's Descent into Vietnam* (New York: Basic Books, 2001), 197; Fall, *Two Viet-Nams*, 175; Lacouture,

Vietnam: Between Two Truces, 46; Guan, *Vietnamese Communists' Relations with China*, 77, 97, 103.

9. Szalontai, "Political and Economic Crisis in North Vietnam," *Cold War History* 5, no. 4 (November 2005): 404, 407–8; Vuong Quan Hoang, "Vietnam's Transition Economy," 5, see Figure 1; Cao Van Vien, *Leadership*, 20; Dong Van Khuyen, *Logistics*, 7; Fall, *Two Viet-Nams*, 291.

10. FRUS, Vietnam, 1955–1957, I, document 372 and Vietnam, 1958–1960, I, documents 4, 58.

11. Vu and Fear, *The Republic of Vietnam, 1955–1975*, 26–7, 29, 31.

12. Timothy Hallinan, "Economic Prospects of the Republic of Vietnam" (Santa Monica: RAND, November 1969), 11–3 and 18 see Table 4; Asselin, *Hanoi's Road*, 98.

13. Pribbenow, *Victory in Vietnam*, 168–70; Chen Jian, "China's Involvement in the Vietnam War, 1964–1969," *The China Quarterly* 142 (June 1995), 371; Xiaoming Zhang, "Vietnam War, 1964–1969: A Chinese Perspective," *The Journal of Military History* 60, no. 4 (October 1996), 756.

14. ORR, "Comparison of Economies," 29, 64–5, 68, 73, 78, 80–1, 85, 88; Dong Van Khuyen, *Logistics*, 7.

15. Fall, *Two Viet-Nams*, 298.

16. Diem, *Major Policy Speeches*, 13.

17. FRUS, Vietnam, 1958–1960, I, document 2; Republic of Vietnam Secretariat of State for Land Property and Land Reform, "Land Reform Program Before 1954 and Land Reform Programs and Achievements Since July 1954," (Saigon: Government of the Republic of Vietnam, 31 July 1959), 7; ORR, "Comparison of Economies," 19; Tuan Hoang, "Ideology in Urban South Vietnam," 334.

18. FRUS, Vietnam, 1958–1960, I, document 4; Cao Van Vien, *Leadership*, 26; ORR, "Comparison of Economies," 2; Fall, *Two Viet-Nams*, 174; Hastings, *Vietnam: An Epic Tragedy*, 112.

19. Bui Tin, *Following Ho Chi Minh*, 25, 27, 39; Szalontai, "Political and Economic Crisis in North Vietnam," 400; Fall, *Two Viet-Nams*, 162; Tongas, *Communist Inferno*, 213; ORR, "Comparison of Economies," 40; Vu. *Vietnam's Communist Revolution*, 134.

20. Szalontai, "Political and Economic Crisis in North Vietnam," 400; Fall, *Two Viet-Nams*, 162; Tongas, *Communist Inferno*, 213; ORR, "Comparison of Economies," 40. Analyzing DRV economic data was challenging as it was manipulated for political purposes often making it unreliable.

21. ORR, "Comparison of Economies," 6, 25; Lacouture, *Vietnam: Between Two Truces*, 37; Larsen, "Agricultural Economy of North Vietnam," vi; Fall, *Two Viet-Nams*, 173–4; Guan, *Vietnamese Communists' Relations with China*, 105; Guan, *Vietnamese Communists' Relations with China*, 212.

22. Tran Van Don, *Our Endless War*, 75; Cao Van Vien, *Leadership*, 27; Fall, *Two Viet-Nams*, 305; Asselin, *Hanoi's Road*, 46.

23. FRUS, Vietnam, 1958–1960, I, document 94.

24. ORR, "Comparison of Economies, 2, 15–6, 19–20; Szalontai, "Political and Economic Crisis

in North Vietnam,"406; Cao Van Vien, *Leadership*, 27; Hallinan, "Economic Prospects of the Republic of Vietnam,"7; FRUS, Vietnam, 1958–1960, I, documents 2, 66.

25. Cao Van Vien, *Leadership*, 27; Hallinan, "Economic Prospects of the Republic of Vietnam," 7, 14; Szalontai, "Political and Economic Crisis in North Vietnam,"406; ORR, "Comparison of Economies," 17.

26. FRUS, Vietnam, 1958–1960, I, document 36.

27. Tran Thi Phuong Hoa, "Franco-Vietnamese Schools," 1, 2, 6, 7, 10, 11; Tuan Hoang, "Ideology in Urban Vietnam, 1950–1975" (Ph.D. diss., University of Notre Dame, 2013), 57, 213; Jonathan D. London, ed. *Education in Vietnam* (Singapore: Institute of Southeast Asian Studies, 2011), 11. (http://jonathanlondon.net/wp-content/uploads/2016/02/EVN_001-London-Education-in-Vietnam.pdf)

28. Karnow, "Interview with Edward Geary Lansdale, 1979, Part 2 of 5."

29. Elliott, *The Sacred Willow*, 3, 6, 30, 34, 231; Vu and Fear, *The Republic of Vietnam, 1955–1975*, 93.

30. Tran Thi Phuong Hoa, "Franco-Vietnamese Schools,"12; Currey, *Victory at Any Cost*, 68; Fall, *Two Viet-Nams*, 305.

31. Tran Thi Phuong Hoa, "Franco-Vietnamese Schools," 7, 11; London, *Education in Vietnam*, 15; Shaw, *The Lost Mandate of Heaven*, 48; Vu and Fear, *The Republic of Vietnam, 1955–1975*, 112.

32. Sara Legrandejacques, "A Colonial University for Southeast Asia? The Indochinese University in Hanoi" *Kyoto Review of Southeast Asia*, 29 (October 2017), (https://kyotoreview.org/yav/indochinese-colonial-university-for-south-east-asia/); Tran Thi Phuong Hoa, "Franco-Vietnamese Schools," 7, 11; London, *Education in Vietnam*, 15; Cao Van Vien, *Leadership*, 26–7; U. Alexis Johnson, *The Meaning of Vietnam* (New Delhi: United States Information Service, 1965), 9; Shaw, *The Lost Mandate of Heaven*, 48; Vu and Fear, *The Republic of Vietnam, 1955–1975*, 112.

33. ORR, "Comparison of Economies."

34. Tongas, *Communist Inferno*, 220.

35. Secretariat of State, "Land Reform Program," 1; Larsen, "Agricultural Economy of North Vietnam," 9.

36. Press Office, *Major Policy Speeches*, 11; Dong Van Khuyen, *Logistics*, 6; Hallinan, "Economic Prospects,"4; FRUS, Vietnam, 1955–1957, I, document 337; Walinsky, *Agrarian Reform as Unfinished Business*, 219–20; Andrew R. Finlayson, *Rice Paddy Recon: A Marine Officer's Second Tour in Vietnam, 1968*–1970 (Jefferson NC: McFarland Publishers, 2014), 149–50.

37. Secretariat of State, "Land Reform Program," 1–3; Miller, *Misalliance*, 162–63; Diem, *Major Policy Speeches*, 11, 31.

38. Secretariat of State, "Land Reform Program,"5; Miller, *Misalliance*, 166–67, 170; Chester L. Cooper, Judith E. Corson, Laurence J. Legere, David E. Lockwood, and Donald M. Weller, *History of Pacification: The American Experience*

with *Pacification in Vietnam* (Washington: Institute of Defense Studies, 1972), 125; Peter Hansen, "Bac Di Cu: Catholic Refugees from the North of Vietnam and Their Role in the Southern Republic, 1954–1959," *Journal of Vietnamese Studies* 4, no. 3 (Fall 2009): 195–6, 198.

39. U.S. Forces, Vietnam, "The Situation in Nam Bo," 12.

40. FRUS, Vietnam, 1955–1957, I, document 337.

41. Walinsky, *Agrarian Reform as Unfinished Business*, 277–8; FRUS, Vietnam, 1955–1957, I, document 340.

42. FRUS, Vietnam, 1955–1957, I, document 340.

43. Walinsky, *Agrarian Reform as Unfinished Business*, 273; Secretariat of State, "Land Reform Program," 8–9; Higgins, *Nightmare*, 228; FRUS, Vietnam, 1955–1957, I, document 354; Stewart, *Vietnam's Lost Revolution*, 106; Lacouture, *Vietnam: Between Two Truces*, 25.

44. Johnson, *The Meaning of Vietnam*, 9; David Wurfel, "Agrarian Reform in the Republic of Vietnam, *The Eastern Survey* 26, no. 6 (June 1957), 81; Walinsky, *Agrarian Reform as Unfinished Business*, 233, 264, 274; Miller, *Misalliance*, 155; Elliott, *Vietnamese War*, 96, 105, 227.

45. David Wurfel, "Agrarian Reform in the Republic of Vietnam, *The Eastern Survey* 26, no. 6 (June 1957), 81; Walinsky, *Agrarian Reform as Unfinished Business*, 233, 264, 274; Miller, *Misalliance*, 155; Elliott, *Vietnamese War*, 96, 105, 227; Phillips, *Why Vietnam Matters*, 211–2; Vatthana Pholsena and Oliver Tappe, eds. *Interactions with a Violent Past: Reading Post Conflict Landscapes in Cambodia, Laos, and Vietnam* (Singapore: NUS Press, 2013), 161.

46. Higgins, *Nightmare*, 161; ORR, "Comparison of Economies,"51 see Table 14, 85, 88, 123, 128; Hallinan, "Economic Prospects," 6; USAID, *Vietnam: Grain Storage and Marketing System*, i. In 1960 South Vietnam exported 340,000 metric tons of rice, earning $27.3 million in revenues.

47. FRUS, East Asia-Pacific Region; Cambodia and Laos, 1958–1960, XVI, document 4; Cao Van Vien, *Leadership*, 27–8; FRUS, Vietnam, 1955–1957, I, document 376 and 1958–1960, I, document 37; Miller, *Misalliance*, 163; Dong Van Khuyen, *Logistics*, 6.

48. Cao Van Vien, *Leadership*, 27–28; Joseph J. Zasloff, "Rural Resettlement in South Viet Nam: The Agroville Program," *Pacific Affairs*, 35, no. 4 (Winter, 1962–1963), 327, 328, 330, 336; Ngo Quang Truong, *Territorial Forces*, 5; Cooper, Corson, Legere, Lockwood, and Miller, *History of Pacification*, 132; Stewart, *Vietnam's Lost Revolution*, 150–1, 180.

49. Zasloff, "Rural Resettlement," 328, 335, 337–8; Cooper, Corson, Legere, Lockwood, and Miller, *History of Pacification*, 133–5; David Halberstam, *The Making of a Quagmire: America and Vietnam during the Kennedy Era* (New York: Rowman and Littlefield, 2008), 179; Ngo Quang Truong, *Territorial Forces* (Washington: U.S.

Army Center of Military History, 1978), 5; U.S. Forces, Vietnam, "The Situation in Nam Bo," 11, 26; Truong Nhu Tang, *Viet Cong Memoir*, 62; Berman, *Perfect Spy*, 149; FRUS, Vietnam, 1958–1960, I, document 271. In addition to his sway within the South Vietnamese government, Thao influenced the opinions of the MSUG, RAND researchers, and journalists.

50. Zasloff, "Rural Resettlement," 330, 332, 334, 335, 336; Berman, *Perfect Spy*, 148–9; Truong Nhu Tang, *Vietcong Memoir*, 42–3, 47; FRUS, Vietnam, 1958–1960, I, document 201; Ngo Quang Truong, *Territorial Forces*, 6; Cooper, Corson, Legere, Lockwood, and Miller, *History of Pacification*, 133–5.

51. ORR, "Comparison of Economies,"14n, 42 see Table 13; Secretariat of State, "Land Reform Program,"12 see Table C; Dong Van Khuyen, *Logistics*, 6, 8; Elliott, *Vietnamese War*, 88.

52. Larsen, "Agricultural Economy of North Vietnam," v, 11, 14; Oliver Tessier, "Le « grand bouleversement » (long troi lo dat): regards croisés sur la réforme agraire en République démocratique du Việt Nam" *Ecole française d'Extrême-Orient* 95/96 (2008–2009), 85. Currey, *Victory at Any Cost*, 219; Fall, *Two Viet-Nams*, 154.

53. Tongas, *Communist Inferno*, 218.

54. Edwin Moise, "Land Reform Errors in North Vietnam," *Pacific Affairs*, 49, no. 1 (Spring 1976), 70–1, 72, 73; 85, Tessier, "The "Great Upheaval," 85, 86–7; Fall, *Two Viet-Nams*, 155, 159; Tongas, *Communist Inferno*, 222–3; Alex-Thai D. Vo. "Nguyen Thi Nam and the Land Reform of North Vietnam, 1953" *Journal of Vietnamese Studies* 10, no. 1 (Winter, 2015), 27–8, 44.

55. Tongas, *Communist Inferno*, 220.

56. Bui Tin, *Following Ho Chi Minh*, 24; Tessier, "The "Great Upheaval," 92; Tongas, *Communist Inferno*, 222; Alex-Thai D. Vo. "Nguyen Thi Nam and the Land Reform of North Vietnam, 1953," 36.

57. Bui Tin, *Following Ho Chi Minh*, 27; Tongas, *Communist Inferno*, 224; Moise, "Land Reform," 76; Fall, *Two Viet-Nams*, 156; Szalontai, "Political and Economic Crisis in North Vietnam," 399, 401; Alex-Thai D. Vo. "Nguyen Thi Nam and the Land Reform of North Vietnam, 1953," 18–9, 27.

58. Alex-Thai D. Vo. "Nguyen Thi Nam and the Land Reform of North Vietnam, 1953," 15, 32, 39.

59. Tongas, *Communist Inferno*, 225; Szalontai, "Political and Economic Crisis in North Vietnam," 399, 401.

60. Fall, *Two Viet-Nams*, 166.

61. Piero Gheddo, *The Cross and the Bo-Tree: Catholics and Buddhists in Vietnam* (New York: Sheed and Ward, 1970), 82.

62. Fall, *Two Viet-Nams*, 156, 157; Tongas, *Communist Inferno*, 219; Tucker, *Encyclopedia of the Vietnam War*, 12; Currey, *Victory at Any Cost*, 222–3; Guan, *Vietnamese Communists' Relations with China*, 35; Alex-Thai D. Vo. "Nguyen Thi Nam and the Land Reform of North Vietnam, 1953," 14.

63. Tongas, *Communist Inferno*, 225; Fall, *Two*

Viet-Nams, 157 see Table 4; Larsen, "Agricultural Economy of North Vietnam," v.

64. Caloric norms based on UK National Health Service figures. See: https://www.nhs.uk/common-health-questions/food-and-diet/what-should-my-daily-intake-of-calories-be/

65. Asselin, *Hanoi's Road*, 83, 98; Larsen, "Agricultural Economy of North Vietnam," vi, 35; Szalontai, "Political and Economic Crisis in North Vietnam,"405; Moise, "Land Reform," 74.

66. FRUS, Vietnam, 1958–1960, I, documents 47, 55, 66.

67. Currey, *Victory at Any Cost*, 223.

Chapter 6

1. Lansdale, *Midst* of Wars, 230; Department of the Army, *The Development and Training of the South Vietnamese Army 1950–1972* (Washington: U.S. Army Center of Military History, 1975), 8. In Vietnamese the armed forces official name was Quan luc Viet Nam Cong hoa (QLVNCH). ARVN was pronounced R-Vin.

2. Nguyen Ngoc Linh, ed. *The Armed Forces of the Republic of Viet Nam* (Saigon: Vietnam Council on Foreign Relations, 1970), 6; Laure Cournil and Pierre Journoud, "Une décolonisation manquée: l'Armée nationale du Vietnam, de la tutelle française à la tutelle américaine (1949–1965)" *Outre-mers*, tome 98, n°370–371, 1er semestre 2011. Le contact colonial dans l'empire français, XIXe–XXe siècles, 67, 68, 70–71; Cao Van Vien, *Leadership*, 10; Ivan Cadeau, "Les unités du génie de l'armée nationale vietnamienne (1951–1954): renfort appréciable ou affaiblissement du genie du corps expéditionnaire? *Revue historique des armées*, no 265 (2011), 2. FRUS, Vietnam, 1955–1957, I, document 123. The joint staff was known as the l'état-major interarmées et des forces terrestres (EMIFT).

3. Cournil and Journoud, "Failed Decolonization," 70; Rettig, "French military policies in the aftermath of the Yen Bay mutiny,"314; Lansdale, *Midst of Wars*, 229; Andrew Wiest, *Vietnam's Forgotten Army: Heroism and Betrayal in the ARVN* (New York: New York University Press, 2008), 21.

4. Lacouture, *Vietnam: Between Two Truces*, p. 116.

5. Phillips, *Why Vietnam Matters*, 20.

6. Cournil and Journoud, "Failed Decolonization," 69; Tran Van Don, *Our Endless War*, 42–3; Lam Quang Thi, *Twenty-Five Year Century*, 37; Lacouture, *Vietnam: Between Two Truces*, 116. The general's full name was Jean de Lattre de Tassigny. He was wounded five times and decorated for valor over a dozen times.

7. FRUS, Vietnam, 1955–1957, I, document 40; Spector, *Advice and Support*, 254.

8. Spector, *Advice and Support*, 228; FRUS, Vietnam, 1955–1957, I, documents 256, 286.

9. Lansdale, "Memorandum for the Record: 'Pacification' in Vietnam,'" 3; Lansdale, *Midst of Wars*, 229, 230–231; Lansdale, "Civic Activities of the Military, Southeast Asia," 5; Spector, *Advice and Support*, 242.

10. Cooper, Corson, Legere, Lockwood, and Miller, *History of Pacification*, 147; Spector, *Advice and Support*, 264, 268, 270; Ngo Quang Truong, *Territorial Force*, 24–5.

11. Ernst, *Fateful Alliance*, 78–9.

12. FRUS, Vietnam, 1955–1957, I, document 326.

13. Lloyd J. Matthews and Dale E. Brown, *Assessing the Vietnam War* (New York: Pergamon and Brassey's, 1987), 82; Spector, *Advice and Support*, 273; FRUS, Vietnam, 1955–1957, I, documents 285, 329.

14. Spector, *Advice and Support*, 131; Cournil and Journoud, "Failed Decolonization," 73; Dong Van Khuyen, *Logistics*, 24; FRUS, Vietnam, 1955–1957, I, documents 7, 12n5, 251; Hoang Ngoc Lung, *Strategy and Tactics*, 4; Cadeau, "engineer units," 3; Cao Van Vien, *Leadership*, 12, 24.

15. Cao Van Vien, *Leadership*, 10, 12, 23, 24, 25; Hoang Ngoc Lung, *Strategy and Tactics*, 14, 19; FRUS, Indochina, 1952–1954, XIII, Part 2, documents 843, 1145 and Vietnam, 1955–1957, I, documents 7, 277; Cao Van Vien et al, *The U.S. Advisor* (Washington: U.S. Army Center of Military History, 1980), 157.

16. Dong Van Khuyen, *Logistics*, 23; Cao Van Vien, *Leadership*, 23, 34; FRUS, Vietnam, 1955–1957, I, documents 123, 208, 215, 275, 375 and 1958–1960, I, documents 51, 258; Department of the Army, *Training of the South Vietnamese Army*, 12, 56; Stur, *Saigon at War*, 156–7. A limited draft by the French had been conducted during the War of Resistance. After 1968, the draft window expanded from ages 20–25 to 18–38.

17. Dong Van Khuyen, *Logistics*, 23; Ha Mai Viet, *Steel and Blood*, 274; Cao Van Vien, *Leadership*, 5, 11, 14. For English speakers, the RVN armed forces were referred to as the RVNAF and invariably confused with the RVN air force.

18. Spector, *Advice and Support*, 290, see Map 7; Ha Mai Viet, *Steel and Blood*, 279–80.

19. Cao Van Vien, *The U.S. Advisor*, 5; Cadeau, "engineer units," 3; Spector, *Advice and Support*, 278; Prados, *Vietnam: The Unwinnable War*, 64.

20. Spector, *Advise and Support*, 242, 264, 296; FRUS, Vietnam, 1955–1957, I, document 227; Lansdale, *Midst of Wars*, 229; Cao Van Vien, *U.S. Advisor*, 2. The first three divisions were numbered the 11th, 21st, and 31st. The field divisions were numbered 1st through 4th while the light division numbers ran from 11th to the 16th. I Corps controlled the 1st and 2nd Field Divisions, and II Corps directed the 3rd and 4th Field Divisions. In 1958, the 1st–4th Field Divisions were redesignated the 1st, 2nd, 5th and 7th Infantry Divisions respectively. The 11th and 13th Light Divisions were combined to form the 21st Infantry Division, the 12th and 14th light Divisions merged into the 22nd Infantry Divisions, while the 15th and 16th Light Divisions formed the 23rd Infantry Division.

21. FRUS, Vietnam, 1955–1957, I, document 123; Dong Van Khuyen, *RVNAF Logistics*, 32; Tran

Van Don, *Our Endless War*, 87; Ha Mai Viet, *Steel and Blood*, 278. The six GMs were: 11, 21, 31, 32, 34 and Nung. GM 34 under Ton That Dinh that became the 1st Field Division, GM 32 became the 2nd Field Division, GM Nung that became the 3rd Field Division. GM 31 became the 4th Field Division. GM 21 evolved into the 11th Light and later the 21st Infantry Division.

22. Ha Mai Viet, *Steel and Blood*, 277; Cao Van Vien, *Leadership*, 11; FRUS, Vietnam, 1955–1957, I, document 241; Spector, *Advice and Support*, 278; J. P. Harris, *Vietnam's High Ground: Armed Struggle for the Central Highlands, 1954–1965* (Lawrence KS: University Press of Kansas, 2016), 16.

23. Cadeau, "engineer units," 4, 7, 9.

24. Ha Mai Viet, *Steel and Blood*, 279. Spector, *Advice and Support*, 221, 264, 296, 297 Chart 3, 298, 299; Department of the Army, *Training the South Vietnamese Army*, 9; Ngo Quang Truong, *Territorial Force*, 25.

25. Ha Mai Viet, *Steel and Blood*, 282–5, 290–1; FRUS, Vietnam, 1958–1960, I, document 23; Ngo Quang Truong, *Territorial Force*, 25; Nguyen Ngoc Linh, *Armed Forces of Viet Nam*, 9. The armored regiments were numbered 1st–4th. General Williams eventually approved training the "special action" companies as "rangers" in 1960.

26. Nathalie Huynh Chau Nguyen, "South Vietnamese Women in Uniform: Narratives of Wartime and Post-War Lives," *Minerva Journal of Women and War*, 3, no. 2 (Fall 2009), 10–3, 16; Yves J. Melanson, "A Brief History of the Academies, Colleges, and Schools of the Central Training Command, RVNAF" (Saigon: MACV HQ Military History Branch, 1969) (TTU), 21; Heather Stur, "South Vietnam's 'Daredevil Girls,'" *New York Times*, 1 August 2017; (https://www.nytimes.com/2017/08/01/opinion/vietnam-war-girls-women.html).

27. Edward J. Marolda and Oscar Fitzgerald, *The United States Navy in the Vietnam Conflict: From Military Assistance to Combat, 1959–1965*, vol. 2 (Washington: Navy Historical Center, 1986), 135–6; Jack Shulimson, *The Marines in Vietnam, 1954–1973: An Anthology and Annotated Bibliography* (Washington: Headquarters, U.S. Marine Corps, 1985), 6, 7, 9; Thomas J. Cutler, *Brown Water, Black Berets: Coastal and Riverine Warfare in Vietnam* (Annapolis: Naval Institute Press, 1988), 23, 24, 53, 44; Nguyen Ngoc Linh, *Armed Forces of Viet Nam*, 8.

28. Robert F. Futrell, *The United States Air Force in Southeast Asia: The Advisory Years to 1965* (Washington: Office of Air Force History, 1981), 36, 49–50; Earl H. Tilford, Jr. *Crosswinds: The Air Force's Set Up in Vietnam* (College Station TX: Texas A & M University Press, 1993), 43; Carl Berger, ed. *The United States Air Force in Southeast Asia, 1961–1973; An Illustrated Account* (Washington: Office of Air Force History, 1984), 8.

29. Cao Van Vien, *Leadership*, 25; Shulimson, *The Marines in Vietnam*, 9; Department of the Army, *Training of the South Vietnamese Army*, 9, 13; Spector, *Advice and Support*, 299.

30. FRUS, Vietnam, 1958–1960, I, document 51. As a comparison, during the same time, the United States had nearly 1,100 generals and admirals commanding about 2.5 million active-duty service members.

31. Ha Mai Viet, *Steel and Blood*, 274; Cao Van Vien, *Leadership*, 12, 14; Indochina War Forum, "le Guerre en Indochine: Groupes Mobiles" http://laguerreenindochine.forumactif.org/t2762-groupes-mobiles.org; FRUS, Vietnam, 1955–1957, II, document 251; "Vietnam: A Television History; Interview with Lawton Collins."

32. Cournil and Journoud, "l'Armée nationale du Vietnam," 70, 72; Cadeau, "engineer units," 3; Department of the Army. *Training of the South Vietnamese Army*, 5; Dong Van Khuyen, *RVNAF Logistics*, 34; FRUS, Indochina, 1952–1954, XIII Part 2, document 1313.

33. Dong Van Khuyen, *RVNAF Logistics*, 32.

34. Hammer, *The Struggle for Indochina*, 130–31; Bui Diem with David Chanoff. *In the Jaws of History* (Bloomington IN: Indiana University Press, 1999), 43, 47; Lacouture, *Vietnam: Between Two Truces*, 124; Department of State, "Biographical Data on Lieutenant General Pham Xuan Chieu" (Washington: Department of State, 21 October 1974), 1–2 (https://www.archives.gov/files/declassification/iscap/pdf/2010-080-doc4.pdf); FRUS, Vietnam, 1955–1957, I, document 44.

35. Lam Quang Thi, *Twenty-Five Year Century*, 84, 87, 119–20, 127; Tran Van Don, *Our Endless War*, 59–60, 128–9; Cao Van Vien, *Leadership*, 59 also see note 8.

36. Spector, *Advise and Support*, 257; Bruce Palmer, Jr., *The 25-Year War: America's Military role in Vietnam* (Lexington KY: University of Kentucky Press, 2002), 37; Nguyen Ngoc Linh, *Armed Forces of Viet Nam*, 15.

37. Department of the Army. *Training of the South Vietnamese Army*, 1, 5; Cutler, *Brown Water, Black Berets*, 71; Spector, *Advise and Support*, 257–8, 259. The five countries were: France, Kingdom of Cambodia, Kingdom of Laos, State of Vietnam, and the United States.

38. Spector, *Advise and Support*, 259, 261; George S. Eckhardt, *Command and Control* (Washington: U.S. Army Center of Military History, 1991), 14–5 and see charts 1 (16) and 3 (18); Spector, *Advice and Support*, 261; Department of the Army, *Development and Training of the South Vietnamese Army*, 7; Ha Mai Viet, *Steel and Blood*, 286, 291, 304; Allen, *None So Blind*, 42.

39. Dong Van Khuyen, *RVNAF Logistics*, 34–5, 37.

40. Futrell, *The Advisory Years to 1965*, 49–50, 52; FRUS, Vietnam, 1958–1960, I, documents 22, 73; Pribbenow, *Victory in Vietnam*, 30;

41. Spector, *Advise and Support*, 262. The AD-4 was redesignated as the A-1 in 1962.

42. Cao Van Vien, *Leadership*, 10; Nguyen Ngoc Linh, *Armed Forces of Viet Nam*, 13; Bui Diem, *Jaws of History*, 77; Allen, *None So Blind*, 31–2; Karnow, "Interview with Edward Geary Lansdale, 1979, Part 1 of 5."

43. Collins, *Development and Training of the South Vietnamese Army*, pp. 14, 16, 132; Nguyen Ngoc Linh, *Armed Forces of Viet Nam*, p. 13; Lacouture, *Vietnam: Between Two Truces*, p. 116; Cournil and Journoud, "Failed Decolonization," 69; Lam Quang Thi, *Twenty-Five Year Century*, 30; Cao Van Vien, *Leadership*, 10; Nguyen Ngoc Linh, *Armed Forces of Viet Nam*, 13; Bui Diem, *Jaws of History*, 77; Melanson, "A Brief History of the Academies, Colleges, and Schools," 3.

44. Ha Mai Viet, *Steel and Blood*, 281; Lam Quang Thi, *Twenty-Five Year Century*, 46; Cao Van Vien, *Leadership*, 11.

45. Cao Van Vien, *Leadership*, 13.

46. Berger, *USAF in Southeast Asia, An Illustrated Account*, 9; Cao Van Vien, *U.S. Advisor*, 3, 199–200; Spector, *Advise and Support*, 221, 240; Ha Mai Viet, *Steel and Blood*, 29; Department of the Army, *Training the South Vietnamese Army*, 132, 141; Allen, *None So Blind*, 14–5. After disbandment, TRIM personnel joined the MAAG's Combat Arms Training and Organization (CATO) division. The armor school moved to Thu Duc in 1952.

47. Spector, *Advice and Support*, 241; Cao Van Vien, *Leadership*, 33–5; Ha Mai Viet, *Steel and Blood*, 289.

48. Cao Van Vien, *U.S. Advisor*, 157; Cao Van Vien, *Leadership*, 36, 37, 38; Lam Quang Thi, *Twenty-Five Year Century*, 85; Melanson, "A Brief History of the Academies, Colleges, and Schools," 8, 22.

49. Department of the Army, *Training the South Vietnamese Army*, 12, 131, 135, 140; Ha Mai Viet, *Steel and Blood*, 289; Cao Van Vien, *Leadership*, 33; Cao Van Vien, *Leadership*, 38; Melanson, "A Brief History of the Academies, Colleges, and Schools," 5–6, 12–3, 17. The VNA took over the French Army artillery school at Phu Hoa (north of Saigon) and moved it to Thu Duc in 1955.

50. Cao Van Vien, *Leadership*, 35; Department of the Army, *Training the South Vietnamese Army*, 13; FRUS, Vietnam, 1955–1957, I, document 325; Spector, *Advice and Support*, 231, 273.

51. Cao Van Vien, *Leadership*, 14.

52. Cao Van Vien, *Leadership*, 14.

53. Spector, *Advise and Support*, 286–7.

54. Pentagon Papers (Gravel Edition), II.4.a; FRUS, Vietnam, 1955–1957, I, documents 123, 208, 215, 375 and 1958–1960, I, document 55; Robert K. Brigham, *ARVN: Life and Death in the South Vietnamese Army* (Lawrence KS: University Press of Kansas, 2006), 30.

55. FRUS, Vietnam, 1955–1957, I, documents 271, 284; Hoang Ngoc Lung, *Strategy and Tactics*, 19; Department of the Army, *Training of the South Vietnamese Army*, 9, 10; Michigan State University Group, "Summary of MSU Police Administration Program, 16 May 1960," (Saigon: Michigan State University Vietnam Technical Assistance Program, 1960), 3; Ngo Quang Truong, *Territorial Forces*, 30.

56. FRUS, Vietnam, 1955–1957, I, documents 271, 284; Hoang Ngoc Lung, *Strategy and Tactics*, 19; Department of the Army, *Training of the South Vietnamese Army*, 9, 10; Michigan State University Group, "Summary of MSU Police Administration Program, 16 May 1960," (Saigon: Michigan State University Vietnam Technical Assistance Program, 1960), 3; Ngo Quang Truong, *Territorial Forces*, 30.

57. Lansdale, *Midst of Wars*, 327.

58. Ernst, *Forging a Fateful Alliance*, 12–3; Lansdale, *Midst of Wars*, 209; MSUG, "Summary of MSU Police Administration Program,"1; FRUS, Vietnam, 1955–1957, I, document 251; Ngo Quang Truong, *Territorial Forces*, 31.

59. Cooper, Corson, Legere, Lockwood, and Miller, *History of Pacification*, 118.

60. FRUS, Vietnam, 1955–1957, I, documents 276, 280, 393. During the early years, the SDC was referred to variously as popular forces, village guards, and auto-defense units.

61. FRUS, Vietnam, 1955–1957, I, document 410.

62. FRUS, Vietnam, 1955–1957, I, document 280 and Vietnam, 1958–1960, I, documents 30, 32, 33, 47; Ngo Quang Truong, *Territorial Force*, 30; Spector, *Advice and Support*, 320; U.S. Forces, Vietnam, "The Situation in Nam Bo," 11.

63. Ngo Quang Truong, *Territorial Forces*, 5; Cao Van Vien, *Leadership*, 8, 27; Hoang Ngoc Lung, *Strategy and Tactics*, 16, 19; Spector, *Advice and Support*, 264 (see Table 1), 271–2, 296; Allen, *None So Blind*, 31.

64. Ernst, *Fateful Alliance*, 78; FRUS, Vietnam, 1955–1957, I, document 280; Howard W. Hoyt, "Report on the Proposed Organization of the Law Enforcement Agencies of the Republic of Viet-Nam, April 1956," (Saigon: Michigan State University Police Advisory Staff, 1956), 12.

65. Ernst, *Fateful Alliance*, 64–5, 69; FRUS, Vietnam, 1955–1957, I, document 315 and Vietnam, 1958–1960, I, document 30; Phillips, *Why Vietnam Matters*, 87–8.

66. Howard W. Hoyt, "Civil Police Administrative Program Semi-Annual Report, 1 July 1957–31 December 1957," (Saigon: Michigan State University Vietnam Technical Assistance Program, 1957), 3.

67. FRUS, Vietnam, 1955–1957, I, documents 360, 365, 399, 400.

68. Ernst, *Fateful Alliance*, 65; U.S. Forces, Vietnam, "The Situation in Nam Bo," 13.

69. FRUS, Vietnam, 1958–1960, I, documents 30, 50; Elliott, *The Vietnamese War*, 107; Spector, *Advice and Support*, 322.

70. FRUS, Vietnam, 1958–1960, I, document 47.

71. FRUS, Vietnam, 1958–1960, I, document 50.

72. FRUS, Vietnam, 1958–1960, I, documents 47, 52; Ernst, *Fateful Alliance*, p. 79; Ngo Quang Truong, *Territorial Forces*, p. 31; Phillips, *Why Vietnam Matters*, 101.

73. Allen, *None So Blind*, 118.

74. FRUS, Vietnam, 1958–1960, I, document 49.

Chapter 7

1. Pike, *PAVN*, 15, 16, 22, 26–7; Currey, *Victory at Any Cost*, 54–5.

2. Currey, *Victory at Any Cost*, 68, 69, 71–3, 80, 82, 91–2, 138.

3. David M. Toczak, *The Battle of Ap Bac: They Did Everything but Learn From It* (Annapolis MD: Naval Institute Press, 2001), 54; Combined Intelligence Center, Vietnam (CICV), "Para-Military Forces in North Vietnam, MACVI 31-2," (Saigon: MACV, 27 July 1972), (TTU), 1; Pike, *PAVN*, 39; Prebbenow, *Victory in Vietnam*, 9; Currey, *Victory At Any Cost*, 213.

4. Giap, *People's War*, 57; Prebbenow, *Victory in Vietnam*, 9, 22; FRUS, Vietnam, 1955–1957, I, document 333. The plan was anachronistically enacted in March 1957.

5. Currey, *Victory at Any Cost*, 157; Pike, *PAVN*, 39.

6. Combined Intelligence Center Vietnam (CICV), "Military Training, in North Vietnam," (Saigon: MACV, 1968), (TTU), 2; Prebbenow, *Victory in Vietnam*, 11.

7. Prebbenow, *Victory in Vietnam*, 10, 29; Pike, *PAVN*, 17–8; Konrad Keller, "Conversations with Enemy Soldiers in late 1968/early 1969: A Study in Motivation and Morale" (Santa Monica CA: RAND, 1970), 34–6.

8. Prebbenow, *Victory in Vietnam*, 11, 12, 28, 29, 41; Ha Mai Viet, *Steel and Blood*, 308; FBIS, *Anti-U.S. Resistance War*, 35–6.

9. Prebbenow, *Victory in Vietnam*, 28, 29, 30, 31; Tucker, *Encyclopedia of the Vietnam War*, 1713–4. It was not until May 1963 that the air force added its first fighter unit, the 921st Fighter Regiment; it was joined by the 923rd Fighter Regiment on 7 December 1965.

10. Prebbenow, *Victory in Vietnam*, 31.

11. Giap, *People's War*, 70, 72; CICV, "Para-Military Forces in North Vietnam," 1; Prebbenow, *Victory in Vietnam*, 38.

12. CICV, "Para-Military Forces in North Vietnam," 2; Prebbenow, *Victory in Vietnam*, 38.

13. FBIS, *Anti-U.S. War*, 40.

14. CICV, "Para-Military Forces in North Vietnam, 1; François Guillemot, "Death and Suffering at First Hand: Youth Shock Brigades during the Vietnam War (1950–1975)" *Journal of Vietnamese Studies*, 4, no. 3 (Fall 2009), 18, 20, 21, 22, 25.

15. Pike, *PAVN*, 183; Prebbenow, *Victory in Vietnam*, 10. The CMPC previously had been known as the General Military Party Committee.

16. Charles R. Shrader, *War of Logistics: Parachutes and Porters in Indochina, 1945–1954* (Lexington KY: University Press of Kentucky, 2015), 41; Pike, *PAVN*, 33–34, 95; Prebbenow, *Victory in Vietnam*, 10, 31, 39–40.

17. Pike, *PAVN*, 193 and see Appendix C: Biographies of Senior Generals; Tucker, *Encyclopedia of the Vietnam War*, 1712.

18. Prebbenow, *Victory in Vietnam*, 33; Pike, *PAVN*, 185–6. The collapse of the PAVN pro–Chinese faction, a consequential event, did not occur until Mao's Cultural Revolution wracked China in the mid 1960s.

19. Lanning and Cragg, *Inside the VC*, 94; Michael Mau, "The Training of Political Cadres in the Lao Dong Party of North Vietnam (1960–1967)," *Asian Survey*, 9, no. 4 (April 1969), 284; Konrad Kellen, "A Profile of the PAVN Soldier in South Vietnam" (Santa Monica CA: RAND, 1966), 38; Konrad Keller, "Conversations with Enemy Soldiers in late 1968/early 1969: A Study in Motivation and Morale" (Santa Monica CA: RAND, 1970), 21; Pike, *PAVN*, 151.

20. Shrader, *War of Logistics*, 159–61, 165, 170; Zhai, "Chinese Military Advisers," 709–10; Allen, *None So Blind*, 50–1.

21. Zhai, "Chinese Military Advisers," 715; Shrader, *War of Logistics*, 128–129, 168, 169. See Table 8.1; Prebbenow, *Victory in Vietnam*, 9–10. The trucks were either of Soviet manufacture or repaired, captured American vehicles.

22. CICV, "Review of NVA Armor and Tactics, MACVI 31-2" (Saigon, MACV, 8 November 1972) (TTU), 1; Prebbenow, *Victory in Vietnam*, 29–30; Tucker, *Encyclopedia of the Vietnam War*, 1713–4; Shrader, *War of Logistics*, 160, 165, 170; Office of Research and Reports, *The Effectiveness of the Air Campaign Against North Vietnam, 1 January–30 September 1966*, (Washington: CIA, 1966), Table D6 "Soviet Military Aid to North Vietnam" (CIA Library). By 1964, the Soviets had sent the DRV 236 artillery pieces (roughly equal to total ARVN artillery in 1959), over 700 AA guns, an additional 60 tanks/self-propelled guns, and 36 aircraft.

23. Noble B. Wonsetler, *The Transformation of the People's Army of Vietnam, 1954–1975* (Fort Leavenworth, KS: U.S. Army Command and Staff College, 2016), 3.; Prebbenow, *Victory in Vietnam*, 9, 29. The Soviets adopted the SKS in 1949.

24. CICV, "Military Training," 1; United States Air Force, "Weekly Air Intelligence Summary (86–32, 10 August 1968)," (TTU), 3–4; Qiang Zhai, "Transplanting the Chinese Model: Chinese Military Advisers and the First Vietnam War, 1950–1954," *The Journal of Military History*, 57, no. 4 (October 1993), 698–9; Guan, *Vietnamese Communists' Relations with China*, 13. The Chinese set up PAVN training bases in Guangxi and Yunnan provinces.

25. CICV, "Military Training,"1; USAF, "Weekly Air Intelligence Summary (86–32, 10 August 1968)," 4; Lanning and Cragg, *Inside the VC and the NVA*, 42; Moore and Galloway, *We Were Soldiers*, 50; Keller, "Profile of the PAVN Soldier,"22.

26. Pike, *PAVN*, 187–8, 192; USAF, "Weekly Air Intelligence Summary (86–32, 10 August 1968)," 41; Keller, "Profile of the PAVN Soldier," 38, 58; CICV, "Military Training,"1; Lanning and Cragg, *Inside the VC and the NVA*, 43; CIA, "SNIE 14.3-67: Capabilities of the Vietnamese Communists for Fighting in South Vietnam, 13 November 1967" (Washington: CIA, 1967), 6.

27. Moore and Galloway, *We Were Soldiers*, 50; Combined Military Interrogation Center, Vietnam (CMICV), "OB [Order of Battle] of SR-1," (Saigon: MACV, 6 April 1970), 2; Pike, *PAVN*, 355; USAF, "Weekly Air Intelligence Summary (86–32, 10 August 1968),"4; Lanning and Cragg, *Inside the VC and the NVA*, 43; CIA, SNIE 14.3-67, 6; CICV, "Review of NVA Armor and Tactics," 1.

28. Keller, "Profile of the PAVN Soldier," 17, 39; Lanning and Cragg, *Inside the VC and the NVA*, 95; Mau, "Training of Political Cadres," 282.

29. Prebbenow, *Victory in Vietnam*, 26; Mau, "Training of Political Cadres," 284, 294–5; Keller, "Conversations with Enemy Soldiers," 23–4, 29, 31; Pike, *PAVN*, 155; Lanning and Cragg, *Inside the VC and the NVA*, 99; Keller, "Conversations with Enemy Soldiers," 21.

30. Combined Document Exploitation Center, Vietnam (CDECV), "A Party Account of the Situation in the Nam Bo Region of South Vietnam, 1954–1960," (TTU), 13.

31. Prebbenow, *Victory in Vietnam*, 29, 94.

32. Prebbenow, *Victory in Vietnam*, 38.

33. Shrader, *War of Logistics*, 95–6, see Map 5.1.

34. Ahern, *Vietnam Declassified*, 7.

35. Ernst, *Forging a Fateful Alliance*, 12–4; Lansdale, *Midst of Wars*, 209, 233; MSUG, "Summary of MSU Police Administration Program,"1; FRUS, Vietnam, 1955–1957, I, documents 32n4, 252; Lansdale, "Civic Activities,"5; Lansdale, "'Pacification' in Vietnam,"12.

36. Ahern, *Vietnam Declassified*, 12, 14, 15–6, 19; Spector, *Advice and Support*, 242–3; Lansdale, *Midst of Wars*, 229, 238–9; Lansdale, "Civic Activities," 5, 6; Lansdale, "'Pacification' in Vietnam," 5, 10; Bui Diem, *Jaws of History*, 77, 100; Phillips, *Why Vietnam Matters*, 40, 41, 53–5, 70.

37. Bringham, *Guerrilla Diplomacy*, 5; CDECV, "The Situation in Nam Bo," 29–30.

38. Ahern, *Vietnam Declassified*, 21–22; CDECV, "The Situation in Nam Bo," 21, 30; Lansdale, *Midst of Wars*, 237–8; Phillips, *Why Vietnam Matters*, 43.

39. Finlayson, *Rice Paddy Recon*, 154.

40. Lansdale, *Midst of Wars*, 208, 237–8; Lansdale, "Civic Activities," 6–7; Lansdale, "'Pacification' in Vietnam," 2; FRUS, Vietnam, 1955–1957, I, document 272; Neese and O'Donnell, *Prelude to Tragedy*, 20–1, 22; Ahern, *Vietnam Declassified*, 18, 27; Colby, *Lost Victory*, 62; Phillips, *Why Vietnam Matters*, 76–7 Stewart, *Vietnam's Lost Revolution*, 57, 59.

41. Stewart, *Vietnam's Lost Revolution*, 30, 32, 39, 41, 54, 58–9, 91; Lansdale, *Midst of Wars*, 208, 237–8; Lansdale, "Civic Activities," 6–7; Lansdale, "Pacification in Vietnam," 2; FRUS, Vietnam, 1955–1957, I, document 272;

42. Lansdale, *Midst of Wars*, 237–8; Lansdale, "'Pacification' in Vietnam," 2; FRUS, Vietnam, 1955–1957, I, document 272 and 1961–1963, II, document 328; Phillips, *Why Vietnam Matters*, 92; Finlayson, *Rice Paddy Recon:*, 150.

43. Stewart, *Vietnam's Lost Revolution*, 27, 29, 68–9, 72.

44. FRUS, Vietnam, 1955–1957, I, document 242; Ha Mai Viet, *Steel and Blood*, 291; Phillips, *Why Vietnam Matters*, 112.

45. Stewart, *Vietnam's Lost Revolution*, 56, 78–9, 80, 83, 104.

46. FRUS, Vietnam, 1955–1957, I, documents 290, 296, 301, 339 (NIE 63–56); FBIS, *Anti-U.S. War*, 22; Ha Mai Viet, *Steel and Blood*, 291; CDECV, "The Situation in Nam Bo," 8; Stewart, *Vietnam's Lost Revolution*, 81–2, 84.

47. Moyar, *Triumph Forsaken*, 79; FRUS, Vietnam, 1955–1957, I, documents 301, 372; CDECV, "The Situation in Nam Bo," 9–10, 31; Ha Mai Viet, *Steel and Blood*, 291; FBIS, *Anti-U.S. War*, 22; Guan, *Vietnamese Communists' Relations with China*, 71;

48. Ahern, *Vietnam Declassified*, 27–28; Miller, *Misalliance*, 132; Ha Mai Viet, *Steel and Blood*, 291; FRUS, Vietnam, 1955–1957, I, document 346.

49. WGBH, "Vietnam: A Television History; Interview with Tran Van Don," 7 May 1981 (WGBH Media Library & Archives); Moyar, *Triumph Forsaken*, 79; FRUS, Vietnam, 1955–1957, I, documents 301, 372; CDECV, "The Situation in Nam Bo," 9–10, 31; Ha Mai Viet, *Steel and Blood*, 291; FBIS, *Anti-U.S. War*, 22; Guan, *Vietnamese Communists' Relations with China*, 71; Stewart, *Vietnam's Lost Revolution*, 109.

50. CDECV, "The Situation in Nam Bo," 11.

51. CDECV, "The Situation in Nam Bo," 10–2, 16; Guan, *Vietnamese Communists' Relations with China*, 98–9, 104.

52. FRUS, Vietnam, 1958–1960, I, documents 72, 76; Neese and O'Donnell, *Prelude to Tragedy*, 247.

Chapter 8

1. Diem, *Major Policy Speeches*, 11; FRUS, 1955–1957, Vietnam, I, document 398 and 1964–1968, Vietnam, I, document 392. To Americans who served, they routinely were designated by the alphanumerical communications code "Victor Charlie" that became "Charlie."

2. Tourison, *Talking with Victor Charlie*, 85.

3. Johnson, *The Meaning of Vietnam*, 10.

4. Chen, "Hanoi's Three Decisions," 249–50; Lien-Hang T. Nguyen, *Hanoi's War*, 52; Truong Nhu Tang, *Viet Cong Memoir*, 58, 71; Lien-Hang T. Nguyen, *Hanoi's War*, 47; Lacouture, *Vietnam: Between Two Truces*, 56.

5. Lien-Hang T. Nguyen, *Hanoi's War*, 52; Truong Nhu Tang, *Viet Cong Memoir*, 56, 66, 69; Asselin, *Hanoi's Road*, 54, 88; Bui Tin, *From Enemy to Friend*, 11; Bringham, *Guerrilla Diplomacy*, 11, 16.

6. Truong Nhu Tang, *Viet Cong Memoir*, 72.

7. Asselin, *Hanoi's Road*, 54–5; Department of State, *A Threat to the Peace*, 97.

8. Heather Marie Stur, *Saigon at War: South Vietnam and the Global Sixties* (New York: Cambridge University Press, 2020), 57–8.

9. FBIS, *Anti-US Resistance War*, 51.

10. Bringham, *Guerrilla Diplomacy*, 61; Asselin, *Hanoi's Road*, 89; Hunt, *A Vietnam War Reader*, 75.

11. Vu. *Vietnam's Communist Revolution*, 123–4, 143–4.

12. Guan, *Vietnamese Communists' Relations with China*, 100, 107, 109–10, 123, 128; Geoffrey C. Stewart, *Vietnam's Lost Revolution: Ngo Dinh*

Diem's Failure to Build an Independent Nation, 1955-1953 (New York: Cambridge University Press, 2017), 48.

13. Bringham, *Guerrilla Diplomacy*, 18; FBIS, *Anti-US Resistance War*, 51; Truong Nhu Tang, *Viet Cong Memoir*, 269.

14. Bringham, *Guerrilla Diplomacy*, 63.

15. Henry Kamm, "How's Vietnam Doing? Doctor Expresses Disgust," *New York Times*, 6 May 1993; Sandra C. Taylor, *Vietnamese Women at War: Fighting for Ho Chi Minh and the Revolution* (Lawrence KS: University Press of Kansas, 1999), 128.

16. Bringham, *Guerrilla Diplomacy*, 129.

17. Truong Nhu Tang, *Viet Cong Memoir*, 147, 218, 269. The "breathtaking pretense" was later extended to the NLF's Provisional Revolutionary Government when it was established in June 1969.

18. Bringham, *Guerrilla Diplomacy*, 128.

19. Mary E. Anderson, Michael E. Arnsten and Harvey A. Averch, *Insurgent Organization and Operations: A Case Study of the Viet Cong in the Delta, 1964-1966* (Santa Barbara CA: RAND, 1967), 18; Pike *Viet Cong*, 136.

20. Department of State, *A Threat to the Peace*, 95; Elliott, *Vietnamese War*, 158; Ben Kiernan, *How Pol Pot Came to Power: Colonialism, Nationalism, and Communism in Cambodia, 1930-1975* (New Haven CT: Yale University Press, 2004), 80. In 1976, the PRP went away, and the majority of its members were accepted into the VWP.

21. Finlayson, *Rice Paddy Recon*, 153.

22. Taylor, *Vietnamese Women at War*, 11, 24, 29, 43, 59, 67, 96, 112-3, 127; Riggs Osborn, "War, Women, Vietnam," 161-2; Tucker, *Encyclopedia of the Vietnam War*, 835; Hunt, *Vietnam's Southern Revolution*, 93, 95.

23. Elliott, *Vietnamese War*, 133, 138; Truong Nhu Tang, *Viet Cong Memoir*, 147n; FBIS, *Anti-U.S. Resistance War*, 50; Bui Tin, *From Enemy to Friend*, 45; Orrin DeForest and David Chanoff, *Slow Burn: The Rise and Bitter Fall of American Intelligence in Vietnam* (New York: Simon and Schuster, 1990), 102, 121.

24. Elliott, *Vietnamese War*, 133; Burton, *North Vietnam's Military Logistics System: Its contribution to the War, 1961-1969*. Fort Leavenworth, Master's Thesis. U.S. Army Command and General Staff College, 1977, 56; George A. Martinez, ed., *The Viet Cong Proselytizing Program in the Saigon-Gia Dinh Special Zone* (McClean VA: Research Analysis Corporation, 1968), 9.

25. CIA, "Working Paper on The Central Office for South Vietnam (COSVN): Its History, Organization and Functions" (Washington: CIA, 1969), 6; Lien-Hang T. Nguyen, *Hanoi's War*, 24-6, 53; Truong Nhu Tang, *Viet Cong Memoir*, 82-83. Three senior North Vietnamese leaders served as secretary during the war. General Ngyuen Chi Thanh replaced Nguyen Van Linh in October 1964 and remained its chief until he unexpectedly died on 7 June 1967. Pham Hung, who had also been a VWP leader in the south during the 1946-1954 War, replaced General Thanh. Hung also assumed military commissar duties and remained secretary through the victory in 1975.

26. Wilkins, *Grab Their Belts to Fight Them*, 52.

27. Lien-Hang T. Nguyen, *Hanoi's War*, 51-3, 71; Bringham, *Guerrilla Diplomacy*, 7, 131; Elliott, *Vietnamese War*, 92-3; Asselin, *Hanoi's Road*, 71; Hunt, *Vietnam's Southern Revolution*, 30-1.

28. Elliott, *Vietnamese War*, 139.

29. Elliott, *Vietnamese War*, 145; DeForest and Chanoff, *Slow Burn*, 224-5; Hunt, *Vietnam's Southern Revolution*, 78-9; Finlayson, *Rice Paddy Recon*, 150, 160.

30. David F. Gordon, ed., *Estimative Products on Vietnam, 1948-1975* (Washington: National Intelligence Council, 2005), 176.

31. Gordon, ed., *Estimative Products*, 177.

32. Currey, *Victory at any Cost*, 239; Tourison, *Talking with Victor Charlie*, 28-9.

33. Lien-Hang T. Nguyen, *Hanoi's War*, 54; Guan, *Vietnamese Communists' Relations with China*, 180.

34. Bui Tin, *From Enemy to Friend*, 15; Robert J. Hanyok, *Spartans in Darkness: American SIGINT and the Indochina War, 1945-1975* (Washington: National Security Agency, 2002), 89, 111, 146-7.

35. Pribbenow, *Victory in Vietnam*, 89; Truong Nhu Tang, *Viet Cong Memoir*, 264-5; Hunt, *Vietnam's Southern Revolution*, 111.

36. Pribbenow, *Victory in Vietnam*, 84-5, 128; Elliott, *Vietnamese War*, 163. Later, South Vietnam was divided into five "B" Fronts, with the Central Highlands becoming the B-3 Front in late 1965 and the rest redesignated in 1966.

37. Elliott, *Vietnamese War*, 191, 215.

38. Martinez, *Viet Cong Proselyting*, 2, 7; John C. Donnell, *Viet Cong Recruitment: Why and How Men Join* (Santa Monica CA: RAND Corporation, 1967), 25, 92, 95, 109-10, 151; Pike *Viet Cong*, 127; DeForest and Chanoff, *Slow Burn*, 102; Lanning and Cragg, *Inside the VC and the NVA*, 187; Hunt, *Vietnam's Southern Revolution*, 116.

39. Elliott, *Vietnamese War*, 105, 207; Martinez, *Viet Cong Proselyting*, 23.

40. Pike *Viet Cong*, 104; FRUS, Vietnam, 1958-1960, I, documents 112, 185 (Special National Intelligence Estimate (SNIE) 63.1-60). The years 1958 and 1959 saw an annual average of over 270 assassinations; in 1960 there were approximately 1,300.

41. Elliott, *Vietnamese War*, 112; FBIS, *Anti-U.S. Resistance War*, 23; Donnell, *Viet Cong Recruitment*, 2; Malcolm W. Browne, *The New Face of War* (Indianapolis: Bobbs-Merrill, 1965), 103; Lanning and Cragg, *Inside the VC and the NVA*, 188; FRUS, Vietnam, 1958-1960, I, document 27; Max Hastings, *Vietnam*, 122, 238; John Prados, *The Blood Road: The Ho Chi Minh Trail and the Vietnam War* (New York: Wiley, 1998), 21; Ahern, *Vietnam Declassified*, 114; Anderson, Arnsten and Averch, *Insurgent Organization and Operations*, xii; Robert Granier Ker Thompson, *Defeating Communist Insurgency: Experiences from Malaya and Vietnam* (New York: McMillan Press, 1966), 25;

Phillips, *Why Vietnam Matters*, 115; Hunt, *Vietnam's Southern Revolution*, 50–1, 53–4.

42. Donnell, *Viet Cong Recruitment*, 7–8, 10, 12, 154; Lanning and Cragg, *Inside the VC and the NVA*, 52; Hunt, *Vietnam's Southern Revolution*, 47; Finlayson, *Rice Paddy Recon*, 153.

43. Elliott, *Vietnamese War*, 172, 197; Donnell, *Viet Cong Recruitment*, 8–9.

44. Pribbenow, *Victory in Vietnam*, 146; Sam Adams, *War of Numbers: An Intelligence Memoir* (South Royalton VT: Steerforth Press, 1994), 55, 66.

45. Martinez, *Viet Cong Proselyting*, 26; DeForest and Chanoff, *Slow Burn*, 99; Donnell, *Viet Cong Recruitment*, 79; Taylor, *Vietnamese Women at War*, 76; Elliott, *Vietnamese War*, 101–2.

46. Donnell, *Viet Cong Recruitment*, 75, 79; DeForest and Chanoff, *Slow Burn*, 99, 174; Martinez, "Proselyting," 24, 26; Elliott, *Vietnamese War*, 101–2.

47. Department of State, *A Threat to Peace*, I, 8, 91; Finlayson, *Rice Paddy Recon*, 158.

48. Lanning and Cragg, *Inside the VC and the NVA*, 53; Anderson, Arnsten and Averch, *Insurgent Organization and Operations*, 15–16; Adams, *War of Numbers*, 55; Pribbenow, *Victory in Vietnam*, 67.

49. Department of State, *Threat to the Peace*, I, 32.

50. Gordon, *Estimative Products*, 190; Donnell, *Viet Cong Recruitment*, 10, 12, 144, 154; Lanning and Cragg, *Inside the VC and the NVA*, 54; Adams, *War of Numbers*, 58.

51. FBIS, *Anti-U.S. Resistance War*, 45–6; Tom Mangold and John Penycate, *The Tunnels of Cu Chi* (New York: Ballantine Book, 1985), 50; Department of State, *Threat to the Peace*, I, 91, 101–2.

52. Elliott, *Vietnamese War*, 176–7, 179; Lanning and Cragg, *Inside the VC and the NVA*, 42, 44, 56; Prados, *The Blood Road*, 28; Trung Nhu Tang, *Viet Cong Memoir*, 117.

53. Lanning and Cragg, *Inside the VC and the NVA*, 42, 44, 54, 55, 57.

54. Lehrack, *First Battle*, 51–2; Pribbenow, *Victory in Vietnam*, 95, 157; David W.P. Elliott and Mai Elliot, *Documents of an Elite Viet Cong Unit: The Demolition Platoon of the 514th Battalion, Part Four: Political Indoctrination and Military Training* (Santa Monica CA: RAND Corporation, 1969), 75–6; Lanning and Cragg, *Inside the VC and the NVA*, 44.

55. Anderson, Arnsten and Averch, *Insurgent Organization and Operations*, 11; Hoang Ngoc Lung, *Intelligence* (Washington: U.S. Army Center of Military History, 1982), 204; DeForest and Chanoff, *Slow Burn*, 134. To allay some confusion, the VC used the word reconnaissance (trinh sat) for both its traditional meaning and as the Western equivalent of military intelligence.

56. Hoang Ngoc Lung, *Intelligence*, 205, 208, 209; Tourison, *Talking with Victory Charlie*, 79–80.

57. U.S. Marine Corps, *Professional Knowledge Gained from Operational Experience in Vietnam, 1965–1966*, NAVMC 2614 (Washington: Government Printing Office, 1967), 214; Hoang Ngoc

Lung, *Intelligence*, 210, 212; Roger P. Fox, *Air Base Defense in the Republic of Vietnam, 1961–1973* (Washington: United States Air Force Office of Air Force History, 1979), 33.

58. Merle L. Pribbenow, "The Sino-Soviet Intelligence Relationship during the Vietnam War: Cooperation and Conflict," *Cold War International History Project*, Working Paper no. 73 (Washington: Woodrow Wilson International Center for Scholars, 2014), 4, 6–7, 12.

59. Halberstam, *Quagmire*, 83; John D. Bergen, *Military Communications: A Test for Technology* (Washington: Center for Military History, 1985), 202, 404; Headquarters, MACV, "Vietnam Lessons Learned No. 79: Enemy Exploitation of Allied Tactical Communications," 8 March 1970 (TTU); 1–2; Hoang Ngoc Lung, *Intelligence*, 205; Marine Corps, *Professional Knowledge*, 214–5, 217; Finlayson, *Rice Paddy Recon*, 34.

60. Asselin, *Hanoi's Road*, 85; Thomas A. Bass, "The Spy Who Loved Us," *The New Yorker* 23 May 2005 (https://www.newyorker.com/magazine/2005/05/23/the-spy-who-loved-us); Lanning and Cragg, *Inside the VC and the NVA*, 43; Anderson, Arnsten and Averch, *Insurgent Organization and Operations*, 20; Hoang Ngoc Lung. *Intelligence*, 201. Lavrentiy Beria was the dreaded head of the Soviet secret police who oversaw the murder of hundreds of thousands during Stalin's purges.

61. Asselin, *Hanoi's Road*, 85; Bass, "The Spy Who Loved Us"; Lanning and Cragg, *Inside the VC and the NVA*, 43; Anderson, Arnsten and Averch, *Insurgent Organization and Operations*, 20; Hoang Ngoc Lung. *Intelligence*, 201.

62. Adams, *War of Numbers*, 98; Mangold and Penycate, *Tunnels of Cu Chi*, 1; Donnell, *Viet Cong Recruitment*, 90.

63. Pribbenow, "The Sino-Soviet Intelligence Relationship during the Vietnam War," 2, 3, 9; Gilbert, *Why the North Won*, 139; Hoang Ngoc Lung, *Intelligence*, 197; CIA, "Central Office for South Vietnam," 24–5; Tuan Hoang, "Ideology in Urban South Vietnam," 86. The COSVN Security Agency was also referred to as the Security Section.

64. Pribbenow, "The Sino-Soviet Intelligence Relationship during the Vietnam War," 3; Pentagon Papers (Gravel Edition), I, document 95.

65. Adams, *War of Numbers*, 98; Lanning and Cragg, *Inside the VC and the NVA*, 187; DeForest and Chanoff, *Slow Burn*, 123, 131. MIS was also known as the Military Intelligence Agency. During the war, General Dao went south to head military intelligence operations in Nam Bo, Cambodia, and the Saigon-Gai Dinh Special Zone. While en route to a COSVN meeting on 24 December 1969, his party was ambushed south of Saigon, and he was killed. Between 1965 and 1972, there were 33,000 assassinations/murders and 58,000 kidnappings.

66. Finlayson, *Rice Paddy Recon*, 37, 77–8, 108, 156–7, 186.

67. Gordon, *Estimative Products on Vietnam*, 191.

68. DeForest and Chanoff, *Slow Burn*, 141; Merle L. Pribbenow, "The Man in the White Cell," (CIA Library); John Prados, *The Hidden History of the Vietnam War* (Chicago: Ivan R. Dee, 1995), 155.

69. Berman, *Perfect Spy*, 131; CMIC, "OB of SR-1," 4; Gilbert, *Why the North Won*, 140. Later in the war, H Section became part of COSVN B-22 Section; human intelligence sections also were referred to as H-2 and Y-16.

70. PAVN, "The Perfect Service in Prison," *People's Army Newspaper*, Spring 2009.

71. FRUS, Vietnam, 1955–1957, I, documents 172, 173n2; Terrance Smith, "Infiltration of Saigon Regime by Communists Is Described as Trial Opens," *New York Times*, 29 November 1969; Hoang Ngoc Lung, *Intelligence*, 217.

72. Truong Nhu Tang, *Vietcong Memoir*, 42–3, 47, 49; Colby, *Lost Victory*, 92–3; Cooper, Corson, Legere, Lockwood, and Miller, *History of Pacification*, 133–5.

73. FRUS, Vietnam, 1961–1963, IV, documents 22, 196, 210, 314; FRUS, Vietnam, 1964–1968, I, documents no. 336, 360 and Vietnam, 1964–1968, II, Persons, 79; Berman, *Perfect Spy*, 127–8, 147–9.

74. Halberstam, *Quagmire*, 141; Berman, *Perfect Spy*, 131, 135, 137, 143, 144, 151; Kelly, "Edward Lansdale and the Saigon Military Mission," 26.

75. DeForest and Chanoff, *Slow Burn*, 140, 141; Berman, *Perfect Spy*, 42, 123, 126, 131; Lanning and Cragg, *Inside the VC and the NVA*, 60–1. Later in the war, the demolition training moved to Cambodia.

76. Adams, *War of Numbers*, 131; George A. Martinez, ed., *Viet Cong Proselyting*, 29; DeForest and Chanoff, *Slow Burn*, 95.

77. Ernst, *Fateful Alliance*, 70, 72; Nguyen Ngoc Linh, *Armed Forces of Viet Nam*, 10; Adams, *War of Numbers*, 119–20.

Chapter 9

1. Douglas Pike, *Viet Cong; The Organization and Techniques of the National Liberation Front of South Vietnam* (Cambridge: The M.I.T. Press, 1966), 83; Moyar, *Triumph Forsaken*, 88–9; Elliott, *Vietnamese War*, 166.

2. Pike, *Viet Cong*, 83; Moyar, *Triumph Forsaken*, 88–9; Elliott, *Vietnamese War*, 166.

3. Fall, *Two Viet-Nams*, 291; Currey, *Victory at Any Cost*, 68–9; Lanning and Cragg, *Inside the VC and the NVA*, 109–10; Robert Wells, *The Invisible Enemy: Boobytraps in Vietnam* (Miami: J. Flores Publications, 1992), 11.

4. Lanning and Cragg, *Inside the VC and the NVA*, 106–8.

5. Marine Corps, *Professional Knowledge*, 165.

6. Giap, *People's War*, 80.

7. Giap, *People's War*, 12.

8. Giap, *People's War*, 52.

9. Marine Corps, *Professional Knowledge*, 166; Hoang, *Strategy and Tactics*, 127; Wells, *Invisible Enemy*, 7.

10. See: Kirk A. Luedeke, "Death on the Highway, The Destruction of Groupement Mobile 100," *Armor Magazine*, 51, no. 1 (January February 2001), 22–9; Allen, *None So Blind*, 10–1, 22, 36; Harris, *Vietnam's High Ground*, 19–20.

11. Pike *Viet Cong*, 102.

12. Anderson, Arnsten and Averch, *Insurgent Organization and Operations*, 102.

13. Lanning and Cragg, *Inside the VC and the NVA*, 126.

14. Hoang, *Strategy and Tactics*, 127; Marine Corps, *Professional Knowledge*, 166, 167, 176, 177; CICV, "What A Platoon Leader Should Know About the Enemy's Jungle Tactics" (Saigon: MACV, 1967), 9.

15. Lanning and Cragg, *Inside the VC and the NVA*, 126; Marine Corps, *Professional Knowledge*, 179; CICV, "Enemy's Jungle Tactics," 5.

16. Lanning and Cragg, *Inside the VC and the NVA*, 183; CICV, "Enemy's Jungle Tactics," 10; Marine Corps, *Professional Knowledge*, 178–9.

17. CICV, "Enemy's Jungle Tactics,"6, 12; Lanning and Cragg, *Inside the VC and the NVA*, 183; Marine Corps, *Professional Knowledge*, 181, 183.

18. Marine Corps, *Professional Knowledge*, 213.

19. CDR JTF-FA, Honolulu Hi, "Oral History Program (OHP-019) Report: MG Vo Van Dan, message dated 10 July 1996" (TTU), 3.

20. Lanning and Cragg, *Inside the VC and the NVA*, 179; Marine Corps, *Professional Knowledge*, 183.

21. Elliott, *Vietnamese War*, 169.

22. Anderson, Arnsten and Averch, *Insurgent Organization and Operations*, 105, 107–8; Marine Corps, *Professional Knowledge*, 183, 184–6; Lanning and Cragg, *Inside the VC and the NVA*, 181–2; Fox, *Air Base Defense*, 48–9.

23. Marine Corps, *Professional Knowledge*, 214; Anderson, Arnsten and Averch, *Insurgent Organization and Operations*, 110; Lanning and Cragg, *Inside the VC and the NVA*, 182; Hoang, *Strategy and Tactics*, 127.

24. Hoang, *Strategy and Tactics*, 127; Marine Corps, *Professional Knowledge*, 183–4; Anderson, Arnsten and Averch, *Insurgent Organization and Operations*, 111; Bui Tin, *From Enemy to Friend*, 117.

25. Marine Corps, *Professional Knowledge*, 185–6. Anderson, Arnsten and Averch, *Insurgent Organization and Operations*, 107–8; Fox, *Air Base Defense*, 49; Lam Quang Thi, *Twenty-Five Year Century*, 56.

26. Anderson, Arnsten and Averch, *Insurgent Organization and Operations*, 59–60, 89, 90; CICV, "Enemy's Jungle Tactics,"17, 18–9; Lanning and Cragg, *Inside the VC and the NVA*, 136–7, 175.

27. Lanning and Cragg, *Inside the VC and the NVA*, 176, 178; Hanyok, *Spartans in Darkness*, 126, 147; CICV, "Enemy's Jungle Tactics," 21.

28. Lanning and Cragg, *Inside the VC and the NVA*, 176, 178; Hanyok, *Spartans in Darkness*, 126, 147; CICV, "Enemy's Jungle Tactics," 21.

29. Anderson, Arnsten and Averch, *Insurgent Organization and Operations*, xii.

30. Lanning and Cragg, *Inside the VC and the NVA*, 136; Anderson, Arnsten and Averch, *Insurgent Organization and Operations*, 63, 69, 75.

31. Gordon Rottman, *Viet Cong and NVA Tunnels and Fortifications of the Vietnam War* (New York: Osprey, 2006), 14–5; Bui Tin, *From Enemy to Friend*, 48, 103.

32. Marine Corps, *Professional Knowledge*, 171.

33. Marine Corps, *Professional Knowledge*, 171–2; Anderson, Arnsten and Averch, *Insurgent Organization and Operations*, 73, 85, 86.

34. Finlayson, *Rice Paddy Recon*, 29, 93.

35. Don A. Starry, *Mounted Combat in Vietnam* (Washington: U.S. Army Center of Military History, 1989), 47; Anderson, Arnsten and Averch, *Insurgent Organization and Operations*, 56–7.

36. Elliott, *Vietnamese War*, 176.

37. FBIS, *Anti-U.S. Resistance War*, 53; Hoang Ngoc Lung, *Strategy and Tactics*, 128; Anderson, Arnsten and Averch, *Insurgent Organization and Operations*, 54–5, 54n1. There were six helicopters in 1961, fifty by 1962, and two hundred by 1964.

38. MACV Historical Branch, *Command History, 1965* (Saigon: Headquarters MACV, 20 April 1966), 10; Elliott, *Vietnamese War*, 179; Marine Corps, *Professional Knowledge*, 171, 219–20; Hoang Ngoc Lung, *Strategy and Tactics*, 128; Wells, *Invisible Enemy*, 137–8. Only an earlier and less effective version of the claymore mine, the M18, was used in Vietnam at this time.

39. Berman, *Perfect Spy*, 136–7, 141.

40. FBIS, *Anti-U.S. Resistance War*, 53–4; Elliott, *Vietnamese War*, 179, 183.

41. Anderson, Arnsten and Averch, *Insurgent Organization and Operations*, 55, 87; Hoang Ngoc Lung, *Strategy and Tactics*, 128.

42. Marine Corps, *Professional Knowledge*, 216, 219; Lanning and Cragg, *Inside the VC and the NVA*, 184.

43. Hoang, *Strategy and Tactics*, 127; Elliott, *Vietnamese War*, 199, 237–8; Lanning and Cragg, *Inside the VC and the NVA*, 185; Hunt, *Vietnam's Southern Revolution*, 127, 129.

44. Wells, *Invisible Enemy*, 8. For the full spectrum of mines, see "Chapter 6, Water, Anti-Tank and Vehicle Mines"; Lanning and Cragg, *Inside the VC and the NVA*, 110; CICV, "Enemy's Jungle Tactics," 23.

45. CICV, "Enemy's Jungle Tactics," 23–4; Jack Shulimson and Charles M. Johnson, *U.S. Marines in Vietnam: The Landing and Buildup, 1965* (Washington: Headquarters Marine Corps History and Museums Division, 1978), 63; Wells, *Invisible Enemy*, 9, 12, 96, 100–1, 104–6.

46. Wells, *Invisible Enemy*, 14, 94–5, 98; Boot, *Road Not Taken*, 345; CICV, "Enemy's Jungle Tactics," 23–4, 25.

47. CICV, "Enemy's Jungle Tactics," 25; Marine Corps, *Professional Knowledge*, 220; Hoang, *Strategy and Tactics*, 127.

48. Bernard F. Fall, *Street Without Joy: The French Debacle in Indochina* (Mechanicsburg, PA: Stackpole Books, 2005), 113–4; Eric M. Bergerud, *The Dynamics of Defeat: The Vietnam War in Hau Nghia Province* (San Francisco: Westview, 1991), 47; Kenneth R. Olsen and Lois Wright Morgan "Why were the Soil Tunnels of Chu Chi and Iron Triangle in Vietnam so Resilient," *Open Journal of Soil Science*, 7, (2017), 38; Lanning and Cragg, *Inside the VC and the NVA*, 135.

49. Rottman, *Tunnels and Fortifications*, 4, 14, 16–7, 19, 21; Olsen and Morgan "Soil Tunnels," 42–3; Marine Corps, *Professional Knowledge*, 200; Lehrack, *First Battle*, 56; Mangold and Penycate, *Tunnels of Cu Chi*, 57; DeForest and Chanoff, *Slow Burn*, 112.

50. Marine Corps, *Professional Knowledge*, 206, 208, 212; Mangold and Penycate, *Tunnels of Cu Chi*, ix; Olsen and Morgan "Soil Tunnels,"43; Mangold and Penycate, *Tunnels of Cu Chi*, viii–ix. For an example of a punji stick pit, see Rottman, *Tunnels and Fortifications*, 60.

51. Olsen and Morgan "Soil Tunnels," 43; Rottman, *Tunnels and Fortifications*, 20.

52. Olsen and Morgan "Soil Tunnels," 44; Mangold and Penycate, *Tunnels of Cu Chi*, viii; Marine Corps, *Professional Knowledge*, 201. The Pathet Lao utilized nearly five hundred limestone caves in the hills of Viengxay in northeastern Laos. See Paul Rogers, "The Secret war in Viengxay" (http://www.laoscaveproject.de/Reports/The_Secret_War_Viengxay.pdf).

53. Olsen and Morgan "Soil Tunnels," 35–7, 41–2; Mangold and Penycate, *Tunnels of Cu Chi*, 24, 56–7; DeForest and Chanoff, *Slow Burn*, 113; Tourison, *Talking with Victor Charlie*, 164, 253.

54. Rottman, *Tunnels and Fortifications*, 32, 35–6, 50; Wells, *Invisible Enemy*, 11; Marine Corps, *Professional Knowledge*, 212; Mangold and Penycate, *Tunnels of Cu Chi*, 4, 15; Olsen and Morgan "Soil Tunnels," 43, 46, 47; DeForest and Chanoff, *Slow Burn*, 113.

55. Rottman, *Tunnels and Fortifications*, 28–9, 32, 33, 41, 50; Marine Corps, *Professional Knowledge*, 206, 209, 212; Olsen and Morgan "Soil Tunnels," 43.

56. Mangold and Penycate, *Tunnels of Cu Chi*, 54;

57. Bui Tin, *From Enemy to Friend*, 47.

Chapter 10

1. Timothy N. Castle, *At War in the Shadow of Vietnam: U.S. Military Aid to the Royal Lao Government, 1954-1975* (New York; Columbia University Press, 1993), 4–5; William J. Rust, *Before the Quagmire: American Intervention in Laos, 1954-1961* (Lexington KY: University Press of Kentucky, 2012), 36; Gregoire Schlemmer, "Questionner la question ethnique: Lecture historique et politique des appurtenances culturelles au Laos," *Moussons* 25 (2015–1), 7–8.

2. A note on Thai and Laotian names: As in the West, Thailand and Laos put the given first and family name last.

3. P.F. Langer and J.J. Zasloff, *Revolution in Laos: The North Vietnamese and the Pathet Lao*

(Santa Monica CA: RAND, 1969), 32, 51–2; Savada and Whitaker, *Laos,* 30–2; Castle, *In the Shadow of Vietnam*, 7; Frederic Benson, "The Unraveling of the 1962 Geneva Accords: Laos 1962–1964, in Stephen Sherman, ed. *Indochina in the Year of the Dragon—1964* (Houston: Radix Press, 2014), 250; Vatthana Pholsena, "The Early Years of the Lao Revolution (1945–1949): Between history, myth and experience" *South East Asia Research* 14, no. 3 (November 2006), 407, 415; Tappe, "Thailand and Laos—A Historical Love-Hatred," 8. The kingdom was not given full independence until 22 October 1953.

4. Langer and Zasloff, *Revolution in Laos*, 34, 49; Pholsena, "The Early Years of the Lao Revolution (1945–1949), 404, 407, 414. Boun Oum also was a prince but of a minor Laotian kingdom, not of the royal family. Outside the spotlight, ICP members Kaysone Eihan and Nouhak Phomsavan continued to lead the Pathet Lao. Houa Phan province was also called Hua Phan and Sam Neua.

5. Elliott, *Vietnamese War*, 152; Savada and Whitaker, *Laos*, 32; Langer and Zasloff, *Revolution in Laos*, 65, 82; Christopher E. Goscha, "Vietnam and the world outside: The case of Vietnamese communist advisors in Laos (1948–62)," *South East Asia Research*, 12, no. 2 (July 2004), 150; Dommen, *Conflict in Laos*, 80.

6. Langer and Zasloff, *Revolution in Laos*, 69.

7. Savada and Whitaker. *Laos*, 30–1, 32; Elliott, *Vietnamese War*, 70; Benson, "The Unraveling of the 1962 Geneva Accords," 252.

8. Michel Bodin, "Les Laotians dans la guerre d'Indochine, 1945–1954," in *Guerres Mondiales et Conflits Contemporains* (Paris: Presses Universitaires de Paris, 2008), 4, 6; Bernard B. Fall, *Hell in a Very Small Place: The Siege of Dien Bien Phu* (New York: Vintage, 1968), 53; Pholsena, "The Early Years of the Lao Revolution (1945–1949), 410, 426. The term "Vietnam People's Volunteers" was an adaptation of the "Chinese People's Volunteer Forces" used by the PLA in Korea during 1950–1953. The howitzers were so deteriorated that they could not even be fired at maximum range.

9. Qiang Zhai, *China and the Vietnam Wars*, 107.

10. Vo Nguyen Giap, *People's War*, 95; Goscha, "Vietnamese communist advisors in Laos," 150; Fall, *Hell in a Small Place*, 116; Fall, *Street Without Joy*, 121; Castle, *At War in the Shadow of Vietnam*, 9; Langer and Zasloff, *Revolution in Laos*, 70–1, 75.

11. Fall, *Street Without Joy*, 117–8; Bodin, "Laotians dans le guerre," 23; Savada and Whitaker. *Laos*, 33; Shrader, *War of Logistics*, 281; Hammer, *The Struggle for Indochina*, 293–4. Muong (or Muang or Mueang) was a centuries-old term for a fortified city-state. By the 20th century it meant district.

12. Fall, *Street Without Joy*, 117–8; Bodin, "Laotians dans le guerre," 23; Savada and Whitaker. *Laos*, 33; Shrader, *War of Logistics*, 281; Hammer, *The Struggle for Indochina*, 293–4.

13. Shrader, *War of Logistics*, 289–90; Fall, *Street Without Joy*, 76–7, 316; Fall, *Hell in a Very*

Small Place, 34, 48. The Plain of Jars gained its name from the hundreds of Neolithic-era stone burial crypts constructed in the form of large jars that cover much of the plain.

14. Victor B. Anthony and Richard R. Sexton, *The War in Northern Laos* (Washington: Center for Air Force History, 1993), p. 8.

15. Fall, *Street Without Joy*, 116, 127; Bodin, "Laotians dans le guerre," 15.

16. Vo Nguyen Giap, *People's War*, 48; Fall, *Street Without Joy*, 315–6. The Seno airfield's name was a French acronym for south, east, north and west (SENO). The paratroops soon departed after being replaced by GMs 6 and 9.

17. Vo Nguyen Giap, *People's War*, 48; Fall, *Street Without Joy*, 315–6; Allen, *None So Blind*, 51–2, 54.

18. Giap, *People's War*, 81, 83, 95.

19. Giap, *People's War*, 79, 95, 99; Shrader, *War of Logistics*, 307–8, 310; *The West Australian* "Rebels Complete Quick Drive Across Laos," 28 December 1953.

20. Christopher E. Gosha, "Une guerre pour Indochina?: Le Laos and le Cambodge dans le conflit Franco-Vietnamien (1958–1954)," in *Guerres Mondiales et Conflits Contemporains* (Paris: Presses Universitaires de Paris, 2008), 41; Giap, *People's War,* 79–80, 100; Shrader, *War of Logistics*, 309; *The West Australian* "Rebels Complete Quick Drive Across Laos," 28 December 1953. The truck-mobile GM 2 was formed around several Moroccan *Tabors* (battalions) and one Foreign Legion battalion. The 18th Regiment also was part of the 325th Division. The 66th Regiment was part of the 304th Division while 101st belonged to the 325th Division.

21. Shrader, *War of Logistics*, 309–10. The paratroop battalions at Seno: 3rd Vietnamese, 1st and 6th Colonial, 2nd Foreign Legion, 2nd Battalion of the 1st Chasseur Paratroop Regiment. Several of the battalions were later lost at Dien Bien Phu.

22. Gosha, "Une guerre pour Indochina?" 42; Vo Nguyen Giap, *People's War*, 79–80, 82, 100; Ami-Jacques Rapin, "Guerrillas, Guerre Secretes et "Covert Operations" au Laos, Essai Historiographique (Lausanne, Center for Asian Interdisciplinary Studies and Research, 1998), 9.

23. Lam, *The Twenty-five Year Century*, 64–5; Vo Nguyen Giap, *People's War*, 82. Shrader, *War of Logistics*, 309. The units were GM 1 composed of three North African battalions and GM 51 contained French paratrooper and armored cavalry battalions.

24. Vo Nguyen Giap, *People's War*, 81–4, 100, 101; Shrader, *War of Logistics*, 308, 310; Gosha, "Une guerre pour Indochina?" 42; Goscha, "Vietnamese communist advisors in Laos," 150.

25. Allen, *None So Blind*, 53, 58; Asselin, *Vietnam's American War*, 67.

26. Fall, *Street Without Joy*, 76–7; Fall, *Hell in a Very Small Place*, 34, 48; Vo Nguyen Giap, *People's War*, 83.

27. Vo Nguyen Giap, *People's War*, 55.

28. FRUS, 1952–1954, Geneva Convention,

XVI, documents 352, 510. British Marshal Harold Alexander told the allies during the Geneva talks that virtually all of Laos was subject to imminent Viet Minh control.

29. FRUS, 1952–1954, Geneva Convention, XVI, documents 275, 491.

30. FRUS, 1952–1954, Geneva Convention, XVI, document 487.

31. Langer and Zasloff, *Revolution in Laos*, 74–5, 77; FRUS, 1952–1954, Geneva Convention, XVI, documents 510, 607, 631.

32. FRUS, 1952–1954, Geneva Convention, XVI, documents 775, 781, 808, 1002; Langer and Zasloff, *Revolution in Laos*, 76; Goscha, "Vietnamese communist advisors in Laos," 164.

33. Langer and Zasloff, *Revolution in Laos*, 78; Porter, *Perils of Dominance*, 37.

34. Goscha, "Vietnamese communist advisors in Laos," 163, 165; Geneva Conference on the Problem of Restoring Peace in Indo-China, "Agreement on the Cessation of Hostilities in Laos, 20 July 1954" (http://avalon.law.yale.edu/20th_century/inch005.asp).

35. Tucker, *Encyclopedia of the Vietnam War*, 1724; Langer and Zasloff, *Revolution in Laos*, 84, 86; Goscha, "Vietnamese communist advisors in Laos," 163–4, 170.

36. Goscha, "Vietnamese communist advisors in Laos," 163, 164, 166.

37. Savada and Whitaker, *Laos*, 33; Goscha, "Vietnamese communist advisors in Laos," 151, 167; Langer and Zasloff, *Revolution in Laos*, 62.

38. CIA, NIE 63.3-55 "Probable Developments in Laos to July 1956," dated 26 July 1955; Goscha, "Vietnamese communist advisors in Laos," 166, 171; FRUS, 1952–1954, Geneva Convention, XVI, document 890; FRUS, East Asian Security; Cambodia, Laos, 1955–1957, XXI, document 329; Langer and Zasloff, *Revolution in Laos*, 78–9, 83–5; Savada and Whitaker, *Laos*, 36.

39. Rust, *Before the Quagmire*, 73.

40. FRUS, East Asian Security; Cambodia, Laos, XXI, 1955–1957, document 505 and 1958–1960, East Asia Pacific Region; Cambodia; Laos; XVI, document 159; Goscha, "Vietnamese communist advisors in Laos," 174–5; Bernard B. Fall, "The Laos Tangle," *International Journal* 16, no. 2 (Spring 1961), 141; Kenneth Conboy, *Shadow War: The CIA's Secret Wars in Laos* (Boulder, CO: Paladin, 1995), 21; Guan, *Vietnamese Communists' Relations with China*, 33, 55, 61.

41. Anthony and Sexton, *War in Northern Laos*, 12; Conboy, *Shadow War*, 14; Bodin, "Laotians dans le guerre," 5, 20, 21.

42. Conboy, *Shadow War*, 14; Bodin, "Laotians dans le guerre," 5, 20, 21; Jared M. Tracy, "Shoot and Salute: U.S. Army Special Warfare in Laos," *Veritas* 14, no. 1 (2018), 44; Stanton, *Green Berets at War*, 16.

43. Langer and Zasloff, *Revolution in Laos*, 87.

44. Langer and Zasloff, *Revolution in Laos*, 84, 87–8; Goscha, "Vietnamese communist advisors in Laos," 175; FRUS East Asian Security, Cambodia, Laos, 1955–1957, XXI, document 512.

45. Rust, *Before the Quagmire*, 89; FRUS, East Asia Pacific Region, Cambodia, Laos, 1958–1960, XVI, documents 166, 172; Savada and Whitaker, *Laos*, 34, 40; Thomas L. Ahern, Jr. *Undercover Armies: CIA and Surrogate Warfare in Laos, 1961-1973* (Washington: Center for the Study of Intelligence, 2006), 5.

46. FRUS, East Asia Pacific Region, Cambodia, Laos, 1958–1960, XVI, documents 166, 172; Savada and Whitaker. *Laos*, 34, 40; Guan, *Vietnamese Communists' Relations with China*, 81.

47. FRUS, East Asia Pacific Region, 1958–1960; Cambodia; Laos; XVI, document 191n2 and Laos Crisis, XXIV, 1961–1963, document 161; Savada and Whitaker, *Laos* 42; William J. Rust, *So Much to Lose: John F. Kennedy and American Policy in Laos* (Lexington: University Press of Kentucky, 2014), 10, 43; Guan, *Vietnamese Communists' Relations with China*, 106; Phillips, *Why Vietnam Matters*, 96.

48. Rust, *Before the Quagmire*, 131, 133; Ahern, *Undercover Armies*, 9.

49. Fall, "Laos Tangle," 142; Prados, *Hidden History*, 222; Tongas, *Communist Inferno*, 209–10; FRUS, East Asia Pacific Region, Cambodia; Laos, 1958–1960, XVI, document 216; Guan, *Vietnamese Communists' Relations with China*, 93–4. Three days later, on 6 January 1959, DRV Prime Minster Pham Van Dong invited Phoui to talks over the Laotian "violations" in the border fighting.

50. Goscha, "Vietnamese communist advisors in Laos," 176.

51. Asselin, *Hanoi's Road*, 64; Goscha, "Vietnamese communist advisors in Laos," 177, 179.

52. Bodin, "Laotians dans le guerre," 5; Fall, *Street Without Joy*, 331–332; FRUS, East Asia Pacific Region, Cambodia, Laos, 1958–1960, XVI, documents 223 note 3 and 228; Fall, "Laos Tangle," 141.

53. Conboy, *Shadow War*, 19; Phillips, *Why Vietnam Matters*, 329–30n17.

54. FRUS, East Asia Pacific Region, Cambodia, Laos, 1958–1960, XVI, documents 223, 228.

55. Tongas, *Communist Inferno*, 210.

56. Guan, *Vietnamese Communists' Relations with China*, 96; Tongas, *Communist Inferno*, 210.

57. Goscha, "Vietnamese communist advisors in Laos," 174, 176; Langer and Zasloff, *Revolution in Laos*, 93; Guan, *Vietnamese Communists' Relations with China*, 195–6.

58. Fall, "Laos Tangle," 142; FRUS, 1958–1960, East Asia Pacific Region, Cambodia, Laos; XVI, documents 207, 223, 227n4; Fall, *Street Without Joy*, 127–8; Anthony and Sexton, *War in Northern Laos*, 23, 27; Rust, *Before the Quagmire*, 111–2; Dommen, *Conflict in Laos*, 102, 119–20.

59. Anthony and Sexton, *War in Northern Laos*, 23, 27; Rust, *Before the Quagmire*, 111–2; Curtis Peebles, *Twilight Warriors: Covert Air Operations Against the USSR* (Annapolis MD: Naval Institute Press, 2005), 229; Conboy, *Shadow War*, 20; Benson, "Genesis of the Hmong-American Alliance, 1949-1962," 22–3; Dommen, *Conflict in Laos*, 102, 119–20; United States Pacific Command.

Commander-in-Chief Pacific (CINCPAC). *CINCPAC Command History 1960.* (FPO San Francisco: Headquarters CINCPAC, 1961). (reproduced by Stephen Sherman), 138–9, 187. The first phase of Project Disallow focused on training Lao officers and NCOs while Phase II moved on to unit training. The Special Forces deployment was called Project Monkhood, and in 1960, the 77th SFG became the 7th SFG. Under another project, called Erawan, by October 1960 Thai PARU officers, with U.S. support, trained 1,000 Lao paratroopers in counter-guerrilla operations. An Operational Detachment A was often referred to as an A-Team.

60. Fall, *Street Without Joy,* 333; Fall, "Laos Tangle," 142; Conboy, *Shadow War,* 19; Goscha, "Vietnamese communist advisors in Laos," 177; Rust, *Before the Quagmire,* 152–3; FRUS, East Asia Pacific Region, Cambodia, Laos, 1958–1960, XVI, document 235.

61. Rust, *Before the Quagmire,* 117; Fall, *Street Without Joy,* p. 334; FRUS, 1958–1960, East Asia Pacific Region; Cambodia; Laos; XVI, documents 234, 236, 252 and Vietnam, 1964–1968, I, document 392; Frederic Benson, *China and Laos, 1945–1979: A Kaleidoscopic Relationship.* Self-published, July 2019. (https://www.academia.edu/39750943/China_and_Laos_1945–1979_A_Kaleidoscopic_Relationship), 33; Dommen, *Conflict in Laos,* 122.

62. Benson, *China and Laos, 1945–1979,* 34; Roger Hilsman, *To Move a Nation: The Politics of Foreign Policy in the Administration of John F. Kennedy* (New York: Doubleday, 1967), 121; FRUS, East Asia Pacific Region, Cambodia, Laos, 1958–1960, XVI, documents 297, 302, 303, 306, 321, Dommen, *Conflict in Laos,* 124.

63. Hilsman, *To Move a Nation,* 121; FRUS, East Asia Pacific Region, Cambodia, Laos, 1958–1960, XVI, documents 297, 302, 303, 306, 321; Ahern, *Undercover Armies,* 10.

64. Lien-Hang T. Nguyen, *Hanoi's War,* 46; Goscha, "Vietnamese communist advisors in Laos," 178–9; FBIS, *Anti-US Resistance War,* 33. As the name implied the group was formed in September 1959.

65. Rust, *Before the Quagmire,* 158; FRUS, 1958–1960, East Asia Pacific Region; Cambodia; Laos; XVI, documents 333, 336, 337, 341, 345; Castle, *Shadow of Vietnam,* 19; FBIS, *Anti-US Resistance War,* 44; Hilsman, *Move a Nation,* 91; Ahern, *Undercover Armies,* 11; Dommen, *Conflict in Laos,* 129.

66. Savada and Whitaker, *Laos,* 55; FRUS, East Asia Pacific Region, Cambodia, Laos, 1958–1960, XVI, documents 368, 369; Guan, *Vietnamese Communists' Relations with China,* 157; Benson, "The Unraveling of the 1962 Geneva Accords," 267–8, 271; Benson, *China and Laos, 1945–1979,* 36; Dommen, *Conflict in Laos,* 29, 310; CINCPAC, *Command History 1960,* 184. Kong Le is also called Kong Lae. At the time of the coup, his commanding officer was in the United States receiving advanced training. Prince Boun Oum's full name was Boun Oum na Champassak, and he was the hereditary ruler of the Kingdom of Champassak in the southern panhandle of Laos.

67. FRUS, East Asia Pacific Region, Cambodia, Laos, 1958–1960, XVI, documents 413, 424, 434n2; Rust, *Before the Quagmire,* 175–6; Allen, *None So Blind,* 123.

68. FRUS, East Asia Pacific Region, Cambodia, Laos, 1958–1960, XVI, documents 450, 453, 462.

69. FBIS, *Anti-US Resistance War,* 44; Hilsman, *Move a Nation,* 91; document 468; Savada and Whitaker, *Laos,* 55; Anthony and Sexton, *War in Northern Laos,* 33; FRUS, East Asia Pacific Region, Cambodia, Laos, 1958–1960, XVI, documents 468, 479, 483; Stanton, *Green Berets at War,* 19–20; CINCPAC, *Command History 1960,* 185–6.

70. Pribbenow, *Victory in Vietnam,* 77.

71. Department of State, *A Threat to the Peace,* II, 31, 62; Pribbenow, *Victory in Vietnam,* 87; Benson, "The Unraveling of the 1962 Geneva Accords," 269, 271.

72. Pribbenow, *Victory in Vietnam,* 41; Daniel C. Koprowski, "John F. Kennedy, the development of counterinsurgency doctrine and American intervention in Laos, 1961–963" Master's Thesis, (Amherst, MA: University of Massachusetts, 2014), 47–8; Anthony and Sexton, *War in Northern Laos,* 33; Goscha, "Vietnamese communist advisors in Laos," 179; Asselin, *Hanoi's Road,* 120–1; Castle, *Shadow of Vietnam,* 23; Hastings, *Vietnam,* 129; Porter, *Perils of Dominance,* 9; Paul F. Langer, *The Soviet Union, China and the Pathet Lao: Analysis and Chronology* (Springfield VA: National Technical Information Service, 1972), 12–3.

73. Goscha, "Vietnamese communist advisors in Laos," 179–80, 182; Paul F. Langer, *The Soviet Union, China and the Pathet Lao: Analysis and Chronology* (Springfield VA: National Technical Information Service, 1972), 52; Anthony and Sexton, *War in Northern Laos,* 44; Fall, "Laos Tangle," 152; FRUS, 1958–1960, East Asia Pacific Region; Cambodia; Laos; XVI, document 485; Castle, *Shadow of Vietnam,* 24–5; Rust, *Before the Quagmire,* 243–4; Benson, "The Unraveling of the 1962 Geneva Accords," 272; Ahern, *Undercover Armies,* 22–3; Dommen, *Conflict in Laos,* 165, 167, 169.

74. Goscha, "Vietnamese communist advisors in Laos," 179–80, 182; Langer, *The Soviet Union, China and the Pathet Lao,* 52; Anthony and Sexton, *War in Northern Laos,* 44; FRUS, 1958–1960, East Asia Pacific Region; Cambodia; Laos; XVI, document 485; Castle, *Shadow of Vietnam,* 24–5; Rust, *Before the Quagmire,* 243–4; Benson, "The Unraveling of the 1962 Geneva Accords," 272; Stanton, *Green Berets at War,* 20–1.

75. Goscha, "Vietnamese communist advisors in Laos," 180; FRUS, Laos Crisis, 1961–1963, XXIV, document 4; FBIS, *Anti-U.S. Resistance War,* 47.

76. Department of State, *Threat to the Peace* II, 62–3, 65; FRUS, Laos Crisis, 1961–1963, XXIV, documents nos. 14, 16; FBIS, *Anti-U.S. Resistance War,* 47; Anthony and Sexton, *War in Northern Laos,* 38–9, 48; Conboy, *Shadow War,* 53.

77. Department of State, *Threat to the Peace,* II, 62–3; FRUS, Laos Crisis, 1961–1963, XXIV,

documents nos. 14, 16; Anthony and Sexton, *War in Northern Laos*, 38–9, 48; Conboy, *Shadow War*, 53; National Security Memorandum [NASM]: "NSAM 29, Re: Meeting with the President on Southeast Asia, dated 9 March 1961." (JFK Library).

78. Vo Nguyen Giap, *People's War*, 82, 101; FRUS, Laos Crisis, 1961–1963, XXIV, documents 52, 70; Anthony and Sexton, *War in Northern Laos*, 47, 51; Pribbenow, *Victory in Vietnam*, 88, 114.

79. Vo Nguyen Giap, *People's War*, 82, 101; FRUS, Laos Crisis, 1961–1963, XXIV, documents 52, 70; Pribbenow, *Victory in Vietnam*, 88, 114.

80. Hilsman, *To Move a Nation*, 91; Pribbenow, *Victory in Vietnam*, 88; Conboy, *Shadow War*, 116; Tucker, *The Encyclopedia of the Vietnam War*, 1744; Goscha, "Vietnamese communist advisors in Laos," 175; Fall, "The Laos Tangle," 138; Pholsena and Tappe, *Interactions with a Violent Past*, 163. The 761st VC Regiment also was referred to as the 721st Regiment.

Chapter 11

1. Asselin, *Hanoi's Road*, 122; John C. Czyzak and Carl F. Salans, "The International Conference on the Settlement of the Laotian Question and the Geneva Agreements of 1962," *The American Journal of International Law*, 57, no. 2 (April 1963), 302; FBIS, *Anti-U.S. Resistance War*, 47.

2. Asselin, *Hanoi's Road*, 122; Rust, *So Much to Lose*, 28; Fall, *Street Without Joy*, 338; Goscha, "Vietnamese communist advisors in Laos," 162; FRUS, Laos Crisis, 1961–1963, XXIV, documents 75, 77, 80; Pentagon Papers (Gravel Edition), IV.B.1, 1.

3. William H. Sullivan, *Obbligato: Notes on a Foreign Service Career* (New York: W.W. Norton, 1984), 162. There were four groups of participants: The Five Powers (U.S., UK, France, USSR, PRC), ICC (India, Poland, Canada) five Border States (RVN, DRV, Cambodia, Thailand, Burma) and representatives of the Three Laotian Princes.

4. FRUS, Laos Crisis, 1961–1963, XXIV, documents 111, 159; Mari Olsen, *Soviet-Vietnam Relations and the Role of China, 1949–1964: Changing Alliances* (New York: Routledge, 2006), 10; Rust, *So Much to Lose*, 42; Ahern, *Undercover Armies*, 85.

5. FRUS, Laos Crisis, 1961–1963, XXIV, document 202; Rudy Abramson, *Spanning the Century: The Life of W. Averell Harriman, 1891–1986* (New York: William Morrow, 1992), 589; Richard H. Schultz, Jr. *The Secret War Against Hanoi: Kennedy's and Johnson's Use of Spies, Saboteurs, and Covert Warriors in North Vietnam* (New York: Harper Collins, 1999), 26; Dommen, *Conflict in Laos*, 79.

6. FRUS, Laos Crisis, 1961–1963, XXIV, document 161; Rust, *So Much to Lose*, 43; Rust, *Before the Quagmire*, 47; Abramson, *Spanning the Century*, 584; Porter, *Perils of Dominance*, 19, 21, 53.

7. FRUS Laos Crisis, 1961–1963, XXIV, documents 88, 97, 180, 198, 202, 210; Rust, *So Much to Lose*, 43.

8. Guan, *Vietnamese Communists' Relations with China*, 208, 209–10.

9. Hilsman, *To Move a Nation*, 140; Asselin, *Hanoi's Road*, 123; Neese and O'Donnell, *Prelude to Tragedy*, 211.

10. Goscha, "Vietnamese communist advisors in Laos," 182; Hilsman, *To Move a Nation*, 140; Asselin, *Hanoi's Road*, 120, 123, 142; Rust, *So Much To Lose*, 113–4; Prebbenow, *Victory in Vietnam*, 106; Guan, *Vietnamese Communists' Relations with China*, 220, 223; Ahern, *Undercover Armies*, 115. A document recovered from a fallen PAVN soldier at Nam Tha noted that the Nam Tha attack was designed to be another Dien Bien Phu. Some sources refer to the 316th Division as a brigade, the 330th Brigade as a division, and 335th Brigade as the 335th Independent Regiment.

11. Guan, *Vietnamese Communists' Relations with China*, 82; Langer, *The Soviet Union, China and the Pathet Lao*, 19–20; Rust, *So Much to Lose*, 113.

12. Langer, *The Soviet Union, China and the Pathet Lao*, 19–20; Rust, *So Much to Lose*, 113; Guan, *Vietnamese Communists' Relations with China*, 107, 213.

13. The GTs normally were composed of police and local auto (self)-defense militia companies (often formed into volunteer battalions [BVs]) backed up by FAR infantry battalions in the GMs.

14. Rust, *So Much to Lose*, 74, 77; Conboy, *Shadow War*, 23, 68; Laos Crisis, FRUS 1961–1963, XXIV, document 280. GM 11 contained the 1st, 2nd and 3rd Infantry Battalions.

15. Benson, *China and Laos, 1945–1979*, 49–50; Rust, *So Much to Lose*, 74; Conboy, *Shadow War*, 23, 68–9, 71; Anthony and Sexton, *War in Northern Laos*, 64–5; FRUS, Laos Crisis, 1961–1963, XXIV, documents 4, 275, 280.

16. Rust, *So Much to Lose*, 74; Conboy, *Shadow War*, 23, 68–9, 71; Anthony and Sexton, *War in Northern Laos*, 64–5; FRUS, Laos Crisis, 1961–1963, XXIV, documents 4, 275, 280; Dommen, *Conflict in Laos*, 214–5.

17. FRUS, Laos Crisis, 1961–1963, XXIV, documents 287, 289; Abramson, *Spanning the Century*, 589, 603.

18. Anthony and Sexton, *War in Northern Laos*, 65; Rust, *So Much to Lose*, 81; Goscha, "Vietnamese communist advisors in Laos," 182; Prebbenow, *Victory in Vietnam*, 106.

19. Prebbenow, *Victory in Vietnam*, 106; Conboy, *Shadow War*, 72; FRUS, Laos Crisis, 1961–1963, XXIV, documents 328–31; Stanton, *Green Berets at War*, 29.

20. Abramson, *Spanning the Century*, 590; FRUS, 1961–1963, Laos Crisis, XXIV, document 341; Rust, *So Much to Lose*, 111; Hilsman, *To Move a Nation*, 141; Dommen, *Conflict in Laos*, 217.

21. Hilsman, *To Move a Nation*, 141; Anthony and Sexton, *War in Northern Laos*, 67; Prebbenow, *Victory in Vietnam*, 107; Dommen, *Conflict in Laos*, 217.

22. FRUS, Laos Crisis, 1961–1963, XXIV, document 343 note 3.

23. Abramson, *Spanning the Century*, 590.

24. Nathan Badenoch and Tomita Shinsuke, "Mountain People of the Muang: Creation and Governance of a Tai Polity in northern Laos" *Southeast Asian Studies*, 2, no. 1 (April 2013), 54.

25. FRUS, Laos Crisis, 1961–1963, XXIV, documents 235, 279, 280; Arthur M. Schlesinger, Jr., "William Averell Harriman Oral History Interview, 1965." (JFK Library), 52; Asselin, *Hanoi's Road*, 120; Rust, *So Much to Lose*, 77.

26. Stanton, *Green Berets at War*, 28; FRUS, Laos Crisis, 1961–1963, XXIV, documents 235, 279, 280; Arthur M. Schlesinger, Jr., "William Averell Harriman Oral History Interview, 1965." (JFK Library), 52; Asselin, *Hanoi's Road*, 120; Rust, *So Much to Lose*, 77.

27. Asselin, *Hanoi's Road*, 123.

28. Pribbenow, *Victory in Vietnam*, 52; Prados, *The Blood Road*, 11.

29. Pribbenow, *Victory in Vietnam*, 126.

30. Hoang Ngoc Lung, *Strategy and Tactics*, 21; FRUS, East Asia-Pacific Region; Cambodia, Laos, XVI, 1958–1960, document 142 The Americans were using the term Ho Chi Minh Trail as early as June 1960.

31. Bui Tin, *From Enemy to Friend*, 76–7.

32. Prados, *Blood Road*, 10, 13; Pribbenow, *Victory in Vietnam*, 52–3; Bui Tin, *From Enemy to Friend*, 76–7.

33. Burton, *North Vietnam's Military Logistics System*, 48; Berman, *Perfect Spy*, 192.

34. Goscha, "Vietnamese communist advisors in Laos," 150; Shrader, *War of Logistics*, 125; Rust, *Before the Quagmire*, 117; FRUS, 1964–1968, Vietnam, I, document 392; Pribbenow, *Victory in Vietnam*, 88. A secondary headquarters also was established later in Laos at an underground tunnel complex in the hills outside Tchepone on Route 9 (50km west of Khe Sanh).

35. Prados, *Blood Road*, 13–4; Anderson, Rainey, Rapping, and Summerfield, *Support Capabilities for Limited War Forces in Laos and South Vietnam*, 118–9; Shrader, *War of Logistics*, 126–7; Lanning and Cragg, *Inside the VC and the NVA*, 73; Truong Nhu Tang, *Viet Cong Memoir*, 240–2; Pribbenow, *Victory in Vietnam*, 53; McElwee, "An Environmental History of the Ho Chi Minh Trail," 4.

36. Pribbenow, *Victory in Vietnam*, 54.

37. Pribbenow, *Victory in Vietnam*, 53–4, 454n10; Lanning and Cragg, *Inside the VC and the NVA*, 73; Truong Nhu Tang, *Viet Cong Memoir*, 240–2.

38. Elliott, *Vietnamese War*, 86; FRUS, Vietnam, 1964–1968, I, document 392; Prados, *Blood Road*, 28; Department of State, *Threat to the Peace*, II, 31–2; Pribbenow, Victory in Vietnam, 11, 80.

39. Bui Tin, *Following Ho Chi Minh*, 42; Elliott, *Vietnamese War*, 119, 167; Pribbenow, *Victory in Vietnam*, 53; Department of State, *Threat to the Peace*, II, 31–32.

40. CICV, "Military Training," A-5; USAF, "Weekly Air Intelligence Summary (86–32, 10 August 1968)," 5; Pribbenow, *Victory in Vietnam*, 53, 79; Gordon, *Estimative Products*, 179; Department of State, *Threat to the Peace, I*, 31–2, 35, 42 and *II*, 35, 36–7; Lanning and Cragg, *Inside the VC and the NVA*, 12, 73; Department of State White Paper "Aggression from the North, 27 February 1965; USAF, "Weekly Air Intelligence Summary (86–32, 10 August 1968)," 5; Prados, *Blood Road*, 13–4; Johnson, *The Meaning of Vietnam*, 14. The most common weapons were French rifles and MAT-49 sub-machineguns.

41. Prados, *The Blood Road*, 28; Pribbenow, *Victory in Vietnam*, 125–6.

42. Pribbenow, *Victory in Vietnam*, 89; Lien-Hang T. Nguyen, *Hanoi's War*, 59, 71.

43. FRUS, Vietnam, 1964–1968, I, document 392; Department of State, *Threat to the Peace, II*, 35, 36; Tucker, *Encyclopedia of the Vietnam War*, 1744; U.S. Army, Vietnam, G-2, "History of the 273 VC Regiment," (Saigon: Headquarters, U.S. Army, Republic of Vietnam, 1970), 6.

44. Burton, *Logistics*, 25; Tucker, *Encyclopedia of the Vietnam War*, 1251; Kellen, "Profile of the PAVN Soldier," 55; Tucker, *Encyclopedia of the Vietnam War*, 1251, 1712; Pribbenow, *Victory in Vietnam*, 115.

45. Pike, *PAVN*, 45, 47.

46. Burton, *North Vietnam's Military Logistics System*, 48; Department of State, *Threat to the Peace, II*, 51–2; Pribbenow, *Victory in Vietnam*, 53; FRUS, Vietnam, 1961–1963, I, documents 42, 149, 152 and II, document 187 and III, document 19.

47. Prebbenow, *Victory in Vietnam*, 29, 83; Burton, *Logistics*, 48.

48. James F. Dunnigan and Alfred A. Nofi, *Dirty Little Secrets of the Vietnam War: Military Information You're Not Supposed to Know* (New York: St. Martin' Griffin, 2000); 150; Pribbenow, *Victory in Vietnam*, 115–6; Victoria Daniels and Judith C. Erdheim, *Game Warden* (Washington: Center for Naval Analyses, 1976) (TTU). A-1.

49. Daniels and Erdheim, *Game Warden*, A-11; Bui Tin, *From Enemy to Friend*, 59; Hoang Ngoc Lung, *Strategy and Tactics*, 4.

50. Pribbenow, *Victory in Vietnam*, 97, 116; Elliott, *Vietnamese War*, 166.

51. Pribbenow, *Victory in Vietnam*, 88; Department of State, *Threat to the Peace, II*, 26, 42, 45; Nguyen, *Hanoi's War*, 55–6; Allen, *None So Blind*, 127.

52. Asselin, *Hanoi's Road*, 124.

53. FRUS 1961–1963, Laos Crisis, XXIV, document 393.

54. Connors, Weiner and Wilson, *Land Border of South Vietnam*, 31–2; Anderson, Rainey, Jr., Rapping, and Summerfield, *Support Capabilities for Limited War Forces in Laos*, 96; McElwee, "An Environmental History of the Ho Chi Minh Trail," 5; Connors, Weiner and Wilson, *Land Border of South Vietnam*, 11, 15–6, 26–7; Pribbenow, *Victory in Vietnam*, 88.

55. Rust, *So Much to Lose*, 51. Pribbenow, *Victory in Vietnam*, 88–89; Department of State, *Threat to the Peace, II*, 42–3.

56. Pribbenow, *Victory in Vietnam*, 114; FRUS, 1964–1968, Vietnam, I, document 392; Bui Tin,

From Enemy to Friend, 77; McElwee, "An Environmental History of the Ho Chi Minh Trail," 5; Pholsena and Tappe, *Interactions with a Violent Past*, 158.

57. Prados, *Blood Road*, 85; Bui Tin, *From Enemy to Friend*, 77; Bui Tin, *Following Ho Chi Minh*, 11.

58. Richard L. Holm, "No Drums, No bugles: Recollections of a Case Officer in Laos, 1962–1964" (CIA Library); Department of State, *Threat to the Peace, II*, 38, 42–3.

59. Pribbenow, *Victory in Vietnam*, 80, 88, 114; Asselin, *Hanoi's Road*, 101, 116; Vo Nguyen Giap, *People's War*, 82, 101.

Chapter 12

1. Richard Nixon, *The Memoirs of Richard Nixon* (New York: Grosset and Dunlap, 1978), 235; Hunt, *A Vietnam War Reader*, 48.

2. McNamara, *In Retrospect*, 35.

3. Rust, *So Much to Lose*, 91; Edmund F. Wehrle, "'A Good, Bad Deal': John F. Kennedy, W. Averell Harriman, and the Neutralization of Laos, 1961–1962" *Pacific Historical Review*, 67, no. 3 (Aug. 1998), 350; Norman B. Hannah, *The Key to Failure: Laos and the Vietnam War.* (New York: Madison Books, 1987), 85; Schlesinger, "William Averell Harriman Oral History Interview, 1965," 51.

4. McNamara, *Retrospect*, 30; Rust, *So Much to Lose*, 42; FRUS, Laos Crisis, 1961–1963, XXIV, document 88; Allen Millett, *The War for Korea, 1950–1951: They Came from the North*, vol. 2 (Lawrence KS: University Press of Kansas, 2010), 45, 48.

5. FRUS, Vietnam, 1961–1963, I, document no, 74.

6. Connors, Weiner and Wilson, *The Land Border of South Vietnam*, 1.

7. Abramson, *Spanning the Century*, 606; Shaw, *Lost Mandate*, 105; Schlesinger, William Averell Harriman Oral History Interview, 1965 (JFK Library), 64; FRUS, Laos Crisis, 1961–1963, XXIV, documents 71, 79; Hammer, *Death in November*, 30–1.

8. Koprowski, "Kennedy and American intervention in Laos," 68n109, 74–5.

9. Vo Nguyen Giap, *People's War*, 31, 82.

10. Asselin, *Hanoi's Road*, 122, 124, 142; Qiang Zhai, *China and the Vietnam Wars*, 107–8.

11. Schlesinger, William Averell Harriman Oral History Interview, 1965 (JFK Library), 60; Nguyen, *Hanoi's War*, 42–3; Asselin, *Hanoi's Road*, 106–7; Qiang Zhai, *China and the Vietnam Wars*, 100, 105–6, 109, 111, 123; Langer and Zasloff, *Revolution in Laos*, 73; Porter, *Perils of Dominance*, 44–5.

12. Nguyen, *Hanoi's War*, 42–3; Asselin, *Hanoi's Road*, 106–7; Qiang Zhai, *China and the Vietnam Wars*, 100, 105–6, 109, 111, 123; Langer and Zasloff, *Revolution in Laos*, 73; Porter, *Perils of Dominance*, 44–5; Guan, *Vietnamese Communists' Relations with China*, 216–7.

13. Guan, *Vietnamese Communists' Relations with China*, 200, 202, 208.

14. Lien-Hang T. Nguyen, *Hanoi's War*, 58; FRUS, Kennedy-Khrushchev Exchanges, 1961–1963, VI, document no, 15.

15. Langer and Zasloff, *Revolution in Laos*, 73; Gaiduk, *The Soviet Union and the Vietnam War*, 4; Wehrle, "A Good, Bad Deal," 359–60; Qiang Zhai, *China and the Vietnam Wars*, 122; Guan, *Vietnamese Communists' Relations with China*, 209.

16. Anthony and Sexton, *War in Northern Laos*, 67–8; CINCPAC, *Command History 1960*, 24–5; Commander-in-Chief Pacific (CINCPAC), *CINCPAC Command History 1962* (FPO San Francisco: Headquarters CINCPAC, 1963), 214–5; FRUS 1961–1963, Laos Crisis, XXIV, document 357; Allen, *None So Blind*, 147–8.

17. Wehrle, "A Good, Bad Deal," 370; CINCPAC, *Command History 1960*, 152–3 and CINCPAC, *Command History 1962*, 213–4; Pricilla Roberts, "The British Royal Air Force Operations over Laos against the Ho Chi Minh Trail, 1962" *Cold War International History Project*, Working Paper no. 89 (December 2018), 4; FRUS, Laos Crisis, 1961–1963, XXIV, documents 356, 360; Anthony and Sexton, *War in Northern Laos*, 67–8; Hilsman, *Move A Nation*, 150–1. "3/9" signified 3rd Battalion 9th Marine Regiment.

18. Rust, *So Much to Lose*, 95.

19. Hilsman, *Move A Nation*, 136; Schlesinger, "William Averell Harriman Oral History Interview, 1965," 52, 74.

20. FRUS, Laos Crisis, 1961–1963, XXIV, document 359.

21. Wehrle, "A Good, Bad Deal," 369.

22. FRUS 1961–1963, Laos Crisis, XXIV, documents 361, 365; Hilsman, *Move A Nation*, 140; Wehrle, "A Good, Bad Deal," 369.

23. FRUS, Laos Crisis, 1961–1963, XXIV, document 358, 368, 370, 374; Rust, *So Much to Lose*, 124; CINCPAC, *Command History 1962*, 201; Guan, *Vietnamese Communists' Relations with China*, 200, 202, 208.

24. FRUS, Laos Crisis, 1961–1963, XXIV, document 395.

25. FRUS, Laos Crisis, 1961–1963, XXIV, document 394; Rust, *So Much to Lose*, 129; Fall, *Street Without Joy*, 339; FBIS, *Anti-U.S. Resistance War*, 52.

26. FRUS 1961–1963, Laos Crisis, XXIV, document 393.

27. Cushman, *External Support of the Viet Cong: An Analysis and a Proposal*, 26.

28. Wehrle, "A Good, Bad Deal," 364; William Conrad Gibbons, *U.S. Government and the Vietnam War: Executive and Legislative Roles and Relationship, II*, (Princeton: Princeton University Press, 1986), 49.

29. Hilsman, *Move A Nation*, 148.

30. Hilsman, *Move A Nation*, 150–1; Rust, *So Much to Lose*, 106.

31. Phillips, *Why Vietnam Matters*, 139.

32. Hannah, *The Key to Failure*, 152.

33. Anderson, Rainey, Rapping and

Summerfield, "Support Capabilities for Limited War Forces in Laos and South Vietnam," 127.

34. FRUS, Laos Crisis, 1961–1963, XXIV, document 369; Wehrle, "A Good, Bad Deal," 371; Hannah, *The Key to Failure*, 52, see note.

35. FRUS, Laos Crisis, 1961–1963, XXIV, document 405.

36. Porter, *Perils of Dominance*, 51.

37. FRUS 1961–1963, Vietnam, II, document 203.

38. FRUS, Laos Crisis, 1961–1963, XXIV, document 408; Wehrle, "A Good, Bad Deal," 364.

39. Shaw, *Lost Mandate*, 104.

40. FRUS, Vietnam, 1961–1963, II, documents 234, 238; Czyzak and Salans, "Geneva Agreements of 1962," 302–3.

41. United Nations, *United Nations Treaty Series, 1963* (New York: United Nations, 1964), 303; Hannah, *The Key to Failure*, 45–6.

42. William J. Rust, *So Much to Lose: John F. Kennedy and American Policy in Laos* (Lexington: University Press of Kentucky, 2014), 3.

43. United Nations, *Treaty Series, 1963*, 324–5; Langer, *The Soviet Union, China and the Pathet Lao*, 14; Porter, *Perils of Dominance*, 63.

44. FRUS 1961–1963, Laos Crisis, XXIV, document 413.

45. FRUS 1961–1963, Laos Crisis, XXIV, document 412.

46. Conboy, *Shadow War*, 96; Roger Warner, *Back Fire: The CIA's Secret War in Laos and Its Link to the War in Vietnam* (New York: Simon Schuster, 1995), 137–8; Porter, *Perils of Dominance*, 37.

47. Conboy, *Shadow War*, 96; Warner, *Back Fire*, 137–8; Porter, *Perils of Dominance*, 37.

48. FRUS, Laos Crisis, 1961–1963, XXIV, document 427, 428, 484; Guan, *Vietnamese Communists' Relations with China*, 191, 215.

49. Rust, *So Much to Lose*, 204.

50. FRUS, East Asia-Pacific Region, Cambodia, Laos, 1958–1960, XVI, document 239; Fox Butterfield, "Laos's Opium Country Resisting Drug Law," *New York Times*, 16 October 1972; Jane Hamilton-Merritt, *Tragic Mountains: The Hmong, the Americans, and the Secret War for Laos, 1942–1992* (Bloomington IN: Indiana University Press, 1999), 28–29. Warner, *Back Fire*, 121; Frederic C. Benson, "Genesis of the Hmong-American Alliance, 1949–1962: Aspirations, Expectations and Commitments during an Era of Uncertainty," *Hmong Studies Journal*, 16 (2015), 2; Benson, *China and Laos, 1945–1979*, 31. Under French rule, private use of opium was legal but distribution was regulated in the 20th century.

51. FRUS, East Asia-Pacific Region, Cambodia, Laos, 1958–1960, XVI, document 239; Fox Butterfield, "Laos's Opium Country Resisting Drug Law," *New York Times*, 16 October 1972; Jane Hamilton-Merritt, *Tragic Mountains: The Hmong, the Americans, and the Secret War for Laos, 1942–1992* (Bloomington IN: Indiana University Press, 1999), 28–9.Warner, *Back Fire*, 121; Frederic C. Benson, "Indochina War Refugee Movements in Laos, 1954–1975: A Chronological Overview

Citing New Primary Sources," *Journal of Lao Studies*, Special Issue, (2015), 25.

52. Savada, *Laos*, 40; Benson, "Genesis of the Hmong-American Alliance, 1949–1962," 14–5, 18, 25, 30; Benson, "The Unraveling of the 1962 Geneva Accords," 291; Benson, "Indochina War Refugee Movements in Laos," 36. CARE stood for Cooperative for American Relief Everywhere.

53. Benson, "The Unraveling of the 1962 Geneva Accords," 273; Benson, "Genesis of the Hmong-American Alliance, 1949–1962," 5, 9, 13; Dommen, *Conflict in Laos*, 75–6.

54. Conboy, *Shadow War*, 23, 60; Savada, *Laos*, 40, 53; Hamilton-Merritt, *Tragic Mountains*, 20–1; Benson, "Genesis of the Hmong-American Alliance, 1949–1962," 13, 17, 19, 23.

55. Fall, *Street Without Joy*, 268; Hamilton-Merritt, *Tragic Mountains*, 55; Conboy, *Shadow War*, 19, 93; Benson, "Genesis of the Hmong-American Alliance, 1949–1962," 13, 24; Benson, "Indochina War Refugee Movements in Laos," 32.

56. FRUS, Laos Crisis, 1961–1963, XXIV, document 6; Benson, "Genesis of the Hmong-American Alliance, 1949–1962," 31–2.

57. NSAM 29, "Meeting with the President on Southeast Asia"; Richard L. Holm, "No Drums, No Bugles"; David Corn, *Blond Ghost: Ted Shackley and the CIA's Crusades* (New York: Simon Shuster, 1994), 127; Savada, *Laos*, 53–4; FRUS, Laos Crisis, 1961–1963, XXIV, documents 6, 125; Koprowski, "Kennedy and American Intervention in Laos," 77; Conboy, *Shadow War*, 58, 88; Anthony and Sexton, *War in Northern Laos*, 54; Ahern, *Undercover Armies*, 30–1.

58. Richard L. Holm, "No Drums, No Bugles"; David Corn, *Blond Ghost: Ted Shackley and the CIA's Crusades* (New York: Simon Shuster, 1994), 127; Savada, *Laos*, 53–4; FRUS, Laos Crisis, 1961–1963, XXIV, documents 6, 125; Koprowski, "Kennedy and American Intervention in Laos," 77; Conboy, *Shadow War*, 58, 88; Anthony and Sexton, *War in Northern Laos*, 54; Benson, "Genesis of the Hmong-American Alliance, 1949–1962," 42; Stanton, *Green Berets at War*, 23–4.

59. Warner, *Back Fire*, 29–30; FRUS, Laos, 1964–1968, XXVIII, documents 179; Benson, "The Unraveling of the 1962 Geneva Accords," 277–8; Benson, "Genesis of the Hmong-American Alliance, 1949–1962," 36, 39, 38, 44; CINCPAC, *Command History 1960*, 141. In 1960, U.S. Special Forces began training PARU officers in ranger tactics.

60. Corn, *Blond Ghost*, 128; FRUS, Laos, 1964–1968, XXVIII, documents 179; Benson, "The Unraveling of the 1962 Geneva Accords," 277–8; Benson, "Genesis of the Hmong-American Alliance, 1949–1962," 36, 39, 38, 44; Tappe, "Thailand and Laos—A Historical Love-Hatred," 6–7.

61. Conboy, *Shadow War*, 120; Hamilton-Merritt, *Tragic Mountains*, 140.

62. Roberts, "The British Royal Air Force Operations over Laos," 10–11, 14; Holm, "No Drums, No Bugles"; Conboy, *Shadow War*, 117.

63. Conboy, *Shadow War*, 86, 97; Prados, *Blood*

Trail, 51; Stanton, *Green Berets at War,* 24. Lao The-ong is also spelled Lao Theung.

64. FRUS, Laos Crisis, 1961–1963, XXIV, document 171; Castle, *Shadow of Vietnam,* 79; Conboy, *Shadow War,* 95–6; Warner, *Back Fire,* 84; Benson, "The Unraveling of the 1962 Geneva Accords," 284–5; Benson, "Genesis of the Hmong-American Alliance, 1949–1962," 46; Ahern, *Undercover Armies,* 114; Holm, "No Drums, No Bugles."

65. Holm, "No Drums, No Bugles."

66. Conboy, *Shadow War,* 118–9; Holm, "No Drums, No Bugles."

67. Goscha, "Vietnamese communist advisors in Laos," 179–180; FRUS, Laos Crisis, 1961–1963, XXIV, document 415; Conboy, *Shadow War,* 96; Douglas S. Blaufarb, *Organizing and Managing Unconventional War in Laos, 1962–1970* (Santa Monica: RAND, 1972), 22; Benson, "Genesis of the Hmong-American Alliance, 1949–1962," 29.

68. Conboy, *Shadow War,* 97; FRUS, Laos Crisis, 1961–1963, XXIV, documents 436, 437, 440; Blaufarb, *Unconventional War in Laos,* 17; Savada, *Laos,* 55; Ahern, *Undercover Armies,* 147–8.

69. FRUS, Laos Crisis, 1961–1963, XXIV, document 440, 489, 490; Anthony and Sexton, *War in Northern Laos,* 81; Benson, "The Unraveling of the 1962 Geneva Accords," 300.

70. FRUS, Laos Crisis, 1961–1963, XXIV, documents 447, 463n6, 490; Conboy, *Shadow War,* 98–9, 112, 138n37; Anthony and Sexton, *War in Northern Laos,* 87; Benson, "The Unraveling of the 1962 Geneva Accords," 287; Ahern, *Undercover Armies,* 153.

71. National Security Memorandum [NASM]: "NSAM 249, Laos Planning, 25 June 1963" (JFK Library); Department of State, "Memorandum for Mr. McGeorge Bundy, The White House: Meeting on Laos, 18 June 1963" (JFK Library), Situation 8–10.

72. "NSAM 249, Laos Planning, 25 June 1963"; Department of State, "Memorandum for Mr. McGeorge Bundy, The White House: Meeting on Laos, 18 June 1963," Situation 8–10. OPLAN 33–63 superseded the Covert Operations Appendix to OPLAN 32–62.

73. Conboy, *Shadow War,* 117, 119, 121, 144; Warner, *Back Fire,* 130–1; Holm, "No Drums, No Bugles."

74. FRUS, 1961–1963, Laos Crisis, XXIV, document 440.

75. Conboy, *Shadow War,* 99–100.

76. Blaufarb, *Unconventional War in Laos,* 24–5; Benson, "The Unraveling of the 1962 Geneva Accords," 295; Benson, *China and Laos, 1945–1979,* 69; Ahern, *Undercover Armies,* 102, 128.

77. Asselin, *Hanoi's Road,* 124–5.

78. Blaufarb, *Unconventional War in Laos,* 20; Rust, *So Much to Lose,* 241; Goscha, "Vietnamese Communist Advisors in Laos," 182; Tucker, *Encyclopedia of the Vietnam War,* 1724; Porter, *Perils of Dominance,* 119.

79. Asselin, *Hanoi's Road,* pp. 123, 124–5, 134–5; Porter, *Perils of Dominance,* 120; Guan, *Vietnamese Communists' Relations with China,* 227–8.

80. FRUS, Vietnam, 1961–1963, III, document 135; Porter, *Perils of Dominance,* 125–26; Dennis J. O'Brien. "William H. Sullivan Oral History, 1970" (JFK Library), 46; Asselin, *Hanoi's Road,* 123; George Washington University National Security Archive (GWUNSA), *New Light in a Dark Corner: Evidence on the Diem Coup in South Vietnam, November 1963.* (https://nsarchive.gwu.edu/briefing-book/vietnam/2020-11-01/new-light-dark-corner-evidence-diem-coup-november-1963?eType=EmailBlastContent&eId=d028c305-87ec-4e63-b938-6e40ae0d7697), document 17; "Vietnam: A Television History; Interview with Madame Ngo Dinh Nhu."

81. O'Brien, "Roger Hilsman Interview," 33.

82. Porter, *Perils of Dominance,* 125–26; O'Brien. "Sullivan Oral History," 46; Luke A. Nichter, *The Last Brahmin: Henry Cabot Lodge, Jr. and the making of the Cold War* (New Haven: Yale University Press, 2020), 198; Asselin, *Hanoi's Road,* 123.

83. Wehrle, "A Good, Bad Deal," 350n3.

84. Sullivan, *Obbligato,* 164.

85. Abramson, *Spanning the Century,* 587.

86. O'Brien, "Roger Hilsman Interview I," 25.

87. Rust, *So Much to Lose,* 149.

Chapter 13

1. Asselin, *Hanoi's Road,* 59–60.

2. CDECV, "The Situation in Nam Bo," 17.

3. Hunt, *A Vietnam War Reader,* 41.

4. Elliott, *Vietnamese War,* 86; Chen, "Hanoi's Three Decisions," 244. As a gauge of the effectiveness of the To Cong campaign, the Nam Bo VWP lost 12,000 of 15,000 members between 1957 and 1959.

5. Lien-Hang T. Nguyen, *Hanoi's War,* 47; Elliott, *The Vietnamese War,* 113; Hunt, *Vietnam's Southern Revolution,* 30.

6. FRUS, Vietnam, 1958–1960, I, documents 47, 49, 60, 63; Palmer, *The McNamara Strategy,* 91.

7. FRUS, Vietnam, 1958–1960, I, documents 61, 62, 64.

8. FRUS, Vietnam, 1958–1960, I, documents 68, 72, 78.

9. *Pentagon Papers,* (NARA), IV.A.5, 61–2; Moyar, *Triumph Forsaken,* 85; FRUS, Vietnam, 1958–1960, I, document 82; Lien-Hang T. Nguyen, *Hanoi's War,* 43; Elliott, *The Vietnamese War,* 104–5.

10. FRUS, Vietnam, 1958–1960, I, document 79; Cooper, Corson, Legere, Lockwood, and Miller, *History of Pacification,* 131; Neese and O'Donnell, *Prelude to Tragedy,* 189, 192.

11. Asselin, *Hanoi's Road,* 59–60.

12. FRUS, Vietnam, 1958–1960, I, documents 122, 271 and 1961–1963, I, document 1; Lien-Hang T. Nguyen, *Hanoi's War,* 47; Elliott, *The Vietnamese War,* 102–3, 113; Hunt, *Vietnam's Southern Revolution,* 30.

13. Sok Udom Deth, Sun Suon, Sekran Bulut, eds. *Cambodia's Foreign Relations and Global Contexts* (Stankt Augostin, GE: Konrad Adenauer

Stiftung, 2017), 10; FRUS, Indonesia, 1958–1960, XVII, documents 243, 246; FRUS, Japan, Korea, 1958–1960, XVIII, documents 288, 289, 298, 307. It was a year of political turbulence as also witnessed by the military coup in Turkey on 27 May 1960. In South Korea, the opposition candidate died of cancer one month before the election, and Syngman Rhee refused to delay or allow the naming of a substitute on the ballot, leading to his undoing after the election.

14. Fall, *Two Viet-Nams*, 432.

15. Colby, *Lost Victory*, 75.

16. Karnow, "Interview with Edward Geary Lansdale, 1979, Part 2 of 5."

17. Colby, *Lost Victory*, 75; Republic of Vietnam, *Violations of the Geneva Agreement by the Viet-Minh Communists, From July 1959 to June 1960* (Saigon: Government of the Republic of Vietnam, 1960).

18. FRUS, Indonesia, 1958–1960, XVII, documents 243

19. FRUS, Vietnam, 1958–1960, I, document 222. Nguyen Chanh Thi was also cited as Nguyen Than Chi.

20. Colby, *Lost Victory*, 76–8; FRUS, Vietnam, 1958–1960, I, documents 230, 232, 233; Neese and O'Donnell, *Prelude to Tragedy*, 24; Demery, *Dragon Lady*, 114; Karnow, "Interview with Edward Geary Lansdale, 1979, Part 4 of 5." The majority of the paratroopers gave up on 12 November, but small groups held out until the next day.

21. Colby, *Lost Victory*, 76–8; FRUS, Vietnam, 1958–1960, I, documents 230, 232, 233; Demery, *Dragon Lady*, 114; Karnow, "Interview with Edward Geary Lansdale, 1979, Part 4 of 5."

22. Elliott, *The Vietnamese War*, 130, 132; Moyar, *Forsaken Triumph*, pp. 88–89.

23. Elliott, *The Vietnamese War*, 114, 130; FRUS, 1958–1960, Vietnam, I, document 185 (SNIE 63.1-60) and 1961–1963, I, document 1; Pike *Viet Cong*, 102; Asselin, *Hanoi's Road*, 64; Pribbenow, *Victory in Vietnam*, 66–7; CINCPAC, *Command History 1960*, 193.

24. *Pentagon Papers* (NARA), IV-A-4-Tab-4, 83; Department of the Army, *Development and Training of the South Vietnamese Army*, 29, 34; Spector, *Advice and Support*, 290 (see Map 7), 298; Tucker, *Encyclopedia of the Vietnam War*, 240; CINCPAC, *Command History 1960*, 140.

25. Guan, *Vietnamese Communists' Relations with China*, 152; Nguyen Van Canh, *Vietnam Under Communism, 1975–1982* (Stanford: Stanford University Press, 1983), 8; Elliott, *The Vietnamese War*, 112–3; Hunt, *Vietnam's Southern Revolution*, 31–2.

26. Elliott, *The Vietnamese War*, 121; Embassy of the Republic of Vietnam, *The Armed Forces of the Republic of Vietnam, Vietnam Information, Series 20*, (Washington: Embassy of the Republic of Vietnam, 1969), 15; Hoang Ngoc Lung, *Strategy and Tactics*, 16; Guan, *Vietnamese Communists' Relations with China*, 152–5; FRUS, Vietnam, 1961–1963, I, documents 1, 167; Ha Mai Viet, *Steel and Blood*, 19; Moyar, *Forsaken Triumph*, 99, 101, 102–3; Harris, *Vietnam's High Ground*, 55–6.

27. Embassy of the Republic of Vietnam, *The Armed Forces of the Republic of Vietnam, Vietnam Information, Series 20*, (Washington: Embassy of the Republic of Vietnam, 1969), 15; Hoang Ngoc Lung, *Strategy and Tactics*, 16; Guan, *Vietnamese Communists' Relations with China*, 152–5; Collins, *Training of the South Vietnamese Army*, 18, 20; FRUS, Vietnam, 1961–1963, I, documents 1, 167; Ha Mai Viet, *Steel and Blood*, 19; Moyar, *Forsaken Triumph*, 99, 101, 102–3; CINCPAC, *Command History 1960*, 139.

28. Pribbenow, *Victory in Vietnam*, 93; Elliott, *The Vietnamese War*, 113, 124; Director Central Intelligence, *The Highlanders of South Vietnam: A Review of Political Developments and Forces* (Washington: CIA, 1966), 31; Harris, *Vietnam's High Ground*, 39–40.

29. FRUS, Vietnam, 1961–1963, I, documents 22, 27, 29, 34, 41, 172.

30. FRUS, Vietnam, 1961–1963, I, document 52; Department of State, *Threat to the Peace, II*, p. 45.

31. Pentagon Papers (NARA), IV.B.1, iv, 10–1, 66; O'Brien. "Sullivan Oral History," 35.

32. Elliott, *The Vietnamese War*, 162, 167; Guan, *Vietnamese Communists' Relations with China*, 203; Hunt, *Vietnam's Southern Revolution*, 47–8. That month the first unit formed up, the 514th Provincial Battalion.

33. Pentagon Papers (NARA), IV.B.1, 11, 62; FRUS, Vietnam, 1961–1963, I, documents 73, 93; Cooper, Corson, Legere, Lockwood, and Miller, *History of Pacification*, 133–5; Zasloff, "Rural Resettlement," 332, 335, 338; Elliott, *The Vietnamese War*, 164.

34. Riggs Osborn, "War, Women, Vietnam," 111.

35. Commander-in Chief Pacific, *CINCPAC Command History 1962*, 174, 261; Riggs Osborn, "War, Women, Vietnam," 111–2.

36. Asselin, *Hanoi's Road*, 59.

37. Pentagon Papers (NARA), IV.B.1, 12–3; DCI, *Highlanders of South Vietnam*, 33; Harris, *Vietnam's High Ground*, 58, 60–1, 68.

38. FRUS, Vietnam, 1961–1963, I, document 210, see Appendix F for the Northwest Frontier Force proposal; Pentagon Papers (NARA), IV.B.1, 16; Porter, *Perils of Dominance*, 149–50; Jack Shulimson, *Joint Chiefs of Staff and the Vietnam War, 1960–1968, Part 1* (Washington, Office of the Chairman of the Joint Chiefs of Staff Office of Joint History, 2011), 101.

39. Commander-in Chief Pacific, *CINCPAC Command History 1962*, 262; Toczek, *Battle of Ap Bac*, 43.

40. FRUS, Vietnam, 1961–1963, I, document 257; Porter, *Perils of Dominance*, 149–50; United States Military Assistance Command Vietnam (MACV), "21st Infantry Division ARVN and 42nd DTA" (Bac Lieu, RVN: MACV Advisory Team 51, 1965), 5; Pentagon Papers (NARA), IV.B.1, 15. The official title was Transportation Company (Light Helicopter).

41. FRUS, Geneva Convention, 1952–1954, XVI, document 1009.

42. Elliott, *The Vietnamese War*, 164.

43. Thomas L. Ahern, Jr. *The Way We Do Things: Black Entry Operations into North Vietnam, 1961–1964* (Washington: Center for the Study of Intelligence, 2004), 10.

44. FRUS, Vietnam, 1961–1963, I, documents 43, 52; National Security Council, "Program of Action to Prevent Communist Domination of South Viet Nam, 9 May 1961" (JFK Library); Conboy, *Shadow War*, 117; Shultz, *The Secret War Against Hanoi*, 3.

45. FRUS, The Intelligence Community, 1950–1955, document 8; McNamara, *In Retrospect*, 129; Schultz, Jr. *The Secret War Against Hanoi*, 21–2.

46. See: NSAM 57 "Responsibility for Paramilitary Operations" (JFK Library).

47. Department of the Army, *Guerrilla Warfare and Special Forces Operations, FM 31-21* (Washington: Department of the Army, September 1961), 14–5. The JUWTF had been conceptualized by 1961 to consist of a commander, joint staff, and a Special Forces Group, but its mission was confined to guerrilla warfare.

48. CINCPAC, *Command History 1962*, 28–9; Maxwell D. Taylor, *Swords and Plowshares* (New York: Random House, 1972), 249; Richard H. Schultz, Jr. "The Great Divide: Strategy and Covert Action in Vietnam," *Joint Forces Quarterly*, 25 (Autumn Winter, 1999–2000), 91–2.

49. Lansdale, *Midst of Wars*, 163–7, 167–8; Anderson, *The Quiet Americans*, 373; Phillips, *Why Vietnam Matters*, 55; William J. Rust, "CIA Operations Officer Lucien Conein: A Study in Contrasts and Controversy" *Studies in Intelligence* 63, no. 4 (Extracts, December 2019): 45–6; Karnow, "Interview with Edward Geary Lansdale, 1979, Part 3 of 5."

50. Pentagon Papers (Gravel Edition), I, document 95, "Lansdale Team Report on Covert Saigon Mission in 1954 and 1955"; Pentagon Papers (NARA), IV.A.4, 6 and IV.A.5, 11; Rust, "CIA Operations Officer Lucien Conein," 48; Kenneth Conboy and Dale Ardradé, *Spies and Commandos: How America Lost the Secret War in North Vietnam* (Lawrence KS: University Press of Kansas, 2000), 7–8, 12–3; Tourison, *Secret Army, Secret War*, 9.

51. Conboy and Ardradé, *Spies and Commandos*, 22, 24; Tourison, *Secret Army, Secret War*, 13, 26–7, 31–2.

52. Nguyen Ngoc Linh, *Armed Forces of Viet Nam*, 9; Fall, *Street Without Joy*, 268–9; Conboy and Ardradé, *Spies and Commandos*, 31–2; Schultz, Jr. *The Secret War Against Hanoi*, 14. The Special Forces were known as the Luc Luong Dac Biet (Airborne Special Forces). GCMAs were later called Combined (Mixed) Intervention Groups.

53. FRUS, Vietnam, 1958–1960, I, documents 110, 113; Andrew F. Krepinevich, *The Army and Vietnam* (Baltimore: John Hopkins University Press, 1986), 25; Conboy, *Shadow War*, 116.

54. Ahern, *Vietnam Declassified*, 45; Schultz, *The Secret War Against Hanoi*, 28; Tourison, *Secret Army, Secret War*, 12, 24–5; Robert M. Gillespie,

Black Ops, Vietnam (Annapolis: Naval Institute Press, 2011), 5; Hoang Ngoc Lung, *Intelligence*, 38; Ahern, *The Way We Do Things*, 8. The Liaison Service changed its name to the Presidential Survey Office in 1962. The service also was known as the Liaison Office.

55. William C. Westmoreland, *A Soldier Reports* (New York: Doubleday, 1976), 127; McNamara, *In Retrospect*, 129; Schultz, Jr. *The Secret War Against Hanoi*, 18; Conboy and Ardradé, *Spies and Commandos*, 52.

56. Schultz, *The Secret War Against Hanoi*, 29.

57. Conboy and Ardradé, *Spies and Commandos*, 32;

58. Tourison, *Secret Army, Secret War*, 120, 132.

59. Ahern, *The Way We Do Things*, 13, 22, 27; Tourison, *Secret Army, Secret War*, 13, 25, 45; Conboy and Ardradé, *Spies and Commandos*, 66–7, 101, 109.

60. United States Military Assistance Command, Vietnam (MACV), Military Assistance Command Studies and Observation Group (MACSOG), *Documentation Study*, 10 July 1970, (TTU), C-d-1; Gillespie, *Black Ops*, 19–20; Ahern, *The Way We Do Things*, 13, 22, 27; Conboy and Ardradé, *Spies and Commandos*, 51; Tourison, *Secret Army, Secret War*, 54–5; Conboy, *Shadow War*, 118. 1st OG was renamed the 77th Special Forces Group in October 1964.

61. Ahern, *The Way We Do Things*, 26–7, 45, 51–2; Gillespie, *Black Ops*, 20; Tourison, *Secret Army, Secret War*, 67; MACSOG, *Documentation Study*, C-d-2.

62. MACSOG, *Documentation Study*, C-b-63, 64; Tourison, *Secret Army, Secret War*, 45, 118; Ahern, *The Way We Do Things*, 14; Gillespie, *Black Ops*, 6.

63. Tourison, *Secret Army, Secret War*, 35–6; Pribbenow, "The Sino-Soviet Intelligence Relationship during the Vietnam War," 4–5; Ahern, *The Way We Do Things*, 57.

64. Conboy and Ardradé, *Spies and Commandos*, 77, 79; Schultz, *The Secret War Against Hanoi*, 130, 135–6, 139–40, 144, 154–5; Tourison, *Secret Army, Secret War*, 21.

65. Schultz, *The Secret War Against Hanoi*, 136–7.

66. Gilespie, *Black Ops*, 58; MACSOG, *Documentation Study*, C-d-20, 21, 37; Schultz, *The Secret War Against Hanoi*, 31, 62–3, 148–9.

67. Clayton D. Laurie and Andres Vaart, *CIA in the Wars of Southeast Asia* (Washington: Center for the Study of Intelligence, 2016), 6; Krepinevich, *The Army and Vietnam*, 64; Rust, "CIA Operations Officer Lucien Conein," 46; Colby, *Lost Victory*, 6, 90–2; Phillips, *Why Vietnam Matters*, 110; DCI, *Highlanders of South Vietnam*, 40, 47; Harris, *Vietnam's High Ground*, 72–3, 76–7, 97.

68. Ahern, *Vietnam Declassified*, 64–5, 68; FRUS, Vietnam, 1961–1963, II, documents 203, 230, 286, 291; Schultz, Jr. *The Secret War Against Hanoi*, 18; DCI, *Highlanders of South Vietnam*, 48; Stanton, *Green Berets at War*, 68; Harris, *Vietnam's High Ground*, 79.

69. FRUS, Vietnam, 1958–1960, I, document 207n3; Gillespie, *Black Ops*, 48; Conboy, *Shadow War*, 116; MACSOG, *Documentation Study*, D-3.

70. MACSOG, *Documentation Study*, D-2; Gillespie, *Black Ops*, 48; Conboy, *Shadow War*, 116. Perhaps the Vietnamese referred to Thunder Shower using its Mandarin Chinese name, Lei-Yu, because many of the local Nung who executed the missions spoke Chinese.

71. FRUS, Laos, 1964–1968, XXVIII, document 43, see note 6; MACSOG, *Documentation Study*, D-2.

72. Peebles, *Twilight Warriors*, 86, 88, 229.

73. MACSOG, *Documentation Study*, C-b-1; Joe F. Leeker, "Air America—Cooperation with Other Airlines" (https://www.utdallas.edu/library/specialcollections/hac/cataam/Leeker/history/Cooperation.pdf), 18, 20, 27; Tourison, *Secret Army, Secret War*, 19–20; Conboy and Ardradé, *Spies and Commandos*, 33; Conboy and Ardradé, *Spies and Commandos*, 43–4; Phillips, *Why Vietnam Matters*, 113.

74. NSAM 29, "Meeting with the President on Southeast Asia"; George R. Hofmann Jr. *Operation Millpond: U.S. Marines in Thailand, 1961* (Quantico VA: U.S. Marine Corps History Division, 2009), 10–1

75. Leeker, "Air America—Cooperation with Other Airlines," 18, 23; NSAM 104, Southeast Asia, 13 October 1961 (JFK Library); Futrell, *The United States Air Force in Southeast Asia: The Advisory Years*, 79; Berger, *United States Air Force in Southeast Asia*, 12; Harris, *Vietnam's High Ground*, 99–100.

76. Graham A. Cosmas, *MACV: The Joint Command Years, 1962–1967* (Washington: U.S. Army Center of Military History, 2006), 55; Berger, *United States Air Force in Southeast Asia*, 13; Futrell, *The United States Air Force in Southeast Asia: The Advisory Years*, 171.

77. Conboy and Ardradé, *Spies and Commandos*, 46–7; Peebles, *Twilight Warriors*, 269; Leeker, "Air America—Cooperation with Other Airlines," 25.

78. Conboy and Ardradé, *Spies and Commandos*, 23.

79. MACSOG, *Documentation Study*, C-b-63, 64; Pribbenow, *Victory in Vietnam*, 127, 171, 456n26.

Chapter 14

1. CINCPAC, *Command History 1962*, 148; Elliott, *The Vietnamese War*, 93; Ha Mai Viet, *Steel and Blood*, 293; Jeffrey J. Clarke, *Advice and Support: The Final Years* (Washington: Center of Military History, 1988), 14.

2. Guan, *Vietnamese Communists' Relations with China*, 216; FRUS, Vietnam, 1961–1963, II, document 42; Gerald Penderghast, *Britain and the Vietnam Wars: The Supply of Troops, Arms and Intelligence, 1945–1975* (Jefferson NC: McFarland, 2015), 53; Stewart, *Vietnam's Lost Revolution*, 193–4.

3. FRUS, Vietnam, 1961–1963, II, document 42; CINCPAC, *Command History 1960*, 152–3.

4. MACV, "Information on the 21st Infantry Division," (Bac Lieu, RVN: MACV Advisory Team 51, 1965), 4; MACV, "21st Infantry Division ARVN and 42nd DTA," 5.

5. FRUS, Vietnam, 1961–1963, III, document 26.

6. Krepinevich, *Army and Vietnam*, 67; Pribbenow, *Victory in Vietnam*, 110; Phillips, *Why Vietnam Matters*, 116.

7. CINCPAC, *Command History, 1962*, 263–4; Moyar, *Victory Forsaken*, 153; Pribbenow, *Victory in Vietnam*, 109; Pentagon Papers (NARA), IV.b.4.II, 13; Elliott, *The Vietnamese War*, 176; Xunhasaba, "The Failure of the 'Special War,' 1961–1965," *Vietnamese Studies (Hanoi)*, 11, (1966) (TTU), 26; Thompson, *Defeating Communist Insurgency*, 129.

8. Elliott, *The Vietnamese War*, 174; Toczek, *Battle of Ap Bac*, 44; CINCPAC, *Command History, 1962*, 264; William R. Fails, *Marines and Helicopters, 1962–1973* (Washington: U.S. Marine Corps History and Museums Division, 1978), 29.

9. Elliott, *The Vietnamese War*, 176–177; FRUS, Vietnam, 1961–1963, II, document 42; MACV, "Information on the 21st Infantry Division," 4; MACV, "21st Infantry Division ARVN and 42nd DTA," 5; Starry, *Mounted Combat in Vietnam*, 24; Ly Tong Ba, "Battle of Ap Bac: Myth and Reality." (https://baovecovang2012.wordpress.com/2013/01/15/tran-ap-bac-thuc-te-va-huyen-thoai-chuan-tuong-ly-tong-ba/).

10. Krepinevich, *Army and Vietnam*, 67; Elliott, *The Vietnamese War*, 76; Pribbenow, *Victory in Vietnam*, 110; Goscha, "A war for Indochina?" 50.

11. FRUS, Vietnam, 1961–1963, II, documents 88, 92, 96; "Vietnam: A Television History; Interview with Lucien Conein," 7 May 1981. (WGBH Media Library & Archives).

12. Elliott, *The Vietnamese War*, 164; Cosmas, *MACV, 1962–1967*, 76; Stewart, *Vietnam's Lost Revolution*, 213–4; Harris, *Vietnam's High Ground*, 83–4.

13. Cable, *Conflict of Myths*, 76, 78–9; Noel Barber, *The War of the Running Dogs: How Malaya Defeated the Communist Guerrillas, 1948–1960* (London: Cassell, 1971), 211; Mao Tse-tung, *On Guerrilla Warfare*, Samuel B. Griffith, trans. (New York: Praeger, 1961), 93.

14. Thompson, *Defeating Communist Insurgency*, 122–3; Phillips, *Why Vietnam Matters*, 111.

15. Phillips, *Why Vietnam Matters*, 122.

16. Neese and O'Donnell, *Prelude to Tragedy*, 96, 101–2, 106–8, 216, 221.

17. Harris, *Vietnam's High Ground*, 122–3, 130–1.

18. Pribbenow, *Victory in Vietnam*, 109; Elliott, *The Vietnamese War*, 178.

19. FRUS, Vietnam, 1961–1963, II, documents 93, 116, 173; Truong Nhu Tang, *A Viet Cong Memoir*, 47; Stanley Karnow, *Vietnam: A History* (New York: Viking, 1983), 257; Jacobs, *Cold War*

Mandarin, 127; Thompson, *Defeating Communist Insurgency*, 138.

20. FRUS, Vietnam, 1961–1963, II, documents 93, 116, 173; Truong Nhu Tang, *A Viet Cong Memoir*, 47; Karnow, *Vietnam: A History*, 257; Jacobs, *Cold War Mandarin*, 127; Thompson, *Defeating Communist Insurgency*, 138; Phillips, *Why Vietnam Matters*, 140.

21. William A. Buckingham, Jr. *Operation Ranch Hand: The Air Force and Herbicides in Southeast Asia, 1961–1971* (Washington: USAF Office of Air Force History, 1982), 11, 16, 28. Ranch Hand initially was to be covert and thus began as a "project" instead of an "operation."

22. Military Assistance Command Vietnam, Historical Branch. *Command History, 1964* (Saigon: Headquarters MACV, 15 October 1965), 103; Buckingham, *Operation Ranch Hand*, 21, 31, 36, 42, 44, 63, 70, 79, 81, 85. The key roads were Highway 1 and routes 13, 14, 15.

23. Berman, *Perfect Spy*, 136–7; Elliott, *The Vietnamese War*, 171, 200; FBIS, *Anti-U.S. Resistance War*, 52. An's cover was as a journalist in *Reuters'* Saigon office at the time.

24. Elliott, *The Vietnamese War*, 171, 200; FBIS, *Anti-U.S. Resistance War*, 52; Buckingham, *Operation Ranch Hand*, 63, 71.

25. Moyar, *Victory Forsaken*, 187; Elliott, *The Vietnamese War*, 179; Sheehan, *Bright Shining Lie*, 119.

26. J.A. Koch, *The Chieu Hoi Program in South Vietnam, 1963–1971* (Santa Monica CA: RAND, 1973), v–vi, xix; Neese and O'Donnell, *Prelude to Tragedy*, 196; FRUS, Vietnam, 1961–1963, III, documents 10, 92, 107, 207 and IV, document 306. In 1966, the U.S. Marines took the program a step further and recruited "Chieu Hoi" Viet Cong soldiers to fight with Marine units in combat. They were called "Kit Carson Scouts" after the famous 19th century Western frontier scout.

27. MACV, "21st Infantry Division ARVN and 42nd DTA," 5; Department of the Army, *Training of the South Vietnamese Army*, 18, 20, 29, 34; Republic of Vietnam, *The Armed Forces of the Republic of Vietnam*, 15; Hoang Ngoc Lung, *Strategy and Tactics*, 16; Spector, *Advice and Support*, 290. See Map 7; Tucker, *Encyclopedia of the Vietnam War*, 240; Harris, *Vietnam's High Ground*, 136, 140.

28. Pribbenow, *Victory in Vietnam*, 110; CINCPAC, *Command History, 1962*, 147, 174; FRUS, Vietnam, 1961–1963, II, documents 68, 328.

29. CINCPAC, *Command History 1962*, 148; Republic of Vietnam, "The Republic of Vietnam Armed Forces, Vietnam Report VIII," (Washington: Embassy of the Republic of Vietnam, 1967), 12, table 1; Nguyen, *Hanoi's War*, 61; Stewart, *Vietnam's Lost Revolution*, 225; Harris, *Vietnam's High Ground*, 82.

30. MACV, "Information on the 21st Infantry Division," 4; MACV, "21st Infantry Division ARVN and 42nd DTA," 5.

31. Hanyok, *Spartans in Darkness*, 135;

Pribbenow, *Victory in Vietnam*, 119; Elliott, *The Vietnamese War*, 180. The title should have been the battle of "Bac" as Americans always omitted the word "Ap" except in this case. Tan Thoi also was cited as Tam Thoi.

32. Toczek, *The Battle of Ap Bac*, 72–4. The Civil Guard was forming combat battalions but none were at Ap Bac.

33. Sheehan, *Bright Shining Lie*, 235; Toczak, *The Battle of Ap Bac*, 68, 72–3; Ha Mai Viet, *Steel and Blood*, 11, 293; Starry, *Mounted Combat in Vietnam*, 21, 24; Ly Tong Ba, "Battle of Ap Bac: Myth and Reality."

34. Toczak, *The Battle of Ap Bac*, 68, 72–3; Ha Mai Viet, *Steel and Blood*, 11, 293; Starry, *Mounted Combat in Vietnam*, 21, 24; Ly Tong Ba, "Battle of Ap Bac: Myth and Reality."

35. Cao Van Vien, *Leadership*, 53; Sheehan, *Bright Shining Lie*, 213; Toczek, *Battle of Ap Bac*, 72–3, 80. Tan Hiep was also called Tam Hiep and located 5km northwest of My Tho.

36. Elliott, *The Vietnamese War*, 183.

37. Ly Tong Ba, "Battle of Ap Bac: Myth and Reality."

38. Sheehan, *Bright Shining Lie*, 210; Moyar, *Triumph Forsaken*, 187; Elliott, *The Vietnamese War*, 119, 180. The 514th Battalion was Nam Bo's best, having been in action since December 1959 when first formed as the My Tho Provincial Armed Unit C211 under Sau Danh, the provincial commander.

39. Elliott, *The Vietnamese War*, 63, 181–2.

40. Sheehan, *Bright Shining Lie*, 222, 262; Hanyok, *Spartans in Darkness*, 136.

41. Cao Van Vien, *Leadership*, 54; Department of State, "10 January 1963 Memorandum for Governor Harriman: Your Conversation with Ken Crawford," (Washington: Department of State, 1963); Sheehan, *Bright Shining Lie*, 211;

42. Sheehan, *Bright Shining Lie*, 258.

43. Toczek, *Battle of Ap Bac*, 78–9.

44. Moyar, *Victory Forsaken*, 190.

45. Sheehan, *Bright Shining Lie*, 213–4.

46. Sheehan, *Bright Shining Lie*, 216.

47. Moyar, *Victory Forsaken*, 189; Toczek, *Battle of Ap Bac*, 87; Elliott, *The Vietnamese War*, 183; Sheehan, *Bright Shining Lie*, 216, 220.

48. Ly Tong Ba, "Battle of Ap Bac: Myth and Reality."

49. Ly Tong Ba, "Battle of Ap Bac: Myth and Reality." The canal also was referred to as the Cong Ba Ky.

50. Sheehan, *Bright Shining Lie*, 236, 247–8, 252–3.

51. Ha Mai Viet, *Steel and Blood*, 13–4; Sheehan, *Bright Shining Lie*, 243, 248–9; Moyar, *Victory Forsaken*, 191–2; Ly Tong Ba, "Battle of Ap Bac: Myth and Reality."

52. Cao Van Vien, *Leadership*, 54; Sheehan, *Bright Shining Lie*, 261–2; Ha Mai Viet, *Steel and Blood*, 14–5; Ly Tong Ba, "Battle of Ap Bac: Myth and Reality."

53. Moyar, *Victory Forsaken*, 188.

54. Starry, *Mounted Combat in Vietnam*, 38,

40–1; Ly Tong Ba, "Battle of Ap Bac: Myth and Reality."

55. Elliott, *The Vietnamese War*, 180; David G. Garr, "Vietnam: Art of the National Liberation Front, An Exhibition, (Cornell: Cornell University, 1970).

56. Palmer, *25-Year War*, 22; Sheehan, *Bright Shining Lie*, 231; Elliott, *The Vietnamese War*, 178.

57. Ha Mai Viet, *Steel and Blood*, 17; Neese and O'Donnell, *Prelude to Tragedy*, 219. Ba continued to excel as a combat commander, eventually being promoted to general and commander of an infantry division.

58. Tourison, *Secret Army, Secret War*, 172; Allen, *None So Blind*, 20.

59. Hastings, *Vietnam*, 164; Moyar, *Victory Forsaken*, 195, 203; Nguyen Manh Hung, "Journalistic Distortions: Neil Sheehan's Portrait of the Vietnamese in *A Bright Shining Lie* (1988)," *Journal of Vietnam Veterans Institute*, 2, no. 1, (1993), 20–1; Phillips, *Why Vietnam Matters*, 141–2.

60. Buckingham, *Operation Ranch Hand*, 96; GWUNSA, *Intelligence and Vietnam (II)*, A-II-4.

61. Elliott, *The Vietnamese War*, 188–9; Pribbenow, *Victory in Vietnam*, 120–1; Harris, *Vietnam's High Ground*, 167–8.

Chapter 15

1. Hammer, *A Death in November*, 83.

2. Higgins, *Nightmare*, 91; FRUS, Vietnam, 1961–1963, III, document 116. This had no connection to the draconian 1959 Decree Ten that allowed summary trials, imprisonment and execution of suspected Viet Cong and Viet Cong sympathizers.

3. Colby, *Lost Victory*, 139.

4. Colby, *Lost Victory*, 130; Miller, *Misalliance*, 264.

5. Colby, *Lost Victory*, 130; Miller, *Misalliance*, 264, Sean Fear, "The Ambiguous Legacy of Ngo Dinh Diem in South Vietnam's Second Republic (1967–1975)" *Journal of Vietnamese Studies*, 11, no. 1 (2106), 7.

6. FRUS, Vietnam, 1961–1963, III, documents 112, 116; Prados, *Hidden History*, 90; Halberstam, *Quagmire*, 117; Higgins, *Nightmare*, 92; Hammer, *A Death in November*, 105, 110. Vesak Day is held on the full moon during the Hindu calendar month of Vaisakha that fell on 8 May in 1963.

7. FRUS, Vietnam, 1961–1963, III, document 116.

8. James McAllister, "'Only Religions Count in Vietnam': Thich Tri Quang and the Vietnam War," *Modern Asia Studies*, 42, 4 (2008), 778; Only after the 1963 Buddhist Crisis did Thich Tri Quang admit that he had deliberately exploited the flag issue to launch what he called a Buddhist-centric "social revolution" in South Vietnam.

9. Hammer, *A Death in November*, 113; FRUS, Vietnam, 1961–1963, III, documents 112, 116, 117; Higgins, *Nightmare*, 90, 93; Moyar, *Triumph Forsaken*, 212–3.

10. FRUS, Vietnam, 1961–1963, III, documents 112, 116, 117; Higgins, *Nightmare*, 90, 93; Hammer, *A Death in November*, 115; Moyar, *Triumph Forsaken*, 212–3.

11. Halberstam, *Quagmire*, 116.

12. Joseph Kraft, "Michael V. Forrestal Oral History Interview, 1964 (JFK Library), 136.

13. Browne, *New Face of War*, 177.

14. Higgins, *Nightmare*, 4; Lacouture, *Vietnam Between Two Truces*, 71–2; Savani, *Face and Images*, 266; Fall, *Street Without Joy*, 342; Gerard Tongas, *Communist Inferno*, 421; "Vietnam: A Television History; Interview with Eldridge Durbrow, Part 2 of 2." For a study on misreporting the Buddhist majority, see Lisa M. Skow and George N. Dionisopoulos, "A struggle to contextualize photographic images: American print media and the 'Burning Monk.'" *Communication Quarterly*, 45, no.4 (Fall 1997); 393–409. (http://enlight.lib.ntu.edu.tw/FULLTEXT/JR-EPT/lisa.htm).

15. Savani, *Face and Images*, 58.

16. Savani, *Face and Images*, 198–9; Nicholas Tarling, ed. *The Cambridge History of Southeast Asia, Volume Two* (Cambridge: Cambridge University Press, 2008), 202; Tai Thu Nguyen, ed., *The History of Buddhism in Vietnam* (Washington DC: Council for Research in Values and Philosophy, 2008), 2; Tongas, *Communist Inferno*, 421; Lacouture, *Vietnam Between Two Truces*, 72; Pike, *Viet Cong*, 12; U.S. Navy Chaplains Division, *The Religions of South Vietnam in Faith and Fact—NAVPERS 15991* (Washington DC: United States Navy, 1967), 17; Tuan Hong, "Ideology in Urban South Vietnam," 225. Attempts at reconciling Buddhism and Confucianism had begun in the 5th century.

17. Hastings, *Vietnam: An Epic Tragedy*, 111; Savani, *Face and Images*, 68; Pike, *Viet Cong*, 2.

18. Higgins, *Vietnam Nightmare*, 43; Tongas, *Communist Inferno*, 419, 421; Stephen Pan and Daniel Lyons, *Vietnam Crisis* (New York, East Asian Research Center, 1966), 115; George McTurnan Kahin, ed. *Government and Politics in Southeast Asia* (Ithaca, NY: Cornell University Press, 1965), 418; Neese and O'Donnell, *Prelude to Tragedy*, 143, 185, 195.

19. FRUS, 1952–1954, Geneva Convention, XVI, document 840.

20. Fall, "Political-Religious Sects," 235, 237; Miller, *Misalliance*, 91; Boot, *Road Not Taken*, 202; Office of Current Intelligence (OCI) Special Report "The Buddhists in South Vietnam, 28 June 1963" (Washington DC: CIA, 1963), 1; Chaplains, *Religions of South Vietnam*, 46–47; Hammer, *A Death in November*, 139; FRUS, Vietnam, 1961–1963, III, document 292 and 1964–1968, I, document 123; Pike, *Viet Cong*, 12; Jerema Swoviak, "The Role of Religion and Politico-Religious Organizations in the South Vietnam During the Ngo Dinh Diem Period," Zeszyty Naukove Tovarzystva Doktorantov Uj Nauki Spoweczne, NR 16 (1/2017), 123; Jeremy Jammes, "Le Saint-Siege Caodaiste de Tay Ninh et le Medium Phan Cong Tac (1890–1959)" *Outre-Mers* T. 94, no. 352–353 (2006), 109.

21. Hansen, "Bac Di Cu: Catholic Refugees," 176–7, 178.

22. Colby, *Lost Victory*, 128–9; Hammer, *A Death in November*, 139; Savani, *Face and Images*, 66.

23. Lacouture, *Vietnam: Between Two Truces*, 109; Hammer, *A Death in November*, 139–40.

24. Kiernan, *How Pol Pot Came to Power*, 3–4.

25. Duiker, "Phan Boi Chau," 86;

26. McAllister, "Only Religions Count," 759, 776; Tai Thu Nguyen, *Buddhism in Vietnam*, 281–2, 290–1; Chaplains, *Religions of South Vietnam*, 53; CIA OCI, "Buddhism," 2; FRUS, Vietnam, 1961–1963, IV, document 75.

27. Moyar, *Triumph Forsaken*, 316; McAllister, "Only Religions Count," 756.

28. CIA, "Buddhist Action in Vietnam: A Special Assessment of the Situation in the Light of Events in March April 1966," dated 29 April 1966 (Washington DC: Central Intelligence Agency, 1966).

29. Hammer, *A Death in November*, 141. The word "sangha" has different meanings. For followers of the Theravada school, the sangha usually refers to only the clerics, but in South Vietnam, dominated by the Mahayana, the sangha included the entire Buddhist community, both clerics and lay people.

30. OCI, "Buddhism," 2–3; Chaplains, *Religions of South Vietnam*, 20.

31. Hammer, *A Death in November*, 84; OCI, "Buddhism," 2–3; Chaplains, *Religions of South Vietnam*, 20.

32. Central Intelligence Agency, Memorandum on "Freedom of Religion in North and South Vietnam, 15 May 1974," (Washington DC: Central Intelligence Agency, 1974), 3; Shaw, *Lost Mandate*, 195; Higgins, *Nightmare*, 45, 18; Prados, *Hidden History*, 90; Tan, "Spiritual Fraternities: Ngo Dinh Diem's Personalist Revolution," 16.

33. Tongas, *Communist Inferno*, 424–5.

34. Tongas, *Communist Inferno*, 424.

35. Tai Thu Nguyen, *Buddhism in Vietnam*, 273; Tongas, *Communist Inferno*, 424; Chaplains, *Religions of South Vietnam*, 20; Lacouture, *Vietnam: Between Two Truces*, 217, 223; Gheddo, *The Cross and the Bo-Tree*, 79.

36. Higgins, *Nightmare*, 46; FRUS, Vietnam, 1961–1963, III, documents 118, 159, 168. At this time, when U.S. officials or the American press referred to the Buddhists, they meant Thich Tri Quang and his coterie.

37. FRUS, Vietnam, 1961–1963, III, documents 116, 118; Zi Jun Toong, "Overthrown by the Press: The US Media's Role in the Fall of Diem," *Australian Journal of American Studies*, 27, no.1 (July 2008), 59.

38. FRUS, Vietnam, 1961–1963, III, documents 117, 118; Halberstam, *Quagmire*, 116. Ironically, U Chan Htoon soon was imprisoned for using his stature as a Buddhist leader to oppose Burma's military dictatorship. Afterwards the World Buddhist Federation headquarters staff fled to Bangkok, Thailand.

39. FRUS, Vietnam, 1961–1963, III, documents 128; Hammer, *A Death in November*, 118–9.

40. FRUS, Vietnam, 1961–1963, III, documents 128, 139, 140, 142.

41. FRUS, Vietnam, 1955–1957, II, documents 44, 49 and 1961–1963, III, document 138.

42. Hammer, *A Death in November*, 136; FRUS, Vietnam, 1961–1963, III, documents 144, 146, 148, 149, 151.

43. Hammer, *A Death in November*, 136; FRUS, Vietnam, 1961–1963, III, documents 146, 148, 149, 151.

44. FRUS, Vietnam, 1961–1963, III, document 142.

45. FRUS, Vietnam, 1961–1963, III, documents 112, 143.

46. FRUS, Vietnam, 1961–1963, III, document 157.

47. Neese and O'Donnell, *Prelude to Tragedy*, 197; Malcolm W. Browne, *Muddy Boots and Red Socks: A Reporter's Life* (New York: Times Books, 1993), 9.

48. Browne, *Muddy Boots and Red Socks*, 9.

49. FRUS, Vietnam, 1961–1963, III, documents 151, 153, 157 and 1964–1968, IV, document 160.

50. FRUS, Vietnam, 1961–1963, III, documents 153, 170.

51. FRUS, Vietnam, 1961–1963, III, document 153.

52. FRUS, Vietnam, 1961–1963, III, documents 155, 170.

53. Hammer, *A Death in November*, 138.

54. See: Video recording of Thich Tam Chau on the self-immolation of Bodhisattva Thich Quang Duc (July 2013) (http://www.youtube.com/watch?v=e7eFkc5XWr4).

55. Tai Thu Nguyen, *Buddhism in Vietnam*, 2, 48–9; Higgins, *Nightmare*, 86–7; Hammer, *A Death in November*, 145–6.

56. Moyar, *Triumph Forsaken*, 221; Halberstam, *Quagmire*, 127–9.

57. Hammer, *A Death in November*, 144.

58. Browne, *Muddy Boots*, 9–10; Hammer, *A Death in November*, 138, 144; Frederick Nolting, *From Trust to Tragedy*, 112.

59. FRUS, Vietnam, 1961–1963, III, document 163.

60. Jacobs, *Cold War Mandarin*, 149.

61. FRUS, Vietnam, 1961–1963, III, document 157, note 2.

62. Demery, *Dragon Lady*, 136.

63. FRUS, Vietnam, 1961–1963, III, document 157, note 2.

64. McAllister, "Only Religions Count in Vietnam," 755, 764, 765, 769; FRUS, Vietnam, 1961–1963, III, document 158.

65. FRUS, Vietnam, 1961–1963, III, document 166.

66. FRUS, Vietnam, 1961–1963, III, document 168.

67. Hammer, *A Death in November*, 145; FRUS, Vietnam, 1961–1963, III, documents 165, 170.

68. FRUS, Vietnam, 1961–1963, III, document 172.

69. Higgins, *Nightmare*, 80.

70. Higgins, *Nightmare*, 41, 87; Hammer, *A*

Death in November, 138; Prados, *Hidden History*, 100.

71. Chaplains, *Religions of South Vietnam*, 53; OCI, "Buddhism," 2; Adams, *War of Numbers*, 32–3.

72. FRUS, Vietnam, 1961–1963, III, document 174.

73. Colby, *Lost Victory*, 131.

74. Colby, *Lost Victory*, 131.

75. "Vietnam: A Television History; Interview with Eldridge Durbrow, Part 2 of 2."

76. Dennis J. O'Brien, "Roger Hilsman Interview I" (JFK Library), 4.

77. FRUS, Vietnam, 1961–1963, III, documents 196, 198; David Halberstam, *Best and Brightest*, (New York: Ballantine, 1992), 256–7; Higgins, *Nightmare*, 43–4; Kraft, "Third Oral Interview with Forrestal," 136; GWUNSA, *Intelligence and Vietnam (II)*, B-RFE-90. The increase in VC incidents after November stemmed directly from COSV orders to exploit the chaos created by Diem's assassination.

78. FRUS, Vietnam, 1961–1963, III, documents 196, 198; Halberstam, *Best and Brightest*, 256–7; Higgins, *Nightmare*, 43–4.

79. FRUS, Vietnam, 1961–1963, III, document 172; CIA Information Report "Thich Tri Quang's Dissatisfaction over Published Statements by American Officials and his Indication of a Continuation of the Buddhist Struggle," 3 August 1963.

80. Higgins, *Nightmare*, 22–3, 45, 81.

81. FRUS, Vietnam, 1961–1963, II, document 304 and III, document 191; CIA Report "Quang's Dissatisfaction," 1, 4.

82. FRUS, Vietnam, 1961–1963, II, document 304 and III, document 191; CIA Report "Quang's Dissatisfaction," 1, 4.

83. FRUS, Vietnam, 1961–1963, III, document 186.

84. Boot, *Road Not Taken*, 356.

Chapter 16

1. FRUS, Vietnam, 1961–1963, III, document 133; Hilsman, *Move A Nation*, 142; Kraft, "Forrestal Oral History," 42; Joshua Kurlantzick, *A Great Place to have a War: American and the Birth of a CIA Military* (New York: Simon and Shuster, 2016), 42.

2. FRUS, Vietnam, 1961–1963, III, document 133.

3. FRUS, Vietnam, 1961–1963, III, document 22.

4. FRUS, Vietnam, 1961–1963, III, documents 195, 196.

5. FRUS, Vietnam, 1961–1963, III, document 198.

6. FRUS, Vietnam, 1961–1963, III, document 208.

7. Nolting, *Trust to Tragedy*, 113.

8. Kraft, "Forrestal Oral History," 48.

9. FRUS, Vietnam, 1961–1963, III, document 205.

10. Vietnam: A Television History: Interview with Lucien Conein."

11. FRUS, Vietnam, 1961–1963, III, document 229.

12. FRUS, Vietnam, 1961–1963, III, document 229.

13. Hunt, *A Vietnam War Reader*, 52; FRUS, Vietnam, 1961–1963, III, document 229.

14. Nolting, *Trust to Tragedy*, 113; FRUS, Vietnam, 1961–1963, IV, documents 96, 215.

15. FRUS, Vietnam, 1961–1963, III, documents 214, 218, 224.

16. FRUS, Vietnam, 1961–1963, III, document 228.

17. FRUS, Vietnam, 1961–1963, III, document 228.

18. FRUS, Vietnam, 1961–1963, III, document 229.

19. FRUS, Vietnam, 1961–1963, III, document 237.

20. Nolting, *Trust to Tragedy*, 114; FRUS, Vietnam, 1961–1963, III, document 241.

21. FRUS, Vietnam, 1961–1963, III, document 243.

22. CIA Information Report "Quang's Dissatisfaction," 1, 4; FRUS, Vietnam, 1961–1963, III, document 243.

23. FRUS, Vietnam, 1961–1963, III, document 246.

24. Neese and O'Donnell, *Prelude to Tragedy*, 276.

25. Higgins, *Nightmare*, 72; FRUS, Vietnam, 1961–1963, III, document 249n6; Karnow, "Interview with Edward Geary Lansdale, 1979, Part 2 of 5."

26. FRUS, Vietnam, 1961–1963, III, document 246.

27. Colby, *Lost Victory*, 133.

28. FRUS, Vietnam, 1961–1963, III, document 246.

29. Hammer, *A Death in November*, 163–4.

30. FRUS, Vietnam, 1961–1963, III, document 248.

31. Halberstam, *Quagmire*, 141.

32. Hammer, *Death in November*, 165; Halberstam, *Quagmire*, 140.

33. Hammer, *Death in November*, 165–6; Halberstam, *Quagmire*, 145–6; FRUS, Vietnam, 1961–1963, III, documents 261, 264.

34. FRUS, Vietnam, 1961–1963, III, document 261.

35. FRUS, Vietnam, 1961–1963, IV, document 80; Hammer, *Death in November*, 166; GWUNSA, *New Light in a Dark Corner*, document 5. The seven generals were, in addition to Don and Tri: Brigadier General Le Van Kim (deputy CJGS and Don's brother-in-law), Major General Tran Van Khiem (ARVN Chief of Staff), Major General Nguyen Khanh (commander II Corps), Ton That Dinh (commander III Corps), Brigadier General Huyen Van Cao (commander IV Corps). General Don became acting Chief of the JGS earlier in August when current CJGS Major General Le Van Ty, a Diem loyalist, was diagnosed with lung cancer and had to undergo extensive medical treatment.

36. Hammer, *Death in November*, 166–7; Halberstam, *Quagmire*, 143–4; FRUS, Vietnam, 1961–1963, III, documents 261, 264.

37. FRUS, Vietnam, 1961–1963, III, document 261.

38. Halberstam, *Quagmire*, 143–4.

39. FRUS, Vietnam, 1961–1963, III, document 275.

40. Halberstam, *Quagmire*, 147.

41. FRUS, Vietnam, 1961–1963, III, document 275.

42. Hilsman *To Move a Nation*, 487; Colby, *Lost Victory*, 136.

43. Nguyen Tien Hung and Jerrold L. Schecter, *The Palace File* (New York: Perennial Library, 1978), 76.

44. Higgins, *Nightmare*, 208.

45. FRUS, Vietnam, 1961–1963, IV, document 48.

46. FRUS, Vietnam, 1961–1963, III, document 281.

47. Neese and O'Donnell, *Prelude to Tragedy*, 44.

48. FRUS, Indochina, 1952–1954, XIII, Part 2, document 1208.

49. "Vietnam: A Television History; Interview with Tran Van Don."

50. FRUS, Vietnam, 1961–1963, III, document 282.

51. Admiral Felt later was formally reprimanded for his actions on 24 August, see FRUS, Vietnam, 1961–1963, III, document 289n7; "Vietnam: A Television History: Interview with Lucien Conein."

52. FRUS, Vietnam, 1961–1963, III, document 280.

53. Hammer, *Death in November*, 174; FRUS, Vietnam, 1961–1963, III, documents 276n3, 281; "Vietnam: A Television History; Interview with Tran Van Don." Hai's "bitterness" toward the Nhus dated back to at least 1962, see: 14 September 1962 Fishel letter (http://vietnamproject.archives.msu.edu/fullrecord.php?kid=6-20-54).

54. Higgins, *Nightmare*, 198–9.

55. Hilsman, *To Move a Nation*, 489; FRUS, Vietnam, 1961–1963, III, document 288.

56. FRUS, Vietnam, 1961–1963, III, document 282.

57. FRUS, Vietnam, 1961–1963, III, documents 282, 309n1; Colby, *Lost Victory*, 138–9.

58. FRUS, Vietnam, 1961–1963, III, document 289. Hilsman paraphrased the President: "Halberstam was a 28-year old kid and he [the President] wanted assurances we were not giving him serious consideration in our decision." According to Higgins, that was exactly what Hilsman was doing, but it is also probable that he and *NYT* correspondent were feeding each other information to their mutual benefit, see: Shaw, *Lost Mandate*, 255.

59. Hilsman, *To Move a Nation*, 490.

60. "Vietnam: A Television History: Interview with Lucien Conein."

61. FRUS, Vietnam, 1961–1963, III, document 290.

62. Phillips, *Why Vietnam Matters*, 205, 226; Boot, *The Road not Taken*, 414–5; Nichter, *The Last Brahmin*, 220; Rust, "CIA Operations Officer Lucien Conein," 51. Conein's post-coup memories were not pleasant. He could not bring himself to look at Diem's corpse. In January 1964 he returned to Washington to receive the CIA Intelligence Star medal for making the coup a success, and it must have been more than awkward, as the entire CIA chain of command from McCone to Colby to Richardson had opposed the coup. A few years later and after a night of drinking, Conein opened up and pleaded with Lansdale to forgive him for his role in Diem's assassination.

63. FRUS, Vietnam, 1961–1963, IV, document 1.

64. FRUS, Vietnam, 1961–1963, IV, document 1.

65. FRUS, Vietnam, 1961–1963, IV, document 1.

66. FRUS, Vietnam, 1961–1963, IV, document 1.

67. VanDeMark, *Road to Disaster*, 171.

68. FRUS, Vietnam, 1961–1963, IV, document 1.

69. Colby, *Lost Victory*, 139; FRUS, Vietnam, 1961–1963, IV, documents 1, 6.

70. Dean Rusk as told to Richard Rusk, *As I Saw It* (New York: W. W. Norton, 1990), 437.

71. FRUS, Vietnam, 1961–1963, IV, document 6; Hilsman, *To Move a Nation*, 492–3; GWUNSA, *New Light in a Dark Corner*, document 6. Neither Hilsman nor Forrestal, who never saw the straightforward cable from Taylor to Harkins (FRUS, Vietnam, 1961–1963, III, document 309) wrongly assumed that Taylor, not Harriman, was the one who displeased the president by twisting facts.

72. Colby, *Lost Victory*, 141; FRUS, Vietnam, 1961–1963, IV, document 22.

73. FRUS, Vietnam, 1961–1963, IV, documents 32, 33.

74. FRUS, Vietnam, 1961–1963, IV, documents 49, 113.

75. Colby, *Lost Victory*, 141.

76. FRUS, Vietnam, 1961–1963, IV, documents 49, 113, GWUNSA, *New Light in a Dark Corner*, document 17.

77. Nichter, *The Last Brahmin*, 199.

78. Colby, *Lost Victory*, 140; FRUS, Vietnam, 1961–1963, IV, documents 72, 94; Nichter, *The Last Brahmin*, 220; Zi, "Overthrown by the Press," 60 (Figure 1), 62–3.

79. FRUS, Vietnam, 1961–1963, IV, document 104.

80. Phillips, *Why Vietnam Matters*, 199; Nichter, *The Last Brahmin*, 218, 231–2; John H. Richardson, "The Spy Left Out in the Cold," *New York Times*, 7 August 2005 (http://www.nytimes.com/2005/08/07/opinion/the-spy-left-out-in-the-cold.html)

81. Neese and O'Donnell, *Prelude to Tragedy*, 149; Demery, *Dragon Lady*, 29, 167; CIA Saigon Report no. DA IN 108950, 24 September 1963, "Tran Kim Tuyen Predicts Dire Prospects for Diem Regime."

82. Demery, *Dragon Lady*, 29, 167; CIA Saigon Report no. DA IN 108950, 24 September 1963, "Tran Kim Tuyen Predicts Dire Prospects for Diem Regime."

83. McNamara, *In Retrospect*, 64.

84. FRUS, Vietnam, 1961–1963, IV, document 114.

85. Hilsman, *To Move a Nation*, 482.

86. FRUS, Vietnam, 1961–1963, IV, document 80.

87. FRUS, Vietnam, 1961–1963, IV, documents 157, 216; Colby, *Lost Victory*, 142–3.

88. Charles Bartlett, "Henry Cabot Lodge, Oral History Interview" (JFK Library), 28.

89. FRUS, Vietnam, 1961–1963, IV, document 155.

90. FRUS, Vietnam, 1961–1963, IV, document 155.

91. FRUS, Vietnam, 1961–1963, IV, document 164.

92. McNamara, *In Retrospect*, 78–9.

93. FRUS, Vietnam, 1961–1963, IV, documents 176, 179, 181, 239; GWUNSA, *New Light in a Dark Corner*, document 20. The full truth about who knew what and when in early October may never be known. A critical message on "Big" Minh's coup machinations, CIA CAS 1448, cannot be found.

94. FRUS, Vietnam, 1961–1963, IV, document 177.

95. FRUS, Vietnam, 1961–1963, IV, document 182.

96. McNamara, *In Retrospect*, 81; FRUS, Vietnam, 1961–1963, IV, document 183; GWUNSA, *New Light in a Dark Corner*, document 19.

97. Nichter, *The Last Brahmin*, 233; FRUS, Vietnam, 1961–1963, IV, document 192.

98. FRUS, Vietnam, 1961–1963, IV, document 192.

99. FRUS, Vietnam, 1961–1963, IV, document 192.

Chapter 17

1. FRUS, Vietnam, 1961–1963, IV, document 200; Higgins, *Nightmare*, 169.

2. Nolting, *From Trust to Tragedy*, 132; FRUS, Vietnam, 1961–1963, IV, document 139.

3. FRUS, Vietnam, 1961–1963, I, document 210 and IV, documents 157, 177, 230.

4. FRUS, Vietnam, 1961–1963, IV, document 206.

5. FRUS, Vietnam, 1961–1963, IV, documents 207, 209; Tran Van Don, *Our Endless War*, 84; GWUNSA, *New Light in a Dark Corner*, documents 21–3.

6. FRUS, Vietnam, 1961–1963, IV, document 213.

7. Tran Van Don, *Our Endless War*, 59–60; FRUS, Vietnam, 1961–1963, IV, document 215; Boot, *Road Not Taken*, 411.

8. FRUS, Vietnam, 1961–1963, IV, document 230.

9. FRUS, Vietnam, 1961–1963, IV, documents 227, 234.

10. FRUS, Vietnam, 1961–1963, IV, documents 227, 232, 233, 234.

11. FRUS, Vietnam, 1961–1963, IV, documents 227, 232, 233, 234.

12. FRUS, Vietnam, 1961–1963, IV, document 234.

13. Rust, "CIA Operations Officer Lucien Conein," 51.

14. McNamara, *In Retrospect*, 81–82.

15. McNamara, *In Retrospect*, 81.

16. FRUS, Vietnam, 1961–1963, IV, documents 235, 236.

17. McNamara, *In Retrospect*, 82.

18. FRUS, Vietnam, 1961–1963, IV, document 236

19. FRUS, Vietnam, 1961–1963, IV, document 13.

20. FRUS, Vietnam, 1961–1963, IV, document 236.

21. Bartlett, "Henry Cabot Lodge Oral Interview," 28; FRUS, Vietnam, 1961–1963, IV, documents 242, 249.

22. FRUS, Vietnam, 1961–1963, IV, document 249.

23. FRUS, Vietnam, 1961–1963, IV, document 247.

24. FRUS, Vietnam, 1961–1963, IV, document 247.

25. Bartlett, "Henry Cabot Lodge Oral Interview," 29.

26. Hilsman, *To Move a Nation*, 518; Phillips, *Why Vietnam Matters*, 203; Nguyen Tien Hung and Schecter, *The Palace File*, 76.

27. GWUNSA, *New Light in a Dark Corner*, document 24.

28. "Vietnam: A Television History: Interview with Lucien Conein."

29. Bartlett, "Henry Cabot Lodge Oral Interview," 29; CIA, "Coup Timeline Sequence (All Times indicated are local Saigon Time, 1 November), 1 November 1963," 1; CIA Report, OCI no. 3238/63, "Progress of the Coup d'État in Saigon (as of 0800 EST); 1; GWUNSA, *New Light in a Dark Corner*, document 26.

30. FRUS, Vietnam, 1961–1963, IV, document 258; Hilsman, *To Move a Nation*, 520; OCI Report, "Progress of the Coup," 1–2. The fates of Diem loyalists varied. Colonel Vien was relieved of his command only to be reinstated a month later. Marine Colonel Khang was sent to Philippines as military attaché. Air Force Colonel Hien was retired. Duong Van Hieu later was sentenced to life in prison but released after a year by the leaders of another coup, while Ngo Trong Hieu also was tried and imprisoned.

31. FRUS, Vietnam, 1961–1963, IV, document 256.

32. CIA, "Coup Timeline Sequence," 2; Westmoreland, *A Soldier Reports*, 115; FRUS, Vietnam, 1961–1963, IV, document 262.

33. FRUS, Vietnam, 1961–1963, IV, document 259.

34. Tran Van Don, *Our Endless War*, 107, 112; Hastings, *Vietnam*, 199–200; Bartlett, "Henry Cabot Lodge Oral Interview," 31; Phillips, *Why Vietnam Matters*, 205.

35. Colby, *Lost Victory*, 158.

36. Moyar, *Triumph Forsaken*, 286.

37. Lien-Hang T. Nguyen, *Hanoi's War*, 49; Currey, *Victory at any Cost*, 243; Elliott, *The Vietnamese War*, 222.

38. Hunt, *A Vietnam War Reader*, 62–3.

39. Moyar, *Triumph Forsaken*, 286–7; Elliott, *The Vietnamese War*, 202; Chen, "Hanoi's Three Decisions," 253; Asselin, *Hanoi's Road*, 165; Lien-Hang T. Nguyen, *Hanoi's War*, 66–7; Asselin, *Vietnam's American War*, 109.

40. Porter, *Perils of Dominance*, 128.

41. Elliott, *The Vietnamese War*, 218; DCI, *Highlanders of South Vietnam*, 1.

42. Martinez, *The Viet Cong Proselytizing Program*, 218, 223; Lien-Hang T. Nguyen, *Hanoi's War*, 65, 74; *Victory Forsaken*, 326; Pribbenow, *Victory in Vietnam*, 125.

43. Lien-Hang T. Nguyen, *Hanoi's War*, 65, 74; Moyar, *Victory Forsaken*, 326; Pribbenow, *Victory in Vietnam*, 125; Porter, *Perils of Dominance*, 132.

44. Elliott, *The Vietnamese War*, 222; Higgins, *Nightmare*, 153, 154; Lien-Hang T. Nguyen, *Hanoi's War*, 65; Porter, *Perils of Dominance*, 132.

45. Lien-Hang T. Nguyen, *Hanoi's War*, 9, 63.

46. VanDeMark, *Road to Disaster*, 217; FRUS, Vietnam, 1961–1963, IV, documents 157, 228; Moyar, *Triumph Forsaken*, 296, 316.

47. FRUS, Vietnam, 1964–1968, I, document 84.

48. Taylor, *Swords and Plowshares*, 302.

49. FRUS, Vietnam, 1961–1963, IV, documents 293, 371 and 1964–1968, I, document 84; Moyar, *Triumph Forsaken*, 296, 303; Allen, *None So Blind*, 178; Harris, *Vietnam's High Ground*, 182.

50. Elliott, *Vietnamese War*, 192.

51. Elliott, *Vietnamese War*, 191–2; MACV, *Command History, 1964*, 49; Harris, *Vietnam's High Ground*, 170–1.

52. McNamara, *In Retrospect*, 84.

53. Finlayson, *Rice Paddy Recon*, 157.

54. Howard Jones, *Death of a Generation: How the Assassination of Diem and JFK Prolonged the Vietnam War* (New York, Oxford University Press, 2003), 435–6.

55. Bui Tin, *From Enemy to Friend*, 155.

56. Shaw, *Lost Mandate*, 272–273.

57. Thomas M. Frank and Laurence D. Cherkis, "The Problem of Fact-Finding in International Disputes," *Case Western Reserve Law Review* 18, no. 5 (1967); 1503.

58. FRUS, Vietnam, 1961–1963, IV, document 165-note 3. Buu Hoi addressed UN issues as neither the DRV nor RVN were officially recognized by that organization.

59. FRUS, Vietnam, 1964–1968, IV, document 245.

60. Frank and Cherkis, "Fact-Finding," 1504–5; CIA "Chronology of Buddhist Crisis in South Vietnam in 1963, 25 October 1963."

61. Frank and Cherkis, "Fact-Finding," 1505; Shaw, *Lost Mandate*, 232; "Vietnam: A Television History; Interview with Madame Ngo Dinh Nhu."

62. Demery, *Dragon Lady*, 146, 214.

63. "Vietnam: A Television History; Interview with Eldridge Durbrow, Part 2 of 2."

64. James McAllister, "Only Religions Count," 756, 778; FRUS, Vietnam, 1961–1963, IV, document 96.

65. McAllister, "Only Religions Count," 756.

66. McAllister, "Only Religions Count," 756, 776.

67. Sullivan, *Obbligato*, 203–4; McAllister, "Only Religions Count," 756, 758; Lacouture, *Vietnam: Between Two Truces*, 208, 214–5; Elliott, *The Sacred Willow*, 270.

68. Lacouture, *Vietnam: Between Two Truces*, 219.

69. FRUS, Vietnam, 1964–1968, IV, document 113; Lacouture, *Vietnam: Between Two Truces*, 209.

70. FRUS, Vietnam, 1964–1968, I, document 324.

71. McAllister, "Only Religions Count," 763; FRUS, Vietnam, 1961–1963, IV, document 75.

72. McAllister, "Only Religions Count," 760–1, 779; FRUS, Vietnam, 1961–1963, IV, document 216 and 1964–1968, I, documents 147, 326, 330.

73. FRUS, Vietnam, 1964–1968, IV, document 96.

74. FRUS, Vietnam, 1964–1968, IV, documents 100, 118, 119.

75. FRUS, Vietnam, 1964–1968, IV, documents 113, 119, 122.

76. FRUS, Vietnam, 1964–1968, IV, document 160; Prados, *The Hidden History*, 155. The Hue police chief was a senior North Vietnamese intelligence officer who had been operating undercover for years. Loan became internationally known after Eddie Adams photographed him in 1968 executing VC terrorist Captain Nguyen Van Lem, who was captured at a mass killing site of civilians and wearing civilian clothes to aid his escape, see: "Eddie Adams' Iconic Vietnam War photo: What happened next," (http://www.bbc.com/news/world-us-canada-42864421).

77. H.R. McMaster, *Dereliction of Duty: Lyndon Johnson, Robert McNamara, the Joint Chiefs of Staff, and the lies that led to Vietnam* (New York: Harper Perennial, 1997), 45; McNamara, *In Retrospect*, 39, 59.

78. Nixon, *The Memoirs of Richard Nixon*, 256–7.

79. Hung and Schecter, *The Palace File*, 79–82, 121, 298.

80. Phillips, *Why Vietnam Matters*, 205.

81. McNamara, *In Retrospect*, 70; Nolting, *From Trust to Tragedy*, xiii.

82. Nolting, *Trust to Tragedy*, 129.

83. Shaw, *Lost Mandate*, 63; Ahern, *House of Ngo*, 116; Moyar, *Triumph Forsaken*, 107–8; Penderghast, *Britain and the Vietnam Wars*, 54; Hammer, *A Death in November*, 38.

84. Mann, *A Grand Delusion*, 297.

Bibliography

Abramson, Rudy. *Spanning the Century: The Life of W. Averell Harriman, 1891–1986*. New York: William Morrow, 1992.

Adams, Sam. *War of Numbers: An Intelligence Memoir*. South Royalton, VT: Steerforth Press, 1994.

Ahern, Thomas L., Jr. "The CIA and the Government of Ngo Dinh Diem: Power Struggles in Saigon," Washington, D.C.: Central Intelligence Agency Center for the Study of Intelligence Library. https://www.cia.gov/library/readingroom/docs/ (hereafter: Center for the Study of Intelligence).

_____. *CIA and the House of Ngo: Covert Action in South Vietnam, 1954–63*. Washington, D.C.: Center for the Study of Intelligence, 2000.

_____. *Undercover Armies: CIA and Surrogate Warfare in Laos, 1961–1973*. Washington, D.C.: Center for the Study of Intelligence, 2006.

_____. *Vietnam Declassified: The CIA and Counterinsurgency*. Lexington: The University Press of Kentucky, 2010.

_____. *The Way We Do Things: Black Entry Operations into North Vietnam, 1961–1964*. Washington, D.C.: Center for the Study of Intelligence, 2004.

Allen, George W. *None So Blind: A Personal Account of the Intelligence Failure in Vietnam*. Chicago: Ivan R. Dee, 2001.

Anderson, David L. *Trapped by Success: The Eisenhower Administration and Vietnam, 1953–61*. New York: Columbia University Press, 1993.

_____. *The Vietnam War*. New York: Palgrave, 2005.

Anderson, Mary E., Michael E. Arnsten, and Harvey A. Averch. *Insurgent Organization and Operations: A Case Study of the Viet Cong in the Delta, 1964–1966*. Santa Barbara, CA: RAND, 1967.

Anderson, Mary E., Richard B. Rainey, Jr., Leonard A. Rapping, and John B. Summerfield, *Support Capabilities for Limited War Forces in Laos and South Vietnam*. Santa Barbara, CA: RAND, 1962.

Anderson, Scott. *The Quiet Americans: Four CIA Spies at the Dawn of the Cold War—A Tragedy in Three Acts*. New York: Doubleday, 2020.

Anthony, Victor B., and Richard R. Sexton, *The War in Northern Laos*. Washington, D.C.: Center for Air Force History, 1993.

Antony, Robert J. "Turbulent Waters: Sea Raiding in Early Modern South East Asia—Abstract." https://www.tandfonline.com/doi/full/10.1080/00253359.2013.766996.

Asselin, Pierre. "The Democratic Republic of Vietnam and the 1954 Geneva Conference: A Revisionist Critique," *Cold War History*, 11, no. 2 (May 2011): 155–195.

_____. *Hanoi's Road to the Vietnam War, 1954–1965*. Berkeley: University of California Press, 2013.

_____. "Le Duan, the American War, and the Creation of an Independent Vietnamese State," *Journal of American-East Asian Relations*, 10, no. 1/2 (Spring–Summer 2001): 1–27.

_____. *Vietnam's American War: A History*. New York: Cambridge University Press, 2018.

Badenoch, Nathan, and Tomita Shinsuke. "Mountain People of the Muang: Creation and Governance of a Tai Polity in Northern Laos," *Southeast Asian Studies*, 2, no. 1 (April 2013): 23–67.

Barber, Noel. *The War of the Running Dogs: How Malaya Defeated the Communist Guerrillas, 1948–1960*. London: Cassell, 1971.

Bass, Thomas A. "The Spy Who Loved Us," *The New Yorker*, 23 May 2005. https://www.newyorker.com/magazine/2005/05/23/the-spy-who-loved-us.

Bazhanov, Boris. *Vospominaniia Byvshego Sekretaria Stalina [Memoirs of the Former Secretary of Stalin]*. Moscow: III Tysiacheletie, 2002. http://lib.ru/MEMUARY/BAZHANOW/stalin.txt.

Benson, Frederic C. *China and Laos, 1945–1979: A Kaleidoscopic Relationship*. Self-published, July 2019. https://www.academia.edu/39750943/China_and_Laos_1945-1979_A_Kaleidoscopic_Relationship.

_____. "Genesis of the Hmong-American Alliance, 1949–1962: Aspirations, Expectations and Commitments during an Era of Uncertainty," *Hmong Studies Journal*, 16 (2015): 1–62.

_____. "Indochina War Refugee Movements in Laos, 1954–1975: A Chronological Overview Citing New Primary Sources," *Journal of Lao Studies*, Special Issue (2015): 24–63.

_____. "The Unraveling of the 1962 Geneva

Accords: Laos 1962–1964" in Stephen Sherman, ed. *Indochina in the Year of the Dragon—1964.* Houston: Radix Press, 2014. https://www.researchgate.net/publication/334454964_The_Unraveling_of_the_1962_Geneva_Accords_Laos_1962-1964.

Bergen, John D. *Military Communications: A Test for Technology.* Washington, D.C.: Center for Military History, 1985.

Berger, Carl, ed. *The United States Air Force in Southeast Asia, 1961–1973; An Illustrated Account.* Washington, D.C.: Office of Air Force History, 1984.

Bergerud, Eric M. *The Dynamics of Defeat: The Vietnam War in Hau Nghia Province.* San Francisco: Westview, 1991.

Berman, Larry. *Perfect Spy: The Incredible Double Life of Pham Xuan An.* Washington, D.C.: Smithsonian Books, 2008.

Blaufarb, Douglas S. *Organizing and Managing Unconventional War in Laos, 1962–1970.* Santa Monica: RAND, 1972.

Bodin, Michel. "Les Laotians dans la guerre d'Indochine, 1945–1954," *Guerres Mondiales et Conflits Contemporains* (Paris: Presses Universitaires de Paris, 2008): 5–21.

Boot, Max. *The Road Not Taken: Edward Lansdale and the American Tragedy in Vietnam.* New York: Liveright, 2018.

Brigham, Robert K. *ARVN: Life and Death in the South Vietnamese Army.* Lawrence: University Press of Kansas, 2006.

_____. *Guerrilla Diplomacy: The NLF's Foreign Relations and the Vietnam War.* Ithaca, NY: Cornel University Press, 1999.

Browne, Malcolm W. *Muddy Boots and Red Socks: A Reporter's Life.* New York: Times Books, 1993.

_____. *The New Face of War.* Indianapolis: Bobbs-Merrill, 1965.

Buckingham, William A. Jr. *Operation Ranch Hand: The Air Force and Herbicides in Southeast Asia, 1961–1971.* Washington, D.C.: USAF Office of Air Force History, 1982.

Bui Diem with David Chanoff. *In the Jaws of History.* Bloomington: Indiana University Press, 1999.

Bui Tin. *Following Ho Chi Minh: Memoirs of a North Vietnamese Colonel.* Judy Stowe and Do Van, trans. Honolulu: University of Hawaii Press, 2003.

_____. *From Enemy to Friend: A North Vietnamese Perspective on the War.* Annapolis: Naval Institute Press, 2002.

Burton, Lance J. *North Vietnam's Military Logistics System: Its Contribution to the War, 1961–1969.* Master's Thesis. U.S. Army Command and General Staff College, 1977.

Butterfield, Fox. "Laos's Opium Country Resisting Drug Law," *New York Times,* 16 October 1972.

Cable, Larry E. *Conflict of Myths: The Development of American Counterinsurgency Doctrine and the Vietnam War.* New York: New York University, 1986.

Cadeau, Ivan. "Les unités du génie de l'armée nationale vietnamienne (1951–1954): renfort appréciable ou affaiblissement du genie du corps expéditionnaire?," *Revue historique des armées,* 265 (2011).

Cao Van Vien. *Leadership.* Washington, D.C.: Department of the Army, 1978.

_____. *The U.S. Advisor.* Washington, D.C.: U.S. Army Center of Military History, 1980.

Cartnal, James. "Dispelling a Myth: The Soviet Note of March 1952," *The History Journal Ex Poste Facto,* 8 (1999). https://history.sfsu.edu/sites/default/files/EPF/1999_James%20Cartnal-ilovepdf-compressed.pdf: 74–89.

Castle, Timothy N. *At War in the Shadow of Vietnam: U.S. Military Aid to the Royal Lao Government, 1954–1975.* New York: Columbia University Press, 1993.

Chapman, Jessica M. *Cauldron of Resistance: Ngo Dinh Diem, the United States, and the 1950s Southern Vietnam.* Ithaca, NY: Cornell University Press, 2013.

_____. "Staging Democracy: South Vietnam's 1955 Referendum to Depose Bao Dai," *Diplomatic History,* 30, no. 4 (September 2006): 1–55.

Chen, King C. "Hanoi's Three Decisions and the Escalation of the Vietnam War," *Political Science Quarterly,* 90, no. 2 (Summer, 1975): pp. 239–259.

Chen Jian, "China's Involvement in the Vietnam War, 1964–1969," *The China Quarterly,* 142 (June 1995): 356–387.

Clarke, Jeffery J. *Advice and Support: The Final Years, 1965–1973.* Washington, D.C.: U.S. Army Center of Military History, 1988.

Clausewitz, Carl Von, *On War,* Michael Howard and Peter Paret, trans. Princeton, NJ: Princeton University Press, 1984.

Colby, William. *Lost Victory: The Firsthand Account of America's Sixteen-Year Involvement in Vietnam.* Chicago: Contemporary Books, 1989.

Communist Party of Vietnam, *Communist Party Documents.* Hanoi: National Publishing House, 2002.

Conboy, Kenneth. *Shadow War: The CIA's Secret Wars in Laos.* Boulder, CO: Paladin, 1995.

Conboy, Kenneth, and Dale Ardradé. *Spies and Commandos: How America Lost the Secret War in North Vietnam.* Lawrence: University Press of Kansas, 2000.

Connors T.T., M.G. Weiner, and J.A. Wilson. *The Land Border of South Vietnam: Some Physical and Cultural Characteristics.* Washington, D.C.: Advanced Research Projects Agency, January 1970.

Conquest, Robert. *The Great Terror: A Reassessment.* New York: Oxford University Press, 1991.

Cooper, Chester L., Judith E. Corson, Laurence J. Legere, David E. Lockwood, and Donald M. Weller. *History of Pacification: The American Experience with Pacification in Vietnam.* Washington, D.C.: Institute of Defense Studies, 1972.

Corn, David. *Blond Ghost: Ted Shackley and the*

CIA's Crusades. New York: Simon & Shuster, 1994.

Cournil, Laure, and Pierre Journoud. "Une décolonisation manquée: l'Armée nationale du Vietnam, de la tutelle française à la tutelle américaine (1949–1965)," *Outre-mers,* tome 98, no. 370–371, 1er semestre (2011).

Currey, Cecil B. *Victory at Any Price: The Genius of Viet Nam's General Vo Nguyen Giap.* Washington, D.C.: Potomac Books, 2005.

Cushman, John H. *External Support of the Viet Cong: An Analysis and a Proposal.* Washington, D.C.: National War College, 1965.

Cutler, Thomas J. *Brown Water, Black Berets: Coastal and Riverine Warfare in Vietnam.* Annapolis: Naval Institute Press, 1988.

Czyzak, John C., and Carl F. Salans. "The International Conference on the Settlement of the Laotian Question and the Geneva Agreements of 1962," *The American Journal of International Law,* 57, no. 2 (April 1963): 300–317.

Daniels, Victoria, and Judith C. Erdheim, *Game Warden.* Washington, D.C.: Center for Naval Analyses, 1976. (TTU).

DeForest, Orrin, and David Chanoff. *Slow Burn: The Rise and Bitter Fall of American Intelligence in Vietnam.* New York: Simon & Schuster, 1990.

Demery, Monique Brinson. *Finding the Dragon Lady: The Mystery of Vietnam's Madame Nhu.* New York: Public Affairs, 2103.

Dommen, Arthur J. *Conflict in Laos: The Politics of Neutralism.* New York: Frederick A. Praeger, 1964.

Dong Van Khuyen. *RVNAF Logistics.* Washington, D.C.: U.S. Army Center for Military History, 1984.

Donnell, John C. *Viet Cong Recruitment: Why and How Men Join.* Santa Monica, CA: RAND Corporation, 1967.

Duiker, William J. *Ho Chi Minh; A Life.* New York: Hyperion, 2000.

_____. "Phan Boi Chau: Asian Revolutionary in a Changing World," *The Journal of Asian Studies* 31, no. 1 (November 1971): 77–88.

Dumbrell, John. *Rethinking Vietnam.* New York: Palgrave McMillan, 2012.

Dunnigan James F., and Alfred A. Nofi. *Dirty Little Secrets of the Vietnam War: Military Information You're Not Supposed to Know.* New York: St. Martin' Griffin, 2000.

Duong, Wendy N. "Gender Equality and Women's issues in Vietnam: The Vietnamese Woman—Warrior and Poet," *Pacific Rim Law and Policy Journal,* 10, no. 2 (Summer 2001): pp. 191–326.

Eckhardt, George S. *Command and Control.* Washington, D.C.: U.S. Army Center of Military History, 1991.

Elliott, David W.P. *The Vietnamese War: Revolution and Social Change in the Mekong Delta, 1930–1975,* concise edition. New York: M.E. Sharpe, 2007.

Elliott, David W.P., and Mai Elliot. *Documents of an Elite Viet Cong Unit: The Demolition Platoon of the 514th Battalion, Part Four: Political Indoctrination and Military Training.* Santa Monica, CA: RAND Corporation, 1969.

Elliott, Mai. *The Sacred Willow: Four Generation in the Life of a Vietnamese Family.* New York: Oxford University Press, 2017.

Ernst, John. *Forging a Fateful Alliance: Michigan State University and the Vietnam War.* East Lansing: Michigan State University Press, 1998.

Fails, William R. *Marines and Helicopters, 1962–1973.* Washington, D.C.: U.S. Marine Corps History and Museums Division, 1978.

Fairbank, John King. *The Great Chinese Revolution: 1800–1985.* New York: Harper & Row, 1986.

Fall, Bernard B. *Hell in a Very Small Place: The Siege of Dien Bien Phu.* New York: Vintage, 1968.

_____. "The Laos Tangle," *International Journal* 16, no. 2 (Spring 1961): 138–157.

_____. "The Political-Religious Sects of Viet-Nam," 26, no. 3, *Pacific Affairs* (September 1955): 235–253.

_____. *Street Without Joy: The French Debacle in Indochina.* Mechanicsburg, PA: Stackpole Books, 2005.

_____. *The Two Viet-Nams: A Political and Military Analysis.* New York: Praeger, 1967.

Fear, Sean. "The Ambiguous Legacy of Ngo Dinh Diem in South Vietnam's Second Republic (1967–1975)," *Journal of Vietnamese Studies,* 11, no. 1 (Winter, 2106): 1–75.

Finlayson, Andrew R. *Rice Paddy Recon: A Marine Officer's Second Tour in Vietnam, 1968–1970.* Jefferson, NC: McFarland, 2014.

Fishel, Wesley R., "Letter to Professor John T. Dorsey, September 14, 1962," Michigan State Vietnam Project Archives. http://vietnam project.archives.msu.edu/fullrecord.php?kid= 6-20-54 (hereafter MSU Project).

Fox, Roger P. *Air Base Defense in the Republic of Vietnam, 1961–1973.* Washington, D.C.: United States Air Force Office of Air Force History, 1979.

Frank Thomas M., and Laurence D. Cherkis. "The Problem of Fact-Finding in International Disputes," *Case Western Reserve Law Review* 18, no. 5 (1967): 1483–1524.

Futrell, Robert F. *The United States Air Force in Southeast Asia: The Advisory Years to 1965.* Washington, D.C.: Office of Air Force History, 1981.

Gaiduk, Ilya V. *The Soviet Union and the Vietnam War.* Chicago: Ivan R. Dee, 1996.

Gelb, Leslie H. and Richard K. Betts. *The Irony of Vietnam: The System Worked.* Washington, D.C.: Brookings Institute Press, 1979.

Geneva Conference on the Problem of Restoring Peace in Indo-China. "Agreement on the Cessation of Hostilities in Laos, 20 July 1954." http://avalon.law.yale.edu/20th_century/inch005.asp.

George Washington University National Security Archive (GWUNSA). *New Light in a Dark Corner: Evidence on the Diem Coup in South Vietnam, November 1963.* https://nsarchive.gwu.edu/briefing-book/vietnam/2020-11-01/new-light-dark-corner-evidence-diem-coup-

november-1963?eType=EmailBlastContent&
eId=d028c305-87ec-4e63-b938-6e40ae0d7697.

Gheddo, Piero. *The Cross and the Bo-Tree: Catholics and Buddhists in Vietnam.* New York: Sheed and Ward, 1970.

Gibbons, William Conrad. *U.S. Government and the Vietnam War: Executive and Legislative Roles and Relationship, Part II.* Princeton: Princeton University Press, 1986.

Gilbert, Marc Jason, ed. *Why the North Won the Vietnam War.* New York: Palgrave, 2002.

Gillespie, Robert M. *Black Ops, Vietnam.* Annapolis: Naval Institute Press, 2011.

Gordon, David F., ed. *Estimative Products on Vietnam, 1948–1975.* Washington, D.C.: National Intelligence Council, 2005.

Goscha, Christopher E. "Une guerre pour Indochina?: Le Laos and le Cambodge dans le conflit Franco-Vietnamien (1958–1954)," *Guerres Mondiales et Conflits Contemporains.* Paris: Presses Universitaires de Paris, 2008.

_____. "Vietnam and the world outside: The case of Vietnamese communist advisors in Laos (1948–62)," *South East Asia Research,* 12, no. 2 (July 2004): 141–185.

Guan, Ang Cheng. *Vietnamese Communist's Relations with China and the Second Indochina Conflict, 1956–1962.* Jefferson, NC: McFarland, 2012.

Guillemot, François. "Death and Suffering at First Hand: Youth Shock Brigades during the Vietnam War (1950–1975)," *Journal of Vietnamese Studies,* 4, no. 3 (Fall 2009): 17–60.

Ha Mai Viet. *Steel and Blood: South Vietnamese Armor and the War for Southeast Asia.* Annapolis: Naval Institute Press, 2008.

Halberstam, David. *The Best and Brightest.* New York: Ballantine, 1992.

_____. *The Making of a Quagmire: America and Vietnam during the Kennedy Era.* New York: Rowman and Littlefield, 2008.

Hallinan, Timothy. "Economic Prospects of the Republic of Vietnam," Santa Monica: RAND, November 1969.

Hamilton-Merritt, Jane. *Tragic Mountains: The Hmong, the Americans, and the Secret War for Laos, 1942–1992.* Bloomington: Indiana University Press, 1999.

Hammer, Ellen J. *A Death in November: America in Vietnam, 1963.* New York: E.P. Dutton, 1987.

_____. *The Struggle for Indochina, 1950–1955.* Stanford: Stanford University Press, 1987.

Hannah, Norman B. *The Key to Failure: Laos and the Vietnam War.* New York: Madison Books, 1987.

Hansen, Peter. "Bac Di Cu: Catholic Refugees from the North of Vietnam and Their Role in the Southern Republic, 1954–1959," *Journal of Vietnamese Studies* 4, no. 3 (Fall 2009): 173–211.

Hanyok, Robert J. *Spartans in Darkness: American SIGINT and the Indochina War, 1945–1975.* Washington, D.C.: National Security Agency, 2002.

Harris, J.P. *Vietnam's High Ground: Armed Struggle for the Central Highlands, 1954–1965.* Lawrence KS: University Press of Kansas, 2016.

Hastings, Max. *Vietnam: An Epic Tragedy, 1945–1975.* New York: HarperCollins, 2018.

Hickey, Gerald Cannon. *Free in the Forest: Ethnohistory of the Vietnamese Central Highlands, 1954–1976.* New Haven: Yale University Press, 1982.

Higgins, Marguerite. *Our Vietnam Nightmare.* New York: Harper and Row, 1965.

Hilsman, Roger. *To Move a Nation: The Politics of Foreign Policy in the Administration of John F. Kennedy.* New York: Doubleday, 1967.

Hoang, Tuan, "Ideology in Urban Vietnam, 1950–1975," Ph.D. diss., University of Notre Dame, 2013.

Hoang Ngoc Lung. *Intelligence.* Washington, D.C.: U.S. Army Center of Military History, 1982.

_____. *Strategy and Tactics.* Washington, D.C.: U.S. Army Center of Military History, 1983.

Hofmann, George R. Jr. *Operation Millpond: U.S. Marines in Thailand, 1961.* Quantico VA: U.S. Marine Corps History Division, 2009.

Holm, Richard L. "No Drums, No Bugles: Recollections of a Case Officer in Laos, 1962–1964." (CIA Library).

Hoyt, Howard W. "Civil Police Administrative Program Semi-Annual Report, 1 July 1957–31 December 1957." Saigon: Michigan State University Vietnam Technical Assistance Program, 1957. (MSU Project)

_____. "Report on the Proposed Organization of the Law Enforcement Agencies of the Republic of Viet-Nam, April 1956." Saigon: Michigan State University Police Advisory Staff, 1956. (MSU Project)

Hunt, David. *Vietnam's Southern Revolution: From Peasant Insurrection to Total War.* Amherst MA: University of Massachusetts Press, 2008.

Hunt, Michael H. *A Vietnam War Reader: A Documentary History from American and Vietnamese Perspectives.* Chapel Hill, NC: University of North Carolina Press, 2010.

Indochina War Forum, "le Guerre en Indochine: Groupes Mobiles," http://laguerreenindochine.forumactif.org/t2762-groupes-mobiles.org.

Jacobs, Seth. *America's Miracle Man in Vietnam: Ngo Dinh Diem, Religion, Race, and U.S. Intervention in Southeast Asia.* Durham NC: Duke University Press, 2004.

_____. *Cold War Mandarin: Ngo Dinh Diem and the Origin of America's War in Vietnam, 1950–1963.* Lanham MD: Rowman and Littlefield, 2006.

Jammes, Jeremy. "Le Saint-Siege Caodaiste de Tay Ninh et le Medium Phan Cong Tac (1890–1959)," *Outre-Mers* T. 94 (2006): 325–53.

Johnson, U. Alexis. *The Meaning of Vietnam.* New Delhi: United States Information Service, 1965.

Jones, Howard. *Death of a Generation: How the Assassination of Diem and JFK Prolonged the Vietnam War.* New York, Oxford University Press, 2003.

Kahin, George McTurnan, ed. *Government and*

Politics in Southeast Asia. Ithaca, NY: Cornell University Press, 1965.

Kamm, Henry. "How's Vietnam Doing? Doctor Expresses Disgust," *New York Times,* 6 May 1993.

Karnow, Stanley. *Vietnam: A History.* New York: Viking, 1983.

Keller, Konrad. *Conversations with Enemy Soldiers in late 1968/early 1969: A Study in Motivation and Morale.* Santa Monica CA: RAND, 1970.

_____. *A Profile of the PAVN Soldier in South Vietnam.* Santa Monica CA: RAND, 1966.

Kelly, Brendan. "Edward Lansdale and the Saigon Military Mission: Nation Building and Counterinsurgency in South Vietnam, 1954–1956," MA thesis, National University of Ireland Maynooth, 2014.

Kennedy, John F. "Remarks of Senator John F. Kennedy at the Conference on Vietnam Luncheon in the Hotel Willard, Washington, D.C., June 1, 1956." John F. Kennedy Presidential Library and Museum (JFK Library).

Kiernan, Ben. *How Pol Pot Came to Power: Colonialism, Nationalism, and Communism in Cambodia, 1930–1975.* New Haven CT: Yale University Press, 2004.

King, John Fairbank. *The Great Chinese Revolution, 1800–1985.* New York: Harper & Row, 1986.

Koch, J.A. *The Chieu Hoi Program in South Vietnam, 1963–1971.* Santa Monica CA: RAND, 1973.

Koprowski, Daniel C. "John F. Kennedy, the development of counterinsurgency doctrine and American intervention in Laos, 1961–1963." Master's Thesis. Amherst, MA: University of Massachusetts, 2014.

Krepinevich, Andrew F. *The Army and Vietnam.* Baltimore: John Hopkins University Press, 1986.

Kurlantzick, Joshua. *A Great Place to Have a War: American and the Birth of a CIA Military.* New York: Simon and Shuster, 2016.

Lacouture, Jean. *Vietnam Between Two Truces,* Konrad Kellen and Joel Carmichael, trans. New York: Random House, 1966.

Lam Quang Thi. *The Twenty-five Year Century: A South Vietnamese General Remembers the Indochina War to the Fall of Saigon.* Denton TX: University of North Texas Press, 2001.

Langer, Paul F. *The Soviet Union, China and the Pathet Lao: Analysis and Chronology.* Springfield VA: National Technical Information Service, 1972.

Langer P.F., and J.J. Zasloff. *Revolution in Laos: The North Vietnamese and the Pathet Lao.* Santa Monica CA: RAND, 1969.

Lanning, Michael Lee, and Dan Cragg. *Inside the VC and the NVA: The Real Story of North Vietnam's Armed Forces.* College Station TX: Texas A&M University Press, 2008.

Lansdale, Edward Geary. "Civic Activities of the Military, Southeast Asia." Washington, D.C.: Anderson-Southeast Asia Subcommittee for the Draper Committee, 13 March 1959. (TTU).

_____. "Memorandum for the Record: 'Pacification in Vietnam.'" Washington, D.C.: Office of

the Secretary of Defense, Special Operations, 1958. (TTU).

_____. *Midst of Wars: An American's Mission to Southeast Asia.* New York: Fordham University Press, 1991.

Larsen, Marion R. "Agricultural Economy of North Vietnam." Washington, D.C.: Department of Agriculture, 1965.

Laurie Clayton D., and Andres Vaart. *CIA in the Wars of Southeast Asia.* Washington, D.C.: Center for the Study of Intelligence, 2016.

Leeker, Joe F. "Air America—Cooperation with Other Airlines." https://www.utdallas.edu/library/specialcollections/hac/cataam/Leeker/history/Cooperation.pdf.

Legrandejacques, Sara. "A Colonial University for Southeast Asia? The Indochinese University in Hanoi," *Kyoto Review of Southeast Asia,* 29 (October 2017). https://kyotoreview.org/yav/indochinese-colonial-university-for-south-east-asia/.

Lehrack, Otto J. *First Battle: Operation Starlite and the Beginning of the Blood Debt in Vietnam.* New York: Presidio Press, 2006.

London, Jonathan D., ed. *Education in Vietnam.* Singapore: Institute of Southeast Asian Studies, 2011. http://jonathanlondon.net/wp-content/uploads/2016/02/EVN_001-London-Education-in-Vietnam.pdf.

Luedeke, Kirk A. "Death on the Highway, The Destruction of Groupement Mobile 100," *Armor Magazine,* 51, no. 1 (January February 2001): 22–29.

Ly Tong Ba. "Battle of Ap Bac: Myth and Reality." https://baovecovang2012.wordpress.com/2013/01/15/tran-ap-bac-thuc-te-va-huyen-thoai-chuan-tuong-ly-tong-ba/.

Mangold, Tom, and John Penycate. *The Tunnels of Cu Chi.* New York: Ballantine Book, 1985.

Mann, Robert. *A Grand Delusion: America's Descent into Vietnam.* New York: Basic Books, 2001.

Mao Tse-tung. *On Guerilla Warfare,* Samuel B. Griffith, trans. New York: Praeger, 1961.

Marolda, Edward J. and Oscar P. Fitzgerald. *The United States Navy in the Vietnam Conflict: From Military Assistance to Combat, 1959–1965,* vol. 2. Washington, D.C.: Navy Historical Center, 1986.

Martinez, George A., ed., *The Viet Cong Proselytizing Program in the Saigon-Gia Dinh Special Zone.* McClean VA: Research Analysis Corporation, 1968.

Matthews. Lloyd J., and Dale E. Brown. *Assessing the Vietnam War.* New York: Pergamon and Brassey's, 1987.

Mau, Michael P. "The Training of Political Cadres in the Lao Dong Party of North Vietnam (1960–1967)," *Asian Survey,* 9, no. 4 (April 1969): 281–296.

McAllister, James. "'Only Religions Count in Vietnam': Thich Tri Quang and the Vietnam War," *Modern Asia Studies,* 42, 4 (2008): 751–782.

McElwee, Pamela. "An Environmental History of

the Ho Chi Minh Trail," *Military Landscapes* (Washington, D.C.: Dumbarton Oaks Press, 2020): 1–28.

McMaster, H.R. *Dereliction of Duty: Lyndon Johnson, Robert McNamara, the Joint Chiefs of Staff, and the Lies That Led to Vietnam.* New York: Harper Perennial, 1997.

McNamara, Robert S. *In Retrospect: The Tragedy and Lessons of Vietnam.* New York: Times Books, 1995.

Melanson, Yves J. "A Brief History of the Academies, Colleges, and Schools of the Central Training Command, RVNAF," Saigon: MACV Headquarters, Military History Branch, 1969. (TTU).

Michigan State University Group. "Summary of MSU Police Administration Program, 16 May 1960," Saigon: Michigan State University Vietnam Technical Assistance Program, 1960.

Miller, Edward G. "Grand Designs: Vision, Power and Nation Building in America's Alliance with Ngo Dinh Diem, 1954–1960." Ph.D. diss., Harvard University, 2004.

_____. *Misalliance: Ngo Dinh Diem, the United States and the Fate of South Vietnam.* Boston: Harvard University Press, 2013.

_____. "Vision, Power and Agency: The Ascent of Ngo Dinh Diem, 1945–54," *Journal of Southeast Asian Studies,* 35, no. 3 (Oct., 2004): 433–58.

Millett, Allen. *The War for Korea, 1945–1950: A House Burning,* vol. 1. Lawrence KS: University Press of Kansas, 2005.

_____. *The War for Korea, 1950–1951: They Came from the North,* vol. 2, Lawrence KS: University Press of Kansas, 2010.

Moise, Edwin E. "Land Reform Errors in North Vietnam," *Pacific Affairs,* 49, no. 1 (Spring 1976): 70–92.

Moore, Harold G., and Joseph L. Galloway. *We Were Soldiers Once ... and Young, Ia Drang: The Battle that Changed the War in Vietnam.* New York: Harper Perennial, 1993.

Moyar, Mark. *Triumph Forsaken: The Vietnam War, 1954–1965.* New York: Cambridge University Press, 2006.

Neese, Harvey, and John O'Donnell, ed. *Prelude to Tragedy: Vietnam, 1960–1965.* Annapolis: Naval Institute Press, 2000.

Ngo Dinh Thuc, Archbishop. "Declaration of Archbishop Ngo-Dinh Thuc." http://www.cmri.org/thucletter.html.

Ngo Quang Truong. *Territorial Forces.* Washington, D.C.: U.S. Army Center of Military History, 1978.

Nguyen, Lien-Hang T. *Hanoi's War: An International History of the War for Peace in Vietnam.* Chapel Hill: University of North Carolina Press, 2012.

Nguyen, Nathalie Huynh Chau. "South Vietnamese Women in Uniform: Narratives of Wartime and Post-War Lives," *Minerva Journal of Women and War,* 3, no. 2 (Fall 2009): pp. 8–33.

Nguyen, Tai Thu, ed. *The History of Buddhism in Vietnam.* Washington, D.C.: Council for Research in Values and Philosophy, 2008.

Nguyen Manh Hung. "Journalistic Distortions: Neil Sheehan's Portrait of the Vietnamese in *A Bright Shining Lie* (1988)," *Journal of Vietnam Veterans Institute,* 2, no. 1 (1993): 17–31.

Nguyen Ngoc Chau. "The potential competitor to Ngo Dinh Diem in 1954," *Việt Nam—L'histoire Politique des deux guerres—Guerre d'indépendance (1858–1954) et guerre idéologique ou Nord Sud (1945–1975),* Editions Nombre 7, France, 2019.

Nguyen Ngoc Linh, ed. *The Armed Forces of the Republic of Viet Nam.* Saigon: Vietnam Council on Foreign Relations, 1970.

Nguyen Ngoc Tan. "New Road, Path of Progress," *Vietnamese National Association,* Special Issue 2007, pp. 132–160. http://hon-viet.co.uk/TsNguyenNgocTan_ChuNghiaNhanViConDuongMoiConDuongCua TienBo.htm.

Nguyen Tien Hung, and Jerrold L. Schecter. *The Palace File.* New York: Perennial Library, 1978.

Nichter, Luke A. *The Last Brahmin: Henry Cabot Lodge, Jr., and the making of the Cold War.* New Haven: Yale University Press, 2020.

Nitz, Kiyoko Kurusu. "Japanese Military Policy Towards French Indochina during the Second World War: The Road to the 'Meigo Sakusen' (9 March 1945)," *Journal of Southeast Asian Studies* 14, no. 2 (1983): 328–353.

Nixon, Richard. *The Memoirs of Richard Nixon.* New York: Grosset and Dunlap, 1978.

Nolting, Frederick. *From Trust to Tragedy: The Political Memoirs of Fredrick Nolting, Kennedy's Ambassador to Diem's Vietnam.* New York: Praeger, 1988.

Olsen, Kenneth R., and Lois Wright Morgan. "Why Were the Soil Tunnels of Chu Chi and Iron Triangle in Vietnam so Resilient?" *Open Journal of Soil Science,* 7 (2017): 34–51.

Olsen, Mari. *Soviet-Vietnam Relations and the Role of China, 1949–1964: Changing Alliances.* New York: Routledge, 2006.

Palmer, Bruce, Jr. *The 25-Year War: America's Military role in Vietnam.* Lexington KY: University of Kentucky Press, 2002.

Palmer, Gregory. *The McNamara Strategy and the Vietnam War: Program Budgeting in the Pentagon, 1960–1968.* Westport, CT: Greenwood Press, 1978.

Pan, Stephen, and Daniel Lyons. *Vietnam Crisis.* New York, East Asian Research Center, 1966.

Peebles, Curtis. *Twilight Warriors: Covert Air Operations Against the USSR.* Annapolis: Naval Institute Press, 2005.

Penderghast, Gerald. *Britain and the Vietnam Wars: The Supply of Troops, Arms and Intelligence, 1945–1975.* Jefferson NC: McFarland, 2015.

Pentagon Papers. National Archives and Records Administration (NARA).

Pentagon Papers (Gravel Edition). Boston: Beacon Press, 1972.

People's Army of Vietnam. "The Perfect Service in Prison," *People's Army Newspaper,* Spring 2009.

Phillips, Rufus. *Why Vietnam Matters: An*

Eyewitness Account of Lessons Not Learned. Annapolis: Naval Institute Press, 2008.

Pholsena, Vatthana. "The Early Years of the Lao Revolution (1945–1949): Between History, Myth and Experience," *South East Asia Research* 14, no. 3 (November 2006): 403–430.

Pholsena, Vatthana, and Oliver Tappe, eds. *Interactions with a Violent Past: Reading Post Conflict Landscapes in Cambodia, Laos, and Vietnam.* Singapore: NUS Press, 2013.

Pike, Douglas. *The PAVN: People's Army of Vietnam.* Novato, CA: Presidio Press, 1984.

_____. *Viet Cong: The Organization and Techniques of the National Liberation Front of South Vietnam.* Cambridge: The M.I.T. Press, 1966.

Porter, Gareth. *Perils of Dominance: Imbalance of Power and the Road to War in Vietnam.* Berkeley: University of California Press, 2006.

Prados, John. *The Blood Road: The Ho Chi Minh Trail and the Vietnam War.* New York: Wiley, 1998.

_____. *The Hidden History of the Vietnam War.* Chicago: Ivan R. Dee, 1995.

_____. *Vietnam: The Unwinnable War, 1945–1975.* Lawrence KS: University Press of Kansas, 2009.

Pribbenow, Merle L. "The Man in the White Cell," Washington, CIA Library, 2008. https://www.cia.gov/library/center-for-the-study-of-intelligence/csi-publications/csi-studies/studies/vol48no1/article06.html.

_____. "The Sino-Soviet Intelligence Relationship during the Vietnam War: Cooperation and Conflict," *Cold War International History Project,* Working Paper no. 73. Washington, D.C.: Woodrow Wilson International Center for Scholars, 2014.

_____. trans. *Victory in Vietnam: The Official History of the People's Army of Vietnam, 1954–1975.* Lawrence KS: University Press of Kansas, 2002.

Quinn-Judge, Sophia. *Ho Chi Minh: The Missing Years, 1919–1941.* Berkeley: University of California Press, 2001.

Rapin, Ami-Jacques. "Guerillas, Guerre Secretes et 'Covert Operations' au Laos, Essai Historiographique." *Center for Asian Interdisciplinary Studies and Research,* Series Red (March 1998): 1–34.

Republic of Vietnam. *The Armed Forces of the Republic of Vietnam, Vietnam Information, Series 20.*

_____. "Land Reform Program Before 1954 and Land Reform Programs and Achievements Since July 1954." Saigon: Secretariat of State for Land Property and Land Reform, 31 July 1959. (TTU).

_____. *Major Policy Speeches by President Ngo Dinh Diem.* Saigon: Press Office, Presidency of the Republic of Vietnam, 1958. (TTU).

_____. "The Republic of Vietnam Armed Forces, Vietnam Report VIII." Washington, D.C.: Embassy of the Republic of Vietnam, 1967. (TTU).

_____. *The Victory of Rung Sat.* Saigon: Government of the Republic of Vietnam, 1955.

_____. *Violations of the Geneva Agreement by the Viet-Minh Communists, From July 1959 to June 1960.* Saigon: Government of the Republic of Vietnam, 1960.

Rettig, Tobias. "French Military Policies in the Aftermath of the Yen Bay Mutiny, 1930: Old Security Dilemmas Return to Surface," *South East Asia Research,* 10, no. 3 (September 2002): 309–331.

Richardson, John H. "The Spy Left Out in the Cold," *New York Times,* 7 August 2005. http://www.nytimes.com/2005/08/07/opinion/the-spy-left-out-in-the-cold.html.

Riggs Osborn, Julie Annette. "War, Women, Vietnam: The Mobilization of Female Images, 1954–1978," Ph.D. diss., University of Washington, 2013.

Roberts, Pricilla. "The British Royal Air Force Operations over Laos against the Ho Chi Minh Trail, 1962," *Cold War International History Project,* Working Paper no. 89 (December 2018): 1–18.

Rogers, Paul. "The Secret War in Viengxay." http://www.laoscaveproject.de/Reports/The_Secret_War_Viengxay.pdf.

Rottman, Gordon L. *Viet Cong and NVA Tunnels and Fortifications of the Vietnam War.* New York: Osprey, 2006.

_____. *Vietnam Airborne.* London: Osprey, 1990.

Rust, William J. *Before the Quagmire: American Intervention in Laos, 1954–1961.* Lexington, KY: University Press of Kentucky, 2012.

_____. "CIA Operations Officer Lucien Conein: A Study in Contrasts and Controversy," *Studies in Intelligence* 63, no. 4 (Extracts, December 2019): 44–57.

_____. *So Much to Lose: John F. Kennedy and American Policy in Laos.* Lexington, KY: University Press of Kentucky, 2014.

Salemink, Oscar. "The Regional Centrality of Vietnam's Central Highlands," *Oxford Research Encyclopedia, Asian History,* 2018 (asianhistory.oxforde.com): 1–30.

Savada, Andrea Matles, and Donald P. Whitaker. *Laos: A Country Study.* Washington, D.C.: Federal Research Division, Library of Congress, 1994.

Savani, A.M. *Visage et Images du Sud Viet-Nam.* Saigon: Imprimerie Francaise d'Outre-Mer, 1955.

Schlemmer, Gregoire. "Questionner la question ethnique: Lecture historique et politique des appurtenances culturelles au Laos," *Moussons* 25 (2015-1): 5–37.

Schultz, Richard H. Jr. "The Great Divide: Strategy and Covert Action in Vietnam," *Joint Forces Quarterly,* 25 (Autumn Winter, 1999–2000): 90–96.

_____. *The Secret War Against Hanoi: Kennedy's and Johnson's Use of Spies, Saboteurs, and Covert Warriors in North Vietnam.* New York: HarperCollins, 1999.

Shaw, Geoffrey D.T. *The Lost Mandate of Heaven: The American Betrayal of Ngo Dinh Diem,*

President of Vietnam. San Francisco: Ignatius Press, 2015.

Sheehan, Neil. *A Bright Shining Lie: John Paul Vann and America in Vietnam.* New York: Vintage Books, 1989.

Shrader, Charles R. *War of Logistics: Parachutes and Porters in Indochina, 1945–1954.* Lexington KY: University Press of Kentucky, 2015.

Shulimson, Jack. *Joint Chiefs of Staff and the Vietnam War, 1960–1968, Parts 1 and 2.* Washington, Office of the Chairman of the Joint Chiefs of Staff Office of Joint History, 2011.

———. *The Marines in Vietnam, 1954–1973: An Anthology and Annotated Bibliography.* Washington, D.C.: U.S. Marine Corps History and Museums Division, 1985.

Shulimson, Jack, and Charles M. Johnson. *U.S. Marines in Vietnam: The Landing and Buildup, 1965.* Washington, D.C.: Headquarters Marine Corps History and Museums Division, 1978.

Skow, Lisa M. and George N. Dionisopoulos. "A Struggle to Contextualize Photographic Images: American Print Media and the 'Burning Monk,'" *Communication Quarterly*, 45, no.4 (Fall 1997); pp. 393–409. http://enlight.lib.ntu.edu.tw/FULLTEXT/JR-EPT/lisa.htm.

Smith, Ralph B. "The Japanese Period in Indochina and the Coup of 9 March 1945," *Journal of Southeast Asian Studies*, 9, no. 2 (September 1978): 268–301.

Smith, Terrance. "Infiltration of Saigon Regime by Communists Is Described as Trial Opens," *New York Times*, 29 November 1969.

Sok Udom Deth, Sun Suon, Sekran Bulut, eds. *Cambodia's Foreign Relations and Global Contexts.* Stankt Augostin, GE: Konrad Adenauer Stiftung, 2017.

Special Operations Research Office Director, *Ethnographic Study Series: Selected Groups in the Republic of Vietnam, The Binh Xuyen.* Washington, D.C.: The American University, 1966.

Spector, Ronald H. *Advice and Support: The Early Years, 1941–1960.* Washington, D.C.: U.S. Army Center of Military History, 1985.

Stanton, Shelby L. *Green Berets at War: U.S. Army Special Forces in Southeast Asia, 1956–1975.* Novato, CA: Presidio Press, 1985.

Starry, Don A. *Mounted Combat in Vietnam.* Washington, D.C.: U.S. Army Center of Military History, 1989.

Stewart, Geoffrey C. *Vietnam's Lost Revolution: Ngo Dinh Diem's Failure to Build an Independent Nations, 1955–1963.* New York: Cambridge University Press, 2017.

Stur, Heather Marie. *Saigon at War: South Vietnam and the Global Sixties.* New York: Cambridge University Press, 2020.

———. "South Vietnam's 'Daredevil Girls,'" *New York Times*, 1 August 2017 https://www.nytimes.com/2017/08/01/opinion/vietnam-war-girls-women.html.

Sullivan, William H. *Obbligato: Notes on a Foreign Service Career.* New York: W.W. Norton, 1984.

Swoviak, Jerema. "The Role of Religion and Politico-Religious Organizations in the South Vietnam During the Ngo Dinh Diem Period," Zeszyty Naukove Tovarzystva Doktorantov Uj Nauki Spoweczne, NR 16 (1/2017): 109–124.

Sydney Morning Herald.

Szalontai, Balazs. "Political and Economic Crisis in North Vietnam, 1955–1956," *Cold War History* 5, no. 4 (November 2005): 395–426.

Tan, Mitchell. "Spiritual Fraternities: The Transnational Networks of Ngo Dinh Diem's Personalist Revolution and the Republic of Vietnam, 1955–1963," *Journal of Vietnamese Studies*, 14, no. 2 (Spring 2019): 1–67.

Tappe, Oliver. "Thailand und Laos—eine historiche Hassliebe [Thailand and Laos—A Historical Love-Hatred]," Orapim Bernart and Holger Warnk, eds. *Thailand—Facetten einer südostasiatischen Kultur [Thailand—Facets of a Southeast Asian Culture].* Munich: East Asia Publishing Company, 2013.

Tarling, Nicholas, ed. *The Cambridge History of Southeast Asia, Volume Two.* Cambridge: Cambridge University Press, 2008.

Taylor, Maxwell D. *Swords and Plowshares.* New York: Random House, 1972.

Taylor, Sandra C. *Vietnamese Women at War: Fighting for Ho Chi Minh and the Revolution.* Lawrence KS: University Press of Kansas, 1999.

Tessier, Oliver. "Le « grand bouleversement » (long troi lo dat): regards croisés sur la réforme agraire en République démocratique du Việt Nam," *Ecole Française d'Extrême-Orient* 95/96 (2008–2009): 73–134.

Thompson, Robert Grainer Ker. *Defeating Communist Insurgency: The Lessons of Malay and Vietnam.* New York: Praeger, 1966.

Tilford, Earl H. Jr. *Crosswinds: The Air Force's Set Up in Vietnam.* College Station TX: Texas A & M University Press, 1993.

Toczak, David M. *The Battle of Ap Bac: They Did Everything but Learn From It.* Annapolis: Naval Institute Press, 2001.

Tongas, Gérald. *J'ai vécu dans L'enfer Communiste au Nord Viet-Nam.* Paris: Nouvelles Editions Debresse, 1960.

Tourison, Sedgewick D. Jr. *Secret Army, Secret War: Washington's Tragic Spy Operations in North Vietnam.* Annapolis: Naval Institute Press, 1995.

———. *Talking with Victor Charlie: An Interrogator's Story.* New York: Ivy Books, 1991.

Tracy, Jared M. "Shoot and Salute: U.S. Army Special Warfare in Laos," *Veritas* 14, no. 1 (2018): 42–54.

Tran Thi Phuong Hoa. "Franco-Vietnamese Schools and the Transition from Confucian to a New Kind of Intellectual in the Colonial Context of Tonkin" (Boston: Harvard-Yenching Institute Working Paper Series, 2009): 1–23.

Tran Van Don. *Our Endless War: Inside Vietnam.* San Rafael CA: Presidio Press, 1978.

Truong Nhu Tang. *A Viet Cong Memoir: An Inside Account of the Vietnam War and its Aftermath.* New York: Vintage, 1986.

Tucker, Spencer T., ed. *Encyclopedia of the Vietnam*

War: A Political, Social and Military History. Oxford: ABC-CLIO, 2011.

Tuong Vu. *Vietnam's Communist Revolution: The Powers and Limits of Ideology.* New York: Cambridge University Press, 2016.

Tuong Vu, and Sean Fear, eds. *The Republic of Vietnam, 1955–1975: Vietnamese Perspectives on Nation Building.* Ithaca NY: Cornell University Press, 2020.

Turner, Robert F., Roger Canfield, and Robert M. Gillespie, eds. *Indochina in the Year of the Dragon—1964.* Houston: Radix Press, 2014.

Ulam, Adam B. *Expansion and Coexistence: Soviet Foreign Policy, 1917–1973.* New York: Praeger, 1977.

United Nations, *United Nations Treaty Series, 1963.* New York: United Nations, 1964.

United States Agency for International Development (USAID). *Vietnam: Grain Storage and Marketing System Economic and Engineering Study.* Toledo OH: Wildman Agricultural Research, March 1970.

United States Air Force. "Weekly Air Intelligence Summary 86–32, 10 August 1968." (TTU).

United States Army. Vietnam, G-2 Intelligence. "History of the 273 VC Regiment." Saigon: Headquarters, U.S. Army, Republic of Vietnam, 1970. (TTU).

United States Central Intelligence Agency. "Buddhist Action in Vietnam: A Special Assessment of the Situation in the Light of Events in March April 1966, 29 April 1966." Washington, D.C.: CIA, 1966.

_____. "Chronology of Buddhist Crisis in South Vietnam in 1963, 25 October 1963." Washington, D.C.: CIA, 1963.

_____. Director Central Intelligence (DCI), *The Highlanders of South Vietnam: A Review of Political Developments and Forces.* Washington, D.C.: CIA, 1966.

_____. Information Report, "Thich Tri Quang's Dissatisfaction over Published Statements by American Officials and his Indication of a Continuation of the Buddhist Struggle," Washington, D.C.: CIA, 3 August 1963.

_____. Memorandum on "Freedom of Religion in North and South Vietnam, 15 May 1974." Washington, D.C.: CIA, 1974.

_____. NIE 63.3–55 "Probable Developments in Laos to July 1956," dated 26 July 1955. Washington, D.C.: CIA, 1955.

_____. OCI, Report, OCI no. 3238/63, "Progress of the Coup d'État in Saigon (as of 0800 EST)." Washington, D.C.: CIA, 1963.

_____. OCI, Special Report, "The Buddhists in South Vietnam, 28 June 1963." Washington, D.C.: CIA, 1963.

_____. OCI. "Coup Timeline Sequence (All Times indicated are local Saigon Time, 1 November), 1 November 1963." Washington, D.C.: CIA, 1963.

_____. Office of Current Intelligence (OCI). "Cast of Characters in South Vietnam, 28 August 1963," Washington, D.C.: CIA, 1963.

_____. Office of Research and Reports (ORR). "A Comparison of the Economies of North and South Vietnam." Washington, D.C.: CIA, 1961.

_____. ORR. *The Effectiveness of the Air Campaign Against North Vietnam, 1 January–30 September 1966.* Washington, D.C.: CIA, 1966. (CIA Library)

_____. Saigon Report no. DA IN 108950, 24 September 1963, "Tran Kim Tuyen Predicts Dire Prospects for Diem Regime." (CIA Library).

_____. "Special National Intelligence Estimate (SNIE) 14.3–67: Capabilities of the Vietnamese Communists for Fighting in South Vietnam," 13 November 1967. Washington, D.C.: CIA, 1967.

_____. "Working Paper on The Central Office for South Vietnam (COSVN): Its History, Organization and Functions." Washington, D.C.: CIA, 1969.

United States Department of State. "Biographical Data on Lieutenant General Pham Xuan Chieu." Washington, D.C.: Department of State, 21 October 1974. (NARA).

_____. *Bulletin,* 12 April 1954, 539–42.

_____. "Memorandum for Mr. McGeorge Bundy, The White House: Meeting on Laos, 18 June 1963" (JFK Library).

_____. *Papers relating to the foreign relations of the United States,* Germany and Austria, 1952–1954, VII; Indochina 1952–1954, XIII Part 2; Geneva Convention, 1952–1954, XVI; Vietnam, 1955–1957, I; East Asian Security, Cambodia, Laos, 1955–1957, XXI; Vietnam, 1958–1960, I; East Asia Pacific Region, Cambodia, Laos, 1958–1960, XVI; Indonesia, 1958–1960, XVII; Japan, Korea, 1958–1960, XVIII; Vietnam 1961–1963, I, II, III, IV; Kennedy-Khrushchev Exchanges, 1961–1963, VI; Southeast Asia, 1961–1963, XXIII; Laos Crisis, 1961–1963, XXIV; Vietnam, 1964–1968, I, II, III; Laos, 1964–1968, XXVIII.

_____. "10 January 1963 Memorandum for Governor Harriman: Your Conversation with Ken Crawford." Washington, D.C.: Department of State, 1963.

_____. *A Threat to Peace: North Viet-Nam's Effort to Conquer South Viet-Nam, Parts I and II.* Washington, D.C.: Government Printing Office, 1961.

United States Department of the Army, *The Development and Training of the South Vietnamese Army, 1950–1972.* Washington, D.C.: U.S. Army Center of Military History, 1975.

_____. *Guerrilla Warfare and Special Forces Operations, FM 31–21.* Washington, D.C.: Department of the Army, September 1961.

United States Forces, Vietnam. "The Situation in Nam Bo since the Restoration of Peace to Date [1961]" (translation of incomplete document captured in Phouc Long province, RVN, on 28 April 1969). (TTU).

United States Foreign Broadcast Information Service, trans. *The Anti-U.S. Resistance War for National Salvation, 1954–1975: Military Events.* Arlington, VA: Joint Publication Research Service, 1982.

United States Marine Corps History and Museums

Division. *The Marines in Vietnam, 1954–1973: An Anthology and Annotated Bibliography.* Washington, D.C.: Headquarters, U.S. Marine Corps, 1985.

———. *Professional Knowledge Gained from Operational Experience in Vietnam, 1965–1966,* NAVMC 2614. Washington, D.C.: Government Printing Office, 1967.

United States Military Advisory Command Vietnam (MACV, CICV), "Military Training, in North Vietnam." Saigon: MACV, 1968. (TTU).

———. CICV, "Review of NVA Armor and Tactics, MACVI 31–2." Saigon: MACV, 8 November 1972. (TTU).

———. Combined Document Exploitation Center, Vietnam (CDECV), "A Party Account of the Situation in the Nam Bo Region of South Vietnam, 1954–1960." Saigon: MACV, undated. (TTU).

———. Combined Intelligence Center, Vietnam (CICV), "Para-Military Forces in North Vietnam, MACVI 31–2." Saigon: MACV, 27 July 1972. (TTU).

———. Combined Military Interrogation Center, Vietnam (CMICV), "OB [Order of Battle] of SR-1." Saigon: MACV, 6 April 1970. (TTU).

———. Historical Branch. *Command History, 1964.* Saigon: Headquarters MACV, 15 October 1965.

———. Historical Branch. *Command History, 1965.* Saigon: Headquarters MACV, 20 April 1966.

———. "Information on 21st Infantry Division," Bac Lieu, RVN: MACV Advisory Team 51, 1965.

———. Military Advisory Command Studies and Observation Group (MACSOG), *Documentation Study,* 10 July 1970. (TTU).

———. "21st Infantry Division ARVN and 42nd DTA," Bac Lieu, RVN: MACV Advisory Team 51, 1965.

———. "Vietnam Lessons Learned No. 79: Enemy Exploitation of Allied Tactical Communications," Saigon: MACV, 8 March 1970. (TTU).

———. "What A Platoon Leader Should Know About the Enemy's Jungle Tactics." Saigon: MACV, 1967. (TTU).

United States National Security Council. "National Security Action Memorandum (NSAM) 29: Re: Meeting with the President on Southeast Asia, 9 March 1961." (JFK Library).

———. "NSAM 104: Southeast Asia, 13 October 1961." (JFK Library).

———. "NSAM 249: Laos Planning, 25 June 1963." (JFK Library).

———. "NSAM 57: Responsibility for Paramilitary Operations, 28 June 1961." (JFK Library).

———. "NSC Memorandum on Communist Problems in South Vietnam During the 1954–1959 'Cease-fire,'" 28 May 1971.

———. "Program of Action to Prevent Communist Domination of South Viet Nam, 9 May 1961" (JFK Library).

United States Navy. Chaplains Division. *The Religions of South Vietnam in Faith and Fact—NAVPERS 15991.* Washington, D.C.: United States Navy, 1967.

United States Pacific Command. Commander-in-Chief Pacific (CINCPAC). CDR JTF-FA, Honolulu HI J2, "Oral History Program (OHP-019) Report: MG Vo Van Dan, message dated 10 July 1996." (TTU).

———. *CINCPAC Command History 1960.* FPO San Francisco: Headquarters CINCPAC, 1961. (reproduced by Stephen Sherman)

———. Commander-in-Chief Pacific. *CINCPAC Command History 1962.* FPO San Francisco: Headquarters CINCPAC, 1963.

VanDeMark, Brian. *Road to Disaster: A New History of America's Descent into Vietnam.* New York: HarperCollins, 2018.

Vietnam Workers Party Central Information Service, *Manifesto and Platform of the Vietnam Lao Dong Party,* April 1952

Vinh Long School, Directory of the. "Biography of Bishop Pierre Martin Ngo Dinh Thuc." http://giaophanvinhlong.net/Duc-Cha-Phero-Ngo-Dinh-Thuc.html.

Vo, Alex-Thai D. "Nguyen Thi Nam and the Land Reform of North Vietnam, 1953," *Journal of Vietnamese Studies* 10, no. 1 (Winter, 2015): 1–62.

Vo Nguyen Giap. *People's War, People's Army.* Hanoi, Foreign Language Publishing House, 1961.

Vu, Tuong. *Vietnam's Communist Revolution: The Powers and Limits of Ideology.* New York: Cambridge University Press, 2016.

Vuong Quan Hoang. "The Vietnam's Transition Economy and Its Fledgling Financial Markets, 1986–2003," *Centre Emile Bernhiem,* Working Paper no. 04/032 (January 2004).

Walinsky, Louis J., ed. *Agrarian Reform as Unfinished Business: The Selected Papers of Wolf Ladejinsky.* Oxford: Oxford University Press, 1977.

Warner, Roger. *Back Fire: The CIA's Secret War in Laos and Its Link to the War in Vietnam.* New York: Simon Schuster, 1995.

Wehrle, Edmund F. "'A Good, Bad Deal': John F. Kennedy, W. Averell Harriman, and the Neutralization of Laos, 1961–1962," *Pacific Historical Review,* 67, no. 3 (August, 1998): 349–377.

Wells, Robert. *Invisible Enemy: Boobytraps in Vietnam.* Miami: J. Flores Publications, 1992.

The West Australian. "Rebels Complete Quick Drive Across Laos," 28 December 1953.

Wiest, Andrew. *Vietnam's Forgotten Army: Heroism and Betrayal in the ARVN.* New York: New York University Press, 2008.

Wilkins, Warren. *Grab their Belts to Fight Them: The Viet Cong's Big Unit War Against the U.S., 1965–1966.* Annapolis: Naval Institute Press, 2011.

Williams, Thomas D. and Jan Olof Bengtsson. "Personalism," *The Stanford Encyclopedia of Philosophy* (Summer 2018 Edition), Edward N. Zalta (ed.). https://plato.stanford.edu/archives/sum2018/entries/personalism/.

Wonsetler, Noble B. *The Transformation of the People's Army of Vietnam, 1954–1975.* Fort

Leavenworth, KS: U.S. Army Command and Staff College, 2016.

Wurfel, David. "Agrarian Reform in the Republic of Vietnam," *The Eastern Survey* 26, no. 6 (June 1957): pp. 81–92.

Xunhasaba, "The Failure of the 'Special War,' 1961–1965," *Vietnamese Studies (Hanoi)*, 11 (1966), p. 26. (TTU).

Yilmaz, Oguzhan, ed. *History of Vietnam and the Socialist Republic of Vietnam*. Konya: University of Selkuc, 2019.

Zasloff, Joseph J. "Rural Resettlement in South Viet Nam: The Agroville Program," *Pacific Affairs*, 35, no. 4 (Winter, 1962–1963): 327–340.

Zhai, Qiang. *China and the Vietnam Wars, 1950–1975*. Chapel Hill NC: University of North Carolina Press, 2000.

_____. "Transplanting the Chinese Model: Chinese Military Advisers and the First Vietnam War, 1950–1954," *The Journal of Military History*, 57, no. 4 (October 1993): 770–785.

Zhang, Xiaoming. "Vietnam War, 1964–1969: A Chinese Perspective," *The Journal of Military History* 60, no. 4 (October 1996): 731–762.

Zi Jun Toong. "Overthrown by the Press: The US Media's Role in the Fall of Diem," *Australian Journal of American Studies*, 27, no.1 (July 2008): 56–72.

Interviews Consulted

Bartlett, Charles. "Henry Cabot Lodge, Oral History Interview, 1966." (JFK Library).

Karnow, Stanley. "Vietnam: A Television History; America's Mandarin (1954–1963); Interview with Edward Geary Lansdale, 1979" (Open Vault, WGBH, http://openvault.wgbh.org/catalog/vietnam-8fe831-interview-with-edward-geary-lansdale-1979). Hereafter: (WGBH Media Library & Archives).

Kraft, Joseph. "Oral History Interviews with Michael V. Forrestal for the John F. Kennedy Library, 1964." (JFK Library).

"Ngo Dinh Luyen interview recounted in 31 January 1979." (WGBH Media Library & Archives).

O'Brien, Dennis J. "Roger Hilsman Oral History, 1970." (JFK Library).

Schlesinger, Arthur M. Jr. "William Averell Harriman Oral History Interview, 1965." (JFK Library).

"Vietnam: A Television History: Interview with Lucien Conein," 7 May1981. (WGBH Media Library & Archives).

"Vietnam: A Television History; Interview with Eldridge Durbrow," 1 February 1979. (WGBH Media Library & Archives).

"Vietnam: A Television History; Interview with Lawton Collins," 29 April 1981. (WGBH Media Library & Archives).

"Vietnam: A Television History; Interview with Lucien Bodard," 18 February 1981. (WGBH Media Library & Archives).

"Vietnam: A Television History; Interview with Madame Ngo Dinh Nhu," 11 February 1982. (WGBH Media Library & Archives).

"Vietnam: A Television History; Interview with Tran Van Don," 7 May 1981. (WGBH Media Library & Archives).

Visuals

British Broadcasting Corporation. "Eddie Adams' Iconic Vietnam War photo: What happened next." http://www.bbc.com/news/world-us-canada-42864421.

British Pathé, "Saigon Revolt, 1955." https://www.britishpathe.com/video/saigon-revolt.

Garr, David G. "Vietnam: Art of the National Liberation Front, An Exhibition." Cornell: Cornell University, 1970.

Video recording of Thich Tam Chau on the self-immolation of Bodhisattva Thich Quang Duc (July 2013). http://www.youtube.com/watch?v=e7eFkc5XWr4.

Index

Numbers in **bold italics** indicate pages with illustrations